Taking Sides: Clashing Views
in Abnormal Psychology,
Eighth Edition

Richard P. Halgin

http://create.mheducation.com

ISBN-10: 1259176746   ISBN-13: 9781259176746

Contents

Preface

The field of abnormal psychology is inherently controversial because we lack a clear delineation between normal and abnormal behavior. Most phenomena in the realm of abnormal psychology fall along continua; the point on a continuum at which behavior moves from being considered "normal" to being considered "abnormal" varies considerably and is influenced by a number of factors. Consider the example of an active boy's behavior. His running around impulsively and shouting out aimless comments would be viewed as normal behavior on a playground but abnormal behavior in a quiet classroom. In a classroom setting, his behavior might be referred to as impulsive and hyperactive, possibly prompting his teacher to refer him to a mental health professional for therapy and medication to help him settle down and pay attention. Although such referrals are commonplace in American schools, some people contend that we pathologize the normal behavior of children when we view their high levels of energy as mental disorders. This is but one of the debates about which you will read in this book, and it is a good example of the kind of controversy found in the field of mental health.

There are many complex issues that arise in the field of abnormal psychology. In this book you will read about controversial matters with which mental health experts struggle, such as: psychological conditions and treatments about which there has been vehement disagreement in recent years, with some experts expressing intense skepticism about the validity of specific clinical problems and interventions that have been in the spotlight, the trend toward biological interventions for an array of psychological problems and mental disorders, pertinent social issues that interface with the field of abnormal psychology, particularly debates about ethical and legal issues that pertain to the field of mental health.

Most students who enroll in a course in abnormal psychology begin the semester with the belief that they will be learning about problems that affect "other people," rather than themselves. In a short period of time, however, they come to realize that they are reading about conditions that have much more personal salience than they had anticipated. Sooner or later, they recognize conditions that they or someone close to them has experienced, and their interest in the topic intensifies. In all likelihood, you will have a similar reaction as you read this book. To capture the essence of each debate, you will find it helpful to connect yourself in a personal way to the issue under consideration; you might imagine yourself dealing with the issue personally, or as the relative of a client with the particular problem, or even as a professional trying to provide mental health assistance.

Plan of the book To assist you in understanding the significance of each issue, every issue begins with an enumeration of learning outcomes which will help you focus on the important lessons contained in the readings. You will then be provided with a thoughtful summary of the major points raised in each reading, with particular attention to the contrasting arguments on each side of the debate. Each issue concludes with a set of questions entitled "Exploring the Issue" which will guide you in the process of critical thinking and reflection. Next comes the section entitled "Is There Common Ground?" which considers shared concerns that emerged from both sides of the controversy. Additional resources are then provided so that you can delve more deeply into the topic in scholarly readings and relevant websites.

Changes to this edition This eighth edition of *Taking Sides: Clashing Views in Abnormal Psychology* includes some significant changes from the seventh edition, containing new topics as well as updates or replacements of articles published in the seventh edition. The new topics address provocative debates which have emerged in recent years, including controversies related to the 2013 publication of DSM-5.

A word to the instructor An *Instructor's Resource Guide with Test Questions* (multiple-choice and essay) is available through the publisher for the instructor using *Taking Sides* in the classroom.

Acknowledgments Very special gratitude goes to research assistants Angela Larochelle, Andrew Gavin, Eric Hughes, and Kathryn Conti, who contributed to the preparation of this volume by conducting bibliographic research and preparing material for publication. Special thanks also go to the research assistants whose contributions to previous editions continue to be evident in the eighth edition: Conor Allen, Wilton Dadmun, Alexander Miller, and Cassandra Treat.

Thanks also to Debra Henricks and the staff at McGraw-Hill, who have contributed in countless ways in making this volume as vibrant and effective as possible.

Richard P. Halgin
University of Massachusetts, Amherst

Editor of This Volume

RICHARD P. HALGIN is a professor of psychology in the Clinical Psychology Program at the University of Massachusetts–Amherst. He is coauthor, with Susan Krauss Whitbourne, of *Abnormal Psychology: Clinical Perspectives on Psychological Disorders,* 6th edition (McGraw-Hill, 2010); and coeditor, with Whitbourne, of *A Casebook in Abnormal Psychology: From the Files of Experts* (Oxford University Press, 1998). His list of publications also includes more than 50 articles and book chapters in the fields of psychotherapy, clinical supervision, and professional issues in psychology. He is a board-certified clinical psychologist, and he has over three decades of clinical, supervisory, and consulting experience. At the University of Massachusetts, his course in abnormal psychology is one of the most popular offerings on campus, attracting more than 500 students each semester. He has also taught the course on a regular basis at Amherst College. His teaching has been recognized at the university and national level: He was honored with the University of Massachusetts Distinguished Teaching Award and the Alumni Association's Distinguished Faculty Award and was also recognized by the Society for the Teaching of Psychology of the American Psychological Association. Upon appointment by the governor, he serves on the Board of Registration of Psychologists in Massachusetts.

> *To my wonderful wife, Lucille, whose love and support provide me with immeasurable amounts of energy, and to our children, Daniel and Kerry, whose values and achievements have been inspiring.*

Academic Advisory Board Members

Members of the Academic Advisory Board are instrumental in the final selection of articles for the *Taking Sides* series. Their review of the articles for content, level, and appropriateness provides critical direction to the editor(s) and staff. We think that you will find their careful consideration reflected in this book.

Correlation Guide

The *Taking Sides* series presents current issues in a debate-style format designed to stimulate student interest and develop critical thinking skills. Each issue is thoughtfully framed with an issue summary, an issue introduction, and a postscript. The pro and con essays—selected for their liveliness and substance—represent the arguments of leading scholars and commentators in their fields.

Taking Sides: Clashing Views in Abnormal Psychology, 8/e is an easy-to-use reader that presents issues on important topics such as *Posttraumatic Stress Disorder, cognitive enhancing medications,* and *forced treatment.* For more information on *Taking Sides* and other *McGraw-Hill Create™* titles, visit www.mcgrawhillcreate.com.

This convenient guide matches the issues in **Taking Sides: Clashing Views in Abnormal Psychology, 8/e** with **Abnormal Psychology, 6/e** by Nolen-Hoeksema.

Abnormal Psychology, 6/e	Taking Sides: Clashing Views in Abnormal Psychology, 8/e
Chapter 1: Looking at Abnormality	Do We Still Need Psychiatrists?
Chapter 2: Theories and Treatment of Abnormality	Do We Still Need Psychiatrists? Is Addiction a Brain Disease? Should Medical Marijuana Be Prescribed for the Treatment of Emotional Disorders? Should Memory-Dampening Drugs Be Used to Prevent and Treat Trauma in Combat Soldiers?
Chapter 3: Assessing and Diagnosing Abnormality	Is Attention-Deficit/Hyperactivity Disorder (ADHD) a Real Disorder? Is Gender Identity Disorder a Mental Illness? Is Posttraumatic Stress Disorder (PTSD) Overdiagnosed and Overtreated? Should Hypersexuality Disorder Be a Diagnosable Mental Disorder?
Chapter 4: The Research Endeavor	Can Positive Psychology Make Us Happier? Does Research Confirm That Abortion Is a Psychologically Benign Experience? Does Research Confirm That Violent Video Games Are Harmful to Minors? Is Forced Treatment of Seriously Mentally Ill Individuals Justifiable? Is Pornography Harmful?
Chapter 5: Trauma, Anxiety, Obsessive-Compulsive, and Related Disorders	Is Posttraumatic Stress Disorder (PTSD) Overdiagnosed and Overtreated? Should Memory-Dampening Drugs Be Used to Prevent and Treat Trauma in Combat Soldiers? Should Medical Marijuana Be Prescribed for the Treatment of Emotional Disorders?
Chapter 6: Somatic Symptom and Dissociative Disorders	Is Posttraumatic Stress Disorder (PTSD) Overdiagnosed and Overtreated?
Chapter 7: Mood Disorders and Suicide	Can Positive Psychology Make Us Happier? Does Research Confirm That Abortion Is a Psychologically Benign Experience? Is Posttraumatic Stress Disorder (PTSD) Overdiagnosed and Overtreated? Overdiagnosed and Overtreated? Should Memory-Dampening Drugs Be Used to Prevent and Treat Trauma in Combat Soldiers? Should Medical Marijuana Be Prescribed for the Treatment of Emotional Disorders?
Chapter 8: Schizophrenia Spectrum and Other Psychotic Disorders	Do We Still Need Psychiatrists? Is Forced Treatment of Seriously Mentally Ill Individuals Justifiable? Is the Use of Aversive Treatment an Inhumane Intervention for Psychologically Disordered Individuals? Must Mentally Ill Murderers Have a Rational Understanding of Why They Are Being Sentenced to Death?
Chapter 9: Personality Disorders	Should the United States Be More Restrictive of Gun Ownership?
Chapter 10: Neurodevelopmental and Neurocognitive Disorders	Are Energy Drinks with Alcohol Dangerous Enough to Ban? Does Research Confirm that Violent Video Games are Harmful to Minors? Is Attention-Deficit/Hyperactivity Disorder (ADHD) a Real Disorder? Must Mentally Ill Murderers Have a Rational Understanding of Why They Are Being Sentenced to Death? Should "Recreational" Drugs Be Legalized? Should "Smart Drugs" Be Used to Enhance Cognitive Functioning?

(Continued)

Abnormal Psychology, 6/e	Taking Sides: Clashing Views in Abnormal Psychology, 8/e
Chapter 11: Disruptive, Impulse Control, and Conduct Disorders	Are Energy Drinks with Alcohol Dangerous Enough to Ban? Does Research Confirm that Violent Video Games are Harmful to Minors? Is Attention-Deficit/Hyperactivity Disorder (ADHD) a Real Disorder? Should "Recreational" Drugs Be Legalized? Should "Smart Drugs" Be Used to Enhance Cognitive Functioning?
Chapter 12: Eating Disorders	
Chapter 13: Sexual Disorders	Is Gender Identity Disorder a Mental Illness? Is Pornography Harmful? Should Gay Conversion Therapy Be Prohibited by Law? Should Hypersexual Disorder Be a Diagnosable Mental Disorder?
Chapter 14: Substance Use and Gambling Disorders	Is Addiction a Brain Disease? Should Medical Marijuana Be Prescribed for the Treatment of Emotional Disorders? Should "Recreational" Drugs Be Legalized?
Chapter 15: Health Psychology	Are Energy Drinks with Alcohol Dangerous Enough to Ban? Can Positive Psychology Make Us Happier? Do We Still Need Psychiatrists? Is Addiction a Brain Disease? Is Forced Treatment of Seriously Mentally Ill Individuals Justifiable? Should Medical Marijuana Be Prescribed for the Treatment of Emotional Disorders? Should "Recreational" Drugs Be Legalized?
Chapter 16: Mental Health and the Law	Are Energy Drinks with Alcohol Dangerous Enough to Ban? Does Research Confirm That Abortion Is a Psychologically Benign Experience? Does Research Confirm that Violent Video Games are Harmful to Minors? Is the Use of Aversive Treatment an Inhumane Intervention for Psychologically Disordered Individuals? Must Mentally Ill Murderers Have a Rational Understanding of Why They Are Being Sentenced to Death? Should Gay Conversion Therapy Be Prohibited by Law? Should Medical Marijuana Be Prescribed for the Treatment of Emotional Disorders? Should "Recreational" Drugs Be Legalized? Should the United States Be More Restrictive of Gun Ownership?

This convenient guide matches the issues in **Taking Sides: Clashing Views in Abnormal Psychology, 8/e** with **Abnormal Psychology: Clinical Perspectives on Psychological Disorders, DSM-5 Update, 7/e** by Whitbourne/Halgin.

Abnormal Psychology: Clinical Perspectives on Psychological Disorders, DSM-5 Update, 7/e	Taking Sides: Clashing Views in Abnormal Psychology, 8/e
Chapter 1: Overview to Understanding Abnormal Behavior	Do We Still Need Psychiatrists?
Chapter 2: Diagnosis and Treatment	Can Positive Psychology Make Us Happier? Do We Still Need Psychiatrists? Is Addiction a Brain Disease? Is Attention-Deficit/Hyperactivity Disorder (ADHD) a Real Disorder? Is Gender Identity Disorder a Mental Illness? Is Posttraumatic Stress Disorder (PTSD) Overdiagnosed and Overtreated? Should Hypersexuality Disorder Be a Diagnosable Mental Disorder? Should Medical Marijuana Be Prescribed for the Treatment of Emotional Disorders? Should Memory-Dampening Drugs Be Used to Prevent and Treat Trauma in Combat Soldiers?
Chapter 3: Assessment	Is Addiction a Brain Disease? Is Attention-Deficit/Hyperactivity Disorder (ADHD) a Real Disorder? Is Posttraumatic Stress Disorder (PTSD) Overdiagnosed and Overtreated? Must Mentally Ill Murderers Have a Rational Understanding of Why They Are Being Sentenced to Death? Should Hypersexuality Disorder Be a Diagnosable Mental Disorder?
Chapter 4: Theoretical Perspectives	Is Addiction a Brain Disease? Should Memory-Dampening Drugs Be Used to Prevent and Treat Trauma in Combat Soldiers? Should Medical Marijuana Be Prescribed for the Treatment of Emotional Disorders?

Abnormal Psychology: Clinical Perspectives on Psychological Disorders, DSM-5 Update, 7/e	Taking Sides: Clashing Views in Abnormal Psychology, 8/e
Chapter 5: Neurodevelopmental Disorders	Are Energy Drinks with Alcohol Dangerous Enough to Ban? Does Research Confirm That Violent Video Games Are Harmful to Minors? Is Addiction a Brain Disease? Is Attention-Deficit/Hyperactivity Disorder (ADHD) a Real Disorder? Should Gay Conversion Therapy Be Prohibited by Law? Should "Recreational" Drugs Be Legalized? Should "Smart Drugs" Be Used to Enhance Cognitive Functioning?
Chapter 6: Schizophrenia Spectrum and Other Psychotic Disorders	Do We Still Need Psychiatrists? Is Forced Treatment of Seriously Mentally Ill Individuals Justifiable? Is the Use of Aversive Treatment an Inhumane Intervention for Psychologically Disordered Individuals? Must Mentally Ill Murderers Have a Rational Understanding of Why They Are Being Sentenced to Death?
Chapter 7: Depressive and Bipolar Disorders	Can Positive Psychology Make Us Happier? Do We Still Need Psychiatrists? Does Research Confirm That Abortion Is a Psychologically Benign Experience? Should Medical Marijuana Be Prescribed for the Treatment of Emotional Disorders?
Chapter 8: Anxiety, Obsessive-Compulsive, and Trauma and Stressor-Related Disorders	Is Posttraumatic Stress Disorder (PTSD) Overdiagnosed and Overtreated? Should Memory-Dampening Drugs Be Used to Prevent and Treat Trauma in Combat Soldiers? Should Medical Marijuana Be Prescribed for the Treatment of Emotional Disorders?
Chapter 9: Dissociative and Somatic Symptom Disorders	Is Posttraumatic Stress Disorder (PTSD) Overdiagnosed and Overtreated?
Chapter 10: Feeding and Eating Disorders; Elimination Disorders; Sleep-Wake Disorders; and Disruptive, Impulse-Control, and Conduct Disorders	Are Energy Drinks with Alcohol Dangerous Enough to Ban? Does Research Confirm that Violent Video Games Are Harmful to Minors? Is Attention-Deficit/Hyperactivity Disorder (ADHD) a Real Disorder? Should "Recreational" Drugs Be Legalized? Should "Smart Drugs" Be Used to Enhance Cognitive Functioning?
Chapter 11: Paraphilic Disorders, Sexual Dysfunctions, and Gender Dysphoria	Is Gender Identity Disorder a Mental Illness? Is Pornography Harmful? Should Gay Conversion Therapy Be Prohibited by Law? Should Hypersexual Disorder Be a Diagnosable Mental Disorder?
Chapter 12: Substance-Related and Addictive Disorders	Are Energy Drinks with Alcohol Dangerous Enough to Ban? Is Addiction a Brain Disease? Should Medical Marijuana Be Prescribed for the Treatment of Emotional Disorders? Should "Recreational" Drugs Be Legalized?
Chapter 13: Neurocognitive Disorders	Must Mentally Ill Murderers Have a Rational Understanding of Why They Are Being Sentenced to Death? Should "Smart Drugs" Be Used to Enhance Cognitive Functioning?
Chapter 14: Personality Disorders	Should the United States Be More Restrictive of Gun Ownership?
Chapter 15: Ethical and Legal Issues	Are Energy Drinks with Alcohol Dangerous Enough to Ban? Does Research Confirm That Abortion Is a Psychologically Benign Experience? Does Research Confirm That Violent Video Games Are Harmful to Minors? Is Forced Treatment of Seriously Mentally Ill Individuals Justifiable? Is the Use of Aversive Treatment an Inhumane Intervention for Psychologically Disordered Individuals? Must Mentally Ill Murderers Have a Rational Understanding of Why They Are Being Sentenced to Death? Should Gay Conversion Therapy Be Prohibited by Law? Should Medical Marijuana Be Prescribed for the Treatment of Emotional Disorders? Should "Recreational" Drugs Be Legalized? Should the United States Be More Restrictive of Gun Ownership?

Topic Guide

This topic guide suggests how the selections in this book relate to the subjects covered in your course.

All issues and their articles that relate to each topic are listed below the bold-faced term.

Abortion

Does Research Confirm That Abortion Is a Psychologically Benign Experience?

Addiction

Is Addiction a Brain Disease?
Should Medical Marijuana Be Prescribed for the Treatment of Emotional Disorders?
Should "Recreational" Drugs Be Legalized?

Attention Deficit/Hyperactivity Disorder (ADHD)

Is Attention-Deficit/Hyperactivity Disorder (ADHD) a Real Disorder?

Cognition

Should "Smart Drugs" Be Used to Enhance Cognitive Functioning?

Deviant Behavior

Does Research Confirm That Violent Video Games Are Harmful to Minors?
Is Pornography Harmful?

Ethics

Is Forced Treatment of Seriously Mentally Ill Individuals Justifiable?
Is the Use of Aversive Treatment an Inhumane Intervention for Psychologically Disordered Individuals?
Must Mentally Ill Murderers Have a Rational Understanding of Why They Are Being Sentenced to Death?
Should Gay Conversion Therapy Be Prohibited by Law?
Should Medical Marijuana Be Prescribed for the Treatment of Emotional Disorders?
Should the United States Be More Restrictive of Gun Ownership?

Health

Are Energy Drinks with Alcohol Dangerous Enough to Ban?
Can Positive Psychology Make Us Happier?
Is Addiction a Brain Disease?
Should Medical Marijuana Be Prescribed for the Treatment of Emotional Disorders?
Should "Recreational" Drugs Be Legalized?

Media

Does Research Confirm That Violent Video Games Are Harmful to Minors?

Medication

Do We Still Need Psychiatrists?
Should Medical Marijuana Be Prescribed for the Treatment of Emotional Disorders?

Should Memory-Dampening Drugs Be Used to Prevent and Treat Trauma in Combat Soldiers?
Should "Recreational" Drugs Be Legalized?
Should "Smart Drugs" Be Used to Enhance Cognitive Functioning?

Mental Illness

Do We Still Need Psychiatrists?
Is Attention-Deficit/Hyperactivity Disorder (ADHD) a Real Disorder?
Is Forced Treatment of Seriously Mentally Ill Individuals Justifiable?
Is Gender Identity Disorder a Mental Illness?
Is Posttraumatic Stress Disorder (PTSD) Overdiagnosed and Overtreated?
Is the Use of Aversive Treatment an Inhumane Intervention for Psychologically Disordered Individuals?
Must Mentally Ill Murderers Have a Rational Understanding of Why They Are Being Sentenced to Death?
Should Hypersexuality Disorder Be a Diagnosable Mental Disorder?

Posttraumatic Stress Disorder (PTSD)

Is Posttraumatic Stress Disorder (PTSD) Overdiagnosed and Overtreated?
Should Memory-Dampening Drugs Be Used to Prevent and Treat Trauma in Combat Soldiers?

Research

Can Positive Psychology Make Us Happier?
Does Research Confirm That Abortion Is a Psychologically Benign Experience?
Does Research Confirm That Violent Video Games Are Harmful to Minors?
Is Forced Treatment of Seriously Mentally Ill Individuals Justifiable?
Is Pornography Harmful?
Should "Smart Drugs" Be Used to Enhance Cognitive Functioning?

Sexuality and Gender

Is Gender Identity Disorder a Mental Illness?
Is Pornography Harmful?
Should Gay Conversion Therapy Be Prohibited by Law?
Should Hypersexual Disorder Be a Diagnosable Mental Disorder?

Therapy

Can Positive Psychology Make Us Happier?
Is Forced Treatment of Seriously Mentally Ill Individuals Justifiable?
Is Posttraumatic Stress Disorder (PTSD) Overdiagnosed and Overtreated?
Is the Use of Aversive Treatment an Inhumane Intervention for Psychologically Disordered Individuals?
Should Medical Marijuana Be Prescribed for the Treatment of Emotional Disorders?
Should Memory-Dampening Drugs Be Used to Prevent and Treat Trauma in Combat Soldiers?

Trauma

Is Posttraumatic Stress Disorder (PTSD) Overdiagnosed and Overtreated?

Introduction

What's "Abnormal" about Abnormal Psychology?

The field of abnormal psychology lends itself well to a discussion of controversial issues because of the inherent difficulty involved in defining the concept of "abnormal." The definition of abnormality is contingent on a myriad of influences that include cultural, historical, geographical, societal, interpersonal, and intrapersonal factors. What is considered everyday behavior in one culture might be regarded as bizarre in another. What was acceptable at one point in time might seem absurd in contemporary society. What seems customary in one region, even in one section of a large city, might be viewed as outrageous elsewhere. Even on a very personal level, one person's typical style of emotional expression might be experienced by another person as odd and disruptive. This introductory essay looks at some of the complex issues involved in defining and understanding abnormality and, in doing so, will set the stage for the controversial issues that follow. With this theoretical foundation, you will be better equipped to tackle the thorny issues in this volume and to develop an approach for reaching your own conclusions about these controversies.

Defining Abnormality

One of the best ways to begin a discussion of the complexity of defining abnormality is by considering our own behavior. Think about an outlandish costume that you wore to a Halloween party and the fun you had engaging in this completely normal behavior. Now imagine wearing the same costume to class the following day, and think about the reactions you would have received. What seemed so normal on the evening of October 31 would have been considered bizarre on the morning of November 1. Only a day later, in a different context, you would have been regarded as abnormal, and your behavior would have been viewed as both disturbed and disturbing. Consider another example: Recall a time in which you were intensely emotional, perhaps weeping profusely at a funeral. If you were to display similar emotionality a few days later in a class discussion, your behavior would cause considerable stir, and your classmates would be taken aback by the intensity of your emotions. Now consider a common behavior that is completely acceptable and expected in American culture, such as shaking a person's hand upon meeting. Did you know that in some cultures such behavior is regarded as rude and unacceptable? These simple examples highlight the ways in which the concept of "normal" is contingent on many factors. Because of the wide variability in definitions of what is abnormal, psychologists have spelled out criteria that can be used in determining abnormal human behavior. These criteria fall into four categories: distress, impairment, risk to self or other people, and socially and culturally unacceptable behavior.

Distress

I begin with the most personal criterion of abnormality because the experience of inner emotional distress is a universal phenomenon and a powerful way in which every person at some point in life feels different from everyone around them. Distress, the experience of emotional pain, is experienced in many ways, such as depression, anxiety, and cognitive confusion. When people feel any of these responses to an extreme degree, they feel abnormal, and they typically look for ways to alleviate their feelings of inner pain. Some of the issues in this book illustrate the various ways in which different people respond to similar life events. For example, people who have been diagnosed with an emotionally devastating case of cancer typically reach out for any and all interventions that will help them battle the disease. One such intervention involves participating in psychotherapy with the aim of extending life, although some experts debate the effectiveness of such treatment. In recent years efforts have been made to find medications that alleviate the memories associated with the experience of a trauma; one issue addresses the possible benefits as well as the disadvantages of dampening memories of a traumatic experience.

Impairment

People who are intensely distressed are likely to find it difficult to fulfill the everyday responsibilities of life. When people are very depressed or anxious, they typically have a difficult time concentrating on their studies, attending to their work responsibilities, or even interacting with other people. Impairment involves a reduction in a person's ability to function at an optimal or even an average level. Although distress and impairment often go hand in hand, they do not always; a person can be seriously impaired but feel no particular distress. This is often the case with substance abuse, in which people are incapable of the basic tasks of physical coordination and cognitive clarity but feel euphoric. Some of the debates in this book address the issue of impairment and the difficulty in assessing the extent to which people are impaired. For example, one issue focuses on the question of whether addiction is a brain disease. This issue has relevance to issues about the extent to which drug-addicted individuals are capable, physiologically and psychologically, of controlling their self-destructive addictive behaviors. Another debate focuses on the question of whether medical marijuana should be prescribed for the treatment of emotional disorders.

Risk to Self or Others

Sometimes people act in ways that cause risk to themselves or others. In this context, risk refers to danger or threat to the well-being of a person. In the case of suicide or self-mutilating behavior, the personal risk is evident. In the case of outwardly directed violence, rape, or even emotional exploitation, the risk is to other people. Although the issue of risk to self or others might not seem controversial on the surface, there are many facets of risk that provoke debate. For example, does an individual have the right to engage in self-injurious, perhaps even life-ending, behavior, or does society have a right, even a responsibility, to intervene? As addressed in two of the issues, do individuals who are at risk of harming other people (i.e., by means of violence) or themselves (i.e., self-starvation) have the right to refuse intervention, or do health professionals have a responsibility to prevent such individuals from engaging in such potentially dangerous behavior? To what extremes should clinicians go in order to behaviorally control the self-injurious, and potentially fatal, behaviors of severely disturbed children and adults? Other potentially harmful behaviors are also discussed, such as engaging in sports such as football which present a considerable risk of concussions. The question is raised about whether such sports should be outlawed for children. Another issue addresses the question of whether harsh aversive treatments are forms of torture or lifesaving interventions.

Socially and Culturally Unacceptable Behavior

Another criterion for defining abnormality pertains to the social or cultural context in which behavior occurs. In some instances, behavior that is regarded as odd within a given culture, society, or subgroup is common elsewhere. For example, some people from Mediterranean cultures believe in a phenomenon called *mal de ojo*, or "evil eye," in which the ill will of one person can negatively affect another. According to this belief, receiving the evil eye from a person can cause a range of disturbing physical and emotional symptoms; consequently, individuals in these cultures often take steps to ward off the power of another person's evil eye. Such beliefs might be regarded as strangely superstitious, almost delusional, in American culture, but they are considered common elsewhere. Even more subtle contexts can influence the extent to which a behavior is defined as abnormal, as illustrated by the example of the Halloween costume mentioned previously. This book features issues related to social and cultural variables, such as whether violent video games promote violent behavior in young people. Some people in society view gender-variant behavior as abnormal. At one extreme are those who consider gender identity disorder a mental illness, and at the other end are those who consider such a perspective to represent a stigmatization of mental illness on people who meet no scientific definition of mental disorder. Also in the realm of sexuality are questions about whether hypersexual behavior should be viewed as a mental disorder and whether gay conversion therapy should be prohibited by law.

What Causes Abnormality?

In trying to understand why people act and feel in ways that are regarded as abnormal, social scientists consider three dimensions: biological, psychological, and sociocultural. Rather than viewing these dimensions as independent, however, experts discuss the relative contribution of each dimension in influencing human behavior, and they use the term *biopsychosocial* to capture these intertwining forces. In the context of abnormality, the biopsychosocial conceptualization of human behavior conveys the sense that abnormal behavior arises from a complex set of determinants in the body, the mind, and the social context.

Biological Causes

During the past several decades scientists have made tremendous progress in discovering ways in which human behavior is influenced by a range of biological variables. In the realm of abnormal psychology, the contributions of the biological sciences have been especially impressive, as researchers have developed increasing understanding of the ways in which abnormal behavior is determined by bodily physiology and genetic makeup. As is the case with many medical disorders, various mental disorders, such as depression, run in families. Mental health researchers have made great efforts to understand why certain mental illnesses are passed from one generation to another and also to understand why certain disorders are not inherited even in identical twin pairs when one of the twins has the condition and the other does not.

In addition to understanding the role of genetics, mental health experts also consider the ways in which physical functioning can cause or aggravate the experience of psychological symptoms. Experts know that many medical conditions can cause a person to feel or act in ways that are abnormal. For example, a medical abnormality in the thyroid gland can cause wide variations in mood and emotionality. Brain damage resulting from a head trauma, even a slight one, can result in bizarre behavior and intense emotionality. Thus the question has been raised about whether concussion-causing sports such as football should be outlawed for children. Similarly, the use of drugs or alcohol can cause people to act in extreme ways that neither they nor those who know them well would have ever imagined. Even exposure to environmental stimuli, such as toxic substances or allergens, can cause people to experience disturbing emotional changes and to act in odd or bizarre ways. Several issues in this book explore conditions in which biology plays a prominent causative role. For example, attention deficit/hyperactivity disorder (ADHD) is regarded as a disorder of the brain that interferes with a person's ability to pay attention or to control behavior.

Psychological Causes

Biology does not tell the entire story about the causes of mental disorders; many forms of emotional disturbance arise as a result of troubling life experiences. The experiences of life, even seemingly insignificant ones, can leave lasting marks on a person. In cases in which an experience involves trauma, such as rape or abuse, the impact can be emotionally disruptive throughout life, affecting a person's thoughts, behaviors, and even dreams.

In trying to understand the psychological causes of abnormality, social scientists and mental health clinicians consider a person's experiences. Not only do they focus on interpersonal interactions with other people that may have left a mark, but they also consider the inner life of the individual—thoughts and feelings that may cause distress or impairment. Some conditions arise from distorted perceptions and faulty ways of thinking. For example, highly sensitive people may misconstrue innocent comments by

acquaintances that cause obsessional worry about being disliked or demeaned. As a result, these people may respond to their acquaintances in hostile ways that perpetuate interpersonal difficulties and inner distress.

Sociocultural Causes

The term *sociocultural* refers to the various circles of social influence in the lives of people. The most immediate circle is composed of people with whom we interact in our immediate environment; for college students, this includes roommates, classmates, and coworkers. Moving beyond the immediate circle are people who inhabit the extended circle of relationships, such as family members back home or friends from high school. A third circle is composed of the people in our environments with whom we interact minimally and rarely by name, such as residents of our community or campus, whose standards, expectations, and behaviors influence our lives. A fourth circle is the much wider culture in which people live, such as American society.

Abnormal behavior can emerge from experiences in any of these social contexts. Troubled relationships with a roommate or family member can cause intense emotional distress. Involvement in an abusive relationship may initiate an interpersonal style in which the abused person becomes repeatedly caught up with people who are hurtful or damaging. Political turmoil, even on a relatively local level, can evoke emotions ranging from intense anxiety to incapacitating fear.

This book discusses several conditions in which sociocultural factors are significant. For example, one issue discusses the ways in which exposure to media violence may promote aggressive behavior.

The Biopsychosocial Perspective

From the discussion so far, it should be evident that most aspects of human behavior are determined by a complex of causes involving an interaction of biological, psychological, and sociocultural factors. As you read about the clinical conditions and mental disorders discussed in this book, it will be useful for you to keep the biopsychosocial perspective in mind, even in those discussions in which the authors seem narrowly focused. For example, a condition may be put forth as being biologically caused, leading the reader to believe that other influences play little or no role. Another condition may be presented as being so psychologically based that it is difficult to fathom the role that biology might play in causing or aggravating the condition. Other issues may be discussed almost exclusively in sociocultural terms, with minimal attention to the roles of biological and psychological factors. An intelligent discussion in the field of abnormal psychology is one that explores the relative importance of biological, psychological, and sociocultural influences. Such a discussion should avoid reductionistic thinking and simplistic explanations for complex human problems.

Why We View Behavior as "Abnormal"

In addition to understanding how to define abnormality and what causes abnormal behavior, it is important to understand how members of society view people who are abnormal and how this view affects people with emotional problems and mental disorders. Many people in our society discriminate against and reject mentally disturbed people. In so doing, they aggravate one of the most profound aspects of dealing with mental disorder—the experience of stigma. A stigma is a label that causes certain people to be regarded as different and defective and to be set apart from mainstream members of society. Today, several decades after sociologist Erving Goffman brought the phenomenon of stigma to public attention, there is ample evidence in American society that people with mental disorders are regarded as different and are often deprived of the basic human right to respectful treatment.

It is common for people with serious psychological disorders, especially those who have been hospitalized, to experience profound and long-lasting emotional and social effects. People who suffer from serious psychological problems tend to think less of themselves because of these experiences, and they often come to believe many of the myths about themselves that are perpetuated in a society that lacks understanding about the nature of mental illness and psychological problems.

Although tremendous efforts have been undertaken to humanize the experiences of people with psychological problems and mental disorders, deeply rooted societal reactions still present obstacles for many emotionally distressed people. Controversies continue to rage about the systems of diagnosis and assessment used by mental health professionals, about the validity of certain clinical conditions, and about the efficacy of various psychotherapeutic and medical interventions. As you read both sides of the debates in this book, it is important that you keep in mind the strong personal beliefs that influence, and possibly bias, the statements of each writer and to consider the ways in which various societal forces are intertwined with the comments of the author.

The most powerful force within the field of mental health during the twentieth century was the medical model, upon which many forms of intervention are based. This book frequently mentions a system of diagnosis developed by the American Psychiatric Association that has been revised several times during the past 50 years. This system is published in a book called the *Diagnostic and Statistical Manual of Mental Disorders*. The most recent version is the fifth edition, which is abbreviated DSM-5. In this medical model diagnostic system, mental disorders are construed as diseases that require treatment. There are both advantages and disadvantages to this approach.

Not only does DSM-5 rely on the medical model, but it also uses a categorical approach for most conditions. A categorical approach assumes that disorders and diseases fall into distinct categories. For example, the medical disease pneumonia is a condition that fits into a category of diseases involving the respiratory system. In corresponding fashion, conditions involving depression fit into a category of depressive disorders, and conditions involving anxiety fit into a category of anxiety disorders. However, there are limitations to the categorical approach. For one thing, psychological disorders are not neatly separable from each other or from normal functioning. For example, where is the dividing line between normal sadness and clinical depression? Furthermore, many disorders seem linked to each other in fundamental ways. In a state of agitated depression, for example, an individual suffers from both anxiety and saddened mood. The editors of DSM-5 struggled with the limitations of the categorical approach and made some changes from previous DSM editions. For example, DSM-5 now includes autism spectrum disorder (ASD) which combines four previously designated categorical disorders, and views them along a spectrum. Also, the most recent diagnostic volume takes a different view of substance related disorders in applying the diagnosis of substance use disorder, which combines previously designated diagnoses of abuse and dependence into a single spectrum of eleven symptoms.

Several of the conditions and interventions discussed in this book have been debated for years. As you read about these issues, it will be helpful for you to keep in mind the context in which these debates have arisen. Some debates arise because of turf battles between professions. For example, psychiatrists may be more inclined to endorse the diagnostic system of the American Psychiatric Association (DSM-5) and to support biological explanations and somatic interventions for mental disorders. Psychologists, on the other hand, may urge mental health professionals to take a broader point of view and to proceed more cautiously in turning to biological explanations and causes.

The Influence of Theoretical Perspective on the Choice of Intervention

Although impressive advances have been achieved in determining why people develop various mental disorders, understanding how best to treat their conditions remains limited and also powerfully influenced by the ideological biases of many clinicians and researchers. For much of the twentieth century, various interventions emerged from markedly different schools of thought, each approach being tied to one of the three major realms—biological, psychological, or sociocultural. But how are biological, psychological, and sociocultural frameworks used in determining choice of intervention?

Within the biological perspective, disturbances in emotions, behavior, and cognitive processes are viewed as being caused by abnormalities in the functioning of the body, such as the brain and nervous system or the endocrine system. Treatments involve a range of somatic therapies, the most common of which is medication, the most extreme of which involves psychosurgery. Several issues in this book focus on debates about reliance on biological explanations and interventions, such as the issue on ADHD, and the issues on medications, including the use of marijuana to treat emotional disorders.

The realm of psychological theories contains numerous approaches, although three schools of thought emerged as most prominent during the second half of the twentieth century: psychodynamic, humanistic, and behavioral. Proponents of the psychodynamic perspective emphasize unconscious determinants of behavior and recommend the use of techniques involving exploration of the developmental causes of behavior and the interpretation of unconscious influences on thoughts, feelings, and behavior.

At the core of the humanistic perspective is the belief that human motivation is based on an inherent tendency to strive for self-fulfillment and meaning in life. Humanistic therapists use a client-centered approach in which they strive to treat clients with unconditional positive regard and empathy. Mental health professionals are called upon to act in ways that are more client-centered as they deal with issues pertaining to gender identity, trauma, or abortion.

According to the behavioral perspective, abnormality is caused by faulty learning experiences, with a subset of behavioral theory focusing on cognitive functions such as maladaptive thought processes. Because behaviorists and cognitive theorists believe that disturbance results from faulty learning or distorted thinking, intervention focuses on teaching clients more adaptive ways of thinking and behaving. Some of the discussions in this book focus on the ways in which behavioral and cognitive approaches might be preferable to medical approaches to conditions such as ADHD, and the use of aversive techniques for treating self-injurious individuals.

Clinicians working within sociocultural models emphasize the ways that individuals are influenced by people, social institutions, and social forces. According to this viewpoint, psychological problems can emerge from social contexts ranging from the family to society. In a corresponding vein, treatments are determined by the nature of the group. Thus, problems rooted within family systems would be treated with family therapy; societal problems caused by discrimination or inadequate care of the mentally ill would be dealt with through enactment of social policy initiatives. Several issues in this volume touch upon sociocultural influences, and how best to respond to survivors of life-threatening trauma.

Keeping the Issues in Perspective

In evaluating the content of the writings in this book, it is important to keep in mind who the writers are and what their agendas might be. Most of the contributors are distinguished figures in the fields of mental health, ethics, and law. They are regarded as clear and influential thinkers who have important messages to convey. However, it would be naive to think that any writer, particularly when addressing a controversial topic, is free of bias.

It is best to read each issue with an understanding of the forces that might influence the development of a particular bias. For example, as physicians, psychiatrists have been trained in the medical model, with its focus on biological causes for problems and somatic interventions. Nonphysician mental health professionals may be more inclined to focus on interpersonal and intrapersonal causes and interventions. Lawyers and ethicists are more likely to be further removed from questions of etiology, focusing instead on what they believe is justified according to the law or right according to ethical standards.

As you read about the issues facing mental health clinicians and researchers, you are certain to be struck by the challenges that these professionals face. You may also be struck by the powerful emotion expressed by the authors who discuss their views on topics in this field. Because psychological stresses and problems are an inherent part of human existence, many discussions about abnormal psychology are emotionally charged. At some point in life, most people have a brush with serious emotional problems, either directly or indirectly. This is a frightening prospect for many people, one that engenders worried expectations and intense reactions. By acknowledging our vulnerability to disruptive emotional experiences, however, we can think about the ways in which we would want clinicians to treat us. As you read the issues in this book, place yourself in the position of an individual in the process of being assessed, diagnosed, and treated for an emotional difficulty or mental disorder.

Before you take a side in each debate, consider how the issue might be personally relevant to you at some point in life. You may be surprised to discover that you respond in different ways to issues that might have special salience to yourself, as opposed to random people somewhere else. By imagining yourself being personally affected by a professional's controversial opinion regarding one or more of the debates in this book, you will find yourself immersed in the discussions about issues for which there is no clear right or wrong.

Richard P. Halgin
University of Massachusetts, Amherst

Unit 1

UNIT

Psychological Conditions and Treatments

*A*t the heart of abnormal psychology are the psychological conditions and mental disorders for which people seek psychological treatment. At the center of many debates regarding psychiatric diagnosis is the Diagnostic and Statistical Manual of Mental Disorders, *Fifth Edition (DSM-5), published in May 2013. Some experts have been harshly critical of DSM-5, contending that its inclusion of new diagnoses may have harmful unintended consequences due to a lack of scientific rigor in the formulation of these diagnoses. Most psychological conditions included in DSM-5 are widely recognized as psychological disorders, but some conditions engender considerable debate. Although symptoms of debilitating depression or disabling anxiety warrant a psychiatric diagnosis, critics have raised issues about the validity of some diagnoses and have questioned the extent to which some conditions are overdiagnosed, and consequently overtreated. For example, are attentional difficulties and high levels of activity reflective of a mental disorder (i.e., ADHD) or reflections of typical childhood behavior, albeit at the far end of the normal spectrum? In light of recent wars, much attention has been given to posttraumatic stress disorder, but questions have arisen as to whether this condition has been overly diagnosed. There is debate about whether gender variant conditions are mental disorders or simply less common presentations of human identity. Questions have also been raised about the extent to which certain behaviors and ways of thinking enhance or detract from quality of life. For example, does positive psychology really make people feel happier?*

Selected, Edited, and with Issue Framing Material by:
Richard P. Halgin, *University of Massachusetts, Amherst*

ISSUE

Should Hypersexual Disorder Be a Diagnosable Mental Disorder?

YES: Robert Weiss, from "Sexual Addiction, Hypersexual Disorder and the DSM-5: Myth or Legitimate Diagnosis?" *Counselor* Magazine (2012)

NO: David J. Ley, from "Is Sex Addiction a Legitimate Disorder?" *Addiction Professional* (2013)

Learning Outcomes
After reading this issue, you will be able to: • Evaluate the arguments for and against including hypersexual disorder in the DSM.   • Discuss the extent to which sexual behavior that is above normal in frequency and pursuit should be viewed as pathological.   • Consider the issue of whether hypersexual disorder has been promoted by some clinicians and publishers as somewhat of a cottage industry to attract clients and customers.   • Discuss the question of whether scientific research supports the validity and reliability of hypersexual disorder.   • Consider criteria for determining the dividing line between normal and abnormal sexual behavior.

ISSUE SUMMARY

YES: Robert Weiss asserts that since the Internet has facilitated access to affordable, easy links to intensely pleasurable sexual content and anonymous sex, mental health professionals are seeing a corresponding increase in the number of people struggling with sexual and romantic addictions. Although the editors of DSM-5 decided against including hypersexual disorder in the nomenclature, Weiss views this condition as a legitimate and serious addictive behavior that leads to a wide array of life problems.

NO: David Ley criticizes the notion of sexual addiction, viewing such labeling as being promoted by the "sex addiction industry," which has benefited from extremely effective and timely marketing efforts. Ley contends that for decades sex addiction proponents have been challenged in the academic press to produce scientific research to back up their theories. The research studies that they have produced, however, are criticized as subject to severe sample bias, and being based largely on anecdotal reports.

In the years leading up to the publication of DSM-5 in 2013, there had been much discussion about whether to reintroduce a diagnosis pertaining to the compulsive pursuit of sexual gratification. A few decades earlier DSM-III-R included sexual addiction as a descriptor under the more general diagnosis of sexual disorders (not otherwise specified), but this was dropped in subsequent editions due to a lack of scientific evidence about the reliability and

validity of this diagnosis. However, in those intervening decades the emergence of the Internet has had a tremendous impact on the pursuit of sexual pleasure in the form of online pornography, social media, and access to sexual interactions with other people. In research and in clinical publications attention was increasingly given by scholars and clinicians to the incidence of cases in which individuals had become overwhelmingly consumed by the pursuit of sexual gratification. Thus, it was not surprising that the editors of DSM-5 assigned a workgroup to develop criteria for this condition which presumably would meet the criteria for being a mental disorder.

Hypersexual disorder was proposed as a DSM-5 diagnosis and consisted of a set of criteria involving recurrent or intense sexual fantasies, urges, or behaviors for at least six months. Individuals with this condition experience clinically significant personal distress or impairment in social, occupational, and general life functioning. Their behavior may focus on masturbation, pornography, sexual behavior with consenting adults, cybersex, telephone sex, strip clubs, prostitutes, etc.

Although the general consensus among mental health professionals and media observers of the DSM-5 development process was that hypersexual disorder would be included in the manual, last-minute politics apparently derailed the effort and the diagnosis was dropped. Additionally surprising was the fact that the condition was not even included in the appendix of the DSM, which is composed of conditions warranting further study. Thus, the question has gained some traction about whether hypersexual disorder should be regarded as a mental disorder, or whether this is a case of pathologizing normal human behavior to fuel an industry of professional clinicians, self-help books, online services that provide advice, and therapy for these individuals.

At the time that social worker Robert Weiss wrote his article supporting the validity of the diagnosis of hypersexual disorder, DSM-5 had not been finalized. Even

though he expressed doubts about this disorder ultimately being included in the diagnostic manual, he explained his rationale for supporting its inclusion. He cites evidence that hypersexual disorder (sexual addiction) is a legitimate, serious, and not uncommon clinical condition for which escalating numbers of men and women seek clinical and self-help support in their effort to alter their out-of-control sexual behavior. Weiss contends that a DSM diagnosis is needed to help clinicians identify individuals who struggle with compulsive, addictive, and impulsive sexual disorders so they can be directed toward appropriate treatments.

David Ley disagrees with the notion that sex addiction is a legitimate disorder, an idea he views as embedded in American culture despite a lack of scientific evidence. He attributes the rise of this behavior as a diagnosable addiction to the mental health and sexuality fields which promote hundreds of self-help books, treatment programs, and 12-step groups that support the idea that sex can be addictive and destructive. Ley asserts that the "sex addiction industry" has benefited from extremely effective and timely marketing efforts which they characterize as public education campaigns. He states that for decades sexual addiction proponents have been challenged to produce scientific research to back up their theories. What they have produced, asserts Ley, are deficient articles based on anecdotal reports lacking in scientific rigor. He states that the term "addiction" is simply too easy to use, when what is needed are empirically supported and culturally sensitive treatments.

YES

Robert Weiss

Sexual Addiction, Hypersexual Disorder and the DSM-5: Myth or Legitimate Diagnosis?

There will always be controversy—as there should be—when any form of inherently healthy human behavior such as eating, exercise or sex is clinically designated as pathological. And while the power to "label" must always be carefully wielded to avoid turning social, religious or moral judgments into diagnoses (as was homosexuality in the *DSM-I* and *DSM-II*), equal care must be taken to not avoid researching and creating diagnostic criteria for non-pathological healthy behaviors should they go awry due to underlying psychological deficits and/or early trauma.

Is Sex Addiction Real?

Preliminary sexual addiction research in the 1980s suggested that approximately 3% to 5% of the adult population then struggled with some form of addictive sexual behavior. The individuals studied at that time were a self-selected, mostly male group who entered residential treatment due to negative consequences experienced from self-described "years of being hooked" on magazine and video porn, multiple affairs, prostitution, old-fashioned phone sex and similar behaviors. More recent peer-reviewed, tier-one research indicates that the problem of sexual addiction is escalating, and sexual addiction therapists today almost universally report that their treatment population is both skewing into younger age groups and becoming more evenly distributed among men and women.

Since the late 1990s, clinical literature has indicated that this increase in addictive sexual behavior is closely correlated to the increasing speed with which we are able to access intensely stimulating graphic pornography and anonymous sexual liaisons via the Internet. Thus, it seems highly likely (though updated research is needed) that today's laptops, smartphones, and other mobile devices are significantly contributing to the escalating numbers of vulnerable adults addicted to both pornography and the casual sexual hookups available anywhere, anytime—thanks to streaming video and "friend finder" smartphone apps. For instance, in 2012 nearly anyone with a smartphone can find a GPS-located sexual partner as readily as he or she can find a nearby Italian restaurant by logging on to Ashley Madison (11 million members) or Grindr (4 million members), two of the more popular friend-finder/sex-locater apps.

The simple fact is our ongoing *tech-connect* boom has dramatically increased the average person's ability to affordably and anonymously access endless amounts of highly graphic pornography, casual sexual experiences and online prostitution. This escalating proliferation of nearly instantaneous, easily accessed, intensely arousing sexual content and connections, while a life-enhancing source of sexual pleasure for some, can and does cause tremendous problems for those with pre-existing addictive disorders, social inhibition, early trauma, and attachment and mood disorders, as well as the more profoundly mentally and developmentally ill.

Ironically, at nearly the very same moment that sexual addiction began its technology generated escalation in the early 1990s, the American Psychiatric Association (APA) removed the term "sexual addiction" as a diagnostic indicator when publishing the *DSM-IV* (and later the *DSM-IV-TR*). Consequently, the past 25 years have wrought a rather anguished, aggressively argued, somewhat personality driven and inconsistent history in the attempts of the psychiatric, addiction, legal and mental health communities to accurately research, label and distinguish the problem of excessive adult consensual sexual behavior. During this period, potentially useful "clinical" diagnostic and treatment models with names such as "Sexual Addiction" (Carnes, 1983; 1991), "Sexual Compulsion" (Coleman, 1990; 2003), "Out-of-Control Sexual Behavior" (Kinsey Institute), and "Sexual Disorder NOS with

Addictive Features" (*DSM-II*, 1968) have been used somewhat interchangeably among informed clinicians, 12-step communities and the general public. But in 2012, without a formal, universally accepted diagnosis, this language has about as much clinical credibility as do "Nymphomania" and "Don Juan-ism," the terms used to describe similar issues over a century ago.

Of related concern is the fact that the sex therapy, sex offender and sex addiction fields, all highly evolved specialties that should be working together with shared knowledge and support, are literally at an unresolved and definitive split over whether sexual addiction even exists! One current example is the recent book that spends 250 or so well-written pages implying that sexual addiction/sexual compulsion/hypersexuality is merely:

a) *a false clinical mirror for a repressive, sex negative and moralistic culture*
b) *a fake diagnosis that uses repressive, moralistic judgments to make money, fame and fortune for savvy but unethical clinicians*
c) *a backlash against healthy male sexuality*
d) *an attempt to use a clinical term to reign in less culturally acceptable consensual sexual choices*
e) *all of the above*

The fact that a book like this has garnered attention highlights the fact that the lack of a formal diagnosis has allowed sexual addiction to become an ongoing catalyst for professional disinformation, clinical acrimony and shared disrespect—all in an area of addiction and mental health care that is in great need of integrative, holistic treatment goals, policy, coordinated research and clinical direction.

Sex Addiction and the DSM: A Brief History

In 1987 the APA's *Statistical Manual of Mental Health Disorders* (*DSM-III-R*) added for the first time the concept of "sexual addiction" as a term that could be applied when useful to clarify the more general diagnosis of "Sexual Disorders NOS (Not Otherwise Specified)." The *DSM-III-R* then explained that this descriptor could be utilized if the individual being assessed displayed "distress about a pattern of repeated sexual conquests or other forms of nonparaphilic sexual addiction, involving a succession of people who exist only as things to be used." While not yet a full diagnosis at that time, as there were no specific criteria offered to detail this phenomenon, this was a documented early acknowledgement by the APA that some

individuals (those not in a manic state and/or influenced by recreational drugs), could nonetheless struggle with addictive sexual behavior patterns.

This early *DSM III-R* descriptor is, by the way, consistent with language commonly used by those clinicians now treating sex addicts and their spouses, who typically define sexual addiction as repetitive and problematic compulsive or impulsive sexual behavior patterns involving excessive shame, secrecy and/or abuse to self and/or others. Active sex addiction is understood to cause relationship, career, legal, emotional and physical health problems. Left untreated, sex addicts will most often continue their problem patterns of consensual sexual behavior despite repeated attempts to limit or eliminate them, even when facing a history of related, often escalating negative life consequences. And sex addicts engage in these behaviors with and without a related mood disorder or substance abuse problem. In other words, just like alcoholics and drug addicts, sex addicts come both with and without pre-existing conditions.

Unfortunately, subsequent and current versions of the *DSM* (the *DSM-IV* and *DSM-IV-TR*) retracted the above descriptor due to "insufficient research" and "lack of expert consensus," a decision that has left addiction specialists, psychotherapists and the burgeoning sexual recovery community with no accurate name for this problem. At present there are no formally acknowledged mental health criteria to accurately assess, diagnose, and treat men and women with problematic patterns of consensual adult sexual behavior. Despite this, American residential and outpatient psychotherapists and addiction counselors today report a marked increase in the number of clients seeking help for self-reported crises like "I find myself disappearing for multiple hours daily into online porn," or, "I feel lost on a never-ending treadmill of anonymous sexual hookups and affairs," or, "Anonymous sex and porn have led me to multiple drug and alcohol relapses."

What Is it Like To Be a Sex Addict?

Sex addicts experience a profound, self-induced neurochemical high when fantasizing about and preparing for a sexual act. They describe these feelings of arousal and intensity as akin to being in a "bubble" or trance. This is a time when intense anticipatory fantasy and euphoric recall induce an adrenaline-fueled, dopamine-driven, tunnel-visioned state during which it is increasingly less possible to think clearly and make good decisions. This excitement (which causes rapid heartbeat, shallow breathing, perspiration, pupil dilatation, feelings of euphoria, etc.) makes it nearly impossible to fully engage our prefrontal lobe, the portion of the brain utilized when making sound, intellectually based decisions. The experience of being "in the bubble" is similar to what drug addicts experience when they are on the way to their dealers' house, cash in hand—jittery, not thinking clearly and already "out of self" long before any substance actually enters their body. This trancelike, fantasy-fueled state does not allow for clear intellectual thought, but it does allow the individual to emotionally detach and dissociate from depression, anxiety and uncomfortable feelings related to past trauma and other life stressors—much like what happens to the alcoholic or drug addict when he or she begins the process of drinking or using. In other words, sex addicts abuse their own neurochemistry in much the same way that alcoholics abuse alcohol and drug addicts abuse cocaine, heroin or crystal meth.

Sex addicts describe this anticipatory state of consciousness as a more powerful experience than the sex itself—and it can certainly last longer. (In the same way, compulsive gamblers say that playing is a more powerful experience than winning.) For sex addicts, actually having sex and the resulting orgasm is not the primary objective of acting out. The subconscious meta-goal is to lose oneself for as long as possible by dissociating into the excitement that comes from playing the game. In fact, achieving orgasm is often delayed for an extended period, as it marks the endpoint of the addict's emotional high. After orgasm the individual's neurochemistry returns to baseline, and he or she is then left with the same emotional challenges and stressors that led to the addict's acting out in the first place. Ultimately, the real goal for the sex addict is to lose himself or herself in the ether of euphoric emotional (as opposed to genital) arousal for as long as possible.

Who Is a Sex Addict?

Being sexually addicted is not positively correlated to being male or female, gay or straight, Asian, African or Caucasian, rich or poor, smart, good-looking, successful or anything else. Sex addicts don't stop acting out when they enter a primary relationship—at least not for long—nor do they stop if they become a parent or find their dream job. In a typical example of addict powerlessness, sex addicts often describe themselves as thinking and saying things like, *This is the last time that I am going to go to this sex shop, download that sex-finder app, see my affair partner, or lose time on that porn site.* But ultimately, because they are "out of control" with their sexual behavior, they return to the same or similar sexual situations despite the fact that these behaviors often produce negative life consequences and frequently go against their underlying values and

beliefs. As such, most sex addicts end up leading secretive "double-lives," keeping their sexual acting out hidden from friends and family alike, and living compartmentalized existences. To tolerate this duality, sex addicts, like all addicted people, create an ever-expanding web of lies, secrecy, manipulation, rationalization and denial. This disintegrated lifestyle often leads to associated mood disorders, relationship dysfunction and eventual life crises.

Typical sexual addict "acting out" behaviors include, but are not limited to, the following:

- Repeated patterns of multiple affairs and brief "serial" relationships
- Endless hours spent abusing Internet and other pornography
- Compulsive masturbation, with or without pornography
- Regularly recurring (and hidden) attendance at strip clubs, adult bookstores and related environments
- Consistent hiring of (or becoming) prostitutes, escorts and sensual massage practitioners
- Seeking to feel loved, adored and special through interaction with prostitutes, multiple affair partners and similar nonintimate encounters
- Obsessive online and smartphone searches for sexual/romantic partners, with or without a subsequent hookup
- Patterns of anonymous or casual sex with people met online, via smartphone hookup apps or in person
- Unsafe and/or physically dangerous sexual practices
- Involvement and/or membership in sexually focused environments (sex clubs, swingers clubs, bathhouses, etc.)
- Seeking out and having sex regardless of potential immediate or long-term consequences to self or others

Sex addicts typically experience:

- Loss of control over escalating sexual fantasies and behaviors
- Increasing frequency and intensity of sexual thoughts and behaviors over time (escalation)
- Significant and escalating amounts of time lost to sexual fantasy and acting out
- Depleted creativity, intimacy and/or recreation (outside of sex and the search for sex)
- Irritability, defensiveness and anger when confronted about or when attempting to stop sexual behaviors (withdrawal)
- Social and emotional isolation

- Related mood and relationship disorders
- Lack of empathy for how sexual behavior may affect spouses and partners
- Negative consequences (relationship, emotional, physical, financial, legal, etc.) directly related to sexual acting out

What Sexual Addiction Is Not

Sexual addiction is not determined utilizing a predetermined moral or religious agenda, nor is it diagnosed simply because one's sexuality lies outside of culturally acceptable norms (monogamy being one such example). Sexual addiction is not delineated by fetishistic or paraphilic patterns (cross-dressing, BDSM, etc.) or by homosexual/bisexual sexual arousal patterns or behavior—even if these arousal patterns are unwanted by the individual (ego-dystonic). Similar to the sex addict, those with ego-dystonic arousal patterns may keep sexual secrets, feel shame or distress, and even feel out of control related to their sexual behavior, but this alone does not make one a sex addict. Sexual addiction is not defined by what or whom the individual finds arousing, nor is it defined by how often they desire to have sex. Sexual addiction is also not defined by the random one-night-stand, marital infidelity or the occasional visit to a strip club with friends.

Sexual addiction is defined by persistent and profound sexual and romantic objectification of self and others, combined with repetitive patterns of sexual urges, fantasies and behaviors that create personal distress and impairment. These sexual and romantic behavior patterns are abused by the individual in a maladaptive attempt to self-medicate and to provide emotional self-stability while offering a sense of control over how the individual meets his or her basic, human dependency needs. Over time these behaviors offer a decreasing return on a profound investment of time, energy, money and focus, including time not spent in self-care, in recreation, with family and in intimate relationships. These patterns persist despite ongoing and related damage to career, education, relationship, family and other important life goals.

How Does Sex Become an Addiction?

Sexual addiction is considered to be a process or behavioral addiction, similar to compulsive gambling, exercise addictions and compulsive spending. Sex addicts typically struggle with underlying emotional or psychological problems often stemming from early life abuse such as physical or sexual trauma and emotional neglect. Male sex addicts more frequently report profound histories of covert childhood emotional abuse (being used emotionally by a parent or caretaker to buoy that parent's ego strength, sense of self and emotional stability), whereas female sex (and relationship) addicts are more likely to report histories of overt childhood sexual and/or physical abuse. In addition to their adult sexual problems, such individuals, while often intellectually intact, report correlated struggles with substance abuse/dependency, anxiety, low self-esteem, poor social skills and mild to major depression, among other mental health concerns. Those with pre-existing social, personality and attachment deficits are highly represented among sex addicts.

Sexual addiction is in essence a symptom of underlying profound adult challenges with intimacy and attachment, stemming both from genetic and environmental sources. Sex addicts have difficulty making use of the soothing containment provided by healthy adult attachment and will instead turn to intensity-based, objectified sexual and romantic experiences for comfort. Alice Miller in her groundbreaking book *The Drama of the Gifted Child* explores the issue in this way: "The child who is used and/or abandoned emotionally by their parent has the chance to develop his intellectual capacities undisturbed, but not the world of his emotions and this will have far-reaching consequences for his well-being."

What Does the Future Hold?

Ironically, at the same time the APA backed away from both defining and providing the research dollars needed to help define addictive sexual behavior, the concept of sex addiction has gained widespread media and public acceptance as well as grudging therapeutic legitimacy. Driven by a combination of media attention, the international rise of 12-step sexual recovery groups, films and television shows focused on sexual addiction (*Shame, Californication*, etc.), and the highly publicized problem sexual behaviors of multiple major political and sports figures, the general public appears to have tentatively embraced the concepts of sex and porn addiction, as well as love or romantic addiction.

Recognizing the need to readdress this issue, the APA has requested and received extensive peer-reviewed, tier-one research data, along with an exhaustive literature review (Shout out to Dr. Marty Kafka of Harvard!) toward its consideration of a potential DSM-5 Hypersexual Disorder diagnosis. While "Hypersexual Disorder" may not be the ideal term for a problem that more accurately involves the lengthy search and pursuit of sexual and romantic intensity rather than just the sex act itself, the proposed criteria as written do point to problem patterns of excessive fantasy and urges that mirror most aspects of what we have come to know more commonly as sexual addiction.

The proposed criteria for Hypersexual Disorder for the DSM-5 read as follows:

A. Over a period of at least six months, recurrent or intense sexual fantasies, sexual urges or sexual behaviors in association with three or more of the following five criteria:

1. Time consumed by sexual fantasies, urges or behaviors repetitively interferes with other important (nonsexual) goals, activities and obligations.
2. Repetitively engaging in sexual fantasies, urges or behaviors in response to dysphoric mood states (e.g., anxiety, depression, boredom, irritability).
3. Repetitively engaging in sexual fantasies, urges or behaviors in response to stressful life events.
4. Repetitive but unsuccessful efforts to control or significantly reduce these sexual fantasies, urges or behaviors.
5. Repetitively engaging in sexual behaviors while disregarding the risk for physical or emotional harm to self or others.

B. There is clinically significant personal distress or impairment in social, occupational or other important areas of functioning associated with the frequency and intensity of these sexual fantasies, urges or behaviors.
C. These sexual fantasies, urges or behaviors are not due to the direct physiological effect of an exogenous substance (e.g., a drug of abuse or a medication).

Specify if:

Masturbation

Pornography

Sexual Behavior with Consenting Adults

Cybersex

Telephone Sex

Strip Clubs

Other: examples—prostitutes, strip clubs/adult bookstores

Thus, hypersexuality is conceptualized as a non-paraphilic sexual desire disorder with an impulsivity com-

ponent. The proposed behavior specifiers are intended to integrate empirically based contributions from numerous perspectives, including dysregulation of sexual arousal and desire, sexual impulsivity, sexual addiction, and sexual compulsivity.

Will the APA Add Hypersexual Disorder to the *DSM-5*?

Documented evidence increasingly points toward Hypersexuality Disorder (sexual addiction) being a legitimate, serious and not uncommon clinical condition associated with the related concerns of disease transmission, family and relationship dysfunction, separation, divorce, anxiety, unplanned pregnancy, mood disorders, job loss and even suicide. Therefore it makes sense that a diagnosis should be imminent and forthcoming. Yet despite the escalating numbers of men and women now seeking both clinical and self-help support in an effort to alter *self-reported patterns of out-of-control sexual behavior*, it seems unlikely that the *DSM-5* Workgroup for Sexual and Gender Identity Disorders will include Hypersexual Disorder as a distinct diagnostic category in the upcoming *DSM-5*. To be fair, it must be acknowledged that the current research literature on hypersexuality/sexual addiction is absent the standards currently utilized to identify an *addictive disorder*, as peer-reviewed, validated research is still lacking in the areas of tolerance and withdrawal—both of which are required to meet all the necessary criteria toward an addictive disorder diagnosis. Significantly more research is also needed related to how this behavioral disorder affects women.

If Not Now, Then When?

A current review of hypersexual disorder research, along with documented evidence offered by treatment providers, demonstrates that the number of researched and reported cases of sexual addiction (as outlined above in the suggested *DSM-5* definition) now greatly exceeds the number of researched and reported cases of several other sexual disorders already classified as DSM diagnoses, such as fetishism and frotteurism. These other disorders, placed in the DSM when standards for inclusion were slightly looser, seem to be grandfathered in, for lack of a better term. That is not to say these aren't legitimate diagnoses, just that hypersexuality as a diagnosis is being held to a higher standard than its sexual disorder predecessors.

In this climate the most ideal outcome would be for the proposed hypersexual disorder diagnosis to be placed in the DSM-5 appendix under "potential diagnoses requiring further research." While this action would not offer a much needed, criteria-based full diagnosis, it would nevertheless be both useful and deeply meaningful, as being a documented DSM "potential diagnosis" brings both intensified interest in legitimate research and a badly needed increase in research funding.

Why Do We Need a Formal Diagnosis?

What a DSM diagnosis would do is help clinicians to clearly identify individuals who struggle with compulsive, addictive and impulsive sexual disorders, diagnose them properly, and direct them toward useful, accurately planned models of treatment. Furthermore, adding hypersexual disorder to the *DSM-5* would go a long way toward removing the same kinds of moral stigma previously applied to alcoholics, drug addicts and compulsive gamblers before those concerns were fully recognized as treatable addictions and legitimate disorders. Let us not forget that prior to proper diagnosis and treatment planning, alcoholics were simply bums, overeaters were fat and lazy, and compulsive gamblers were too sociopathic to not gamble away the family rent. A legitimate diagnosis removes moral stigma and lessens the chance that a sex addict will be misdiagnosed or have problematic sexual behavior inadvertently normalized.

It should be noted that the proposed hypersexual disorder diagnosis, were it included in the *DSM-5*, would neither add to our nation's tax burden nor raise health insurance rates, as most mental health coverage already excludes psychological treatment for sexual issues. Nor would the diagnosis "take off the hook" or "give excuses for bad behavior to" those men and women whose sexual activities have caused harm to self, loved ones and others. Hypersexuality as a diagnostic criteria also will not and was never intended to provide sexual offenders an easy way out of the consequences (legal and otherwise) for their nonconsensual, violating sexual patterns.

Whether we call it hypersexual disorder, sexual addiction or something else altogether, the problem itself has never been an excuse for bad behavior, nor is it a fun pastime. Sex addicts are absolutely responsible for the hurt and loss left in the wake of their sexual acting out, but having the problem also does not make them bad or unworthy people. A diagnosis would bring a useful retort to those emotionally and psychologically damaging terms such as *nympho*, *slut*, and *pervert*, replacing them with a legitimate, informed diagnostic category from which useful treatment planning and outcome studies can then be drawn.

References

American Psychiatric Association. *Diagnostic and statistical manual of mental disorders*. 2nd ed. Washington, DC, 1968.

American Psychiatric Association. *Diagnostic and statistical manual of mental disorders*. 3rd ed. Washington, DC, 1980.

American Psychiatric Association. *Diagnostic and statistical manual of mental disorders*. 3rd ed., revised. Washington, DC, 1987.

American Psychiatric Association. *Diagnostic and statistical manual of mental disorders*. 4th ed. Washington, DC, 1994.

Bancroft, J., Janssen, E., Strong, D. & Vukadinovic, Z. (2003). The relation between mood and sexuality in gay men. *Archives of Sexual Behavior*, 32, 231–242.

Carnes, P. (1983). *Out of the shadows: Understanding sexual addiction*. Minneapolis, MN: CompCare.

Carnes, P. (1991). *Don't call it love: Recovery from sexual addiction*. New York: Bantam Books.

Carnes, P. & Delmonico, D. (1996). Childhood abuse and multiple addictions: Research findings in a sample of self-identified sexual addicts. *Sexual Addiction & Compulsivity*, 3, 258–268.

Coleman, E. (1990). The obsessive-compulsive model for describing compulsive sexual behavior. *American Journal of Preventive Psychiatry & Neurology*, 2, 9–14.

Coleman, E., Raymond, N. & McBean, A. (2003). Assessment and treatment of compulsive sexual behavior. *Minnesota Medicine*, 86, 42–47.

Cooper, A. (1998). Sexuality and the internet: Surfing into the new millennium. *CyberPsychology & Behavior*, 1, 181–187.

Cooper, A., Delmonico, D. & Burg, R. (2000). Cybersex users, abusers, and compulsives: New findings and implications. *Sexual Addiction & Compulsivity*, 7, 5–29.

Epstein, A. (1973). The relationship of altered brain states to sexual psychopathology. In J. Zubin (Ed.), *Contemporary sexual behavior: Critical issues in the 1970s* (pp. 297–310). Baltimore, MD: Johns Hopkins University Press.

Kafka, M. P. (2000). The paraphilia-related disorders: Nonparaphilic hypersexuality and sexual compulsivity/addiction. In S. R. Leiblum & R. C. Rosen (Eds.),

Principles and practice of sex therapy (3rd ed., pp. 471–503). New York: Guilford Press.

Kafka, M. P. (2010). Hypersexual Disorder: a proposed diagnosis for DSM-5. *Archives of Sexual Behavior*, 39, 377–400.

Kaplan, H. S. (1995). *The sexual desire disorders: Dysfunctional regulation of sexual motivation*. New York: Brunner/Mazel Publishers.

Krueger, R. B. & Kaplan, M. S. (2000). Disorders of sexual impulse control in neuropsychiatric conditions. *Seminars in Clinical Neuropsychiatry*, 5, 266–274.

Krueger, R. B. & Kaplan, M. S. (2001). The paraphilic and hypersexual disorders. *Journal of Psychiatric Practice*, 7, 391–403.

Ley, David. (2012). *The myth of sex addiction* London: Rowman & Littlefield.

Miller, Alice. (1981). *The drama of the gifted child: The search for true self*. New York: Basic Books.

Raymond, N. C., Coleman, E. & Miner, M. H. (2003). Personality characteristics of sexual addicts and gamblers. *Journal of Gambling Studies*, 9, 17–30.

Reid, R. C. (2007). Psychiatric comorbidity and compulsive/impulsive traits in compulsive sexual behavior. *Comprehensive Psychiatry*, 44, 370–380.

Reid R.C., Carpenter B.N., Hook J.N., Garos S., Manning J.C., et al. Report of findings in a DSM-5 field trial for hypersexual disorder. *The Journal of Sexual Medicine*, 2868–2877.

Stein, D. J., Black, D. W. & Pienaar, W. (2000). Sexual disorders not otherwise specified. *CNS Spectrums*, 5, 60–64.

Stein, D. J., Black, D. W., Shapira, N. A. & Spitzer, R. L. (2001). Hypersexual disorder and preoccupation with Internet pornography. *American Journal of Psychiatry*, 158, 1590–1594.

Voon V., Mole T.B., Banca P., Porter L., Morris L., et al. Neural correlates of sexual cue reactivity in individuals with and without compulsive sexual behaviours. *PLoS ONE* 9(7): e102419.

Weiss, Robert. (2012). *Cruise control: Understanding sex addiction in gay men*. Carefree, AZ: Gentle Path Press.

Weiss, Robert & Scheider, J. (2012). *Untangling the web: Sex, porn and fantasy addiction in the internet age*. Carefree, AZ: Gentle Path Press.

Author's Note

Since this article was written and published, two significant studies have appeared, both supporting the idea of sexual addiction (or hypersexuality) as a legitimate and treatable disorder. The first study, "Report of Findings in a DSM-5 Field Trial for Hypersexual Disorder," found that Dr. Kafka's proposed criteria are indeed well constructed. His proposed diagnosis correctly identified 88% of the self-identified sexual addicts included in the study. More importantly, the diagnosis was 93% accurate in terms of negative results. This level of accuracy is actually quite high in comparison to most other psychiatric diagnoses. The second and much more notable study, "Neural Correlates of Sexual Cue Reactivity in Individuals With and Without Compulsive Sexual Behaviours," compared the brain activity of self-identified sex addicts to the brain activity of non-sex addicts, and also to the brain activity of drug addicts. Here the researchers found that when sex addicts are shown pornographic imagery their brains "light up" in three specific areas—the ventral striatum, the dorsal anterior cingulate, and the amygdala—while the brains of non-sex addicts do not. Furthermore, when sex addict's brains light up they do so in the same places and to the same degree as the brains of drug addicts when they are exposed to drug-related stimuli. In short, the parts of the brain in charge of things like pleasure, mood, memory, and decision-making are activated in sex addicts exactly as they are with drug addicts. Other variables in this study also linked sex addiction with other forms of addiction, though brain reactivity was by far the most important measure.

Robert Weiss, LCSW, is the founding director of the Sexual Recovery Institute and the director of Sexual Disorders Services for Elements Behavioral Health, whose programs include The Ranch in Tennessee, Promises Treatment Center and Sexual Recovery Center in California. He is the co-author of several books including *Cruise Control: Understanding Sex Addiction in Gay Men*, *Untangling the Web: Sex, Porn, and Fantasy Obsession in the Internet Age*, and *Cybersex Exposed: Simple Fantasy or Obsession?*

David J. Ley   **NO**

Is Sex Addiction a Legitimate Disorder?

Sex addiction has been a powerful and enduring phenomenon of pop psychology, but its privileged status may be coming to an end. Since the early 1980s, the idea that sex can be addictive has become embedded in American popular culture and media, despite a consistent lack of scientific evidence or endorsement of the concept by behavioral health professionals. Sweeping changes in the social, healthcare and scientific communities signal that the field of sex addiction treatment might have to change quickly or face increasing marginalization.

Young counselors in the addiction, mental health and sexuality fields face a dilemma when it comes to sex addiction. On the one side, there is a powerful and vocal industry promulgating sex addiction and its treatment, with hundreds of self-help books, treatment programs and 12-Step groups supporting the idea that sex can be addictive and destructive. Conferences on the topic are well-attended, and professional organizations have certified hundreds of providers to treat sex addiction. In 2012, the American Society of Addiction Medicine (ASAM) included sexuality in its new definition of addiction, framing sex as a behavior that can become destructive and can affect the brain of sufferers.

The sex addiction industry has benefited from extremely effective and timely marketing efforts, though it prefers to term these "public education" campaigns. For several years, savvy sex addiction treatment providers used sex scandals in the media to further their agenda. Breaking news involving public figures caught with their pants down triggered press releases describing the dangers of sex addiction and implying that the "scandal du jour" might be the result of untreated sex addiction. These education efforts offered advice on seeking sex addiction treatment for oneself or loved ones.

Oftentimes, these scandals led to sex addiction therapists being invited to discuss the issue on national news and talk shows. Under such a media onslaught, it is no wonder that young therapists, not to mention the general public, are often confused as to whether sex addiction constitutes a legitimate disorder.

The wake-up call for young counselors comes when they see a patient and attempt to render a diagnosis of sex addiction. Simply put, there isn't one. The American Psychiatric Association (APA) has played what I call the "hokey pokey dance" with sex addiction, including it in one edition of the DSM and removing it in the next. Since the DSM-IV, the only available, related diagnosis has been "sexual disorder not otherwise specified," which includes language regarding clients who view sexual relationships as "conquests."

This language harkens back to dark days when the condition was called Don Juanism in men and nymphomania in women. This long, often tragic, history is one reason for traditional mental health's resistance to the concept of sex addiction. Carol Groneman's excellent work *The History of Nymphomania* details the disturbing history of the use of the nymphomania diagnosis to suppress and pathologize female sexuality. Modern psychiatry is understandably loath to take up the issue without substantial scientific arguments, and evidence that this is not merely a moral debate.

Society's acceptance of the concept of sex addiction has not swayed the APA or most other traditional institutions. For decades, sex addiction proponents have been challenged in the academic press to produce scientific research to back up their theories. Thirty years later, the sex addiction field has produced countless articles, but these articles are roundly criticized as subject to severe sample bias, based largely on anecdotal reports, with no "gold standard" studies employing randomized designs and control groups where sex addiction-specific approaches could be compared with traditional therapy techniques such as cognitive-behavioral therapies.

In early 2013, the APA completely rejected the concept of sex addiction, and the related concept of hypersexual disorder, in finalizing the newly released DSM-5. The majority of sex addiction clinicians saw this as merely another example of the degree to which they, and their patients, are misunderstood by the mental health system. Most sex addiction providers argue that the fact that sex addiction is not a recognized diagnosis has no impact on their practices, and that they will continue providing services the way they have for decades. The overwhelming majority of sex addiction treatment is provided outside traditional funding, usually on a self-pay basis.

Challenging the Industry

In 2012, I published *The Myth of Sex Addiction*, the first book to challenge the sex addiction industry aggressively. The book followed my own attempt to answer this question: "Is sex addiction real, and if it's not, does it matter?" Ultimately, I concluded that the sex addiction concept is subject to dangerous levels of moral and social bias. Numerous sex addiction therapists have acknowledged to me that their belief in sex addiction is more akin to a faith.

Patients and family members have shared with me that challenges to the validity of the sex addiction diagnosis often result in shaming and threats from their therapists. Patients who question the concept are told they are "in denial" about their addiction. Even therapists who use the sex addiction label in their work report that their own attempts to reform or modernize sex addiction theory or practices within their organizations have resulted in aggressive warnings to maintain the status quo.

I stand in a unique position, as a critic of the sex addiction industry. I provide sexuality-related therapies, and see many of the same types of clients who seek out sex addiction treatment. Without a sex addiction case formulation or diagnosis, patients can and do receive appropriate, effective and ethical services to treat their complaints. Sexual behavior problems are treated similarly to other complex problem behaviors (which are typically symptoms of other issues).

Like most individuals in the healthcare industry, I'm gearing up for major changes in business practices. These changes might have a great impact on the sex addiction industry's ability to continue business as usual, and will force the industry either to change or to become excluded from mainstream healthcare.

Evidence-Based Challenge

One of the most significant areas of healthcare change lies in the drive for evidence-based treatments. Strategies used in my agency, such as Motivational Interviewing, the Community Reinforcement Approach, Dialectical Behavioral Therapy and Integrated Dual Diagnosis Treatment, are just a few of the approaches demonstrated to produce positive results. Funders, including managed care organizations, government agencies, employers and individual patients, are increasingly savvy with their money, demanding services with measurable outcomes. To date,

there are no peer-reviewed empirical studies supporting the approaches used by the sex addiction treatment industry.

The overwhelming majority of sex addiction programs provide services under a 12-Step model of treatment pioneered by Patrick Carnes. While there is evidence supporting 12-Step facilitation and 12-Step support groups in the treatment of substance use disorders, the effectiveness of 12-Step approaches for sex-related problems is untested.

Under healthcare reform, patients and funders will expect their service provider to offer not only evidence-based treatments, but treatments reimbursable under managed care. Without an accepted diagnosis, and lacking evidence-based treatment research, sex addiction treatment may get lumped in with alternative services such as massage therapy or naturopathy—services that are often valued by individuals but occupy a limited role in the overall healthcare system.

Population Demographics

Our society is becoming increasingly comfortable with a range of sexual expression, from homosexuality and non-monogamous relationships to open discussion of bondage. The social changes apparent in the gay marriage debate and the bestselling popularity of *Fifty Shades of Grey* signal only the most public aspects of this social shift. The field of sex addiction treatment has long declared that many forms of sexual behavior are dangerous and addictive. Sexual fantasy, desire for infidelity, use of pornography, and interest in fetishistic behaviors have all been classified as symptoms of sex addiction, representing behaviors that are potentially destructive. The sex addiction concept has explicitly been used by religious and social conservatives, who consider homosexuality a disease.

Research from UCLA in 2012 investigated the characteristics of those in sex addiction clinics around the country. Their results revealed that men in treatment for sex addiction are more than three times more likely to be gay or bisexual, when compared with those in substance abuse treatment. Speculation on this has suggested that these rates reflect unique male homosexual practices such as the use of "bathhouses" and the common acceptance of anonymous sex.

A competing interpretation is that this high percentage of gay and bisexual males in sex addiction programs represents the effects of stigma against male homosexuality. During the 2007 sex scandal involving U.S. Sen. Larry Craig, leaders of the sex addiction industry publicly labeled Craig as a man who was "acting out," without acknowledgment of the complex social bias faced by bisexual or same-sex attracted individuals. The secrecy and shame of Craig's actions were blamed on sexual addiction, rather than on the social pressures that same-sex attracted men experience in our society.

Countless gay and bisexual men have told me that their sexual desires have been similarly characterized as "acting out behaviors" by their sex addiction therapists and treatment programs. Some psychiatric facilities routinely add "hypersexuality" as a problem area to the treatment plans of any gay or bisexual patient in order to justify room restrictions or one-to-one monitoring, under the assumption that these men will be inappropriately sexual on the unit.

There are some public figures in the sex addiction industry who stand up for gay rights and argue that being gay is not a disease. But based on current research, the sex addiction treatment industry as a whole cannot effectively defend itself against charges that the sex addiction concept reflects outdated and morally based cultural biases against male homosexuality.

Reflection of Therapists' Views

During the publicity effort for my book, a Brazilian news reporter began an interview with a fascinating question: "Is sex addiction just another example of the American optimistic tendency to believe that every problem has both a name and a solution?" Her skepticism highlighted the culturally bound nature of the sex addiction concept.

The large, for-profit sex addiction treatment industry that exists in the United States is unique. While 12-Step sex addiction programs have proliferated in other countries, residential and inpatient treatment programs specifically for sex addiction are rare outside the U.S.

In 2011, French politician Dominique Strauss-Kahn was charged with rape. Within hours of the allegation, he was labeled as a sex addict in the American media. And yet, despite Strauss-Kahn's long history of alleged sexual misbehaviors, it was only as these allegations occurred in American culture that these behaviors were labeled evidence of a disease. In many other cultures, a man's social status is enhanced, not hurt, by indications of his promiscuity and virility. In the U.S., these same issues often drive men into sexual addiction treatment.

Many sex addiction therapists are poorly trained in the area of normative human sexuality. They are not alone in this—mental health therapists and medical doctors often are poorly trained in sexuality as well. But when clinicians work directly with sexuality issues, they inevitably make judgments based on their own subjective experiences and standards. That subjectivity impedes the effectiveness of sex addiction counselors in treating the range of normal sexuality, particularly when counselors may be working from the perspective of their own personal recovery from an experience of sex addiction.

Further, these clinicians are making these judgments based on their own experiences of sexuality within a narrow, sexually conservative cultural framework that idealizes monogamy and romantic love and that treats male sexuality as inherently dangerous.

What Do the Data Show?

One last significant industry shift posing a challenge to the business-as-usual approach to sex addiction lies in the increased pressure to make data-driven decisions in clinical care and administration. More and more, it is only through the use of data regarding client needs, characteristics, outcomes and services that we can effectively defend our services to funders. There is developing data regarding issues in sex addiction, and the sex addiction industry must consider it.

First, it is likely that there are far fewer people actually struggling with controlling their sexual behaviors than has been previously reported. Based solely on anecdotal experience, the sex addiction movement has commonly claimed that as much as 6 to 12% of the U.S. population struggles with sexual behavior problems. But recent studies suggest that fewer than 1 to 2% of people report actually having problems resulting from regulating their sexual behaviors, as opposed to having problematic sexual fantasies.

These studies also suggest that there may be many people who feel their sexual desires are difficult to control, but that there are very few who actually cannot control their desires or choices. The experience of a feeling of lack of control over one's sexual desires may be a normative experience, which may explain why the sex addiction concept is so popular.

Also, among the many people seeking sex addiction treatment, there are different problems and etiologies. But sex addiction is commonly presented as a homogenous phenomenon that follows a predictable pattern of addiction, regardless of the behaviors involved. This presentation supports the use of one-size-fits-all group therapy approaches. . . .

DAVID J. LEY, PhD, is a clinical psychologist based in Albuquerque, NM. He is the executive director of New Mexico Solutions, a nonprofit behavioral health agency providing substance abuse and mental health services. He is the author of *Insatiable Wives: Women Who Stray and the Men Who Love Them* and *The Myth of Sex Addiction.*

EXPLORING THE ISSUE

Should Hypersexual Disorder Be a Diagnosable Mental Disorder?

Critical Thinking and Reflection

1. How should clinicians respond to a client seeking help for sexual behavior considered excessive by the client?
2. What criteria should professionals use in determining whether sexual behavior is excessive to the point that it would meet the criteria for mental disorder?
3. What are your thoughts about David Ley's assertion that there is a "sex addiction industry" which is responsible for promoting the diagnosis and treatment of hypersexual disorder?
4. What factors may have played a role in influencing the editors of DSM-5 to ultimately drop hypersexual disorder from the final version of the manual?
5. What kind of research could be developed to assess the validity of hypersexual disorder?

Is There Common Ground?

Robert Weiss and David Ley would concur that the decision to include the diagnosis of hypersexual disorder in DSM-5 involved many complex issues, with strong voices being heard on both sides of the argument. They would probably also agree with the idea that many people are troubled by the extent to which the pursuit of sexual gratification consumes an inordinate amount of time and energy in their lives. In addition, they would support the right of individuals to self-determination as it affects personal choices about the decision to seek help for a problem considered distressing in their lives.

Where Weiss and Ley disagree, however, pertains to the notion of what is pathological. Weiss speaks about the reports of mental health professionals who are seeing an increase in the number of people with sexual and romantic addictions. Ley, however, contends that some of these mental health professionals are playing a role in causing many people to characterize their high level of sexuality as pathological, and thus warranting professional help or the purchase of self-help resources.

Weiss and Ley would probably agree that scientifically sound research is needed in order to determine the validity of hypersexual disorder, because a reliance on anecdotal reports is insufficient for determining the extent of this condition.

Create Central

www.mhhe.com/createcentral

Additional Resources

Bower, M., Hale, R., & Wood, H. (2013). *Addictive States of Mind*. London: Karnac Books.

Carnes, P. J., & Adams, K. M. (2013). *Clinical Management of Sex Addiction*. Hoboken, NJ: Taylor & Francis.

Hall, P. (2013). *Understanding and Treating Sex Addiction: A Comprehensive Guide for People Who Struggle with Sex Addiction and Those Who Want to Help Them*. London: Routledge.

Internet References . . .

Hypersexual Disorders

    http://www.hypersexualdisorders.com/

American Association of Sexuality Counselors Educators and Therapists (AASECT)

    http://www.aasect.org/

Medical News Today

    http://www.medicalnewstoday.com/articles/182473.php

Sexual Recovery Institute

    http://www.sexualrecovery.com/

The Society for the Advancement of Sexual Health

    http://www.sash.net/

Selected, Edited, and with Issue Framing Material by:
Richard P. Halgin, *University of Massachusetts, Amherst*

ISSUE

Is Attention-Deficit/Hyperactivity Disorder (ADHD) a Real Disorder?

YES: National Institute of Mental Health (NIMH), from "Attention Deficit Hyperactivity Disorder (ADHD)," National Institute of Mental Health (2014)

NO: Tim O'Shea, D.C., from "ADD: A Designer Disease," The Chiropractic Resource Organization (2014)

Learning Outcomes

After reading this issue, you will be able to:

- Understand the diagnostic criteria generally associated with the DSM diagnosis of ADHD.
- Discuss the scientifically supported theories about the causes of ADHD, as well as the etiological theories that have been discredited.
- Understand the kinds of interventions most commonly used for treating ADHD.
- Evaluate the argument that ADHD is a "designer disease" that is promoted by various constituencies in ways that harm rather than help millions of children.
- Discuss the benefits of accurate diagnosis, as well as the risks of inappropriate diagnosis of ADHD.

ISSUE SUMMARY

YES: The National Institute of Mental Health concurs with DSM-5 in viewing ADHD as a valid disorder that warrants thoughtful diagnosis and effective intervention.

NO: Tim O'Shea, Doctor of Chiropractic, views the diagnosis of ADD/ADHD as representing an invidious assault on American children that is promoted by parents, teachers, psychiatrists, school personnel, lobbyists, and the pharmaceutical industry.

Anyone who has set foot in an American classroom has observed a range of children whose behaviors and compliance span a relatively wide continuum. At one end are well-behaved children who listen attentively to their teachers, cooperate, and follow instructions. At the other end are children who seem to be completely out of control. They show a constellation of behaviors characterized by inattention and/or hyperactivity. These children are referred to by teachers and special educators as having attention-deficit/hyperactivity disorder (ADHD), as described in the *Diagnostic and Statistical Manual of Mental Disorders*, Fifth Edition (DSM-5). According to DSM-5, their inattention is evidenced by a range of behaviors such as the following:

They fail to attend to details or they make careless mistakes; they have difficulty sustaining attention in tasks or play; they often seem like they're not listening when spoken to; they have difficulty organizing tasks and activities; they often avoid, dislike, or resist tasks that require sustained mental effort; they often lose things; they are easily distracted; and they are often forgetful in daily activities. DSM-5 also enumerates a range of behaviors that characterize hyperactivity. Hyperactive individuals often fidget, tap, or squirm; they often leave their seats when expected to sit; they run about or climb in inappropriate situations; they are often unable to play or engage quietly in leisure activities; they seem to be "on the go" and acting as if "driven by a motor;" they often talk excessively; they may blurt out or complete the sentences of others; they may have difficulty waiting their turn; and they often interrupt others. In the ADHD diagnostic group, individuals can be classified as having a predominantly hyperactive, or inattentive, or combined presentation of symptoms.

A few decades ago, these hyperactive and impulsive children might have been labeled as having "minimal brain dysfunction," a label that suggested that an underlying neurological problem was the basis for their disruptive behavior. As times have changed, so have the labels, such that the terms ADHD and ADD (attention deficit disorder, a label in popular usage) have become commonplace, not only in describing many children, but also many adults.

In the first selection, the National Institute of Mental Health (NIMH) views ADHD as a very real disorder, referring to this condition as "one of the most common childhood brain disorders" that can continue through adolescence and adulthood. In discussing ADHD, NIMH approaches the discussion from a medical model vantage point, noting that "like many other illnesses" ADHD probably results from a combination of factors, with many studies suggesting that genes play a large role, and some studies also pointing to the contributing role of toxic environmental factors.

According to NIMH, ADHD symptoms usually appear early in life, between the ages of 3 and 6. Parents may notice that their child loses interest sooner than other children or seems constantly out of control. Although no single test is used to diagnose ADHD, health professionals can gather information about the child's behavior and environment in an effort to rule out competing diagnostic hypotheses.

NIMH discusses various treatment options for individuals with ADHD. Medications in the form of stimulants are the most common medications used, although as NIMH notes, some of these medications can have significant side effects such as decreased appetite, sleep problems, and in some rare cases alarming effects including suicidal thoughts. Psychotherapeutic interventions include behavioral therapy to help the individual organize tasks, complete schoolwork, work through emotionally difficult events, and develop better social skills.

NIMH states that some children with ADHD continue to have this condition as adults. It is also stated that many adults who have ADHD don't know it; they just feel that it is impossible to get organized, stick to a job, or remember appointments. The simple tasks of daily life such as getting up on time, preparing to leave for work, getting to the job on time, and being productive prove to

be challenging for them. As is the case with children, these individuals are likely to have a history of failure at school, problems at work, or difficulties in relationships. Adults with ADHD, according to NIMH, may benefit from cognitive behavioral therapy in which they work to change their poor self-image, give more effort to thinking before acting, and resist taking unnecessary risks.

In the second selection, Tim O'Shea, Doctor of Chiropractic, characterizes ADHD as a "designer disease" that has been advanced by the "billion dollar Ritalin industry." Dr. O'Shea views the rampant diagnosis of this condition as "an invidious assault on American children" which is promoted by parents, teachers, American psychiatrists, school personnel, and lobbyists, all of whom benefit from the proliferation of this diagnosis. He asserts that no verifiable physical changes have ever been identified as causative of this condition.

In discussing the various constituencies who derive benefit from the ADD/ADHD diagnosis, Dr. O'Shea first focuses on psychiatrists, specifically the American Psychiatric Association, which in 1980 decided to "re-medicalize" the profession. According to O'Shea, psychiatrists "needed a new disease within their specialty which could be cured by drugs." Second, the pharmaceutical industry developed a booming market for psychostimulants which have been prescribed to millions of children; furthermore, the drug companies donate millions of dollars annually to CHADD: Children and Adults with ADD, which O'Shea views as a public relations initiative that promotes these drugs. Third, O'Shea points to teachers who are able to remove disorderly children from their classrooms and put them into Learning Disabilities classes because of their diagnosis. Fourth, school counselors and school psychologists are given the privilege of assigning diagnoses. Fifth, the schools receive millions of dollars to implement "learning programs" for these children. Sixth, parents appreciate the diagnosis of their children, so they themselves don't have to feel responsible for misbehavior. Lastly, the children who are given this diagnosis appreciate the lowered pressure on them when they underperform.

Dr. O'Shea expresses alarm about the personal and societal costs of psychostimulants. The physical side effects as well as the emotional problems associated with these medications are considerable. Furthermore, O'Shea contends that society pays a cost because normal emotions of frustration and elation are muted in children and adolescents who take these drugs, and these young people fail to learn adaptive ways of coping with life stress.

YES

National Institute of Mental Health

Attention Deficit Hyperactivity Disorder(ADHD)

What Is Attention Deficit Hyperactivity Disorder?

Attention deficit hyperactivity disorder (ADHD) is one of the most common childhood brain disorders and can continue through adolescence and adulthood. Symptoms include difficulty staying focused and paying attention, difficulty controlling behavior, and hyperactivity (overactivity). These symptoms can make it difficult for a child with ADHD to succeed in school, get along with other children or adults, or finish tasks at home.

Brain imaging studies have revealed that, in youth with ADHD, the brain matures in a normal pattern but is delayed, on average, by about 3 years.[1] The delay is most pronounced in brain regions involved in thinking, paying attention, and planning. More recent studies have found that the outermost layer of the brain, the cortex, shows delayed maturation overall,[2] and a brain structure important for proper communications between the two halves of the brain shows an abnormal growth pattern.[3] These delays and abnormalities may underlie the hallmark symptoms of ADHD and help to explain how the disorder may develop.

Treatments can relieve many symptoms of ADHD, but there is currently no cure for the disorder. With treatment, most people with ADHD can be successful in school and lead productive lives. Researchers are developing more effective treatments and interventions, and using new tools such as brain imaging, to better understand ADHD and to find more effective ways to treat and prevent it.

What Are the Symptoms of ADHD in Children?

Inattention, hyperactivity, and impulsivity are the key behaviors of ADHD. It is normal for all children to be inattentive, hyperactive, or impulsive sometimes, but for children with ADHD, these behaviors are more severe and occur more often. To be diagnosed with the disorder, a child must have symptoms for 6 or more months and to a degree that is greater than other children of the same age. Children who have symptoms of **inattention** may:

- Be easily distracted, miss details, forget things, and frequently switch from one activity to another
- Have difficulty focusing on one thing
- Become bored with a task after only a few minutes, unless they are doing something enjoyable
- Have difficulty focusing attention on organizing and completing a task or learning something new
- Have trouble completing or turning in homework assignments, often losing things (e.g., pencils, toys, assignments) needed to complete tasks or activities
- Not seem to listen when spoken to
- Daydream, become easily confused, and move slowly
- Have difficulty processing information as quickly and accurately as others
- Struggle to follow instructions.

Children who have symptoms of **hyperactivity** may:

- Fidget and squirm in their seats
- Talk nonstop
- Dash around, touching or playing with anything and everything in sight
- Have trouble sitting still during dinner, school, and story time
- Be constantly in motion
- Have difficulty doing quiet tasks or activities.

Children who have symptoms of **impulsivity** may:

- Be very impatient
- Blurt out inappropriate comments, show their emotions without restraint, and act without regard for consequences
- Have difficulty waiting for things they want or waiting their turns in games
- Often interrupt conversations or others' activities.

ADHD CAN BE MISTAKEN FOR OTHER PROBLEMS

Parents and teachers can miss the fact that children with symptoms of inattention have ADHD because they are often quiet and less likely to act out. They may sit quietly, seeming to work, but they are often not paying attention to what they are doing. They may get along well with other children, whereas children who have more symptoms of hyperactivity or impulsivity tend to have social problems. But children with the inattentive kind of ADHD are not the only ones whose disorders can be missed. For example, adults may think that children with the hyperactive and impulsive symptoms just have disciplinary problems.

What Causes ADHD?

Scientists are not sure what causes ADHD, although many studies suggest that genes play a large role. Like many other illnesses, ADHD probably results from a combination of factors. In addition to genetics, researchers are looking at possible environmental factors, and are studying how brain injuries, nutrition, and the social environment might contribute to ADHD.

Genes. Inherited from our parents, genes are the "blueprints" for who we are. Results from several international studies of twins show that ADHD often runs in families. Researchers are looking at several genes that may make people more likely to develop the disorder.[4,5] Knowing the genes involved may one day help researchers prevent the disorder before symptoms develop. Learning about specific genes could also lead to better treatments.

A study of children with ADHD found that those who carry a particular version of a certain gene have thinner brain tissue in the areas of the brain associated with attention. This research showed that the difference was not permanent, however, and as children with this gene grew up, the brain developed to a normal level of thickness. Their ADHD symptoms also improved.[6]

Researchers are also studying genetic variations that may or may not be inherited, such as duplications or deletions of a segment of DNA. These "copy number variations" (CNVs) can include many genes. Some CNVs occur more frequently among people with ADHD than in unaffected people, suggesting a possible role in the development of the disorder.[7,8]

Environmental factors. Studies suggest a potential link between cigarette smoking and alcohol use during pregnancy and ADHD in children.[9,10] In addition, preschoolers who are exposed to high levels of lead, which can sometimes be found in plumbing fixtures or paint in old buildings, have a higher risk of developing ADHD.[11]

Brain injuries. Children who have suffered a brain injury may show some behaviors similar to those of ADHD. However, only a small percentage of children with ADHD have suffered a traumatic brain injury.

Sugar. The idea that refined sugar causes ADHD or makes symptoms worse is popular, but more research discounts this theory than supports it.[12] In one study, researchers gave children foods containing either sugar or a sugar substitute every other day. The children who received sugar showed no different behavior or learning capabilities than those who received the sugar substitute.[13] Another study in which children were given higher than average amounts of sugar or sugar substitutes showed similar results.[14]

In another study, children who were considered sugar-sensitive by their mothers were given the sugar substitute aspartame, also known as Nutrasweet. Although all the children got aspartame, half their mothers were told their children were given sugar, and the other half were told their children were given aspartame. The mothers who thought their children had gotten sugar rated them as more hyperactive than the other children and were more critical of their behavior, compared to mothers who *thought* their children received aspartame.[15]

Food additives. There is currently no research showing that artificial food coloring causes ADHD. However, a small number of children with ADHD may be sensitive to food dyes, artificial flavors, preservatives, or other food additives. They may experience fewer ADHD symptoms on a diet without additives, but such diets are often difficult to maintain.[12,16]

How Is ADHD Diagnosed?

Children mature at different rates and have different personalities, temperaments, and energy levels. Most children get distracted, act impulsively, and struggle to concentrate at one time or another. Sometimes, these normal factors may be mistaken for ADHD. ADHD symptoms usually appear early in life, often between the ages of 3 and 6, and because symptoms vary from person to person, the disorder can be hard to diagnose. Parents may first notice that their child loses interest in things sooner than other children, or seems constantly "unfocused" or "out of control." Often, teachers notice the symptoms first, when a child has trouble following rules, or frequently "spaces out" in the classroom or on the playground.

No single test can diagnose a child as having ADHD. Instead, a licensed health professional needs to gather information about the child, and his or her behavior and environment. A family may want to first talk with the child's pediatrician. Some pediatricians can assess the child themselves, but many will refer the family to a mental health specialist with experience in childhood brain disorders such as ADHD. The pediatrician or mental health specialist will first try to rule out other possibilities for the symptoms. For example, certain situations, events, or health conditions may cause temporary behaviors in a child that seem like ADHD.

Between them, the referring pediatrician and specialist will determine if a child:

- Is experiencing undetected seizures that could be associated with other medical conditions
- Has a middle ear infection that is causing hearing problems
- Has any undetected hearing or vision problems
- Has any medical problems that affect thinking and behavior
- Has any learning disabilities
- Has anxiety or depression, or other psychiatric problems that might cause ADHD-like symptoms
- Has been affected by a significant and sudden change, such as the death of a family member, a divorce, or parent's job loss.

A specialist will also check school and medical records for clues, to see if the child's home or school settings appear unusually stressful or disrupted, and gather information from the child's parents and teachers. Coaches, babysitters, and other adults who know the child well also may be consulted.

The specialist also will ask:

- Are the behaviors excessive, and do they affect all aspects of the child's life?
- Do they happen more often in this child compared with the child's peers?
- Are the behaviors a continuous problem or a response to a temporary situation?
- Do the behaviors occur in several settings or only in one place, such as the playground, classroom, or home?

The specialist pays close attention to the child's behavior during different situations. Some situations are highly structured, some have less structure. Others would require the child to keep paying attention. Most children with ADHD are better able to control their behaviors in situations where they are getting individual attention and when they are free to focus on enjoyable activities. These types of situations are less important in the assessment. A child also may be evaluated to see how he or she acts in social situations, and may be given tests of intellectual ability and academic achievement to see if he or she has a learning disability.

Finally, after gathering all this information, if the child meets the criteria for ADHD, he or she will be diagnosed with the disorder.

How Is ADHD Treated?

Currently available treatments aim at reducing the symptoms of ADHD and improving functioning. Treatments include medication, various types of psychotherapy, education and training, or a combination of treatments.

Medications

Stimulants such as methylphenidate and amphetamines are the most common type of medication used for treating ADHD. Although it may seem counterintuitive to treat hyperactivity with a stimulant, these medications actually activate brain circuits that support attention and focused behavior, thus reducing hyperactivity. In addition, a few non-stimulant medications, such as atomoxetine, guanfacine, and clonidine, are also available. For many children, ADHD medications reduce hyperactivity and impulsivity and improve their ability to focus, work, and learn. Medications also may improve physical coordination.

However, a one-size-fits-all approach does not apply for all children with ADHD. What works for one child might not work for another. One child might have side effects with a certain medication, while another child may not. Sometimes several different medications or dosages must be tried before finding one that works for a particular child. Any child taking medications must be monitored closely and carefully by caregivers and doctors.

Stimulant medications come in different forms, such as a pill, capsule, liquid, or skin patch. Some medications also come in short-acting, long-acting, or extended release varieties. In each of these varieties, the active ingredient is the same, but it is released differently in the body. Long-acting or extended release forms often allow a child to take the medication just once a day before school, so he or she doesn't have to make a daily trip to the school nurse for another dose. Parents and doctors should decide together which medication is best for the child and whether the child needs medication only for school hours or for evenings and weekends, too.

For more information about stimulants and other medications used for treating mental disorders, see the booklet, *Mental Health Medications*, on the National Institute of Mental Health (NIMH) website (http://www.nimh.nih.gov/). The Food and Drug Administration (FDA) website (http://www.fda.gov/) has the latest information on medication approvals, warnings, and patient information guides.

What are the side effects of stimulant medications?

The most commonly reported side effects are decreased appetite, sleep problems, anxiety, and irritability. Some children also report mild stomachaches or headaches. Most side effects are minor and disappear over time or if the dosage level is lowered.

- **Decreased appetite.** Be sure your child eats healthy meals. If this side effect does not go away, talk to your child's doctor. Also talk to the doctor if you have concerns about your child's growth or weight gain while he or she is taking this medication.
- **Sleep problems.** If a child cannot fall asleep, the doctor may prescribe a lower dose of the medication or a shorter-acting form. The doctor might also suggest giving the medication earlier in the day, or stopping the afternoon or evening dose. Adding a prescription for a low dose of a blood pressure medication called clonidine sometimes helps with sleep problems. A consistent sleep routine that includes relaxing elements like warm milk, soft music, or quiet activities in dim light, may also help.
- **Less common side effects.** A few children develop sudden, repetitive movements or sounds called tics. Changing the medication dosage may make tics go away. Some children also may have a personality change, such as appearing "flat" or without emotion. **Talk with your child's doctor if you see any of these side effects.**

Are stimulant medications safe?

Under medical supervision, stimulant medications are considered safe. Stimulants do not make children with ADHD feel high, although some kids report feeling slightly different or "funny."

Preschoolers are more sensitive to the side effects of methylphenidate, and some may experience slower than average growth rates. Very young children should be closely monitored while taking ADHD medications.[17,18,19]

FDA warning on possible rare side effects

In 2007, the FDA required that all makers of ADHD medications develop Patient Medication Guides that contain information about the risks associated with the medications. The guides must alert patients that the medications may lead to possible cardiovascular (heart and blood) or psychiatric problems. The agency undertook this precaution when a review of data suggested that ADHD patients with existing heart conditions had a slightly higher risk of strokes, heart attacks, and/or sudden death when taking the medications. Recently published studies, however, have not found evidence that using stimulants to treat ADHD increases the risk for cardiovascular problems.[20,21]

The FDA review also found a slight increased risk, about 1 in 1,000, for medication-related psychiatric problems, such as hearing voices, having hallucinations, becoming suspicious for no reason, or becoming manic (an overly high mood), even in patients without a history of psychiatric problems. The FDA recommends that any treatment plan for ADHD include an initial health history, including family history, and examination for existing cardiovascular and psychiatric problems.

One ADHD medication, the non-stimulant atomoxetine (Strattera), carries another warning. Studies show that children and teenagers who take atomoxetine are more likely to have suicidal thoughts than children and teenagers with ADHD who do not take it.[22] **If your child is taking atomoxetine, watch his or her behavior carefully. A child may develop serious symptoms suddenly, so it is important to pay attention to your child's behavior every day.** Ask other people who spend a lot of time with your child to tell you if they notice changes in your child's behavior. Call a doctor right away if your child shows any unusual behavior. While taking atomoxetine, your child should see a doctor often, especially at the beginning of treatment, and be sure that your child keeps all appointments with his or her doctor.

Do medications cure ADHD?

Current medications do not cure ADHD. Rather, they control the symptoms for as long as they are taken. Medications can help a child pay attention and complete schoolwork. It is not clear, however, whether medications can help children learn better. Adding behavioral therapy, counseling, and practical support can help children with ADHD and their families to better cope with everyday problems. NIMH-funded research has shown that medication works best when treatment is regularly monitored by the prescribing doctor and the dose is adjusted based on the child's needs.[23]

Psychotherapy

Different types of psychotherapy are used for ADHD. Behavioral therapy aims to help a child change his or her behavior. It might involve practical assistance, such as help organizing tasks or completing schoolwork, or working through emotionally difficult events. Behavioral therapy also teaches a child how to monitor his or her behavior. Learning to give oneself praise or rewards for acting in a desired way, such as controlling anger or thinking before acting, is another goal of behavioral therapy. Parents and teachers also can give positive or negative feedback for certain behaviors. In addition, clear rules, chore lists, and other structured routines can help a child control his or her behavior.

Therapists may teach children social skills, such as how to wait their turn, share toys, ask for help, or respond to teasing. Learning to read facial expressions and the tone of voice in others, and how to respond appropriately can also be part of social skills training.

How can parents help?

Children with ADHD need guidance and understanding from their parents and teachers to reach their full potential and to succeed in school. Before a child is diagnosed, frustration, blame, and anger may have built up within a family. Parents and children may need special help to overcome bad feelings. Mental health professionals can educate parents about ADHD and how it impacts a family. They also will help the child and his or her parents develop new skills, attitudes, and ways of relating to each other.

Parenting skills training helps parents learn how to use a system of rewards and consequences to change a child's behavior. Parents are taught to give immediate and positive feedback for behaviors they want to encourage, and ignore or redirect behaviors they want to discourage. In some cases, the use of "time-outs" may be used when the child's behavior gets out of control. In a time-out, the child is removed from the upsetting situation and sits alone for a short time to calm down.

Parents are also encouraged to share a pleasant or relaxing activity with the child, to notice and point out what the child does well, and to praise the child's strengths and abilities. They may also learn to structure situations in more positive ways. For example, they may restrict the number of playmates to one or two, so that their child does not become overstimulated. Or, if the child has trouble completing tasks, parents can help their child divide large tasks into smaller, more manageable steps. Also, parents may benefit from learning stress-management techniques to increase their own ability to deal with frustration, so that they can respond calmly to their child's behavior.

Sometimes, the whole family may need therapy. Therapists can help family members find better ways to handle disruptive behaviors and to encourage behavior changes. Finally, support groups help parents and families connect with others who have similar problems and concerns. Groups typically meet regularly to share frustrations and successes, to exchange information about recommended specialists and strategies, and to talk with experts.

TIPS TO HELP KIDS STAY ORGANIZED AND FOLLOW DIRECTIONS

- **Schedule.** Keep the same routine every day, from wake-up time to bedtime. Include time for homework, outdoor play, and indoor activities. Keep the schedule on the refrigerator or on a bulletin board in the kitchen. Write changes on the schedule as far in advance as possible.
- **Organize everyday items.** Have a place for everything, and keep everything in its place. This includes clothing, backpacks, and toys.
- **Use homework and notebook organizers.** Use organizers for school material and supplies. Stress to your child the importance of writing down assignments and bringing home the necessary books.
- **Be clear and consistent.** Children with ADHD need consistent rules they can understand and follow.
- **Give praise or rewards when rules are followed.** Children with ADHD often receive and expect criticism. Look for good behavior, and praise it.

What Conditions Can Coexist with ADHD?

Some children with ADHD also have other illnesses or conditions. For example, they may have one or more of the following:

- **A learning disability.** A child in preschool with a learning disability may have difficulty understanding certain sounds or words or have problems expressing himself or herself in words. A school-aged child may struggle with reading, spelling, writing, and math.
- **Oppositional defiant disorder.** Kids with this condition, in which a child is overly stubborn or

rebellious, often argue with adults and refuse to obey rules.

- **Conduct disorder.** This condition includes behaviors in which the child may lie, steal, fight, or bully others. He or she may destroy property, break into homes, or carry or use weapons. These children or teens are also at a higher risk of using illegal substances. Kids with conduct disorder are at risk of getting into trouble at school or with the police.
- **Anxiety and depression.** Treating ADHD may help to decrease anxiety or some forms of depression.
- **Bipolar disorder.** Some children with ADHD may also have this condition in which extreme mood swings go from mania (an extremely high elevated mood) to depression in short periods of time.
- **Tourette syndrome.** Very few children have this brain disorder, but, among those who do, many also have ADHD. People with Tourette syndrome have nervous tics, which can be evident as repetitive, involuntary movements, such as eye blinks, facial twitches, or grimacing, and/or as vocalizations, such as throat-clearing, snorting, sniffing, or barking out words inappropriately. These behaviors can be controlled with medication, behavioral interventions, or both.

ADHD also may coexist with a sleep disorder, bedwetting, substance abuse, or other disorders or illnesses. For more information on these disorders, visit the NIMH website.

Recognizing ADHD symptoms and seeking help early will lead to better outcomes for both affected children and their families.

How Can I Work with My Child's School?

If you think your child has ADHD, or a teacher raises concerns, you may be able to request that the school conduct an evaluation to determine whether he or she qualifies for special education services.

Start by speaking with your child's teacher, school counselor, or the school's student support team, to begin an evaluation. Also, each state has a Parent Training and Information Center and a Protection and Advocacy Agency that can help you get an evaluation. A team of professionals conducts the evaluation using a variety of tools and measures. It will look at all areas related to the child's disability.

Once your child has been evaluated, he or she has several options, depending on the specific needs. If special education services are needed and your child is eligible under the Individuals with Disabilities Education Act, the school district must develop an "individualized education program" specifically for your child within 30 days.

If your child is considered not eligible for special education services—and not all children with ADHD are eligible—he or she still can get "free appropriate public education," available to all public-school children with disabilities under Section 504 of the Rehabilitation Act of 1973, regardless of the nature or severity of the disability.

For more information on Section 504, consult the U.S. Department of Education's Office for Civil Rights, which enforces Section 504 in programs and activities that receive Federal education funds.

Visit the Department of Education website for more information about programs for children with disabilities.

Transitions can be difficult. Each school year brings a new teacher and new schoolwork, a change that can be especially hard for a child with ADHD who needs routine and structure. Consider telling the teachers that your child has ADHD when he or she starts school or moves to a new class. Additional support will help your child deal with the transition.

Do Teens with ADHD Have Special Needs?

Most children with ADHD continue to have symptoms as they enter adolescence. Some children are not diagnosed with ADHD until they reach adolescence. This is more common among children with predominantly inattentive symptoms because they are not necessarily disruptive at home or in school. In these children, the disorder becomes more apparent as academic demands increase and responsibilities mount. For all teens, these years are challenging. But for teens with ADHD, these years may be especially difficult.

Although hyperactivity tends to decrease as a child ages, teens who continue to be hyperactive may feel restless and try to do too many things at once. They may choose tasks or activities that have a quick payoff, rather than those that take more effort, but provide bigger, delayed rewards. Teens with primarily attention deficits struggle with school and other activities in which they are expected to be more self-reliant.

Teens also become more responsible for their own health decisions. When a child with ADHD is young, parents are more likely to be responsible for ensuring that their child maintains treatment. But when the child reaches adolescence, parents have less control, and those with ADHD may have difficulty sticking with treatment.

To help them stay healthy and provide needed structure, teens with ADHD should be given rules that are clear and easy to understand. Helping them stay focused and organized—such as posting a chart listing household chores and responsibilities with spaces to check off completed items—also may help.

Teens with or without ADHD want to be independent and try new things, and sometimes they will break rules. If your teen breaks rules, your response should be as calm and matter-of-fact as possible. Punishment should be used only rarely. Teens with ADHD often have trouble controlling their impulsivity and tempers can flare. Sometimes, a short time-out can be calming.

If your teen asks for later curfews and use of the car, listen to the request, give reasons for your opinions, and listen to your child's opinion. Rules should be clear once they are set, but communication, negotiation, and compromise are helpful along the way. Maintaining treatments, such as medication and behavioral or family therapy, also can help with managing your teenager's ADHD.

What about teens and driving?

Although many teens engage in risky behaviors, those with ADHD, especially untreated ADHD, are more likely to take more risks. In fact, in their first few years of driving, teens with ADHD are involved in nearly four times as many car accidents as those who do not have ADHD. They are also more likely to cause injury in accidents, and they get three times as many speeding tickets as their peers.[24]

Most states now use a graduated licensing system, in which young drivers, both with and without ADHD, learn about progressively more challenging driving situations.[25] The licensing system consists of three stages—learner's permit, during which a licensed adult must always be in the car with the driving teen; intermediate (provisional) license; and full licensure. Parents should make sure that their teens, especially those with ADHD, understand and follow the rules of the road. Repeated driving practice under adult supervision is especially important for teens with ADHD.

Can Adults Have ADHD?

Some children with ADHD continue to have it as adults. And many adults who have the disorder don't know it. They may feel that it is impossible to get organized, stick to a job, or remember and keep appointments. Daily tasks such as getting up in the morning, preparing to leave the house for work, arriving at work on time, and being productive on the job can be especially challenging for adults with ADHD.

These adults may have a history of failure at school, problems at work, or difficult or failed relationships. Many have had multiple traffic accidents. Like teens, adults with ADHD may seem restless and may try to do several things at once, most of them unsuccessfully. They also tend to prefer "quick fixes," rather than taking the steps needed to achieve greater rewards.

How is ADHD diagnosed in adults?

Like children, adults who suspect they have ADHD should be evaluated by a licensed mental health professional. But the professional may need to consider a wider range of symptoms when assessing adults for ADHD because their symptoms tend to be more varied and possibly not as clear cut as symptoms seen in children.

To be diagnosed with the condition, an adult must have ADHD symptoms that began in childhood and continued throughout adulthood.[26] Health professionals use certain rating scales to determine if an adult meets the diagnostic criteria for ADHD. The mental health professional also will look at the person's history of childhood behavior and school experiences, and will interview spouses or partners, parents, close friends, and other associates. The person will also undergo a physical exam and various psychological tests.

For some adults, a diagnosis of ADHD can bring a sense of relief. Adults who have had the disorder since childhood, but who have not been diagnosed, may have developed negative feelings about themselves over the years. Receiving a diagnosis allows them to understand the reasons for their problems, and treatment will allow them to deal with their problems more effectively.

How is ADHD treated in adults?

Much like children with the disorder, adults with ADHD are treated with medication, psychotherapy, or a combination of treatments.

Medications. ADHD medications, including extended-release forms, often are prescribed for adults with ADHD.[27]

Although not FDA-approved specifically for the treatment of ADHD, antidepressants are sometimes used to treat adults with ADHD. The antidepressant bupropion (Wellbutrin), which affects the brain chemical dopamine, showed benefits for adults with ADHD.[28] Older antidepressants, called tricyclics, sometimes are used because they, like stimulants or atomoxetine, affect the brain chemical norepinephrine.

Adult prescriptions for stimulants and other medications require special considerations. For example, adults often require other medications for physical problems, such as diabetes or high blood pressure, or for anxiety and depression. Some of these medications may interact badly with stimulants. An adult with ADHD should discuss potential medication options with his or her doctor. These and other issues must be taken into account when a medication is prescribed.

Education and psychotherapy. A professional counselor or therapist can help an adult with ADHD learn how to organize his or her life with tools such as a large calendar or date book, lists, reminder notes, and by assigning a special place for keys, bills, and paperwork. Large tasks can be broken down into smaller, more manageable steps so that completing each part of the task provides a sense of accomplishment.

Psychotherapy, including cognitive behavioral therapy, also can help change one's poor self-image by examining the experiences that produced it. The therapist encourages the adult with ADHD to adjust to the life changes that come with treatment, such as thinking before acting, or resisting the urge to take unnecessary risks.

What Efforts Are Under Way to Improve Treatment?

This is an exciting time in ADHD research. The expansion of knowledge in genetics, brain imaging, and behavioral research is leading to a better understanding of the causes of the disorder, how to prevent it, and how to develop more effective treatments for all age groups.

NIMH-funded researchers studied ADHD treatments for school-aged children in a large-scale, long-term study called the Multimodal Treatment Study of Children with ADHD (MTA study). Though the study has been completed, a recent follow-up found that, over a 10-year period, children with ADHD who were treated with methylphenidate had, on average, higher heart rates compared to children who received other treatments. That this effect on heart rate could be detected even after years of use, suggests that the body does not get completely used to stimulants. Children taking stimulants over the long-term should be monitored regularly for potential cardiovascular complications.[29]

NIMH also funded the Preschoolers with ADHD Treatment Study (PATS), which involved more than 300 preschoolers who had been diagnosed with ADHD. The study found that low doses of the stimulant methylphenidate are safe and effective for preschoolers. Preschoolers diagnosed with ADHD are less likely to respond to methylphenidate treatment if they also have three or more coexisting disorders, highlighting the need for new and better treatments.[30]

NIMH-sponsored scientists continue to look for the biological basis of ADHD, and how differences in genes and brain structure and function may combine with life experiences to produce the disorder.

References

1. Shaw P, Eckstrand K, Sharp W, Blumenthal J, Lerch JP, et al. Attention-deficit/hyperactivity disorder is characterized by a delay in cortical maturation. *Proc Natl Acad Sci U S A. 2007* Dec 4;104(49):19649–54. Epub 2007 Nov 16. PubMed PMID: 18024590; PubMed Central PMCID: PMC2148343.

2. Shaw P, Malek M, Watson B, Sharp W, Evans A, Greenstein D. Development of cortical surface area and gyrification in attention-deficit/hyperactivity disorder. *Biol Psychiatry.* 2012 Aug 1;72(3):191–7. Epub 2012 Mar 13. PMID: 22418014.

3. Gilliam M, Stockman M, Malek M, Sharp W, Greenstein D, et al. Developmental trajectories of the corpus callosum in attention-deficit/hyperactivity disorder. *Biol Psychiatry.* 2011 May 1;69(9):839–46. Epub 2011 Jan 17. PMID: 21247556.

4. Faraone SV, Mick E. Molecular genetics of attention deficit hyperactivity disorder. *Psychiatr Clin North Am.* 2010 Mar;33(1):159–80. Review. PubMed PMID: 20159345; PubMed Central PMCID: PMC2847260.

5. Gizer IR, Ficks C, Waldman ID. Candidate gene studies of ADHD: a meta-analytic review. *Hum Genet.* 2009 Jul;126(1):51–90. Epub 2009 Jun 9. Review. PubMed PMID: 19506906.

6. Shaw P, Gornick M, Lerch J, Addington A, Seal J, et al. Polymorphisms of the dopamine D4 receptor, clinical outcome, and cortical structure in attention-deficit/hyperactivity disorder. *Arch Gen Psychiatry.* 2007 Aug;64(8):921–31. PMID: 17679637.

7. Elia J, Glessner JT, Wang K, Takahashi N, Shtir CJ, et al. Genome-wide copy number variation study associates metabotropic glutamate receptor gene networks with attention deficit hyperactivity disorder. *Nat Genet.* 2011 Dec 4;44(1):78–84. doi: 10.1038/ng.1013. PMID: 22138692.

8. Williams NM, Franke B, Mick E, Anney RJ, Freitag CM, et al. Genome-wide analysis of copy number variants in attention deficit hyperactivity disorder: the role of rare variants and duplications at 15q13.3. *Am J Psychiatry.* 2012 Feb;169(2):195–204. PMID: 22420048.

9. Nomura Y, Marks DJ, Halperin JM. Prenatal exposure to maternal and paternal smoking on attention deficit hyperactivity disorders symptoms and diagnosis in offspring. *J Nerv Ment Dis.* 2010 Sep;198(9):672–8. PubMed PMID: 20823730; PubMed Central PMCID: PMC3124822.

10. Millichap JG. Etiologic classification of attention-deficit/hyperactivity disorder. *Pediatrics*. 2008 Feb; 121(2):e358–65. Review. PubMed PMID: 18245408.

11. Froehlich TE, Lanphear BP, Auinger P, Hornung R, Epstein JN, Braun J, Kahn RS. Association of tobacco and lead exposures with attention-deficit/hyperactivity disorder. *Pediatrics*. 2009 Dec;124(6):e1054–63. Epub 2009 Nov 23. PubMed PMID: 19933729; PubMed Central PMCID: PMC2853804.

12. Millichap JG, Yee MM. The diet factor in attention-deficit/hyperactivity disorder. *Pediatrics*. 2012 Feb;129(2):330–7. Epub 2012 Jan 9. Review. PubMed PMID: 22232312.

13. Wolraich M, Milich R, Stumbo P, Schultz F. Effects of sucrose ingestion on the behavior of hyperactive boys. *J Pediatr*. 1985 Apr;106(4):675–82. PMID: 3981325.

14. Wolraich ML, Lindgren SD, Stumbo PJ, Stegink LD, Appelbaum MI, Kiritsy MC. Effects of diets high in sucrose or aspartame on the behavior and cognitive performance of children. *N Engl J Med*. 1994 Feb 3;330(5):301–7. PMID: 8277950.

15. Hoover DW, Milich R. Effects of sugar ingestion expectancies on mother-child interactions. *J Abnorm Child Psychol*. 1994 Aug;22(4):501–15. PMID: 7963081.

16. Nigg JT, Lewis K, Edinger T, Falk M. Meta-analysis of attention-deficit/hyperactivity disorder or attention-deficit/hyperactivity disorder symptoms, restriction diet, and synthetic food color additives. *J Am Acad Child Adolesc Psychiatry*. 2012 Jan;51(1):86–97.e8. PMID: 22176942.

17. Wigal T, Greenhill L, Chuang S, McGough J, Vitiello B, et al. Safety and tolerability of methylphenidate in preschool children with ADHD. *J Am Acad Child Adolesc Psychiatry*. 2006 Nov;45(11):1294–303. PubMed PMID: 17028508.

18. Swanson J, Greenhill L, Wigal T, Kollins S, Stehli A, et al. Stimulant-related reductions of growth rates in the PATS. *J Am Acad Child Adolesc Psychiatry*. 2006 Nov;45(11):1304–13. PubMed PMID: 17023868.

19. Greenhill L, Kollins S, Abikoff H, McCracken J, Riddle M, et al. Efficacy and safety of immediate-release methylphenidate treatment for preschoolers with ADHD. *J Am Acad Child Adolesc Psychiatry*. 2006 Nov;45(11):1284–93. Erratum in: *J Am Acad Child Adolesc Psychiatry*. 2007 Jan;46(1):141. PubMed PMID: 17023867.

20. Cooper WO, Habel LA, Sox CM, Chan KA, Arbogast PG, et al. ADHD drugs and serious cardiovascular events in children and young adults. *N Engl J Med*. 2011 Nov 17;365(20):1896–904. Epub 2011 Nov 1. PMID: 22043968.

21. Vitiello B, Elliott GR, Swanson JM, Arnold LE, Hechtman L, et al. Blood pressure and heart rate over 10 years in the multimodal treatment study of children with ADHD. *Am J Psychiatry*. 2012 Feb;169(2):167–77. PMID: 21890793.

22. Warning on Strattera for attention-deficit hyperactivity disorder. *FDA Consum*. 2005 Nov–Dec;39(6):4. PubMed PMID: 16671156.

23. The MTA Cooperative Group. A 14-month randomized clinical trial of treatment strategies for attention-deficit/hyperactivity disorder. *Arch Gen Psychiatry*. 1999 Dec;56(12):1073–86. PMID: 10591283.

24. Cox DJ, Merkel RL, Moore M, Thorndike F, Muller C, Kovatchev B. Relative benefits of stimulant therapy with OROS methylphenidate versus mixed amphetamine salts extended release in improving the driving performance of adolescent drivers with attention-deficit/hyperactivity disorder. *Pediatrics*. 2006 Sep;118(3):e704–10. PMID: 16950962.

25. U.S. Department of Transportation, National Highway Traffic Safety Administration, Legislative Fact Sheets. Traffic Safety Facts, Laws. Graduated Driver Licensing System. January 2006.

26. Post RE, Kurlansik SL. Diagnosis and management of adult attention-deficit/hyperactivity disorder. *Am Fam Physician*. 2012 May 1;85(9):890–6. PMID: 22612184.

27. Ramos-Quiroga JA, Corominas M, Castells X, Bosch R, Casas M. OROS methylphenidate for the treatment of adults with attention-deficit/hyperactivity disorder. *Expert Rev Neurother*. 2009 Aug;9(8):1121–31. Review. PubMed PMID: 19673602.

28. Wilens TE, Haight BR, Horrigan JP, Hudziak JJ, Rosenthal NE, Connor DF, Hampton KD, Richard NE, Modell JG. Bupropion XL in adults with attention-deficit/hyperactivity disorder: a randomized, placebo-controlled study. *Biol Psychiatry*. 2005 Apr 1;57(7):793–801. PubMed PMID: 15820237.

29. Vitiello B, Elliott GR, Swanson JM, Arnold LE, Hechtman L, Abikoff H, Molina BS, Wells K, Wigal T, Jensen PS, Greenhill LL, Kaltman JR, Severe JB, Odbert C, Hur K, Gibbons R. Blood pressure and heart rate over 10 years in the multimodal treatment study of children with ADHD. *Am J Psychiatry*. 2012 Feb;169(2):167–77. PMID: 21890793.

30. Ghuman JK, Riddle MA, Vitiello B, Greenhill LL, Chuang SZ, et al. Comorbidity moderates response to methylphenidate in the Preschoolers with Attention-Deficit/Hyperactivity Disorder Treatment Study (PATS). *J Child Adolesc Psychopharmacol*. 2007 Oct;17(5):563–80. PMID: 17979578.

THE NATIONAL INSTITUTE OF MENTAL HEALTH (NIMH) is one of 27 constituents that comprise the National Institutes of Health (NIH), which is part of the U.S. Department of Health and Human Services. The mission of NIMH is to transform the understanding and treatment of mental illnesses through basic and clinical research, paving the way for prevention, recovery, and cure.

Tim O'Shea, D.C.

 **NO**

ADD: A Designer Disease

Designer jeans, designer shirts, designer handbags, designer watches, jewelry, perfumes, neckties, shoes,— what are they? Take an ordinary item, put a name on it, a couple million in marketing and promotion, and voilà, its value is raised tenfold, or more. How? By skillfully creating an illusion of worth in the malleable, fickle, public "consciousness."

Same with ADD. Everyone gets mildly depressed from time to time. That's ordinary. Kids get rowdy sometimes. That's ordinary too. Our attention wanders, we get distracted, we have difficulty finishing a task. So what? Welcome to life. But to turn these everyday experiences into diseases that can be compared with cancer or diabetes, actual medical entities that takes real marketing and dog-wagging mastery.

So what do we need? A new disease, but we don't have time to discover one? No problema. We do have the most advanced marketing machine in human history already in place. We can create a disease out of almost nothing. But it won't be a real disease. It will be A Designer Disease. Even before I started researching the topic, I had instinctively doubted the existence of ADD from the time when I first began hearing about it.

Sounded very suspicious to me. I wondered, why does ADD only exist in the U.S. and not in Scandinavia, not in The Netherlands, not in France, not in Fiji, and not in Japan? A disease that respects geographic borders? Where has it come from all of a sudden, to go from nothing to being a household word in just a few short years? Like Jack Nicholson says, faced with a basic question, following the money usually brings you closer to the truth. Even a superficial glance at the billion-dollar Ritalin industry raises that red flag.

What I was not prepared for was the invidious systematic assault on American children and the shared benefit for so many players: parents, teachers, American psychiatrists, school personnel, lobbyists, the drug empire, a convoluted dynamic that has taken on a life of its own and blanketed the public consciousness with the requisite superficial line of junk science and PC doubletalk. If the reader had unlimited time, in order to place the following chapter in proper perspective, I would recommend that he stop reading at this point and only continue after a complete re-reading of two classics: *1984* by George Orwell and *Brave New World* by Aldous Huxley.

One needs to be reminded from time to time of man's capacity for calculated treachery and for keeping the truth that lies just beneath the surface so well hidden, when great fortunes are at stake. Doing a net search for ADD is a revelation: thousands of articles and websites spring up onto the screen, 99% of them parroting the same tired, recycled spin on the safety, efficacy, and necessity of drug intervention to "control" this "new" "epidemic." Most of them are one or two pages, unreferenced, unsubstantiated, going around in circles, written at the compulsory 9th grade level, almost making me believe that ADD must really exist, because this is how its sufferers write.

Only with persistence can one come up with the body of work composing the attached reference list. A new point of view is tenable, it is consistent, and in my opinion self-evident after one resolves to answer the questions which follow.

What exactly is ADD? **Attention Deficit Disorder**, according to the American Psychiatry Association, hereinafter noted as the APA, is a recent disease that supposedly afflicts over 5 million Americans, mostly young boys. ADD is generally characterized by hyperactivity, with tendencies toward fidgeting, loud outbursts, learning disabilities, and generally unruly behavior. It is perhaps the only disease in American history which may be legally diagnosed by people with no medical credentials whatsoever, including teachers, school counselors, aides, principals, even parents. No lab tests, blood tests, microscope studies, or definitive diagnostic tests exist for ADD. No consistent genetic basis or organic neurological lesions, or any verifiable physical changes have ever been identified as causative of ADD. There is no objective scientific proof that the disease exists.

On the contrary, overwhelming evidence suggests that ADD was invented in 1980 by the American Psychiatric Association in order to bolster the position of its failing profession. Politics and economics took over almost immediately, seeing a way to allocate billions of dollars in drugs and professional fees to "combat" the new "epidemic."

When reading anything about ADD, I have noted that is seems essential to keep one central notion clearly in mind: ADD is not a medical entity; it is economic and political. I soon discovered I was not alone in this sentiment:

"ADD does not exist. These children are not disordered." Thomas Armstrong, PhD *The Myth of the ADD Child.*

"Both the FDA and the DEA have acknowledged that ADD is not a disease, or anything organic or biologic." Fred Baughman, MD *The Future of ADD.*

"We have invented a new disease, given it medical sanction, and now we must disown it." Diane McGuiness *The Limits of Biologic Treatment for Psychiatric Distress.*

"Research does not confirm the existence of an ADD syndrome. There is no medical, neurological, or psychiatric justification for the ADD diagnosis."—Peter Breggin, MD *Toxic Psychiatry* p 281.

"Be forewarned that ADD is not a real disease, but rather a contrived illusion of a disease, a marketplace tool."—Fred Baughman, MD.

Whoa! I wasn't ready for all that!

Why did ADD appear? To address this question, it is necessary to take a brief look at the American Psychiatry Association in the past century. In Chapter I of his remarkable work, *A Dose of Sanity*, psychiatrist Sidney Walker gives an illuminating historical summary of his profession during the past 150 years. Psychiatrists are MDs who specialize in mental disorders. Classically, they study organic, physical causes of mental illnesses such as brain tumors, infections, and other diseases that might have a psychological component.

The father of American psychiatry was Benjamin Rush, a signer of the Declaration of Independence. His book *Diseases of the Mind*, 1812, dealt with biological causes of mental illness. In other words, mental illness was seen generally as the result of another disease, such as tuberculosis, syphilis, or a tumor.

In the 1800s, psychiatrists like Griesinger, Alzheimer, and Kraeplin concentrated on brain anatomy and nerve cell irregularities as the cause of mental disorders. For over a century psychiatrists sought the underlying physical causes of mental illness. Microscope study of brain slices was employed by world class psychiatrists like Adolph Meyer in the late 30s, looking for brain lesions that could be linked with mental problems.

This scientific approach began to change with the emergence and prevalence of the notions of Sigmund Freud around 1940. Although Freud's ideas about sexuality and the unconscious mind have made a lasting impact on the study of the human mind, Sidney Walker feels that for the first time, the brain was left out of the picture. Physical disease processes were no longer considered as the first place to look for the cause of mental illness. Freudian psychology concentrated on "the mind" itself, as if the mind were separate from the brain. For the first time in its history, the direction of psychiatry was no longer guided by medical physicians. Instead, psychologists took over the field, with their focus on "the psyche."

Most mental illness, they said, resulted from "adverse events," such as childhood trauma, parent relationships, and early experiences. Never before has a medical specialty been assumed by "non-medical participants." This was a mistake from which it would take psychiatrists 40 years to recover. In the 1950s and 1960s we saw the rise of psychoanalysis: the talking doctors. Their promise was to cure mental illness by psychotherapy. Sidney Walker attributes the decline of psychiatry before 1980 to the failure of psychoanalysis and psychotherapy to deliver.

By and large they didn't work that well. Ignoring the biological and organic causes of mental disease was the reason, according to Dr. Walker. The profession had abandoned its roots, which held that mental illness was generally "in reaction to" some underlying physical disorder. They had traded a scientific approach for a non-scientific one. The 1970s saw the emergence of the fore-runner of ADD: minimal brain disorder.

Same pseudo-scientific underpinnings as ADD vague rationales for targeting a vulnerable new market for "treatment," supported by the drug companies. Same opportunities for liberal, socialistic expansion and job creation to "diagnose" and monitor the newly discovered epidemic. Nixon's own psychologist, a Dr. Hutschnecker, penned a now-famous memo in 1970 in which he recommended mass testing of very young children in order to ascertain possible "pre-delinquent" behavior patterns. Even though the memo was discredited by the APA itself, political support snowballed and became the focus for policy for the coming decade.

The new magic words were "disability" and "intervention." It was the dawn of the age of the Professional Victim. The story is told with detail and clarity in Peter Schrag's *The Myth of the Hyperactive Child*. Having failed to reform the malfunctioning institutions, the new game was to reform the individual. With no scientific basis, new words came into use: "pre-delinquent" "dyslexia" and "learning disabled."

By 1995, over 50% of American children are identified as either "learning disabled" or ADD! Schrag outlines how an entire empire of social, educational, political, medical and economic power willed itself into existence in a few short years.

The shoddiest of scientific studies were thrown together, funded by the drug companies, in support of the new politics of the state's new right to determine "normal" emotions and behavior. Though all the studies were eventually discredited, they served as a foundation for similar "scientific documentation" during the 1980s, in which nonconformity suddenly became a medical condition requiring treatment.

During the 1970s, people were going to family doctors, psychologists, social workers, priests, and marriage counselors for their problems, none of whom were prescribing drugs for minor complaints of depression. Year by year, psychiatrists were failing to attract voluntary patients, simply because the need was not perceived by most people.

So with the stock of the APA at an all-time low, we come to 1980 and the now famous APA Committee meeting. It was at this meeting that the APA decided to "re-medicalize." That meant giving up on this talking-cure psychoanalysis stuff which was pushing the profession into the basement, and reasserting themselves as real medical professionals with the right to be successful and sell a ton of drugs.

As you might imagine, no one was happier to hear this news than the pharmaceutical industry, but we'll get to that. Maybe they couldn't get voluntary patients, but what about involuntary ones? The only problem was, if the psychiatrists were to successfully reestablish themselves as medical doctors, they needed a new disease within their specialty which would be cured by drugs.

Enter ADD stage left, first named as a disorder by the APA in their 1980 meeting. Forget the fact that ADD had been around for almost a century under 25 different names, listed on p 8 of Dr. Armstrong's book. That didn't matter. What was of major significance was that now ADD had reality: it was finally named and described in the APA's bible, the *Diagnostic and Statistical Manual*, known hereinafter as the DSM.

Breggin, Armstrong, Wiseman, and Baughman go on for pages about the significance of the Diagnostic and Statistical Manual. I direct the reader to them for a fuller understanding of the insidious role this book has played in catapulting a declining profession into a position of wealth and respectability, at the expense of the well-being of millions of defenseless children.

If that sounds harsh or strident, I've got a feeling it's an understatement. Don't take my word for it.

Now, about the Manual. The *Diagnostic and Statistical Manual* was first published by the APA in 1952. The DSM is a catalogue of mental disorders. Each disorder has a list of symptoms under it. A patient may be "diagnosed" as having a particular mental disorder if enough of the listed symptoms are present. Although the instructions in the DSM caution psychiatrists against using the DSM as a "cookbook" because there is so much overlap and so many other factors to consider before a supportable diagnosis can be made, in actual practice the cookbook method is precisely the way DSM is most commonly used. Psychiatrists have been very busy since 1952.

Each new edition of the DSM is bigger:

Title	Year	# of Mental Disorders
DSM	1952	112
DSM-II	1968	163
DSM-III	1980	224
DSM-III-R	1987	253
DSM-IV	1994	374
DSM-5	2013	374

Lest the reader assume that each of these "illnesses" was researched and studied in the same scientific manner as a physical illness, before it appears in pathology textbooks, here are what a few professionals have to say:

Renee Garfinkel, a psychologist and representative of the APA who attended DSM meetings, told *Time* magazine: "the low level of intellectual effort was shocking. Diagnoses were developed by majority vote on the level we would use to choose a restaurant. You feel like Italian. I feel like Chinese. So let's go to a cafeteria. Then it's typed into a computer. It may reflect on our naivete, but it was our belief that there would be an attempt to look at things scientifically." (Walker p 22)

Al Parides, MD, a psychiatrist, states that the DSM is not scientific at all, but a masterpiece of political maneuvering, in which the normal problems of life are turned into psychiatric conditions. (Wiseman, p 357)

How a mental disorder winds up in the DSM in the first place is a long and enlightening story, for which the reader is directed to the studies by Walker and also by Louise Armstrong.

"To read about the evolution of the DSM is to know this: it is an entirely political document. What it includes, what it does not include, are the result of intensive campaigning, lengthy negotiating, infighting, and power plays."
—Louise Armstrong

An unsuspecting neophyte like myself might expect that for a mental disorder to appear in the primary handbook of the profession licensed to treat mental disorders, years of research, experimentation, and double blind studies would have had to come first, right? Guess again.

Armstrong cites the story of the origin of a disorder called "self-defeating personality disorder." The chairman of the DSM committee, Robert Spitzer, thought up the disorder on a fishing trip, and when he returned, persuaded enough of the committee to include it in the Manual. It goes on from there. (*And They Call It Help*)

The DSM is the only way that ADD is diagnosed. Here's how it's done. In the DSM-IV, ADD has nine symptoms listed under it. If a child has any six of them, in the opinion of the doctor (or the teacher!) that child may be diagnosed as having ADD. That's it! Funny thing is, it seems like most of these entries on the list are not symptoms of a mental disorder, but just symptoms of being a kid:

1. Often fidgets with hands or feet or squirms in seat
2. Often leaves seat in classroom or in other situations in which remaining seated is expected
3. Often runs about or climbs excessively in situations in which it its inappropriate
4. Often has difficulty playing or engaging in leisure activities quietly
5. Is often on the go or often acts as if driven by a motor
6. Often talks excessively
7. Often blurts out answers before questions have been completed
8. Often has difficulty awaiting turn
9. Often interrupts or intrudes on others

Sound like anyone you've ever known? Some may ask if there are any kids who would not fit six of these criteria. The reader should understand that this is the only "diagnostic" "testing" that exists for determining ADD. Six out of nine. No lab test, no blood tests, no physical examination whatsoever, no standardized batteries of written or verbal psychological testing. Just these nine.

And unlike any other disease in history, the diagnosis may be made by anyone in authority, with no medical credentials or training whatsoever: the school nurse, school counselor, a teacher, the principal, a coach.

DSM cookbook diagnosis of any disease is a ridiculous oversimplification and the primary reason so many modern psychiatrists are embarrassed by their own profession. Differential diagnosis of any disease, especially a mental disorder, requires time-consuming, thorough testing, analysis and thoughtful consideration, ruling out several possibilities, one by one, before arriving at the final diagnosis, which itself is still subject to change.

DSM cookbook diagnosis, by contrast, which is standard in the profession according to most sources, is quick and easy and absurdly oversimplifying. Many patients are often labeled ADD after a 15-minute interview with a pediatrician, who has no training in mental disorders at all.

As Dr. Walker says, DSM is usually a "substitute for diagnosis" not part of any scientific differential process of ruling out likely possibilities. As we approach the millennium, psychiatry has lost its identity as a profession, according to psychiatrists like Peter Breggin, MD. Today psychiatry has sold most of its traditional values in exchange for being "dominated by the interests of the multi-billion dollar pharmaceutical industry as the profession becomes wholly dependent on the drug companies for its survival."

In the meantime, several million Americans "will suffer permanent brain damage from psychiatric drugs and electroshock while the profession denies it is happening." (*Toxic Psychiatry*, p 17). Labeling is the new game, the new psychiatry, the new bait and switch. Labeling is what psychiatrists now offer in place of diagnosis.

Take a moment to understand the difference. When a patient with a mental disorder presents to a doctor for the first time, there are literally dozens of possible physical, organic disease processes which could be the cause. If the doctor misses the underlying disease, because it is subclinical (only beginning) or because standard physical examination is glossed over in favor of the 15-minute DSM cookbook approach, it is doubtful whether another doctor will take the trouble to look for another cause. Why bother?

DSM diagnostic labels, like "depression" or "delusional dominating personality disorder" remain on a patient's chart for life. These labels are too frequently the end of the line, as far as trying to diagnose the cause of the mental problem. Most doctors will hesitate to challenge the diagnosis of a colleague, especially if it requires a lot of new work.

The result is that a patient may be labeled "depressed" but in actuality be depressed because of one of the following:

rickettsial infection

hypoglycemia

brain tumor

brain infection

hypothyroid

toxic poisoning

anemia

malnutrition

parasites

vitamin deficiency

to name just a few.

Once labeled, powerful psychoactive drugs are prescribed, which cover up the depression. Meanwhile the underlying disease may progress unchecked, often to the point where years of illness will result.

Rare? Think again. Standard physical exams are not routinely done by today's psychiatrists. A comprehensive study in the *American Review of Medicine* by Dr. Erwin Koranyi estimates misdiagnosis of easily detectable physical illness and labeling them as mental illness occurs half the time!

Koryani's study of 2090 psychiatric patients showed that **43%** of them had an undiagnosed underlying major illness. Dr. Koryani explains that once a patient is labeled a psychiatric case, physical complaints are assumed to be "psychosomatic" and are routinely ignored. Neurologist Sir Francis Walshe describes mental hospitals as "living museums of undiscovered bodily disease . . . undiagnosed."

For a person who has ever been diagnosed as depressed or having ADD, health insurance may be denied for life. If the person is ever injured, and litigation becomes necessary to document the injury, these labels are powerful tools that are often used against the person's case, to undermine credibility and the reality of the injury. It gets worse.

The reader again is directed to further explore the tip of this iceberg. The bottom line is that labeling doesn't cure anything. Misdiagnosis and cookbook labeling commonly delay appropriate treatment for hundreds of thousands of patients. Labeling is not treatment.

Who Benefits From ADD? Simple answer: almost everyone involved.

First the **psychiatrists**. To really understand the role of psychiatry in the modern world, one must come to terms with the information contained in works such as *Psychiatry: The Ultimate Betrayal*. Wiseman thoroughly documents the contributions of psychiatrists to the world over the past 150 years:

- Extermination of 375,000 mental patients in Germany, prior to the Holocaust
- Providing Hitler with the rationale and method for the Holocaust itself
- Over 100,000 lobotomies between 1936 and 1970

- Millions of worthless and unnecessary electro-shock treatments of the brain
- Replacing the idea that the citizen is personally responsible for his actions with the notion that other factors are always to blame
- Addicting large segments of the population to dangerous drugs like Ritalin, Elavil, Valium, and Prozac
- Infecting the courtrooms of the nation with absurdities like "recovered memory," "irresistible impulse," "urban stress syndrome," and "temporary insanity"

As cited above, in 1980 the APA was at low ebb. The rest of the medical profession no longer respected psychiatrists because by allowing their direction to be determined by non medical personnel, the failures of psychotherapy were pre-eminent. After 18 years of aggressive public relations ramjetting ADD into the public consciousness, psychiatrists found themselves back in the driver's seat.

Each of the 5 million ADD children requires some $1200 in diagnostics, although not all of them receive it. Perhaps only 1 million are being treated by 2002. So that's only about $12 billion, although with a potential of $60 billion. And that's not even including medications.

So the immediate financial future of cookbook-toting psychiatrists looks fairly bright. The majority of them will be riding ADD into the millennial sunset, accounting for 99% of the current "informative" websites on the topic. Not all doctors are that impressed by the scientific validity of the psychiatric profession when it comes to the ethics of their intent toward children.

Thomas Szasz, MD, in his book *Cruel Compassion*, tells us: "This elementary fact makes the child psychiatrist one of the most dangerous enemies not only of children, but also of adults who care for the two precious and valuable things in life: children and liberty. Child psychology and child psychiatry cannot be reformed. They must be abolished."

Don't sugar-coat it like that, Tom. Bruce Wiseman, author of *Psychiatry: the Ultimate Betrayal*, concurs:

"All vestiges of psychiatry and psychology should be removed from our schools. Schools are for learning. They are not for psychiatric experiments on young minds." p 385. Definitely a 21st century opinion.

Second, the **pharmaceutical industry**. Ciba-Geigy, the producer of Ritalin has found itself at the center of a boom market. In 1974, a prescription for 100 Ritalin tablets was $12. By 2000 it's $150. For this one drug alone, 6 million prescriptions were written annually at a cost of about $150 each. That's $900 million annually, and that's only the domestic market.

There are also several other drugs for ADD, bringing in other millions, including Cylert, Dexedrine, Disipramine. Some estimates by "studies" funded by Ciba-Geigy and backed by the APA are now saying that as much as **30% of the child population** may be in "need" of drug treatment for this new disease which has just been miraculously discovered. The current 1 million kids on Ritalin—that's only the beginning!

To keep the ball rolling, Ciba donates millions of dollars every year to a "community" organization known as CHADD: Children and Adults with ADD. CHADD now has over 35,000 members in 600 chapters nationwide. It has become the de facto PR branch of Ciba for disseminating promotional information about Ritalin, describing it as "safe and effective" for treatment of ADD.

Third, **teachers**. It doesn't take much study to discover the deplorable condition of today's American education system, especially grade schools and high schools. Most studies assessing overall literacy at about 50%. (Wiseman) In 1900, illiteracy was about 1.9%!

Here's a graph of SAT scores from 1966-1994:

YEAR	VERBAL SKILLS	MATH
1966	466	492
1976	429	470
1986	435	476
1992	424	476

Source: US Dept of Education
US Dept of Education Digest of Education Statistics, 1997 p 133
http://www.finaid.org/educators/educstat.pdf

In a nation where half of high school graduates cannot competently read or write, consider what a blessing ADD has been to beleaguered school teachers. We're off the hook! It's not our fault! These kids are disordered—there's something wrong with them. Blame the victims.

Besides removing blame, an overstressed teacher may now get to remove the student as well: a diagnosis of ADD frequently gets a disorderly student out of the class and into a special Learning Disabilities class. This is another gigantic contrived social invention, along with dyslexia, but it is beyond the scope of this chapter.

At the very least, the child will be prescribed Ritalin and will now be manageable. The best news for teachers is that they don't even have to wait for a psychiatrist to pronounce a kid ADD. In our modern Orwellian setting, the teachers can do it! All they have to do is check off six of the nine DSM "symptoms" and the student may be out of there.

"The vast majority of teachers have become true believers. Between 88 and 96 per cent of teachers believe they can diagnose a hyperactive child. And three-fourths feel that they have an obligation to recommend that a doctor be informed" —*The Myth of the Hyperactive Child* p 8

"Teachers who no longer know how to teach claim the children are defective." —*Psychiatry: The Ultimate Betrayal* p 283

Other teachers benefiting from the new epidemic are the "ADD" teachers. Any doubts about Orwell's accuracy about the future will soon be erased if one takes the time to research the bizarre and experimental "teaching methods" which have had to be invented so quickly to handle the new "epidemic."

Larry Brown, MD is not letting anyone off the hook. He describes the widespread use of Ritalin as a "low point in professional ethics."

"Where drugs are used as a cheap alternative to reform of the schools, then the practice of drugging children must be seen as a political act." "Drugging children . . . represents an ominous step along the Orwellian continuum of social control through psychotechnology."—*Toxic Psychiatry* pp. 313, 293.

Orwell and Huxley, over and over are cited by doctors who criticize the new psychiatry.

Fourth, the **school counselors**, some of whom may only have undergrad degrees in social work or psychology, but none of whom has medical credentials. For them ADD may be a dream come true. School psychologists have suddenly been raised to the level of a psychiatrist. Everyone can diagnose!

In 1950, there were only about 1000 psychologists in American schools. When ADD was invented in 1980, there were about 10,000. By 1990 there were over 22,000 psychologists in American schools! (Thomas Fagan, PhD Memphis State University)

By 2008, there were 35,400. (Charvat: www.nasponline.org/advocacy/SP_Workforce_Estimates_9.08.pdf)

Fifth, **the schools**. A school evaluation to determine eligibility for Special Ed costs $1270. If an estimated 5 million cases are supposedly out there, that's $6 billion for the schools. Hundreds of "learning programs," tests, and materials have been designed for ADD. It is a growth industry. It must be real!

Special Education programs ballooned from $1 billion in 1977 to $30 billion in 1994! (*U.S. News and World Report*, 13 Dec 93) Ever wonder where all these "handicapped" kids appeared from, suddenly in the 80s?

Sixth, **the parents**. Parents benefit in several ways from the creation of ADD. The underlying causes of unruly children today are not difficult to discover. By the time he is in the 8th grade, the average kid has seen some 8,000 murders on TV.

Children's diets are extremely sensitizing and allergenic, with the emphasis on sugar and dairy. Who does the shopping? Single parents, absent parents, drugged parents abound in our society. Too often no one's driving the bus at home. Unrestricted TV intake is not a substitute for raising a child. For all these reasons, unruly, disturbed kids are a natural consequence.

Ultimately the responsibility lies with parents, and they are failing. Sure they have excuses; parents have problems of their own. So here comes this brand new "disease" which will again take the blame off the parents, because "my child has a disorder" for the parents, the payoff comes in the alleviation of guilt. —*The Myth of the Hyperactive Child* p 65

And the best news is, he can be drugged into submission! Next problem. But the difficulty wasn't really resolved; it was just shelved, put on hold, incubated. Know what they say about payback. Finally, the "patient."

Once a child has been diagnosed ADD, the pressure's off. He's told he has a disability, and is put into a category of students who are no longer expected to perform. Adapting to expectation, he slacks off, having found the excuse he needed to glide along without working to his capacity. He makes his contribution to the above chart on SAT performance.

Many children have calmed down with just the label ADD. And a sugar pill they thought was Ritalin. Academic standards are lowered; glib and trendy pop psychology excuses are made. At the snap of the fingers suddenly everything's all set. Few things are as permanent as a temporary solution. Other benefits for the ADD child are more time allotted to take SATs, as well as entry tests for med school and law school. Eligibility for many state and federal disability programs is on the rise. For an already confused adolescent, ADD certainly has its compensations.

How does Ritalin fit in? Ritalin (methylphenidate) is an amphetamine made by Ciba-Geigy which today accounts for about 90% of medication provided to ADD "patients." Ritalin is an addictive drug, classed by the DEA as a Schedule II controlled substance, same as narcotics like heroin, morphine and cocaine.

Ritalin is also as an illegal street drug where a profit of about $400 can be made from an average prescription. It can be crushed up and snorted, or else mixed with heroin to enhance a junkie's high. The U.S. uses 90% of the world's Ritalin, and Canada most of the remaining 10%.

The theory is that kids are so hyperactive, give them speed and they'll be normal—the famous Paradoxical Effect. The reality is, long-term effects of Ritalin given to children have never been studied, according to the 2003 PDR. No known biochemical imbalance in these children has ever been proven.

As far as learning disability is concerned, Ritalin has never been shown to improve it even slightly. (Armstrong p 47) Moreover there is absolutely no evidence to show that the emotional stability of adult life can be promoted or even influenced by childhood experience with Ritalin. (*A Dose of Sanity*, p 141)

Childhood use of Ritalin does show a high correlation with adolescent abuse of street drugs an easy transition. Ritalin brings with it the psychotic tendencies which can be brought on by the advanced drugs, like heroin, cocaine, and speed.

In light of the immense social and economic forces promoting explosive market growth of this wonder drug, it wouldn't be so bad if it were harmless. Unfortunately most parents don't know about the PDR. The Physician's Desk Reference is an annual publication by the drug companies which is a general catalogue of all drugs sold in the U.S., their effects, recommended dosages, and adverse effects. The PDR is a legal protection for the pharmaceutical industry more than anything else; it is fair warning about side effects of drugs: 3200 pages of CYA. But parents are rarely told what it says.

Here are some of the side effects the 2003 PDR, 57th edition lists for Ritalin:

nervousness

skin rash

seizures

decreased growth

nausea

Tourette's syndrome

insomnia

nausea

glaucoma

gastric pain

weight loss

emotional swings

headache

visual problems

suicidal tendency

dizziness

irregular heart

tardive dyskinesia

fatigue

visual problems

decreased appetite

moodiness

high blood pressure

Outside of that, it should be fine.

Tourette's syndrome is a condition characterized by inappropriate, sometimes obscene vocal outbursts, and unpredictable and strange physical movements. It may be long term. Tardive dyskinesia is a permanent condition characterized by involuntary facial tics, jerky movements of the head and arms; in short, a movement disorder that can involve any of the voluntary muscles of the body.

A 1986 study published in *Psychiatric Research* found brain pathology in the form of tissue shrinkage in more than half the subjects taking Ritalin. Ritalin has also caused cancer in lab animals. FDA's response? "People are not mice." —*Detroit News* 13 Jan 96

The emotional problems listed from Ritalin use may include: drug-induced neurosis, psychosis, addiction, clinical depression. In addition, the most stupid finding of all may be that long term Ritalin use can actually cause the very conditions it is supposed to cure: inattention, hyperactivity, and impulsivity! Hello! Anybody out there?

The PDR specifically states that Ritalin should not be used for children under 6. Nevertheless American psychiatrists ignore Ciba's own warning and prescribe Ritalin for some 200,000 pre-school children! What are we doing?

Many doctors, like Carl Kline, MD, see no need for Ritalin at all: "It is my belief that if these drugs were outlawed, children would not be at all deprived of essential medication, but that doctors would be forced to make more accurate diagnoses and seek better means of handling the hyperactive behavior of a certain small percentage of their little patients."

Probably the most detrimental of all Ritalin's side effects are decreased growth and suicidal tendencies. During childhood, all the systems of the body are under the control of growth hormone for their normal development. The organs of the body have not reached their full size and strength. Ritalin interferes with growth hormone. Permanent organic and skeletal deficits are likely to result even after Ritalin is discontinued.

Remember, no long-term studies of this drug's lasting side effects have ever been done. Are parents routinely informed about all these possible side effects before the doctor writes the prescription? What do you think?

Do you think this information might be helpful to a parent making a decision? The chance for suicidal tendencies is that something for which to put your child at risk just because he has a lot of energy? Kurt Cobain was a Ritalin patient as a teenager.

No long-term statistical studies have ever been done on suicide resulting from Ritalin use, or from Prozac, for that matter. Yet all doctors and Ciba will admit that for the 20 million Americans on these two drugs, suicide is a possible result. Individual stories number in the thousands, but who is keeping track? No one wants to rock the boat, too many political interest are in place, too much money changing hands.

Virtually all the recent school shooters have been on psych meds. [CCHR International, John Spagnola]

The darkest aspect of the whole ADD scam, in my opinion is the totalitarian leveling effect that is being perpetrated on American children and docilely accepted by American adults. Children may still be able to function and to attend classes on Ritalin. But any teacher or parent will attest that creativity is usually gone. The light in their eyes goes out. Children develop at different rates, with varying degrees of stress and the ability to cope with it. As Dr. Walker says, stress and confusion are a necessary part of adolescence, essential to the learning process. Character formation.

To mute these normal emotions of frustration and elation with drugs is to steal these kids' childhood and adolescence from them. What's a kid like coming off Ritalin at age 14, after several medicated years? . . . they come off drugs at 14 or so and suddenly they're big, strong people who've never had to spend any time building any controls in learning how to cope with their own daily stress.

Then the parents who have forgotten what the child's real personality was like without the mask of the drug, panic and say Help me. I don't know what to do with him. They can only deal with the medicated child. [Schrag, p 94]

Of course childhood and adolescence are confusing periods of growth—there's no dress rehearsal. First time through's a take. But what we're doing with these psychotropic drugs is erasing footage that can never be replaced. Each lost stressful experience was an opportunity for growth and learning that was drugged out of existence, stolen from the child forever. High and lows are clipped; elation and depression are merged together as one, and the victim cruises through his formative years an insensate robot.

Huxley's prevision accuracy is scary: in *Brave New World* the Ritalin of the future is a drug called **soma**. Soma sees to it that "no one is ever sad or angry." An entire branch of the government is reserved for "Emotional Conditioning" and another for "Malthusian Engineering."

Extraordinary that nearly 80 years ago this author predicted the trend toward government assuming the regulation of its citizens' emotions.

In many school districts where the parents or the child has resisted the administration of Ritalin, the authorities have actually taken custody of the student and forced this dangerous experimental drug to be administered. At least the World Controllers in Brave New World, even though they knew what they were doing, had a convincingly paternal explanation about taking away people's freedom to experience life as being "for their own good."

Today this pretense is not even bothered with. Our totalitarian victimization of unsuspecting children is pure politics and economics. The science is so thin as to be ludicrous, behind both ADD and Ritalin. There is nothing scientific about modern bio-psychiatry; and there is certainly nothing scientific about Ritalin. Laws are being passed making "psychiatric care" (read "drugs") to be required whenever possible: public schools, the Medicare system, welfare, mental institutions—anywhere the state can legally intrude into the life and mind of the individual.

This is not Orwellian paranoia; it's happening every day.

Now we certainly can't maintain that no children (or adults) have mental disorders which require treatment. It's obvious enough that children today can be under extreme duress, from dietary influences, from dysfunctional home life, from drugs, from dysfunctional school life, from MTV, or any TV, and from several dozen underlying physical conditions, many of which may manifest as mental disorders. Don't miss the point here. Of course there are some troubled kids out there today who need professional help. But that help is not a 15-minute interview and diagnosis whose purpose is to feed another passenger onto a self-serving, political freight train, rolling down the tracks out of control, trying to legislate more power, more money to the furtherance of its own economic momentum. Is this your child?

What do you think his problem stems from? What do you gain from a shotgun diagnosis? Peace of mind? Exemption from responsibility? Group acceptance? Sympathy? What about the kid and his future? Have you informed yourself about Ritalin? What if you're just covering up some serious underlying pathology in favor of the quick fix, something that's going to smolder, to incubate, to develop, undiagnosed?

Does the child get enough exercise? Does he ever get any exercise? Sugar and dairy? Do you know that such foods are sensitizing allergens which may provide the entire biochemical explanation for chronic misbehavior? What about discipline? Wild horses run wild.

Calling someone ADD doesn't really solve anything, unless you belong to one of the above benefiting groups. But long-term, everyone loses, except the drug companies. Alternative (non-drug) cures for the student with "too much energy" abound. They work because they don't approach the problem from a primarily political point of view. Alternative methods focus on resolution of the problem; rather than finding excuses to prolong it, for ancillary and ulterior agendas.

For hyperactivity, the most commonly effective holistic approach would be dietary: eliminate the sensitizing allergens: milk, cheese, ice cream, white sugar, white flour, soft drinks. These are non-foods; virtually devoid of nutritive value, empty, devitalizing "foods of commerce." In the body they have druglike, antigenic effects especially with years of daily intake. This is not a theory. Try the 60-day Program. [thedoctorwithin.com]. No change, keep doing it.

Next, **exercise**. According to the National Institutes of Health, **only 4%** of Americans exercise. Often physical education programs are the first to be trimmed by budget cutbacks. Many excuses, but children need an hour of vigorous exercise every day, especially if they are being criticized for something as ill-defined as hyperactivity. Their musculoskeletal systems are developing rapidly. Such growth is inhibited by inactivity, i.e., "normal" behavior, like sitting immobile at a desk for eight hours. Try the 60-day test. The word is vigorous.

Then there is gross **nerve blockage**. Upper neck trauma from falls and accidents, or even from childbirth, may go uncorrected for years. Thousands of documented cases of "ADD," as well as learning disorders, have resolved employing this simple biomechanical corrective approach: spinal adjustment.

Rarely, true thyroid imbalance may be a factor. If all the above more common approaches have failed, a thyroid panel may be considered.

Moderate doses of the amino acid phenylalanine, available in any health food store, have also proven effective. Simply getting the kid away from TV for a few months may have profound results. It's not enough that television is a medium which caters to the lowest possible common denominator of intelligence, and that its primary purpose is not entertainment or information, but control. All that is a given.

What is much more subtle is the assiduous effect of having no image remain on the screen for more than three seconds. Except for MTV, when it's much less than a second. This type of incessant hypnotic bombardment of the watcher's psyche imprints a unassailably superficial view of the world. The illusion is: I saw it on TV, now I understand it. Complex issues are reduced to flashes of data—wrapped in that homogenized, canny, controlled little format. No need to do further research or actually read something on a topic. Oh yeah, I know all about that: it was on TV.

The idea of actually learning something about a subject is an alien concept. Lastly, if all the above actually have been tried and have met with no success, the child might be evaluated by a traditional, slow-to-drug psychiatrist who would first of all go through the painstaking process of ruling out underlying physical causes. The doctor might then actually run standardized psychiatric test batteries, which are taught in the psychiatric curriculum, even including psychoanalysis (shudder! how very retro!). Happy dinosaur hunting.

In the long run, delaying normal adolescent development with Ritalin and the ADD diagnosis do not serve the child. Nobel prize winner Dr. Alexis Carrel in 1939 saw the notable disadvantages of the unchallenged child:

"Irresponsible also is the youth brought up in modern schools by teachers ignorant of the necessity for effort, for intellectual concentration, for moral discipline. Later on in life, when these young men and women encounter the indifference of the world, the material and mental difficulties of existence, they are incapable of adaptation, save by asking for relief for protection, for doles, and if relief can not thus be obtained, by crime." —*Man, The Unknown* p 146

The ideas presented in this chapter only scratch the surface of what is really going on in the field of psychiatry, pharmacology and the politics of ADD. The reality of the situation is probably much worse than we have hinted at here. The reader is urged to use this chapter as a starting point for further investigation, beginning with the attached references, especially if there are children involved who have been diagnosed ADD. Remember, all scientific data indicates that there is no such thing. But no such equivocation exists for the side effects of the psychotropics.

The point of view put forth in this chapter is expressed by perhaps 1% of what is being written and published on the topic of ADD today. But in the words of George Orwell, "sanity is not statistical." Our children are the future. To allow them to be victimized for economic and political gain, supported only by some very shaky pseudo-science drug-funded studies, erodes the fabric of society by subtly and gradually surrendering the constitutional rights of the individual. The state should not tell you what degree of "hyperactivity" or energy is acceptable in your child. That is personal. That is individual. That's your business. That's over the line. We never granted them that right.

There's no medical, scientific, or legal basis for it. But they're doing it because we're letting them. If the doctors and the drug empires and the social servants need another disease to make a few more trillion dollars from, let them figure out how to cure the diseases we've already got, instead of trying to pretend that nonconformity is a medical condition.

Living things mature at different rates, even within the same species. That's a law of nature, not something that needs to be "treated." Plant a dozen trees in the same soil. After a year are you going to ask yourself what's wrong with the shorter ones? Or the thinner ones? Or the taller ones? What would you know about the way this tree should grow to maturity? How about trusting in its own inner wisdom?

Living things are not like PC boards in an assembly line. There's a lot of room for normal variation. Eccentricity does not require medical treatment. Most creative people are eccentric in some way: Bill Gates, Einstein, Audrey Hepburn, Linus Pauling, John Lennon, Mozart, Elton John, Michelangelo, Picasso, Nikola Tesla, Benjamin Franklin, Edward Van Halen, BJ Palmer, Sam Kinison, A.P. Hill, Madonna, A.P. Hill, Gandhi, Tony Robbins, Galileo, Versace, Steve Jobs, Elon Musk etc. What if some teacher had diagnosed these people ADD and put them on Ritalin? What would have been lost?

This chapter has been the sketchiest of overviews whose purpose has been to point the reader in the direction of further study, and to plant a seed of doubt, that the overwhelming majority of the conventional wisdom about ADD may be false, unsubstantiated, unscientific, malevolent, and motivated primarily by political and economic agenda. "Experts" will tell you this chapter is wrong, but aren't they the ones making their livelihood by drugging your child? You don't need them; I've included a list of experts that you can use to make up your own mind. That is, if you're still the one who does that.

References

Walker, Sidney, MD — *A Dose of Sanity* Wiley 1996.

Breggin, Peter, MD — *Toxic Psychiatry* St. Martins Press 1994.

Armstrong, Thomas PhD — *The Myth of the ADD Child* Penguin 1997.

Barkley, Russell, PhD — "Safer Than Aspirin."

Physicians Desk Reference — Medical Economics 57th edition 2003.

Baughman, Fred, MD — "The Future of Mental Health" *USA Today* 3/1/97.

Wiseman, Bruce — *Psychiatry: The Ultimate Betrayal* — Freedom 1995.

Baughman, Fred, MD — "What Every Parent Needs to Know About ADD."

McGuiness, Diane PhD "The Limits of Biologic Treatment for Psychiatric Distress."

Koranyi, Erwin MD Undiagnosed physical illness in psychiatric patients *Am Rev Med*, vol 33, 1982.

Schrag, Peter — The Myth of the Hyperactive Child.

Brown, Larry MD — Children's Rights and the Mental Health Profession.

Szasz, Thomas MD — Cruel Compassion.

American Psychiatry Assn. — *Diagnostic and Statistical Manual of Mental Disorders*, Revised Edition III-R, 1987.

Walshe, Sir Francis — Psychiatric Signs and Symptoms Due To Medical Problems — 1967.

Armstrong, Louise — And They Call It Help: The Psychiatric Policing of America's Children 1993.

Huxley, Aldous — Brave New World — Harper 1932.

Orwell, George — 1984 — Signet — 1949.

Carrel, Alexis MD — Man, the Unknown MacFadden — 1939.

U.S. Dept of Education — National Center For Education Statistics: Digest of Education Statistics p 133 1997.

Batmandjlif, F MD — The Body's Many Cries for Water Global Health Solutions 1994.

United Nations — REPORT OF THE INTERNATIONAL NARCOTICS CONTROL BOARD FOR 1995 — E/INCB/1995/1 — UNITED NATIONS PUBLICATION ISBN 92-1-148096-5 ISSN 0257-371

Breggin, P MD — Reclaiming Our Children Perseus — 2000.

Fallon, J — "Caring for the Child with PDD" ICA Review Aug 1999.

Coyle, J MD — Psychotropic Drug Use in Very Young Children — JAMA 23 Feb 2000, p 1059

Giesen, Center, Leach — "An Example of Chiropractic Manipulation" JMPT p 353 vol 12, no 5 Oct 1989.

Barnes, T — "Chiropractic Management of the Specific Needs Child" Topics in Clinical Chiropractic — p 9 — Dec 1997.

Liesman, N — Case Study of ADHD from Kentuckiana — ICA Review p 55 Oct 1998.

Plaugher & Anrig — Pediatric Chiropractic Williams & Wilkins, p 563, 1998.

Barnes, T — A Multi-Faceted Approach to ADHD — ICA Review Feb 1995, p 41.

Brzozowski, W, Walton, E — The effect of chiropractic treatment on students with learning and behavioral impairments ACCA Journal of Chiropractic — 14(12) p 5127 — Dec 1977.

US House of Representatives Hearing on Autism and Vaccines—6 Apr 2000—Dan Burton, Chairman.

Wiseman, B — Psychiatry and the Creation of Senseless Violence — CCHRI — 2000. —1-800-869-2247.

US Dept of Education Digest of Education Statistics, 1997 p 133 http://www.finaid.org/educators/educstat.pdf

Upledger, J — Autism — Observation, Experiences, and Concepts.

Jeffrey L. Charvat, PhD Estimates of the School Psychology Workforce September 2008 www.nasponline.org/advocacy/SP_Workforce_Estimates_9.08.pdf

Begley, S *Scientists' Bible Finally Unveiled* 16 May 2013. www.huffingtonpost.com/2013/05/17/dsm-5-unveiled-changes-disorders-_n_3290212.html

Tim O'Shea, a Doctor of Chiropractic, is the author of several books and articles on nutrition and holistic health, including *The Sanctity of Human Blood: Vaccination Is Not Immunization*, a book about the risks and limitations of vaccines. He conducts seminars nationally and internationally and sponsors a website www.thedoctorwithin.com which addresses various issues pertaining to holistic health.

EXPLORING THE ISSUE

Is Attention-Deficit/Hyperactivity Disorder (ADHD) a Real Disorder?

Critical Thinking and Reflection

1. To what extent should conditions involving inattention and hyperactivity be regarded as medical, as opposed to emotional disorders?
2. What are the minimal behavioral criteria that should be met before recommending that an inattentive and easily distracted individual should be prescribed medication?
3. What might motivate some individuals to want to be diagnosed with the ADHD label?
4. How would you go about designing a research study aimed at differentiating normal characteristics such as occasional inattentiveness from diagnosable conditions such as ADHD?
5. A common style in contemporary society is to multitask, in which attention is divided among several simultaneous tasks (e.g., word processing, checking email, talking on the phone). To what extent does multitasking cause people to believe that they have ADHD because they feel unable to process all the information coming their way?

Is There Common Ground?

Although Tim O'Shea is harshly critical of the diagnosis of ADD/ADHD in the *Diagnostic and Statistical Manual of Mental Disorders,* he concedes the fact that DSM cautions against using the manual as a "cookbook" because there is so much overlap and so many other factors to consider before a supportable diagnosis can be made. Nevertheless, he notes that in actual practice the cookbook method is precisely the way DSM is most commonly used.

NIMH highlights some myths about causes of ADHD, such as the erroneous belief that ADHD can be caused by high levels of sugar intake or food additives. Careful differential diagnosis is also important to rule out conditions that may cause behavior suggestive of ADHD such as undetected seizures, middle ear infection, anxiety or depression, and major life changes.

Dr. O'Shea and NIMH would concur regarding the importance of differentiating typical childhood behaviors from those that would represent a diagnosable mental disorder. For example, NIMH recommends an evaluation that asks whether a child's behaviors are excessive, significantly different from the behavior of peers, continuous versus temporary, and situational versus pervasive. Dr. O'Shea states that once all nonmedical efforts have proved ineffective in helping a misbehaving or inattentive child, a "traditional, slow-to-drug psychiatrist" may be consulted who would go through the painstaking process of ruling out underlying physical causes.

Create Central

www.mhhe.com/createcentral

Additional Resources

Association of Youth Children and Natural Psychology (2013). *Overcoming ADHD Without Medication: A Parent and Educator's Guidebook.* Newark, NJ: Newark Educational and Psychological Publications.

Brown, R. P., & Gerbarg, P. L. (2012). *Non-Drug Treatments for ADHD: New Options for Kids, Adults and Clinicians.* New York, NY: W. W. Norton.

Bruchmüller, K., Margraf, J., & Schneider, S. (2012). "Is ADHD Diagnosed in Accord with Diagnostic Criteria? Overdiagnosis and Influence of Client Gender on Diagnosis." *Journal of Consulting and Clinical Psychology*, 80(1), 128–138. doi:10.1037/a0026582.

Hallowell, E. M., & Ratey, J. J. (2011). *Driven to Distraction: Recognizing and Coping with Attention Deficit Disorder from Childhood Through Adulthood.* New York, NY: Anchor Books.

Internet References . . .

Pediatric Psychopharmacology Research Unit, Department of Psychiatry, Massachusetts General Hospital

http://medapps.med.harvard.edu/psych/redbook/
redbook-family-child-02.htm

American Academy of Child and Adolescent Psychiatry ADHD Resource Center

http://www.aacap.org/AACAP/Families_and_Youth/
Resource_Centers/ADHD_Resource_Center/Home.
aspx

Centers for Disease Control and Prevention—ADHD

http://www.cdc.gov/ncbddd/ADHD/

GoodTherapy.org—Top 10 websites for ADHD

http://www.goodtherapy.org/blog/best-adhd
-resources-2012-0114137

Selected, Edited, and with Issue Framing Material by:
Richard P. Halgin, *University of Massachusetts, Amhersty*

ISSUE

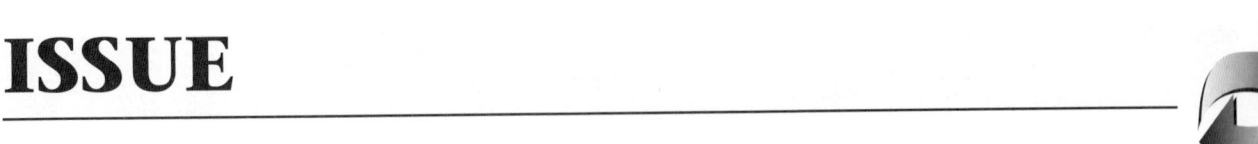

Is Gender Identity Disorder a Mental Illness?

YES: Traditional Values Coalition, from "A Gender Identity Disorder Goes Mainstream: Cross-Dressers, Transvestites, and Transgenders Become Militants in the Homosexual Revolution," *Traditional Values Coalition* (2005)

NO: Kelley Winters, from "Diagnosis vs. Treatment: The Horns of a False Dilemma" and "Top Ten Problems with the GID Diagnosis," *GID Reform Weblog* (2008)

Learning Outcomes

After reading this issue, you will be able to:

- Discuss the DSM diagnostic criteria for Gender Dysphoria (GD) in Adults and Adolescents.
- Critically evaluate the justification for including the diagnosis of GD in the *Diagnostic and Statistical Manual of Mental Disorders*.
- Understand the ways in which a diagnostic label can cause gender-variant people to feel stigmatized.
- Evaluate the extent to which the political ideologies play a role in the definition of what constitutes a mental disorder.
- Assess the extent to which the change in DSM terminology from "Gender Identity Disorder" to "Gender Dysphoria" represents significant change in thinking about gender-variant conditions.

ISSUE SUMMARY

YES: The Traditional Values Coalition argues that gender-variant people are psychologically disturbed individuals who need professional help, and that their condition should be viewed as a mental disorder.

NO: Kelley Winters asserts that the GID diagnosis imposes the stigma of mental illness upon people who meet no scientific definition of mental disorder.

For decades vehement debates have raged about what is normal and what is abnormal when it comes to human sexual behavior. For much of the twentieth century, homosexuality was regarded as a mental disorder and was listed in the *Diagnostic and Statistical Manual of Mental Disorders* (DSM). In 1973, following great controversy and upheaval within the American Psychiatric Association, homosexuality was deleted from the list of mental disorders. Similar controversy emerged about the inclusion of Gender Identity Disorder (GID) in DSM-IV. In response to that debate, DSM-5 has modified the diagnosis by referring to "Gender Dysphoria" (GD). Regardless of the specific terminology,

the debate continues about the inclusion of a gender-variant condition in a diagnostic manual of mental disorders. Even though the articles selected for this issue use the term GID, most of the arguments for and against pathologizing gender variance apply. In fact, some people would argue that the diagnostic label should not have been changed from GID to GD, thus making the articles in this issue relevant, even though the official terminology has changed in DSM-5.

DSM-5 contains two diagnoses in this category: (1) Gender Dysphoria in Children, and (2) Gender Dysphoria in Adolescents and Adults. Criteria for the adolescent/adult condition include a marked incongruence between one's experienced/expressed gender and assigned gender, as evidenced by two of the following: (1) a marked incongruence between one's experienced/expressed gender and primary and/or secondary sex characteristics; (2) a strong desire to get rid of one's primary and/or secondary sex characteristics; (3) a strong desire for the primary and/or secondary sex characteristics of the other gender; (4) a strong desire to be of the other gender; and (5) a strong conviction that one has the typical feelings and reactions of the other gender. In addition, the individual experiences significant distress or impairment, or a significantly increased risk of suffering distress or disability. Subtypes include (1) GD with a disorder of sex development and (2) GD without a disorder of sex development. The diagnosis of GD can be further specified as post transition for individuals who have transitioned to full-time living in the desired gender, and who have undergone or are undergoing at least one cross-sex medical procedure or treatment regimen (i.e., regular cross-sex hormone treatment or gender reassignment surgery, e.g., penectomy, vaginoplasty in a born male, mastectomy, phalloplasty in a born female).

Those who argue that such gender variance should be viewed as a mental disorder, such as members of the Traditional Values Coalition, assert that transgender people are psychologically disturbed individuals who need professional help, rather than societal approval or affirmation. They contend that maleness and femaleness are unchangeable because they exist in a person's DNA; surgical efforts to change a person's sex result in little other than bodily mutilation. According to the Coalition, a man who has his sex organ removed and takes hormone treatments to grow female breasts is still genetically a male.

He is simply a mutilated man, not a woman. This fiction, however, is being perpetrated by a perverted sexual ideology—not by biological facts or science. Homosexuals and their transgender allies believe that "gender" is a cultural invention, not a biological reality. Gender-confused individuals need long-term counseling, not approval for what is clearly a mental disturbance.

In a two-part publication, Kelley Winters argues that diagnosing gender variance as a mental disorder has imposed the stigma of mental illness and sexual deviance upon people who meet no scientific definition of mental disorder. Because of this stigmatization, many gender-variant people fear losing their families, homes, jobs, civil liberties, and access to medical care. Such diagnostic labels, Winters argues, imply that the inner identities of gender-variant individuals are not legitimate, but represent perversion, delusion, or immature development. Those who support such labeling do not acknowledge the existence of many healthy, well-adjusted transsexual and gender-variant people or justify why they are labeled as mentally ill. Identification with the "other sex," meaning other than assigned birth sex, is described as symptomatic regardless of an individual's satisfaction and happiness with that identification. The DSM diagnosis of gender-variant conditions undermines and even contradicts social transition and the medical necessity of hormonal and surgical treatments that relieve the distress of gender dysphoria, defined here as a persistent distress with one's current or anticipated physical sexual characteristics or current ascribed gender role. Furthermore, the DSM diagnosis fails to distinguish the intrinsic distress of gender dysphoria from that caused by external societal intolerance.

A Gender Identity Disorder Goes Mainstream: Cross-Dressers, Transvestites, and Transgenders Become Militants in the Homosexual Revolution

Lesbian, Gay, Bisexual, and Transgender (LGBT) activists are working to add "sexual orientation," "gender," and "gender identity" to federal legislation. If this legislation is passed, cross-dressers, transsexuals, and drag queens will have federally protected minority status equal to minority groups.

What Is a Transgender?

The term Transgender is an umbrella term coined by transgender activists to describe the following individuals: heterosexual cross-dressers, homosexual transvestites or drag queens, and transsexuals (individuals undergoing so-called sex change operations) and she-males.

Some of these individuals live their lives as she-males with both female and male sexual characteristics. These are deeply troubled individuals who need professional help, not societal approval or affirmation.

A History Lesson: Gender Bill of Rights?

In Houston, in August 1993, at a meeting of the Second International Conference on Transgender Law and Employment Policy, transgender activists passed the "International Gender Bill of Rights."

Here is the text of the Gender Bill of Rights:

> All human beings carry within themselves an ever-unfolding idea of who they are and what they are capable of achieving. The individual's sense of self is not determined by chromosomal sex, genitalia, assigned birth sex, or initial gender role. Thus the

individual's identity and capabilities cannot be circumscribed by what society deems to be masculine or feminine behavior.

It is fundamental that individuals have the right to define, and to redefine as their lives unfold, their own gender identity, without regard to chromosomal sex, genitalia, assigned birth sex, or initial gender role.

The Right to Free Expression of Gender Identity—Given the right to define one's own gender identity, all human beings have the corresponding right to free expression of their self-defined gender identity.

The Right to Control and Change One's Own Body—All human beings have the right to control their bodies, which includes the right to change their bodies cosmetically, chemically, or surgically, so as to express a self-defined gender identity.

The Right to Competent Medical and Professional Care—Given the individual right to define one's gender identity, and the right to change one's own body as a means of expressing a self-defined gender identity, no individual should be denied access to competent medical or other professional care on the basis of chromosomal sex, genitalia, assigned birth sex, or initial gender role.

The Right to Freedom from Psychiatric Diagnosis or Treatment—Given the right to define one's own gender identity, individuals should not be subject to psychiatric diagnosis or treatment solely on the basis of their gender identity or role.

The Right to Sexual Expression—Given the right to a self-define gender identity, every consenting adult has a corresponding right to free sexual expression.

The Right to Form Committed, Loving Relationships and Enter into Marital Contracts—Given that all human beings have the right to free expression of a self-defined gender identity, and the right to sexual expression as a form of gender expression, all human beings have a corresponding right to form committed, loving relationships with one another and to enter into marital contracts, regardless of either partner's chromosomal sex, genitalia, assigned birth sex, or initial gender role.

The Right to Conceive or Adopt Children; the Right to Nurture and Have Custody of Children and Exercise of Parental Rights—Given the individual's right to form a committed, loving relationship with another, and to enter into marital contracts with another, together with the right to sexual expression of one's gender identity, all individuals have a corresponding right to conceive or adopt children, to nurture children and to have custody of children, and to exercise parental rights with respect to children, natural or adopted, without regard to chromosomal sex, genitalia, assigned birth sex, or initial gender role.

Transgenders Are Mentally Disordered

The American Psychiatric Association (APA) still lists transsexualism and transvestism as paraphilias or mental disorders in the *Diagnostic and Statistical Manual* (*DSM-IV-TR*). However, homosexual groups such as the Human Rights Campaign (HRC) and GenderPac are pushing hard to have this classification removed from the *DSM*. The objective is to normalize a mental disorder in the same way that homosexuality was normalized in 1973 when psychiatrists removed this sexual dysfunction from the *DSM*. In fact, when the APA met in May 2003 in San Francisco, Dr. Charles Moser with the Institute for Advanced Study of Human Sexuality argued that sadomasochism, transsexualism/transvestism, and even bestiality (sex with animals) should be removed from the *DSM*. According to Moser, psychiatry no longer has a "base line" to judge what constitutes normal behavior, so these categories should be removed.

Media Is Aiding Transgender Movement

Hollywood and the liberal media are doing their part to normalize this serious mental illness. In 2001, for example, the Los Angeles Times published "Era of the Gender Crosser," that portrayed transgendered individuals as a misunderstood and persecuted minority. According to author Mary McNamara, individuals who believe they are the opposite sex should be treated as if they have a medical condition, not a mental condition.

The Discovery Health Channel repeatedly runs "What Sex Am I?" which questions the reality of male and female.

Hollywood is pushing the transgender agenda in various ways. HBO ran "Normal," in March 2003. This show described a middle-aged married man who decided he was really a woman and sought a sex change. Networks are also running "Brandon Teena," about a poor sexually confused girl who dressed like a boy. She was eventually murdered by two angry young men when they discovered who she was. Teena Brandon has become a martyr for the transgender cause.

The latest martyr for transgender activists is a boy named Justin Zapata, who dressed like a girl and called himself "Angie."

Justin was brutally murdered in 2008 by a Mexican gang member who briefly "dated" Justin until he found out that "Angie" was actually an 18-year-old boy. The gang member has been sentenced to life in prison without parole—plus an extra sentence for committing a "hate crime" against Zapata.

Hollywood, which is dominated in many areas by homosexual activists, will continue to introduce transgender themes into its movies and TV shows.

Transgender activists are also receiving help from journalists. The National Lesbian and Gay Journalists Association, for example, has distributed to media outlets a "Stylebook Supplement." It encourages journalists to cater to the transgender agenda by referring to transgendered persons by their self-identification, not their actual birth sex.

Psychiatrists and Pediatricians Are Pushing Transgender Confusion on Kids

The transgender movement is also being helped by psychiatrists and pediatricians who are pushing the view that children should be free to choose their own "genders."

In May 2006, the Pediatric Academic Societies held a conference in San Francisco to promote this bizarre viewpoint.

A member of the National Association for Research and Therapy of Homosexuality (NARTH) was an eyewitness at this conference and described what occurred at this conference.

Two of the attendees were Irene N. Sills and Arlene Istar Lev. They presented a paper titled, "Gender-Variant Youth—The Role Of The Pediatrician." They outlined a "non-pathological model for transgender expression" designed to "help identify the gender-variant child as one who simply marches to the beat of a different drummer."

Pro-transgender activists like these are referring to children with serious Gender Identity Disorders as merely "gender variant."

Some pro-transgender pediatricians are actually injecting preteens with hormones to keep them from developing into adult males or females—until these kids "decide" what sex they wish to be.

This is child abuse, yet the transgender agenda is well-advanced in academia and in the medical and mental health professions.

No One Can Change Their Sex

The reality is that no person can actually change into a different sex. Maleness and femaleness are in the DNA and are unchangeable. A man who has his sex organ removed and takes hormone treatments to grow female breasts is still genetically a male. He is simply a mutilated man, not a woman. This fiction, however, is being perpetrated by a perverted sexual ideology—not by biological facts or science.

Homosexual groups such as the Human Rights Campaign and the National Gay and Lesbian Task Force have provided transgender activists with credibility and political power as they pursue their agenda.

The transgender movement's philosophy is based on the writings of several transsexuals. Among them are Nancy Nangeroni, founder of the International Foundation for Gender Education, Martine Rothblatt, and Marxist radical Leslie Feinberg, author of *Transgender Warrior,* and an editor with the Workers World Party, a Communist splinter group that aligns itself with North Korea.

Nancy Nangeroni claims that Western Civilization is "sick" because it pathologizes any person who wants a sex change operation. Martine Rothblatt is author of *The Apartheid of Sex: A Manifesto on the Freedom of Gender.* According to Rothblatt, our culture's practice of dividing people into two sexes is as evil as racial apartheid. He argues that there are actually several sexes, not just male and female. Those who oppose transgenderism are "transphobic" and intolerant.

The Human Rights Campaign, one of the most aggressive homosexual groups in the United States, is allied with transgender activists and has actually developed workplace guidelines for how businesses should handle men and women who are undergoing sex change operations.

In addition, Parents and Friends of Lesbians and Gays (PFLAG) has a special Transgender Special Outreach Network, which includes coordinators in more than 170 chapters. It also distributed 12,000 copies of "Our Trans Children" to schools and to parents of these sexually confused children.

The leading transgender group is GenderPac, headed by male-to-female transgender Riki Wilchins. He is author of *READ MY LIPS: Sexual Subversion & the End of Gender.* Wilchins works closely with the NGLTF to get the APA to remove transsexualism as a mental disorder. Patricia Ireland, former head of the YWCA, is a member of the board of GenderPac and helps lobby Congress for passage of legislation protecting the "gender identity" of individuals in the workplace and in our culture.

Be Whatever You Wish

Homosexuals and their transgender allies believe that "gender" is a cultural invention, not a biological reality. According to these activists, a person can self-identify and be whatever he or she wishes to be sexually. One pro-transgender activist, Professor Anne Fausto-Sterling, for example, has said that "Complete maleness and complete femaleness represent the extreme ends of a spectrum of possible body types."

Fausto-Sterling published "The Five Sexes: Why Male and Female Are Not Enough," in The Sciences, March/April 1993. In fact, many of these sexually confused individuals decide that they wish to be neither male nor female, but to exist as she-males with female sexual characteristics from the waist up and male sexual characteristics from the waist down.

One of these individuals actually set up a web site to describe herself. Della Grace on her web site "Body Politic," says she is a she-male and former lesbian photographer and visual artist. Grace says she willingly purchased a "one-way ticket" to "no man's land," to inhabit the "nether world" where she is neither male nor female. She calls herself a "pansexual, which means I don't discriminate on the basis of gender or species." She also describes herself as a "gender variant" mutant who has decided against being male or female.

Deconstructing Male and Female

The NARTH has published numerous articles on various Gender Identity Disorders. One is by Dale O'Leary, author of *The Gender Agenda.* In the NARTH paper, "Destabilizing The Categories Of Sex And Gender," O'Leary notes: Patients who suffer from the belief that they are men trapped in the bodies of women (or women trapped in the bodies of men) need real help. . . . The promotion of 'sex changes,' and the normalizing of severe Gender Identity Disorders by radical feminists, pro-same-sex attraction disorder activists, and sexual revolutionaries is part of their larger agenda—namely, the destabilization of the categories of sex and gender."

O'Leary notes that radicals and medical professionals who promote sex change operations are operating under the delusion that one's gender is changeable. One cannot change into a different sex. It is genetically and medically impossible. Gender-confused individuals need long-term counseling, not approval for what is clearly a mental disturbance.

Dr. Martin Silverman, a member of NARTH, has written extensively on Gender Identity Disorders. In a NARTH paper, "Gender Identity Disorder In Boys: A Complemental Series?" he notes that a boy who has developed a Gender Identity Disorder, such as homosexuality or transvestism, typically comes from a home where the mother is smothering in her love and where the father is passive and feels powerless to overcome his wife's dominance in the family. NARTH has more information on this disorder on its web site: www.narth.com.

What Can Be Done?

If the transgender movement is not already active in your community, it will be. Wherever there are homosexual activist groups, you will find transgendered individuals working alongside them to establish policies and recruitment programs in public schools and to change laws to redefine what it means to be male or female. Here are some suggestions for action:

Monitor city and state legislative proposals that contain the word "gender" in them. Gender is code for cross-dressers, transvestites, and transsexuals. Inform your local politicians of this cultural agenda so they will recognize it when activists attempt to push through legislation.

Oppose Gay Straight Alliance clubs on school campuses. These are recruitment programs to lure children into sexually destructive lifestyles.

These GLSEN-sponsored groups are now promoting cross-dressing for children.

Use TVC, NARTH, and other materials in fighting homosexual/transgenderism.

TRADITIONAL VALUES COALITION (TVs), founded in 1980 by Reverend Louis P. Sheldon, is "the largest nondenominational, grassroots church lobby in America." TVC focuses on issues such as marriage, religious liberties, pornography, education, family tax relief, and what the Coalition calls "the right to life" and "the homosexual agenda." The organization emphasizes on "the restoration of the values needed to maintain strong, unified families," providing information on these topics to Christians and pastors.

Kelley Winters

 **NO**

Diagnosis vs. Treatment:
The Horns of a False Dilemma

The transgender community has been divided by fear that we must choose between access to corrective hormonal and surgical procedures to support transition and the stigma of mental illness imposed by the current diagnosis of Gender Identity Disorder (GID).[1] This schism has allowed little dialogue and no progress on GID reform in nearly three decades. However, the GID diagnosis has failed our community on both points. Transsexual individuals are poorly served by a diagnosis that both stigmatizes us as mentally deficient and sexually deviant *and at the same time* undermines the legitimacy of social transition and medical procedures that are often dismissed as "elective," "cosmetic," or as reinforcing mental disorder.

Gender Identity Disorder in the *Diagnostic and Statistical Manual of Mental Disorders*[2] has imposed stigma of mental illness and sexual deviance upon people who meet no scientific definition of mental disorder.[3] It does not acknowledge the existence of many healthy, well-adjusted transsexual, and gender variant people or justify why we are labeled as mentally ill.

I have heard countless narratives of suffering inflicted by the stereotype of mental illness and "disordered" gender identity, and I have experienced it myself. We lose our families, our children, our homes, jobs, civil liberties, access to medical care, and our physical safety. With each heartbreak, we're almost invariably told the same thing—that we're "nuts," that our identities and affirmed roles are madness and deviance. The following statement by Dr. Robert Spitzer at the 1973 annual meeting of the American Psychiatric Association remains as true today for transgender people as it was for gay and lesbian people then:

> "In the past, homosexuals have been denied civil rights in many areas of life on the ground that because they suffer from a 'mental illness' the burden of proof is on them to demonstrate their competence, reliability, or mental stability."[4]

The current GID diagnosis places a similar burden of proof upon gender variant individuals to prove our competence, with consequences of social stigma and denied civil rights. It harms those it was intended to help. For example,

> "Transsexuals suffer from 'mental pathologies,' are ineligible for admission to Roman Catholic religious orders and should be expelled if they have already entered the priesthood or religious life, the Vatican says in new directives."[5]

Simultaneously, GID in the DSM-IV-TR undermines and even contradicts social transition and the medical necessity of hormonal and surgical treatments that relieve the distress of gender dysphoria, defined here as a persistent distress with one's current or anticipated physical sexual characteristics or current ascribed gender role.[6] For example, Paul McHugh, M.D., former psychiatrist-in-chief at Johns Hopkins Hospital, used GID diagnosis as a key reason to eliminate gender confirming surgeries there:

> "I concluded that to provide a surgical alteration to the body of these unfortunate people was to collaborate with a mental disorder rather than to treat it."[7]

Dr. Paul Fedoroff of the Centre for Addiction and Mental Health (formerly the Clarke Institute of Psychiatry) cited the psychiatric diagnosis to urge elimination of gender confirming surgeries in Ontario in 2000,

> "TS [transsexualism, in reference to the GID diagnosis] is also unique for being the only psychiatric disorder in which the defining symptom is facilitated, rather than ameliorated, by the 'treatment.' . . . It is the only psychiatric disorder in which no attempt is made to alter the presenting core symptom."[8]

Paradoxically, the GID diagnosis has been defended as necessary for access to hormonal and surgical transition procedures. It is required by Standards of Care of the World Professional Association for Transgender Health,[9] and GID is cited in legal actions to gain access to these procedures. Attorney Shannon Minter, head counsel for the National Center for Lesbian Rights, was quoted in *The Advocate*,

"'When we go to court to advocate for transsexual people to get medical treatment in a whole variety of circumstances, from kids in foster care to prisoners on Medicaid,' the GID diagnosis is used to show that treatment is medically necessary."[10]

Dr. Nick Gorton echoed long-standing fears that access to hormonal and surgical procedures would be lost if the GID were removed entirely,

"Loss of the DSM diagnostic category for GID will endanger the access to care, psychological well being, and in some cases, the very life of countless disenfranchised transgender people who are dependent on the medical and psychiatric justification for access to care."[11]

Gender dysphoric transpeople have therefore assumed that we must suffer degradation and stigma by the current GID diagnosis or forfeit lifesaving medical transition procedures. But has our community been impaled on the horns of a false dilemma?

Are hormonal and surgical procedures available to transitioning individuals because of the current diagnosis of "disordered" gender identity or in spite of it? Because the GID criteria and supporting text are tailored to contradict transition and pathologize birth-role nonconformity[3], affirming and tolerant professionals are burdened to reconstrue GID in more positive and supportive way for transitioning clients. For example, last month the American Medical Association passed a historic resolution, "Removing Financial Barriers to Care for Transgender Patients." It reinterpreted GID to emphasize distress and de-emphasize difference:

". . . a persistent discomfort with one's assigned sex and with one's primary and secondary sex characteristics, which causes intense emotional pain and suffering."[12]

The AMA statement is perhaps a model for what the GID diagnosis should become.

The current GID diagnosis and its doctrine of "disordered" gender identity have failed the transcommunity on both issues of harmful psychosexual stigma *and* barriers to medical care access. The DSM-V Sexual and Gender Identity Disorders work group has an opportunity to correct both failures with new diagnostic nomenclature based on scientific standards of distress and impairment rather than intolerance of social role nonconformity and difference from assigned birth sex.

Notes

1. This essay is expanded from K. Winters, "Harm Reduction for Gender Disorders in the DSM-V," Philadelphia Trans Health Conference, May 2008.

2. American Psychiatric Association, *Diagnostic and Statistical Manual of Mental Disorders,* Fourth Edition, Text Revision, Washington, D.C., 2000.

3. K. Winters, "Gender Dissonance: Diagnostic Reform of Gender Identity Disorder for Adults," *Sexual and Gender Diagnoses of the Diagnostic and Statistical Manual* (DSM), Ed. Dan Karasic, MD, and Jack Drescher, MD, Haworth Press, 2005; co-published in *Journal of Psychology & Human Sexuality,* vol. 17 issue 3, pp. 71–89, 2005.

4. R. Spitzer, "A Proposal About Homosexuality and the APA Nomenclature: Homosexuality as an Irregular Form of Sexual Behavior and Sexual Orientation Disturbance as a Psychiatric Disorder," *American Journal of Psychiatry,* Vol. 130, No. 11, November 1973, p. 1216.

5. N. Winfield, Associated Press, "Vatican Denounces Transsexuals," *Newsday,* Jan 2003.

6. Working definition of Gender Dysphoria by Dr. Randall Ehrbar and I following our panel presentations at the 2007 convention of the American Psychological Association. It is defined in glossary of the DSM-IV-TR as "A persistent aversion toward some of all of those physical characteristics or social roles that connote one's own biological sex." (p. 823)

7. P. McHugh, "Surgical Sex," *First Things* 147: 34–38, http://www.firstthings.com/ftissues/ft0411/articles/mchugh.htm, 2004.

8. J. Fedoroff, "The Case Against Publicly Funded Transsexual Surgery," *Psychiatry Rounds,* Vol. 4, Issue 2, April 2000.

9. World Professional Association for Transgender Health (formerly HBIGDA), "Standards of Care for The Hormonal and Surgical Sex Reassignment of Gender Dysphoric Persons," http://wpath.org/Documents2/socv6.pdf, 2001.

10. S. Rochman, "What's Up, Doc?" *The Advocate*, http://www.advocate.com/issue_story_ektid50125.asp, Nov 2007.

11. R.N. Gorton, "Transgender as Mental Illness: Nosology, Social Justice, and the Tarnished Golden Mean," www.Nickgorton.org/misc/work/private_research/transgender_as_mental_illness.pdf, 2006.

12. American Medical Association, "Resolution 122, Removing Financial Barriers to Care for Transgender Patients," http://www.ama-assn.org/ama1/pub/upload/mm/16/a08_hod_resolutions.pdf, June 2008.

Top Ten Problems with the GID Diagnosis

What are the problems with the Gender Identity Disorder diagnosis in the *Diagnostic and Statistical Manual of Mental Disorders* (DSM)[1]? How are overarching issues of psychiatric stigma and access to medical transition procedures related to specific flaws in the diagnostic criteria[2] and supporting text? The philosopher Jiddu Krishnamurti said

If we can really understand the problem, the answer will come out of it, because the answer is not separate from the problem.[3]

This is my personal list of the most egregious problems with the current Gender Identity Disorder diagnosis. While far from comprehensive, it is perhaps a starting point for dialogue about how harm reduction of gender nomenclature might be possible in the DSM-V.

1. **Focus of pathology on nonconformity to assigned birth sex in disregard to the definition of mental disorder, which comprises distress and impairment.**
   Recent revisions of the DSM increasingly target gender identity and expression that differ from natal or assigned sex as disordered. The current diagnostic criteria for GID in the DSM-IV-TR are preoccupied with social gender role nonconformity, especially for children. Identification with the "other sex," meaning other than assigned birth sex, is described as symptomatic regardless of our satisfaction and happiness with that identification [p. 581].

2. **Stigma of mental illness upon emotions and expressions that are ordinary or even exemplary for nontransgender children, adolescents and adults.**
   Criterion A for Gender Identity Disorder highlights a desire to be treated as, or "frequently passing as," our affirmed gender as pathological. For children, criteria A and B stress ordinary masculine or feminine expression in clothing, play, games, toys, and fantasy as symptoms of mental "disturbance" [p. 581]. The supporting text disparages innocent childhood play as disorder, including Barbie dolls, playing house, Batman and "rough-and-tumble" activity, if they violate stereotypes of assigned birth sex [pp. 576–577]. Incredulously, knitting is implicated as a focus of sexual perversion for adult transwomen in the supporting text [p. 579].

3. **Lacks clarity on gender dysphoria, defined here as clinically significant distress with physical sex characteristics or ascribed gender role.[4]**
   The distress of gender dysphoria that necessitates medical intervention is inadequately described in criterion B of the GID diagnosis in the DSM-IV-TR as "discomfort" or "inappropriateness." For children, this often-debilitating pain is obfuscated in the diagnostic criterion, which emphasizes nonconformity to gender stereotypes of assigned birth sex rather than clinically significant distress. Adolescents and adults who believe that we were "born in the wrong sex" meet criterion B on the basis of their belief, even if our gender dysphoria has been relieved by transition or related medical procedures [p. 581].

4. **Contradicts transition and access to hormonal and surgical treatments, which are well proven to relieve distress of gender dysphoria.**
   Social role transition, living and passing in our affirmed gender roles, and desiring congruent anatomic sex characteristics are listed as "manifestation" of mental pathology in criterion A of Gender Identity Disorder. Requests for

hormonal or surgical treatment to relieve gender dysphoria are disparaged as "preoccupation" in criterion B and supporting text rather than medical necessity [p. 581]. Evidence of medical transition treatment, such as breast development for transwomen or chest reconstruction for transmen, is described in a negative context as "associated features and disorders" of mental illness in the supporting text [p. 579].

5. **Encourages gender-conversion therapies, intended to change or shame one's gender identity or expression.**

The DSM is intended as a diagnostic guide without specific treatment recommendations [p. xxxvii]. Nevertheless, the current GID diagnostic criteria are biased to favor punitive gender-conversion "therapies." For example, gender variant youth, adolescents or adults who have been shamed into the closet, forced into concealing our inner gender identities, no longer meet the diagnostic criteria of Gender Identity Disorder and are emancipated from a label of mental illness.

6. **Misleading title of "Gender Identity Disorder," suggesting that gender identity is itself disordered or deficient.**

The name, Gender Identity Disorder, implies "disordered" gender identity—that the inner identities of gender variant individuals are not legitimate but represent perversion, delusion or immature development. In other words, the current GID diagnosis in the DSM-IV-TR implies that transwomen are nothing more than mentally ill or confused "men" and vice versa for transmen.[5]

7. **Maligning terminology, including "autogynephilia," which disrespects transitioned individuals with inappropriate pronouns and labels.**

Maligning language labels gender variant people by our assigned birth sex in disregard of our gender identity. In other words, affirmed or transitioned transwomen are demeaned as "he" and transmen as "she." It appears throughout the diagnostic criteria and supporting text of the GID diagnosis in the current DSM-IV-TR, where affirmed roles are termed "other sex" [p. 581], transsexual women are called "males" and "he" [p. 577], and transsexual men as "females" [p. 579]. Such demeaning terms deny our social legitimacy and empower defamatory social stereotypes like "a man in a dress," in the press, the courts, our workplace, and our families.

8. **False positive diagnosis of those who are no longer gender dysphoric after transition and of gender nonconforming children who were never gender dysphoric.**

There is no exit clause in the diagnostic criteria for individuals whose gender dysphoria has been relieved by transition, hormones or surgical treatments, regardless of how happy or well adjusted with our affirmed gender roles. The diagnosis is implied "to have a chronic course" for adults [p. 580], despite transition status or absence of distress. Children may be diagnosed with Gender Identity Disorder, solely on the basis of gender role nonconformity, without evidence of gender dysphoria. Criterion A requires only four of five listed attributes, and four of those describe violation of gender stereotypes of assigned birth sex, The fifth, describing unhappiness with birth sex, is not required to meet criterion A. Criterion B may be met by "aversion toward rough-and-tumble play and rejection of male stereotypical toys . . ." for natal boys and "aversion toward normative feminine clothing" for natal girls [p. 581].

9. **Conflation of impairment caused by prejudice with distress intrinsic to gender dysphoria.**

Criterion D of the GID diagnosis, the clinical significance criterion [p. 581], was intended to require clinically significant distress or impairment to meet the accepted definition of mental disorder [p. xxxi]. Unfortunately, it fails to distinguish intrinsic distress of gender dysphoria from that caused by external societal intolerance. Lacking clarity in criterion D, prejudice, and discrimination can be misconstrued as psychological impairment for gender variant individuals who are not distressed by our physical sex characteristics or ascribed gender roles.

10. **Placement in the class of sexual disorders.**

In 1994, Gender Identity Disorders were moved from the class of "Disorders Usually First Evident in Infancy, Childhood or Adolescence," to the section of sexual disorders in the DSM-IV, renamed "Sexual and Gender Identity Disorders".[6] This reinforces stereotypes of sexual deviance for gender variant people.

The DSM-V Task Force has an opportunity to address these shortcomings in the current GID diagnosis. I hope that this list can help provide a way to evaluate proposals for less harmful diagnostic nomenclature in the fifth edition of the DSM.

Notes

1. American Psychiatric Association, *Diagnostic and Statistical Manual of Mental Disorders,* Fourth Edition, Text Revision, Washington, D.C., 2000, pp. 576–582.

2. DSM-IV-TR Diagnostic criteria for Gender Identity Disorder of Adults and Adolescents are available online at http://www.gidreform.org/gid30285.html and for children at http://www.gidreform.org/gid3026.html

3. "Krishnamurti Quotes," http://www.krishnamurti.org.au/articles/krishnamurti_quotes.htm

4. Working definition of Gender Dysphoria by Dr. Randall Ehrbar and I, following our panel presentations at the 2007 convention of the American Psychological Association. It is defined in glossary of the DSM-IV-TR as "A persistent aversion toward some of all of those physical characteristics or social roles that connote one's own biological sex." (p. 823)

5. K. Winters, "Gender Dissonance: Diagnostic Reform of Gender Identity Disorder for Adults," *Sexual and Gender Diagnoses of the Diagnostic and Statistical Manual (DSM),* Ed. Dan Karasic, MD. and Jack Drescher, MD., Haworth Press, 2005; co-published in *Journal of Psychology & Human Sexuality,* vol. 17, issue 3, pp. 71–89, 2005.

6. American Psychiatric Association, *Diagnostic and Statistical Manual of Mental Disorders,* Fourth Edition, 1994.

KELLEY WINTERS is the founder of GID Reform Advocates as well as a writer on issues of transgender medical policy. Winters is the author of *Gender Madness in American Psychiatry: Essays from the Struggle for Dignity* (2008), and her articles have appeared in a number of books and journals. She is also on the advisory board for TransYouth Family Advocates and the Matthew Shepard Foundation.

EXPLORING THE ISSUE

Is Gender Identity Disorder a Mental Illness?

Critical Thinking and Reflection

1. To what extent should the mental health profession be concerned about personal issues of gender identity, particularly in people who do not view themselves as psychologically disturbed?
2. With the diagnosis of Gender Dysphoria being included in *DSM-5*, the assumption would be that this is a "treatable condition." What kind of "treatment" should be recommended?
3. How would you go about designing a research study of the psychological difficulties experienced by gender variant individuals?
4. If you were designing an educational program to inform the public about gender variant individuals, what message would you want to convey?
5. *DSM-5* includes the diagnosis of Gender Dysphoria in Children. What issues should be considered before assigning this diagnosis to a child?

Is There Common Ground?

Although it is difficult to find areas of agreement between the Traditional Values Coalition and Kelley Winters, there does seem to be agreement about the powerful role of psychiatric diagnosis in our society. The Coalition views gender variant people as deeply troubled people who are psychologically disturbed and in need of professional help. The Coalition sees efforts of various lobbying groups as sharing the objective to "normalize a mental disorder in the same way that homosexuality was normalized in 1973 when psychiatrists removed this sexual dysfunction [sic] from *DSM*."

Kelley Winters also takes note of the pathologizing of gender variant conditions, although their inclusion in the *DSM* is viewed as imposing the stigma of mental illness and sexual deviance upon people who meet no scientific definition of mental disorder. Thus, it seems that in their divergence, both parties in this debate seem to be challenging the very definition of what constitutes a mental disorder. Even the *DSM-5* relabeling of gender variance in terms of "Gender Dysphoria" raises questions about what aspects of gender variance make such conditions mental disorders per se.

Create Central

www.mhhe.com/createcentral

Additional Resources

Drescher, J., & Byne, W. (2012, March 1). Gender dysphoric/gender variant (gd/gv) children and adolescents: Summarizing what we know and what we have yet to learn. *Journal of Homosexuality*, 59(3), 501–510.

Kreukels, B. P. C., Steensma, T. D., & De, V. A. L. C. (2014). *Gender Dysphoria and Disorders of Sex Development: Progress in Care and Knowledge*. Dordrecht: Springer.

Teich, N. M. (2012). *Transgender 101: A Simple Guide to a Complex Issue*. New York, NY: Columbia University Press.

Internet References . . .

Gender Spectrum

https://www.genderspectrum.org/

PFLAG—Parents, Families, Friends and Allies United with LGBT People to Move Equality Forward!

http://community.pflag.org/transgender

World Professional Association for Transgender Health

http://www.wpath.org/

Selected, Edited, and with Issue Framing Material by:
Richard P. Halgin, *University of Massachusetts, Amherst*

ISSUE

Is Posttraumatic Stress Disorder (PTSD) Overdiagnosed and Overtreated?

YES: Stephen Joseph, from "Has PTSD Taken Over America?," "What Is Trauma?," "Changing How We Think about Psychological Trauma," and "Therapy for Posttraumatic Growth: Car Mechanics and Gardeners," psychologytoday.com (2011–2012)

NO: U.S. Department of Veterans Affairs, National Center for PTSD, from "What Is PTSD?," "How Common Is PTSD?," and "Treatment of PTSD," ptsd.va.gov (2012)

Learning Outcomes
After reading this issue, you will be able to: • Discuss the symptoms of PTSD and the characteristics of PTSD that distinguish it from expectable stress following exposure to an upsetting experience. • Critically evaluate the question of whether "trauma" has become too broadly defined, and the diagnosis of PTSD applied too liberally. • Understand the differences between two treatment approaches to PTSD: an intervention based on facilitating growth and an intervention focused on reforming how one thinks about the traumatic experience. • Discuss how the criteria for PTSD have evolved over time and consider the forces contributing to changes in this diagnosis. • Understand the concept of posttraumatic growth.

ISSUE SUMMARY

YES: Dr. Stephen Joseph argues that since the development of posttraumatic stress disorder (PTSD) as a diagnosis, the definition of trauma has been altered from its 1980 definition in DSM-III, and has been applied so loosely that everyday experiences can now be considered traumatic.

NO: The Department of Veterans Affairs (VA) states that PTSD can develop in any individuals who have gone through a life-threatening event that caused them to fear for their lives, see horrible things, and feel helpless. The VA urges therapists to help individuals with PTSD identify what triggers their stressful memories, find ways to cope with intense feelings about the past, become aware of their feelings and reactions in order to change their reactions, and raise their self-esteem.

Most people would acknowledge that involvement in the horrors of war leaves an indelible psychological mark on the soldiers who have risked their own lives or witnessed the death and injury of others. Although the experience of life-threatening trauma can take place in any human context, research efforts and clinical intervention have focused primarily on the condition known as posttraumatic stress disorder (PTSD) associated with military combat. In fact, the label PTSD was only added to the *Diagnostic and Statistical Manual of Mental Disorders* in 1980 when DSM-III was published by the American Psychiatric Association, in great part due to the growing awareness of the psychological casualties reported by veterans of the Vietnam War. In DSM-5, the PTSD diagnosis continues to evolve with the addition of more specificity about operationalizing some of the criteria, and by adding new symptoms (e.g., negative cognitions and mood). Even a new subtype is being added: Posttraumatic Stress Disorder in Preschool Children.

Because of all that was learned from the Vietnam era about PTSD, major efforts were made from the outset of the Afghanistan and Iraq wars on the part of the Department of Defense and the U.S. Department of Veterans Affairs to assess the impact of combat and to develop interventions aimed at reducing long-standing psychological disturbance. The research initiatives of the VA as well as the studies being conducted in other research programs have also made valuable contributions to the literature on PTSD arising from nonmilitary traumas, such as the diagnosis and treatment of people surviving trauma in noncombat situations: the national trauma of the September 11 attacks, the regional traumas caused by natural disasters such as hurricanes and tornadoes, and the personal traumas experienced by people who have been assaulted, raped, abused, or devastated by accident or injury.

Along with the justifiable attention to the nature of trauma and the development of effective interventions for trauma survivors has come some scrutiny, particularly about the possibility that PTSD is being overdiagnosed. More specifically, the question has been proposed about the extent to which individuals who experience distressing and possibly traumatizing experiences are being inappropriately labeled with a psychiatric *disorder,* rather than an expectable response to stress. Are such individuals being led to psychotherapy to treat their *disorder* instead of being given the tools to use their harrowing experience as an opportunity for posttraumatic growth?

Dr. Stephen Joseph challenges us to change how we think of trauma, and he expresses concern that PTSD may be taking over America. In considering the diagnosis of PTSD, he notes that the current definition is far more wide-ranging than that published in 1980 in DSM-III, and he asserts that the current definition is fraught with problems. According to Dr. Joseph, it is a normal process following traumatic events to suffer from intrusive thoughts, upsetting memories, and nightmares accompanied by attempts at emotional numbing and problems sleeping, difficulties with concentration, and feelings of being on edge. In this natural response

lies the opportunity for personal transformation as the person works through the significance of what has happened and what it means.

Dr. Joseph believes that over the past three decades, the diagnosis of PTSD has undergone "bracket creep" such that the diagnosis of PTSD is now much more common than it would have been 30 years ago. Not only is it more common, it has also become more widely used to describe what previously would have been viewed as normal human distress. The task for therapists, then, is to facilitate posttraumatic growth.

Contrasting with the view of Dr. Joseph is the Department of Veterans Affairs, which has been facing the challenge of responding to the needs of millions of soldiers returning from war and combat. During the first decade of the twenty-first century, the VA has played a tremendously important role in tending to the needs of soldiers returning from combat, particularly those who served in Iraq and Afghanistan. With the numbers of soldiers returning with physical injury and psychological trauma reaching an all-time high, the VA has become a major player in responding to these men and women. Cynics might view the VA as having a vested interest in perpetuating the diagnosis of PTSD so that billions of dollars of funding will continue to be directed to the VA, which is the U.S. government's second largest department (after the Department of Defense). On the other side of that argument, however, is the fact that the budget of the VA is indeed limited, and therefore tremendous effort must be invested in ensuring the validity of every single diagnosis of PTSD among soldiers and veterans, so that financial resources are directed to those individuals whose lives have been so detrimentally affected by trauma.

In the VA's materials, acknowledgment is made of the fact that going through trauma does not mean that a person will develop PTSD. The VA states that although approximately half of all Americans go through some type of trauma, only 7–8 percent of the population develops PTSD. As for the most appropriate response, the VA does not discuss posttraumatic growth, but rather advocates interventions that help traumatized individuals change their cognitions. In cognitive therapy, the therapist helps the client understand how certain thoughts about the trauma cause an increase in stress and a worsening of symptoms. Clients are taught how to identify thoughts about the world and themselves which are causing fear and upset, and to replace these thoughts with more accurate and less distressing thoughts.

YES

Stephen Joseph

Has PTSD Taken Over America?

Last week I was interviewed by Alice Karekezi for Salon. Com. She asked me if I thought PTSD was over diagnosed.

There are actually two questions rolled up into this I think. The first is whether people are being inappropriately diagnosed with PTSD as defined by DSM. The second is whether the concept of PTSD has been over applied.

So, the first question; I think the vast majority of psychologists and psychiatrists are responsible professional people and are using the diagnostic category as it is meant to be used. Overall they are doing what it says on the tin.

It's what it says on the tin I wonder about. To the second question I wonder whether the concept of PTSD has been applied too widely.

It is my view that posttraumatic stress occurs in people following all sorts of threatening events and that these reactions are on a spectrum ranging from mild to severe levels. The job of psychiatric classification is to draw a line somewhere on that spectrum. Above the line, the person is suffering from a disorder, below the line they are not. I'm not saying that this is how it should be, simply that this is what is happening when a diagnosis is made. In my view the line has been drawn in such a way that a clear cut distinction is not made between those who are suffering from PTS and those who are suffering from PTSD.

To me it seems that to suffer from intrusive thoughts, upsetting memories and nightmares accompanied by attempts at avoidance, emotional numbing and problems sleeping, concentrating, and feelings of being on edge and tense, and so on following traumatic events is a normal and natural process—of personal transformation as the person works through the significance of what has happened to them and what it means. As distressing as such an experience may be it is not an illness. As such the term PTS seems appropriate.

The problem is if people who are suffering from PTS are given the diagnosis of PTSD. This happens because the diagnositic criteria do not make a distinction between PTS and PTSD.

So, when does the label PTSD become appropriate? In my view the label PTSD should be applied when it is clear that there is a dysfunction of these normal and natural mental mechanisms such that the person is unable to cognitively-emotionally process their experiences. We know that there are brain correlates but that line of research needs to go further and show that PTSD is a disorder of the brain.

In the context of psychiatric classification I simply think we ought to be cautious with the word disorder and to make sure that it means more than being distressed, different or difficult.

***

What Is Trauma?

Is it time to dump the diagnosis of PTSD?

My dictionary defines trauma as a deeply distressing or disturbing experience. Defined like that the events which can be considered traumatic are wide ranging indeed—from what might be considered the stuff of ordinary life such as divorce, illness, accidents and bereavement to extreme experiences of war, torture, rape and genocide.

Insofar as we adopt this wide ranging definition trauma is the stuff of everyday life.

The American Psychiatric Association's current definition of posttraumatic stress disorder (PTSD), introduced in 1994, states that a person must have experienced or witnessed an event or events that involved actual or threatened death or serious injury, or a threat to the physical integrity of self or others, and which involved fear, helplessness, or horror.

While the American Psychiatric Association's definition is more restrictive than my dictionary definition it is still far more wide ranging than the original 1980 definition of PTSD which stated that an event had to be outside the range of usual human experience. Then, only the most horrific events would qualify.

Looking to the future, debate rages in clinical and scientific circles about whether the next definition of trauma in DSM-V should be more or less restrictive.

Should we go back to something closer to the original idea that a trauma was an experience than when encountered would psychologically overwhelm all who encountered it? Or should we move in the direction of thinking that all life events have the potential to be perceived as traumatic?

Not surprisingly the elastic nature of the concept of trauma over the years has caused a great deal of public confusion.

And the topic of PTSD seems charged with emotion. There are two points of view.

First is the view that PTSD results from a stressor that is so overwhelming that no matter what the person's resources they will develop PTSD. As such the diagnosis of PTSD does not reflect any personal vulnerability.

The second is that people who develop PTSD are vulnerable in some way. As such the diagnosis of PTSD does reflect inner vulnerability. Those who do not develop PTSD are resilient.

And sometimes people who take the former view are dismissive of those who have received a diagnosis of PTSD following more everyday events as if their PTSD is somehow less valid. It is claimed that PTSD is being over-diagnosed.

But the fact is that since the 1994 definition, research has defined PTSD in such a way that trauma is necessary but not always sufficient to produce PTSD—so both these points of view are right.

The current definition has it both ways by understanding PTSD as the outcome of an interaction between trauma intensity and personal vulnerability.

An extreme event may be sufficient to produce PTSD in all who experience it so that personal vulnerability is not a factor. But a less extreme event may only produce PTSD in those who are already vulnerable.

Not surprisingly, in a culture in which mental illness is stigmatized, the issue of whether PTSD is caused by an event or by personal vulnerability is one which is charged with emotion. As the public understanding seems closer to the original definition of PTSD, the current definition is fraught with problems.

***

Changing How We Think about Psychological Trauma

The possibility of posttraumatic growth has become one of the most exciting topics in modern clinical psychology and psychotherapy.

Many commentators have talked about how trauma can be a catalyst to positive psychological change. Often,

people's philosophies of life change; perhaps becoming wiser, less materialistic, or more able to live in the present. Their sense of self changes too; perhaps becoming more patient, compassionate or grateful. And people's relationships change; perhaps with a new depth of quality, the ability to make time for others, or becoming more giving.

Certainly, the study of posttraumatic growth is fascinating.

But what I find so compelling about this topic, and what most commentators haven't spotted yet, is that posttraumatic growth turns on its head how we think about psychological trauma.

For the last thirty years, the idea of posttraumatic stress disorder (PTSD) has been the big idea in the field of psychological trauma. But PTSD has increasingly come under fire by its critics.

Critics point to how PTSD has become scientifically meaningless. Psychiatric classification demands that a line is drawn that separates people into two groups: those without the disorder and those with the disorder. The question is where to draw that line.

Since the diagnosis of PTSD was formally introduced in 1980 the line has moved twice—in a manner some authors have referred to as bracket creep—so that the diagnosis of PTSD is now much more common than it would have been thirty years ago.

But not only is it more common, it has also become evident that it is widely used to describe what might previously have been viewed as normal human distress. This can't continue without devaluing the idea of PTSD.

The challenge therefore is for the next edition of the Diagnostic and Statistical Manual (DSM) to demonstrate when these normal processes of posttraumatic stress become disordered, so that the term PTSD is used clearly to describe dysfunction of some mental mechanism.

And it becomes increasingly clear that for most people trauma is simply not an illness.

For many years humanistic psychologists have argued against the illness ideology in psychology with little success. But now it is also becoming obvious to the wider audience that what is needed is a new non-pathological understanding of the normal processes that trauma triggers.

This is the cutting edge of posttraumatic growth research and theory. It is why I think posttraumatic growth is one of the most important topics in contemporary psychology. Posttraumatic growth shows that what we need is neither a negative psychology, nor a positive psychology, but an integrative psychology that understands that trauma and transformation, suffering and joy, go hand in hand.

***

Therapy for Posttraumatic Growth: Car Mechanics and Gardeners

What sort of therapy facilitates posttraumatic growth?

The best starting point is to examine the deep seated philosophical assumptions of therapy.

Therapists often talk about having a toolbox in which they have various exercises, techniques and suggestions that they can pull out in the service of the client. For sure, it is important to have a range of tools, but more important is to understand the job that needs to be done.

Look in a car mechanic's toolbox and you see a particular set of tools. Look in a gardener's toolbox and you see a different set. Each of these workers has a different task in mind.

I choose these two workers deliberately because they represent two different mindsets of the therapy world.

A car breaks down. You look under the hood but you have no idea yourself what the problem is. You need to take it to the appropriate expert mechanic who will then diagnose the problem. The mechanic knows about cars. He knows how they work. He knows what sounds to listen out for that mean something is wrong. He knows what the right levels of fluids should be. After a time the mechanic looks up. He tells you what is wrong and what needs to be done to get the car back into working order. You agree, and the mechanic gets to work.

Therapists who adopt the illness ideology to psychological problems are like the car mechanic. They know what normal functioning is and the different ways a person can be disordered. They listen attentively to what you tell them in order to diagnose the particular disorder that is causing you not to work properly. It's important to get the diagnosis right because only then can they be sure to provide the right treatment to cure the illness. If someone has a stomach upset they need indigestion tablets but if they have a broken leg they need a brace. After all, you wouldn't give indigestion tablets to heal a broken leg! Once the disorder is correctly identified, the right treatment can be provided to get you back to normal.

On the other hand, the gardener adopts the growth ideology. She turns the soil around the new plant making sure that it gets the right nutrients, is not too cold in winter and not too warm in summer, and is getting the right balance of light and shade. With trees whose growth has been stunted by a lack of nutrients, twisted at an angle having strained to get at the sunlight, or damaged in a storm, the gardener sets out to feed the tree, remove the barriers to sunlight, or provide support to grow anew. She trusts in the plant to grow as healthily as it can if all these barriers to growth are removed.

Therapists who are like gardeners don't need to direct growth or define what it will look like, for once the barriers to psychological growth are removed they trust that growth will happen.

Sometimes we need therapists to be like car mechanics and sometimes we need them to be like gardeners. In this sense I would argue that therapy is not so much about what you do as how you do it.

Therapists can make suggestions to their clients, offer advice, provide the opportunity for various exercises and so on, but how any therapist does these things ultimately rests on what they think they are doing—their fundamental assumptions—whether they think of themselves as car mechanics or as gardeners.

Both sets of assumptions have their roles to play in helping people. But we need to know when to be like car mechanics and when to be like gardeners.

To help people suffering from posttraumatic stress disorder (PTSD) it may be that therapists need to be like car mechanics, but to facilitate posttraumatic growth perhaps they need to be more like gardeners.

STEPHEN JOSEPH, PhD, is a professor of psychology, health, and social care in the School of Sociology and Social Policy at the University of Nottingham, UK. He specializes in traumatic stress, psychotherapy, and positive psychological functioning. He is the co-director of the Centre for Trauma, Resilience, and Growth. He has written *What Doesn't Kill Us: The New Psychology of Posttraumatic Growth* and has co-written and co-edited several professional books including *Understanding Post-Traumatic Stress; Positive Psychology in Practice; Person-Centred Psychopathology; Positive Therapy; Person-Centred Practice; Trauma, Recovery and Growth;* and *Post-Traumatic Stress: The Facts.*

U.S. Department of Veterans Affairs, National Center for PTSD

NO

What Is PTSD?

Posttraumatic Stress Disorder (PTSD) can occur after you have been through a traumatic event. A traumatic event is something terrible and scary that you see, hear about, or that happens to you, like:

- Combat exposure
- Child sexual or physical abuse
- Terrorist attack
- Sexual or physical assault
- Serious accidents, like a car wreck
- Natural disasters, like a fire, tornado, hurricane, flood, or earthquake

During a traumatic event, you think that your life or others' lives are in danger. You may feel afraid or feel that you have no control over what is happening around you. Most people have some stress-related reactions after a traumatic event; but, not everyone gets PTSD. If your reactions don't go away over time and they disrupt your life, you may have PTSD.

How Does PTSD Develop?

Most people who go through a trauma have some symptoms at the beginning. Only some will develop PTSD over time. It isn't clear why some people develop PTSD and others don't.

Whether or not you get PTSD depends on many things:

- How intense the trauma was or how long it lasted
- If you were injured or lost someone important to you
- How close you were to the event
- How strong your reaction was
- How much you felt in control of events
- How much help and support you got after the event

What Are the Symptoms of PTSD?

PTSD symptoms usually start soon after the traumatic event, but they may not appear until months or years later. They also may come and go over many years. If the symptoms last longer than four weeks, cause you great distress, or interfere with your work or home life, you might have PTSD.

There are four types of symptoms of PTSD:

1. **Reliving the event (also called re-experiencing symptoms)**
   You may have bad memories or nightmares. You even may feel like you're going through the event again. This is called a flashback.
2. **Avoiding situations that remind you of the event**
   You may try to avoid situations or people that trigger memories of the traumatic event. You may even avoid talking or thinking about the event.
3. **Negative changes in beliefs and feelings**
   The way you think about yourself and others may change because of the trauma. You may feel fear, guilt, or shame. Or, you may not be interested in activities you used to enjoy. This is another way to avoid memories.
4. **Feeling keyed up (also called hyperarousal)**
   You may be jittery, or always alert and on the lookout for danger. Or, you may have trouble concentrating or sleeping. This is known as hyperarousal.

Can Children Have PTSD?

Children can have PTSD too. They may have symptoms described above or other symptoms depending on how old they are. As children get older, their symptoms are more like those of adults. Here are some examples of PTSD symptoms in children:

- Children age birth to 6 may get upset if their parents are not close by, have trouble sleeping, or suddenly have trouble with toilet training or going to the bathroom.
- Children age 7 to 11 may act out the trauma through play, drawings, or stories. Some have nightmares or become more irritable or aggressive. They may also want to avoid school or have trouble with schoolwork or friends.
- Children age 12 to 18 have symptoms more similar to adults: depression, anxiety, withdrawal, or reckless behavior like substance abuse or running away.

What Other Problems Do People with PTSD Experience?

People with PTSD may also have other problems. These include:

- Feelings of hopelessness, shame, or despair
- Depression or anxiety
- Drinking or drug problems
- Physical symptoms or chronic pain
- Employment problems
- Relationship problems, including divorce

In many cases, treatments for PTSD will also help these other problems, because they are often related. The coping skills you learn in treatment can work for PTSD and these related problems.

Will I Get Better?

"Getting better" means different things for different people, and not everyone who gets treatment will be "cured." Even if you continue to have symptoms, however, treatment can help you cope. Your symptoms don't have to interfere with your everyday activities, work, and relationships.

What Treatments Are Available?

When you have PTSD, dealing with the past can be hard. Instead of telling others how you feel, you may keep your feelings bottled up. But treatment can help you get better. There are two main types of treatment, psychotherapy (sometimes called counseling) and medication. Sometimes people combine psychotherapy and medication.

Psychotherapy for PTSD

Psychotherapy, or counseling, involves meeting with a therapist. There are different types of psychotherapy:

- Cognitive behavioral therapy (CBT) is the most effective treatment for PTSD. There are different types of CBT, such as cognitive therapy and exposure therapy.
  - One type is Cognitive Processing Therapy (CPT) where you learn skills to understand how trauma changed your thoughts and feelings.
  - Another type is Prolonged Exposure (PE) therapy where you talk about your trauma repeatedly until memories are no longer upsetting. You also go to places that are safe, but that you have been staying away from because they are related to the trauma.
- A similar kind of therapy is called Eye Movement Desensitization and Reprocessing (EMDR), which involves focusing on sounds or hand movements while you talk about the trauma.

Medications for PTSD

Medications can be effective too. A type of drug known as a selective serotonin reuptake inhibitor (SSRI), which is also used for depression, is effective for PTSD. Another medication called Prazosin has been found to be helpful in decreasing nightmares related to the trauma. IMPORTANT: Benzodiazepines and atypical antipsychotics should generally be avoided for PTSD treatment because they do not treat the core PTSD symptoms.

How Common Is PTSD?

Posttraumatic stress disorder (PTSD) can occur after you have been through a trauma. A trauma is a shocking and scary event that you see or that happens to you. During this type of event, you think that your life or others' lives are in danger. You may feel afraid or think that you have no control over what is happening.

Going through trauma is not rare. About 6 of every 10 (or 60%) of men and 5 of every 10 (or 50%) of women experience at least one trauma in their lives. Women are more likely to experience sexual assault and child sexual abuse. Men are more likely to experience accidents, physical assault, combat, disaster, or to witness death or injury.

Going through a trauma does not mean you'll get PTSD, though. Even though over half of us go through some type of trauma, a much smaller percent develop PTSD.

Here are some facts (based on the U.S.):

- About 7 or 8 out of every 100 people (or 7–8% of the population) will have PTSD at some point in their lives.

- About 5.2 million adults have PTSD during a given year. This is only a small portion of those who have gone through a trauma.
- Women are more likely than men to develop PTSD. About 10% of women develop PTSD sometime in their lives compared with 5% of men.

Who Is Most Likely to Develop PTSD?

Although most people who go through trauma will not get PTSD, you are more likely to develop PTSD if you:

- Were directly exposed to the trauma as a victim or a witness
- Were seriously hurt during the event
- Went through a trauma that was long-lasting or very severe
- Believed that you were in danger
- Believed that a family member was in danger
- Had a severe reaction during the event, such as crying, shaking, vomiting, or feeling apart from your surroundings
- Felt helpless during the trauma and were not able to help yourself or a loved one

You are also more likely to develop PTSD if you:

- Had an earlier life-threatening event or trauma, such as being abused as a child
- Have another mental health problem
- Have family members who have had mental health problems
- Have little support from family and friends
- Have recently lost a loved one, especially if it was not expected
- Have had recent, stressful life changes
- Drink a lot of alcohol
- Are a woman
- Are poorly educated
- Are younger

Some groups of people, including African-Americans and Hispanics, may be more likely than whites to develop PTSD. This may be because these groups are more likely to go through a trauma. For example, in Veterans who survived Vietnam, a larger percent of African-Americans, Hispanics, and Native Americans were in combat than whites.

Your culture may also affect how you react to trauma. For example, people from groups that are open and willing to talk about problems may be more willing to seek help.

PTSD and the Military

If you are in the military, you may have seen combat. You may have been on missions that exposed you to horrible and life-threatening experiences. You may have been shot at, seen a buddy shot, or seen death. These are types of events that can lead to PTSD.

Experts think PTSD occurs:

- In about 11–20% of Veterans of the Iraq and Afghanistan wars (Operations Iraqi and Enduring Freedom), or in the range of 11–20 Veterans out of 100 who served in OEF/OIF.
- In as many as 10% of Gulf War (Desert Storm) Veterans, or in 10 Gulf War Veterans out of 100.
- In about 30% of Vietnam Veterans, or about 30 out of 100 Vietnam Veterans.

Other factors in a combat situation can add more stress to an already stressful situation. This may contribute to PTSD and other mental health problems. These factors include what you do in the war, the politics around the war, where the war is fought, and the type of enemy you face.

Another cause of PTSD in the military can be military sexual trauma (MST). This is any sexual harassment or sexual assault that occurs while you are in the military. MST can happen to both men and women and can occur during peacetime, training, or war.

Among Veterans who use VA health care, about:

- 23 out of 100 women (or 23%) reported sexual assault when in the military.
- 55 out of 100 women (or 55%) and 38 out of 100 men (or 38%) have experienced sexual harassment when in the military.

There are many more male Veterans than there are female Veterans. So, even though military sexual trauma is more common in women Veterans, over half of all Veterans with military sexual trauma are men.

Treatment of PTSD

Today, there are good treatments available for PTSD. When you have PTSD, dealing with the past can be hard. Instead of telling others how you feel, you may keep your feelings bottled up. But talking with a therapist can help you get better.

Cognitive behavioral therapy (CBT) is one type of counseling. Research shows it is the most effective type of counseling for PTSD. The VA is providing two forms of cognitive behavioral therapy to Veterans with PTSD: Cognitive Processing Therapy (CPT) and Prolonged Exposure (PE) therapy.

There is a similar kind of therapy called Eye Movement Desensitization and Reprocessing (EMDR) that is used for PTSD. Also, medications have been shown to be effective. A type of drug known as a selective serotonin reuptake inhibitor (SSRI), which is also used for depression, is effective for PTSD.

Types of Cognitive Behavioral Therapy

What Is Cognitive Therapy?

In cognitive therapy, your therapist helps you understand and change how you think about your trauma and its aftermath. Your goal is to understand how certain thoughts about your trauma cause you stress and make your symptoms worse.

You will learn to identify thoughts about the world and yourself that are making you feel afraid or upset. With the help of your therapist, you will learn to replace these thoughts with more accurate and less distressing thoughts. You will also learn ways to cope with feelings such as anger, guilt, and fear.

After a traumatic event, you might blame yourself for things you couldn't have changed. For example, a soldier may feel guilty about decisions he or she had to make during war. Cognitive therapy, a type of CBT, helps you understand that the traumatic event you lived through was not your fault.

What Is Exposure Therapy?

In exposure therapy your goal is to have less fear about your memories. It is based on the idea that people learn to fear thoughts, feelings, and situations that remind them of a past traumatic event.

By talking about your trauma repeatedly with a therapist, you'll learn to get control of your thoughts and feelings about the trauma. You'll learn that you do not have to be afraid of your memories. This may be hard at first. It might seem strange to think about stressful things on purpose. But over time, you'll feel less overwhelmed.

With the help of your therapist, you can change how you react to the stressful memories. Talking in a place where you feel secure makes this easier.

You may focus on memories that are less upsetting before talking about worse ones. This is called "desensitization," and it allows you to deal with bad memories a little bit at a time. Your therapist also may ask you to remember a lot of bad memories at once. This is called "flooding," and it helps you learn not to feel overwhelmed.

You also may practice different ways to relax when you're having a stressful memory. Breathing exercises are sometimes used for this.

What Is EMDR?

Eye movement desensitization and reprocessing (EMDR) is another type of therapy for PTSD.

Like other kinds of counseling, it can help change how you react to memories of your trauma.

While thinking of or talking about your memories, you'll focus on other stimuli like eye movements, hand taps, and sounds. For example, your therapist will move his or her hand, and you'll follow this movement with your eyes.

Experts are still learning how EMDR works, and there is disagreement about whether eye movements are a necessary part of the treatment.

Medication

Selective serotonin reuptake inhibitors (SSRIs) are a type of antidepressant medicine. These can help you feel less sad and worried. They appear to be helpful, and for some people they are very effective. SSRIs include citalopram (Celexa), fluoxetine (such as Prozac), paroxetine (Paxil), and sertraline (Zoloft).

Chemicals in your brain affect the way you feel. For example, when you have depression you may not have enough of a chemical called serotonin. SSRIs raise the level of serotonin in your brain.

There are other medications that have been used with some success. Talk to your doctor about which medications are right for you.

Other Types of Treatment

Some other kinds of counseling may be helpful in your recovery. However, more evidence is needed to support these types of treatment for PTSD.

Group Therapy

Many people want to talk about their trauma with others who have had similar experiences.

In group therapy, you talk with a group of people who also have been through a trauma and who have PTSD. Sharing your story with others may help you feel more comfortable talking about your trauma. This can help you cope with your symptoms, memories, and other parts of your life.

Group therapy helps you build relationships with others who understand what you've been through. You learn to deal with emotions such as shame, guilt, anger, rage, and fear. Sharing with the group also can help you build self-confidence and trust. You'll learn to focus on your present life, rather than feeling overwhelmed by the past.

Brief Psychodynamic Psychotherapy

In this type of therapy, you learn ways of dealing with emotional conflicts caused by your trauma. This therapy helps you understand how your past affects the way you feel now.

Your therapist can help you:

- Identify what triggers your stressful memories and other symptoms
- Find ways to cope with intense feelings about the past
- Become more aware of your thoughts and feelings, so you can change your reactions to them
- Raise your self-esteem

Family Therapy

PTSD can affect your whole family. Your kids or your partner may not understand why you get angry sometimes, or why you're under so much stress. They may feel scared, guilty, or even angry about your condition.

Family therapy is a type of counseling that involves your whole family. A therapist helps you and your family to communicate, maintain good relationships, and cope with tough emotions. Your family can learn more about PTSD and how it is treated.

In family therapy, each person can express his or her fears and concerns. It's important to be honest about your feelings and to listen to others. You can talk about your PTSD symptoms and what triggers them. You also can discuss the important parts of your treatment and recovery. By doing this, your family will be better prepared to help you.

You may consider having individual therapy for your PTSD symptoms and family therapy to help you with your relationships.

How Long Does Treatment Last?

CBT treatment for PTSD often lasts for three to six months. Other types of treatment for PTSD can last longer. If you have other mental health problems as well as PTSD, treatment may last for one to two years or longer.

What If Someone Has PTSD and Another Disorder? Is the Treatment Different?

It is very common to have PTSD at that same time as another mental health problem. Depression, alcohol or drug abuse problems, panic disorder, and anxiety disorders often occur along with PTSD. In many cases, the PTSD treatments described above will also help with the other disorders. The best treatment results occur when both PTSD and the other problems are treated together rather than one after the other.

What Will We Work On in Therapy?

When you begin therapy, you and your therapist should decide together what goals you hope to reach in therapy. Not every person with PTSD will have the same treatment goals. For instance, you might focus on:

- Reducing your PTSD symptoms
- Learning the best way to live with your symptoms
- Learning how to cope with other problems associated with PTSD, like feeling less guilt or sadness, improving relationships at work, or communicating with friends and family

Your therapist should help you decide which of these goals seems most important to you, and he or she should discuss with you which goals might take a long time to achieve.

What Can I Expect from My Therapist?

Your therapist should help you decide which of these goals seems most important to you, and he or she should discuss with you which goals might take a long time to achieve.

The two of you should agree at the beginning that this plan makes sense for you. You should also agree on what you will do if it does not seem to be working. If you have any questions about the treatment, your therapist should be able to answer them.

You should feel comfortable with your therapist and feel you are working as a team to tackle your problems. It can be difficult to talk about painful situations in your life, or about traumatic experiences that you've had. Feelings that emerge during therapy can be scary and challenging. Talking with your therapist about the process of therapy, and about your hopes and fears in regards to therapy, will help make therapy successful.

If you do not like your therapist or feel that the therapist is not helping you, it might be helpful to talk with another professional. In most cases, you should tell your therapist that you are seeking a second opinion.

THE DEPARTMENT OF VETERANS AFFAIRS is a U.S. government-run military veteran benefit system established in 1930 which covers disability compensation, pension, education, home loans, life insurance, vocational rehabilitation, survivors' benefits, medical benefits, and burial benefits. In recent years, the Department of Veterans Affairs has worked to spread knowledge about PTSD and the appropriate treatments for this condition.

EXPLORING THE ISSUE

Is Posttraumatic Stress Disorder (PTSD) Overdiagnosed and Overtreated?

Critical Thinking and Reflection

1. In light of the differing definitions of trauma, how can consensus be reached in determining the definition of a disorder that results from the experience of trauma?
2. What is the dividing line between posttraumatic *stress* and posttraumatic stress *disorder*?
3. Consider the fact that not all people who experience trauma develop PTSD. To what extent might there be personal variables that predispose some people to develop PTSD, and how might researchers determine what these variables are?
4. In what ways could the different therapeutic approaches be integrated, namely an intervention aimed at facilitating posttraumatic growth and an intervention that employs cognitive techniques?
5. DSM-5 contains a subtype of PTSD called Posttraumatic Stress Disorder in Preschool Children. What are the risks and benefits of such a diagnosis being applied to young children?

Is There Common Ground?

Both sets of articles accept the fact that posttraumatic stress disorder is a debilitating condition experienced by countless numbers of people who have experienced life-threatening or horrifying experiences. Dr. Joseph expresses concern that PTSD is being overdiagnosed. Although the VA does not make this argument so explicitly, the professionals who work in the VA system are committed to precision in diagnosis of PTSD, so that treatments (as well as disability benefits) are adequately provided to those who truly have a disorder and are in dire need of intervention. The wisdom derived from the extensive research conducted by the VA on the nature and treatment of PTSD will prove beneficial to all survivors of trauma, both in the military and in the general public.

Both sets of articles also acknowledge the benefits of obtaining help from professionals to find ways in which the distress resulting from such exposure can be understood and controlled. There also seems to be agreement with the premise that traumatized individuals will benefit from an intervention in which they revise the ways in which they view the traumatic experience and take cognitive control over what can be debilitating symptoms. The VA recommends cognitive therapeutic techniques such as cognitive exposure techniques aimed at reducing the emotional impact of intrusive thoughts and memories. Dr. Joseph recommends an approach, which could also be construed as being cognitively based, in which the

trauma survivor views the experience as an opportunity for growth.

Create Central

www.mhhe.com/createcentral

Additional Resources

Bryant, R. A., Friedman, M. J., Spiegel, D., Ursano, R., & Strain, J. (2011, September 1). A review of acute stress disorder in DSM-5. *Depression and Anxiety, 28*(9), 802–817.

Hoge, C. W. (2010). *Once a Warrior, Always a Warrior: Navigating the Transition from Combat to Home—Including Combat Stress, PTSD, and mTBI.* Guilford, CT: GPP Life.

Joseph, S. (2011). *What Doesn't Kill Us: The New Psychology of Posttraumatic Growth.* New York, NY: Basic Books.

Williams, M. B., & Poijula, S. (2013). *The PTSD Workbook: Simple, Effective Techniques for Overcoming Traumatic Stress Symptoms.* Oakland, CA: New Harbinger.

Zayfert, C., & DeViva, J. C. (2011). *When Someone You Love Suffers from Posttraumatic Stress: What to Expect and What You Can Do.* New York, NY: Guilford Press.

Internet References . . .

Gateway to Post Traumatic Stress Disorder Information

http://www.ptsdinfo.org/

Heal My PTSD

http://healmyptsd.com/

National Center for PTSD

http://www.ptsd.va.gov/

U.S. Department of Veterans Affairs

http://www.mentalhealth.va.gov/ptsd.asp

Selected, Edited, and with Issue Framing Material by:
Richard P. Halgin, *University of Massachusetts, Amherst*

ISSUE

Can Positive Psychology Make Us Happier?

YES: Stephen M. Schueller and Acacia C. Parks, from "The Science of Self-Help: Translating Positive Psychology Research into Increased Individual Happiness" *European Psychologist* (2014)

NO: Laurel C. Newman and Randy J. Larsen, from "How Much of Our Happiness Is Within Our Control?" Original Work, (2009)

Learning Outcomes
After reading this issue, you will be able to:
• Determine if it is possible to adapt strategies to improve one's happiness.
• Discuss how the manipulation of environmental variables could impact happiness.
• Discuss what it means to be "happy" and determine if it is the sort of thing that can actually be manipulated.

ISSUE SUMMARY

YES: Positive psychologists Stephen M. Schueller and Acacia C. Parks present a summary of the current state of positive psychological interventions as they pertain to self-help, interventions that have been shown to lead to increases in individual happiness.

NO: Psychologists Laurel Newman and Randy Larsen challenge the external validity and sustainability of the effects of these strategies, arguing that most of what influences our long-term happiness is outside our control.

Who wants to be happy? Or perhaps the more empirical question is, how *can* we be happy? The U.S. Declaration of Independence lists the pursuit of happiness as an unalienable right, but no psychological researcher was around in 1776 to teach U.S. citizens how best to pursue it. Nor is the quest for happiness an exclusively U.S. business; the country Bhutan, for instance, has a Gross National Happiness (GNH) index to help guide government policy. Still, in the Western world of psychological research, Maslow's hierarchy of needs seems to be at play. In Maslow's hierarchy, we must satisfy our most basic needs (e.g., hunger) before we can concern ourselves with higher level needs, such as happiness and flourishing. If this is true, then only the more affluent countries, those that have satisfied their citizens' more basic needs, can even afford to ask the happiness question.

With this affluence, the positive psychology movement has risen during the last decade with the study of human flourishing as its major aim. Its focus on examining and nurturing what is best in humans is grounded in ancient Greek philosophies and more recent humanistic psychological theories, such as that of Carl Rogers. Recently, happiness has become a popular emphasis of the movement, with a host of psychological researchers attempting to answer many important questions. Is happiness biologically based? Is it environmental? How much is under our personal control? Sonja Lyubomirsky's early book described research that she contended would achieve lasting happiness, but many critics examined her results with skepticism. Is the research now substantial enough for psychologists to finally tell people how they can become happy?

Stephen M. Schueller and Acacia C. Parks seem to think so. In the YES article, they argue that previous research has provided substantial evidence that individual happiness can increase. Schueller and Parks believe that this increase in individual happiness can be achieved by imitating the behaviors of those who are "naturally" happy. They hold that current research shows small-to-moderate increases in well-being and decreasing depressive symptoms result from the teaching and encouraging of unhappy people to learn and apply these "happy" behaviors. They contend that less happy people can not only learn strategies (e.g., savoring, gratitude, kindness, and creating meaning), but also apply these strategies to increase their levels of happiness. Indeed, psychological studies seem to show that careful interventions can be effective in facilitating happiness.

Laurel Newman and Randy Larsen, in contrast, believe that psychologists should be cautious before making public announcements about how people can make ourselves happier. According to Newman and Larsen, psychologists are misleading when they say that 40 percent of happiness is within our control. Although they do agree that roughly half of the difference in happiness scores (within a group) may be attributed to genetics, they also believe that most life-changing events (those that affect happiness) are out of a person's control. This means, perhaps most important, that strategies and techniques for increasing happiness are not likely to endure, because people have a surprising tendency to return to preexisting levels of happiness after good and bad events have produced temporary changes in happiness levels. Moreover, Newman and Larsen contend that the experimental effects of the most oft-cited happiness interventions are at best weak and require very specific circumstances to produce any effect.

POINT

- According to some models, 40 percent of happiness may be within our control.
- Circumstantial factors do not adequately explain different levels of happiness.
- Studies with happiness-inducing strategies show people can increase their levels of happiness.
- Individual differences in adaptation show that people can use strategies to help themselves stay happy, even after a less-than-happy event.

COUNTERPOINT

- Heritability estimates describe variations in groups and do not apply to individuals.
- A variety of environmental variables predict happiness, and many of them are uncontrollable.
- These strategies have weak statistical effects that show up only under very specific circumstances.
- People adapt quickly to negative and positive changes, returning to previous levels of happiness.

YES

Stephen M. Schueller and Acacia C. Parks

The Science of Self-Help: Translating Positive Psychology Research into Increased Individual Happiness

A recent initiative by Martin Seligman, the founder of positive psychology, aims to increase global well-being, with the goal being 51% of the world population "flourishing" by 2051. Considerable evidence supports that effective interventions exist to help achieve this goal. Many of these interventions, however, use resources (such as therapists' and coaches' time) that can only benefit one person at a time. Promoting the flourishing of 51% of the world population by 2051, however, requires developing resources that can aid multiple people without additional investment of professional time. Indeed, psychological researchers have long acknowledged that psychosocial interventions can be disseminated via various less traditional approaches and this notion has been echoed in recent calls for the translation of in-person psychosocial interventions into new, more innovative, and cost-effective modes of delivery.

One mode is to provide resources directly to those who are interested without professional assistance, known simply as self-help. Although evidence supports that self-help can be efficacious, a majority of the current self-help resources are not based on scientifically supported principles or have not been evaluated. Thus, happiness-seekers have to sort through an array of resources to try to find evidence-based techniques. With regard to increasing happiness, many people use a "do-it-yourself" approach, drawing on ancient wisdom, scientific evidence, and lessons from popular approaches without professional guidance. Although this may work for some people, others might need more guidance, and it is thus important to help those interested in pursuing happiness to identify what is most likely to work based on the current scientific evidence.

This paper aims to provide the current state of research in increasing happiness especially as it pertains to self-help in order to help scientists and therapists interested in contributing to the study and application of positive psychology for self-help purposes.

We begin by briefly defining happiness and discussing its mutability, and then turn to defining a positive psychological intervention (hereafter: PPI) and to describing the current evidence base for a selection of evidence-based PPIs. We . . . highlight specific concerns related to developing self-help interventions based on positive psychology principles. We close with future directions and conclusions for the field.

What Is Happiness and Can It Change?

The predominant conception of happiness in Western cultures is that happiness is characterized by positive subjective appraisals and feelings. This conception, deemed the hedonic approach, preferences emotions and subjective evaluations rather than character, achievements, or objective life circumstances (which is deemed a eudaimonic approach). Thus, one is happy if he or she says so. These subjective states include two key components: (1) a cognitive appraisal that one's life is good, and (2) reports of frequently experiencing positive emotions and infrequently experiencing negative emotions. Accordingly, increasing happiness is a combination of helping people to view the circumstances of their lives more positively, as well as to experience more positive emotions and fewer negative emotions.

Although whether individual happiness could increase used to be a major debate, research throughout the past decade has provided substantial evidence that it can. Furthermore, research findings overwhelmingly support that the best way to do so is to change what one does to be more aligned with the behaviors of happy people. Self-help should therefore teach these scientifically supported behaviors to help people increase their own happiness.

     . . . Some theories have . . . emerged to help explain the underlying mechanisms that drive the efficacy of PPIs. For example, Fredrickson's Broaden and Build Model posits that deliberately increasing positive emotions leads to greater resources (e.g., creativity, resilience, and openness to new experiences), which in turn can spur individuals to engage in behaviors that further promote well-being (Fredrickson, 2001). This cycle results in a positive feedback loop that might improve cognitive appraisals, positive emotions, and possibly even life circumstances. While not specific to any particular PPI, the model provides a solid empirical justification for the goal of increasing happiness and describes a cascade of benefits that is empirically testable. It has only been in very recent years, however, that questions of mechanisms and potential moderators of particular PPIs' effectiveness have started to receive empirical attention. . . .

Defining Positive Psychological Interventions

Behaviors related to happiness have been translated into several PPIs. . . . The most comprehensive and exclusive definition of a PPI . . . posits that an intervention can only be deemed a PPI if evidence exists that it successfully increases positive feelings, behaviors, and/or cognitions. Therefore, while many interventions could be potentially considered PPIs, they may not qualify as a PPI due to the lack of an empirical basis. . . .

     Based upon our review of the literature, the resulting interventions can be classified into five categories: (1) savoring experiences and sensations, (2) cultivating (and sometimes expressing) gratitude, (3) engaging in kind acts, (4) promoting positive relationship processes, and (5) pursuing hope and meaning. Thus, these categories are a description of the evidence-base rather than a theoretical proposal of what could exist. We do not include strengths, a prominent research area within positive psychology, as a category itself because each of the identified categories corresponds to specific strengths and research suggests that mere strength-identification is an insufficient strategy to promote well-being. From this research, it appears as though strength-identification may not be valuable above and beyond the specific strategies it inspires. In the context of self-help, thus, we focus on these specific strategies as included in the categories above.

     It is also important to note that whether or not a specific activity will actually lead to increased happiness is related to additional factors of the activity (e.g., dosage and variety) or the person (e.g., personality, strengths, and motivation); we will return to some of these issues at the end of the paper, as they provide additional layers of complexity to the somewhat simple story that disseminating an effective intervention leads to increased happiness.

Evidence for Positive Psychological Interventions

A considerable evidence base for PPIs exists. Two recently published meta-analyses suggest that on average PPIs lead to small-to-moderate increases in well-being and decreases in depressive symptoms. We review specific studies and PPIs below, but rather than present effect sizes for each study, we believe the effect sizes found in these meta-analyses provide a more useful summary of the field and the degree to which well-being might change over time in response to PPIs. Sin and Lyubomirsky (2009) found average increases in well-being of $r = .29$ and decreases in depressive symptoms of $r = .31$. Bolier and colleagues (2013), with their more restricted definition and fewer studies, however, found smaller effects of $d = 0.34$ for measures of subjective well-being, $d = 0.20$ for psychological well-being, and $d = 0.23$ for depressive symptoms. One reason we believe that it is useful to view these summary effect sizes rather than the effect sizes from individual studies is that characteristics of the application of the interventions were more predictive of differences in the effect sizes obtained than the specific techniques used. Longer intervention duration, greater degree of participant self-selection, and high level of initial participant distress (i.e., depression or other psychosocial problems) all corresponded to larger effect sizes. Most relevant to this review, however, is that supported interventions were more efficacious than self-help. We return to issues related to the widespread implementation of self-help after our review of specific PPI strategies. Overall, however, it appears that one can reasonably expect small but significant and lasting changes in well-being resulting from engaging in PPIs and even smaller effects when doing so on one's own. We now turn to a review and description of the specific PPIs that align with the definition of PPIs we offered.

Positive Psychology Interventions

Savoring

Savoring aims to intensify (through focused awareness) and prolong (through elaboration skills) momentary pleasurable experiences. The concept of savoring is derived from one of the most basic activities in mindfulness meditation wherein one deliberately and systematically attends to every aspect of an experience. While easiest to apply to a sensory experience, such as eating, savoring can be used with any type of experience, including memories. Individuals who engage in savoring more often have higher levels of happiness, life satisfaction, optimism, and perceived control, and lower levels of depression. Several factors have been proposed to increase the savoring of experiences including savoring in the presence of others, writing about the experience, considering counterfactuals, incorporating humor, focusing on the meaning of the activity, and maintaining an awareness of the fleeting nature of the experience. Savoring interventions fall into two categories: (1) those that teach and encourage the practice of the general principles of savoring and (2) those that teach a specific savoring skill and encourage the use of that skill.

Teaching a wide range of savoring strategies and encouraging the application of these strategies in one's life is an effective way to promote well-being. For example, Schueller (2010) instructed participants to reflect daily for at least 2–3 min on two pleasurable experiences and to make the pleasure last as long as possible. For example, when drinking hot chocolate, one might prolong that experience by focusing first on the various features of the whipped cream (i.e., the taste, texture, and temperature), then on the drink itself, and lastly, on the interplay of those flavors, textures, and temperatures together. Participants who engaged in this simple exercise reported higher levels of happiness one week later. More structured instruction in savoring also appears to contribute to well-being. An intervention taught participants savoring strategies through a 20-min audio recording and then instructed them to brainstorm ways they could have savored three positive activities they experienced within the past week. Participants were instructed to use these skills throughout the week and track the number of times they savored events in a savoring log. Participants who completed this savoring intervention experienced significant reductions in negative emotions but no significant boosts in positive emotions. Thus it might be that savoring serves to buffer against negative life events.

Another way to promote savoring is to teach specific strategies to enhance a person's focus and recall of pleasant aspects in one's environment and life. In "mindful photography," people spend at least 15 min daily taking photographs that are creative, beautiful, and hold personal meaning. Participants who took mindful photographs for a two-week period reported significantly more positive mood compared to participants who took photographs but received no specific instruction to the types of photographs to take. Similar strategies have been used for savoring positive memories, referred to as reminiscence. Reminiscence has been used particularly for older populations with positive benefits on life satisfaction.

Gratitude

Gratitude refers to the emotional response accompanying the acknowledgment that some outside force is responsible for something good that has happened to oneself. Gratitude interventions include both grateful reflection and gratitude-motivated activities. Both have demonstrated efficacy at increasing well-being including increasing positive emotions, reducing depressive symptoms, and improving physical health. Grateful reflection, exemplified by gratitude journaling, refers to listing things for which one is grateful. In gratitude journaling, people write down what they are thankful for, most often completing this in private. Some instructions emphasize the importance of writing both the thing that one is grateful for as well as the reason why that thing happened, however, benefits have been found with only noting the events. Gratitude-motivated activities encourage public expressions of gratitude. In a direct comparison of expressing gratitude versus merely promoting positive thoughts toward a relationship partner, it was found that grateful expressions were considerably more effective at enhancing the strength of the relationship. The PPI known as the "gratitude letter" instructs an individual to express gratitude to another person that he or she has never had a proper chance to thank. The instructions emphasize the importance of conducting a gratitude visit (i.e., a face-to-face meeting) after writing the letter; however, studies suggest that this is not the essential component and that simply writing a letter may also boost well-being, albeit perhaps to a slightly lesser degree.

Kindness

Common wisdom states that one of the most reliable ways to feel better is to do good for someone else. Indeed, happier people tend to act more kindly, and performing kind acts, in turn, boosts happiness. Furthermore, happiness and kindness appear to exist in some kind of "positive feedback loop" such that one encourages the other. In this way, acts of kindness interact with gratitude to create reciprocity between givers and recipients. Even more interesting, reflecting on one's acts of kindness, even without deliberately increasing the frequency of kind acts, also increases happiness.

Kindness research has examined a variety of kind acts, ranging from brief, cost-free behaviors, such as holding the door or complimenting a stranger to behaviors that come at a personal cost, such as buying a gift or helping a colleague with a project at work. One type of kind act that has received particular research attention is prosocial spending – that is, spending money on other people. Compared to spending money on oneself, spending money on others leads to increases in happiness. This line of research suggests that while, on average, money does not "buy" happiness, using money to promote kindness provides an important exception. Even interventions, however, that promote kindness more generally appear to lead to significant boosts in well-being. In a study by Lyubomirsky, Tkach, and Sheldon (2004) undergraduate students who performed five kind acts weekly for 6 weeks experienced significant increases in well-being compared to a no-treatment control group, but only if these kind acts were performed all in one day rather than spread throughout the week.

Promoting Positive Relationship Processes

In his three-word summary of positive psychology, "Other people matter," Chris Peterson (2006) emphasizes the centrality of positive relationships for happiness. Indeed, robust findings support this claim. In fact, relationships are so central to happiness that one analysis of the happiest people led to the conclusion that "good social relationships might be a necessary condition for high happiness" (Diener & Seligman, 2002, p. 82). Thus, increasing the amount of social contact a person has and improving the quality of one's interpersonal relationships are both strong pathways to promoting happiness.

One intervention designed to improve a positive process in one's social interactions is active-constructive responding. This intervention draws on research that noted that individuals respond to good news in either an active versus passive and constructive versus destructive manner and that couples that use more active-constructive responding have more satisfying and stable relationships. Active-constructive responding means reacting to the good news with authentic displays of excitement and expanding the discussion of the event through active questioning. For example, if one's spouse received a job promotion, an active-constructive response would be "That is great news! I am so happy for you! We should go out to dinner to celebrate. Tell me exactly what happened when you found out." In many ways, this is similar to savoring as it serves to intensify and elongate a positive experience through encouraging, retelling, and re-experiencing, but

is circumscribed to the interpersonal domain and the sharing of positive news. Instruction in active-constructive responding has been provided as a standalone exercise and incorporated into programs such as Group Positive Psychotherapy and the Masters of Resilience Training (MRT) Program. Although, active-constructive responding is well liked, it has limited support for its efficacy as a standalone exercise. More research needs to assess whether it can increase its impact on happiness when delivered experimentally.

Creating Meaning

Various conceptualizations of meaning in life exist, encompassing an understanding of relationships among people, things, and events to a general sense that one's life is significant. Despite these various definitions, empirical findings have consistently indicated that meaning in life predicts well-being, happiness, and life satisfaction. Thus, interventions aimed at facilitating the construction of meaning and purpose can contribute to individual happiness.

One way that PPIs seek to promote meaning is through expressive writing paradigms. Life narratives have a powerful influence over people's construction of meaning and their individual happiness. The cognitive change theory of expressive writing posits that writing can enhance well-being and emotional adjustment through facilitating the construction of a coherent and meaningful narrative of the event. In the basic paradigm underlying this research, people write about a past trauma on consecutive days with instructions to facilitate specific styles of expression; participants instructed to include both the facts of the trauma and their emotions experienced fewer illness-related doctor's visits in the weeks to follow compared to other styles of writing. While the expressive writing paradigm is not itself a PPI, research examining the effects of writing expressively about positive events is, and has found similar benefits. Expressive writing is a useful tool for self-help because it can be done independently with minimal instruction and has demonstrated benefits even when the writing is repeated over several days. An important caveat is the same style of writing might not be useful for both positive and negative events. In a series of studies, Lyubomirsky, Sousa, and Dickerhoof (2006) found that analyzing events, facilitated through writing, improved well-being and health with negative but not positive events. For positive events, on the other hand, participants benefited more from talking through the event aloud or adopting an approach where they replayed but did not analyze the event.

Another way in which meaning can be promoted is through increasing hope for the future – and more specifically, the belief that one's goals are within one's reach. The more abstract idea of pursuing hope has typically been operationalized as the formulation and pursuit of personally meaningful goals, which according to Self-Determination Theory contributes substantially to one's happiness. Writing about life goals, for instance, can bring about greater clarity and awareness to those goals. [T]he "Best Possible Self" intervention increases focus on one's life goals by requiring people to visualize and write about their "ideal future life," in as much detail as possible. Participants who completed this writing assignment over a 4-week period experienced increases in positive emotions and displayed more interest and higher degrees of motivation compared with a control group who merely wrote about life details. It is worth noting that although this exercise is useful at bringing clarity and awareness of goals, it does not provide support at putting those goals into action.

Other research has demonstrated that teaching people goal setting and planning skills is an effective way to increase happiness. Goal setting and planning relate to the other major component of Snyder's (2002) conceptualization of hope, "pathways thinking." "Pathways thinking" involves brain-storming and planning the specific routes one can use to achieve a given goal. The first portion of MacLeod and colleagues' (2008) intervention is similar to the "Best Possible Self" intervention; participants receive instructions to envision their goals. However, participants are also instructed on how to select and refine goals, to plan to achieve those goals, to address obstacles and potential solutions to achieving those goals, and lastly to review the implementation of the plan. This program was effective in both group and individual self-directed formats.

. . .

Concerns and Caveats Regarding the Widespread Implementation of Self-Administered PPIs

Thus far, we have told a simple story: effective PPIs exist, and if individuals can access them – and we believe that self-help is the best vehicle by which this access will occur in a scalable and sustainable way – they will become happier. However, in reality, this story is much more complex; compared to professionally-delivered or supported interventions, self-help has several unique challenges, which must be addressed.

Motivation and Engagement

When people seek out self-help resources, their motivation is often quite high, however this motivation often drops over time resulting in a reduced use of the techniques. Indeed, with regard to the *Live Happy* iPhone app, only a small portion of the people who downloaded the app used it and left enough data to allow analysis of the changes in their mood scores. This is quite consistent with other work that finds that an overwhelming number of people who begin an Internet intervention drop out, with very few even progressing past a first lesson. Thus self-help interventions need to be designed to help hook people in early and facilitate long-term behavior change.

The Fogg Behavior Model (FBM) offers several insights into design considerations to do so. In the FBM, three factors influence one's performance of a target behavior: motivation, ability, and triggers. When motivation is high, people are able to complete more difficult behaviors (i.e., finding a self-help resource). When motivation is low, however, people's ability to complete difficult behaviors drops. In order to be successful, self-help programs should provide structure such that when motivation drops people will continue to practice a target behavior. . . . Having a scheduled, weekly activity will promote follow through in the future, even when motivation drops, because of the commitment made and the social reinforcement of getting together with a friend. Another insight from the FBM is that behavior change should begin with small behaviors that through repeated practice will increase one's ability to complete larger behaviors. Thus, a person might begin by gratitude journaling a single thing each day and begin to challenge himself by noting more and more things he is grateful for as time goes on.

Motivation is a critical element of intervention efficacy as well. Indeed, some research suggests that only those motivated to increase their happiness benefit from PPIs. In a study by Lyubomirsky and colleagues (2011), they compared participants recruited either through advertisements for a happiness intervention or cognitive exercises. Recruitment source was deemed to be a proxy for motivation. All participants, regardless of the recruitment ad that attracted them, were randomly assigned to one of three conditions: two included previously supported active PPIs (gratitude or optimism) and one a control condition (listing experiences of the week). Both the gratitude and optimism conditions led to increases in well-being compared to the control condition but only for the "motivated" participants who were recruited into the study with the "happiness intervention" ad. The results of this study provide both reservations and promise for

PPIs. First, the lack of efficacy within the "unmotivated" group expecting to receive "cognitive exercises" demonstrates the PPIs may not be effective for all people. One could interpret these findings to be suggestive of possible placebo effects for PPIs; however, it seems unlikely given that well-being did not improve among the "motivated" group who received the control condition. Lyubomirsky and colleagues (2011) took these findings to illustrate the critical importance of motivation. They concluded the PPIs require both a proper "way" and the "will" to follow through and do the suggested technique. Fortunately, PPIs are well-liked and compared to other strategies with the same goal (i.e., promoting a better mood) are viewed as more useful and used more often. So although motivation is an important concern for self-help, PPIs might be particularly effective at overcoming this concern.

Variety and Flexibility

Variety appears to be a critical factor in supporting both initial and sustained benefits of any life changes related to increased happiness. Professionals often adapt interventions to consider a person's current needs and capacities, as well as offering suggestions to continue to challenge a person to apply their skills in new ways to promote growth. Self-help interventions can, *and should*, be designed to support long-term practice. For example, to add variety to the "Best Possible Self" intervention, Lyubomirsky and colleagues (2011) modified the instructions to include writing about different topics each week (i.e., romantic life, educational attainment, hobbies or personal interests, family life, career situation, social life, community involvement, and physical/mental health). Variations such as these should be developed drawing on the current theories of happiness and tested to ensure they contribute to sustainable benefits in happiness.

Person-Activity Fit

Perhaps the most important caveat to the proposal that widespread dissemination of PPIs would be beneficial to the general population is the need for a more nuanced approach that considers person-activity fit. Initial work in the PPI literature looking at individual differences suggests substantial variation exists among happiness-seekers – Parks and colleagues (2012) identified two distinct "clusters" that differ substantially in their baseline levels of life satisfaction, positive emotion, and depressive symptom levels. One of these subgroups was consistent with population norms reported in other research: reasonably happy, experiencing few or no depressive symptoms. The other,

however, reported well-being scores low enough to suggest clinical depression. While self-help approaches can be effective even for people suffering from mental disorders, presumably, these two subgroups might require different self-help techniques. For instance, individual differences in depression levels have practical significance when it comes to gratitude. In one study, a gratitude intervention was ineffective, and in some cases led to reduced well-being, among depressed individuals who were also interpersonally "needy." Given the existence of cases where the efficacy of PPIs varies by individual differences, we recommend that the widespread dissemination of PPIs to the general population be balanced with further attention to questions of person-activity fit.

Rigorous Designs

Rigorous scientific research studies on self-help are limited. Indeed, as previously mentioned, many self-help resources do not draw on empirically-based principles and lack validation on their own. This issue is mirrored in positive psychology research, where PPIs are often not tested against rigorous control conditions. Furthermore, results suggest that although PPIs are efficacious when compared to no-treatment controls, the effects are considerably lower when compared to "treatment as usual" or placebo controls. Positive findings for PPIs may be circumscribed within specific groups (e.g., motivated individuals) and differences among samples may result in an inability to replicate key findings. Thus, although we have presented considerable evidence that PPIs do work, we provide the caveat – not always. Although, we believe further exploration of factors such as motivation, variety, and person-activity fit will help explain some of these inconsistences, it is nevertheless critical that investigations use high-quality methods to examine the limits of the effectiveness of these techniques.

Future Directions and Conclusions

Positive psychology has helped develop a variety of intervention strategies that can reliably boost individual happiness. An important next step is to research important questions of what interventions work for whom, under what circumstances, and in what contexts to ensure that when interventions are provided as self-help, people will receive the most effective and relevant techniques. Some research has begun to address these questions but much additional work is needed to fully disentangle these issues. In order to do so, however, studies should evaluate the effectiveness of these methods when provided in real-world settings and the complications and nuances that arise when doing so. Indeed, promoting the flourishing of the world population requires bringing resources directly to people as opposed to assuming they will find these resources themselves.

In conclusion, PPIs can lead to reliable boosts in well-being, yet these benefits are smaller when provided as self-help resources. In this paper, we have outlined specific positive psychological strategies including savoring, gratitude, kindness, promoting positive relationship processes, and pursuing hope and meaning. Beyond their efficacy, PPIs are useful for self-help not merely because they increase well-being but because they are also well liked. Effectively using PPIs for self-help, however, requires a consideration of the role that motivation and engagement, variety and flexibility, and person-activity fit play in supporting long-term behavior change.

Moreover, in order to begin to achieve Seligman's goal of promoting flourishing worldwide, PPI researchers must think beyond questions of efficacy and begin to tackle the problem of dissemination. What are the best modalities for distributing PPIs to the general population? How can PPIs be made available in a way that is affordable and accessible for all? How will we accurately assess whether PPIs "work" in the more inherently messy real-world environments through which they will ultimately be offered to users? . . . We hope . . . that readers will be inspired to do that work, as we believe it will ultimately benefit a substantial portion of the world population.

References

Bolier, L., Haverman, M., Westerhof, G. J., Riper, H., Smit, F., & Bohlmeijer, E. (2013). Positive psychology interventions: A meta-analysis of randomized controlled studies. *BMC Public Health, 13*, 119. Retrieved from http://www.biomedcentral.com/1471-2458/13/119.doi:10.1186/1471-2458-13-119

Diener, E., & Seligman, M. E. (2002). Very happy people. *Psychological Science, 13*, 81–84.

Fredrickson, B. L. (2001). The role of positive emotions in positive psychology: The broaden-and-built theory of positive emotions. *American Psychologist, 56*, 218–226.

Lyubomirsky, S., Dickerhoof, R., Boehm, J. K., & Sheldon, K. M. (2011). Becoming happier takes both a will and a proper way: An experimental longitudinal intervention to boost well-being. *Emotion, 11*, 391–402.

Lyubomirsky, S., Sousa, L., & Dickerhoof, R. (2006). The costs and benefits of writing, talking, and thinking about life's triumphs and defeats. *Journal of Personality and Social Psychology, 90*, 692–708.

Lyubomirsky, S., Tkach, C., & Sheldon, K. M. (2004). *Pursuing sustained happiness through random act of kindness and counting one's blessings: Tests of two six-week interventions.* Unpublished manuscript, University of California, Riverside.

MacLeod, A. K., Coates, E., & Hetherton, J. (2008). Increasing well-being through teaching goal-setting and planning skills: Results of a brief intervention. *Journal of Happiness Studies, 9*, 185–196.

Parks, A. C., Della Porta, M. D., Pierce, R. S., Zilca, R., & Lyubomirsky, S. (2012). Pursuing happiness in everyday life: The characteristics and behaviors of online happiness seekers. *Emotion, 12*, 1222–1234.

Peterson, C. (2006). *A primer in positive psychology.* New York, NY: Oxford University Press.

Schueller, S. M. (2010). Preferences for positive psychology exercises. *Journal of Positive Psychology, 5*, 192–203.

Sin, N. L., & Lyubomirsky, S. (2009). Enhancing well-being and alleviating depressive symptoms with positive psychological interventions: A practice-friendly metaanalysis. *Journal of Clinical Psychology, 65*, 467–487.

Snyder, C. R. (2002). Hope theory: Rainbows in the mind. *Psychological Inquiry, 13*, 249–275.

STEPHEN M. SCHUELLER, PhD, is a research assistant professor in the Department of Preventive Medicine at Northwestern University's Feinberg School of Medicine and a faculty member of the Center for Behavioral Intervention Technologies (CBITs). His research focuses on the use of Internet and mobile interventions for the treatment and prevention of depression and the promotion of happiness and well-being.

ACACIA C. PARKS, PhD, is an assistant professor of psychology at Hiram College. Her research focuses on the efficacy of positive psychological interventions and the psychological and behavioral characteristics of individuals who use them.

Laurel C. Newman and Randy J. Larsen    **NO**

How Much of Our Happiness Is Within Our Control?

In reviewing articles for the "no" side of this issue, there were several individual perspectives on why we psychologists should take caution before announcing to the public that we know how to make people happier. However, there was no culminating piece containing the variety of lines of logic and research that inspire this warning. Thus, the purpose of this piece is not to insist that we have absolutely zero control over our own happiness. Rather, it is to summarize the evidence suggesting that we have much less control over it than positive psychologists typically espouse.

1. **The heritability of happiness:** In 1989, a group of researchers began a wildly ambitious and comprehensive study of twins called the Minnesota Twin Family study. They used comparisons of identical twins, fraternal twins, and other family members to determine the proportion of the variation in the public's happiness scores that is caused by genetic factors, which is called the *heritability* of happiness. In 1996, two of the researchers (David Lykken and Auke Tellegen) published a paper reporting that the heritability is around .50, which means about half of the variability we see in the population's happiness scores is caused by people's genes, and about half by other things. Most psychologists would concede that a person cannot change his or her genes, so it follows that at least one major cause of happiness lies outside of our control.
2. **The hedonic treadmill:** In 1978, Brickman, Coates, and Janoff-Bulman published a well-cited study showing that people who had befallen great fortune (lottery winners) or great tragedy (recent paraplegics) returned to their preexisting levels of happiness within a year following the event. A re-analysis of the data from the study showed that the paraplegics' level of happiness really never fully returned to baseline.

Nevertheless, follow-up research has been done on the topic, and most psychologists agree that people do adapt emotionally to most of the good and bad events in life and have a surprising tendency to remain very near their preexisting level of happiness despite life's slings and arrows. This has been called the "hedonic treadmill theory" because no matter how fast or slow people "run," they stay in the same place (emotionally, of course). This is good news because it means we have the capacity to adapt to the inevitable tragedies and problems of life, but it is also bad news because, for most people, it precludes ever attaining everlasting bliss.

The two points made thus far comprise the portion of this "no we cannot make ourselves happier" argument that is generally accepted, and even pointed out, by most positive psychologists. The points that follow may be viewed as more controversial.

3. **The famous 40 percent:** Sonja Lyubomirsky is most often cited by positive psychologists and the media as the person who has cracked the happiness code and made the fruits available to all. In her book, *The How of Happiness: A New Approach to Getting the Life You Want,* she summarizes the research showing that happiness is 50 percent heritable and 10 percent due to well-studied demographic variables. She claims *that means* the remaining 40 percent of happiness is within our control. To illustrate this concept, the cover of her book contains a pie with 40 percent removed and the claim, "this much happiness—up to 40 percent—is within your power to change." Her book has been touted by many as scientific evidence of great news: We have a surprisingly high level of control over our own happiness. There are a few problems with this conclusion, though.

An original essay written for this volume.

a. She misuses heritability estimates. Heritability estimates estimate the proportion of individual differences, or variation, in scores *among a group of people* that can be attributed to their genes. They describe variation in a group, and cannot be applied to any individual person.[1] There are undoubtedly people whose happiness lies largely within their control, and others who suffer from life circumstances that will likely cause lasting and inescapable misery. It is the job of positive psychologists to study these sorts of distinctions rather than making the misleading claim that everyone has an equal capacity for increasing his or her happiness.

b. Even if the 40 percent estimate were valid (which, as I just explained, it isn't), it is not accurate to claim that whatever portion of our happiness is not due to genetics and not due to as-of-yet carefully studied demographic variables is by default within our control. That 40 percent estimate would simply include *everything else*—everything besides genes and the demographic variables that have been carefully studied. That leaves room for many situational and personality variables that likely have a strong impact on our emotional state. Home foreclosures, lost jobs, unfaithful spouses, chronic illness, unplanned pregnancies, miscarriages, broken down cars and other daily hassles, work/life conflict, marital discord—the list is practically endless of things that would be included in that "everything else" portion, and the very important question remains as to which of those variables matter most, and to what extent those variables are actually within our control.

c. The evidence for the effectiveness of existing happiness interventions is shaky and unclear. Several positive psychologists have their own prescriptions for how to increase one's own happiness. These prescriptions are generally based on scientific research,[2] and most involve happiness exercises you can do easily at home to boost your happiness. There are currently two lines of research that have received the most attention that claim to increase happiness. In her book, Sonja Lyubomirsky describes exercises such as a *gratitude exercise* (wherein you contemplate 5 things you are grateful for at the end of each week), committing regular acts of kindness toward others, and distracting yourself when things are going badly rather than ruminating. Seligman and colleagues have tested 5 similar strategies and found scattered effects with 3 of them (though they also found temporary effects with an unconvincing placebo exercise). Although these interventions are often referred to by positive psychologists as promising evidence that we can boost our own happiness, the actual effects of these interventions are unimpressive. Though Lyubomirsky's book does not include actual data from her studies, a careful reading of the original journal articles reporting her results shows that many of the strategies have weak, improperly derived, or even unreported statistical effects that only show up at all under a very specific set of circumstances. Her 2005 paper is most commonly cited as scientific evidence that happiness-boosting interventions can work. However, in the actual paper, the *gratitude exercise* only mattered for people who did it once per week (not three times per week) and the *acts of kindness* exercise only mattered for people who did 5 acts of kindness all in one day for 6 weeks straight (not people who spread the acts out). Additionally, I use the term "mattered" rather than "worked" because the data were not reported in the article, nor were the results of any statistical tests.[3] Indeed, Boehm and Lyubomirsky's chapter in the *Handbook of Positive Psychology* reviews 8 studies, each testing several of what they call successful activities for increasing happiness. But the whole of the chapter contains mention of only one statistically significant result. The situation is surprisingly bleak considering the methodological features of her studies that should stack the results in her favor.[6] Nevertheless, her book has been translated into 11 languages and she is cited by positive psychologists and the media alike as having uncovered lasting keys to happiness. Several crucial questions remain: Do these exercises really increase happiness at all? If so, what boundary conditions are necessary for them to work? Are they ineffective for some people, and can they even have drawbacks?[4] Will any boost to happiness resulting from these exercises be long-lasting?[5] Given what we know about the hedonic treadmill, and given that emotional adaptation is even faster for good events than for bad ones, it seems likely that any benefits that people might gain from these interventions would dissipate quickly over time.

4. **The trouble with the denominator:** It might be surprising to most people to learn that personality

psychologists have found that positive and negative affect (PA and NA) are independent of each other. This means the people who experience the most positive emotions are not necessarily the people who experience the least negative emotions. Furthermore, most psychologists accept the proposition that our subjective well-being is defined, in emotional terms, as our ratio of positive to negative affect. So to make a person happier, you could increase the numerator (PA) *or* decrease the denominator (NA). Unfortunately, there is also a well-documented pattern of findings across various subfields of psychology that "bad is stronger than good." Bad events have a deeper and longer lasting impact on us emotionally than good events. This is called the *negativity bias*, and it is interpreted by most as having an evolutionary purpose: avoiding threats helps us survive; relishing accomplishments does not. What all this suggests is that people would get more bang for their buck by trying to eliminate the causes of negative emotion in their lives than by trying to increase the positive. This has been pointed out in the positive psychology literature,[7] but it remains largely ignored or even dismissed by most positive psychologists, as their "declaration of independence" depends on their determination to focus on increasing the positive and not dwelling on the negative. To make matters worse, while bad is stronger than good, it also seems evident that many key sources of negative affect (such as those listed in paragraph 3b) are largely if not fully outside of people's control. Indeed, Diener and colleagues recently stressed the need for a *revised adaptation (hedonic treadmill) theory* based on results from a large longitudinal study investigating whether or not people's life satisfaction levels are stable across time. They concluded that most people's were largely stable (which fits with hedonic treadmill theory), but that a portion of people (about 25 percent) have more fluctuating levels of life satisfaction. What variables did they find have a significant and lasting impact on life satisfaction? Unemployment and widowhood (both negative and outside of our control) had the strongest effects, with divorce having significant but smaller effects (an event most people view as negative and often outside of their control). It was in this article that they pointed out that paraplegics and other disabled people (again, negative and outside of their control) actually do not return fully to baseline. The lottery winners did not gain any lasting happiness from their wins (a positive event outside of their control). In fact, almost all the data cited in their review shows that,

though life satisfaction may fluctuate, it seems to be lastingly influenced primarily by events that are negative and outside of our control. Another comprehensive study by Diener and colleagues compared well-being data from large samples of people from 55 nations and found that subjective well-being was higher among people who lived in nations that were wealthier, individualistic, and that protected their citizens' human rights. Few people in countries that lack these characteristics are there by choice.

There is some debate as well among psychologists as to whether we *should* be trying to increase happiness in the American public, most of whom report being pretty happy already. That is an issue for another day. The question here is, *if* we concede that boosting happiness is a worthwhile goal to pursue for psychologists, to what extent is doing so *possible*? Careful research has shown that happiness is by no means predetermined or "fixed" by genetics. Psychologists have uncovered a variety of environmental variables that predict (correlate with or cause) happiness. However, we must not confuse prediction with control. Nobody chooses to become a widow, be confined to a wheelchair, live in an impoverished nation, or lose their job. Many of the most influential environmental variables in our lives are every bit as uncontrollable as our genes.

In the field of psychology, unbridled enthusiasm often gives way to skepticism, and this is a good thing for the field. Psychology has a long history of demonstrating that people like to be in control of their surroundings, and they like to be happy. It comes as no surprise that they would embrace the finding that they are in control of making themselves happy. But the job of psychologists is to make claims based on objective interpretation of scientific evidence. Objective interpretation seems to point more to the idea that most of what influences our happiness in large and lasting ways lies outside the realm of the controllable.

Notes

1. See Diener, 2008, for a lengthier explanation of this concept.
2. Psychologists agree that any finding in the field of psychology as well as any claims for treatment or intervention must be based on scientific research, so this is a good thing. However, claiming that one's opinions are based on scientific research has become somewhat of a free pass to say whatever you want as long as there is at least some trend

in your data that is consistent with your theory. Most psychologists are not going to take the time to sift through the details of others' (often unpublished) data and publish purposeful criticisms of others' work, and most laypersons do not have the skills to judge the quality of research. Therefore, whether or not the quality and results of the research actually warrant the claims being made is a question that often goes unchecked.

3. The results were described by bar graphs, which showed increases in well-being of .4 points for the acts of kindness exercise and .15 points (identical to the magnitude of change for the control group, incidentally) for the gratitude exercise. However, because there was no information on the scale or its end points and no statistical analyses were presented, it is impossible to judge what these values mean. One can only assume the results were not statistically significant, in which case it is misleading to refer to this article as evidence that these two activities increase happiness.

4. For example, the advice to stop ruminating probably has a lot of cash value for a chronic ruminator, but for most normal, well-adjusted people, ruminating can signal to us that we need to do something about a problem in our environment. Indeed, evolutionary and personality psychologists agree that negative emotions exist because they serve a purpose. Stifling the emotion, though more affectively pleasant, may not always be in our best interest.

5. Occasionally, researchers do conduct follow-up studies several months down the road. When they do, they often find mixed success, meaning that people are still a little happier who engaged in some of the exercises, but people who completed other exercises have returned to baseline (if they ever budged at all).

6. For example, lack of a convincing placebo control group (even though there is evidence that placebos have an effect in these types of studies), multiple measures of happiness and subjective well-being as dependent variables (which increases the overall probability of finding a significant result due to chance), and instructions telling participants that the researchers *expect* the exercises to boost people's moods (which can influence participants' responses).

7. Larsen and Prizmic estimate that bad events impact us about 3.14 times as strongly as good events.

LAUREL C. NEWMAN is an assistant professor and director of psychology at Fontbonne University in St. Louis. She received a BA from Lindenwood University in Missouri and her MS and PhD from Washington University. She conducts research on the influence of self-perceptions, values, and goals.

RANDY J. LARSEN is a personality psychologist interested in emotion. He does research on such topics as emotion/cognition interactions, emotional aging, emotion regulation, and subjective well-being. He currently serves as a member of the Publication Committee of the Society for Personality and Social Psychology. Additionally, he is a fellow of both APA and APS, serves on several journal editorial boards, and is currently serving as Chair of the Psychology Department at Washington University.

EXPLORING THE ISSUE

Can Positive Psychology Make Us Happier?

Critical Thinking and Reflection

1. Imagine you are an unhappy person who wishes to become happier. How would each of the viewpoints presented in these articles influence your decision whether or not to seek therapy? What might you expect to gain from therapy in each case?
2. Which of these viewpoints do you agree with most? How does your choice make a difference in how you, as a hypothetical therapist, might address an unhappy client's needs?
3. What does it mean to be "happy" in each of the views expressed in these two articles? Does defining happiness have an impact on whether or not positive psychology techniques? If yes, how so? If no, then why not?
4. Psychologists debate whether or not we should try to increase happiness in the American public. What arguments might either side make?
5. Larsen and Newman argue that psychologists should take caution before making public announcements about how we can make ourselves happier. What problems might result from a lack of caution?

Is There Common Ground?

Being able to determine how to increase happiness and relieve suffering is one of the main goals of psychology, especially psychotherapy. Additionally, happiness is widely held to be an essential component of individual well-being. Most people can agree that if an individual is able to increase their happiness, his or her quality of life will also improve as a result. Indeed, the authors of both articles agree that those who are happier tend to have particular behavioral characteristics (gratitude, kindness, promoting positive relationships, etc.) related to their perceived happiness. However, whether or not an increase in happiness is within our personal control is still very much up for debate.

Both articles agree that there are limitations to using positive psychology interventions to increase happiness, although they may not agree on the severity of these limitations. Some of the less severe limitations include flexibility and variability of interventions, person-activity fit, and motivation to be happy. Some of the more severe limitations indicate that happiness is really outside of our control, including the heritability of happiness and the "hedonic treadmill theory" of happiness. If happiness is truly outside

of our control, could it be possible that positive changes in the environment can promote happiness, just as negative changes in the environment (e.g., loss of job and death of loved one) decrease happiness?

Create Central

www.mhhe.com/createcentral

Additional Resource

Boehm, J. K., and Lyubomirsky, S. (2009). The promise of sustainable happiness. In *The Oxford Handbook of Positive Psychology*, 2nd ed. Oxford University Press.

Held, B.S. (2004). The negative side of positive psychology. *Journal of Humanistic Psychology, 44*(1), 9–41.

McMahon, D. M. (2006). *Happiness: A History*. Boston, MA: Atlantic Monthly Press.

Niemiec, R., and Wedding, D. (2008). *Positive Psychology at the Movies: Using Films to Build Virtues and Character Strengths*. Cambridge, MA: Hogrefe.

Internet References . . .

ABC News

http://abcnews.go.com/Health/story?id=4115033&page=1&singlePage=true

New York Times

http://www.nytimes.com/2010/06/01/health/research/01happy.html?_r=1

U.S. News

http://health.usnews.com/health-news/family-health/brain-and-behavior/articles/2009/06/24/positive-emotional-psychology-have-a-daily-diet-of-positive-emotions

Unit 2

UNIT

The Trend Toward Biological Interventions

*A*lthough *the medical model has been prominent in the field of mental health for the past century, in recent years the trend toward biological explanations and interventions for psychological problems has become increasingly evident. For example, debate has intensified about the extent to which drug addiction should be viewed as a disease of the brain or a maladaptive behavior pattern under volitional control. The field of psychopharmacology has mushroomed to such an extent that billions of dollars are spent each year on medications for a wide array of emotional and behavioral problems. Medications are being tried in ways that would have been regarded as quite unlikely only a decade ago, as is the case in the use of drugs to dampen memories of a traumatic experience such as combat, or the case of "smart drugs" being used to enhance cognitive functioning in normal individuals. Also evoking considerable debate is the question of whether medical marijuana should be prescribed for the treatment of mental disorders. Major proponents of the medical model are the psychiatrists who belong to the association that publishes the* Diagnostic and Statistical Manual of Mental Disorders, *Fifth Edition (DSM-5). Critics, including some psychiatrists, believe that some psychiatrists have overstepped the boundaries of their position by mislabeling and mistreating countless people by virtue of their rigid adherence to the medical model.*

Selected, Edited, and with Issue Framing Material by:
Richard P. Halgin, *University of Massachusetts, Amherst*

ISSUE

Do We Still Need Psychiatrists?

YES: **Steven Moffic**, from "Why We Still Need Psychiatrists!" madinamerica.com (2012)

NO: **Steven Balt**, from "Yes, We Still Need Psychiatrists, but for What?" *The Carlat Psychiatry Report,* (2012)

Learning Outcomes
After reading this issue, you will be able to:
• Critically evaluate the influence of psychiatrists on society, and discuss what steps they can take to move beyond traditional methods of providing mental health care.
• Evaluate the advantages and disadvantages of the model in which a single provider prescribes medication and also conducts psychotherapy, as opposed to a model in which a psychiatrist prescribes the medication, but psychotherapy is provided by another mental health professional.
• Consider the influence of pharmaceutical companies that provide "education" to psychiatrists about the effectiveness of their products. To what extent should this influence be monitored by the government?
• Discuss the communication skills that psychiatrists and other mental health professionals should be expected to have, and the ways in which these skills should be evaluated during the years of training.
• Address the criticism that psychiatry has built a scientific façade for a profession that is not really based on rigorous science.

ISSUE SUMMARY

YES: Psychiatrist Steven Moffic states that psychiatrists play critically important roles in the field of mental health care because they are extensively trained and well-versed in understanding the functioning of the human body and the treatment of mental disorders. He urges psychiatrists to accept constructive criticism and to take steps to move forward in developing innovative intervention models such as collaborating on-site with primary care physicians in offering integrated care.

NO: Psychiatrist Steven Balt believes that psychiatrists have overstepped the boundaries of their position, and doing so has often led to mislabeling and mistreating countless people. He contends that much of what psychiatrists do is pseudoscience, but that most people nevertheless buy into the psychiatric model. He argues that psychiatrists, with their years of scientific education, can use their influence to change the current state of affairs in the field of mental health.

For the past half century, a certain tension has existed between the professions of psychiatry and clinical psychology. Psychiatrists, who are physicians, have been trained in the medical model. Although many psychiatrists conduct psychotherapy, their training has been heavily influenced by four years of broad medical training followed by residency training in psychiatry, which usually takes place in a medical center. By contrast, clinical psychologists earn a doctorate in psychology, either at a university or at a professional school of psychology, and are generally more influenced by psychological theories and interventions. Because clinical psychologists (and professionals in several other mental health disciplines) do not prescribe medication, they often work collaboratively with psychiatrists or primary care physicians when treating patients needing psychotropic medication. In fact, in recent years, an increasing number of prescriptions for these medications have been provided by primary care physicians. The benefit of this trend is the fact that such medications are more readily available, and in a context that some patients view as less stigmatizing than that of a mental health provider's office. The disadvantage, however, is that primary care physicians are not as likely as psychiatrists to have specialized knowledge about these medications, and may therefore be less attuned to the benefits and risks of the meds they prescribe.

The influence of psychiatry as a profession has been especially marked in the realm of psychiatric diagnosis. The American Psychiatric Association publishes the *Diagnostic and Statistical Manual of Mental Disorders,* the most recent edition being DSM-5. The DSM is widely used by mental health professionals for diagnosing patients and for justifying health insurance coverage for treatment of these conditions. All editions of the DSM have generated considerable controversy over issues of what constitutes a disease, illness, or disorder. Despite its limitations, DSM serves an important function in promoting a common language for characterizing various psychological conditions, although some critics assert that its influence is too great, and that the research underlying the determination of diagnoses is flawed.

The influence of clinical psychology has been especially notable in the development and promotion of evidence-based interventions. Evidence-based practice refers to clinical decision making that integrates the best available research evidence and clinical expertise in the context of the cultural background, preferences, and characteristics of the patient. Because psychologists undergo extensive graduate training in research methods, their expertise is often tapped for research on diagnosis and treatment.

Because of their medical training, psychiatrists would presumably have a distinct professional advantage in terms of their understanding the various ways in which bodily functioning is related to psychological disturbance. They would also presumably have an advanced understanding of somatic interventions ranging from medication to brain procedures such as electroconvulsive therapy and deep brain stimulation. With such sophisticated knowledge, psychiatrists are in a position to have tremendous influence on the patients they treat, and as a consequence on their loved ones, the community, and society as a whole.

Yet the question arises about the extent of their positive influence, and whether psychiatry in its current form is as good as it can be. Stated in a more extreme form, the question can be asked whether we still need psychiatrists.

Psychiatrist Steven Moffic argues that we do indeed need psychiatrists, but perhaps the profession needs to redefine itself in ways that are more responsive to the needs of contemporary society. He urges his colleagues to listen to criticism, and begin to take steps forward along new paths of service provision. For example, he urges more collaboration between psychiatrists and primary care physicians at the point of service—the medical offices to which patients turn for help with physical as well as emotional symptoms. In such a setting, the best potential exists for making accurate diagnoses and decisions about interventions.

Dr. Moffic contends that psychiatrists have a lengthy and comprehensive medical education and are therefore best equipped to attend to abnormal bodily functioning that might affect emotional experiences (e.g., an underactive thyroid or a brain tumor that could be related to a person's experience of anxiety, depression, or psychotic symptoms). Dr. Moffic states that, because psychiatrists can provide both psychotherapy and medication, their services can be more cost-effective than is the case in which *two* professionals treat a patient.

Psychiatrist Steven Balt does not advocate an end to the profession of psychiatry but rather urges significant changes in the ways in which psychiatrists go about their work. Dr. Balt believes that psychiatry has overstepped its bounds, and has mislabeled and mistreated countless numbers of people. He even muses about the innumerable times he has been asked to prescribe a medication that would have dubious therapeutic value for the patient. The implication is that for some prescribers it would be easier to write the prescription than to engage the patient in a dialogue about the pros and cons of the medication option. Rather than pointing the finger of responsibility solely at psychiatrists, Dr. Balt takes a broader view, and urges his colleagues to challenge the "disability" system that makes people "too demoralized to give a damn."

Dr. Balt views the process of bringing about change an uphill battle, which is made particularly difficult because psychiatrists tenaciously hold onto a status quo, which for some is foisted upon them by their employers (e.g., hospitals, clinics). Dr. Balt recommends that psychiatrists develop a new mindset in which they are taught to *interact* more and intervene less. He is critical of the scientific façade that psychiatry has built on the basis of scant scientific evidence in order to keep itself relevant. With attention to effective communication, psychiatrists can explain to their patients how they can overcome their "illnesses" and help patients realize that some of their complaints are not actually illnesses in the first place.

Concurring with Dr. Moffic, Dr. Balt appreciates the extensive medical training of psychiatrists, but urges them to use their unique position to change the state of affairs.

Thus, the question at hand is less about whether we need psychiatrists at all, but whether we need or want the kind of services offered by many psychiatrists at the present time. Psychiatrists have a special opportunity to use their sophisticated understanding of bodily systems to develop and refine comprehensive integrative interventions in which they effectively treat the whole person.

YES

Steven Moffic

Why We Still Need Psychiatrists!

"It is really quite incredible to me that some . . . are willing to denigrate the 8 years of training that it takes to become sophisticated about pathophysiology of the whole body, understand the intricate play of medical and mental problems and really master complex diagnosis, pharmacotherapy, and psychotherapy, as I feel I did in my training."

—A psychiatrist colleague, personal e-mail communication, 4/2/12

This blog, and many to follow, will try to analyze why we are in this "incredible" state of affairs and what to do about it.

The Siege on Psychiatrists

In many ways, this situation has been building over many years. We can start with the middle of the last century, when psychologists and social workers started to provide more and more of the psychotherapy that psychiatrists like Freud had developed. And, wouldn't you know it, and just as Freud had predicted, not only have their results been pretty good, but they helped develop more evidence-based psychotherapies like Cognitive-Behavioral Therapy. So, it turned out we don't really need psychiatrists to purely do psychotherapy, do we?

Then, around 1990, the promising new wave of psychopharmacology provided a new direction for psychiatrists. In fact, with Prozac for clinical depression, it all seemed so easy and safe that primary care physicians soon became the major prescribers of psychiatric medications. Just pop a pill like you might a daily vitamin. Patients seemed to like that, too, as it seemed less stigmatizing to go to your general doctor instead of a "shrink."

More recently, the book by Robert Whitaker, *Anatomy of an Epidemic,* strongly suggested that we may have been led down a path mined with unexpected risks for long-term use of most of these new medications. Convincing evidence, which seemed to fit my own personal experience, was presented about how some of our "thought leaders" in psychiatry may have been swayed by pay from the pharmaceutical companies.

To top this all off, a colleague just advertised two jobs for a psychiatrist and/or nurse practitioner, as if there wasn't any difference between the two professions. Similarly, not a week goes by that I don't have a patient ask what the difference is between a psychiatrist and a psychologist. Hint (if you don't know the answer): psychologists cannot yet generally prescribe medication. Adding to this confusion, although anyone with a Ph.D. in any field can call themselves a "doctor," only psychiatrists are medical doctors specializing in mental disorders. Besides confusing psychiatrists with psychologists, "psychiatry" is often confused with all mental healthcare. Technically speaking, "psychiatry" should just refer to what psychiatrists do.

Outside of our profession, scientologists have led an anti-psychiatry movement for decades. More gently and helpfully, many of our patients have formed a consumer movement to achieve more of a voice and remind us that recovery is more than just taking a medication.

We psychiatrists also do not get paid nowadays nearly as much as one may imagine. How about $25 from Medicare or Medicaid to do a medication review for the most seriously symptomatic, a reimbursement which doesn't compare well to what many plumbers make.

Psychiatric Advances and Retreats

Fortunately, our current state of affairs hasn't always been the case, otherwise the profession would not have developed and continued to serve a societal need in the first place. A highly selective view of some of psychiatry's glory days, followed by retrenchments, would include the following.

Back in the 1800s, in the early days of state psychiatric hospitals, inmates with mental illness were able to leave jails and prisons to receive "moral treatment" in attractive new facilities. Imagine how proud these early psychiatrists must have been to be able to increase the dignity and safety of these patients. Unfortunately, over time, these state hospitals started to become overpopulated and in need of repair.

Then, the theories of Sigmund Freud seemed to promise a new way to treat mental illness. Just think of what made this so exciting in the early 1900s. The pride and promise to disclose unknown and unconscious conflicts! Unfortunately, though as Freud himself anticipated, the psychotherapies derived from his theories have major limitations, especially for the most seriously mentally ill.

There is more. The promise of mental healthcare for all with the federally-funded community mental health centers, supplanted by cost-cutting for-profit managed care systems. Therapeutic communities and housing led by such psychiatrists as Loren Mosher, only to give way to scores of homeless mentally ill. But you get the picture by now. One wave of promise supplanted by another, and not one way necessarily complementing and being integrated with the other. Two steps forward, then one step back.

Stepping into an Integrated Future

Fortunately, all of these prior treatments and settings are alive and partially well in one way or another. And therein lies the hope for the future: integrating the best of the past in new ways. If we accept constructive criticism, we should be poised to take another two steps forward. One of these emerging new paths leads to clinics that integrate psychiatrists on-site with primary care physicians. It is here, given enough time, where there is the best potential to make accurate diagnoses and more carefully prescribe psychiatric medication when it is needed.

Who has the best potential to lead this advance? By now, you should know the answer. It is still only psychiatrists that have the most comprehensive education and training in all aspects of mental health and mental illness. In the loving spirit of Shakespeare, let us count some of the many ways they can add unique value to those in need.

- Psychiatrists, alone among all the mental healthcare professionals, still take some version of the Hippocratic Oath, dedicating ourselves to the patient first and foremost.
- Psychiatrists, alone among mental healthcare professionals, have worn the white coat of medicine, which forever will infuse our professional identity.

- Psychiatrists, alone and unlike any other mental healthcare discipline, have had direct responsibility for life and death decisions in medical school and internship.
- Psychiatrists by far have the longest and most comprehensive education, with at least 8 years of graduate school.
- Psychiatrists have studied the brain extensively, and know why it is the hardest organ to study in the body, let alone how the brain may differ from our "mind" and "spirit."
- Psychiatrists know that deficits in the frontal lobes of the brain can cause a condition called Anosognosia, which leaves many prospective patients unable to even realize and accept that they have a mental problem in the first place.
- Psychiatrists, by our medical school training, are best equipped to make sure that an underactive thyroid gland or brain tumor is not causing one's anxiety, depression, or psychosis.
- Psychiatrists know best that people with psychiatric illness have much poorer overall health than the general population, and why.
- Psychiatrists are leading the way in understanding that disorders like PTSD and Major Depression may turn out to be not just brain diseases, but whole body illnesses.
- Psychiatrists best understand the medical language of other physicians.

Sure, we have "bad apples" among us, just like any other profession. And we, too, are subject to social forces that limit what we can do. Nevertheless, one might heed the advice of another hard-hitting and truth-finding investigative journalist, Mike Wallace, who just recently died. He had a serious suicide attempt and suffered periodic depressions. When asked once what advice he would give others suffering from depression, he simply recommended to find a "good psychiatrist." Note that he did not say, find any psychiatrist. How to find that good psychiatrist will be the subject of future blogs. If you have any recommendations on how to do so, let us know.

[Additional Statements of Dr. Moffic in Response to Posted Comments]

. . . What we do know is that when psychiatrists provide combined psychotherapy and medication, instead of a patient seeing both a therapist and a psychiatrist, that it is more cost-effective (saves money and is more therapeutic). We do know that in for-proft managed care healthcare systems led by business people, patients get much less care.

I'm with you for having others providing the same services that psychiatrists can for cheaper and less training. That is how I led, and why I was early to advocate for paraprofessionals and peer specialists. But there are some things that psychiatrists should be able to do better, just like one might only go to dermatologists or surgeons. No excuse if that care is not provided humbly, compassionately, and respectfully.

***

. . . I did not write the blog to defend psychiatry and psychiatrists. It was to try to improve what we can do, if that is possible. We indeed may need a paradigm shift, as some have suggested. For that, I appreciate all the comments on what we are doing wrong or where we are wrong about what we are thinking.

Sometimes it is clear we do well. That is why I gave the Mike Wallace example. For whatever information he shared publicly, whoever was his psychiatrist saved his life, a life that he dedicated to finding the truth and exposing fraud to millions on the *60 Minutes* TV show.

I'm all for other ways of helping than medications. Loren Mosher was a friend and colleague and model of a brave psychiatrist, and I know well what happened to him. [Editor's note: Dr. Mosher was an American psychiatrist who spent his career seeking more humane treatment for people with schizophrenia, including a residential treatment model which did not rely on drugs. He was dismissed from NIMH and resigned from the American Psychiatric Association in 1998 as a protest against the influence of psychiatric companies on psychiatric practice.]

***

It is certainly true that medications can do harm, and more than we realized at first. There are also many other things that do mental harm: racism, sexism, trauma (physical, sexual, and mental), substance abuse, environmental pollution, loss of jobs, poverty. . . .

STEVEN MOFFIC is a professor in the Department of Psychiatry and Behavioral Medicine as well as the Department of Family and Community Medicine at the Medical College of Wisconsin. He is interested in psychiatric ethics, cultural psychiatry, ecopsychiatry, prison psychiatry, and the nature of evil. He has devoted considerable attention during his career to exploring ethics within the practice of psychiatry.

Steven Balt

→ **NO**

Yes, We Still Need Psychiatrists, but for What?

If anyone's looking for a brief primer on the popular perception of psychiatry and the animosity felt by those who feel hurt or scarred by this (my) profession, a good place to start would be a recent post by Steven Moffic entitled "Why We Still Need Psychiatrists!" on Robert Whitaker's site, Mad in America.

Moffic, a psychiatrist at the Medical College of Wisconsin, is a published author, a regular contributor to *Psychiatric Times*, and a member of the Group for the Advancement of Psychiatry. Whitaker is a journalist best known for his books *Mad in America* and *Anatomy of an Epidemic*, both of which have challenged modern psychiatric practice.

Moffic's thesis is that we still "need" psychiatrists, particularly to help engineer necessary changes in the delivery of psychiatric care (for example, integration of psychiatry into primary care, incorporating therapeutic communities and other psychosocial treatments into the psychiatric mainstream, etc.). He argues that we are the best to do so by virtue of our extensive training, our knowledge of the brain, and our "dedication to the patient."

The reaction by readers was, predictably, swift and furious. While Whitaker's readers are not exactly a representative sample (one reader, for example, commented that "the search for a good psychiatrist can begin in the obituary column"—a comment which was later deleted by Mr. Whitaker), their comments—and Moffic's responses—reinforce the idea that, despite our best intentions, psychiatrists are still *not* on the same page as many of the people we intend to serve.

As I read the comments, I find myself sympathetic to many of Moffic's critics. There's still a lot we don't know about mental illness, and much of what we do might legitimately be called "pseudoscience." However, I am also keenly aware of one uncomfortable fact: For every patient who argues that psychiatric diagnoses are fallacies and that medications "harm" or "kill" people, there are dozens—if not hundreds—of others who not only disagree, but who INSIST that they DO have these disorders and who don't just accept but REQUEST drug treatment.

For instance, consider this response to Moffic's post:

> Stop chemically lobotomizing adults, teens, children, and infants for your imaginary psychiatric "brain diseases." Stop spreading lies to the world about these "chronic" (fake) brain illnesses, telling people they can only hope to manage them with "appropriate" (as defined by you and yours) "treatments," so that they are made to falsely believe in non-existent illnesses and deficiencies that would have them "disabled" for a lifetime and too demoralized about it to give a damn.

I don't know how Moffic would respond to such criticism. If he's like most psychiatrists I know, he may just shrug it off as a "fringe" argument. But that's a dangerous move, because despite the commenter's tone, his/her arguments are worthy of scientific investigation.

Let's assume this commenter's points are entirely correct. That still doesn't change the fact that lots of people have already "bought in" to the psychiatric model. In my practice, I *routinely* see patients who want to believe that they have a "brain disease." They ask me for the "appropriate treatment"—often a specific medication they've seen on TV, or have taken from a friend, and *don't want* to hear about the side effects or how it's not indicated for their condition. (It takes more energy to say "no" than to say "yes.") They often appreciate the fact that there's a "chemical deficiency" or "imbalance" to explain their behavior or their moods. (Incidentally, family members, the criminal justice system, and countless social service agencies also appreciate this "explanation.") Finally, as I've written about before, many patients don't see "disability" as such a bad thing; in fact, they *actively pursue it*—sometimes even *demanding* this label—despite my attempts to convince them otherwise.

Reprinted with permission from *The Carlat Psychiatry Report,* Steven Balt, April 12, 2012. www.thecarlatreport.com

In short, I agree with many of the critics on Whitaker's site—and Whitaker himself—that psychiatry has far overstepped its bounds and has mislabeled and mistreated countless people. (I can't tell you how many times I've been asked to prescribe a drug for which I think to myself "what in the world is this going to do????") But the critics fail to realize is that this "delusion" of psychiatry is not just in psychiatrists' minds. It's part of society. Families, the legal system, Social Security, Medicaid/Medicare, Big Pharma, Madison Avenue, insurance companies, and employers of psychiatrists (and, increasingly, non-psychiatrists) like me—all of them see psychiatry the same way: as a way to label and "pathologize" behaviors that are, oftentimes, only slight variants of "normal" (whatever *that* is) and seek to "treat" them, usually with chemicals.

Any attempt to challenge this status quo (this "shared delusion," as I wrote in my response to Moffic's post) is met with resistance, as illustrated by the case of Loren Mosher, whom Moffic discusses briefly. The influence of the APA and drug companies on popular thought—not to mention legislation and allocation of health-care resources—is far more deeply entrenched than most people realize.

But the good thing is that Moffic's arguments for why we need psychiatrists can just as easily be used as arguments for why psychiatrists *are* uniquely positioned to change this state of affairs. Only psychiatrists—with their years of scientific education—can dig through the muck (as one commenter wrote, "to find nuggets in the sewage") and appropriately evaluate the medical literature. Psychiatrists *should* have a commanding knowledge of the evidence for all sorts of treatments (not just "biological" ones, even though one commenter lamented that she knew more about meds than her psychiatrist!) and argue for their inclusion and reimbursement in the services we provide.

Psychiatrists can (or should) also have the communication skills to explain to patients how they can overcome "illnesses" or, indeed, to educate them that their complaints are not even "illnesses" in the first place. Finally, psychiatrists should command the requisite authority and respect amongst policymakers to challenge the broken "disability" system, a system which, I agree, *does* make people "too demoralized to give a damn."

This is an uphill battle. It's particularly difficult when psychiatrists tenaciously hold on to a status quo which, unfortunately, is also foisted upon them by their employers. (And I fear that Obamacare, should it come to pass, is only going to intensify the overdiagnosis and ultrarapid biological management of patients—more likely by providers with even *less* education than the psychiatrist). But it's a battle we *must* fight, not just for the sake of our jobs, but—as Whitaker's readers emphasize—for the long-term well-being of millions of patients, and, quite possibly, for the well-being of our society as a whole.

[Additional Statements of Dr. Balt in Response to Posted Comments]

It's truly unfortunate that the good psychiatrists I know . . . piece together pathology and psychiatry and human health and disease . . . "with nutrition, lifestyle, sleep modification, exercise, stress reduction, and . . . medication." Even though most psychiatrists would welcome the opportunity to practice in this manner, most of us don't have luxury of time to do so . . . and, moreover, most patients have little *interest* in any of the above.

BTW, before anyone accuses me of "blaming the patient," I would invite you to spend a day trying to talk patients *out of* a non-indicated benzo, stimulant, sleeper, or Seroquel, or an SSRI for "stress."

***

I have worked in three county mental health systems (and three private-practice settings, plus a VA clinic); I have seen, in my own experience, literally hundreds of people who have come to me and who, in my opinion, do not have a clear psychiatric diagnosis (which begs the question: what is a psychiatric diagnosis anyway?) but who insist that they do and, moreover, who demand the same drugs that people on sites like Whitaker's and Surviving Antidepressants regularly denounce. It's a very interesting quandary.

***

[There are] patients who demand medications even when (a) there is no clear evidence of a mental illness (and never was one); (b) other, less dangerous alternatives exist to manage whatever "symptoms" the patient complains about; (c) the natural course of their disorder precludes the need for ongoing medication; and/or (d) the patient has received a full explanation (i.e., informed consent) about potential risks and dangers.

Early in the course of an illness, when symptoms *do* exist to warrant a diagnosis, the risk/benefit ratio often favors the medication. Furthermore, this is the standard of care, so docs like me avoid any malpractice risks by prescribing the drug, regardless of whether we think it's the best option. But as you know, each illness has its own natural course, and symptoms wax and wane. What's appropriate upon initial presentation is often not appropriate later on (which is why I always work out a tentative "taper" or "discontinuation" strategy at the outset with each patient—for *every* drug). Unfortunately, many of our drugs have addictive qualities (or street value), and many patients are too heavily invested in the belief that the drugs "fix them," both of which lead to their demands for more.

***

Regarding involuntary detention/forced treatment. . . . In my experience at three different hospitals, I can say that the vast majority, if not all, patients who were involuntarily hospitalized truly *did* need to be briefly sequestered for the safety of themselves or others (or were obviously disorganized and incapable of managing their own affairs). I don't think many disinterested observers would disagree with that assessment. Now, whether that was due to mental illness is an entirely *different* question. (Most of the time, drug/ETOH intoxication or withdrawal was a major contributor.) As a result, one could argue that forced drugging was unnecessary and inappropriate, and yes, simply "calming down" was often interpreted as "insight" or "acceptance of treatment."

***

. . . I'm reminded about the training program in which I currently work. The first-year residents (whose psychiatry exposure is limited to the inpatient psych units) spend most of their time (a) writing notes . . . , and (b) learning to argue in favor of involuntary detention. Indeed, twice a week at "probable cause" hearings, the residents argue for continued involuntary treatment of their patients in front of a county judge and a patients' rights advocate (who represents the patients). The residents consider it not only a "badge of honor" to "win" their cases, but an important part of their education. More important, in fact, than proper diagnosis and treatment (which, [in my humble opinion], is virtually impossible in the chaotic environment of the inpatient unit).

***

. . . I'm reminded of an exercise I used to give my students (psychiatry trainees): Go into a room with a patient and forget everything you know about the DSM, psychiatric diagnosis, and medications. Instead, talk to the patient as a fellow human being. Get to know him as you would a new acquaintance. Pretend you're meeting him for coffee or at a social gathering. Try to understand the nature of his suffering, but also his personal strengths and ways in

which he can use those strengths or develop new ones. Treat him as a teammate or partner, and identify some goals to achieve together. And so on. . . .

Interestingly, when one approaches patients in this nonjudgmental, unbiased way, true mental "illness" (as much as some commenters here may disagree with that term), when it exists, *does* present itself, and often quite convincingly. On the other hand, many patients start to be seen as pretty "normal," with certain quirks or idiosyncrasies, but nothing too foreign or disturbing.

Indeed, the DSM tells us how to think about human behavior; the drug companies tell us precisely which neurotransmitters are responsible for sadness, elation, irritability, and fatigue; and our practice & payment arrangements effectively prevent us from using any other construct with which to understand our patients. But this simple exercise—sort of like trying to write with one's non-dominant hand—sheds a great deal of light on the biases we bring to the everyday practice of psychiatry. Moreover, it shows us how easy it would be to do things differently.

***

. . . If only we were taught to *interact* more and intervene less. Or, better yet, some strategies for effective interaction. Unfortunately, those are hard to define. They also seem to be skills that some people just seem to have from birth and just can't be taught. (Yes, I know about the literature on common factors of good therapists or effective psychotherapies. . . .)

***

. . . [P]sychiatry has built [a] scientific facade (on the basis of very scant evidence) in order to keep itself relevant in modern medicine. In reality, what's truly relevant (at least until we have better "interventions") is not scientific at all. It's what we say and do, and how we do it.

STEVEN BALT is a researcher, working psychiatrist, and editor-in-chief of the online newsletter, *The Carlat Psychiatry Report: An Unbiased Monthly Covering All Things Psychiatric.* He is a practicing psychiatrist at North Bay Psychiatric Associates in San Rafael, California. He is experienced in psychopharmacology, cognitive behavior therapy, dialectical behavior therapy, and community psychiatry, with a special interest in addiction psychiatry and process addictions such as eating disorders.

EXPLORING THE ISSUE

Do We Still Need Psychiatrists?

Critical Thinking and Reflection

1. Although some patients may suffer due to mislabeling and a failure to receive appropriate medication from psychiatrists, what aspects of the current psychiatric model are worth saving?
2. What are some of the advantages of integrating psychiatric care with care provided by a primary care physician? Any disadvantages?
3. During the past two decades, pharmaceutical companies have engaged in direct marketing of psychotropic medications for anxiety, depression, and other emotional symptoms. What are some advantages and disadvantages of this marketing?
4. Many psychiatrists limit their practice to prescribing medications, with the expectation that psychotherapy will be provided by another mental health professional. What are the advantages and disadvantages of this model?
5. Psychiatrists are urged to develop more sensitive and effective styles of communicating with their patients. What are some of the characteristics and behaviors that should be expected in a mental health professional?
6. What can psychologists contribute in terms of developing valid and reliable diagnostic procedures as well as effective therapeutic interventions?

Is There Common Ground?

Despite the way that the issue was framed by the authors, neither is proposing an end to the profession of psychiatry. Rather, they are expressing ardent viewpoints with the intention of sparking change and innovation in the field of mental health. Dr. Moffic calls for a paradigm shift, and Dr. Balt contends that psychiatrists are uniquely positioned to change the current state of affairs.

In challenging psychiatrists to change the status quo (and by implication, other mental health professionals as well), a number of issues emerge that warrant consideration. First, there is the question of science. To what extent are psychiatric diagnoses valid and reliable characterizations of the disorders they label? The development of the fifth edition of the *Diagnostic and Statistical Manual of Mental Disorders* (DSM-5) has been fraught with years of controversy and debate about what characterizes various psychological disorders. Not only have battles raged over diagnostic labels, but so also have debates emerged about what treatments are really effective for specific disorders. Psychiatrists can continue collaborating with psychologists and other mental health researchers in conducting research on the many conditions and treatments still needing investigation.

Professionals from all the mental health disciplines have an opportunity to touch the lives of all the patients they treat, to provide guidance to their loved ones, and to play a role of leadership in society. To maximize this potential, specialists from the various disciplines must come together in collaborative efforts that will benefit the lives of all those with whom they interact professionally.

Create Central

www.mhhe.com/createcentral

Additional Resources

Carlat, D. J. (2010). *Unhinged: The Trouble with Psychiatry—A Doctor's Revelations about a Profession in Crisis.* New York, NY: Free Press.

Greenberg, G. (2013). *The Book of Woe: The DSM and the Unmaking of Psychiatry.* New York, NY: Blue Rider Press/Penguin.

Wallace, E. R., & Gach, J. (2008). *History of Psychiatry and Medical Psychology: With an Epilogue on Psychiatry and the Mind-Body Relation.* New York, NY: Springer.

Whitaker, R. (2010). *Anatomy of an Epidemic: Magic Bullets, Psychiatric Drugs, and the Astonishing Rise of Mental Illness in America.* New York, NY: Crown Publishers.

Internet References . . .

American Psychiatric Association

www.psych.org

American Psychological Association

www.apa.org

MentalHealth.gov

http://www.mentalhealth.gov/

National Alliance on Mental Illness

www.nami.org

Selected, Edited, and with Issue Framing Material by:
Richard P. Halgin, *University of Massachusetts, Amherst*

ISSUE

Should "Smart Drugs" Be Used to Enhance Cognitive Functioning?

YES: Barbara J. Sahakian and Sharon Morein-Zamir, from "Neuroethical Issues in Cognitive Enhancement," *Journal of Psychopharmacology* (2011)

NO: Helia Garrido Hull, from "Regression by Progression: Unleveling the Classroom Playing Field Through Cosmetic Neurology," *University of Hawaii Law Review* (2010)

Learning Outcomes

After reading this issue, you should be able to:

- Understand the appropriate and inappropriate uses of cognitive enhancing drugs.
- Discuss the risks as well as the benefits of cognitive enhancing drugs by healthy individuals without cognitive disabilities.
- Consider the responsibilities of society to limit the unauthorized use of prescription drugs by people who take them without medical oversight.
- Evaluate the extent to which people with legitimate need for cognitive enhancing medications may be placed at a disadvantage if nonimpaired individuals are prescribed "smart drugs" which will give them an even greater advantage in academic performance.
- Discuss whether cognitive enhancing drugs should be classified as controlled substances.

ISSUE SUMMARY

YES: Professor Barbara J. Sahakian and Dr. Sharon Morein-Zamir note that cognitive enhancing medications provide considerable benefits to individuals with cognitive disabilities, and can also serve as "smart drugs" for healthy individuals for the purpose of cognitive enhancement. While more research is needed into the long-term effects of these drugs on healthy individuals, responsible use of these drugs is recommended in order to gain maximum benefits with minimal harm to the individual and to society as a whole.

NO: Attorney and Professor Helia Garrido Hull explains that the use of cognitive enhancing drugs by healthy individuals can have a negative impact on individuals with disabilities. The use of such drugs in competitive environments such as classrooms creates an imbalance between students without cognitive disabilities and those with disabilities for whom the drugs were originally intended. She asserts that the government has a responsibility to enforce the law in order to maintain the integrity of decades of legal precedent intended to protect individuals with disabilities from becoming disadvantaged again. Although many of these drugs are listed as controlled substances, their use without a prescription has become widespread and viewed as morally acceptable.

In 2012 various articles and news stories appeared in the national media about the shortage of psycho-stimulant medications such as Adderall (amphetamine-dextroamphetamine) and Ritalin (methylphenidate). These substances fall under federal regulations of the Drug Enforcement Agency (DEA), which oversees issues pertaining to their manufacture and distribution. The DEA tightly regulates the quantity of psychostimulants produced each year based on what is viewed as the country's legitimate need. However, that "need" seems to be rising exponentially each year. For example, in 2010 more than 18 million prescriptions were written for Adderall, but this figure was more than 13 percent higher than the number of prescriptions written the year before. Millions of individuals, including children, adolescents, and adults, rely on these medications to help them deal with their symptoms of attention-deficit/hyperactivity disorder as well as other neuropsychiatric conditions, and some are finding it more and more difficult to find a pharmacy that has inventory of their prescribed medication. These individuals rely on psychostimulant medications to help them control their hyperactivity and/or enhance their concentration and attentional functioning. People with other psychiatric conditions such as chronic psychotic disorders find these medications beneficial because they result in improved cognitive functioning that can be instrumental in living independently. Rather than referring to these medications as psychostimulants, some prefer terms such as cognitive enhancers or "smart drugs" because they have been shown to improve various aspects of cognitive functioning.

A primary reason for the limited availability of psychostimulant medication pertains to the reality of their illicit use. As "controlled substances" they are considered to be habit-forming and therefore likely to be abused. The major question relating to the shortage of these medications pertains to the extent to which these drugs are being used by people without prescriptions. For example, it is common among college students to "borrow" a friend's prescribed psychostimulant medication, particularly during periods of intense study. These drugs have also become increasingly common in the workplace, particularly by those in stressful and competitive jobs. More worrisome, however, are the instances in which these drugs are being illegally diverted in the distribution system and are being sold as recreational drugs.

Because psychostimulant drugs can be addictive, American society takes a relatively strong stance in terms of trying to control the distribution and use of these drugs. However, in recent years, some critics have questioned the wisdom of restricting availability of medications that might be beneficial to many people, and consequently yield considerable advantages to society in terms of increased success in academics, greater productivity in the workplace, and enhanced cognitive functioning in everyday life. Improved performance in all these areas would likely result in greater self-esteem for individuals, and as a result, a happier society.

Those in favor of loosening the grips on the availability of psychostimulant medication argue that these drugs are not all that different from the caffeine consumed daily by most Americans, sometimes in very high quantities and at a cost to physical health and well-being. Instead of drinking a half-dozen cups of coffee or cans of caffeinated soda, why not just take a pill that will help you stay more alert, focus more effectively, and get your work done more efficiently? Would not it be advantageous for surgeons, military personnel, shift workers, and airline pilots to take a prescribed medication to help them do their jobs better?

In addition to the personal and societal benefits of increased productivity and self-esteem, proponents of smart drugs contend that cognitive enhancement could lead to the reduction of unfair disparity in society. For example, individuals with neuropsychiatric disorders, debilitating medical conditions, brain injury, or ADHD could benefit from the use of cognitive enhancing medications which would enable them to function and compete more effectively in society.

Those opposed to the wider use of smart drugs express alarm about this trend, expressing particular concern that, rather than making people smarter, reliance on such drugs may actually reduce creativity, imagination, and motivation. Rather than viewing psychostimulants as smart drugs, critics label these agents as a form of cosmetic neurology. They also attempt to bring the discussion into the realm of a dialogue about ethics, which is called the field of neuroethics. Critics of these agents also take exception to the argument that smart drugs can level the playing field such that individuals with lower intellectual capacity or those from deprived backgrounds will be better able to compete with those not dealing with such deficits. How is the playing field leveled if the non-disadvantaged are taking these same drugs, and therefore leaping proportionally ahead of their less fortunate peers?

The article for the YES position affirms the need for and value of smart drugs. Professor Barbara J. Sahakian and research associate Sharon Morein-Zamir are prominent researchers in the field of brain functioning. While acknowledging some of the risks of smart drugs, they contend that these agents have considerable potential for improving the lives of countless numbers of people, particularly those with serious brain dysfunction. Regarding the wider use of smart drugs in society, they encourage responsible use, and assert that mentally competent adults should be able to engage in cognitive enhancement, and that regulatory agencies should allow this. At the same time, they urge scientists, physicians, and policymakers to ensure easy access to information about the benefits and risks of using these drugs.

The article for the NO position by law professor Helia Garrido Hull opposes the nontherapeutic use of powerful prescription stimulants because of the significant risks involved, and because such use places disabled individuals at a competitive disadvantage in the classroom. In addition to concerns about equity, Professor Helia Garrido Hull also expresses alarm about the potential detrimental effects on individuals who may experience the unwelcome effect of having their creativity sapped.

YES

Barbara J. Sahakian and Sharon Morein-Zamir

Neuroethical Issues in Cognitive Enhancement

Why Are Smart Drugs Needed?

Cognitive-enhancing drugs, also known as smart drugs, are needed to treat cognitive disabilities and improve the quality of life for patients with neuropsychiatric disorders and brain injury. Cognitive-enhancing drugs are used in treating cognitive impairment in disorders such as Alzheimer's disease (AD), schizophrenia and Attention Deficit Hyperactivity Disorder (ADHD). In neurodegenerative diseases, such as AD, cognitive-enhancing drugs are used to slow down or compensate for the decline in cognitive and behavioural functioning that characterizes such disorders. There are currently 700,000 people with dementia in the UK, most of whom have AD. Each year, 39,400 new cases are diagnosed in England and Wales, translating to a new case every 14 minutes. Current costs of long-term care for dementia in the UK are estimated at £4.6 billion, and with an increasing aging population, this estimate is expected to rise to £10.9 billion by the year 2031 (Knapp and Prince, 2007). Likewise, the number of people placed in institutions is expected to rise from 224,000 in 1998 to 365,000 in 2031. Cognitive-enhancing drugs are important in this context as it has been suggested that a treatment that would reduce severe cognitive impairment in older people by just 1% a year would cancel out all estimated increases in the long-term care costs due to the aging population in the UK (Knapp and Prince, 2007).

Cognitive enhancers may be beneficial not just in neurodegenerative disorders but also in neuropsychiatric disorders for which they are not yet routinely prescribed. For instance, though it is common knowledge that people with schizophrenia typically suffer from hallucinations and delusions, it is the long-term cognitive impairments that often impede everyday function and quality of life for many patients. Twenty four million people world wide suffer from schizophrenia (World Health Organization, 2008). In the USA, direct and indirect costs were estimated at over $60 billion in the year 2000 (Wu et al., 2005). It has been suggested that even small improvements in cognitive functions could help patients make the transition to independent living (Davidson and Keefe, 1995).

However, it is not only adults suffering from neuropsychiatric disorders that benefit from cognitive-enhancing drugs. ADHD affects 3 to 7% of all children worldwide, and is the most prevalent neuropsychiatric disorder of childhood (American Psychiatric Association, 2000). ADHD is a highly heritable and disabling condition characterized by core cognitive and behavioural symptoms of impulsivity, hyperactivity and/or inattention. It has important implications for education provision, long-term social outcomes and economic impact. For example, long-term studies indicate it is associated with poorer long-term outcomes, including increased educational dropout, job dismissal, criminal activities, substance abuse, other mental illness and increased accident rates (Barkley, 2006). The annual excess cost of ADHD in the USA in 2000 was estimated to be $42.5 billion (Pelham et al., 2007).

Whilst it is pharmacological cognitive enhancers (PCEs) that we will consider in this paper, there are numerous methods of boosting one's brain power. Some additional methods under development are neuroprosthetics for cognition, and transcranial magnetic stimulation. Importantly, there are many others such as education, physical exercise and neurocognitive activation or cognitive training that are commonly being used (Beddington et al., 2008; Hilman et al., 2008; Willis et al., 2006).

Research on Cognitive Enhancers

Despite the fact that much research has been dedicated to the development and understanding of various cognitive enhancers, we still have limited knowledge as to how specific cognitive functions are modulated by neurotransmitters. For example, whilst we know that methylphenidate improves symptoms of ADHD and improves performance on objective behavioural tasks, such as spatial working memory and stop signal, we have yet to determine conclusively whether dopamine, noradrenaline or both neurotransmitters are required for these effects on cognition. Some of the most notable PCEs being explored to assist individuals with neurological or neuropsychiatric disorders with executive function and attention difficulties include methylphenidate, atomoxetine and modafinil (Stahl, 2008). Methylphenidate, also commonly known as Ritalin, increases the synaptic concentration of dopamine and noradrenaline by blocking their reuptake. Atomoxetine (Strattera) on the other hand, is a relatively selective noradrenaline reuptake inhibitor. In the case of modafinil (Provigil), despite considerable research its precise mechanism of action is unclear, although it has been found to exhibit a multitude of effects including potentiation of noradrenaline and, to a degree, dopamine neurotransmission (Volkow et al., 2009), elevation of extracellular glutamate, serotonin and histamine levels, and decreased extracellular GABA (Minzenberg and Carter, 2008). Recent evidence suggests that some of its cognitive effects may be modulated primarily by noradrenaline transporter inhibition (Minzenberg et al., 2008).

An effective method of testing the effects of cognitive enhancers on cognition is by using double-blind placebo-controlled studies where participants undergo a battery of objective cognitive tasks targeted at measuring various facets of cognition, including memory, attention and executive functions. For example, in the CANTAB Spatial Working Memory task (SWM), a number of coloured boxes are shown on the screen (Owen et al., 1990). The aim of this task is that, by touching the boxes and using a process of elimination, the subject should find one blue 'token' in each of a number of boxes. The number of boxes is gradually increased, until it is necessary to search a total of eight boxes. SWM is a test of the subject's ability to retain spatial information and to manipulate remembered items in working memory. It is a self-ordered task, which also assesses heuristic strategy. This test is sensitive to frontal lobe and 'executive' dysfunction (Owen et al., 1990) and is impaired in childhood and adulthood ADHD (Kempton et al., 1999; McLean et al., 2004; Mehta et al., 2004).

It has been demonstrated that methylphenidate improves spatial working memory performance both in young volunteers with ADHD and in adult patients with ADHD, whereby patients make fewer task-related errors when on methylphenidate (Mehta et al., 2004; Turner et al., 2005). The neural substrates mediating SWM task performance have been examined using imaging techniques such as positron emission topography (PET) and indicate that the dorsolateral and mid-ventrolateral prefrontal cortex are particularly recruited (Owen et al., 1996). Studies using PET and contrasting [(11)C] raclopride binding, with the subject on versus off methylphenidate, have further indicated that methylphenidate influences dopaminergic

function, particularly in the striatum (Wang et al., 1999). Methylphenidate has been found to improve both performance and efficiency in the spatial working memory neural network involving the dorsolateral prefrontal cortex and posterior parietal cortex in healthy volunteers (Mehta et al., 2000).

Similar studies using the double-blind, randomized placebo-controlled methodology have reported that additional drugs such as modafinil and atomoxetine can improve performance in some tasks of executive functioning. Thus, modafinil has been found to improve spatial planning and response inhibition in ADHD patients, as measured by a variant of the Tower of London task and the stop signal task, respectively (Turner et al., 2004). It has been further demonstrated that modafinil produced improvements in performance in a group of healthy volunteers on tests of spatial planning, response inhibition, visual recognition and short-term memory (Turner et al., 2003). Likewise, administration of an acute dose of atomoxetine has been found not only to improve response inhibition in ADHD patients (Chamberlain et al., 2007), but also in healthy adults (Chamberlain et al., 2006). Using functional Magnetic Resonance Imaging (fMRI), the brain mechanisms by which atomoxetine exerts its effects in healthy volunteers has been examined in a double-blind placebo-controlled study (Chamberlain et al., 2009). Atomoxetine led to increased activation in the right inferior frontal gyrus when participants attempted to inhibit their responses in the stop signal task. Inhibitory motor control has been shown previously to depend, at least in part, on the function of this brain region (Aron et al., 2003).

Such results demonstrate the potential of drugs to enhance certain domains of cognition. At the same time, psychopharmacological research entails the consideration of several complex factors (Morein-Zamir et al., 2008). These include neurotransmitter function at times following an inverted U-shaped curve, with deviations from optimal level in either direction impairing performance (e.g., Ramos and Arnsten, 2007; Tannock et al., 1995). Likewise, different neurotransmitter levels can be found across brain regions, suggesting a complex interplay between baseline levels and drug administration. While some cognitive functions may improve following drug administration, others may worsen, as they depend on different optimum neurotransmitter levels (Cools and Robbins, 2004). These and related findings strongly suggest that drug-induced neurotransmitter increases may improve functioning in some groups but have no effect or even impair performance in others, already at optimum. In accordance, it is not uncommon for PCEs to improve performance primarily or exclusively in individuals with greater impairment

(Mehta et al., 2000). With increasing understanding of the brain's neurochemistry, using imaging techniques and animal models, the complex roles of pre-existing baseline levels, drug dosage and individual differences are becoming more apparent (Morein-Zamir et al., 2008).

The Interest in Cognitive Enhancement

There is a clear trend in many western countries towards increasing prescriptions of methylphenidate (Farah, 2005). With the advent of psychiatric medications with greater tolerability and fewer side effects (though see Swanson et al., 2007), these trends are set to continue. However, it is not only those who suffer from neuropsychiatric and neurological disorders who are appearing to use PCEs. The use of stimulants, including methylphenidate and amphetamines, by students has been rising as well. Trends suggest that between 1993 and 2001 there was a clear increase in the life-time and 12-month prevalence rates of non-medical use of prescription drugs in college students (McCabe et al., 2007). In the USA, studies indicate that up to 16% of students on some college campuses use stimulants (Babcock and Byrne, 2000; McCabe et al., 2005), while 8% of university undergraduates report having illegally used prescription stimulants (Teter et al., 2005). Surveys on students indicate that most illicit use of prescription stimulants reported in the past year involve amphetamine-dextroamphetamine combination agents (e.g., Adderall), with higher use amongst Caucasians and Hispanics compared with African-Americans and Asians, and with considerable variations between colleges (Teter et al., 2006). The most commonly reported motives for use were to aid concentration, help study and increase alertness (Teter et al., 2006). There is also a trend for increasingly younger students to use such drugs, with one report indicating that 2.4% of eighth graders (13–14 years old) abused methylphenidate, as did 3.4% of tenth graders and 4.4% of twelfth graders (Johnston et al., 2006; see also McCabe et al., 2004). The trends are also not reserved solely for North America, as prescriptions rates in England of stimulants have been rising steadily from 220,000 in 1998 to 418,300 in 2004 (Niyadurupola, 2007; see also Turner and Sahakian, 2006). Though drugs such as modafinil are prescribed off-label in North America, they can be freely obtained without prescription via the internet from multiple websites in various countries. In fact, a recent survey identified 159 sites offering drugs for sale, only two of which were regulated, and 85% not requiring a physician's prescription from the patient (Califano, 2008). Another cognitive domain of great interest is memory. Given the aging population in the UK and elsewhere,

and the fact that the lifespan of individuals is being extended, it is highly likely that cognitive-enhancing drugs that can improve memory in healthy elderly people will prove to be in demand.

The popular media has reported extensively both on studies finding improved performance in healthy individuals and on the rising use of PCEs in healthy individuals. For example, the results of the study by Turner and colleagues (2003) on modafinil were reported in the media, including papers, magazines and radio. Papers ranging from The Guardian to The New Yorker and Nature, as well as the BBC, have discussed their potential for widespread use (Ghosh, 2007; Maher, 2008; Meikle, 2002; Talbot, 2009). Maintaining an optimum level of alertness, arousal and attention might be expected to prove valuable in a range of work and leisure activities. Indeed, the use of PCEs is not restricted to academia, and American sprinter Kelli White received a two-year ban in 2004 due to the use of modafinil when competing in the world championships and other US nationals.

These trends of growing use are likely set to increase as presently there are also novel cognitive enhancers under development, many of which are aimed at improving memory and learning. For example, ampakines, which work by enhancing the AMPA receptor's response to glutamate, improve cognition in healthy aged volunteers (Lynch, 2004). Novel compounds such nicotinic alpha-7 receptor agonists are now in phase 2 of clinical trials in Alzheimer's disease and schizophrenia (e.g., MEM 3454 Memory Pharmaceuticals/Roche; Mazurov et al., 2006).

The Neuroethics of Cognitive Enhancement

The study of cognitive-enhancing drugs, and their influence both on patients with neuropsychiatric and neurological disorders and healthy adults, raises numerous neuroethical issues. Neuroethics is defined as the study of the ethical, legal and social questions that arise when scientific findings about the brain are carried into medical practice, legal interpretations and health and social policy (Marcus, 2004). In response to the advances in cognitive neuroscience and neuropsychiatry and their increasing potential for broader application in the 'real world', and in part to the use of PCEs in healthy individuals, the Neuroethics Society (www.neuroethicssociety.org) was established (Nature Editorial, 2006). Neuroethics is a subfield within the broader domain of bioethics, which encompasses the ethical and moral implications of all biological and medical advances. Neuroethics was established to address the rapid developments within cognitive neuroscience and neuropsychiatry, and addresses findings relating specifically to the sciences of the mind, encompassing the central nervous system and the underlying brain mechanisms of human behaviour.

It is clear that research conducted by neuroscientists is now eliciting profound ethical implications: there are a whole range of ethical issues being raised due to neuroethical research from the use of PCEs in healthy individuals to the use of fMRI technology in military, civil and legal domains (Farah et al., 2004). We have advocated elsewhere that these ethical considerations in regard to societal issues should be part of training in neuroscience courses (Sahakian and Morein-Zamir, 2009). Neuroethics instruction to students is important because these future researchers should have some responsibility, as scientists and as members of society, as to the consequences of their research and how it may impact on society. We will now consider the 'rights' and 'wrongs' of cognitive enhancement in healthy people.

There are many potential positive outcomes for the use of cognitive enhancers in healthy adults. In addition to scientific and clinical advances, cognitive enhancement may lead to the removal of unfair disparity in society. Likewise, such drugs may lead to increased performance in both pleasurable and competitive activities. In an attempt to increase discussion on the topic and understand the subjective effects of healthy individuals taking modafinil for cognitive enhancement purposes, Sahakian and Morein-Zamir (2007) interviewed several scientists who have taken modafinil. The subjective effects ranged from moderate to 'mild but very valuable to me,' and the academics interviewed reported varied effects on cognition including global effects on attention, working memory, word finding, improved sustained hard thinking and increases in mental energy. Better performance may in particular be valuable for individuals working in military roles, as shift workers or in positions that entail responsibility for the safety of many such as air traffic controllers. The Research and Development organization for the US Department of Defence (DARPA) has stated that

eliminating the need for sleep during an operation, while maintaining the high level of both cognitive and physical performance of the individual, will create a fundamental change in war fighting and force employment. Such capability has the potential to disrupt enemy operations tempo, increase the effectiveness of small footprint military forces and shorten the duration of conflict.

(Moreno, 2004, 2006).

Similar cognitive enhancement effects may seem desirable also in others, such as surgeons. However, long-term studies by the pharmaceutical industry to ensure safety and efficacy in healthy people are still required. Part of ensuring the safety of the use of these drugs long-term would be to address their potential for substance abuse, as there is also the potential for abuse of certain PCEs, such as methylphenidate (Bright, 2008).

Indeed, the potential harms of cognitive enhancement in healthy individuals must not be overlooked. Namely, there could be long-term side effects or risks, which would be unacceptable given that this is not medical treatment. Patients with debilitating symptoms will often tolerate the side effects of drug treatment because improvements in symptoms outweigh the negative aspects, but this is not the case for cognitive enhancers in healthy individuals (Turner and Sahakian, 2006). Safety concerns are particularly pertinent in the developing brain. Administering drugs to children, who are more vulnerable, may elicit additional harms not apparent in adults (Swanson et al., 2007). Clinical monitoring in this group is even more vital than in adults given the necessary prevalent off-label use, at times the potential for abuse, and the lack of clinical trials in this population (Zito et al., 2008). Additional safety concerns include drug–drug interactions and the presence of contraindications, which may become even more challenging with the increasing availability of PCEs via the internet (Sahakian and Morein-Zamir, 2007).

Another concern is the possibility of people being coerced or even forced into taking cognitive enhancers. This may occur explicitly, for example requiring that workers be alert during a night shift; or it may take on more subtle forms, such as providing a competitive environment where incentives are offered for best performance (Farah et al., 2004). In accordance, surveys indicate that the majority of college students overestimate the prevalence of non-medical use of prescription stimulants, leading to misperceived norms which in turn may promote such behaviour (McCabe et al., 2008). This may result in an overworked 24/7 society where people are pressured into working ever longer hours to the detriment of their own and their family's wellbeing. Concerns have also been raised regarding the possibility of greater inequality with the increased use of cognitive enhancers, if access is dependent on wealth (Chatterjee, 2004; Farah et al., 2004). This is true both between individuals (due to socioeconomic status and financial means), and between nations, as has occurred in the past with some medical advances (Ashcroft, 2005). Alternatively, given the likelihood that some PCEs may be affordable, costing about the same as a cup of coffee (Lennard, 2009), they could be adopted in disadvantaged populations, as was the case of mobile phones. Nevertheless, it is uncertain how the allocation and funding of various cognitive enhancers should be controlled and what the decision-making process should be.

This leads to another concern regarding how healthy individuals may obtain PCEs, ensuring both fair and safe access. Presently, in the USA and the UK, drugs such as modafinil, atomoxetine and methylphenidate require a doctor's prescription as these drugs are regulated for administration in psychiatric or medical conditions (Niyadurupola, 2007). Off-label prescriptions, or the prescription of a medication for a condition not described in the approved labelling, are very common and legal (Radley et al., 2006), and there is very limited regulation of off-label drugs with prescriptions, relying largely on the physician's discretion (Hampton, 2007). Hence modafinil, for instance, can be prescribed for people complaining of jetlag (Sahakian and Morein-Zamir, 2007). It is likely that physicians will face increasing pressure to prescribe PCEs to healthy individuals, and those who view the role of medicine as helping patients live better or achieve their goals may be open to considering such requests (Chatterjee, 2004; Greely et al., 2008). It is the physicians' responsibility to detect malingerers, decide whether or not to prescribe drugs for cognitive enhancement off-label, prescribe and monitor appropriately (Hampton, 2007). Otherwise, they risk that patients may decide to approach other doctors or less safe means of obtaining enhancers such as via friends, colleagues or the internet, where little regulation or monitoring is available and safety can be compromised (Califano, 2008; McCabe and Boyd, 2005). In the UK, the Academy of Medical Sciences workgroup specifically identified cognitive enhancers as a topic to be addressed by the Food Standards Agency and the Medicines and Health Care Regulatory Authority (Academy of Medical Sciences, 2008).

Another concern is that the use of cognitive enhancers may be considered cheating, allocating an unfair advantage over others in particular circumstances such as in competitive situations or test taking. Already the popular press has reported the negative opinions of some college students against their peers who use PCEs when studying for exams. Additional concerns pertain to the possibility of being 'overenhanced', for example being plagued by unwanted memories. Likewise, given that the effectiveness of PCEs will likely increase in the future, concerns have been raised over alternations in personhood and the risk of becoming a homogeneous society (President's Council on Bioethics, 2003). Furthermore, our perception of ourselves could change from mechanistic

beings, as we may become unable to take credit for our achievements. Additional concerns relate to the fact that PCEs are 'unnatural' and that virtues such as motivation and hard work could become outdated with the expectation that everyone could just 'take a drug' (for additional discussion of these concerns, please see Chatterjee, 2004; Greely et al., 2008; Wolpe, 2002).

Whilst many of the concerns are already very relevant with the increasing off-label and illicit use of PCEs by young people, such drugs are one method by which individuals can perform better and more effectively and so consequently enjoy more achievements and success. However, we would not want to preclude other methods, for example, extra help in the classroom, smaller classes, and a greater consideration for life/work balance (Sahakian and Morein-Zamir, 2007; Turner and Sahakian, 2006). Currently, PCEs (in particular pharmaceuticals such as modafinil, atomoxetine and methylphenidate) have the potential to provide important clinical benefits and further development in this area is worthy of pursuit. Pharmacogenomics will make it possible to target individuals with safe and effective cognitive enhancers. Pharmacogenomics is the discipline behind how genes influence the body's response to drugs, which is important for enhancing the efficacy of individualized treatments and reducing medication side effects (see also Roiser et al. 2005). This raises the possibility in future of allowing PCEs to subsets of people who will experience benefits but will likely not experience the adverse effects. Presently, scientists are working together with social scientists, philosophers, ethicists, policy makers and the general public to actively discuss the ethical and moral consequences of cognitive enhancement (Sahakian and Morein-Zamir, 2007). This will go some way to ensuring that technological advances are put to maximal benefit and minimal harm.

Several position and discussion papers have been featured in scientific journals and in the media discussing PCE in the healthy (Greely et al., 2008; Maher, 2008; Sahakian and Morein-Zamir, 2007). With the increased awareness of the ever-growing popularity of cognitive-enhancing drugs, many scientists have expressed positive and negative views on the issue, reflecting the complexity of the debate. Amongst them, Martha Farah of the University of Pennsylvania has commented that 'It would without question improve my quality of life' but also considered that others may wonder whether improving productivity through artificial means would undermine the value of hard work. Likewise, as reported in an article in the Daily Mail, scientists such as Michael Gazzaniga, Director for the SAGE Center for the Study of Mind at the University of California Santa Barbara has stated, 'If we can boost our abilities to make up for the ones Mother Nature didn't give us, what is wrong with that?'. Other scientists view PCEs in the general population negatively, including Eric Kandel from Columbia University who has stated that using drugs to boost exam scores is 'awful'. The drugs 'are designed for people with serious problems who really need help.' Howard Gardner, from Harvard University, has expressed concern that "We have no idea what these drugs do to other forms of intelligence" (e.g., emotional intelligence; Burne, 2007). Furthermore, Anjan Chatterjee, from the University of Pennsylvania, has raised the valid argument that 'No one has conducted thorough studies about how brain-boosting drugs would affect healthy people after weeks or months of use.'

The discussion led to Nature conducting an online poll which collected data from 1400 respondents from 60 countries (Maher, 2008). Interestingly, one in five respondents said they had used drugs for non-medical reasons as cognitive enhancers. Of those responding, 52% obtained cognitive-enhancing drugs by prescription, 34% by the internet and 14% by pharmacy. It was unclear whether the prescribed enhancers were diverted from other people's prescriptions, prescribed for different purposes or at different doses for the user, although in the UK a greater proportion obtained the drugs over the internet compared with the USA. In another online survey conducted in the USA, friends and peers were identified by the majority of university student respondents as the source of prescription drugs (McCabe and Boyd, 2005). This latter finding dovetails with a recent survey reported in the UK amongst Cambridge University students (Lennard, 2009). In the Nature poll, the most popular drug reported in the survey was methylphenidate (Ritalin) with 62% of users, 44% reported taking modafinil, and 15% reported taking beta-blockers (but see Teter et al., 2006 for different findings).

The respondents' opinions were also informative, with 96% of all respondents thinking that people with neuropsychiatric disorders should be given cognitive-enhancing drugs. In marked contrast, 86% of respondents thought that healthy children under the age of 16 should be restricted from taking cognitive-enhancing drugs. However, 33% of respondents said they would feel pressure to give cognitive-enhancing drugs to their children if other children at school were taking them. The Cambridge Varsity survey, completed by 1000 students, revealed that 1 in 10 had taken a prescription drug for cognitive enhancement (Lennard, 2009). The survey further found large differences between students of the different colleges within the university, as well as between areas of study, with Science and Engineering students being the least likely to take the drugs modafinil, methylphenidate or an amphetamine–

dextroamphetamine combination agent (Adderall). This survey complements the attitudes reported in the Nature survey in that a third of respondents said that given the opportunity, they would take a drug to enhance their cognition. Though suggestive, the data above are likely to suffer from selection bias and so should be interpreted with caution.

Conclusions and Outstanding Questions

In summary, we would like to stress that PCEs have considerable potential for improving the lives of individuals with neuropsychiatric and medical disorders, such as AD, schizophrenia, ADHD and those with brain injury. Therefore, PCEs are likely to be developed further and we expect their use to increase. At the same time caution must be exerted, particularly as studies of long-term effects in healthy humans regarding safety and efficacy are urgently required. Moreover, the potential use of PCEs in children with developing brains and the potential for abuse in certain populations must be considered, together with broader societal concerns such as coercion and inequality of access.

Thus, rather than advocate for overall inclusion or exclusion of PCE use in healthy individuals, we would encourage their responsible use. This includes scientists, physicians and policy makers ensuring that easy access to information about the advantages and dangers of using PCEs is available to the public (Sahakian and Morein-Zamir, 2007). Moreover, the public should be encouraged to use other non-pharmacological methods of cognitive enhancement, such as education. Greely and colleagues (2008) recommend that at present policies and limits should be created at the level of professional societies, such as physicians and educators, rather than the law. They further suggest that mentally competent adults should be able to engage in cognitive enhancement using drugs and that regulatory agencies should allow this given the availability of data for safety and efficacy (Greely et al., 2008). However, in order to do this, an evidence-based approach to the assessment of the risks and benefits of cognitive enhancement must be adopted. Additionally, there is a need for large-scale and refined surveys that do not focus necessarily on addiction, and that target populations beyond college students (see also Boyd and McCabe, 2008). However, others propose the formation of new laws and indeed regulatory structures to protect against the potential harms (Fukuyama, 2002).

Careful and critical evaluation of PCEs for the healthy population continues to be a key challenge to policymakers and regulators (Foresight Mental Capital and Wellbeing

Project, 2008) This can be viewed within the context of the wider phenomenon of healthy adults taking drugs for other reasons, such as to enhance mood or sleeping habits. The potential for the development of better treatments for the cognitive symptoms in neuropsychiatric disorders and brain injury means that novel PCEs that are safe and effective have the potential to be of significant benefit to such individuals within society. Yet, enforceable policies concerning the use of PCEs to support fairness, protect individuals from coercion and minimize enhancement-related socioeconomic disparities are critical (Greely et al., 2008). This has also been recognized in the Foresight Mental Capital and Wellbeing Report as 'Novel PCEs may prove of great benefit in the future, particularly given the rapidly developing field of pharmacogenomics and the aging population' (Foresight Mental Capital and Wellbeing Project, 2008). Ultimately, we too advocate a rational approach to the use of PCEs in order to gain maximum benefits with minimum harms to the individual and to society as a whole. The use of PCE is relevant to everyone and particularly to members of the psychopharmacology scientific community. We hope that by raising the neuroethical issues accompanying the scientific findings, and presenting some of the social implications already taking place, the reader will consider these issues.

References

Academy of Medical Sciences (2008) *Brain Science, Addiction and Drugs*. Working group report chaired by Professor Sir Gabriel Horn. Foresight Brain Science, Addiction and Drugs Project. London: Office of Science and Technology.

American Psychiatric Association (2000) *Diagnostic and Statistical Manual of Mental Disorders, IV-Text Revision edn*. American Psychiatric Association, American Psychiatric Association.

Aron AR, Fletcher PC, Bullmore ET, Sahakian BJ, Robbins TW (2003) Stop-signal inhibition disrupted by damage to right inferior frontal gyrus in humans. *Nat Neurosci* 6: 115–116.

Ashcroft RE (2005) Access to essential medicines: a Hobbesian social contract approach. *Develop World Bioeth* 5: 121–141.

Babcock Q, Byrne T (2000) Student perceptions of methylphenidate abuse at a public liberal arts college. *J Am Coll Health* 49: 143–145.

Barkley RA (2006) *Attention-Deficit Hyperactivity Disorder: A Handbook for Diagnosis and Treatment*, 3rd edn. New York: The Guilford Press.

Beddington J, Cooper CL, Field J, et al. (2008) The mental wealth of nations. *Nature* 455: 1057–1060.

Boyd CJ, McCabe SE (2008) Coming to terms with the nonmedical use of prescription medications. *Subst Abuse Treat Prev Policy* 3: 22.

Bright GM (2008) Abuse of medications employed for the treatment of ADHD: results from a large-scale community survey. *Medscape Journal of Medicine* 10: 111.

Burne J (2007) Can taking a pill make you brainy? London: Daily Mail, 64–65.

Califano J (2008) *You've Got Drugs! V: Prescription Drug Pushers on the Internet*. New York, Columbia University: The National Center on Addiction and Substance Abuse.

Chamberlain SR, Del Campo N, Dowson J, et al. (2007) Atomoxetine improved response inhibition in adults with attention deficit/hyperactivity disorder. *Biol Psychiat* 62: 977–984.

Chamberlain SR, Hampshire A, Muller U, et al. (2009) Atomoxetine modulates right inferior frontal activation during inhibitory control: a pharmacological functional magnetic resonance imaging study. *Biol Psychiat* 65: 550–555.

Chamberlain SR, Muller U, Blackwell AD, Clark L, Robbins TW, Sahakian BJ (2006) Neurochemical modulation of response inhibition and probabilistic learning in humans. *Science* 311: 861–863.

Chatterjee A (2004) Cosmetic neurology: the controversy over enhancing movement, mentation, and mood. *Neurology* 28: 968–974.

Cools R, Robbins TW (2004) Chemistry of the adaptive mind. *Philosophical Transactions. Series A Mathematical Physical and Engineering Sciences* 362: 2871–2888.

Davidson M, Keefe RS (1995) Cognitive impairment as a target for pharmacological treatment in schizophrenia. *Schizophr Res* 17: 123–129.

Farah MJ (2005) Neuroethics: the practical and the philosophical. *Trends Cog Sci* 9: 34–40.

Farah MJ, Illes J, Cook-Deegan R, et al. (2004) Neurocognitive enhancement: what can we do and what should we do? *Nat Rev Neurosci* 5: 421–425.

Foresight Mental Capital and Wellbeing Project (2008) *Final Project Report*. London: The Government Office for Science.

Fukuyama F (2002) *Our Posthuman Future: Consequences of the Biotechnology Revolution*. USA: Farrar, Straus and Giroux.

Ghosh P (2007) Drugs may boost your brain power. London: BBC News.

Greely H, Sahakian B, Harris J, et al. (2008) Towards responsible use of cognitive-enhancing drugs in the healthy. *Nature* 456: 702–705.

Hampton T (2007) Experts weigh in on promotion, prescription of off-label drugs. *J Am Med Assoc* 297: 683–684.

Hilman CH, Erickson KI, Kramer AF (2008) Be smart, exercise your heart: exercise effects on brain and cognition. *Nat Rev Neurosci* 9: 58–65.

Johnston LD, O'Malley PM, Bachman JG, Schulenberg JE (2006) *Monitoring the Future National Results on Adolescent Drug Use: Overview of Key Findings,* 2005. (NIH Publication No. 06-5882). Bethesda, MD: National Institute on Drug Abuse.

Kempton S, Vance A, Maruff P, Luk E, Costin J, Pantelis C (1999) Executive function and attention deficit hyperactivity disorder: stimulant medication and better executive function performance in children. *Psychol Med* 29: 527–538.

Knapp M, Prince M (2007) *Dementia UK: Summary of Key Findings*. London, UK: Alzheimer's Society, 1–12.

Lennard N (2009) One in ten takes drugs to study. *Varsity* 693: 1. Available at: http://www.varsity.co.uk/home/.

Lynch G (2004) AMPA receptor modulators as cognitive enhancers. *Curr Opin Pharmacol* 4: 4–11.

Maher B (2008) Poll results: look who's doping. *Nature* 452: 674–675.

Marcus SJ (2004) *Neuroethics: Mapping the Field*. Dana Press, New York, NY.

Mazurov A, Hauser T, Miller CH (2006) Selective alpha7 nicotinic acetylcholine receptor ligands. *Curr Med Chem* 13: 1567–1584.

McCabe SE (2008) Misperceptions of non-medical prescription drug use: a web survey of college students. *Addict Behav* 33: 713–724.

McCabe SE, Boyd CJ (2005) Sources of prescription drugs for illicit use. *Addict Behav* 30: 1342–1350.

McCabe SE, Brower KJ, West BT, Nelson TF, Wechsler H (2007) Trends in non-medical use of anabolic steroids by U.S. college students: results from four national surveys. *Drug Alcohol Depen* 90: 243–251.

McCabe SE, Schulenberg JE, Johnston LD, O'Malley PM, Bachman JG, Kloska DD (2005) Selection and socialization effects of fraternities and sororities on US college student substance use: a multi-cohort national longitudinal study. *Addiction* 100: 512–524.

McCabe SE, Teter CJ, Boyd CJ, Guthrie SK (2004) Prevalence and correlates of illicit methylphenidate use among 8th, 10th, and 12th grade students in the United States, 2001. *J Adolescent Health* 35: 501–504.

McLean A, Dowson J, Toone B, et al. (2004) Characteristic neurocognitive profile associated with adult attention-deficit/hyperactivity disorder. *Psychol Med* 34: 681–92.

Mehta MA, Goodyer IM, Sahakian BJ (2004) Methylphenidate improves working memory and set-shifting in AD/HD: relationships to baseline memory capacity. *J Child Psychol and Psyc* 45:293–305.

Mehta MA, Owen AM, Sahakian BJ, Mavaddat N, Pickard JD, Robbins TW (2000) Methylphenidate enhances working memory by modulating discrete frontal and parietal lobe regions in the human brain. *J Neurosci* 20: RC65.

Meikle J (2002) Scientists wake up to brain stimulant. London: The Guardian.

Minzenberg MJ, Carter CS (2008) Modafinil: a review of neurochemical actions and effects on cognition. *Neuropsychopharmacol* 33: 1477–1502.

Minzenberg MJ, Watrous AJ, Yoon JH, Ursu S, Carter CS (2008) Modafinil shifts human locus coeruleus to low-tonic, high-phasic activity during functional MRI. *Science* 322: 1700–1702.

Morein-Zamir S, Robbins TW, Turner D, and Sahakian, B. J. (2008). *State-of-Science Review: SR-E9, Pharmacological Cognitive Enhancement*. UK Government Foresight Mental Capital and Mental Wellbeing Project.

Moreno JD (2004) DARPA on your mind. *Cerebrum* 6: 91–99.

Moreno JD (2006) Juicing the brain: research to limit mental fatigue among soldiers may foster controversial ways to enhance any person's brain. *Scientific American Mind* 17: 66–73.

Nature Editorial (2006) Neuroethics needed. *Nature* 441: 907.

Niyadurupola G (2007) *Better Brains. Postnote 285*. London: The Parliamentary Office of Science and Technology.

Owen AM, Downes JJ, Sahakian BJ, Polkey CE, Robbins TW (1990) Planning and spatial working memory following frontal lobe lesions in man. *Neuropsychologia* 28: 1021–1034.

Owen AM, Morris RG, Sahakian BJ, Polkey CE, Robbins TW (1996) Double dissociations of memory and executive functions in working memory tasks following frontal lobe excisions, temporal lobe excisions or amygdalo-hippocampectomy in man. *Brain* 119: 1597–1615.

Pelham WE, Foster EM, Robb JA (2007) The economic impact of attention-deficit/hyperactivity disorder in children and adolescents. *J Pediatr Psychol* 32: 711–727.

Radley DC, Finkelstein SN, Stafford RS (2006) Off-label prescribing among office-based physicians. *Arch Int Med* 166: 1021–1026.

Ramos BP, Arnsten AF (2007) Adrenergic pharmacology and cognition: focus on the prefrontal cortex. *Pharmacol Therapeut* 113: 523–536.

Roiser JP, Cook LJ, Cooper JD, Rubinsztein DC, Sahakian BJ (2005) Association of a functional polymorphism in the serotonin transporter gene with abnormal emotional processing in ecstasy users. *Am J Psychia* 162: 609–612.

Sahakian B, Morein-Zamir S (2007) Professor's little helper. *Nature* 450: 1157–1159.

Sahakian B, Morein-Zamir S (2009) Neuroscientists need neuroethics teaching. *Science* 325(5937): 147.

Stahl SM (2008) *Stahl's Essential Psychopharmacology*, 3rd edn. Cambridge: Cambridge University Press.

Swanson JM, Elliott GR, Greenhill LL, et al. (2007) Effects of stimulant medication on growth rates across 3 years in the MTA follow-up. *J Am Acad Child Adolesce Psychiatry* 46: 1015–1027.

Tannock R, Schachar R, Logan GD (1995) Methylphenidate and cognitive flexibility: dissociated dose effects in hyperactive children. *J Abnorm Child Psych* 23: 235–266.

Talbot M (2009) Brain gain: the underground world of "neuroenhancing" drugs. New York: The New Yorker.

Teter CJ, McCabe SE, Cranford JA, Boyd CJ, Guthrie SK (2005) Prevalence and motives for illicit use of prescription stimulants in an undergraduate student sample. *J Am Coll Health* 53: 253–262.

Teter CJ, McCabe SE, LaGrange K, Cranford JA, Boyd CJ (2006) Illicit use of specific prescription stimulants among college students: prevalence, motives, and routes of administration. *Pharmacotherapy* 26: 1501–1510.

The President's Council on Bioethics (2003) *Beyond Therapy: Biotechnology and the Pursuit of Happiness*. Washington, D.C. Available at: http://www.bioethics.gov/reports/beyondtherapy/index.html.

Turner DC, Blackwell AD, Dowson JH, McLean A, Sahakian BJ (2005) Neurocognitive effects of methylphenidate in adult attention-deficit/hyperactivity disorder. *Psychopharmacology* 178: 286–295.

Turner DC, Clark L, Dowson J, Robbins TW, Sahakian BJ (2004) Modafinil improves cognition and response inhibition in adult attention-deficit/hyperactivity disorder. *Biol Psychia* 55: 1031–1040.

Turner DC, Robbins TW, Clark L, Aron AR, Dowson J, Sahakian BJ (2003) Cognitive enhancing effects of modafinil in healthy volunteers. *Psychopharmacology* 165: 260–269.

Turner DC, Sahakian BJ (2006) Neuroethics of cognitive enhancement. *BioSocieties* 1: 113–123.

Volkow ND, Fowler JS, Logan J, et al. (2009) Effects of modafinil on dopamine and dopamine transporters in the male human brain: clinical implications. *J Am Med Assoc* 301: 1148–1154.

Wang GJ, Volkow ND, Fowler JS, et al. (1999) Reproducibility of repeated measures of endogenous dopamine competition with [11C]raclopride in the human brain in response to methylphenidate. *J Nucl Med* 40: 1285–1291.

Willis SL, Tennstedt SL, Marsiske M, et al. (2006) Long-term effects of cognitive training on everyday functional outcomes in older adults. *J Am Med Assoc* 296: 2805–2814

Wolpe PR (2002) Treatment, enhancement, and the ethics of neurotherapeutics. *Brain Cognition* 50: 387–395.

World Health Organization (2008) Available at: http://www.who.int/mental_health/management/schizophrenia/en/.

Wu EQ, Birnbaum HG, Shi L, et al. (2005) The economic burden of schizophrenia in the United States in 2002. *J Clin Psych* 66: 1122–1129.

Zito JM, Derivan AT, Kratochvil CJ, Safer DJ, Fegert JM, Greenhill LL (2008) Off-label psychopharmacologic prescribing for children: history supports close clinical monitoring. *Child and Adolescent Psychiatry and Mental Health* 2: 24.

Barbara J. Sahakian is a professor in the Department of Psychiatry at the University of Cambridge School of Clinical Medicine in England. Her research is aimed at understanding the neural basis of cognitive, emotional, and behavioral dysfunction in order to develop more effective pharmacological and psychological treatments. Her lab focuses on early detection, differential diagnosis, and proof of concept studies using cognitive enhancing drugs.

Sharon Morein-Zamir is a research associate in the Department of Psychiatry at the University of Cambridge School of Clinical Medicine in England. She is interested in action control and executive function and in the different facets of compulsivity as instances in which control may be impaired. Recently she has become interested in the social and ethical considerations that result from neuroscience research, such as the debate surrounding the use of cognitive enhancing drugs.

Helia Garrido Hull

Regression by Progression: Unleveling the Classroom Playing Field Through Cosmetic Neurology

"[H]ow much happier that man is who believes his native town to be the world, than he who aspires to become greater than his nature will allow."[1]

Introduction

In the novel *Frankenstein,* Victor Frankenstein exceeds the natural order of reality by creating life and learns to regret his desire to become something greater than his own nature allowed. Although the story is fiction, for many, the desire to exceed their own physical, emotional, or intellectual limitations is very real. Today, medical advances intended to improve the quality of life for those suffering from disease, disorders, or disabilities are routinely employed by healthy individuals to enhance their natural abilities. The illicit use of prescription drugs for non-therapeutic purposes has sparked an ethical debate within the academic and medical communities regarding the propriety of enhancing performance through cosmetic neurology.[2] For some, using prescription drugs for non-therapeutic use is both morally wrong and socially unjustified. As one author opined, "the original purpose of medicine is to heal the sick, not turn healthy people into gods."[3] For others, using prescription drugs to increase attention span, improve learning, or to augment productivity is both morally acceptable and culturally desirable.[4] Nowhere is this more evident than on high school and college campuses throughout the United States, where healthy, intelligent students are increasingly using controlled drugs without prescriptions to enhance academic performance. Lost in this debate, however, is the significant negative impact that illicit use of certain prescription drugs by healthy individuals has on those individuals for whom the drugs were originally intended.

High school and college students across the country are increasingly using methylphenidate and amphetamines to increase cognition, improve grades, and gain a competitive edge over their classmates; they also use these substances recreationally. Both stimulant drugs are prescribed to treat individuals suffering from Attention Deficit Hyperactivity Disorder (ADHD), a psychological disorder that places millions of students at a competitive disadvantage within the learning environment.[5] Due to their high potential for abuse, methylphenidate and amphetamines are listed as controlled substances under U.S. law; therefore, they can only be used legally with a prescription.[6] The non-medical use of either stimulant is a crime punishable by imprisonment and the imposition of substantial monetary fines, but the lack of enforcement coupled with moral acceptance of such use among students has led to an increase in illicit use of each stimulant.[7]

The use of methylphenidate and amphetamines by students without ADHD is both dangerous to the user and unfair to those individuals who require the stimulants to compete with other students in the classroom. When healthy individuals utilize stimulants to enhance their natural cognitive abilities, the gap that use of the medicine was intended to close between students with and without ADHD reemerges. As a result, the classroom playing field once again becomes unlevel, placing certain individuals at a competitive disadvantage while destroying decades of legal precedent intended to protect those individuals from such an imbalance.

This article addresses the increasing use of methylphenidate and amphetamines by high school and college students and argues that states have a responsibility to prevent the uncontrolled, non-therapeutic, and injury-causing use of stimulants by students under their supervision and to protect the rights of individuals with ADHD.

[The second section] provides a brief overview of ADHD, the dangers associated with the use of methylphenidate and amphetamines to treat the disorder, and the Food and Drug Administration's response to risks posed by the use of each drug. [The third section] explores the increasing non-medical use of methylphenidate and amphetamines by students across the United States and considers the short-term and long-term implications of such use. [The fourth section] argues that the current regulatory structure is inadequate and negatively impacts students with legitimate medical needs by un-leveling the playing field created by existing laws. [The fifth section] presents recommendations to level the academic playing field.

ADHD: Diagnosis, Regulation, and Risk

Student misconduct in the classroom severely constrains the ability of schools to effectively educate students and has become a common reason for referring students to mental health services.[8] Often, student misconduct is linked to inattention, hyperactivity, or impulsivity that are the hallmarks of ADHD.[9] Once a student is diagnosed with ADHD, teaching strategies, unique learning environments, and adaptive or assistive technologies can be employed to prevent classroom disruptions and assist students with ADHD to compete on a level playing field with their fellow students.[10]

ADHD

ADHD is the current diagnostic label for a developmental disorder that has been known over the last century as "brain-damaged syndrome," "minimal brain dysfunction (MBD)," "hyperkinetic impulsive disorder," or "attention deficit disorder (ADD)."[11] ADHD affects between five to eight percent of school-age children and is the most common reason for referral of children to mental health services.[12] Individuals with ADHD often experience substantial impairment in family, social, and educational functioning.[13] In a classroom environment, individuals with ADHD may have difficulty controlling their behavior and staying focused and may experience periods of hyperactivity.[14] As a result, otherwise simple classroom tasks can become extremely challenging.[15] ADHD symptoms first appear between the ages of three and six, but no single test has proven effective at identifying the disorder.[16] Typically, individuals undergo a battery of tests by physicians and mental health specialists to rule out other possibilities for the symptoms exhibited.[17] Although it is normal for young children to experience periods of inattention, hyperactivity, or impulsivity, children with ADHD exhibit these behaviors more frequently and with greater severity.[18] Thus, ADHD is typically determined upon proof that the child has exhibited such symptoms for at least six months at a degree greater than that expected from children of similar age.[19] Although treatment may temporarily relieve many of the disorder's symptoms to help individuals lead productive lives, no cure exists.[20] ADHD can continue into adulthood.[21] Approximately two to four percent of adults have ADHD.[22] Although diagnostic criteria exist for children, there are currently no age-appropriate diagnostic criteria for adults.[23] Many adult patients are self-referred.[24] Because it is difficult for doctors to accurately diagnose ADHD even in adults, students who understand the testing protocol can easily manipulate the process to obtain a prescription.[25]

Once diagnosed, individuals with ADHD may be treated with one of a number of psychoactive stimulants. However, only two substances are widely utilized by American physicians to treat children: methylphenidate and amphetamines.[26] Stimulants work by increasing dopamine levels in the brain, a chemical associated with pleasure, movement, and attention.[27] These stimulants pass through the blood-brain barrier to affect brain function that manifests in changes in perception, mood, consciousness cognition, and behavior.[28] For individuals with ADHD, the stimulants act to reduce hyperactivity and impulsivity and to improve the individual's ability to focus, work, and learn.[29] Because these medications may pose significant dangers to individuals with cardiovascular (heart and blood) or psychiatric problems, however, physicians should examine individuals diagnosed with ADHD to assess their cardiovascular and psychiatric health and warn them of the dangers associated with using the particular drug.[30]

The use of stimulants has been shown to improve attention span, concentration, compliance, handwriting, fine motor skills, and interactions with other students.[31] Although methylphenidate and amphetamines are effective at treating the symptoms of ADHD, their ability to bring about short-term beneficial changes in consciousness and mood creates a high potential for abuse that can lead to addiction.[32] Congress has addressed this problem by placing strict controls on these and other psychoactive drugs.[33]

Regulation of Psychoactive Drugs

The United Nations Convention on Psychotropic Substances (UNCPS) was signed by the United States on February 21, 1971 and ratified on April 16, 1980. The goal of the Convention is to encourage stricter regulation over the illegal importation, manufacture, distribution, possession, and improper use of controlled substances.[34] The U.S. Drug Enforcement Agency (DEA) was designated as the authority responsible for meeting the United States' obligations under the treaty.[35] However, because the Convention is not self-executing, implementation of its terms required additional action by Congress. Recognizing the "substantial and detrimental effect on the health and general welfare of the American people" caused by such activities, Congress enacted the Controlled Substances Act (CSA) to implement the UNCPS.[36] The Act created five Schedules (classifications) that categorize drugs based on multiple factors including the drug's medical utility and its risk of harm. Schedule I drugs include drugs that have the highest potential for abuse, offer no recognized medical utility, and cannot be used safely.[37] Examples include LSD, PCP, heroin, marijuana, and crack cocaine. Schedule II includes drugs that have a high potential for abuse, the use of which may lead to severe psychological or physical dependence.[38] However, Schedule II drugs do have currently accepted medical use as part of treatment plans.[39] Examples include morphine, cocaine, oxycodone, methylphenidate, and amphetamine mixtures.[40] Drugs listed on Schedules III, IV, and V have decreasing potential for abuse, medical utility, and risk of physical dependence or psychological dependence relative to the drugs and other substances in higher Schedules.[41] The DEA is charged with enforcing the CSA, but the Food and Drug Administration (FDA) also plays a critical role as the primary authority for regulating controlled drugs that are prescribed for therapeutic use.[42]

The CSA created penalties for the unlawful manufacturing, distribution, and dispensing of controlled substances, with penalties that vary based on several factors, including the Schedule of the substance. In 1988, Congress passed the Anti-Drug Abuse Act (ADAA), which imposes penalties on both the seller and the purchaser of the drug.[43] Unless otherwise authorized by law, it is unlawful to knowingly or intentionally distribute a controlled substance.[44] The penalty for such action is imprisonment for up to one year, a minimum fine of $1000, or both.[45] If the distribution is to someone under twenty-one years of age, or occurs within 1000 feet of a private or public school, college, or university, the penalty is twice the maximum punishment normally authorized.[46] It is also unlawful for any person to knowingly or intentionally possess a controlled substance without a valid prescription for the substance.[47] Any individual found to illegally possess such drugs may be imprisoned for up to one year

and shall be fined a minimum of $1000.[48] The penalty for such distribution or possession is particularly harsh for students. In addition to the criminal penalties that may be imposed, distributors of controlled substances are ineligible to receive federal benefits for up to five years and possessors are ineligible to receive these benefits for up to one year.[49] This includes student loans and grants.[50] Despite these substantial penalties, students across the country continue to illegally use or distribute methylphenidate and amphetamines. In many cases, individuals who use the drugs illegally are unaware of the risks posed by such use.

Methylphenidate

Methylphenidate shares many of the pharmacological effects of amphetamine, methamphetamine, and cocaine.[51] It is commonly known by a variety of names, including "Diet Coke," "Kiddie Cocaine," "Vitamin R," "Poor Man's Cocaine," "Skittles," and "Smarties."[52] The names reflect the effects that users experience. Both animal and human studies comparing the effects of cocaine with that of methylphenidate showed that subjects could not tell the difference because each produced the same physiologic effects.[53] Methylphenidate acts on the central nervous system (CNS) to reduce symptoms of ADHD by "blocking the neuronal dopamine transporter, and to a lesser extent, norepinephrine."[54] Use of methylphenidate produces "dose-related increases in blood pressure, heart rate, respiration and body temperature, appetite suppression and increased alertness."[55] Chronic use can inhibit growth and result in weight loss.[56] If abused, methylphenidate may cause "excessive CNS stimulation, euphoria, nervousness, irritability," agitation, psychotic episodes, violent behavior, and severe psychological dependence.[57]

Methylphenidate is most commonly marketed under the brand name Ritalin, and its beneficial effects on individuals with ADHD are well documented.[58] The drug's success led to its widespread administration beginning in the 1990s. Between 1990 and 2000, the production of Ritalin increased nearly 500 percent.[59] Today, Ritalin is the most widely prescribed Schedule II stimulant to treat ADHD.[60] According to the United Nations, the United States produces and consumes approximately 75 percent of the world's Ritalin.[61] Although these drugs have helped many individuals with ADHD, their use has become so widespread that questions exist as to whether the drug has been over-prescribed and over-used.[62]

Amphetamines

Amphetamines are potent stimulants that affect the CNS by increasing levels of dopamine and norepinephrine in the brain to produce increased alertness and focus, while decreasing fatigue and hunger.[63] Its actions resemble those of adrenaline, the body's fight or flight hormone.[64] The drug was widely used by soldiers in World War II to combat fatigue and increase alertness on the battlefield. After the war, easy access for the general public led to increased use that culminated in widespread abuse of the drug in the 1960s.[65] In 1971, Congress listed the drug as a Schedule II drug based on its potential for abuse, but it has reemerged as the drug of choice for many students.[66] One of the most common amphetamines used to treat ADHD is marketed under the trade name of Adderall.[67]

Amphetamines act on the brain to "increase alertness, reduce fatigue, heighten concentration, decrease appetite, and enhance physical performance."[68] They may produce a feeling of well-being, euphoria, and loss of inhibitions.[69] Misuse may result in "seizures, hypertension, tachycardia, hyperthermia, psychosis, hallucinosis, stroke, and fatality."[70]

For individuals with cardiovascular risk factors, amphetamine use is particularly dangerous.[71] Blood pressure may elevate to a point where blood vessels in the brain rupture and cause a stroke.[72] Some individuals, even young athletes, have suffered heart attacks as a result of amphetamine use.[73] In other cases, users may become "extremely paranoid, violent, and out of control."[74] In the United States, Adderall use continues to climb. Between 1990 and 2000, the production for Adderall increased by 2000 percent.[75]

FDA Response to Risk of Methylphenidate and Amphetamine Misuse

In 2005, Canada pulled Adderall off the market, citing reports linking it to twenty deaths between 1999 and 2003.[76] In that same period, twenty-five people died suddenly in the United States and fifty-four others suffered serious, unexplained heart problems while taking ADHD stimulants.[77] The FDA responded by announcing that it found no need to make immediate changes to the marketing or labeling of drugs used to treat ADHD.[78] The FDA noted that most of the victims had existing heart defects that increased the risk for sudden death.[79] It also noted that the overall risk associated with Adderall was only slightly higher than that associated with methylphenidate products used to treat ADHD.[80]

The FDA did acknowledge, however, that use of stimulants presents the potential for rare fatal and non-fatal cardiovascular events.[81] In 2006, the FDA's Drug Safety and Risk Management Advisory Committee voted unanimously to recommend the distribution of Medical Guides to warn of potential cardiovascular risks associated with using ADHD stimulants.[82] The Committee also recommended requiring black box warnings—the strongest warning required by the FDA—to alert users of the significant cardiovascular risks associated with such use.[83] The Committee's decision was based on the proven relationship between elevated blood pressure and cardiovascular risk in adults, and the fact that the number of prescriptions for ADHD increased significantly over the previous fifteen years, including in the adult population.[84] Even those who disagreed with the recommendation noted the need for a broader, more effective means of communicating these risks to patients.[85]

Later that year, the FDA's Pediatric Advisory Committee recommended the implementation of stronger warnings regarding the use of the stimulants in patients with underlying structural cardiovascular defects or cardiomyopathies;[86] however, the Pediatric Advisory Committee opposed requiring a black box warning to the labeling of stimulants.[87] They recommended that the FDA modify information in other sections of the product labeling to address the potential harms.[88] The FDA adopted that recommendation.[89] Product labeling on ADHD stimulants now caution on:

> (1) use in patients with structural cardiac abnormalities or other serious heart problems; (2) the potential for increasing blood pressure and exacerbating preexisting conditions such as hypertension, heart failure, recent myocardial infarction, or ventricular arrhythmia; (3) the need to conduct a careful history (including assessment for a family history of sudden death or ventricular arrhythmia); (4) a physical examination to assess for the presence of cardiac disease, and further cardiac evaluation if warranted; (5) the potential for causing or exacerbating psychotic, manic, or "aggressive" symptoms or seizures; (6) the potential for growth suppression in continuously medicated youth; and (7) the potential for visual disturbances.[90]

The FDA also directed manufacturers of all drug products approved for the treatment of ADHD to develop Patient Medication Guides to alert patients to potential cardiovascular risks and risks of adverse psychiatric symptoms associated with the use of stimulants.[91] The FDA, however, refused to require pharmaceutical companies to place black box warnings on these drugs as it had done for other dangerous drugs used to treat children and adolescents for depression.[92] Patients, families, and caregivers receive the guides when a medicine is dispensed.[93] The problem with this approach is that its efficacy is based on the assumption that information about the drug's risks is effectively conveyed to the user.

A black box warning is the strongest warning required by the FDA, and it is typically required when (1) "[t]here is an adverse reaction so serious in proportion to the potential benefit from the drug that it is essential that it be considered in assessing the risks and benefits of using a drug," (2) "[t]here is a serious adverse reaction that can be prevented or reduced in frequency or severity by appropriate use of the drug," or (3) where the FDA has approved the drug with restrictions to assure safe use.[94] Although black box warnings are typically mandated based on observed adverse reactions, the FDA has acknowledged that "there are instances when a boxed warning based on an expected adverse reaction would be appropriate."[95]

The FDA's failure to require black box warnings on ADHD stimulants is problematic for several reasons. First, stimulant misuse has increased among school-aged children, and studies show that an increasing number of students obtain the drugs illegally from a friend or acquaintance with a legal prescription.[96] Many students who use the drugs illegally are unaware of the risks associated with taking the drugs.[97] This strongly suggests that the dangers associated with sharing these drugs with others is not being effectively conveyed to those who have a prescription for the drug. Having a black box warning posted on the prescription vial could increase the likelihood that legal users will warn the illegal user of potential serious side effects of non-therapeutic use.

Second, statistically significant increases in heart rate and blood pressure occur in adults treated with stimulant use, and blood pressure is strongly and directly correlated with vascular and overall mortality in adults.[98] Placing a black box warning on the prescription vial could increase awareness of the risks associated with use by individuals with heart conditions and increase the chance that those at serious risk are informed of the dangers. Given the increased distribution of stimulants and the resultant excess supply of the drugs that can be diverted to illegal use, it would be prudent to place additional warnings on stimulants. As the United States becomes more interested in the potential for cognitive enhancement, there is a growing urgency to increase awareness of the harms of illicit stimulant use.

The Decade of the Brain: Better Learning Through Chemistry

Congress declared the 1990s as the "Decade of the Brain" in an effort to increase the scientific study of debilitating neural diseases and conditions that plagued society.[99] The declaration stimulated research that led to breakthroughs in fundamental knowledge on how to treat debilitating neurological disorders and neuropsychiatric diseases.[100] For some, such breakthroughs encouraged the increased acceptance of science as a means to improve the human condition and the expectation that treatments for currently incurable diseases would become available.[101] Moreover, once those cures become available, some individuals with those disorders will seek to do what they wish with their body free from government interference.[102] For others, however, artificial enhancement of humanity through application of human invention is both morally wrong and spiritually corrupt.[103] The argument cuts across science, religion and law with no clear answers, and the classroom has emerged as the epicenter of the debate. As the next section reveals, an increasing number of students are turning to stimulants to gain a competitive edge on peers in the classroom.

Illicit Stimulant Use by Students

The United States continues to be the world's largest market for illicit drugs and a major destination of illicit drug consignments.[104] In 2008, an estimated 35.5 million persons in the United States, or 14.2 percent of the population aged twelve or older, reported the use of illicit drugs at one point in their lives.[105] Of these, an estimated 22.2 million persons were classified with substance dependence or abuse.[106] That number is likely to increase, as more than 20 million Americans acknowledged being drug users in 2008.[107] Perhaps more troubling is the increase in abuse of prescription drugs.

In 2008, the number of individuals who abused prescription drugs in the United States exceeded the total number of individuals who abused cocaine, heroin, hallucinogens, and inhalants.[108] Prescription drug abuse now ranks second only to cannabis abuse.[109] Young adults aged eighteen to twenty-five years exhibited twice the level of prescription drug abuse than youth aged twelve to seventeen years, and more than triple the level of abuse among adults aged twenty-six years and older.[110] This trend is likely to continue in the United States because individuals are increasingly turning to prescription drugs to fulfill a need. In 2008, 2.5 million individuals abused prescription drugs for the first time.[111] This is 300,000 more than the number of first-time cannabis users.[112] Of those individuals who used illicit drugs for the first time in 2008, nearly one third (29.6 percent) initiated their use with psychotherapeutics, including pain relievers, tranquilizers, stimulants, and sedatives.[113] Of these, approximately 600,000 individuals initiated their illicit drug use through use of prescription stimulants.[114] More than half of these individuals acknowledged that they received the prescription drugs from friends or relatives for free.[115] Illicit stimulant use begins as early as middle school, extends through high school and college, and continues into the workforce.

Illicit Stimulant Use in Middle School and High School

The misuse and abuse of stimulants used to treat ADHD is common among youth. For example, one study reported that 23.3 percent of middle and high school students taking prescribed stimulants had been solicited to give, sell, or trade their medication to friends.[116] The rate increased as the student moved from middle school to high school.[117] A Wisconsin study reported that of 161 elementary and high school students prescribed the stimulant methylphenidate, 16 percent had been asked to give or sell their medications to others.[118] Another study from Canada reported that of a random sample of middle and high school students who were using legally prescribed stimulants, 14.7 percent gave their medications to others, 7.3 percent sold their medication to others, and 4.3 percent had their medications stolen by others.[119] This early use continues in college.

Illicit Stimulant Use in Post-Secondary Education

In 2008, college-aged students (eighteen to twenty-five years old) had the highest rate (19.6 percent) of illicit drug use among all age groups.[120] In this age group, the use of psychotherapeutics (5.9 percent) was almost four times greater than the use of cocaine (1.5 percent).[121] This data shows that illicit use of prescription stimulants has become a major problem in post-secondary education.[122] In a recent study of 1811 undergraduate students at a large public university, thirty-four of the students questioned admitted to the illegal use of ADHD stimulants.[123] Most of the students questioned acknowledged that they used the drugs during periods of high academic stress because the stimulants increased reading comprehension, interest, cognition, and memory.[124] Furthermore, most students acknowledged that they possessed little knowledge of the drug or its potential to cause harm.[125] In another study of 1550 college students, of those responding who were not diagnosed with ADHD, almost half (43 percent) reported illegally using prescription stimulants.[126] Approximately 16 percent to 29 percent of students with ADHD stimulant prescriptions were asked to give, sell, or trade their medications.[127] Perhaps more troubling, students have acknowledged they find it easy to obtain prescription drugs on campus and that they do not perceive any stigma attached to their use.[128] Rather, many students believe such use is physically harmless, morally acceptable, and even a necessary predicate to success.[129] This perspective has led to an increased illicit use of stimulants in the workforce.

Illicit Stimulant Use in the Workplace

The abuse of drugs has also filtered over into the workforce. In 2008, of the 17.8 million illicit drug users aged eighteen or older, 12.9 million (72.7 percent) were employed either full- or part-time.[130] Today, doctors, lawyers, and other professionals use stimulants such as Ritalin and Adderall to compete in increasingly stressful, competitive work environments.[131] Recent reports suggest the declining economy may be a key factor behind the increasing number of individuals using these inexpensive stimulants.[132]

While stimulants like Ritalin and Adderall increase the user's attention and productivity, they may have the unwelcome effect of sapping the person's creativity. Memory, attention, and creativity represent three different cognitive domains that are interconnected and contribute to the "mental performance" of an individual.[133] As one psychologist noted, individuals taking Ritalin act "like a horse with blinders, plodding along . . . moving forward, getting things done, but . . . less open to inspiration."[134] Many entrepreneurs, performers, politicians, and communicators alike attribute their success to untreated ADHD.[135] Some argue that living with untreated ADHD allows them to think unconventionally and believe that ADHD medications dampen inspiration, leaving them to think like everyone else.[136] This view may have some merit, given that some of the greatest figures in history—including Albert Einstein, Thomas Edison, Salvador Dali, and Winston Churchill—exhibited classic ADHD traits, but were never treated for the disorder.[137]

Although no long-term career studies exist to determine whether stimulants actually dampen creativity and imagination, at least one study has found anecdotal evidence that taking Ritalin renders some children less interested in pursuing creative opportunities.[138] Psychologists have acknowledged that there may be a trade-off between the ability to focus and creativity for individuals using ADHD drugs, where individuals capable of focusing on a single thing while filtering out distractions may be less creative.[139] As Martha Farah, a psychologist and director of the University of Pennsylvania's Center for Cognitive Neuroscience opined, "I'm a little concerned that we could be raising a generation of very focused accountants."[140] Farah, however, also believes cosmetic neurology will be as commonplace as cosmetic surgery, as it may lead to improvements in the world.[141] As another author indicates, despite increased use of stimulants by academics, "so far no one is demanding that asterisks be attached to Nobels, Pulitzers or Lasker awards" like those associated with the possible enhanced performances of professional athletes.[142] The apparent acceptance of cognitive enhancement by professionals in the workplace has raised a number of ethical dilemmas, the answers to which have the potential to change what it means to be successful in or out of the classroom.

The Ethics of Brain Enhancement

The use of ADHD stimulants is just the beginning. Today, scientists are actively investigating memory enhancement drugs to help millions of baby boomers suffering from age-related memory loss. If such a "Viagra for the brain" is discovered, how should it be used?[143] Should it be administered, for example, to the elderly population if it improves their quality of life? No consensus likely exists on this question, given the divergent views on the use of brain enhancers. An affirmative answer would generate important questions and challenge notions about human meaning and its limitations. A negative answer would generate equally important questions about the role of medicine to humanity and challenge notions about the purpose of human intellect. From a purely scientific viewpoint, it makes little sense to wait patiently for evolution to improve brain function. Human intellect has evolved to the point at which it is now capable of creating technology that increases brain capacity.[144] Arguably, using brain enhancement technology to improve the quality of life of modern-day man is no different than the use of rudimentary stone tools by early humans 2.6 million years ago.[145] Such tools were the product of human intellect and dramatically improved early man's quality of life, allowing individuals to perform activities the human body was not equipped to perform.[146] For some, the development of simple tools parallels the development of brain enhancing drugs and represents another step in the evolutionary process that should be embraced. For others, however, the use of technology to enhance natural abilities raises profound questions about the moral status of nature and the proper stance of human beings toward the natural world.[147] Thus, the fundamental question is not whether improvement is possible, but whether humans should aspire to improve their natural state at all.[148]

Much of the debate has focused on the equality of access to enhancers. In 2007, for example, the British Medical Association argued for the equal access to brain enhancement drugs.[149] The authors of that paper acknowledged that equality of opportunity is an explicit goal of the educational system, and requires that individuals are given "the best chance of achieving their full potential and of competing on equal terms with their peers."[150] The best way to achieve this goal, according to the authors, is through selective use of neuroenhancers among individuals with lower intellectual capacity or those who have deprived backgrounds.[151] However, this argument misses the larger problem. From a legal and societal perspective, the question should be whether the use of such brain enhancement drugs by healthy individuals to increase normal abilities is consistent with the goal of leveling the playing field so that *all* students, including those suffering from ADHD, have an equal opportunity to receive an appropriate education.

Unleveling the Playing Field Through Cognitive Enhancement

In 1970, U.S. public schools educated only one in five children with disabilities.[152] In many states, it was illegal for any deaf, blind, emotionally disturbed, or mentally retarded individual to attend public school.[153] That changed after two landmark decisions. In *Pennsylvania Association for Retarded Children v. Commonwealth of Pennsylvania (PARC)*,[154] plaintiffs challenged the constitutionality of state laws that denied mentally retarded children access to a free public education because of their disabilities. *PARC* ended in a consent decree that enjoined the state from denying disabled individuals "access to a free public program of public education and training."[155] In *Mills v. Board of Education of the District of Columbia*,[156] seven children labeled by school personnel as having behavioral problems or mental retardation, or as emotionally disturbed or hyperactive, were denied admission to public school or excluded after admission with no provision for an alternative educational placement or review.[157] The court, relying on a Supreme Court mandate that states provide public education on equal terms, held that the state must provide a free public education to the students.[158]

PARC and *Mills* established that the Equal Protection Clause of the Fourteenth Amendment to the United States Constitution guarantees every child with a disability the right to appropriate public education. In 1975, Congress enacted the Education for All Handicapped Children Act (EHA), to help states protect the educational rights and meet the needs of students with disabilities.[159] The EHA is now codified as the Individuals with Disabilities Education Act (IDEA).[160]

In promulgating the EHA, Congress found that state and local agencies have a responsibility to provide education for all disabled students.[161] Congress also found it in the country's interest for the federal government to assist state and local efforts to provide education for all disabled individuals.[162] The EHA codified existing law by requiring states to provide access for every disabled individual to a Free Appropriate Public Education (FAPE).[163] To be eligible for federal financial assistance under the EHA, states must develop and implement policies assuring access to a FAPE for all children with disabilities.[164] Congress expressly intended that states provide a *full* educational opportunity to ensure that disabled individuals between the ages of three and twenty-one have equal opportunities in the learning environment.[165] Today, challenges to these mandates are brought under the IDEA.

Under the IDEA, a child is considered disabled if that child suffers from "other health impairments . . . [and] by reason thereof, needs special education and related services."[166] Implementing regulations promulgated by the U.S. Department of Education provide:

> *Other health impairment* means having limited strength, vitality, or alertness, including a heightened alertness to environmental stimuli, that results in limited alertness with respect to the educational environment, that
>
> (i) [i]s due to chronic or acute health problems such as . . . attention deficit disorder or attention deficit hyperactivity disorder . . . and
>
> (ii) [a]dversely affects a child's educational performance.[167]

Once a child is evaluated and determined to be learning disabled under the IDEA, states are required to ensure that an individualized education program (IEP) is developed for the student.[168] Academic success is an important factor in determining whether an IEP is reasonably calculated to provide educational benefits.[169] The IEP considers, for example, accommodations provided to the student to help him attain identified academic goals in a regular classroom.[170] Those goals are measured through classroom performance and by state administered standardized test results.[171] Congress added procedural safeguards that permit re-evaluation of state plans to measure their effectiveness in providing a free and appropriate education to all disabled individuals.[172] The Act requires the state or Secretary of Interior to conduct studies, investigations, and evaluations that are necessary to ensure the effective

implementation of the Act.[173] Collectively, these provisions were intended to ensure that disabled individuals have a fair chance to compete academically with individuals who do not suffer from a disability.

Studies have demonstrated that the Intelligent Quotients (IQ) of individuals with ADHD are normally distributed and that the academic deficits of ADHD may be a consequence of it rather than a core feature.[174] This suggests that students with ADHD are just as smart and capable as their peers but are hindered by their disorder. Prescription stimulants, therefore, play a critical role in maintaining equality of opportunity. Advances in cognitive neurology, however, threaten to turn back the hands of time and once again place disabled students at a competitive disadvantage in the classroom. The non-therapeutic use of stimulant drugs designed to help disabled individuals compete in the classroom is inconsistent with United States disability policy and must be prevented. Efforts to prevent illicit use in post-secondary education have largely failed; the legal and financial obligations imposed on states related to primary and secondary education, however, offer an effective means to address the problem.

Analysis and Recommendations

The misuse of stimulant drugs is frequently a prelude to chronic abuse or drug dependence.[175] The diversion of prescription drugs for non-therapeutic use begins as early as middle school and continues into high school, college, and the workplace.[176] States have diminishing levels of responsibility and control over students as they progress from primary and secondary education to post-secondary education and into the workforce.[177] As such, states should act early to prevent the illicit drug abuse.

Re-Evaluate Success in the Classroom Under IDEA

Congress exercised its authority under the Spending Clause of the Constitution to enact the IDEA with the express goal of providing a free and appropriate public education to students who are disadvantaged because of a disability.[178] In 2010, the federal government authorized almost $24 billion in funding for the IDEA.[179] To receive federal funds under the IDEA, a state must comply with the extensive goals and procedures set forth in the Act as they apply to state and local educational agencies that accept funds for K-12 programs.[180] Because the IDEA is an entitlement statute, school districts must identify children with disabilities and provide a free and appropriate public education.[181] Unlike other federal disability laws that are designed to ensure equality of access for disabled individuals at all levels, the IDEA was intended to ensure that students are successful in the K-12 system.[182] That success is evaluated in large part on student performance in the classroom and on state-administered standardized tests, where a student's achievement is reflected in relation to how well that student performs relative to other students taking the same test.[183] When healthy individuals use performance enhancing stimulant drugs to perform well on tests, the value of the testing protocol is significantly diminished and test scores may not accurately reflect student achievement.

For many students with debilitating mental or physical disabilities, the IDEA provides help through the provision of educational plans that help modify personal behavior and other aspects of the classroom environment. For students with ADHD, however, the IDEA can do more. Individuals with ADHD are as intelligent as individuals without ADHD, but they require assistance to be successful in the classroom. Like many of their non-disabled peers, students with ADHD are fully capable of performing well in post-secondary education. In fact, individuals with ADHD often move well beyond the basic goals of the IDEA to lead very productive lives. In many ways, the success of students with ADHD reflects the underlying goal of United States disability policy—equality of opportunity through accommodation. Yet, absent change, existing law will act to set back decades of progress in the field of disability law. States must be required to take action to prevent healthy students from using performance enhancing drugs that provide a competitive advantage over individuals with ADHD on standardized tests.

While the IDEA currently does not require states to provide services that maximize each child's potential, it does require states to level the playing field by providing services that are appropriate to ensure the success of the student. For standardized tests, the appropriate environment is one that provides an otherwise capable student with ADHD to compete fairly with students who do not have ADHD. Absent this procedural safeguard, the test scores are rendered meaningless and cannot accurately reflect student progress as required under the IDEA.

In enacting the IDEA, Congress expressly provided for the re-evaluation of state plans to measure their effectiveness in providing appropriate education to all disabled individuals.[184] Given the increasing illicit use of performance enhancing drugs by healthy middle and high school-aged students, the effective implementation of the Act is at risk. As part of any state education plan approved for funding under the IDEA, the state should be required to take appropriate measures to ensure that illicit drug use by healthy students does not detrimentally impact the ability of disabled students to compete in the classroom or on state-administered standardized tests.

Implement Social Norm Educational Programs

Many students who misuse drugs do so because they are unaware of the medical, psychological, and legal consequences of illicit drug use and abuse.[185] One of the most effective ways to address the problem of illicit drug use by students is through targeted educational campaigns that address misconceptions of such use.[186] Through early state-wide intervention, states can counter the potential adverse effects of illicit drug use while promoting student health and protecting the rights of disabled individuals. To be effective, any educational campaign must recognize that illicit stimulant use has become an accepted part of the academic experience for many students.[187] Unlike other forms of drug use, there is little stigma attached to the non-therapeutic use of stimulants. The culture of some schools may actually encourage students to use stimulants.[188] As one student at Columbia University acknowledged, "[a]s a kid, I was made to feel different for taking these drugs . . . [n]ow it's almost cool to take them."[189] Today, students with legal stimulant prescriptions routinely sell or give pills to others, without regard for the consequences of their actions.[190]

The most effective means to prevent illicit stimulant use is to dispel misconceptions students have regarding the drugs. For example, one college used a social norms marketing campaign to target prescription drug misuse in college.[191] Of the students surveyed at the completion of the campaign, 36.6 percent acknowledged that they would be more cautious in using prescription drugs.[192] Other targeted social norms campaigns have documented significant reductions in risky behaviors among students within a few years of the campaign.[193] To effectively address illicit stimulant use, states should implement educational campaigns aimed at addressing both the physiological harm that may occur to individuals who use drugs without a prescription, and the impact illicit drug use has on disabled individuals who require assistance to succeed in the classroom.

Social norm campaigns should elicit student input and use appropriate visual media mat bring credibility to the presentation to improve the likelihood that the message will be received. States must be proactive in addressing student perceptions of stimulant use. Early intervention through education is an essential first step, but states that receive federal funds under the IDEA must also take steps to ensure that student assessment is fair and accurately reflects the performance of disabled students. The state's power to take appropriate steps to protect the health of students and to protect the rights of the disabled is strongest when school authorities act in loco parentis.[194]

Protecting the Rights and Safety of Students

Unemancipated minors are subject to the control of their parents or guardians.[195] Minors placed in private or public schools for their education are subject to the care and control of the teachers and administrators of those schools who stand in loco parentis.[196] The nature of that power is both custodial and tutelary, and it permits school officials a degree of supervision and control that cannot be exercised over adults.[197] Indeed, "a proper educational environment requires close supervision of schoolchildren, as well as the enforcement of rules against conduct that would be perfectly permissible if undertaken by an adult."[198] While schools do not have an absolute duty to protect students from harm in all circumstances, schools do have a responsibility to protect students entrusted to their care from health risks.[199] As the United States Supreme Court has noted, states have a compelling interest in deterring illicit drug use by students in primary and secondary education because "[s]chool years are the time when the physical, psychological and addictive effects of drugs are most severe."[200]

The misuse of stimulants such as Ritalin and Adderall pose significant risk to school-aged students who may not be aware of the strong contraindications to their use. Indeed, the Court itself has noted that amphetamines produce an "'artificially induced heart rate increase, [p]eripheral vasoconstriction, [b]lood pressure increase, and [m]asking of the normal fatigue response,' making them a 'very dangerous drug when used during exercise of any type.'"[201] For students with undiagnosed heart defects, the risk is even greater. Dangerous complications, including death, may result from use of stimulants. Many students overdose as result of misuse and must seek medical intervention.[202]

The Supreme Court has acknowledged that "[t]he effects of drug-infested schools are visited not just upon the users, but upon the entire student body and faculty, as the educational process is disrupted."[203] The illicit use of prescription stimulants by healthy students harms disabled individuals who must use the stimulants to compete in the classroom. Such use interferes with the school's ability to provide an appropriate education to individuals with ADHD and should not be tolerated. When a state accepts funding under the IDEA, it effectively agrees to take all reasonable steps to provide each disabled student with an education that is appropriate for the individual.[204]

Illicit stimulant use interferes with that requirement and places students with ADHD at a competitive disadvantage in the classroom, in direct contravention of United States disability policy.

In view of the increased misuse of stimulants among students and the harm it causes to the user and to disabled individuals, state action to protect students from harm is warranted. States must ensure that student assessment accurately and fairly reflects student progress. Since student achievement is largely determined based on the results of standardized tests, states should implement random drug testing procedures prior to administering standardized tests.

Suspicionless drug testing in the middle school and high school environment is constitutional. In *Board of Education of Independent School District No. 92 of Pottawatomie County v. Earls*,[205] high school students challenged the constitutionality of the schools' suspicionless urinalysis drug testing policy. The school district's policy required all middle and high school students to consent to drug testing in order to participate in any competitive extracurricular activity, such as the Academic Team, Future Farmers of America, Future Homemakers of America, band, or choir.[206] The test was designed to detect use of illegal drugs, including amphetamines.[207] After considering the reasonableness of the policy,[208] the privacy interest affected,[209] the character of the intrusion imposed by the policy,[210] and the ability of the policy to meet its stated goals,[211] the Court held that the policy was constitutional.[212]

The Court began its analysis by noting that in the context of safety, a search unsupported by probable cause may be reasonable "when special needs, beyond the normal need for law enforcement, make the warrant and probable-cause requirement impracticable."[213] Special needs inhere in the public school context.[214] The Court placed great emphasis on the fact that the school district's policy was undertaken in furtherance of the district's responsibilities as guardian and tutor of the children entrusted to its care. Thus, the relevant question became whether the policy allowing for suspicionless searches was one that a reasonable guardian and tutor might undertake.[215] The Court found that the policy was reasonable because it was implemented to address the general nationwide epidemic of drug use, and because of the specific evidence of increased drug use in the school district.[216]

In assessing the students' privacy interest, the Court noted that students have a diminished expectation of privacy in public schools where the state is responsible for maintaining discipline, health, and safety.[217] It noted that students are routinely required to submit to physical examinations and vaccinations against disease.[218]

Respondents attempted to draw a distinction between individuals engaged in extracurricular athletic activities who had a diminished expectation of privacy under existing law, and individuals engaged in non-athletic extracurricular activities who are not subject to regular physicals and communal undress.[219] The Court disagreed, noting that its prior decision allowing for suspicionless drug testing of high school athletes depended primarily upon the school's custodial responsibility and authority.[220]

Next, the Court considered the character of the intrusion.[221] The Court noted that the degree of the intrusion on privacy associated with sample collection largely depends on the way in which production of the urine sample is monitored.[222] Students were required to fill a sample cup behind closed doors and deliver the sample to an official stationed outside the bathroom.[223] The sample was not released to law enforcement officials, and it was only used to determine eligibility to continue participating in the activity.[224] In view of the non-intrusive mode of collection used by the district, the Court found that the intrusion was negligible.[225]

Finally, the Court considered the nature and immediacy of the government's concerns and the efficacy of the policy in meeting them.[226] The Court noted that "the nationwide drug epidemic makes the war against drugs a pressing concern in every school."[227] The need for state action is magnified, according to the Court, when the threat affects children "for whom [the state] has undertaken a special responsibility of care and direction."[228] The school district's evidence of increased drug use among students, coupled with rising drug use nationwide, convinced the Court that the school district's drug testing policy was a necessary and appropriate means to address the drug problems.

In view of the rising misuse of prescription stimulants by middle and high school students across the country, the substantial risk of harm associated with misuse of stimulants, and the negative impact such use has on the opportunities of disabled individuals to compete in the classroom, it is likely that the United States Supreme Court would uphold any carefully tailored, state-sponsored drug testing of students taking standardized tests. Although standardized tests are not technically extracurricular activities, they are competitive by design and the test results have significant consequences for students intending to continue their education in college. Randomly testing students for illicit use of stimulants to protect students from harm and to preserve the rights of disabled individuals is no less reasonable than testing students involved in Academic Team, Future Farmers of America, Future Homemakers of America, band, choir, or other activities.

Conclusion

Over the last 35 years, the IDEA and other laws have increased educational opportunities for individuals with disabilities and their families.[229] Despite this, a significant threat has emerged that threatens to undo decades of progress. On school campuses across the nation, an increasing number of students illegally use prescription drugs to enhance their natural ability in the classroom. The non-therapeutic use of powerful prescription stimulants poses significant risks for students and places disabled individuals at a competitive disadvantage in the classroom in direct contravention of United States disability policy. Breakthroughs in neuroscience present humanity with a promise and a predicament. Brain enhancement therapeutics has the potential to improve the quality of life for those living with neurological disorders or impairment, and forces humans to address the propriety of artificially elevating human capabilities. The use of stimulants to elevate abilities in the classroom raises difficult questions about nature, science, and fundamental fairness. Given the United States' express goal of providing equal opportunities for disabled individuals, policies and activities directed to the use of enhancement technology must be based on a sound consideration of the impact such use will have on the rights of disabled individuals.

Notes

1. Mary Shelly, Frankenstein; or, The Modern Prometheus 47 (Barnes and Noble Books 2003) (rev. ed. 1831).

2. See generally Anjan Chatterjee, Cosmetic Neurology: The Controversy Over Enhancing Movement, Mentation, and Mood, 63 Neurology 968, 968 (2004) (defining cosmetic neurology as the use of medicine to artificially improve brain function by modulating motor, cognitive, and affective systems to enhance performance and improve quality of life).

3. Chatterjee, supra note 2, at 969 (citing Francis Fukuyama, Our Posthuman Future: Consequences of the Biotechnology Revolution 208 (2002)).

4. Henry Greely et al., Towards Responsible Use of Cognitive-Enhancing Drugs by the Healthy, 456 Nature 702 (2008), available at http://www.nature.com/nature/journal/v456/n7223/full/456702a.html.

5. Attention Deficit Hyperactivity Disorder (ADHD), Nat'l Inst. of Mental Health, http://www.nimh.nih.gov/health/publications/attention-deficit-hyperactivity-disorder/complete-index.shtml (last visited Sept. 5, 2010) [hereinafter NIMH].

6. 21 C.F.R. §1308.12 (2010).

7. *See* 21 U.S.C. § 841(a)(1) (2006) (imposing penalties for the unauthorized distribution of a controlled substance); *see also* Sean Esteban et al., *Non-medical Use of Prescription Stimulants Among US College Students: Prevalence and Correlates from a National Survey,* 99 ADDICTION 96 (2005), *available at* http://www.wellcorps.com/files/NonMedicalUseOf-PrescriptionStimulants.pdf.

8. *Strategies for Teaching Students With Attention Deficit Disorder,* W. VA. UNIV., http://www.as.wvu.edu/~scidis/add.html (last updated Apr. 10, 2007).

9. *See* NIMH, *supra* note 5.

10. *Strategies for Teaching Students With Attention Deficit Disorder, supra* note 8.

11. *What is ADHD or ADD?,* NAT'L RES. CTR. ON AD/HD, http://www.help4adhd.org/en/about/what (last visited Sept. 5, 2010).

12. *Id.*

13. Am. Med. Ass'n, *Attention Deficit Hyperactivity Disorder,* http://www.ama-assn.org/ama1/pub/upload/mm/443/csaphl0a07-fulltext.pdf (last visited Sept. 5, 2010).

14. NIMH, *supra* note 5.

15. *Id.*

16. *Id.*

17. *Id.*

18. American Acad. of Pediatrics, *ADHD and Your School-Aged Child* (Oct. 2001),http://pediatrics.aap-publications.org/cgi/data/108/4/1033/DCI/l.

19. *Id.*

20. NIMH, *supra* note 5.

21. *Id.*

22. NAT'L RESOURCE CTR. ON AD/HD, *supra* note 11.

23. ADHD diagnosis in children is based on meeting the criteria of the *Diagnostic and Statistical Manual of Mental Disorders* (DSM-IV-TR). These criteria require evidence of inattention, or hyperactivity and impulsivity, or both.

24. *Adult ADHD: Issues and Answers,* NYU SCHOOL OF MEDICINE ADULT ADHD NEWSLETTER (N.Y.U. Sch. of Med., New York, N.Y.), Spring 2005, *available at* http://webdoc.nyumc.org/nyumc/files/psych/attachments/adult_adhd_l_l.pdf.

25. *Id.* (noting that ADHD can be diagnosed in adults who exhibit criteria used to diagnose children as long as the adult can recollect such symptoms in childhood).

26. *Ritalin Use Among Youth: Examining the Issues and Concerns: Hearing Before the Subcomm. on Early Childhood, Youth and Families of the H. Comm. on Education and the Workforce,* 106th Cong. 12-14, 79-98 (2008) (statement of Terrance W. Woodworth, Deputy Dir., Office of Diversion Control, Drug Enforcement Admin., U.S. Dep't of Justice), *available at* http://www.justice.gov/dea/pubs/cngrtest/ct051600.htm [hereinafter Woodworth Statement].

27. Nat'l Inst. on Drug Abuse, Nat'l Insts. of Health, U.S. Dep't of Health & Human Servs., *NIDA Info-Facts: Stimulant ADHD Medications: Methylphenidate and Amphetamines* (June 2009), *available at* http://drugabuse.gov/pdf/lnfofacts/ADHD09.pdf.

28. *Id.*

29. NIMH, *supra* note 5.

30. Victoria L. Vetter et al., *Cardiovascular Monitoring of Children and Adolescents with Heart Disease Receiving Medications for Attention Deficit/Hyperactivity Disorder,* 117 CIRCULATION 2407, 2418 (2008), http://circ.ahajournals.org/cgi/content/full/l17/18/2407 ("The consensus of the committee is that it is reasonable to obtain ECGs as part of the evaluation of children being considered for stimulant drug therapy.").

31. Jay D. Tarnow, *Pharmacological Treatment of Attention Deficit Disorders,* ADHD SELF-MGMT. CTR. ONLINE, http://www.adhdselfmanagement.com/pharmacological_treatment_add.html (last visited May 24, 2010).

32. *Id.*

33. *See infra* Part II.B.

34. Convention on Psychotropic Substances, E.S.C. Res. 1474 (XLVIII), U.N.Doc.A/RES/1474 (XLVIII) (Mar. 24, 1970).

35. *Continuing Concerns Over Imported Pharmaceuticals: Hearing Before the Subcomm. on Oversight and Investigations of the H. Comm. on Energy and Commerce,* 107th Cong. 37-40 (2001) (statement of Laura M. Nagel, Deputy Assistant Adm'r, Office of Diversion Control, Drug Enforcement Admin.), *available at* http://ftp.resource.org/gpo.gov/hearings/107h/73737.pdf.

36. Controlled Substances Act, Pub. L. No. 91-513, 84 Stat. 1236, 1242 (1970) (codified at 21 U.S.C. §§ 801-904 (2006)).

37. 21 U.S.C. § 812(b)(1) (2006).

38. *Id.* § 812(b)(2).

39. *Id.*

40. *Id.*

41. *Id.* § 812(b)(3)-(5).

42. 21 C.F.R. § 290.1 (2010).

43. Anti-Drug Abuse Act of 1988, Pub. L. No. 100-690, 102 Stat. 4181.

44. 21 U.S.C. § 841(a)(1) (2006).

45. *Id.* § 844(a).

46. *Id.* §§ 859(a), 860(a).

47. *Id.* § 844(a).

48. *Id.*

49. *Id.* § 862(a)(1)(A), (b)(1)(A).

50. *Id.* § 862(d)(1)(A).

51. Drug Enforcement Agency, U.S. Dep't of Justice, Methylphenidate (A Background Paper) (Oct. 1995), *available at* http://www.methylphenidate.net/.

52. Drug Free World, The Truth About Ritalin Abuse (2009), http://www.drugsalvage.com.au/downloads/kiddie_cocaine.pdf.

53. *Id.*

54. Am. Med. Ass'n, *supra* note 13, at 8.

55. Drug Enforcement Agency, *supra* note 51.

56. *Id.*

57. *Id.*

58. *See, e.g., id; see also* Howard Abikoff et al., *Symptomatic Improvement in Children With ADHD Treated With Long-Term Methylphenidate and Multimodal Psychosocial Treatment,* 43 J. Am. Acad. Child & Adolescent Psychiatry 802 (2004) (reporting significant benefits from methylphenidate use in children with ADHD).

59. Woodworth Statement, *supra* note 26, at fig.l.

60. U.N. Int'l Narcotics Control Bd., Report of the International Narcotics Control Board for 2009, at 13 (Feb. 24, 2010), *available at* http://www.incb.org/pdf/annual-report/2009/en/AR_09_English.pdf.

61. *Id.* at 26.

62. Gene R. Haislip, Deputy Assistant Adm'r, Drug Enforcement Admin., ADD/ADHD Statement of Drug Enforcement Administration, Address at the Conference on Stimulant Use in the Treatment of ADHD (Dec. 10-12,1996), *available at* http://www.add-adhd.org/ritalin.html.

63. Susan Jones et al., *Amphetamine Blocks Long-Term Synaptic Depression in the Ventral Tegmental Area,* 20 J. Neurosci. 5575, 5575-80 (2000).

64. Alcoholism & Drug Addiction Research Found., *Amphetamines* (1991), http://www.xs4all.nl/~4david/amphetam.html.

65. Everett H. Ellinwood et al., *Chronic Amphetamine Use and Abuse* (2000), http://www.acnp.org/g4/GN401000166/CH162.htm.

66. Woodworth Statement, *supra* note 26, at fig. 1.

67. Nat'l Inst. on Drug Abuse, *supra* note 27.

68. Patrick G. O'Connor, *Amphetamines, in* The Merck Manual Home Edition (Online Version) (last updated Jan. 2009), *available at* http://www.merckmanuals.com/home/sec25/ch312/ch312c.html.

69. *Id.*

70. Neal Handly, *Toxicity, Amphetamine* (last updated Oct. 21, 2009), *available at* http://emedicine.medscape.com/article/812518-overview.

71. O'Connor, *supra* note 68.

72. *Id.*

73. *Id.*

74. *Id.*

75. Woodworth Statement, *supra* note 26, at fig. 1.

76. Matt McMillen, *Adderall: A Stroke of Bad News,* Wash. Post, Feb. 15, 2005, at HE02.

77. Gardiner Harris, *Deaths Cited in Reports on Stimulant Drugs, But Their Cause is Uncertain,* N.Y. Times, Feb. 9, 2006, at A19.

78. U.S. Food & Drug Admin., *Statement on Adderall* (Feb. 9, 2005), http://www.fda.gov/NewsEvents/Newsroom/PressAnnouncements/2005/ucml08411.htm.

79. U.S. Food & Drug Admin., *Public Health Advisory for Adderall and Adderall XR* (Feb. 9, 2005), *available at* http://www.fda.gov/Drugs/DrugSafety/PostmarketDrugSafetyInformationforPatientsandProviders/DrugSafetyInformationforHealthcareProfessionals/PublicHealthAdvisories/ucm051672.htm.

80. *Id.*

81. U.S. Food & Drug Admin., *Drug Safety and Risk Management Advisory Committee Minutes* (Feb. 9, 2006), www.fda.gov/ohrms/dockets/ac/06/minutes/2006-4202MI_FINAL-Minutes.pdf.

82. *Id.* at 4.

83. *Id.*

84. *Id.*

85. *Id.*

86. U.S. Food & Drug Admin., *Minutes of the Pediatric Advisory Committee 6* (Mar. 22, 2006), http://www.fda.gov/ohrms/dockets/ac/06/minutes/2006-4210m_Minutes%20PAC%20March%2022%202006.pdf.

87. *Id.*

88. *Id.*

89. U.S. Food & Drug Admin., *FDA Directs ADHD Drug Manufacturers to Notify Patients about Cardiovascular Adverse Events and Psychiatric Adverse Events* (Feb. 21, 2007), http://www.fda.gov/NewsEvents/

Newsroom/PressAnnouncements/2007/ucml08849.htm.

90. American Med. Ass'n, *supra* note 13, at 12.

91. U.S. Food & Drug Admin., *supra* note 89.

92. *Antidepressant Medications for Children and Adolescents: Information for Parents and Caregivers,* NAT'L INST. ON MENTAL HEALTH (Dec. 3, 2010), http://www.nimh.nih.gov/health/topics/child-and-adolescent-mental-health/antidepressant-medications-for-children-and-adolescents-information-for-parents-and-caregivers.shtml.

93. U.S. Food & Drug Admin., *supra* note 81.

94. *See* U.S. Food & Drug Admin., *Guidance for Industry: Warnings and Precautions, Contraindications, and Boxed Warning Sections of Labeling for Human Prescription Drug and Biological Products—Content and Format 9* (Jan. 2006), http://www.fda.gov/downloads/Drugs/GuidanceComplianceRegulatoryInformation/Guidances/ucm075096.pdf; *see also* 21 C.F.R. § 314.520 (2010).

95. U.S. Food & Drug Admin., *supra* note 94, at 9.

96. *Id.*

97. Margaret Marrer, Adderall *Use and Abuse: Is Georgetown Part of a Growing Trend?,* GEORGETOWN INDEP. (Jan. 2, 2010), http://www.thegeorgetownindependent.com/2.14589/adderall-use-and-abuse-l.2081595.

98. Joseph Biederman et al., *A Randomized, Placebo-Controlled Trial of OROSMethylphenidate in Adults With Attention-Deficit/Hyperactivity Disorder,* 59 BIOLOGICAL PSYCHIATRY 829 (2006). *See also* Richard H. Weisler et al., *Long-Term Cardiovascular Effects of Mixed Amphetamine Salts Extended Release in Adults With ADHD,* 10 CNS SPECTRUMS 35 (2005), *available at* http://www.cnsspectrums.com/aspx/articledetail.aspx?articleid=492 (finding statistically significant increases in blood pressure and heart rate after use of stimulants).

99. *See* Edward G. Jones & Lorne M. Mendell, *Assessing the Decade of the Brain,* 284 SCIENCE 739 (1999).

100. *id.*

101. *Id.*

102. Personal autonomy and the right to privacy is viewed by some as a liberty, protected by the Due Process Clause of the Fourteenth Amendment, that allows the individual to choose what to do with his or her own body free from government restrictions that prevent such action.

103. *See, e.g.,* Benedict Carey, *Smartening Up: Brain Enhancement Is Wrong, Right?,* N.Y. TIMES, Mar. 9, 2008, at WK1.

104. U.N. INT'L NARCOTICS CONTROL BD., *supra* note 60, at 66.

105. *Id.* at 72.

106. OFFICE OF APPLIED STUDIES, SUBSTANCE ABUSE & MENTAL HEALTH SERVS. ADMIN., U.S. DEP'T OF HEALTH & HUMAN SERVS., RESULTS FROM THE 2008 NATIONAL SURVEY ON DRUG USE AND HEALTH: NATIONAL FINDINGS (2009), *available at* http://www.oas.samhsa.gov/nsduh/2k8nsduh/2k8Results.pdf.

107. *Id.*

108. U.N. INT'L NARCOTICS CONTROL BD., *supra* note 60, at 72.

109. *Id.* at 72-73.

110. *Id.* at 73.

111. *Id.*

112. *Id.* at 73, 74.

113. OFFICE OF APPLIED STUDIES, *supra* note 106, at 52.

114. *Id.*

115. *Id.* at 30.

116. Sean Esteban McCabe et al., *The Use, Misuse and Diversion of Prescription Stimulants Among Middle and High School Students,* 39 SUBSTANCE USE & MISUSE 1095, 1103 (2004).

117. *Id.*

118. C. J. Musser et al., *Stimulant Use and the Potential for Abuse in Wisconsin as Reported by School Administrators and Longitudinally Followed Children,* J. DEVELOPMENTAL & BEHAVIORAL PEDIATRICS 187, 192 (1998).

119. Christine Poulin, *Medical and Nonmedical Stimulant Use Among Adolescents: From Sanctioned to Unsanctioned Use,* 165 CAN. MED. ASS'N J. 1039, 1039 (2001).

120. OFFICE OF APPLIED STUDIES, *supra* note 106, at 2.

121. *Id.*

122. Sean E. McCabe, *Medical Use, Illicit Use and Diversion of Prescription Stimulant Medication,* 38 J. PSYCHOACTIVE DRUGS 45, 45-46 (2006).

123. Alan D. DeSantis et al., *Illicit Use of Prescription ADHD Medications on a College Campus: A Multimethodological Approach,* 57 J. AM. COLL. HEALTH 315, 316 (2008).

124. *Id.*

125. *Id.* at 317.

126. Claire D. Advokat et al., *Licit and Illicit Use of Medications for Attention-Deficit Hyperactivity Disorder in Undergraduate College Students,* 56 J. AM. COLL. HEALTH 601, 602 (2008).

127. Timothy E. Wilens et al., *Misuse and Diversion of Stimulants Prescribed for ADHD: A Systematic Review*

of the Literature, 47 J. Am. Acad. Child Adolescent Psychiatry 21(2008).

128. DeSantis, *supra* note 123, at 322.

129. *Id.*

130. Office of Applied Studies, *supra* note 106, at 2.

131. *Popping Pills a Popular Way to Boost Brain Power,* CBS News (Apr. 25, 2010), http://www.cbsnews.com/stories/2010/04/22/60minutes/main6422159.shtnil.

132. Matt Manning, *Sandusky County Officials: No Decline Seen in Drug Use,* News-Messenger (Fremont, Ohio), Aug. 6, 2009 (on file with author) (noting that many new cases of illicit drug use involve the use of less expensive prescription medicines like Adderall and Ritalin).

133. Christina Lanni et al., *Cognition Enhancers Between Treating and Doping the Mind,* 57 Pharmacological Research 196 (2008).

134. Jeffrey Zaslow, *What if Einstein had Taken Ritalin? ADHD's Impact on Creativity,* Wall St. J., Feb. 3, 2005, at Dl.

135. *Id.*

136. *Id.*

137. *Id.*

138. *Id.*

139. Margaret Talbot, *Brain Gain: The Underground World of "Neuroenhancing" Drugs,* New Yorker, Apr. 27, 2009, *available at* http://www.newyorker.com/reporting/2009/04/27/090427fa_fact_talbot?currentPage=all.

140. *Id.*

141. *Popping Pills a Popular Way to Boost Brain Power, supra* note 131.

142. Carey, *supra* note 103.

143. *See* Pew Forum on Religion & Pub. Life, *The Pursuit of Perfection: A Conversation on the Ethics of Genetic Engineering* (Mar. 31, 2004), *available at* http://pewforum.org/Science-and-Bioethics/The-Pursuit-of-Perfection-A-Conversation-on-the-Ethics-of-Genetic-Engineering.aspx [hereinafter Pew Forum].

144. Michael S. Gazzaniga, *Smarter on Drugs,* Sci. Am. Mind, Oct. 2005.

145. Sileshi Semaw et al., *2.6-Million-year-old Stone Tools and Associated Bones from OGS-6 and OGS-7, Gona, Afar, Ethiopia,* 45 J. Hum. Evolution 169 (2003).

146. *Id.*

147. Michael J. Sandel, *The Case Against Perfection.* Atl. Monthly, Apr. 2004, at 50.

148. *Id.*

149. Med. Ethics Dep't, British Med. Ass'n, *Boosting Your Brainpower: Ethical Aspects of Cognitive Enhancements* 19 (2007), *available at* http://www.bma.org.uk/images/Boosting_brainpower_tcm41-147266.pdf.

150. *Id.*

151. *Id.*

152. Office of Special Educ. Programs, Office of Special Educ. & Rehab. Servs., U.S. Dep't of Educ., History: Twenty-Five Years of Progress in Educating Children With Disabilities Through IDEA (2005), *available at* http://www2.ed.gov/policy/speced/leg/idea/history.pdf.

153. *Id.*

154. 334 F. Supp. 1257 (E.D. Pa. 1971).

155. *Id.* at 1258.

156. 348 F. Supp. 866 (D.D.C. 1972).

157. *Id.* at 868.

158. *Id.* at 874 (citing Brown v. Bd. of Educ., 347 U.S. 483, 493 (1954)).

159. Education for All Handicapped Children Act of 1975, Pub. L. No. 94-142, 89 Stat. 773.

160. 20 U.S.C. §§ 1400-1482 (2006).

161. *Id.* § 1400(3).

162. *Id.* § 1400(6).

163. *Id.* § 1400(3).

164. *Id.*

165. *Id.* § 1412(a)(1)(A).

166. *Id.* § 1401(3)(A)(i)-(ii).

167. 34 C.F.R. § 300.8(c)(9) (2010).

168. 20 U.S.C. §§ 1412(a)(4), 1414(d)(1)(a) (2006); 34 C.F.R. § 300.347 (2010).

169. 20 U.S.C. §§ 1401(14), 1412(a)(4), 1414(d) (2006).

170. *Id.* § 1414(c)(l)(A)(ii), (d)(l)(A)(i)(II)-(IV).

171. *Id.* § 1412(a)(16)(A).

172. *Id.* § 1418(a).

173. *Id.* § 1418(b).

174. Bonnie J. Kaplan et al., *The IQs of Children with ADHD are Normally Distributed,* 33 J. Learning Disabilities 410, 425-32 (2000); *see also* T.P. Ho et al., *Situational Versus Pervasive Hyperactivity in a Community Sample,* 26 Psychol. Med. 309 (1996).

175. Donald E. Greydanus, *Stimulant Misuse: Strategies to Manage a Growing Problem* (June 2007), http://www.acha.org/prof_dev/ADHD_docs/ADHD_PDprogram_Article2.pdf.

176. *See generally* Nat'l Ctr. on Addiction & Substance Abuse, Colum.Univ., National Survey of American

ATTITUDES ON SUBSTANCE ABUSE XV: TEENS AND PARENTS (Aug. 2010), http://www.casacolumbia.org/upload/2010/20100819teensurvey.pdf (discussing the use of prescription drugs for non-therapeutic use by middle and high school students).

177. *See, e.g.,* Guckenberger v. Boston Univ., 974 F. Supp. 106 (D. Mass. 1997) (citing Se. Cmty. Coll. v. Davis, 442 U.S. 397, 401 (1979)) (noting that federal disability laws do not compel educational institutions to make substantial modifications in their program to allow disabled persons to participate).

178. *See* 20 U.S.C. § 1400(d)(1)(A) (2006); *see also* Arlington Cent. Sch. Dist. Bd. of Educ. v. Murphy, 548 U.S. 291 (2006).

179. Office of Special Educ. Programs, U.S. Dep't of Educ., IDEA Regulations: State Funding (2006), http://idea.ed.gov/object/fileDownload/model/TopicalBrief/field/Pdf/file/primary_key/18.

180. *See* 20 U.S.C. §§ 1412-1414 (2006).

181. *Id.*

182. *Id.* §1400(d)(1)(A).

183. For example, Arizona mandates use of a "state-wide nationally standardized norm-referenced achievement test in reading, language arts and mathematics[.]" ARIZ. REV. STAT. § 15-741 (West, Westlaw through 2010 legislation).

184. *See* 20 U.S.C. §1418(d)(2)(A)-(C) (2006).

185. *See* DeSantis, *supra* note 123, at 317.

186. *See, e.g.,* Cal. Dep't of Alcohol & Drug Programs, Preventing Prescription Drug Abuse: Colleges (2011), http://www.prescriptiondrugmisuse.org/index.php?page=colleges.

187. *See, e.g.,* Higher Educ. Ctr. for Alcohol & Other Drug Abuse & Violence Prevention, Fraternity and Sorority Members and Alcohol and Other Drug Use (Aug. 2008), http://www.higheredcenter.org/files/product/fact_sheet5.pdf (recommending social norm marketing to combat the widespread drug and alcohol culture on college campuses).

188. Andrew Jacobs, *The Adderall Advantage,* N.Y. TIMES, July 31, 2005, *available at* http://www.nytimes.com/2005/07/31/education/edlife/jacobs31.html.

189. *Id.*

190. See *id.*

191. *See* Cal. Dep't of Alcohol & Drug Programs, *supra* note 186 (referencing a social norm study conducted by Western Washington University).

192. *Id.*

193. *See generally* Nat'l Social Norms Inst., Univ. of Va., *Articles on the Social Norms Approach—Measuring Misperceptions and Behavior,* http://www.socialnorm.org/ (last visited Sept. 5, 2010) (cataloging studies on social marketing campaigns to students).

194. Vernonia Sch. Dist. 47J v. Acton, 515 U.S. 646, 654 (1995). In *Vernonia,* the Supreme Court noted that during the school day the teacher or school serves "in loco parentis" or "in the place of the parent." *See id.* at 654-55.

195. *Id.* at 654 (citing 59 Am. Jur. 2d *Parent and Child* § 10 (1987)).

196. *Id.*

197. New Jersey v. T.L.O., 469 U.S. 325, 336-337 (1985).

198. *Id.* at 339.

199. *Vernonia,* 515 U.S. at 656 (noting that "[f]or their own good and that of their classmates, public school children are routinely required to submit to various physical examinations, and to be vaccinated against various diseases").

200. *Id.* at 662.

201. *Id.* (quoting Jerald Hawkins, *Drugs and Other Ingesta: Effects on Athletic Performance, in* HERB APPENZELLER, MANAGING SPORTS and RISK MANAGEMENT STRATEGIES 90, 90-91 (1993)).

202. Beth Beavers, *Campus ADHD Prescription Abuse Increases,* UNIV. DAILY KANSAN, Sept. 2, 2009, *available at* http://www.kansan.com/news/2009/Sep/02/ADHD.

203. *Vernonia,* 515 U.S. at 662.

204. 20 U.S.C. § 1412(a) (2006).

205. 536 U.S. 822 (2002).

206. *Id.* at 826.

207. *Id.*

208. *Id.* at 828-30.

209. *Id.* at 830-31.

210. *Id.* at 832-34.

211. *Id.* at 834-38.

212. *Id.* at 838.

213. *Id.* at 829 (quoting Griffin v. Wisconsin, 483 U.S. 868, 873 (1987)) (internal quotation marks omitted).

214. Vernonia Sch. Dist. 47J v. Acton, 515 U.S. 646, 653 (1995).

215. *Earls,* 536 U.S. at 830.

216. *Id.* at 825.

217. *Id.* at 830.

218. *Id.* at 830-31.

219. *Id.* at 831.

220. *Id.*

221. *Id.* at 832.

222. *Id.*

223. *Id.*

224. *Id.* at 833.

225. *Id.*

226. *Id.* at 834.

227. *Id.*

228. Vernonia Sch. Dist. 47J v. Acton, 515 U.S. 646, 662 (1995).

229. *See, e.g.,* Elementary and Secondary Education Act of 1965, Pub. L. No. 89-10, 79 Stat. 27 (providing grant assistance to help educate children with disabilities); Elementary and Secondary Education Act Amendments of 1965, Pub. L. No. 89-313, 79 Stat. 1158; *see also* Handicapped Children's Early Education Assistance Act of 1968, Pub. L. No. 90-538, 82 Stat. 901 (authorizing support for exemplary early childhood programs); Economic Opportunities Amendments of 1972, Pub. L. No. 92-424, 86 Stat. 688 (authorizing support for increased Head Start enrollment for young children with disabilities).

HELIA GARRIDO HULL is an associate professor of law and the associate dean for student affairs at Barry University in Miami Shores, Florida. She also practices law at Disability Rights Florida, a statewide, not-for-profit corporation that is the designated protection and advocacy system for individuals with disabilities in Florida.

EXPLORING THE ISSUE

Should "Smart Drugs" Be Used to Enhance Cognitive Functioning?

Critical Thinking and Reflection

1. If researchers determine that there are no dangerous effects of prolonged use of cognitive enhancing drugs, what role should moral considerations play in evaluating the question of widespread availability of these drugs?
2. How would you respond to those who assert that the use of smart drugs by healthy individuals gives them an even greater advantage over cognitively impaired individuals who rely on these drugs to play on an even field?
3. Should the illicit use of drugs such as Ritalin or Adderall be treated as harshly as abuse of drugs such as methamphetamine and heroin?
4. Would you accept a job where the use of cognitive enhancing drugs is recommended or even required? Why or why not?
5. Consider this quotation: "The original purpose of medicine is to heal the sick, not turn healthy people into gods." To what extent do you view the use of smart drugs an attempt to become superhuman?

Is There Common Ground?

In considering the positions taken by the authors of the YES and the NO publications, some points of agreement are evident. There seems to be consensus that psychostimulant medications serve an important role for individuals with various cognitive impairments and neuropsychiatric disorders. Individuals with serious forms of ADHD find that these medications help them control their hyperactivity and assist them in cognitive tasks such as attention and concentration.

The authors of both articles also point out the possible risks of these drugs, and advocate research regarding their long-term effects, with particular attention to issues of safety and efficacy. Especially careful consideration should be given to the use of these drugs with children whose brains are still developing.

Both sides also agree that these drugs should be regulated. The YES authors state that enforceable policies are needed regarding the use of these drugs in order to support fairness, protect individuals from coercion, and minimize enhancement-related socioeconomic disparities. The NO author asserts that, in light of the U.S. goal of providing equal opportunities for the disabled, policies should take into consideration the ways in which enhancement technology will affect the rights of disabled individuals.

Create Central

www.mhhe.com/createcentral

Additional Resources

Buchanan, A. E. (2011). *Beyond Humanity?: The Ethics of Biomedical Enhancement.* Oxford: Oxford University Press.

Farah, M. J. (2010). *Neuroethics: An Introduction with Readings.* Cambridge, MA: MIT Press.

Fröding, B. (2013). *Virtue Ethics and Human Enhancement.* Dordrecht: Springer.

Hildt, E., & Franke, A. G. (2013). *Cognitive Enhancement: An Interdisciplinary Perspective.* Dordrecht: Springer.

Illes, J., & Sahakian, B. J. (2011). *The Oxford Handbook of Neuroethics.* Oxford: Oxford University Press.

Internet References . . .

The Cognitive Enhancement Research Institute (CERI)

www.ceri.com

Partnership for Drug-Free Kids

http://www.drugfree.org/

SharpBrains

www.sharpbrains.com

Selected, Edited, and with Issue Framing Material by:
Richard P. Halgin, *University of Massachusetts, Amherst*

ISSUE

Should Memory-Dampening Drugs Be Used to Prevent and Treat Trauma in Combat Soldiers?

YES: Elise Donovan, from "Propranolol Use in the Prevention and Treatment of Posttraumatic Stress Disorder in Military Veterans: Forgetting Therapy Revisited," *Perspectives in Biology and Medicine* (2010)

NO: The President's Council on Bioethics, from "Happy Souls," in *Beyond Therapy: Biotechnology and the Pursuit of Happiness,* The President's Council on Bioethics (2003)

Learning Outcomes
After reading this issue, you should be able to:
• Evaluate the therapeutic advantages and disadvantages of prescribing memory-dampening drugs to soldiers who have experienced combat-related trauma.
• Understand the three phases of memory (i.e., formation, acquisition, and encoding), and how memory-dampening drugs might be used during each phase.
• Consider the extent to which posttraumatic growth might be limited as a result of taking memory-dampening drugs following the experience of trauma.
• Address the question of whether society has a responsibility to help combat veterans suppress the psychological symptoms arising from the trauma of war.
• Critically evaluate the role of the federal government in formulating bioethical standards such as those pertaining to the use of memory-dampening drugs.

ISSUE SUMMARY

YES: Research scientist Elise Donovan states that an alarming and rising number of soldiers are returning from combat suffering from PTSD, and that medications such as the beta-blocker propranolol can alleviate their symptoms. Propranolol, she argues, will help soldiers with PTSD who have essentially lost "their sense of self" reintegrate into society. Because the drug causes memory dampening, rather than memory loss, it will create an opportunity for veterans to better cope with everyday life upon returning from combat. She believes that symptoms and consequential behaviors associated with PTSD (i.e., suicide, domestic abuse, alcohol or drug abuse) will be greatly reduced in PTSD patients who take propranolol. Dr. Donovan also states that use of propranolol will foster an experience of posttraumatic growth.

NO: The President's Council on Bioethics, chaired by Dr. Leon Kass, criticizes the use of memory-dampening drugs to treat the symptoms of trauma by asking, "What kind of society are we likely to have when the powers to control memory, mood, and mental life through drugs reach their full maturity?" The Council asserts that identities are formed by what people do and what they undergo or suffer. Escaping painful memories would necessarily result in a change in the identity of who the person is, as well as the person's perception and understanding of significant life events.

Traumatic experiences are disastrous or extremely painful events that have severe psychological and physiological effects that can last for years. Trauma survivors experience a constellation of disruptive and possibly disabling symptoms associated with posttraumatic stress disorder. They may re-experience the traumatic event through recurring intrusive recollections, dreams, flashbacks, or physiological reactivity to cues that remind them of the trauma. Because of their heightened sense of vulnerability, trauma survivors avoid stimuli associated with the traumatic event in various ways. They may avoid thoughts, feelings, or conversations associated with the trauma; they may choose to stay away from activities, places, or people that remind them of the event. They may become distant and detached from other people, show little affect, and become pessimistic about life. At the same time, they are likely to experience persistent symptoms of arousal such as difficulty sleeping, irritability, hypervigilance, concentration difficulty, or an exaggerated startle response. In light of this disturbing symptom picture, it is understandable that people who have survived a trauma would go to great lengths to reduce their symptoms and alleviate their profound distress. Preliminary research has pointed to the possibility that the beta-blocker drug propranolol can dampen the memory of trauma, and thereby make life more bearable for some trauma survivors. With the emerging possibility that a drug can dampen the memory of trauma, a controversy has arisen about whether this intervention is really as beneficial as it sounds.

During the past decade, in which the U.S. military has been engaged in the wars in Iraq and Afghanistan, the number of combat soldiers suffering from posttraumatic stress disorder has been stunning. Some estimates suggest that as many as 20% of American soldiers serving in these wars have developed PTSD (www.ptsd.va.gov/public/pages/how-common-is-ptsd.asp). In light of the potentially devastating effects on the lives of these veterans, and the lives of their loved ones, researchers and clinicians have devoted tremendous effort to developing interventions that can alleviate the symptoms of PTSD. One area of investigation has focused on the beta-blocker drug propranolol. Assuming that this drug can dampen the memory, and the emotional impact of the trauma, might it serve as a useful component of interventions for combat veterans suffering from PTSD?

Dr. Elise Donovan takes issue with a report published in 2003 by the President's Council on Bioethics, which was critical of this intervention and contended that it disrupts one's sense of self. She asserts that veterans who cannot function in society have essentially lost their sense of self. If we have an intervention that can assist them in their return to healthier functioning, she argues, it would not be justifiable to withhold research and treatment that may alleviate their distressing symptoms. Dr. Donovan notes that individuals taking propranolol will still remember the "facts" of the trauma, but their appraisal of these facts will change. Because propranolol targets fear-based memories, even if the experience of fear is reduced, an individual could still retain other emotional reactions to the event such as disgust or sadness. Dr. Donovan also describes another benefit of propranolol, namely its effect in fostering posttraumatic growth, the beneficial transformations that occur as a result of trauma, including the reevaluation of life goals and feelings of increased self-reliance, empathy, social support, and intimacy.

Although Dr. Donovan argues against administering propranolol prior to combat situations due to possible effects that could impair a soldier's cognitive and physiological functioning, she asserts that we do have a moral and ethical obligation to military service members to maximize efforts to alleviate PTSD symptoms in veterans who have been traumatized by the atrocities of war and combat.

Arguing against the use of memory-dampening drugs for alleviating symptoms of trauma, the Council contends that, as we reminisce from a greater distance and with more life experience, even our most painful experiences can often acquire for us a meaning that we did not foresee when the experiences occurred. The Council asserts that our identities are formed both by what we do and by what we undergo or suffer. Although we may regret the shadows that unchosen memories cast over our pursuit of happiness, we cannot simply escape them while remaining who we really are. Those who endure bad memories should not use the new biotechnical powers to ease the psychic pain of bad memories. Using such medications does not preserve memories' truth, but attempts instead to make the problem go away, and with it the truth of the experience in question.

The Council purports that altering the formation of emotionally powerful memories risks falsifying our perception and understanding of the world, making shameful acts seem less shameful, or terrible acts less terrible. Thus, the inference can be made from the Council's arguments that combat veterans might actually benefit from the experience of dealing with traumatic memories, possibly in the form of posttraumatic growth in which they mature emotionally as a result of surviving traumatic events. Furthermore, the Council contends that these drugs are effective only when administered during or shortly after a traumatic event. Thus, it would be necessary to make a predictive judgment as to which traumatized individuals should be treated with these drugs. Would this be possible in the field of combat?

YES ↵

Elise Donovan

Propranolol Use in the Prevention and Treatment of Posttraumatic Stress Disorder in Military Veterans: Forgetting Therapy Revisited

An Army Ranger medic in Afghanistan fractured several vertebrae in a fall after enemy shrapnel disabled his parachute. He medicated himself and proceeded to treat the other injured soldiers around him. Four years after his return to the United States, he had such a vivid flashback to combat that he physically attacked his own mother and father at a lake house vacation, while his wife watched helplessly. Between 17 and 25% of soldiers returning from Iraq suffer from posttraumatic stress disorder (PTSD). These are documented cases; if unreported cases were included, this number would likely be much higher. Other reports indicate that 20.3% of active soldiers and 42.4% of soldiers who have returned from active service require mental health treatment (Hoge et al. 2004; Milliken, Auchterlonie, and Hoge 2007). During proceedings of a 2008 class-action lawsuit on behalf of nearly 2 million veterans against the Department of Veterans Affairs, it was reported that approximately 1,000 veterans receiving care attempt suicide monthly. Experiences such as that of the Army Ranger accompanied by these alarming statistics demonstrate the severity and prevalence of this problem, but the impact it has on the lives of those afflicted and their loved ones is often unnoticed by those who have not witnessed it firsthand. Exploration of treatments for PTSD is crucial, but because PTSD is a neuropsychological condition and some treatments include possible mindaltering pharmacological agents, ethical issues exist regarding PTSD research and treatment.

During the past decade, research on the use of drugs to prevent and treat PTSD has been accompanied by discussion and argument of the ethical issues surrounding treatments that may alter emotion and memory (Henry, Fishman, and Youngner 2007; President's Council on Bioethics 2003). Recently, however, research has progressed in a new direction. This new research directly impacts the ethical issues and alters the previous arguments, especially with regard to PTSD in military members returning from active combat. This essay will review the scientific research in this area, discuss the previous ethical issues and arguments, and present a new perspective considering the advances in research and the ethical discussion with a focus on use in military veterans.

Posttraumatic Stress Disorder and Propranolol

Multiple definitions of PTSD exist, but the *Diagnostic and Statistical Manual of Mental Disorders-IV-TR* states:

> The essential feature of Posttraumatic Stress Disorder is the development of characteristic symptoms following exposure to an extreme traumatic stressor involving direct personal experience of an event that involves actual or threatened death or serious injury, or other threat to one's physical integrity . . . or witnessing an event that involves death, injury, or a threat of physical integrity to another person. . . . The person's response to the event must involve intense fear, helplessness or horror. The full symptom picture must be present for more than 1 month. (p. 463)

In veterans, symptoms include disturbing memories and dreams related to stressful military experiences, acting or feeling like a military experience is happening again, having physical and emotional responses to things that remind the veteran of a military experience, loss of interest in things that used to be pleasurable, alcohol abuse, sleep disturbances including both insomnia and excessive sleeping, distancing from loved ones, and many others (McGhee et al. 2009).

From *Perspectives in Biology and Medicine*, vol. 53, no. 1, Winter 2010, pp. 61–74. Copyright © 2010 by Johns Hopkins University Press. Reprinted by permission.

While memory is a complex and integrated process, three phases are applicable to this discussion. These include formation, acquisition, and encoding of the memory; emotional response to and consolidation of the memory; and reconsolidation, reinstatement, and retrieval of the memory, which includes recall and the emotional responses triggered by later stimuli. The neuroendocrine involvement in memory formation and response to trauma has been extensively studied and well reviewed, and the role of stress hormones is established (Bremner et al. 2008; Mathew, Price, and Charney 2008; Roozendaal, Barsegyan, and Lee 2008; van Stegeren 2008; Zohar et al. 2008). Adrenal stress hormones, including glucocorticoids and adrenergic signals (epinephrine and norepinephrine), are released in response to stressful or emotionally arousing events and interact to facilitate memory formation and consolidation. Beta-adrenergic stimulation and the subsequent physiological cascade are an integral part of the fight-or-flight response and play a major role in response to trauma in conjunction with glucocorticoids. Not all memories are modulated by stress hormones; rather, there is preferential modulation during consolidation of emotionally arousing memories (Roozendaal, Barsegyan, and Lee 2008). Van Stegeren (2008) has discussed the role of epinephrine and norepinephrine in emotional memory formation:

> Increased noradrenalin levels lead to better memory performance, whereas blocking the noradrenergic receptors with a beta blocker attenuates this enhanced memory for emotional information. Noradrenalin appears to interact with cortisol in emotional memory processes, varying from encoding to consolidation and retrieval. (p. 532)

The primary pharmacological agent that has been examined for treatment of PTSD is propranolol, a beta-adrenergic receptor antagonist, and the Department of Veterans Affairs is currently recruiting volunteers for clinical trials. While many beta-antagonists exist—including some that are now prescribed more often and are more potent than propranolol—the majority of research in this area has used propranolol, and it will be the focus of discussion. Research has examined propranolol treatment in each of the three phases of memory mentioned above. If it is known an event will be stressful, such as rescuers responding to a disaster, administration of propranolol would influence formation, acquisition, and encoding. Administration immediately after a traumatic event, such as in the emergency room after a rape, would influence response and consolidation. Administration

later—for example, during stimulated arousal of PTSD in those who have been diagnosed—may influence the later stage during recall, retrieval, and reconsolidation. The beta-adrenergic system is involved not only with response and memory formation, but also the conditioning of the emotional response associated with the memory, so propranolol may both dampen memory formation and dissociate the memory from the emotional response. Although this treatment has been termed "forgetting therapy," it isn't designed to make individuals forget their physical experiences but rather to dissociate the emotions and fears from the memories.

Because they slow heart rate and inhibit arterial vasoconstriction, beta-blockers have been administered for years to treat hypertension and other cardiovascular diseases. Memory loss is listed as a potential side effect of propranolol use for cardiovascular conditions (Henry, Fishman, and Youngner 2007). Although propranolol can also interfere with hippocampal centers involved in memory storage, including dampening memory of a trauma and enhancing memory of the events preceding the trauma (Bell 2008), there have been no reported cases of severe memory loss due to the use of propranolol for cardiovascular conditions. In addition, in the transcripts from the proceedings of the President's Council on Bioethics (2002), Dr. James McGaugh states: "The clinically used doses, let's say, propranolol, 20 milligrams, is not going to induce retrograde amnesia."

The first paper reporting experimental results of propranolol use in modulation of memory and emotion in humans was published by Cahill et al. in 1994. Subjects received either propranolol or placebo one hour prior to exposure to an emotional arousal or neutral stimulus, and then recall and emotional response were measured. No differences were observed between groups for neutral stimulus, but with an emotional arousal stimulus, recall in the placebo group was significantly higher than in the propranolol group. These data suggest that the beta-adrenergic system is involved in memory formation, particularly when emotional arousal is involved; this system is central to enhanced memory formation.

Other early results are somewhat contradictory. While one study saw no difference in recall response to emotional arousal one week following initial stimuli with or without propranolol administration (van Stegeren, Everaerd, and Gooren 2002), other data do indicate effectiveness of treatment. Propranolol given during contextual fear conditioning was found to decrease emotional arousal upon subsequent exposure to stimulus (Grillon et al. 2004). Propranolol use in individuals diagnosed with PTSD has also been examined in this context. Propranolol was given during stimuli, and different responses were observed between arousal and neutral stimuli, but no differences were observed between controls and those with PTSD. However, nearly 75% of the PTSD subjects were taking psychotropic medications, which may have altered the observed effects (Reist et al. 2001). Collectively, these data suggest that propranolol use prior to a substantially traumatic exposure may be effective in reducing emotional and fear responses.

Research on the effect of propranolol immediately following trauma or to disrupt formation and consolidation has focused on administration to individuals in the emergency room. Fewer individuals treated with propranolol within six hours following a traumatic event developed PTSD than those receiving placebo. In addition, and when subjected to imagery trials three months later, no individuals who received propranolol experienced physiologic responses, compared to 43% of controls (Pitman et al. 2002). Despite several subjects not returning for follow-up in this study, these are encouraging results. A subsequent study examined a time course treatment with propranolol in individuals reporting to the emergency room after trauma. Follow-up two months after the trauma indicated that PTSD rates were significantly higher in subjects who refused propranolol (Vaiva et al. 2003).

More recently, research has shifted to examine propranolol use during memory reconsolidation after development of PTSD. Individuals with diagnosed PTSD were examined to determine whether reactivation of traumatic event memory would provide an opportunity for propranolol modulation and subsequent weakened emotional association. Subjects diagnosed with PTSD triggered by a variety of events recalled and described their experiences in detail and received either propranolol or placebo immediately and again two hours later. One week later subjects came back and listened to the accounts of their trauma from the previous week, while physiological indicators of stress were recorded. Responses in subjects who received propranolol were significantly lower on all physiological measurements than those who received placebo (Brunet et al. 2008).

Subsequent studies have shown similar results. Possible weakening or alleviation of the fear response, and prevention of its return by propranolol during reconsolidation were examined by treating subjects with propranolol prior to stimulation and reactivation of their fear memory. According to Kindt et al. (2009): "one reactivation trial combined with the administration of propranolol completely eliminated the behavioral expression of the fear memory 24 hours later" (p. 257). The propranolol did not erase the memory; rather, it dampened the emotional response to subsequent stimuli. These results have

profound potential for service members with PTSD, whose condition is often triggered by everyday stimuli such as a car backfire.

Because these data indicate an effectiveness of propranolol both immediately after trauma and during reconsolidation, McGhee et al. (2009) performed a retrospective study on burned service members to examine whether those who had received propranolol during treatment of their physical injuries had different rates of PTSD development. Propranolol is given during treatment of some burn victims to decrease the hypermetabolic and cardiovascular effects associated with the autonomic response to severe burns. No difference was seen in PTSD development in those burned service members who received propranolol and those who didn't, but neither the time between the injury and propranolol administration nor the propranolol dose were reported. The soldiers who received propranolol also had significantly higher burn areas, received significantly more morphine, and had significantly more surgeries during treatment, all of which could confound interpretation. These results do not correlate with those showing effectiveness of propranolol use, but this study was retrospective and not well controlled. Clearly, additional well-controlled prospective studies are needed to adequately address dose, timing, optimal safety, and efficacy of propranolol as a treatment for PTSD.

Ethics and Propranolol Use

While research is not conclusive on the most effective timing and use of propranolol in prevention and treatment of PTSD, results are promising and clinical trials are underway. The major ethical opposition to "forgetting therapy" has come from the President's Council on Bioethics report, *Beyond Therapy: Biotechnology and the Pursuit of Happiness* (2003). In addition, the September 2007 edition of the *American Journal of Bioethics* featured a target article followed by commentary responses that filled nearly half the issue and focused on ethical issues surrounding "forgetting therapy." Both of these sources were published prior to much of the research on propranolol use during memory reconsolidation. *Beyond Therapy* cites only the work by Cahill and Pitman described earlier.

I will begin the discussion of the ethical issues surrounding "forgetting therapy" with excerpts from *Beyond Therapy* and the transcripts of the President's Council proceedings. The President's Council places the debate in the setting of the pursuit of happiness and sense of self. *Beyond Therapy* suggests that because we seek happiness for ourselves and "our soul," not for our material body, our happiness is connected to our personhood and identity. We would not seek happiness if achieving it meant we would lose ourselves or our identity in the process, and memory is essential to this process. "If experiencing our happiness depends upon experiencing a stable identity, then our happiness depends also on our memory, on knowing who we are in relation to who we have been" (p. 238).

The Council's primary objection to propranolol therapy is that use for memory alteration disrupts sense of self. *Beyond Therapy* asserts that our memory preserves us and who we are and where we have been, furnishes our sense of self, and is a combination of happy moments and shameful acts. To be ourselves we cannot abandon or forget who we once were: "To alter or numb our remembrance of things past cuts to the heart of what it means to remember in a human way, and it is this biotechnical possibility that we focus on here" (p. 245). It asserts further that if we sacrifice the accuracy of our memories in order to ease pain and suffering and expand control of our lives, we will ultimately sever ourselves from reality and leave our identity or sense of self behind. The Council suggests that if we treat those who suffer bad memories, we will compromise the truthfulness of how they remember and risk having them live falsely, despite the acknowledgment that some memories are so painful and intrusive as to preclude the possibility for normal life and experience.

The Council acknowledges that those who experience events so traumatic as to be debilitating would benefit from this type of treatment. Nonetheless, it expresses concerns, including treatment of criminals or those who intentionally committed "awful deeds" to dull their pain, treating soldiers before battle to turn them into "killing machines" who would have no cares about their actions, or allowing ready access to the drug to persons who may take it any time they think an event will result in painful memory. An additional concern is whether having the power to dull memories of terrible things will render individuals and society unmoved by suffering, wrongdoing, and cruelty: "Armed with new powers to ease the suffering of bad memories, we might come to see all psychic pain as unnecessary and in the process come to pursue a happiness that is less than human: an unmindful happiness, unchanged by time and events, unmoved by life's vicissitudes" (p. 258). These concerns are legitimate, but they are directed more towards use in everyday occasions in the general public, not in military veterans.

Beyond Therapy's closing statement encapsulates the Council's conclusion regarding alteration of memory:

> Nothing would trouble us, but we would probably be shallow people, never falling to the depths of despair because we have little interest in the

heights of human happiness or in the complicated lives of those around us. In the end, to have only happy memories is not to be happy in a truly human way. It is simply to be free of misery—an understandable desire given the many troubles of life, but a low aspiration for those who seek a truly human happiness. (p. 264)

Bell (2008) quotes the Council on the issue of our sense of self: "our memories make us who we are and by rewriting memories pharmacologically we might succeed in easing real suffering at the risk of falsifying our perception of the world and undermining our true identity" (p. 3). Bell's response to this statement acknowledges the Council's concern in that memories affect our life in society, and that by altering memories we may desensitize ourselves to our actions and lose empathy for others who have experienced trauma. Bell continues to suggest that individuals taking propranolol will still remember facts and the traumatic effect, but that their evaluation and appraisal will change:

> Patients taking propranolol will still remember the "facts" as it were, of the traumatic effect. Only their appraisal of these facts will change. Furthermore, propranolol is designed to specifically target fear-based memories, so even if the experience of fear was reduced, one could still retain other emotional reactions to the event such as disgust or sadness, which could serve to remind us why certain behaviours are wrong. (p. 3)

The Council report does not address the idea that normal memory evolution includes a certain amount of decay. This was presented, however, by Dr. James McGaugh in the transcripts of the proceedings of the Council (President's Council 2002). As we age we tend to forget or become less aware of our past memories, particularly those from the more distant past. In addition, anesthetics and analgesics are regularly administered to prevent patients from feeling pain during medical procedures. This is not conceptually different from dulling PTSD-associated emotional pain. The Council does acknowledge that self and sense of self naturally evolve and change over time. An individual of 30 is neither physically, emotionally, nor cognitively the same as he or she was at age one. Thus, sense of self is not a static quality that can only be changed by pharmacological intervention.

Additional relevant points for discussion were presented in the commentaries responding to the target article. Overmedication is a problem in our society, as is "disease mongering"—the labeling of normal human behaviors, adaptations, or responses as medical conditions, and then treating those conditions pharmacologically. This issue is an important concern of the Council, who present the scenario of an individual who witnesses a murder and immediately takes propranolol to render the memory less painful (President's Council 2003). While this scenario is worthy of consideration—and I agree that use in this manner is inappropriate—it is also somewhat unrealistic, as these drugs would not be available like aspirin or Tylenol, which people might carry in their pockets for use at any time. However, emotional experience and response is an aspect of human life. By using propranolol to prevent or treat PTSD, are we disease mongering as suggested by the Council? Trachman (2007) discusses the converse side of the argument in detail. A traumatic experience is a causal event outside a person's control. Some people can assimilate these events, come to terms with them, and be strengthened by them. However, not all people react in this manner. Some people are so affected by the painful experience that rational insight and actions may be impaired. For these people, Trachman reasons, "interventions that help control their passions should ultimately result in improved self-understanding, personal behavior, and well being" (p. 22). The key in this argument in support of use is in the triggering of PTSD by events outside of the control of the individual. This is different from behaviors such as cigarette smoking, where the individual knowingly chooses to engage in a behavior that will likely result in the need for treatment. Trachman supports propranolol use but advocates research to better predict individuals who will develop PTSD, so it will be clearer whom to treat in the ER (see also Bell 2007). Consideration of use during reconsolidation would alter this argument.

Beyond Therapy argues not only against the use of memory-altering pharmacotherapy, but also against research into its effectiveness. There is resistance to this stance. For example, Hall and Carter (2007) note that: "[The] President's Council on Bioethics (PCB) involve a series of speculative harms that do not provide good reasons to oppose trials to assess the safety and effectiveness of propranolol. Nor does the PCB make a case for proscribing the clinical use of propranolol if the clinical trials indicate that it is effective" (p. 23). Hall and Carter also point out that use of propranolol in PTSD patients may reduce their abuse of alcohol and other recreational drugs to self-medicate. Between 35 and 40% of veterans have used alcohol more than they intend to, and nearly 30% of that same cohort report wanting or needing to cut down on alcohol consumption (Hoge et al. 2004). Obviously unreported cases are not included here, which would surely increase the prevalence.

Another argument is that this treatment is still being studied, that ethical content of memories is "highly debat-able and contingent on individual valuations," and that ethicists should simply consider relief of human suffering (Rosenberg 2007). Some agree with the Council that grief and stress following a traumatic situation are normal, and that over time these tend to subside (Bell 2007). This line of argument states that the experience of trauma and stress and the subsequent response make us who we are as people and are thus essential to personal growth. However, I contend that the essence of PTSD is these emotions *not* subsiding, and that therefore these arguments don't hold against the idea of using propranolol to dissociate emotional response from memory in individuals diagnosed with PTSD.

Another argument against the use of propranolol is that the effects of propranolol on cognition, or conscious decision-making, are unknown. Would altering memory and emotion have an effect on decision-making? Craigie (2007) reports that propranolol has been shown to influence decision-making in different paradigms, with contradictory results. It would be helpful to determine whether—and how—propranolol may cause this effect. If it does, then the risk/benefit ratio of administering propranolol must be reconsidered.

A topic not discussed in *Beyond Therapy* is the effect of propranolol on posttraumatic growth (PTG). PTG refers to the beneficial transformations that occur as a result of trauma, including the reevaluation of life goals and increased self-reliance, empathy, social support, and levels of intimacy. Warnick (2007) reports that PTG occurs more frequently than PTSD, and that the two can occur concurrently, but states there are no data on the effects of propranolol on PTG: "If propranolol diminishes emotion-laden memory, it thus appears reasonable to assume it could drastically reduce the amount of rumination on an emotional event and prevent the development of PTG" (p. 37). In fact, one therapy for people who have experienced traumatic events is an attempt to induce PTG. If, however, an individual with PTSD is afflicted to the point of functional loss or self-harm, he or she may be incapable of experiencing PTG. Propranolol administration and disruption of reconsolidation may aid in induction of PTG as well as relieve PTSD. Warnick rightly suggests expanding research to include effects on PTG.

Discussion Regarding Propranolol Use

While it is imperative that more research be conducted to determine the efficacy of propranolol use in military members suffering from PTSD, the ethical stance against propranolol use is questionable. We have a moral and ethical obligation to military service members to maximize efforts to alleviate PTSD. The consensus seems to be that the President's Council's arguments are unfounded, and that using propranolol to treat PTSD is not unethical. However, independent of arguments regarding the ethical issues, the timing of propranolol use in military service members warrants discussion and should influence the direction of future research.

Using any beta-blocker prior to combat to prevent PTSD in military personnel should not be considered, as it would likely be more detrimental than beneficial. First, the beta-adrenergic signaling system is mediated by the catecholamines epinephrine and norepinephrine. These hormones are central to the fight-or-flight response, and they trigger the heightened awareness necessary for soldiers to survive in combat situations. Propranolol causes slowed heart rate and impairs the ability of the body to raise heart rate; in addition, it inhibits vasoconstriction (thus its effectiveness in treating high blood pressure). It also inhibits exercise performance, because many of the physiological adaptations that occur during exercise to accommodate the increased demand on body systems are facilitated by epinephrine. Therefore, propranolol administration prior to combat situations would not only dampen soldiers' awareness and fight-or-flight response, but it would also impair their ability to respond physiologically and meet the physical demands of combat. Second, the use of propranolol on soldiers before battle to get them to forget what they are being submitted to, to make them forget what they have done to others, or to make them not care would certainly be morally and ethically wrong (Evars 2007; Henry, Fishman, and Youngner 2007; President's Council 2003). The fact that giving soldiers propranolol prior to battle would inhibit their physiological ability to perform and would be counterproductive renders this ethical argument moot.

Ethical issues surrounding propranolol can be separated into two categories, those related to research, and those related to clinical use. Nearly all publications on this issue state that more research on the effects and efficacy of propranolol use is needed. It has been difficult to decipher the proper time, dose, and administration of propranolol in part because of the different paradigms used to examine it: results don't translate between experiments because conditions differ greatly between them. Furthermore, research into which areas of the brain are involved in traumatic memory formation must rely on models, rather than subjecting animals or individuals to actual trauma. It may therefore be impossible to design experiments that truly test the human response to trauma and the effect of propranolol on that response. In addition, many service members don't develop PTSD for three to five years following return from duty, which presents a difficult timeline for study and decisions as to who should be examined.

Most of the ethical issues presented in the literature are in reference to clinical use. When considering treating people before a potentially traumatic experience, or immediately after trauma, one must consider whether the individual in question will actually develop PTSD. Individuals respond differently to traumatic experiences, and not all subsequently suffer from PTSD. Thus the two following questions are posed. Does the mere possibility of developing PTSD warrant preventive treatment, particularly when data suggest that propranolol can successfully dissociate the emotional response from the memory after development of PTSD? And would individuals be capable of informed consent following a traumatic event?

Because of the current widespread use of propranolol for other conditions and the mildness of its side effects, we can conclude there is no harm in using it for preventative therapy. If propranolol use proves to be effective in treatment of PTSD during the reconsolidation phase, then the argument against using the drug to prevent PTSD because we don't know who will actually develop it becomes moot, because only those who do develop PTSD would be treated. This would also alleviate the concern about people taking propranolol because they feel bad. Regulation could hinge on the concept presented earlier: that cases in which a causal event outside the person's mind, and outside the realm of normal human adaptation, should be treated. It also seems reasonable that the use of propranol would be inappropriate in less severe cases of PTSD, but this is a judgment best left to the clinicians. While the statement is not included in *Beyond Therapy*, McGaugh states in the transcripts that in circumstances in which an event is "really so horrible, it's going to flash into my head, recur and recur so that it begins to take over my life; then that would be a case, I think, in which a little propranolol, if the studies bear out, might be of value" (President's Council 2002).

The Council's major argument against propranolol use to suppress memory is that this action would violate identity and sense of self, and that altering individual memories would affect society, cause people to lose empathy for fellow sufferers, and desensitize people to their actions. Memory is an intrinsic human quality, so does pharmacologically tampering with memory infringe on basic human qualities? In response to this, I present the following two scenarios. Take first the case of a 30-year-old veteran who has completed a tour in Kosovo in addition to three tours in Iraq. Upon walking past a cemetery on the way to a 4th of July BBQ, he is overtaken by grief at the sight of veterans' graves decorated for the holiday. The grief, guilt, and memories triggered by this sight result in his spending over an hour sobbing uncontrollably in the cemetery on the grave of a deceased veteran, while sounds of civilians enjoying their holiday can be heard in the distance. On this same 4th of July, a Vietnam veteran drives miles into an isolated mountain campground because the sounds of the fireworks set off in celebration trigger his flashbacks to combat experiences. When PTSD has reached the point that it impairs daily function and affects relationships as in these two cases, and when PTG is not possible, affected individuals have already lost their sense of self and identity. Society should feel morally and ethically obligated to assist them to regain "normal" life in society, particularly because their condition was caused by their service to their country.

The President's Council states that if experiencing happiness depends upon experiencing a stable identity, then happiness also depends on memory. Individuals with PTSD are neither stable nor happy, and if the members of society are not affected by the sight or knowledge of these soldiers, they have lost their empathy. Those who have suffered and been helped would have more empathy and support and would relate to those who continue to suffer. The Council asks: "could we be happy in the absence of happy memories? Conversely, could we be happy in the presence of terrible memories, memories so traumatic and so life-altering that they cast a deep shadow over all that we do, today and tomorrow?" (p. 241) Does knowing that 18 Iraqi war veterans commit suicide every month as a consequence of their service answer these questions? I am not arguing that any memory evoking a challenging or emotional response should be blunted, but that when emotions associated with memories alter and destroy lives, considering treatments is a moral necessity.

While substantive ethical issues attend both research and clinical use of memory-altering therapies, the central consideration is the development of treatments to help PTSD patients live normal, productive lives. Since death associated with war is considered ethically acceptable, and the risk of death in war is outweighed by the benefits of fighting that war, helping those who carried out the agenda, risked death, and suffer with a condition associated with their service should be considered an ethical obligation. In the very least, research into the use and effectiveness of propranolol in treating soldiers who have been diagnosed with PTSD is warranted. If it proves to be ineffective, so be it—but if it does prove to be effective and the benefits outweigh the risks, its use should be encouraged. Hall and Carter (2007) also support this view: "If it is reasonable to ask these individuals

to engage in life threatening and emotionally distressing activities, then it would be wrong to deny them access to medications that may reduce their considerable risk of developing PTSD" (p. 24). If propranolol use disrupts our sense of self, why do we prescribe it so widely for cardiovascular disease? One cannot argue that use of a drug in the same dose but for different conditions is ethically acceptable in one case and not the other, when the physiological effects in both cases are the same.

Beyond Therapy argues that propranolol use presents risks to episodic memory, to the memory of actual events, and potentially to emotionally positive memory (Henry, Fishman, and Youngner 2007). "Forgetting therapy" is an inappropriate label, as treatment does not induce memory loss per se; rather, it dissociates emotions from memory. Therefore, arguments that loss of episodic memory of events is a risk become moot. This may also indicate a disconnection between the science and scientific research on the one hand, and the ethics community on the other, in that individuals in different academic and educational fields construe different meanings from the same terms.

I will close with the following excerpt from Kolber's (2007) commentary. Kolber quotes a PTSD victim as saying: "I have severe posttraumatic stress disorder and would sell my soul to the devil himself to be rid of my 24/7 hellish flashbacks and night terrors" (p. 25). We have an ethical and moral obligation to treat PTSD. Opinions on propranolol treatment in military veterans should be revised in light of the recent advances in research and updated discussions of ethical issues.

References

American Psychiatric Association (APA). 2000. *Diagnostic and statistical manual of mental disorders*, 4th ed. text revision (DSM-IV-TR). Washington, DC: APA.

Bell, J. 2007. Preventing post-traumatic stress disorder or pathologizing bad memories? *Am J Bioeth* 7(9):29–30.

Bell, J. 2008. Propranolol, post-traumatic stress disorder and narrative identity. *J Med Ethics* 34(11):e23.

Bremner, J. D., et al. 2008. Structural and functional plasticity of the human brain in post-traumatic stress disorder. *Prog Brain Res* 167:171–83.

Brunet, A., et al. 2008. Effect of post-retrieval propranolol on psychophysiological responding during subsequent script-driven traumatic imagery in post-traumatic stress disorder. *J Psychiatr Res* 42(6):503–6.

Cahill, L., et al. 1994. Beta-adrenergic activation and memory for emotional events. *Nature* 371(6499): 702–4.

Craigie, J. 2007. Propranolol, cognitive biases, and practical decision-making. *Am J Bioeth* 7(9):31–32.

Evars, K. 2007. Perspectives on memory manipulation: Using beta-blockers to cure post-traumatic stress disorder. *Camb Q Healthc Ethics* 16(2):138–46.

Grillon, C., et al. 2004. Effects of the beta-blocker propranolol on cued and contextual fear conditioning in humans. *Psychopharmacology* 175(3):342–32.

Hall, W., and A. Carter. 2007. Debunking alarmist objections to the pharmacological prevention of PTSD. *Am J Bioeth* 7(9):23–25.

Henry, M., J. R. Fishman, and S. J. Youngner. 2007. Propranolol and the prevention of post-traumatic stress disorder: Is it wrong to erase the sting of bad memories? *Am J Bioeth* 7(9):12–20.

Hoge, C. W., et al. 2004. Combat duty in Iraq and Afghanistan, mental health problems, and barriers to care. *N Engl J Med* 351 (l):13–22.

Kindt, M., M. Soeter, and B. Vervliet. 2009. Beyond extinction: Erasing human fear responses and preventing the return of fear. *Nat Neurosci* 12(3):256–58.

Kolber A. 2007. Clarifying the debate over therapeutic forgetting. *Am J Bioeth* 7(9):25–27.

Mathew, S. J., R. B. Price, and D. S. Charney. 2008. Recent advances in the neurobiology of anxiety disorders: Implications for novel therapeutics. *Am J Med Genet C Semin Med Genet* 15:89–98.

McGhee, L. L., et al. 2009. The effect of propranolol on posttraumatic stress disorder in burned service members. *J Burn Care Res* 30(1):92–97.

Milliken, C. S., J. L. Auchterlonie, and C. W Hoge. 2007. Longitudinal assessment of mental health problems among active and reserve component soldiers returning from the Iraq war. *JAMA* 298(18):2141–48.

Pitman, R. K., et al. 2002. Pilot study of secondary prevention of posttraumatic stress disorder with propranolol. *Biol Psychiatry* 51(2):189–92.

President's Council on Bioethics. 2002. Proceedings transcripts. www.bioethics.gov/topics/memory_index.html.

President's Council on Bioethics. 2003. *Beyond therapy: Biotechnology and the pursuit of happiness.* Washington, DC: President's Council on Bioethics; Dana Press.

Reist, C., et al. 2001. Beta-adrenergic blockade and emotional memory in PTSD. *Int J Neuropsychopharmacol* 4(4):377–83.

Roozendal, B., A. Barsegyan, and S. Lee. 2008. Adrenal stress hormones, amygdala activation, and memory for emotionally arousing experiences. *Prog Brain Res* 167:79–97.

Rosenberg, L. 2007. Necessary forgetting: On the use of propranolol in post-traumatic stress disorder management. *Am J Bioeth* 7(9):27–28.

Trachman, H. 2007. Spinoza's passions. *Am J Bioeth* 7(9):21–23.

Vaiva, G., et al. 2003. Immediate treatment with propranolol decreases posttraumatic stress disorder two months after trauma. *Biol Psychiatry* 54(12):947–49.

van Stegeren, A. H. 2008. The role of the noradrenergic system in emotional memory. *Acta Physiol* 127:532–41.

van Stegeren, A. H., W. Everaerd, and L. J. G. Gooren. 2002. The effect of beta-adrenergic blockade after encoding on memory of an emotional event. *Psychopharmacology* 163(2):202–12.

Warnick, J. 2007. Propranolol and its potential inhibition of positive post-traumatic growth. *Am J Bioeth* 7(9):37–38.

Zohar, J., et al. 2008. Post-traumatic stress disorder: Facts and fiction. *Curr Opin Psychiatry* 21:74–77.

ELISE DONOVAN began a postdoctoral fellowship at the Liggins Institute in Auckland, New Zealand, following completion of her PhD in health and exercise science at Colorado State University in 2011. At Colorado State, she studied obesity-associated coronary artery disease under the mentorship of Benjamin Miller and Karyn Hamilton, and also explored issues in philosophy under the direction of distinguished Professor Bernie Rollin. At the Liggins Institute, she has been studying the developmental origins of chronic disease and evolutionary medicine.

The President's Council on Bioethics    **NO**

Beyond Therapy: Biotechnology and the Pursuit of Happiness

Chapter Five

Who has not wanted to escape the clutches of oppressive and punishing memories? Or to calm the burdensome feelings of anxiety, disappointment, and regret? Or to achieve a psychic state of pure and undivided pleasure and joy? The satisfaction of such desires seems inseparable from our happiness, which we pursue by right and with passion.

In these efforts at peace of mind, human beings have from time immemorial sought help from doctors and drugs. In a famous literary instance, Shakespeare's Macbeth entreats his doctor to free Lady Macbeth from the haunting memory of her own guilty acts:

> *Macbeth.*   Canst thou not minister to a mind
> diseas'd,
> Pluck from the memory a rooted sorrow,
> Raze out the written troubles of the brain,
> And with some sweet oblivious antidote
> Cleanse the stuff'd bosom of that perilous
> stuff
> Which weighs upon the heart?
>
> *Doctor.*   Therein the patient
> Must minister to himself.

Ministering to oneself, however, is easier said than done, and many people have found themselves unequal to the task without some outside assistance. For centuries, they have made use of external agents to drown their sorrows or lift their spirits.

The burgeoning field of neuroscience is providing new, more specific, and safer agents to help us combat all sorts of psychic distress. Soon, doctors may have just the "sweet oblivious antidote" that Macbeth so desired: drugs (such as beta-adrenergic blockers) that numb the emotional sting typically associated with our intensely bad memories[.]

To be sure, these agents—and their better versions, yet to come—are, for now at least, being developed not as means for drug-induced happiness but rather as agents for combating major depression or preventing posttraumatic stress disorder (PTSD). Yet once available for those purposes, they could also be used to ease the soul and enhance the mood of nearly anyone.

By using drugs to satisfy more easily the enduring aspirations to forget what torments us and approach the world with greater peace of mind, what deeper human aspirations might we occlude or frustrate? What qualities of character may become less necessary and, with diminished use, atrophy or become extinct, as we increasingly depend on drugs to cope with misfortune? How will we experience our incompleteness or understand our mortality as our ability grows to medically dissolve all sorts of anxiety? Will the availability of drug-induced conditions of ecstatic pleasure estrange us from the forms of pleasure that depend upon discipline and devotion? And, going beyond the implications for individuals, what kind of a society are we likely to have when the powers to control memory, mood, and mental life through drugs reach their full maturity and are widely used?

I. What Are "Happy Souls"?

Because the happiness we seek we seek for *ourselves*—for *our* self, not for someone else's, and for our *self* or embodied soul, not for our bodies as material stuff—our happiness is bound up with our personhood and our identity. We would not want to attain happiness (or any other object of our desires) if the condition for attaining it required that we become someone else, that we lose our identity in the process.

The importance of identity for happiness implies necessarily the importance of memory. If experiencing our happiness depends on experiencing a stable identity, then our happiness depends also on our memory, on knowing who we are in relation to who we have been.

But if enfeebled memory can cripple identity, selectively altered memory can distort it. Changing the content

From the President's Council on Bioethics, October 2003.

of our memories or altering their emotional tonalities, however desirable to alleviate guilty or painful consciousness, could subtly reshape who we are, at least to ourselves. With altered memories we might feel better about ourselves, but it is not clear that the better-feeling "we" remains the same as before. Lady Macbeth, cured of her guilty torment, would remain the murderess she was, but not the conscience-stricken being even she could not help but be.

[A]n unchecked power to erase memories, brighten moods, and alter our emotional dispositions could imperil our capacity to form a strong and coherent personal identity. To the extent that our inner life ceases to reflect the ups and downs of daily existence and instead operates independently of them, we dissipate our identity, which is formed through engagement with others and through immersion in the mix of routine and unpredictable events that constitute our lives.

II. Memory and Happiness

Our identity or sense of self emerges, grows, and changes. Yet, despite all the changes, thanks to the integrating powers of memory, our identity also, remarkably, persists *as ours*.

We especially want our memories to be not simply a sequence of disconnected experiences, but a narrative that seems to contain some unfolding purpose, some larger point from beginning to end, some aspiration discovered, pursued, and at least partially fulfilled.

Memory is central to human flourishing, in other words, precisely because we pursue happiness in time, as time-bound beings. We have a past and a future as well as a present, and being happy through time requires that these be connected in a meaningful way. If we are to flourish as ourselves, we must do so without abandoning or forgetting who we are or once were. Yet because our lives are time-bound, our happiness is always incomplete—always not-yet and on-the-way, always here but slipping away, but also always possible again and in the future. Our happiest experiences can be revivified. And, as we reminisce from greater distance and with more experience, even our painful experiences can often acquire for us a meaning not in evidence when they occurred.

The place of memory in the pursuit of happiness also suggests something essential about human identity, a theme raised in various places and in different ways throughout this report: namely, our identities are formed both by what we do and by what we undergo or suffer. We actively choose paths and do deeds fit to be remembered. But we also live through memorable experiences that we would never have chosen—experiences we often wish never happened at all. To some extent, these unchosen memories constrain us; though we may regret the shadows they cast over our pursuit of happiness, we cannot simply escape them while remaining who we really are. And yet, through the act of remembering—the act of discerning and giving meaning to the past as it really was—we can shape, to some degree, the meaning of our memories, both good and bad.

The capacity to alter or numb our remembrance of things past cuts to the heart of what it means to remember in a human way, and it is this biotechnical possibility that we focus on here. Deciding when or whether to use such biotechnical power will require that we think long and hard about what it means to remember truthfully, to live in time, and to seek happiness without losing or abandoning our identity. The rest of this discussion of "memory and happiness" is an invitation to such reflection.

Good Memories and Bad

[T]he significance of past events often becomes clear to us only after much rumination in light of later experience, and what seems trivial at one time may appear crucial at another. Neither can an excellent memory be one that remembers only what we *want* to remember: sometimes our most valuable memories are of events that were painful when they occurred, but that on reflection teach us vital lessons.

Biotechnology and Memory Alteration

It is a commonplace observation that, while some events fade quickly from the mind, emotionally intense experiences form memories that are peculiarly vivid and long-lasting. Not only do we recall such events long after they happened, but the recollection is often accompanied, in some measure, by a recurrence of the emotions aroused during the original experience.

When a person experiences especially shocking or violent events (such as a plane crash or bloody combat), the release of stress hormones may be so intense that the memory-encoding system is over-activated. The result is a consolidation of memories both far stronger and more persistent than normal and also more apt, upon recollection, to call forth the intense emotional response of the original experience. In such cases, each time the person relives the traumatic memory, a new flood of stress hormones is released, and the experience may be so emotionally intense as to be encoded as a new experience. With time, the memories grow more recurrent and intrusive, and the response—fear, helplessness, horror—more incapacitating.

As we shall see, drugs that might prevent or alleviate the symptoms of PTSD are among the chief medical benefits that scientists expect from recent research in the neuro-chemistry of memory formation.

In fact, the discovery of hormonal regulation of memory formation was quickly followed up by clinical studies on human subjects demonstrating that memory of emotional experiences can be altered pharmacologically. In one particularly interesting series of experiments, Larry Cahill and his colleagues showed that injections of beta-blockers can, by inhibiting the action of stress hormones, suppress the memory-enhancing effects of strong emotional arousal.

[T]aking propranolol appears to have little or no effect on how we remember everyday or emotionally neutral information. But when taken at the time of highly emotional experiences, propranolol appears to suppress the normal memory-enhancing effects of emotional arousal—while leaving the immediate emotional response unaffected. These results suggested the possibility of using beta-blockers to help survivors of traumatic events to reduce their intrusive—and in some cases crippling—memories of those events.

[A]lthough the pharmacology of memory alteration is a science still in its infancy, the significance of this potential new power—to separate the subjective experience of memory from the truth of the experience that is remembered—should not be underestimated. It surely returns us to the large ethical and anthropological questions with which we began—about memory's role in shaping personal identity and the character of human life, and about the meaning of remembering things that we would rather forget and of forgetting things that we perhaps ought to remember.

Memory-Blunting: Ethical Analysis

If we had the power, by promptly taking a memory-altering drug, to dull the emotional impact of what could become very painful memories, when might we be tempted to use it? And for what reasons should we yield to or resist the temptation?

At first glance, such a drug would seem ideally suited for the prevention of PTSD, the complex of debilitating symptoms that sometimes afflict those who have experienced severe trauma. These symptoms—which include persistent reexperiencing of the traumatic event and avoidance of every person, place, or thing that might stimulate the horrid memory's return[1] can so burden mental life as to make normal everyday living extremely difficult, if not impossible.[2] For those suffering these disturbing

symptoms, a drug that could separate a painful memory from its powerful emotional component would appear very welcome indeed.

Yet the prospect of preventing (even) PTSD with beta-blockers or other memory-blunting agents seems to be, for several reasons, problematic. First of all, the drugs in question appear to be effective only when administered during or shortly after a traumatic event—and thus well before any symptoms of PTSD would be manifested. How then could we make, and make on the spot, the *prospective* judgment that a particular event is sufficiently terrible to warrant preemptive memory-blunting? Second, how shall we judge *which* participants in the event merit such treatment? After all, not everyone who suffers through painful experiences is destined to have pathological memory effects. Should the drugs in question be given to everyone or only to those with an observed susceptibility to PTSD, and, if the latter, how will we know who these are? Finally, in some cases merely witnessing a disturbing event (for example, a murder, rape, or terrorist attack) is sufficient to cause PTSD-like symptoms long afterwards. Should we then, as soon as disaster strikes, consider giving memory-altering drugs to all the witnesses, in addition to those directly involved?

If the apparent powers of memory-blunting drugs are confirmed, some might be inclined to prescribe them liberally to all who are involved in a sufficiently terrible event. After all, even those not destined to come down with full-blown PTSD are likely to suffer painful recurrent memories of an airplane crash, an incident of terrorism, or a violent combat operation. In the aftermath of such shocking incidents, why not give everyone the chance to remember these events without the added burden of painful emotions? This line of reasoning might, in fact, tempt us to give beta-blockers liberally to soldiers on the eve of combat, to emergency workers en route to a disaster site, or even to individuals requesting prophylaxis against the shame or guilt they might incur from future misdeeds—in general, to anyone facing an experience that is likely to leave lasting intrusive memories.

Yet on further reflection it seems clear that not every intrusive memory is a suitable candidate for prospective pharmacological blunting. As Daniel Schacter has observed, "attempts to avoid traumatic memories often backfire":

> Intrusive memories need to be acknowledged, confronted, and worked through, in order to set them to rest for the long term. Unwelcome memories of trauma are symptoms of a disrupted psyche that requires attention before it can resume

healthy functioning. Beta-blockers might make it easier for trauma survivors to face and incorporate traumatic recollections, and in that sense could facilitate long-term adaptation. Yet it is also possible that beta-blockers would work against the normal process of recovery: traumatic memories would not spring to mind with the kind of psychological force that demands attention and perhaps intervention. Prescription of beta-blockers could bring about an effective trade-off between short-term reductions in the sting of traumatic memories and long-term increases in persistence of related symptoms of a trauma that has not been adequately confronted.[3]

The point can be generalized: in the immediate aftermath of a painful experience, we simply cannot know either the full meaning of the experience in question or the ultimate character and future prospects of the individual who experiences it. We cannot know how this experience will change this person at this time and over time. Will he be cursed forever by unbearable memories that, in retrospect, clearly should have been blunted medically? Or will he succeed, over time, in "redeeming" those painful memories by actively integrating them into the narrative of his life? By "rewriting" memories pharmacologically we might succeed in easing real suffering at the risk of falsifying our perception of the world and undermining our true identity.

Finally, the decision whether or not to use memory-blunting drugs must be made in the absence of clearly diagnosable disease. The drug must be taken right after a traumatic experience has occurred, and thus before the different ways that different individuals handle the same experience has become clear. In some cases, these interventions will turn out to have been preventive medicine, intervening to ward off the onset of PTSD before it arrives—though it is worth noting that we would lack even post hoc knowledge of whether any particular now-unaffected individual, in the absence of using the drug, would have become symptomatic.[4] In other cases, the interventions would not be medicine at all: altering the memory of individuals who could have lived well, even with severely painful memories, without pharmacologically dulling the pain. Worse, in still other cases, the use of such drugs would inoculate individuals in advance against the psychic pain that *should* accompany their commission of cruel, brutal, or shameful deeds. But in all cases, from the defensible to the dubious, the use of such powers changes the character of human memory, by intervening directly in the way individuals "encode," and thus the way they understand, the happenings of

their own lives and the realities of the world around them.

Remembering Fitly and Truly

Altering the formation of emotionally powerful memories risks severing what we remember from how we remember it and distorting the link between our perception of significant human events and the significance of the events themselves. It risks, in a word, falsifying our perception and understanding of the world. It risks making shameful acts seem less shameful, or terrible acts less terrible, than they really are.

Imagine the experience of a person who witnesses a shocking murder. Fearing that he will be haunted by images of this event, he immediately takes propranolol (or its more potent successor) to render his memory of the murder less painful and intrusive. Thanks to the drug, his memory of the murder gets encoded as a garden-variety, emotionally neutral experience. But in manipulating his memory in this way, he risks coming to think about the murder as more tolerable than it really is, as an event that should not sting those who witness it. For our opinions about the meaning of our experiences are shaped partly by the feelings evoked when we remember them. If, psychologically, the murder is transformed into an event our witness can recall without pain—or without *any* particular emotion—perhaps its moral significance will also fade from consciousness. If so, he would in a sense have ceased to be a genuine witness of the murder. When asked about it, he might say, "Yes, I was there. But it wasn't so terrible."

This points us to a deeper set of questions about bad memories: Would dulling our memory of terrible things make us too comfortable with the world, unmoved by suffering, wrongdoing, or cruelty? Does not the experience of hard truths—of the unchosen, the inexplicable, the tragic—remind us that we can never be fully at home in the world, especially if we are to take seriously the reality of human evil? Further, by blunting our experience and awareness of shameful, fearful, and hateful things, might we not also risk deadening our response to what is admirable, inspiring, and lovable? Can we become numb to life's sharpest sorrows without also becoming numb to its greatest joys?

There seems to be little doubt that some bitter memories are so painful and intrusive as to ruin the possibility for normal experience of much of life and the world. In such cases the impulse to relieve a crushing burden and restore lost innocence is fully understandable: If there are some things that it is better never to have experienced at all—things we would avoid if we possibly could—why not erase them from the memory of those unfortunate enough to have suffered them? If there are some things it is better never to have known or seen, why not use our power over memory to restore a witness's shattered peace of mind? There is great force in this argument, perhaps especially in cases where children lose prematurely that innocence that is rightfully theirs.

And yet, there may be a great cost to acting compassionately for those who suffer bad memories, if we do so by compromising the truthfulness of how they remember. We risk having them live falsely in order simply to cope, to survive by whatever means possible.

The Obligation to Remember

Having truthful memories is not simply a personal matter. Strange to say, our own memory is not merely our own; it is part of the fabric of the society in which we live. Consider the case of a person who has suffered or witnessed atrocities that occasion unbearable memories: for example, those with firsthand experience of the Holocaust. The life of that individual might well be served by dulling such bitter memories,[5] but such a humanitarian intervention, if widely practiced, would seem deeply troubling: Would the community as a whole—would the human race—be served by such a mass numbing of this terrible but indispensable memory? Do those who suffer evil have a duty to remember and bear witness, lest we all forget the very horrors that haunt them?

Surely, we cannot and should not force those who live through great trauma to endure its painful memory *for the benefit of the rest of us*. But as a community, there are certain events that we have an obligation to remember—an obligation that falls disproportionately, one might even say unfairly, on those who experience such events most directly.[6] What kind of people would we be if we did not "want" to remember the Holocaust, if we sought to make the anguish it caused simply go away? And yet, what kind of people are we, especially those who face such horrors firsthand, that we can endure such awful memories?

The answer, in part, is that those who suffer terrible things cannot or should not have to endure their own bad memories alone. If, as a people, we have an obligation to remember certain terrible events truthfully, surely we ought to help those who suffered through those events to come to terms with their worst memories. Of course, one might see the new biotechnical powers, developed precisely to ease the psychic pain of bad memories, as the mark of such solidarity: perhaps it is our new way of meeting the obligation to aid those who remember the hardest things, those who bear witness to us and for us. But such solidarity may, in the end, prove false: for it exempts us from the duty to suffer-with (literally, to feel *com*-passion

for) those who remember; it does not demand that we preserve the truth of their memories; it attempts instead to make the problem go away, and with it the truth of the experience in question.

The Soul of Memory, the Remembering Soul

[W]e might often be tempted to sacrifice the accuracy of our memories for the sake of easing our pain or expanding our control over our own psychic lives. But doing so means, ultimately, severing ourselves from reality and leaving our own identity behind; it risks making us false, small, or capable of great illusions, and thus capable of great decadence or great evil, or perhaps simply willing to accept a phony contentment. We might be tempted to alter our memories to preserve an open future—to live the life we wanted to live before a particular experience happened to us. But in another sense, such interventions assume that our own future is not open—that we cannot and could never redeem the unwanted memory over time, that we cannot and could never integrate the remembered experience with our own truthful pursuit of happiness.

To have only happy memories would be a blessing—and a curse. Nothing would trouble us, but we would probably be shallow people, never falling to the depths of despair because we have little interest in the heights of human happiness or in the complicated lives of those around us. In the end, to have only happy memories is not to be happy in a truly human way. It is simply to be free of misery—an understandable desire given the many troubles of life, but a low aspiration for those who seek a truly human happiness.

Notes

1. These symptoms are observed especially among combat veterans; indeed, PTSD is the modern name for what used to be called "shell shock" or "combat neurosis." Among veterans, PTSD is frequently associated with recurrent nightmares, substance abuse, and delusional outbursts of violence. There is controversy about the prevalence of PTSD, with some studies finding that up to 8 percent of adult Americans have suffered the disorder as well as a third of all veterans of the Vietnam War. See Kessler, R. C., et al., "Post-Traumatic Stress Disorder in the National Comorbidity Survey," *Archives of General Psychiatry* 52(12): 1048–1060, 1995; Kulka, R. A., et al., *Trauma and the Vietnam War Generation: Report of Findings from the National Vietnam Veterans Readjustment Study*, New York: Brunner/Mazel, 1990.

2. There is already ongoing controversy about excessive diagnosis of PTSD. Many psychotherapists believe that a patient's psychic troubles are generally based on some earlier (now repressed) traumatic experience which must be unearthed and dealt with if relief is to be found. True PTSD is, however, generally transient, and the search for treatment is directed against the symptoms of its initial (worst) phase—the sleeplessness, the nightmares, the excessive jitteriness.

3. Of course, many Holocaust survivors managed, without pharmacological assistance, to live fulfilling lives while never forgetting what they lived through. At the same time, many survivors would almost certainly have benefited from pharmacological treatment.

4. There is no definitive diagnostic criterion for PTSD, but the core symptoms are thought to include persistent re-experiencing of the traumatic event, avoidance of associated stimuli, and hyperarousal. See *Diagnostic and Statistical Manual of Mental Disorders, Fourth Edition, text revision*, Washington, D.C.: American Psychiatric Association, 2000, pp. 463–486.

5. Schacter, D., *The Seven Sins of Memory: How the Mind Forgets and Remembers*, New York: Houghton Mifflin, 2001, p. 183.

6. For a discussion of memory-altering drugs and the meaning of "bearing witness," see the essay by Cohen, E., "Our Psychotropic Memory," *SEED*, no. 8, Fall 2003, p. 42.

THE PRESIDENT'S COUNCIL ON BIOETHICS was a group of individuals appointed by President George W. Bush in November 2001 to advise his administration on bioethical issues that may emerge as a consequence of advances in biomedical science and technology.

EXPLORING THE ISSUE

Should Memory-Dampening Drugs Be Used to Prevent and Treat Trauma in Combat Soldiers?

Critical Thinking and Reflection

1. Assuming that a medication is effective in alleviating the symptoms of combat-related PTSD, what are some of the risks and costs of using such an intervention?
2. Consider societal responsibility pertaining to the use of memory-dampening drugs in treating combat-related PTSD. Namely, to what extent does society have a responsibility to try to alleviate these symptoms?
3. Some experts assert that for some people, the experience of trauma can lead to posttraumatic growth in which the trauma survivor has a greater appreciation of life and relationships. If memory-dampening drugs are found to reduce the potential for posttraumatic growth, how should that consideration be weighed in determining the appropriateness of these drugs?
4. Assuming that memory-dampening drugs are effective in reducing PTSD symptoms, who should make the decision about their appropriateness in a given case, a physician, the trauma survivor, or a team of experts? Also, when should they be administered to combat soldiers, on the field, back at base, or upon returning home?
5. How should researchers go about studying the effects of memory-dampening drugs on survivors of combat trauma? What are some of the methodological challenges involved in this kind of research? What are some of the ethical considerations that must be weighed?

Is There Common Ground?

Dr. Elise Donovan and the President's Council on Bioethics acknowledge that the experience of trauma can have debilitating effects on people who are exposed to such horrifying experiences. Posttraumatic stress disorder has justifiably received increasing attention in America as a result of the alarming numbers of soldiers diagnosed with this condition who have fought in the wars in Iraq and Afghanistan. American society has a responsibility to respond to the devastating effects of PTSD on combat soldiers, on their loved ones, and on the country as a whole. Dr. Donovan and the Council agree that drugs such as propranolol can be effective in alleviating some of the debilitating symptoms of PTSD. Dr. Donovan contends that it is justifiable and ethical to use these drugs to treat soldiers who have been traumatized by combat. The Council, however, expresses strong reservations about these drugs on ethical grounds, contending that individuals who take these drugs to alleviate symptoms of trauma would possibly be deprived of the opportunity to grow as a result of

their traumatic experience. Dr. Donovan is also concerned about ethical and moral issues, but asserts that for those who have risked their lives to serve the country, and who suffer with PTSD as a result, there is an ethical obligation to try to alleviate their psychological distress.

Create Central

www.mhhe.com/createcentral

Additional Resources

Chu, J. A. (2011). *Rebuilding Shattered Lives: Treating Complex PTSD and Dissociative Disorders*. Hoboken, NJ: John Wiley & Sons.

Farah, M. J. (2010). *Neuroethics: An Introduction with Readings*. Cambridge, MA: MIT Press.

Hurley, E. (2010, August 1). "Combat Trauma and the Moral Risks of Memory Manipulating Drugs." *Journal of Applied Philosophy*, 27(3), 221–245.

Kolber, A. (2011, January 1). "Give Memory-Altering Drugs a Chance: The Ethical Challenges of Memory-Dampening Drugs Are Likely to Be Manageable and the Pay-Offs Considerable." (COMMENT) (Report). *Nature*, 476 (7360).

Newman, E. J., Berkowitz, S. R., Nelson, K. J., Garry, M., & Loftus, E. F. (2011, September 1). "Attitudes about Memory Dampening Drugs Depend on Context and Country." *Applied Cognitive Psychology*, 25(5).

Internet References . . .

Journal of Medical Ethics

http://jme.bmj.com/content/early/2014/05/02/
medethics-2013-101972.full

National Institute of Mental Health

http://www.nimh.nih.gov/health/topics/
post-traumatic-stress-disorder-ptsd/index.shtml

The Oxford Centre for Neuroethics

http://www.neuroethics.ox.ac.uk/bio-ethics_bites

Selected, Edited, and with Issue Framing Material by:
Richard P. Halgin, *University of Massachusetts, Amherst*

ISSUE

Is Addiction a Brain Disease?

YES: National Institute on Drug Abuse, from *Drugs, Brain, and Behavior: The Science of Addiction,* National Institute on Drug Abuse (2007)

NO: Steven Slate, from "Addiction Is NOT a Brain Disease, It Is a Choice," thecleanslate.org (Accessed April 24, 2014)

Learning Outcomes
After reading this issue, you will be able to: • Understand the concept of "brain disease" as it applies to behaviors such as addiction.   • Critically evaluate the contrasting view that addiction is a brain disease versus the notion that addictive behavior is a choice.   • Consider the extent to which addiction is influenced by the biological makeup of the individual.   • Understand the bodily systems that are affected by drug abuse, and the ways in which drugs work on the brain to produce feelings of pleasure.   • Discuss the extent to which addiction is influenced by environmental factors.

ISSUE SUMMARY

YES: In the NIDA publication, the argument is made that addiction is indeed a disease, and that scientific information is available about the nature, prevention, and treatment of this disease.

NO: On his website, The Clean Slate Addiction Site, Steven Slate argues that addiction to drugs and alcohol is not a disease, and to call it such we must either overlook the major gaps in the disease argument, or we must completely redefine the term "disease." He states, "In a true disease, some part of the body is in a state of abnormal physiological functioning, and this causes the undesirable symptoms.... In addiction there is no such physiological malfunction."

In the National Institute on Drug Abuse (NIDA) publication, the argument is made that addiction is indeed a disease, and that scientific information is available about the nature, prevention, and treatment of this disease. NIDA promotes the idea that it is important for scientists to study the effects that drugs have on the brain and on behavior, so that this information can be used to develop drug abuse prevention and treatment programs. NIDA highlights the fact that, although the initial decision to take drugs is voluntary, over time drug-addicted individuals show physical changes in areas of the brain that are critical to judgment, decision making, learning and memory, and behavior control.

NIDA views addiction as a chronic, relapsing brain disease that is characterized by compulsive drug seeking and use, despite harmful consequences. Over time, if drug use continues, pleasurable activities become less pleasurable, and drug abuse becomes necessary for abusers to simply feel "normal." Drug abusers reach a point where they seek and take drugs, despite the tremendous problems caused for themselves and their loved ones. Some individuals may start to feel the need to take higher or more frequent doses, even in the early stages of their drug use.

NIDA contends that the initial decision to take drugs is mostly voluntary. However, when drug abuse takes over, a person's ability to exert self-control can become seriously impaired. Brain imaging studies from drug-addicted individuals show physical changes in areas of the brain that are critical to judgment, decision making, learning and memory, and behavior control. The overall risk for addiction is influenced by the biological makeup of the individual. According to NIDA, addiction can even be influenced by gender or ethnicity, a person's developmental stage, and the surrounding social environment. Scientists studying the effects that drugs have on the brain and on people's behavior use this information to develop programs for preventing drug abuse and for helping people recover from addiction.

Steven Slate vehemently objects to the view that addiction is a brain disease, resting his argument on the premise that substance use is a choice. He contends that in a real disease, some part of the body is in a state of abnormal physiological functioning with the result of undesirable symptoms. However, in addiction there is no such physiological malfunction.

Slate criticizes the conclusion drawn by NIDA that brain changes provide evidence for the argument that addiction is a physical disease associated with compulsive drug seeking and use. He asserts that brain scans of heavy substance users do not represent a malfunctioning brain, but rather are normal reflections of brain neuroplasticity. Slate provides several examples of how the brain changes as a result of routine activities such as playing a piano or driving a taxi, or just about any other sustained mental activity. Thus, if a person's brain can change as a result of addicted thoughts and choices, then it can be further changed by engaging in opposing thoughts and behaviors. In other words, the choice to refrain from substances would bring about changes in brain functioning. Conditions that can be remedied by freely chosen thoughts and behaviors just do not fit into the general understanding of disease.

Slate is also critical of research that is cited by proponents of the disease model of addiction who point to differences in brain scans associated with prolonged recovery. In criticizing a graphic used to support the premise that addiction is a brain disease, Slate contends that there was no medical treatment of disease that would explain the brain changes; rather, the brain changes can be attributed to the fact that the addicts "chose abstinence." When people choose to stop using drugs, their brain activity will follow such a choice. When addicts are presented with a clear and immediately rewarding alternative to substance use and an incentive not to use, they are likely to make the choice with the greater payoff. When they can see other options for happiness as more appealing, more attainable, and as taking a level of effort they're willing to expend, then they will choose such options instead of substances. He objects to the characterization of addiction as "compulsive drug seeking and use," insisting that drug use is not compulsive, but instead a choice with unfortunate consequences.

YES

National Institute on Drug Abuse

Drugs, Brain, and Behavior:
The Science of Addiction

Drug Abuse and Addiction

What Is Drug Addiction?

Addiction is defined as a chronic, relapsing brain disease that is characterized by compulsive drug seeking and use, despite harmful consequences. It is considered a brain disease because drugs change the brain—they change its structure and how it works. These brain changes can be long lasting, and can lead to the harmful behaviors seen in people who abuse drugs.

Is Continued Drug Abuse a Voluntary Behavior?

The initial decision to take drugs is mostly voluntary. However, when drug abuse takes over, a person's ability to exert self control can become seriously impaired. Brain imaging studies from drug-addicted individuals show physical changes in areas of the brain that are critical to judgment, decision making, learning and memory, and behavior control. Scientists believe that these changes alter the way the brain works, and may help explain the compulsive and destructive behaviors of addiction.

Why Do Some People Become Addicted to Drugs, While Others Do Not?

As with any other disease, vulnerability to addiction differs from person to person. In general, the more risk factors an individual has, the greater the chance that taking drugs will lead to abuse and addiction. "Protective" factors reduce a person's risk of developing addiction.

What Factors Determine If a Person Will Become Addicted?

No single factor determines whether a person will become addicted to drugs. The overall risk for addiction is impacted by the biological makeup of the individual—it can even be influenced by gender or ethnicity, his or her developmental stage, and the surrounding social environment (e.g., conditions at home, at school, and in the neighborhood).

Which Biological Factors Increase Risk of Addiction?

Scientists estimate that genetic factors account for between 40 and 60 percent of a person's vulnerability to addiction, including the effects of environment on gene expression and function. Adolescents and individuals with mental disorders are at greater risk of drug abuse and addiction than the general population.

The Brain Continues to Develop into Adulthood and Undergoes Dramatic Changes During Adolescence

One of the brain areas still maturing during adolescence is the prefrontal cortex—the part of the brain that enables us to assess situations, make sound decisions, and keep our emotions and desires under control. The fact that this critical part of an adolescent's brain is still a work-in-progress puts them at increased risk for poor decisions (such as trying drugs or continued abuse). Thus, introducing drugs while the brain is still developing may have profound and long-lasting consequences.

Drugs and the Brain

Introducing the Human Brain

The human brain is the most complex organ in the body. This three-pound mass of gray and white matter sits at the center of all human activity—you need it to drive a car, to enjoy a meal, to breathe, to create an artistic masterpiece, and to enjoy everyday activities. In brief, the brain regulates your basic body functions; enables you to interpret and respond to everything you experience, and shapes your thoughts, emotions, and behavior.

Published by National Institutes of Health, NIH Pub no. 07-5605, April 2007, pp. 5, 7, 8, 10, 15–20.

The brain is made up of many parts that all work together as a team. Different parts of the brain are responsible for coordinating and performing specific functions. Drugs can alter important brain areas that are necessary for life-sustaining functions and can drive the compulsive drug abuse that marks addiction. Brain areas affected by drug abuse—

- *The brain stem* controls basic functions critical to life, such as heart rate, breathing, and sleeping.
- *The limbic system* contains the brain's reward circuit—it links together a number of brain structures that control and regulate our ability to feel pleasure. Feeling pleasure motivates us to repeat behaviors such as eating—actions that are critical to our existence. The limbic system is activated when we perform these activities—and also by drugs of abuse. In addition, the limbic system is responsible for our perception of other emotions, both positive and negative, which explains the mood-altering properties of many drugs.
- *The cerebral cortex* is divided into areas that control specific functions. Different areas process information from our senses, enabling us to see, feel, hear, and taste. The front part of the cortex, the frontal cortex or forebrain, is the thinking center of the brain; it powers our ability to think, plan, solve problems, and make decisions.

How Does the Brain Communicate?

The brain is a communications center consisting of billions of neurons, or nerve cells. Networks of neurons pass messages back and forth to different structures within the brain, the spinal column, and the peripheral nervous system. These nerve networks coordinate and regulate everything we feel, think, and do.

- *Neuron to Neuron*
  Each nerve cell in the brain sends and receives messages in the form of electrical impulses. Once a cell receives and processes a message, it sends it on to other neurons.
- *Neurotransmitters—The Brain's Chemical Messengers*
  The messages are carried between neurons by chemicals called neurotransmitters. (They transmit messages between neurons.)
- *Receptors—The Brain's Chemical Receivers*
  The neurotransmitter attaches to a specialized site on the receiving cell called a receptor. A neurotransmitter and its receptor operate like a "key and lock," an exquisitely specific mechanism that ensures that each receptor will forward the appropriate message only after interacting with the right kind of neurotransmitter.
- *Transporters—The Brain's Chemical Recyclers*
  Located on the cell that releases the neurotransmitter, transporters recycle these neurotransmitters (i.e., bring them back into the cell that released them), thereby shutting off the signal between neurons.

How Do Drugs Work in the Brain?

Drugs are chemicals. They work in the brain by tapping into the brain's communication system and interfering with the way nerve cells normally send, receive, and process information. Some drugs, such as marijuana and heroin, can activate neurons because their chemical structure mimics that of a natural neurotransmitter. This similarity in structure "fools" receptors and allows the drugs to lock onto and activate the nerve cells. Although these drugs mimic brain chemicals, they don't activate nerve cells in the same way as a natural neurotransmitter, and they lead to abnormal messages being transmitted through the network.

Other drugs, such as amphetamine or cocaine, can cause the nerve cells to release abnormally large amounts of natural neurotransmitters or prevent the normal recycling of these brain chemicals. This disruption produces a greatly amplified message, ultimately disrupting communication channels. The difference in effect can be described as the difference between someone whispering into your ear and someone shouting into a microphone.

How Do Drugs Work in the Brain to Produce Pleasure?

All drugs of abuse directly or indirectly target the brain's reward system by flooding the circuit with dopamine. Dopamine is a neurotransmitter present in regions of the brain that regulate movement, emotion, cognition, motivation, and feelings of pleasure. The overstimulation of this system, which rewards our natural behaviors, produces the euphoric effects sought by people who abuse drugs and teaches them to repeat the behavior.

How Does Stimulation of the Brain's Pleasure Circuit Teach Us to Keep Taking Drugs?

Our brains are wired to ensure that we will repeat life-sustaining activities by associating those activities with pleasure or reward. Whenever this reward circuit is activated, the brain notes that something important is happening that needs to be remembered, and teaches us to do it again and again, without thinking about it. Because drugs of abuse stimulate the same circuit, we learn to abuse drugs in the same way.

Why Are Drugs More Addictive Than Natural Rewards?

When some drugs of abuse are taken, they can release 2 to 10 times the amount of dopamine that natural rewards do. In some cases, this occurs almost immediately (as when drugs are smoked or injected), and the effects can last much longer than those produced by natural rewards. The resulting effects on the brain's pleasure circuit dwarfs those produced by naturally rewarding behaviors such as eating and sex. The effect of such a powerful reward strongly motivates people to take drugs again and again. This is why scientists sometimes say that drug abuse is something we learn to do very, very well.

What Happens to Your Brain If You Keep Taking Drugs?

Just as we turn down the volume on a radio that is too loud, the brain adjusts to the overwhelming surges in dopamine (and other neurotransmitters) by producing less dopamine or by reducing the number of receptors that can receive and transmit signals. As a result, dopamine's impact on the reward circuit of a drug abuser's brain can become abnormally low, and the ability to experience any pleasure is reduced. This is why the abuser eventually feels flat, lifeless, and depressed, and is unable to enjoy things that previously brought them pleasure. Now, they need to take drugs just to bring their dopamine function back up to normal. And, they must take larger amounts of the drug than they first did to create the dopamine high—an effect known as tolerance.

How Does Long-Term Drug Taking Affect Brain Circuits?

We know that the same sort of mechanisms involved in the development of tolerance can eventually lead to profound changes in neurons and brain circuits, with the potential to severely compromise the long-term health of the brain. For example, glutamate is another neurotransmitter that influences the reward circuit and the ability to learn. When the optimal concentration of glutamate is altered by drug abuse, the brain attempts to compensate for this change, which can cause impairment in cognitive function. Similarly, long-term drug abuse can trigger adaptations in habit or nonconscious memory systems. Conditioning is one example of this type of learning, whereby environmental cues become associated with the drug experience and can trigger uncontrollable cravings if the individual is later exposed to these cues, even without the drug itself being available. This learned "reflex" is extremely robust and can emerge even after many years of abstinence.

What Other Brain Changes Occur with Abuse?

Chronic exposure to drugs of abuse disrupts the way critical brain structures interact to control behavior—behavior specifically related to drug abuse. Just as continued abuse may lead to tolerance or the need for higher drug dosages to produce an effect, it may also lead to addiction, which can drive an abuser to seek out and take drugs compulsively. Drug addiction erodes a person's self-control and ability to make sound decisions, while sending intense impulses to take drugs.

NATIONAL INSTITUTE ON DRUG ABUSE (NIDA) was established in 1974 and became part of the National Institutes of Health, Department of Health and Human Services in October 1992. Since then it has been a federal focal point for research on drug abuse and addiction. NIDA's aim is to use the power of science to analyze drug abuse and addiction. NIDA addresses the most fundamental and essential questions about drug abuse, from detecting and responding to emerging drug abuse trends, and understanding how drugs work in the brain and body, to developing and testing new treatment and prevention approaches.

Steven Slate  **NO**

Addiction Is NOT a Brain Disease, It Is a Choice

They're screaming it from the rooftops: "addiction is a disease, and you can't stop it without medical treatment"! But why are they screaming it so loud, why are they browbeating us about it, why is it always mentioned with a qualifier? You don't hear people constantly referring to cancer as "the disease of cancer"—it's just "cancer", because it's obvious that cancer is a disease, it's been conclusively proven that the symptoms of cancer can't be directly stopped with mere choices—therefore no qualifier is needed. On the other hand, addiction to drugs and alcohol is not obviously a disease, and to call it such we must either overlook the major gaps in the disease argument, or we must completely redefine the term "disease."

Real Diseases versus the Disease Concept or Theory of Drug Addiction

In a true disease, some part of the body is in a state of abnormal physiological functioning, and this causes the undesirable symptoms. In the case of cancer, it would be mutated cells which we point to as evidence of a physiological abnormality, in diabetes we can point to low insulin production or cells which fail to use insulin properly as the physiological abnormality which create the harmful symptoms. If a person has either of these diseases, they cannot directly choose to stop their symptoms or directly choose to stop the abnormal physiological functioning which creates the symptoms. They can only choose to stop the physiological abnormality indirectly, by the application of medical treatment, and in the case of diabetes, dietetic measures may also indirectly halt the symptoms as well (but such measures are not a cure so much as a lifestyle adjustment necessitated by permanent physiological malfunction).

In addiction, there is no such physiological malfunction. The best physical evidence put forward by the disease proponents falls totally flat on the measure of representing a physiological malfunction. This evidence is the much touted brain scan[1]. The organization responsible for putting forth these brain scans, the National Institute on Drug Abuse and Addiction (NIDA), defines addiction in this way:

> Addiction is defined as a chronic relapsing brain disease that is characterized by compulsive drug seeking and use, despite harmful consequences. It is considered a brain disease because drugs change the brain—they change it's structure and how it works. These brain changes can be long lasting, and can lead to the harmful behaviors seen in people who abuse drugs.

The NIDA is stating outright that the reason addiction is considered a disease is because of the brain changes evidenced by the brain scans they show us, and that these changes cause the behavior known as addiction, which they characterize as "compulsive drug seeking and use". There are three major ways in which this case for the disease model falls apart:

- the changes in the brain which they show us are not abnormal at all
- people change their behavior IN SPITE OF the fact that their brain has changed in response to repeated substance use
- there is no evidence that the behavior of addicts is compulsive (compulsive meaning involuntary) (point two addresses this, as well as some other research that will be presented)

This all applies equally to "alcoholism" as well. If you're looking for information on alcoholism, the same theories and logic discussed here are applicable; wherever you see the term addiction used on this site, it includes alcoholism.

Brain Changes in Addicts Are Not Abnormal, and Do Not Prove the Brain Disease Theory

On the first count—the changes in the brain evidenced by brain scans of heavy substance users ("addicts") do not represent a malfunctioning brain. They are quite normal, as research into neuroplasticity has shown us. Whenever we practice doing or thinking anything enough, the brain changes—different regions and neuronal pathways are grown or strengthened, and new connections are made; various areas of the brain become more or less active depending upon how much you use them, and this becomes the norm in your brain—but it changes again as you adjust how much you use those brain regions depending on what you choose to think and do. This is a process which continues throughout life, there is nothing abnormal about it. But don't take my word for it, listen to Sharon Begley, science writer for the Wall Street Journal, who has spent years investigating it and writing both newspaper columns and books on neuroplasticity[2].

The term refers to the brain's recently discovered ability to change its structure and function, in particular by expanding or strengthening circuits that are used and by shrinking or weakening those that are rarely engaged. In its short history, the science of neuroplasticity has mostly documented brain changes that reflect physical experience and input from the outside world.

So, when the NIDA's Nora Volkow and others show us changes in the brain of a substance user as compared to a non-substance user, this difference is not as novel as they make it out to be. They are showing us routine neuroplastic changes which every healthily functioning person's brain goes through naturally. The phenomenon of brain changes isn't isolated to "addicts" or anyone else with a so-called brain disease—non-addicted and non-depressed and non-[insert brain disease of the week here] people experience brain changes too. One poignant example was found in the brains of London taxi drivers, as Begley and neuroscientist Jeffrey Schwartz pointed out in *The Mind and The Brain*. [4]

Is Being a Good Taxi Driver a Disease?

A specific area of the brain's hippocampus is associated with creating directional memories and a mental map of the environment. A team of researchers scanned the brains of London taxi drivers and compared their brains to non-taxi drivers. There was a very noticeable difference, not only between the drivers and non-drivers, but also between the more experienced and less experienced drivers:

There it was: the more years a man had been a taxi driver, the smaller the front of his hippocampus and the larger the posterior. "Length of time spent as a taxi driver correlated positively with volume in...the right posterior hippocampus," found the scientists. Acquiring navigational skills causes a "redistribution of gray matter in the hippocampus" as a driver's mental map of London grows larger and more detailed with experience.

So, the longer you drive a cab in London (that is, the longer you exert the mental and physical effort to quickly find your way around one of the world's toughest to navigate cities), the more your brain physically changes. And the longer you use drugs, the more your brain changes. And indeed, the longer and more intensely you apply yourself to any skill, thought, or activity—the more it will change your brain, and the more visible will be the differences between your brain and that of someone who hasn't been focused on that particular skill. So, if we follow the logic of the NIDA, then London's taxi drivers have a disease, which we'll call taxi-ism. But the new diseases wouldn't stop there.

Learning to play the piano well will change your brain—and if you were to compare brain scans of a piano player to a non-piano player, you would find significant differences. Does this mean that piano playing is a disease called Pianoism? Learning a new language changes your brain, are bilingual people diseased? Athletes' brains will change as a result of intensive practice—is playing tennis a disease? Are soccer players unable to walk into a sporting goods store without kicking every ball in sight? We could go on and on with examples, but the point is this— when you practice something, you get better at doing it, because your brain changes physiologically—and this is a normal process. If someone dedicated a large portion of their life to seeking and using drugs, and their brain didn't change—then that would be a true abnormality. Something would be seriously wrong with their brain.

It's not just physical activity that changes our brains, thoughts alone can have a huge effect. What's more, whether the brain changes or not, there is much research which shows that the brain is slave to the mind. As Begley points out elsewhere, thoughts alone can create the same brain activity that would come about by doing things[2]:

Using the brain scan called functional magnetic resonance imaging, the scientists pinpointed regions that were active during compassion meditation. In almost every case, the enhanced activity was greater in the monks' brains than the novices'. Activity in the left prefrontal cortex (the seat of positive emotions such as happiness) swamped activity in the right prefrontal (site of negative emotions and anxiety), something never before seen from purely mental activity. A sprawling circuit that switches on at the sight of suffering also showed greater activity in the monks. So did regions responsible for planned movement, as if the monks' brains were itching to go to the aid of those in distress.

So by simply practicing thinking about compassion, these monks made lasting changes in their brain activity. Purely mental activity can change the brain in physiologically significant ways. And to back up this fact we look again to the work of Dr Jeffrey Schwartz[3], who has taught OCD patients techniques to think their way out of obsessive thoughts. After exercising these thought practices, research showed that the brains of OCD patients looked no different than the brains of those who'd never had OCD. If you change your thoughts, you change your brain physically—and this is voluntary. This is outside the realm of disease, this shows a brain which changes as a matter of normality, and can change again, depending on what we practice choosing to think. There is nothing abnormal about a changing brain, and the type of changes we're discussing aren't necessarily permanent, as they are characterized to be in the brain disease model of addiction.

These brain change don't need to be brought on by exposure to chemicals. Thoughts alone, are enough to rewire the very circuits of the human brain responsible for reward and other positive emotions that substance use and other supposedly "addictive" behaviors ("process addictions" such as sex, gambling, and shopping, etc.) are connected with.

The Stolen Concept of Neuroplasticity in the Brain Disease Model of Addiction

Those who claim that addiction is a brain disease readily admit that the brain changes in evidence are arrived at through repeated choices to use substances and focus on using substances. In this way, they are saying the disease is a product of routine neuroplastic processes. Then they go on to claim that such brain changes either can't be remedied, or can only be remedied by outside means (medical treatment). When we break this down and look at it step by step, we see that the brain disease model rests on an argument similar to the "stolen concept". A

stolen concept argument is one in which the argument denies a fact on which it simultaneously rests. For example, the philosophical assertion that "reality is unknowable" rests on, or presumes that the speaker could know a fact of reality, it presumes that one could know that reality is unknowable—which of course one couldn't, if reality truly was unknowable—so the statement "reality is unknowable" invalidates itself. Likewise, the brain disease proponents are essentially saying "neuroplastic processes create a state called addiction which cannot be changed by thoughts and choices"—this however is to some degree self-invalidating, because it depends on neuroplasticity while seeking to invalidate it. If neuroplasticity is involved, and is a valid explanation for how to become addicted, then we can't act is if the same process doesn't exist when it's time to focus on getting un-addicted. That is, if the brain can be changed into the addicted state by thoughts and choices, then it can be further changed or changed back by thoughts and choices. Conditions which can be remedied by freely chosen thoughts and behaviors, don't fit into the general understanding of disease. Ultimately, if addiction is a disease, then it's a disease so fundamentally different than any other that it should probably have a completely different name that doesn't imply all the things contained in the term "disease"—such as the idea that the "will" of the afflicted is irrelevant to whether the condition continues.

People Change Their Addictive Behavior in Spite of the Fact That Their Brain Is changed—And They Do So Without Medication or Surgery (added 4/18/14)

In the discussion above, we looked at some analogous cases of brain changes to see just how routine and normal (i.e. not a physiological malfunction) such changes are. Now we're going to look directly at the most popular neuroscientific research which purports to prove that these brain changes actually cause "uncontrolled" substance use ("addiction").

The most popular research is Nora Volkow's brain scans of "meth addicts" presented by the NIDA. The logic is simple. We're presented with the brain scan of a meth addict alongside the brain scan of a non-user, and we're told that the decreased activity in the brain of the meth user (the lack of red in the "Drug Abuser" brain scan presented) is the cause of their "compulsive" methamphetamine use. Here's how the National Institute on Drug

Abuse (NIDA) explains the significance of these images in their booklet—Drugs, Brains, and Behavior: The Science of Addiction:

> Just as we turn down the volume on a radio that is too loud, the brain adjusts to the overwhelming surges in dopamine (and other neurotransmitters) by producing less dopamine or by reducing the number of receptors that can receive signals. As a result, dopamine's impact on the reward circuit of a drug abuser's brain can become abnormally low, and the ability to experience any pleasure is reduced. This is why the abuser eventually feels flat, lifeless, and depressed, and is unable to enjoy things that previously brought them pleasure. Now, **they *need* to take drugs just to try and bring their dopamine function back up to normal....**

They go on that these same sorts of brain changes:

> . . . may also lead to addiction, which can drive an abuser to seek out and take drugs compulsively. Drug addiction erodes a person's self-control and ability to make sound decisions, while sending intense impulses to take drugs....

That image is shown when NIDA is vaguely explaining how brain changes are responsible for "addiction." But later on, when they try to make a case for treating addiction as a brain disease, they show [an] image, which tells a far different story if you understand more of the context than they choose to mention:

Again, this graphic is used to support the idea that we should treat addiction as a brain disease. However, the authors mistakenly let a big cat out of the bag with this one—because the brain wasn't treated at all. Notice how the third image shows a brain in which the red level of activity has returned almost to normal after 14 months of abstinence. That's wonderful—but it also means that the NIDA's assertions that "Addiction means *being unable to quit,* even in the face of negative consequences"(LINK) and "It is considered a brain disease because drugs change the brain. . . . These brain changes . . . can *lead to the harmful behaviors* seen in people who abuse drugs" are *dead wrong*.

When these studies were done, **nobody was directly treating the brain of methamphetamine addicts**. They were not giving them medication for it (there is no equivalent of methadone for speed users), and they weren't sticking scalpels into the brains of these meth addicts, nor were they giving them shock treatment. So what did they do?

These methamphetamine addicts were court ordered into a treatment program (whose methodology wasn't disclosed in the research) which likely consisted of a general mixture of group and individual counseling with 12-step meeting attendance. I can't stress the significance of this enough: their brains were not medically treated. ***They talked to counselors. They faced a choice between jail and abstinence. They CHOSE abstinence (for at least 14 months!)—even while their brains had been changed in a way that we're told robs them of the ability to choose to quit "even in the face of negative consequences."*** [5]

Even with changed brains, people are capable of choosing to change their substance use habits. They choose to stop using drugs, and as the brain scans above demonstrate—their brain activity follows this choice. If the brain changes caused the substance using behavior, i.e. if it was the other way around, then a true medical intervention should have been needed—the brain would've needed to have changed first via external force (medicine or surgery) before abstinence was initiated. They literally wouldn't have been able to stop for 14 months without a real physical/biological medical intervention. But they did....

Substance Use Is Not Compulsive, It Is a Choice

There doesn't seem to be any evidence that substance use is involuntary. In fact, the evidence, such as that presented above, shows the opposite. Nevertheless, when the case for the disease is presented, the idea that drug use is involuntary is taken for granted as true. No evidence is ever actually presented to support this premise, so there isn't much to be knocked down here, except to make the point I made above—is a piano player fundamentally incapable of resisting playing the piano? They may love to play the piano, and want to do it often, they may even be obsessive about it, but it would be hard to say that at the sight of a piano they are involuntarily driven by their brain to push aside whatever else they need to do in order to play that piano.

There is another approach to the second claim though. We can look at the people who have subjectively claimed that their substance use is involuntary, and see if the offer of incentives results in changed behavior. Gene Heyman covered this in his landmark book, Addiction: A Disorder of Choice[3]. He recounts studies in which cocaine abusers were given traditional addiction counseling, and also offered vouchers which they could trade in for modest rewards such as movie tickets or sports equipment—if they proved through urine tests that they were abstaining from drug use. In the early stages of the study, 70% of those in the voucher program remained abstinent, while only 20% stayed abstinent in the control group which didn't receive the incentive of the vouchers. This demonstrates that substance use is not in fact compulsive or involuntary, but that it is a matter of choice, because these "addicts" when presented with a clear and immediately rewarding alternative to substance use and incentive not to use, chose it. Furthermore, follow up studies showed that this led to long term changes. A full year after the program, the voucher group had double the success rate of those who received only counseling (80% to 40%, respectively). This ties back in to our first point that what you practice, you become good at. The cocaine abusers in the voucher group practiced replacing substance use with other activities, such as using the sports equipment or movie passes they gained as a direct consequence of abstaining from drug use—thus they made it a habit to find other ways of amusing themselves, this probably led to brain changes, and the new habits became the norm.

Long story short, there is no evidence presented to prove that substance use is compulsive. The only thing ever offered is subjective reports from drug users themselves that they "can't stop", and proclamations from treatment professionals that the behavior is compulsive due to brain changes. But if the promise of a ticket to the movies is enough to double the success rate of conventional addiction counseling, then it's hard to say that substance users can't control themselves. The reality is that they can control themselves, but they just happen to see substance use as the best option for happiness available to them at the times when they're abusing substances. When they can see other options for happiness as more attractive (i.e. as promising a greater reward than substance use), attainable to them, and as taking an amount of effort they're willing to expend—then they will absolutely choose those options instead of substance use, and will not struggle to "stay sober", prevent relapse, practice self-control or self-regulation, or any other colloquialism for making a different choice. They will simply choose differently.

But wait . . . there's more! (Added 4/21/14) Contrary to the claims that alcoholics and drug addicts literally lose control of their substance use, a great number of experiments have found that they are really in full control of themselves. Priming dose experiments have found that alcoholics are not triggered into uncontrollable craving after taking a drink. Here's a link to the evidence and a deeper discussion of these findings: Alcoholics Do Not Lose Control. Priming dose experiments of cocaine, crack, and methamphetamine users found that after being given a hit of their drug of choice (primed with a dose) they are

capable of choosing a delayed reward rather than another hit of the drug. Here's a link to a discussion of these findings: Drug addicts don't lose control of their drug use.

Three Most Relevant Reasons Addiction Is Not a Disease

So to sum up, there are at least two significant reasons why the current brain disease theory of addiction is false.

- A disease involves physiological malfunction, the "proof" of brain changes shows no malfunction of the brain. These changes are indeed a normal part of how the brain works—not only in substance use, but in anything that we practice doing or thinking intensively. Brain changes occur as a matter of everyday life; the brain can be changed by the choice to think or behave differently; and the type of changes we're talking about are not permanent.
- The very evidence used to demonstrate that addicts' behavior is caused by brain changes also demonstrates that they change their behavior while their brain is changed, without a real medical intervention such as medication targeting the brain or surgical intervention in the brain—and that their brain changes back to normal AFTER they VOLITIONALLY change their behavior for a prolonged period of time
- Drug use in "addicts" is not compulsive. If it was truly compulsive, then offering a drug user tickets to the movies would not make a difference in whether they use or not—because this is an offer of a choice. Research shows that the offer of this choice leads to cessation of substance abuse. Furthermore, to clarify the point, if you offered a cancer patient movie tickets as a reward for ceasing to have a tumor—it would make no difference, it would not change his probability of recovery.

Addiction is NOT a disease, and it matters. This has huge implications for anyone struggling with a substance use habit.

References:

NIDA, Drugs Brains and Behavior: The Science of Addiction, sciofaddiction.pdf

Sharon Begley, Scans of Monks' Brains Show Meditation Alters Structure, Functioning, Wall Street Journal, November 5, 2004; Page B1, http://psyphz.psych. wisc.edu/web/News/Meditation_Alters_Brain_ WSJ_11-04.htm

Gene Heyman, Addiction: A Disorder of Choice, Harvard University Press, 2009

Sharon Begley and Jeffrey Schwartz, The Mind And The Brain, Harper Collins, 2002

Links to the 2 methamphetamine abuser studies by Nora Volkow:

http://www.jneurosci.org/cgi/content/full/21/23/9414

http://ajp.psychiatryonline.org/cgi/reprint/158/3/377

STEVEN SLATE, is the author of the website. The Clean Slate Addiction Site, which is dedicated to providing helpful information about addiction and substance abuse. He heads the New York office of the Baldwin Research Institute, which describes itself as an independent alcoholism and drug addiction research organization.

EXPLORING THE ISSUE

Is Addiction a Brain Disease?

Critical Thinking and Reflection

1. Imagine that you are a researcher who initiated a study assessing the relative contributions of biology and personality to the development of drug addiction. How would you go about studying this complex question?
2. Put yourself in the place of a clinician who is beginning to treat a drug-addicted individual. What questions would you ask in order to assess the extent to which the client is taking personal responsibility for the addiction?
3. Imagine that you are an educator with the goal of helping young people understand why drugs can be so addictive. Which points would you emphasize in your lecture?
4. What are the pros and cons of viewing drug addiction as a brain disease?
5. If unlimited funds were available for a program designed to reduce drug addiction, what initiatives would you imagine as the most effective?

Is There Common Ground?

In discussing the phenomenon of addiction, we turn first to accepted definitions of substance dependence, which is defined by behavior consisting of at least three of the following symptoms during a 12-month period: tolerance; symptoms of withdrawal; use of the substance in larger amounts or over a longer period than intended; persistent desire or unsuccessful attempts to cut down or control use; extensive time devoted to activities involved in obtaining, using, or recovering from substance use; a giving up or reduction in important activities because of substance use; and continued use despite knowledge of a substance-caused physical or psychological problem.

Over time, substance dependence evolves into addiction that is chronic and debilitating, and very difficult to shake. Both NIDA and Steven Slate understand that addiction can play a powerful role in a person's life, and both parties see that the initial decision to take drugs is voluntary. They differ, however, with regard to the individual's capacity for self-control once dependence on the

substance develops. NIDA focuses on the brain changes that take place, whereas Slate focuses on an individual's capacity to make choices.

Create Central

www.mhhe.com/createcentral

Additional Resources

Dunnington, K. (2011). *Addiction and Virtue: Beyond the Models of Disease and Choice.* Downers Grove, IL: IVP Academic.

Heyman, G. M. (2009). *Addiction: A Disorder of Choice.* Cambridge, MA: Harvard University Press.

Poland, J. S., & Graham, G. (2011). *Addiction and Responsibility.* Cambridge, MA: MIT Press.

Ross, D. (2010). *What Is Addiction?* Cambridge, MA: MIT Press.

Internet References . . .

National Council on Alcoholism and Drug Dependence, Inc.

http://www.ncadd.org/

National Institute on Drug Abuse

http://www.drugabuse.gov/

Partnership for Drug-Free Kids

http://www.drugfree.org/

Substance Abuse and Mental Health Services Administration

http://www.samhsa.gov/

Selected, Edited, and with Issue Framing Material by:
Richard P. Halgin, *University of Massachusetts, Amherst*

ISSUE

Should Medical Marijuana Be Prescribed for the Treatment of Emotional Disorders?

YES: Ron Marczyk, from "Worth Repeating: Marijuana Treats Anxiety and Depression," tokesignals.com (2013)

NO: Robert Berezin, from "It's Time to Address the Marijuana Issue," *Psychology Today* (2014)

Learning Outcomes

After reading this issue, you should be able to:

- Discuss the costs to society of endorsing the acceptance of marijuana as a medication for emotional disorders.
- Evaluate the physical and psychological risks for individuals who are prescribed marijuana for emotional disorders.
- Compare and contrast the risks of traditional medications vs. medical marijuana for treating emotional disorders.
- Consider limitations that should be defined regarding the prescription of medical marijuana for emotional disorders (e.g., age of the patient).
- Discuss methods for assessing the effectiveness of medical marijuana for treating emotinal disorders.

ISSUE SUMMARY

YES: Registered Nurse Ron Marczyk asserts that the "cannabinoid homeostatis healing perspective" has quietly been gathering evidence over the last 10 years, which overwhelmingly supports the need for human trials to test the use of medical marijuana as a psychiatric treatment. Medical evidence points strongly to a new treatment paradigm in which medical cannabinoids heal the brain in ways that shut down anxiety and depression while resetting the system.

NO: Psychiatrist Robert Berezin contends that the alleged beneficial properties of cannabis are fundamentally phony and have been put out there by the marijuana lobby in the service of promoting legalization. He views marijuana as causing a "destructive alteration of consciousness, which makes users passive, removed, intellectualized, falsely special, and not equipped to take on the challenges of life."

For the past century debate has raged about the detrimental vs. beneficial effects of marijuana (cannabis). The components of cannabis, cannabinoids including tetrahydrocannabinol (THC) and cannabidiol (CBD) have been used to treat an array of health problems for thousands of years, yet American society has struggled for decades with questions about legitimizing medical marijuana. Over the past few decades, many reports have emerged about the effectiveness of marijuana for treating severe pain or nausea associated with chemotherapy in cancer and AIDS patients. More and more states have decriminalized the recreational use of marijuana, and some states including Colorado and Washington have legalized its sale and use. In line with decreased public negativity about the recreational use of marijuana, approximately half the states have approved the prescription of marijuana for various illnesses and medical conditions. If marijuana is permissible, and even recommended, for the treatment of physical health problems, should this substance also be available for the treatment of psychological health problems such as anxiety and depression?

On the national scene, politicians and media personalities have joined the debate about medical marijuana and have thrown considerable fuel on the fire. Particularly noteworthy was the CON-then-PRO stance of Dr. Sanjay Gupta, a neurosurgeon at Emory Medical School and media correspondent for CNN and other major media outlets. In 2009 Dr. Gupta wrote an article in *Time* magazine strongly opposing the use of marijuana, which he recanted in 2013 (http://www.cnn.com/2013/08/08/health/gupta-changed-mind-marijuana/), explaining that he had come to realize that the drug does not have a high potential for abuse, and that for some medical conditions such as intractable pain it is the only intervention that works.

Although public acceptance has increased for the prescription of marijuana for physical health problems, the jury is still out on its use for psychological symptoms and disorders. In fact, some concern has been raised about the potential for long-term marijuana use resulting in severe psychological disturbance in some individuals. In the United Kingdom, the Royal College of Psychiatrists (http://www.rcpsych.ac.uk/mentalhealthinformation/mentalhealthproblems/alcoholanddrugs/cannabisand mentalhealth.aspx) notes that there is growing evidence that people with serious mental illness such as depression and psychosis are more likely to use cannabis, while also citing research that the drug increases the risk of developing a psychotic episode or schizophrenia, particularly in individuals with a genetic vulnerability to these conditions. Thus, the question emerges about the risks of prescribing marijuana to individuals struggling with symptoms of intense anxiety or depression.

Registered Nurse Ron Marczyk, a retired high school health teacher, states that growing evidence over the past decade supports the need for human trials to test the use of medical marijuana as a psychiatric treatment. He asserts that the "75 years of (mis)information we have been fed" is unequivocally untrue. Marczyk explains that medical evidence now points to a new treatment paradigm in which medical cannabinoids are seen as healing the brain by strengthening the tone of CB1 and CB2 receptors, perhaps by boosting retrograde signal strength that shuts down anxiety and depression and resets the system. Marczyk characterizes cannabinoid-based medicines as a new generation of psychiatric medications, contending that the safety of cannabis is unparalleled, with no reported deaths attributed to its medical use.

Psychiatrist Robert Berezin is strongly critical of the view that marijuana is a substance with little potential for harm. Rather, he views it as a component of a substance abuse epidemic that has become incredibly destructive to the well-being of society. He highlights the irony of a society going to great lengths to curtail the use of nicotine while legalizing the "far more destructive" substance of marijuana. Highlighting the fact that contemporary marijuana is much more potent than the drug of previous decades, he objects to the characterization of marijuana as a "junior drug" which has slid under the radar. Rather than viewing this drug as innocuous, Berezin expresses alarm about the psychotropic effects that are destructive to an individual's personality and the processing of experience.

Dr. Berezin discusses the clinical case of Eddie who turned to marijuana to treat his feelings of emptiness and loneliness. Rather than alleviating Eddie's symptoms, marijuana contributed to his emotional shutdown, and evoked serious problems in his psychological functioning. Eddie purportedly became dependent on marijuana "to inflate his burgeoning and false sense of superiority. . . . [It] also amplified his sensations, which gave him a false feeling of participation and engagement in life." Berezin speaks about Eddie as having developed "marijuana brain" from which it took him a full year to recover. Generalizing from the case of Eddie and from his extensive clinical experience as a psychiatrist, Dr. Berezin expresses concern that the legalization of marijuana represents a sanctioning of a destructive "alteration in consciousness, which makes users passive, removed, intellectualized, falsely special, and not equipped to take on the challenges of life." He is especially alarmed about the use of marijuana by teens whose brains are still developing.

YES

Ron Marczyk

Worth Repeating: Marijuana Treats Anxiety and Depression

Welcome to Room 420, where your instructor is Mr. Ron Marczyk and your subjects are wellnesss, disease prevention, self actualization, and chillin'.

This post is dedicated to these two great medical researchers. The fathers of homeostatic cannabinoid based medicine:

Lumír Ondřej Hanuš, discoverer of the endogenous ligand, anandamide, from the brain (1992) and Raphael Mechoulam, discoverer of the psychoactive compound, THC, from Cannabis sativa (1964). Both compounds bind to the CB1 and 2 cannabinoid receptors in the brain.

These two men need to be nominated and awarded the 2012 Nobel Prize in medicine for discovering the healing potential of cannabis. Their discoveries will save the human race a great deal of suffering. Thank you for your gift to humanity, gentlemen.

Nobel ballots open this summer!

The "cannabinoid homeostatic healing perspective" has quietly been gathering evidence over the last 10 years which overwhelmingly supports the need for human trials to test the use of medical marijuana as a psychiatric treatment. The 75 years of (mis)information we have been fed is now being shown to be unequivocally untrue.

Yes, Big Pharma pushes drugs on us, but is there a large, legitimate need for an agent to heal our modern anxieties? Is this really a problem? Yes! The need for newer, second generation, nontoxic psychiatric medicines clearly exists, as seen in these health stories.

"One in Five American Adults Takes Psychiatric Drugs" (*Wall Street Journal*)

Epidemic? Half of US teens 'meet criteria for mental disorder' (*Raw Story*)

"Drugs Found Ineffective for Veterans stress" (*New York Times*)

"Medical marijuana: medical necessity versus political agenda" (*Medical Science Monitor*)

"Despite supporting evidence, the DEA refuses to reclassify marijuana as a Schedule II drug, which would allow physicians to prescribe marijuana to suffering patients," and . . .

"After reviewing relevant scientific data and grounding the issue in ethical principles like beneficence and nonmaleficence, there is a strong argument for allowing physicians to prescribe marijuana. *Patients have a right to all beneficial treatments and to deny them this right violates their basic human rights.*"

Government prejudice and bias aside, here is what the latest research has concluded . . .

From "The therapeutic potential of the endocannabinoid system for the development of a novel class of antidepressants" *Trends in Pharmacological Sciences*/2009—Laboratory of Neuroendocrinology, The Rockefeller University, New York

"Substantial evidence has accumulated implicating a deficit in endocannabinoid in the etiology of depression; accordingly, pharmacological augmentation of endocannabinoid signaling could be a novel target for the pharmacotherapy of depression."

"Within preclinical models, facilitation of endocannabinoid neurotransmission evokes both antidepressant and anxiolytic effects. Similar to the actions of conventional antidepressants, enhancement of endocannabinoid signaling can enhance serotonergic and noradrenergic transmission; increase cellular plasticity and neurotrophin expression (brain growth factor) within the hippocampus; and dampen activity within the neuroendocrine stress axis."

"Furthermore, limbic endocannabinoid activity is increased by both pharmacological and somatic treatments for depression, and, in turn, appears to contribute to some of the neuroadaptive alterations elicited by these treatments." (*Read = cannabinoids heal the brain*)

"These preclinical findings support the rationale for the clinical development of agents which inhibit the cellular uptake and/or metabolism of endocannabinoids in the treatment of mood disorders."

From "Endocannabinoids and stress" *Stress: The International Journal on the Biology of Stress*/July 2011—Max Planck Institute of Psychiatry Munich, Germany

"Endocannabinoid (eCB) signaling serves to maintain HPA-axis homeostasis, by buffering basal activity as well as by mediating glucocorticoid fast feedback mechanisms. Following chronic stressor exposure." . . .

"Investigation into the role of the endocannabinoid system in allostatic states and recovery processes may give insight into possible therapeutic manipulations of the system in treating chronic stress-related conditions in humans."

Conclusions from "Endocannabinoid-mediated modulation of stress responses: physiological and pathophysiological significance" *Immunobiology*/August 2010.

"The endogenous cannabinoid (endocannabinoid) system has emerged as an important lipid signaling system playing a key role in mediating and/or modulating behavioural, neurochemical, neuroendocrine, neuroimmune and molecular responses to stress."

". . . The goal now should be to exploit our understanding of the role of the endocannabinoid system in fundamental stress physiology and pathophysiological processes to better understand and treat a range of stress-related disorders including anxiety, depression and pain."

And beyond healing the brain, can cannabinoids therapy through plasticity create optimal human emotional wellness by stimulating flow, and peak experiences which lead to personal self-actualization?

First, some health background.

Allostasis is the process of achieving *stability, or homeostasis*, through physiological or behavioral change.

In addition, it is a process of reestablishing homeostasis. This theory suggests that both homeostasis and allostasis are endogenous systems responsible for maintaining the internal stability of an organism.

Allostatic load is defined as the physiological consequences of chronic exposure to fluctuating or heightened neural or neuroendocrine response that results from repeated or chronic stress.

This term is used to explain how frequent activation of the body's stress response, essential for managing acute threats, can in fact damage the body in the long run. Allostatic load is generally measured through a composite index of indicators (stressors) of cumulative strain on several organs and tissues, but especially on the cardiovascular system (HPA) and immune system.

The biological organism that you are has an internal environment necessary for life that must find a homeostatic relationship with the outside environment. When these two environments are in balance, so are you.

Because these two environments are moving targets, maintaining this synchronization is constant work. There are many things you must do on a daily basis to maintain your health: being a human is very high maintenance!

The daily physical, emotional, and cognitive energy one must generate to maintain this balanced allostatic load is the very definition of health.

Humans experience stress, or perceive things as threatening, when they do not believe that their resources for coping with obstacles (stimuli, people, situations, etc.) are enough for what the circumstances demand. Remember, attitude is everything.

Stress is defined as anything that causes an organism to change or adapt to a new challenge from one or both of these environments.

Two major systems controlled by the ECS are the reaction to stress and control of your immune system. These two systems function in tandem.

The multitude of events changing around you and to which you must adapt every day are called stressors. Evidence shows that prolonged, unrelieved stress down-regulates the ECS over time.

Long-term, unresolved stress and anxiety leads to depression, represented by exhaustion in the chart.

On the day you can no longer maintain ongoing homeostasis with the environment you start to decline in overall health and, over time, die.

Researchers are starting to use the phrase CB1/CB2 "tone" to describe how well this retrograde feedback loop "anandamide-FAAH-CB1-CB2 receptor pathway" is doing its job.

The "tone" of the CB1 and CB2 receptors is controlled by a naturally named molecule called anandamide. The endocannabinoid system (ECS) controls every major body system. It is a major feedback master control system whose job it is to bring homeostasis to individual systems and to all body systems together/ It's that important.

The medical evidence that has gathered in the last 10 years points strongly to a new treatment paradigm in which medical cannabinoids heal the brain by strengthening the tone of CB1 and CB2 receptors; it is perhaps the boost in this retrograde signal strength that shuts down anxiety and depression and resets the system.

Will plant-based cannabinoids become front-line medications to treat mood disorders, anxiety, PTSD in the near future? Clearly, the evidence supports cannabinoid-based medicines as the new second generation psychiatric medications.

Big Phama thinks so, too, and is already positioning itself to step in. By the way, just how many sprays of Sativex under your tongue do you think it will take to relieve anxiety and depression?

The job of the endocannabinoid system has now been firmly established as that of a "gatekeeper" that maintains homeostasis in every major body system.

It has now been verified that CB2 receptors are widely distributed throughout the brain.

"We demonstrated that CB2 receptors and their gene transcripts are widely distributed in the brain. This multifocal expression of CB2 immunoreactivity in brain suggests that CB2 receptors may play broader roles in the brain than previously anticipated and may be exploited as new targets in the treatment of depression and substance abuse."

CB1 and CB2 receptors found at the synaptic cleft monitor electrical traffic being transmitted along the axon of the neuron and send a "retrograde" or backwards signal to dampen down impulses that would overload the system. It has been described as a neural circuit breaker "by buffering basal activity as well as by mediating glucocorticoid fast feedback mechanisms."

From "Functional interactions between stress and the endocannabinoid system: from synaptic signaling to behavioral output" *The Journal of Neuroscience*/November 2010 Laboratory of Neuroendocrinology, the Rockefeller University, New York.

"*Endocannabinoid signaling is distributed throughout the brain, regulating synaptic release of both excitatory and inhibitory neurotransmitters.*"

"The evidence reviewed here demonstrates that endocannabinoid signaling is involved in both repeated stress and activating and terminating the hypothalamic-pituitary-adrenal axis (below) response to both acute and repeated stress."

"In addition to neuroendocrine function, however, endocannabinoid signaling is also recruited by stress and glucocorticoid hormones to modulate cognitive and emotional processes such as memory consolidation and extinction." (Important for PTSD)

"*Collectively, these data demonstrate the importance of endocannabinoid signaling at multiple levels as both a regulator and an effector of the stress response*".

Cannabinoids acting though the ECS dampen down glutamate, which excites cells in your muscle to contract when alarmed. The flight or flight reaction is correctly called the "general adaptive syndrome."

Cannabis's safety profile is unparalleled. Its use has caused *zero deaths* since they have been keeping records! It should be the medicine all others are measured against for producing harm.

Again, for the US government to block research and deny free access to medical marijuana is a violation of basic human rights. To ignore empirically based medical proof in order to protect special interests and to play politics with people's lives is the very definition of ignorance.

Pain in life is inevitable, but suffering is optional. Right view! Right view!

Every day is a ganja day! Maintain—Ron

Ron Marczyk is a retired high school health education teacher, a former New York City police office, a registered nurse with six years of ER/critical care experience in New York City hospitals, and currently focuses on how evolutionary psychology explains human behavior.

Robert Berezin

 **NO**

It's Time to Address the Marijuana Issue

To Put It Simply, "What Are We Thinking?"

The substance abuse epidemic is so incredibly destructive to the well-being of our society—to our children, our adolescents, as well as adults. It is problematic enough to deal with the hard drugs—heroin, cocaine, etc.; prescription drug abuse—the opiates, amphetamines; never mind the psychiatric pharmaceuticals—the antidepressants, benzodiazepines, sleeping pills, etc.; and of course alcoholism. While we are going to great lengths to curtail cigarettes and nicotine, we are legalizing marijuana which is far more destructive. We in the psychiatric, psychological, and social work professions need to be active and clear in addressing this pressing issue.

I am limiting my focus to marijuana itself—THC and other cannabinoids, not to the social issues. Marijuana is a psychoactive drug. It is a mild to moderate hallucinogen. While not physically addictive it is powerfully habituating. And the marijuana of today is not your father's marijuana. It is far, far stronger.

As a psychiatrist I have treated all of the addictions. And marijuana usage has gotten a pass. It has slid under the radar and is somehow considered a junior drug, so it doesn't count. In fact, because of its psychotropic effects it is very distorting and destructive to the personality. Habitual marijuana use affects the brain. It affects the processing of experience by our consciousness. The altered top-down processing affects the play of consciousness itself. In order for psychotherapy to proceed, a patient has to be marijuana free. I will give an example of the marijuana issue in psychotherapy from my book about my patient, Eddie.

Eddie said that for some time, smoking pot had made him "paranoid." This was actually a marijuana anxiety state. Even though it no longer worked and despite the amplification of anxiety, Eddie had kept right on smoking, trying to recapture his earlier positive experiences. Since he was such a veteran smoker, he also felt ashamed of the marijuana anxiety itself.

Eddie turned to marijuana to fortify himself, to fill his emptiness and loneliness, and to inflate his ego. Cigarettes worked up to a point. Always a smoker, Eddie increased his smoking to over a pack a day. The process of smoking, filling the lungs, coincides with the physical location in the body for the feeling of emptiness. It is felt in the chest. Eddie filled his emptiness with a drug. Nicotine also has the drug effect of constricting the arterioles all over the body. This physical shutdown at every capillary mimicked a physical holding, which fortified and fed his emotional shutdown. Marijuana worked even better—a psychotropic, also inhaled. His lungs, full of THC smoke, was a full-filling experience. He felt that it stimulated his creativity. He believed it made him a deeper and creative thinker, the very attributes he felt were missing in himself. Marijuana fostered his specialness, which had already become the criteria for his value as a person. And he quickly became dependent on it to inflate his burgeoning and false sense of superiority. Marijuana also amplified his sensations, which gave him a false feeling of participation and engagement in life. He often smoked before social situations to undo being exposed as lacking and worthless, and to diminish his social anxiety. Eddie had no access to an inner voice saying, "Wait a minute—what am I doing?" He went the other way: "This stuff is great." He was actively seeking a drug to enhance his sense of specialness. Marijuana fortified his decision to harden himself emotionally, by numbing himself from human feeling. I feel good. I feel great. I don't need anybody. I'm superior.

Marijuana has a characteristic effect on consciousness itself. It promotes a disjunction between thinking and feeling. It distanced Eddie from participation in his feelings, which he was wont to do in the first place. His thinking, ungrounded in feeling, was free to roam, untethered. In its early phases, this promoted a sense of creativity, due to the liberated ability of his mind to roam free and unanchored. It also fostered obsessional and intellectualized "insights." Marijuana intellectualization was disconnected from feeling. And as we know, feeling is the anchor of the characterological play. This became an organizing feature of the neuronal loops of his experience and warped the workings of his consciousness. Through habitual usage, this "marijuana mind," was established in him, whether he was smoking or not.

Eddie took for granted that therapy was about intellectualized insights. (This is a common assumption, which is unfortunately all too frequently shared by many therapists.) This decidedly is not the case. Eddie's pride in his intellectualized insights was problematic for the therapy because it interfered with real engagement. Eddie valued his insights as special and impressive. His compensatory identity as superior was attached to being a user of not only marijuana but the other hallucinogens as well. And finally, marijuana served to heighten his senses. As a result, Eddie felt super-participatory in sensory experience. This was compensatory for Eddie's sense of removal as the observer/outsider he normally felt himself to be.

As is typical, in order for Eddie's brain to work right again, it took him a full year to recover from habitual marijuana usage. This was not about detoxing it out of his system—that took place fairly quickly. Likewise, it was not a physiological dependence. The issue was marijuana's effects on his consciousness and a psychological dependence on this valued cast of mind which I call "marijuana brain."

Now it is certainly true that not every smoker gets marijuana anxiety, but it is very common. And even more important, this psychotropic drug effects the brain of every smoker. With the legalization of marijuana we are sanctioning this destructive alteration of consciousness, which makes users passive, removed, intellectualized, falsely special, and not equipped to take on the challenges of life with our full and unadulterated where-with-all. This is especially so in the developing brain and consciousness of teenagers, never mind the altered brains of adults. As a society we are supposed to foster the full and best development of our children into capable, responsible, caring adults. We need to oppose the use of marijuana, not foster it.

Robert Berezin, MD, is the author of *Psychotherapy of Character: The Play of Consciousness in the Theater of the Brain.*

EXPLORING THE ISSUE

Should Medical Marijuana Be Prescribed for the Treatment of Emotional Disorders?

Critical Thinking and Reflection

1. What criteria should be used in determining the appropriateness of marijuana vs. traditional medications for the treatment of emotional disorders?
2. What risk factors should be considered when prescribing marijuana for emotional disorders (e.g., genetic vulnerability to psychosis, etc.)?
3. How would you design a research program to assess the therapeutic benefits of marijuana for treating emotional disorders?
4. What social costs, if any, might develop as a result of promoting marijuana as a treatment for emotional disorders?
5. What factors may have contributed to the reluctance of society to legalize marijuana?

Is There Common Ground?

Ron Marczyk and Robert Berezin would concur with the premise that considerable misinformation has been disseminated over the past several decades about marijuana. However, Marczyk contends that the misinformation has involved exaggerated assertions about the risks of marijuana, while Berezin believes that many people in society have been led to believe that contemporary marijuana is as innocuous of that distributed decades earlier. Both authors would probably support scientifically sound research efforts to assess the benefits as well as the risks of marijuana use, particularly in individuals struggling with emotional disorders.

Both Marczyk and Berezin would support efforts to find interventions for alleviating distress for individuals suffering with serious emotional disorders such as debilitating anxiety and depression. They would disagree, however, about the appropriateness of a substance such as marijuana as an intervention of choice for such individuals.

Create Central

www.mhhe.com/createcentral

Additional Resources

Backes, M. (2013). *Cannabis Pharmacy: The Practical Guide to Medical Marijuana*. New York, NY: Black dog & Leventhal Publishers.

Campos, A. C., Moreira, F. A., Gomes, F. V., Del Bel, E. A., & Guimarães, F. S. (2012). Multiple mechanisms involved in the large-spectrum therapeutic potential of cannabidiol in psychiatric disorders. *Philosophical Transactions of the Royal Society B: Biological Sciences*, *367*(1607), 3364–3378. doi:10.1098/rstb.2011.0389

Castle, D. J., Murray, R. M., & D'Souza, D. C. (2012). *Marijuana and Madness*. Cambridge: Cambridge University Press.

Kweskin, S. (2013, July 1). The dope on medical cannabis: Results of a survey of psychiatrists. *Psychiatric Times*. Retrieved April 28, 2014, from http://www.psychiatrictimes.com/substance-use-disorder/dope-medical-cannabis-results-survey-psychiatrists

Martin, M., Rosenthal, E., & Carter, G. T. (2011). *Medical Marijuana 101*. Oakland, CA: Quick American Archives.

Spiegel, J. (2013, March 11). Medical marijuana for psychiatric disorders. *Psychology Today*. Retrieved April 28, 2013, from http://www.psychologytoday .com/blog/mind-tapas/201303/medical-marijuana-psychiatric-disorders

Zaman, T., Rosenthal, R., Jr., J. R., Kleber, H., & Millin, R. (2013, November 25). Resource document on marijuana as medicine. *APA Position Statements*. Retrieved April 28, 2014, from http://www .psych.org/advocacy--newsroom/position-statements

Internet References . . .

American Psychiatric Association

http://www.psychiatry.org/

National Institute of Mental Health

http://www.nimh.nih.gov/index.shtml

National Institute on Drug Abuse

http://www.drugabuse.gov

Unit 3

UNIT

Social, Ethical, and Legal Issues

*M*any issues in the field of abnormal psychology interface with social issues, ethical concerns, and legal matters, with heated debate emerging about topics pertaining to efforts to protect personal rights while also being responsive to societal concerns. Some of these issues are serious, and find their way to the judicial system where debates about psychological experiences provide the basis for arguments in court, as has been the case with lawsuits about limiting the sale of violent video games to minors, the ability of mentally ill convicts to understand why they are being sentenced to death, the use of aversive treatments for people who engage in self-harming behaviors, or the forced medicating of severely mentally ill individuals. Legal and legislative battles have also raged about abortion, and psychologists have been called upon to present evaluative summaries of research on potential psychological effects on a woman who undergoes an abortion. Legislative debates have also focused on whether gay conversion therapy should be outlawed, gun ownership should be restricted, recreational drugs should be legalized, and whether energy drinks containing alcohol should be banned.

Selected, Edited, and with Issue Framing Material by:
Richard P. Halgin, *University of Massachusetts, Amherst*

ISSUE

Does Research Confirm That Violent Video Games Are Harmful to Minors?

YES: Leland Y. Yee and Steven F. Gruel, from "Brief of *Amicus Curiae* in Case of *Brown v. Entertainment Merchants Association*," U.S. Supreme Court (2010)

NO: Patricia A. Millett, from "Brief of *Amici Curiae* in *Brown v. Entertainment Merchants Association*," U.S. Supreme Court (2010)

Learning Outcomes

After reading this issue, you should be able to:

- Discuss and critically evaluate the arguments about the strength of scientific evidence that either supports or discredits the relationship between playing violent video games and engaging in aggressive behavior among youth.
- Understand the ways in which playing video games can influence neurological structure and functioning.
- Evaluate the extent to which playing violent video games by young people can lead to academic problems.
- Compare the rationale used by the government to regulate other media such as television and radio and the arguments made for and against the regulation of violent video game sales to children.
- Consider the similarities and differences between passively watching a violent movie and actively participating in a violent video game.

ISSUE SUMMARY

YES: California State Senator Leland Yee and Attorney Steven F. Gruel (Counsel of Record for the professional associations in pediatrics and psychology) contend that substantial research shows that violent video games can cause psychological or neurological harm to minors. Studies have shown that, in addition to fostering aggressive thought and behavior, ultra-violent video games can lead to reduced activity in the frontal lobes of the brain as well as behavioral problems such as antisocial behavior and poor school performance. Senator Yee and Attorney Gruel believe that the government has a duty to protect children, and that the First Amendment of the U.S. Constitution, with regard to free speech, should not be used to place at risk immature children who cannot discern the difference between fantasy and reality.

NO: Attorney Patricia A. Millett (Counsel of Record for the amicus curiae submitted on behalf of the Entertainment Merchants Association) argues that there is insufficient evidence to show that violent video games can cause psychological or neurological harm to minors. Attorney Millett claims that the various studies cited in the opposing amicus curiae are either flawed or have been discredited. She also asserts that studies have shown no compelling causal connections between playing violent video games and aggressive or antisocial behavior in youths.

In recent years, video games have caught the attention of the public because of various reports about violent and sexually explicit imagery contained in products sold to young people. The debate about the potential impact of exposure to aggressive or sexually explicit media has raged for decades, with social critics expressing great concern about the impact on young people who seem to be flooded with images that would have been unimaginable 30 years ago. American society has become increasingly tolerant of violent movies, some of which have developed cult-like followings. Violent movies with scenes of maiming, torture, sexual assault, and murder, which might have been censored in the twentieth century, are now common, and some have even become the basis of cinematic parody.

As society seems to have become desensitized to violence in the movies, shifts have also taken place in the extremity of violence in video games. Social science researchers and neuroscientists have been recruited to study the extent to which playing such games negatively influences behavior and causes changes in the brain. Special concern has focused on the effects on children for whom perceptual experiences influence the development of personality as well as brain functioning. The challenges of conducting such research are understandably formidable. How does a social science researcher determine that Joey's misbehavior in school on Monday is related to his playing a violent video game the day before? How does a neuroscientist assess the relationship between Jane's abnormal brain functioning and her exposure to video game violence? Lacking clear answers to such questions, legislators face a difficult task in any attempt to regulate the sale of violent video games to minors. Critics of such proposed legislation, such as companies that develop and sell these games, are likely to employ two arguments: (1) research cannot demonstrate a causal connection between playing violent video games and aggressive behavior or abnormal brain functioning, and (2) the U.S. Constitution protects the dissemination of media that has not been proven to be harmful.

Senator Leland Yee, who has a doctorate in developmental psychology, has long opposed the sale of violent video games to children. In his role on the San Francisco Board of Education and through his work in various mental health settings, Dr. Yee has had a long history of working on behalf of children and becoming aware of the forces in society that can have detrimental impact on them. Thus, it is not surprising that he would submit a brief reflecting efforts to protect minors from harm that could result from playing violent video games. The argument is made that research demonstrates that participating in the playing of violent video games by children increases aggressive thought and behavior, increases antisocial behavior and delinquency, engenders poor school performance, and desensitizes the game player to violence.

In the brief submitted by Senator Yee, neuroscience research is also cited about brain effects resulting from exposure to violent video games. For example, functional magnetic resonance imaging (fMRI) research points to a relationship between alterations in brain functioning and exposure to media violence. Namely, teenagers who played a violent video game exhibited increased activity in a part of the brain that governs emotional arousal, and decreased activity in the parts of the brain involved in focus, inhibition, and concentration.

One argument against the sale of violent video games to minors highlights the difference between passive exposure to violence, such as watching a movie, and the active engagement involved in playing a video game in which the participant is a shooter who personally decides whether to pull the trigger and whether to kill or not. The implication is that a young person who is "shooting" and "assaulting" via a role play is much more powerfully affected by this behavior than would be a young person watching such behaviors in a movie.

Aside from the debate about the psychological and neurological effects of playing violent video games, there is debate about the legality of restricting their sale to any person, including a minor. Does the U.S. Constitution view the distribution of violent video games as being protected by the First Amendment? Senator Yee points to restrictions on the sale of alcohol, tobacco, and firearms to minors as providing justification for such restrictions on the sale of violent video games to impressionable young people.

The NO side of the argument emerges primarily from the premise that research is seriously deficient in demonstrating a causal relationship between the playing of violent video games and aggressive behavior or brain changes. As any beginning psychology student knows, correlation does not equal causation. In other words, is Joey aggressive because he plays violent video games, or is Joey an aggressive boy by nature who finds that playing violent video games is fun? In the brief submitted by Attorney Millett on behalf of the Entertainment Merchants Association, the argument is made that the courts should reject the studies submitted as evidence of a relationship between violent video games and aggressive behavior, contending that those studies do not even establish correlation, much less causation. Thus, arguers on this side of the debate assert that, in order to demonstrate such a relationship, substantial scientific evidence must be presented in order to validate the claim that violent video games cause psychological harm or neurological effects to minors. Attorney Millett contends that the scientific evidence submitted has failed to substantiate those claims.

In criticizing research pointing to a relationship between violent video games and changes in brain functioning, Attorney Millett asserts that, while fMRI studies may indicate areas of the brain that decrease in activation during a task, it is not yet understood how brain activation is influenced by neural development in children. Furthermore, because fMRI studies depend on statistical analysis, it is possible that errors in the procedure of analysis may undermine the reliability of the results.

YES

Leland Y. Yee and Steven F. Gruel

Brief of *Amicus Curiae* in Case of *Brown v. Entertainment Merchants Association*

Summary of Argument

By any measure, California has a compelling interest in protecting the physical and psychological care of minors. When juxtaposed against the backdrop of protecting the First Amendment, this Court has held that the Constitution does not confer the protection on communication aimed at children as it does for adults. When weighing the conflicting concerns of minors this Court correctly carved a flexible standard of review and not a strict scrutiny approach. We know, of course, that a state can prohibit the sale of sexually-explicit material to minors under a "variable obscenity" or "obscenity as to minors" standard. *Ginsberg v. New York*, 390 U.S. 629 (1968). Just as it was rational for the State to conclude that that type of material was harmful to minors, the restrictions to assist parents in protecting their children's well-being is, in a practical sense, no different than the concerns supporting California's enactment of California Civil Code Sections 1746–1746.5.

Indeed, restricting the sale and rental of extremely violent interactive videos to minors advances the very same societal interests understood in *Ginsberg*. Contrary to the Ninth Circuit's perception, *Ginsberg* was not meant to exclusively apply to sexually explicit materials, but can and should apply to equally harmful materials depicting violence. *Video Software Dealers Association v. Schwarzenegger*, 556 F.3d 950 (9th Cir. 2009).

Needless to say, the world is much different today than it was in 1968 when *Ginsberg* was decided. What *has* remained for the past 40 years, however, is the common-sense understanding that the First Amendment does not protect materials harmful to minors.

In 2006, a Federal Trade Commission study revealed that nearly 70 percent of 13 to 16 year olds are able to successfully purchase Mature or M-rated video games. These M-rated games, labeled by the industry as such in an attempt to voluntarily "police" the distribution of harmful videos, are designed specifically for adults. The content in these types of games enable the user to murder, burn, and maim law enforcement officers, racial minorities, and members of clergy as well as sexually assault women.

In his March 29, 2006 testimony submitted to the Subcommittee on the Constitution, Civil Rights, and Property Rights of the United States Senate Judiciary Committee, Senator Yee noted that the interactive nature of video games is vastly different than passively listening to music, watching a movie, or reading a book. With interactive video games, the child becomes a part of the action which serves as a potent agent to facilitate violence, and over time learns the destructive behavior. This immersion results in a more powerful experience and potentially dangerous learned behavior in children and youth. In fact, often times it is the same technology that our military and police use to simulate and train for real life battle conditions and violent law enforcement confrontations in the community.

Moreover, there is a practical side in favor of the State's effort to regulate the sale or rental of violent video games to children. Parents can read a book, watch a movie or listen to a CD to discern if it is appropriate for their child. These violent video games, on the other hand, can contain up to 800 hours of footage with the most atrocious content often reserved for the highest levels that can be accessed only by advanced players after hours upon hours of progressive mastery.

Just as the technology of video games improves at astonishing rates, so too does the body of research consistently demonstrate the harmful effects these violent interactive games have on minors. Hundreds of peer-reviewed studies, produced over a period of 30 years documenting the effects of screen violence (including violent video games), have now been published in the professional journals of the American Academy of Pediatrics, American

U.S. Supreme Court, 2010.

Academy of Child and Adolescent Psychiatry, American Psychological Association, American Medical Association, American Academy of Family Physicians, and the American Psychiatric Association and others.

This *amicus* brief includes some of the most recent research addressing this serious concern including a meta-analysis of approximately 130 studies pertaining to the effects of playing violent video games which was published in March 2010.

These data continually and strongly suggest that participating in the playing of violent video games by children increases aggressive thought and behavior; increases antisocial behavior and delinquency; engenders poor school performance; and desensitizes the game player to violence.

Notably, extended play has been observed to depress activity in the frontal cortex of the brain which controls executive thought and function, produces intentionality and the ability to plan sequences of action, and is the seat of self-reflection, discipline and self-control.

Also, United States Surgeon General David Satcher warned in his Report on Youth Violence (2000) of a demonstrated link between screen violence and subsequent physical aggression in children and adolescents that is stronger than the link between secondhand smoke and cancer.

Finally, new data shows that the intensity of interactive video games may be habituating and that 2 to 3 hour sessions of intense interactions with video games raise adrenaline levels in children and produces extended physiological arousal. In the medical community concern has been raised at prolonged and regularly repeated states of adrenalized arousal and hyper-vigilance involved in children watching violent video games and the possible harmful effects on still developing bodies and brains.

These studies demonstrate that playing ultra-violent games can cause automatic aggressiveness, increase aggressive thoughts and behavior, antisocial behavior, desensitization, poor school performance and reduced activity in the frontal lobes of the brain.

As a society, we understand the clear unequivocal commonsense reasons to prohibit the sale of alcohol, tobacco, firearms, driver's licenses and pornography to minors. That same reasoning applies in the foundation and enactment of California Civil Code Sections 1746–1746.5. Given that the First Amendment does not protect the State's restriction on the sale or rental of harmful violent video games to minors, the Court should reverse the decision of the Ninth Circuit Court of Appeals and uphold the California law as a statutory safeguard necessary in this modern day world.

Argument

I. This Court Has Acknowledged Society's Rational and Compelling Interest in Distinguishing and Limiting the Rights Enjoyed by Minors.

This Court has long agreed that there is an overriding justification in protecting children from conduct pervasive in society. Without question, restricting a minor's access to gambling, smoking and alcohol serve the community's interest in both protecting a minor's development as well as safeguarding against the individual and widespread collateral consequences which flow from a minor's early addiction to these vices.

As a general proposition, many constitutional rights vary in the degree to which the exercise of the right by minors is protected from government abridgment. For example, minors do not have the right to exercise the franchise. Similarly, a minor's right to have an abortion may be subject to regulations that would be rejected as unduly burdensome if they were applied to adult women. Thus, there is a recognized foundation for distinguishing between minors and adults in analyzing the constitutionality of regulations.

This foundation comports with the commonsense intuition that, because children lack maturity to make wise judgments, their autonomy deserves less respect from the state than does the autonomy of adults. While paternalistic state regulations are correctly viewed as demeaning when applied to adults, there are considered appropriate, if not necessary, for children.

In *Ginsberg,* of course, this Court concluded that the State had greater authority to limit the exercise of protected freedoms because children were involved and, in relying on its precedents, recognized that "the State has an interest 'to protect the welfare of children' and to see that they are 'safeguarded from abuses' which might prevent 'their growth into free and independent well-developed men and citizens.'"

As it relates to expressive materials, there is no language from this Court suggesting that the State's interest in protecting minors from such material *is limited* to speech with sexual content. In *Erznoznik v. City of Jacksonville,* a case concerning restrictions on films depicting nudity from being shown in drive-in movies, the Court was unwilling to protect minors from brief exposure to such images.

However, the alleged harm caused by the minimal exposure to nude images a child passing by a drive-in theater might witness cannot realistically be compared to harm resulting from repeated and long-term exposure to violent video games. In fact, in *FCC v. Pacifica Foundation,*

438 U.S. 726 (1978), this Court supported an FCC determination that the radio broadcast of a George Carlin monologue containing "filthy words" could be restricted precisely because it was accessible to young children.

Children, this Court has acknowledged, are different in the eyes of the law because of brain development. *Ropers v. Simmons,* 543 U.S. 551 (2005). Under the "evolving standards of decency" test, the *Ropers* Court held that it was cruel and unusual punishment to execute a person who was under the age of 18 at the time of the murder. Writing for the majority, Justice Kennedy cited a body of sociological and scientific research that found that juveniles have a lack of maturity and sense of responsibility compared to adults. Adolescents were found to be over-represented statistically in virtually every category of reckless behavior.

In *Ropers,* the Court noted that in recognition of the comparative immaturity and irresponsibility of juveniles, almost every state prohibited those under age 18 from voting, serving on juries, or marrying without parental consent. The studies also found that juveniles are also more vulnerable to negative influences and outside pressures, including peer pressure. They have less control, or experience with control, over their own environment. More recently, in *Graham v. Florida,* 130 S.Ct. 2011 (2010) this Court used the same rationale in finding that some life sentences without parole for minors were unconstitutional. This unequivocal commonsense approach by the Court to constitutional matters and children should be likewise applied in addressing the deepening dangers to minors from violent video games.

In sum, "[A] state or municipality can adopt more stringent controls on communicative materials available to youths than on those available to adults." *Erznoznik,* at 212.

Here, California's marginal control on the sale or rental of violent video games to minors is within the permissible advancement of a significant, if not compelling, public interest in protecting the development and mental health of minors.

California's concern for its minors in the modern violent video game world is not fanciful or without basis. Science supports the legislative public policy determination.

    II. Science Confirms That Violent Video Games Are Harmful to Minors Allowing the State Clear Justification in Regulating Children's Access to These Materials.
    1. Overview of Scientific Research Confirms Harmful Effects to Minors from Violent Video Games.

Testimony before Congress has elicited a large body of testimony by national experts, medical and mental health professional associations and others, the gist of which is that there is a significant relationship between exposure to media violence and aggressive behavior, and that repeated exposure leads to general increases in aggressiveness over time. The following testimony is typical:

> "Though there are many complexities in this realm of behavioral research, there is one clear and simple message that parents, educators, and public policy makers such as yourselves need to hear: Playing violent video games can cause increases in aggression and violence."

In October 2009, the American Academy of Pediatrics (AAP) issued its Policy Statement on Media Violence. The AAP, after considering the evidence from the extensive research on the effects of media violence, concluded that exposure to media violence, including playing violent video games, "represents a *significant risk to the health of children and adolescents.*" (emphasis added). Indeed, both before and since California's enactment of the statutes in this case, there have been hundreds of studies in the area of the effects of playing violent video games on children.

In fact, as part of this *amicus* brief, leading researchers, scholars and scientists from around the United States, Germany and Japan, who have studied the harmful effects of violent video game playing on minors, are submitting their Statement on Video Game Violence for this Court's consideration. *See* Appendix. Nearly 100 other leading researchers and scholars from around the globe have endorsed this Statement. *See* Endorsement list in Appendix. These researchers have clearly found harmful effects to minors in playing violent video games.

Repeatedly thinking about violent characters, choosing to be aggressive, enacting that aggressive choice, and being rewarded for it can be conceived as a series of learning trials influencing a variety of types of aggressive knowledge structures. *"Violent Video Games: Specific Effects of Violent Content on Aggressive Thoughts and Behavior,"* Advances in Experimental Social Psychology, Vol. 36 (2004).

The American Academy of Pediatrics also, with numerous others, concludes that exposure to violence in media, including violent video games, can contribute to aggressive behavior, desensitization to violence, nightmares and fear of being harmed. *"Media Violence,"* American Academy of Pediatrics, Volume 108, Number 5 (November 2001). The American Academy of Pediatrics found that American children between 2 and 18 years of age spend an average of 6 hours and 32 minutes each day using media, including video games.

Predicated on years of studies and research, in August 2005, the American Psychological Association formally recognized the serious negative impact of violent video games on this nation's children and passed its Resolution "On Violence in Video Games and Interactive Media."

These prestigious associations of experts concluded not only that there are long-term negative effects on children in playing these violent video games, but that the industry, the public, parents, caregivers and educational organizations had a responsibility to intercede in this epidemic.

The statute authored by Senator Yee which California enacted into law was a direct response to that alarm for state assistance given our children's unfettered access to violent video games. The First Amendment does not preclude the state action carefully crafted in this case.

2. A Minor's Exposure to Violent Video Games—
   More Time Spent Playing Games with Increasing Graphic Violence.

A minor's exposure to the avalanc[h]e of violent video games is staggering. Video games first emerged in the 1970s, but it was during the 1990s that violent games truly came of age. In 1992, *Wolfenstein 3D*, the first major "first-person shooter" game was released. In a first-person shooter, one "sees" the video game world through the eyes of the player, rather than seeing it as if looking on from afar. The player is the one fighting, killing, and being killed. Video game historian Steven Kent noted that "part of *Wolfenstein 3D* popularity sprang from its shock value. In *Wolfenstein 3D*, enemies fell and bled on the floor."

With ever changing advancements in technology, the dramatic increases in speed and graphic capability have resulted in more realistic violence. As an example, in the video game *Soldier of Fortune*, the player/shooter can wound an enemy causing exposed bone and sinew.

As the video games became more graphically violent, the average time children played these games continued to climb. In the book, *Violent Video Game Effects on Children and Adolescents*, the authors note that in the early 1990s, boys averaged 4 hours a week and girls 2 hours a week playing video games. In a few years these averages jumped to 7.1 and 4.5, respectively. In a recent survey of over 600 eighth-and ninth-grade students, children averaged 9 hours per week with boys averaging 13 hours per week and girls averaging 5 hours per week.

In 1993, United States Senators Joseph Lieberman and Herbert Kohl noticed the increasing violence in video games and held hearings to examine the issue. Although there was much less research on the effects of violent video games, the senators put pressure on the video game industry to create a rating system. The goal of the rating system was to provide information to parents about the content of games so that they could make informed decisions about which games their children could play. However, these industry "voluntary" labels rating video games are inherently flawed and have failed due to "invalid assumptions about what is safe versus harmful."

In 2003, more than 239 million computer and video games were sold in the United States; that is almost two games for every household in the United States. More than 90% of all U.S. children and adolescents play video games. The National Youth Violence Prevention Resource Center (2004) has stated that a 2001 review of the 70 top-selling video games found 49% contained serious violence. In 41% of the games, violence was necessary for the protagonists to achieve their goals. There is no doubt, violent video games are among the most popular entertainment products for teens and adolescents, especially for boys.

New generation violent video games contain substantial amounts of increasingly realistic portrayals of violence. Elaborate content analyses revealed that the favored narrative is a "human perpetrator engaging in repeated acts of justified violence involving weapons that results in some bloodshed to the victim."

3. Scientific Studies Confirm That Violent Video Games Have Harmful Effects [on] Minors.

In a nutshell, teens and adolescents play video games frequently, and a significant portion of the games contain increasingly realistic portrayals of violence. Viewing violence increases aggression and greater exposure to media violence is strongly linked to increases in aggression.

Playing a lot of violent games is unlikely to turn a normal youth with zero, one or even two other risk factors into a killer. But regardless of how many other risk factors are present in a youth's life, playing a lot of violent games is likely to increase the frequency and the seriousness of his or her physical aggression, both in the short term and over time as the youth grows up. These long-term effects are a consequence of powerful observational learning and desensitization processes that neuroscientists and psychologists now understand to occur automatically in the human child. Simply stated, "adolescents who expose themselves to greater amounts of video game violence were more hostile, reported getting into arguments with teachers more frequently, were more likely to be involved in physical fights, and performed more poorly in school.

In a recent book, researchers once again concluded that the "active participation" in all aspects of violence: decision-making and carrying out the violent act, result in a greater effect from violent video games than a violent movie. Unlike a passive observer in movie watching, in first-person shooter and third-person shooter games, you're the one who decides whether to pull the trigger or not and whether to kill or not. After conducting three very different kinds of studies (experimental, a cross-sectional correlational study, and a longitudinal study) the results confirmed that violent games contribute to violent behavior.

The relationship between media violence and real-life aggression is nearly as strong as the impact of cigarette smoking and lung cancer: not everyone who smokes will get lung cancer, and not everyone who views media violence will become aggressive themselves. However, the connection is significant.

In an upcoming publication concerning children and violent video games, three complementary theoretical perspectives are discussed when contemplating the effects of playing video games. The *General Aggression Model* and its offshoot the *General Learning Model* describe the basic learning processes and effects involved in both short-term and long-term effects of playing various types of games. The *Five Dimensions of Video Game Effects* perspective describes different aspects of video games and video game play that influence the specific effects likely to occur. The *Risk and Resilience* perspective describes the effects of video game play—prosocial, antisocial, and other—take place within a complex set of social and biological factors, each of which contribute to development of the individual's thoughts, feelings, and behaviors.

The main findings can be succinctly summarized: playing violent video games causes an increase in the likelihood of physically aggressive behavior, aggressive thinking, aggressive affect, physiological arousal, and desensitization/low empathy. It also decreases helpful or prosocial behavior. With the exception of physiological arousal (for which there are no cross-sectional or longitudinal studies), all of the outcome variables showed the same effects in experimental, cross-sectional, and longitudinal studies. The main effects occurred for both males and females, for participants from low-violence collectivistic type Eastern countries (*e.g.*, Japan), and from high-violence individualistic type Western countries (*e.g.*, USA, Europe).

Research also indicates that the aggression carried out by video game characters is usually portrayed as justified, retributional, necessary to complete the game, rewarded and followed by unrealistic consequences. The overall level and realism of violent depictions, use of guns and likelihood of being killed by a gun has risen substantially over time; additionally, female victims and police officer victims rose significantly across time.

Many researchers have begun studying the concept of video game "addiction" and most researchers studying the pathological use of computer or video games have defined it similarly to how pathological gambling is defined—based on damage to family, social, school, occupational, and psychological functioning. The pace of studies has increased greatly in the past decade. In 2007, the American Medical Association released a report on the "addictive potential" of video games. The report concluded with a recommendation that the "AMA strongly encourage the consideration and inclusion of 'Internet/video game addiction' as a formal diagnostic disorder in the upcoming revision of the *Diagnostic and Statistical Manual of Mental Disorders*-IV" (p. 7).

The most comprehensive study to date in the US used a national sample of over 1,100 youth aged 8 to 18, in which 8.5% of video game players were classified as pathological demonstrates that it is not a trivial number of people who are suffering damage to their lives because of their game play.

School Performance

Several studies have documented a negative relation between amount of time playing video games and school performance among children, adolescents, and college students. The displacement hypothesis, that games displace time on other activities, is the most typical explanation for this relation. It could be argued, however, that the relation might be due to the children themselves, rather than to game time. It is highly likely that children who perform more poorly at school are likely to spend more time playing games, where they may feel a sense of mastery that eludes them at school. Nevertheless, each hour a child spends playing entertainment games (in contrast to educational games, which have been demonstrated to have educational benefits) is an hour not spent on homework, reading, exploring, creating, or other things that might have more educational benefit. Some evidence has been found to support the displacement hypothesis. In one nationally representative US sample of 1,491 youth between 10 and 19, gamers spent 30% less time reading and 34% less time doing homework. Therefore, even if poor school performance tends to cause increases in time playing video games, large amounts of video game play are likely to further hurt their school performance.

In short, the recent explosion in research on video game effects has greatly improved our understanding of how this medium affects its consumers. Several conclusions can be drawn without any reasonable doubt. First, there are many different effects of playing video games on the player. Some of these are short term, whereas others are long term. Second, the specific effects depend on a host of factors, including the content, structure, and context of the game. Third, the same game can have multiple effects on the same person, some of which may be generally beneficial whereas others may be detrimental. Fourth, playing violent video games is a causal risk factor for a host of detrimental effects in both the short and the long term, including increasing the likelihood of physically aggressive behavior.

Negative Effects on the Brain

Studies have shown evidence that exposure to violent video games reduces the player's use of some brain areas involved in higher order thought and impulse control.

In addition to behavioral-psychological theories explaining the relationship between media violence exposure and aggressive behavior, recently attention has turned to neuro-psychological theories. These theories attempt to identify areas of brain functioning that may be affected by media violence exposure and that may underlie aggressive behavior.

As recently as June 2010, another study of violent video game effects on frontal lobe activity was published wherein it was concluded that playing a violent video game for only 30 minutes immediately produced lower activity levels (compared to a nonviolent video game) in prefrontal regions thought to be involved in cognitive inhibition. This study shows that playing a violent video game for 30 minutes causes a decrease in brain activity in a region of the frontal lobe that is known to be important in the ability to inhibit impulsive behavior. The study also suggested that that violent games may also impair emotional functioning when it noted that "an impaired role of DLPFC (dorsolateral prefrontal cortex) in inhibition, therefore, may yield impaired emotional functioning following violent video game play."

Other studies of the neurological underpinnings of aggressive behavior, for example, indicate that a neural circuit that includes parts of the frontal cortex, amygdala

and temporal lobes is important in emotional regulation and violence. Research strongly suggests an underactivity of brain inhibitory mechanisms in the frontal cortex and striatum, coupled with hyperarousal of the amygdala and temporal lobe regions, is responsible for chronic, explosive and/or severe aggressive behavior.

Research clearly indicates that areas in the frontal lobe and amygdale may be activated by viewing violent television and playing violent video games.

With the use of functional magnetic resonance imaging (fMRI), research has shown a direct alteration in brain functioning from exposure to media violence. Researchers found that teenagers who played a violent video game exhibited increased activity in a part of the brain that governs emotional arousal and the same teenagers showed decreased activity in the parts of the brain involved in focus, inhibition and concentration.

Youth who play a lot of violent video games (but who have not been diagnosed with a behavioral disorder) show a similar pattern of brain activity when doing complex executive control tasks as youth who have been diagnosed with some type of aggression-related behavior disorder. This pattern is very different from control-group youth who do not play a lot of violent games (and who have not been diagnosed with a behavioral disorder).

Youth who play a lot of violent video games show a deficit in a specific type of executive control known as proactive control. Proactive control is seen as necessary to inhibit impulsive reactions. This difference shows up in the brain wave patterns as well as in behavioral reactions.

Additionally, video game violence exposure and aggressive behavior to brain processes have been linked reflecting a desensitization in the aversive motivational system. Repeated exposure to media violence reduces its psychological impact and eventually produced aggressive approach-related motivational states theoretically leading to a stable increase in aggression.

Finally, in a functional magnetic resonance imaging study on players of the first-shooter game *Tactical Ops: Assault on Terror,* the violent portions of a video game activated the regions in the brain known to be active in fight-or-flight situations. In other words, the brain reacted to the fictional violence of a video game in much the same way as it reacts to real violence.

In short, neuroscience research supports a critical link between perpetration of virtual violence with reduced activation of a neural mechanism known to be important for self-control and for evaluation of affect. These findings strongly suggest that focusing on the activity of prefrontal cortical structures important for executive control could provide important mediational links in the relationship between exposure to violent media and increased aggression.

4. Recent Studies and Researchers Continue to Find Harmful Effects to Minors from Playing Violent Video Games

In March 2010, leading researchers in the area of media violence from the United States and Japan worked together to conduct a meta-analytic procedure testing the effects of violent games on aggressive behavior, aggressive cognition, aggressive affect, physiological arousal, empathy/desensitization, and prosocial behavior. In conducting [the] meta-analysis on the effects of video game violence, these researchers retrieved over 130 research reports which entailed scientific tests on over 130,000 participants. This study has been described as "probably about as exhaustive a sampling of the pre-2009 research literature as one could obtain and far more than that used in any other review of violent video game effects."

This extensive meta-analysis of the effects of violent video games confirms what many theories predicted and what prior research about other violent mass media found: that violent video games stimulate aggression in the players in the short run and increase the risk for aggression behaviors by the players later in life. The effects occur for males and females and for children growing up in Eastern and Western cultures. Also, the effects were stronger for more violent than less violent outcomes.

From their overarching analysis, these researchers concluded that the scientific debate should move beyond the simple question whether violent video game play is a causal risk factor for behavior because "scientific literature has effectively and clearly shown the answer to be 'yes.'"

Regardless of research method (experimental, correlational, or longitudinal) and regardless of cultures tested (East and West), the same effects are proven: exposure to violent video games is a causal risk factor for aggressive thoughts and behavior, and decreased empathy and prosocial behavior in youths. In fact, Dr. Anderson, one of three 2010 American Psychological Association Distinguished Scientist Lecturers, has stated that this recent meta-analysis on violent video games may be his last because of its "definitive findings."

5. The Shortcomings of Purported "Research" Contesting the Scientific Studies Showing the Harmful Effects to Minors Playing Violent Video Games

The Video Software Dealers Association and the Entertainment Software Association will likely contest the science showing the harmful effects of violent video games on minors. Apart from the self-serving motive for such opposition, one need only consider a professional organization that clearly does not doubt the serious aggression-teaching abilities of violent video games—the United States Department of Defense. Both the U.S. Army and U.S. Marines have their own video games used to train soldiers as tactical "first-person shooters" leading teams in "close-quarters urban combat." Many of these military combat training videos, such as *Full Spectrum Warrior* and *First To Fight* have been adapted and placed on the commercial market for minors to play.

Also, alleged "scientific" studies may be suggested by Respondents to argue that there are no harmful effects from violent video game playing. These "findings" can be explained by small sample size, poor test conditions and chance. The simple response to these studies is the recent and clear findings of the meta-analysis comprising 130 studies of the effects of violent video games showing the like between violent video games and aggression.

Conclusion

The scientific debate about whether exposure to media violence causes increases in aggressive behavior is over. All major types of research methodologies have been used, including experiments, cross-sectional correlational studies, longitudinal studies, intervention studies and meta-analyses. For each category, exposure to media violence was significantly associated with increased aggressions or violence. Likewise, the harmful effects on minors from playing violent video games are documented and not seriously contested.

Much research over several decades documents how witnessing violence and aggression leads to a range of negative outcomes for children. Negative outcomes result both from witnessing real violence as well as from viewing media violence. The most recent comprehensive review of the media violence literature documents the ". . . unequivocal evidence that media violence increases the likelihood of aggressive and violent behavior in both immediate and long-term contexts."

In the end, we need only to circle back from this rising ocean of research and return to simple common-sense. Society has a direct, rational and compelling reason in marginally restricting a minor's access to violent video games. Indeed, under the statute any parent remains completely free to provide any video game for their children.

Although this Court has never directly dealt with this precise issue, the Court's clear and understandable precedent in protecting children establishes that the lower court should be reversed and given the scientific findings by the community of mental health professions, the California statute upheld.

Respectfully submitted,

Steven F. Gruel
Counsel of Record
July 19, 2010
Counsel for Amicus Curiae

Appendix

Statement on Video Game Violence

"Both the American Psychological Association and the American Academy of Pediatrics have issued formal statements stating that scientific research on violent video games clearly shows that such games are causally related to later aggressive behavior in children and adolescents. Extensive research has been conducted over many years using all three major types of research designs (experimental, cross-sectional, and longitudinal). Numerous original empirical research studies have been conducted on children and adolescents. Overall, the research data conclude that exposure to violent video games causes an increase in the likelihood of aggressive behavior. The effects are both immediate and long term. Violent video games have measurable and statistically significant effects on both males and females. Theoretically important effects of violent video games have been confirmed by many empirical studies. The effects have been replicated by researchers in different settings and in numerous coun-

tries. The psychological processes underlying such effects are well understood and include: imitation, observational learning, priming of cognitive, emotional and behavioral scripts, physiological arousal, and emotional desensitization. These are general processes that underlie all types of social behavior, not just aggression and violence; they have been confirmed by countless studies outside of the media violence domain. In addition to causing an increase in the likelihood of aggressive behavior, violent video games have also been found to increase aggressive thinking, aggressive feelings, physiological desensitization to violence, and to decrease pro-social behavior."

LELAND Y. YEE is a member of the California State Senate. He earned a doctorate in developmental psychology from the University of Hawaii, and then worked in various educational and mental health settings. As a former member and president of the San Francisco Unified School District Board of Education and as a therapist in the Mental Health Department of San Francisco, he has long opposed the sale of violent video games to children. During his tenure as a member of the State Senate, Yee has fought for, among many other things, children and mental health services. Yee authored a statute that prohibited stores in California from selling violent or M-rated video games to minors based on the potential psychological harm they might cause. His statute was eventually overturned by the Supreme Court of the United States in 2011.

STEVEN F. GRUEL is a high-profile defense attorney in California. He runs a private law firm in San Francisco, where he specializes in criminal defense law. Attorney Gruel is the counsel of record for the *amicus* brief of Senator Leland Yee.

Patricia A. Millett

 **NO**

Brief of *Amici Curiae* in *Brown v. Entertainment Merchants Association*

Introduction and Summary of Argument

As respondents explain, California's ban on the sale and rental of certain video games to minors is subject to strict scrutiny because it directly regulates video games based on the content of a game, *i.e.,* whether the game is deemed "violent." California asserts that its law is necessary to "prevent psychological or neurological harm to minors who play violent video games." Pet. App. 23a. Under strict scrutiny, California must both provide "substantial evidence" that the video games it regulates cause psychological or neurological harm to minors who play them, and demonstrate that the restriction will "alleviate these harms in a direct and material way." *Turner Broadcasting Sys., Inc. v. FCC,* 512 U.S. 622, 664, 666 (1994). *See Ashcroft v. Free Speech Coalition,* 535 U.S. 234, 253 (2002).

California has done neither. Indeed, California does not offer any reliable evidence, let alone substantial evidence, that playing violent video games causes psychological or neurological harm to minors. California confesses it cannot prove causation, but points to studies that it says show a "correlation" between the two. Pet. Br. 52. But the evidence does not even do that.

California and Senator Yee also cite studies that purport to show a link between the playing of violent video games and violent, aggressive, and antisocial behavior by minors. But in the court of appeals, California expressly disclaimed any interest in regulating video games sales and rentals to minors to prevent such conduct, Pet. App. 23a–24a, and therefore these studies are waived because the argument was waived. The studies are of no help to California in any event because they document neither a causal connection nor a correlation between the playing of violent video games and violent, aggressive, or antisocial behavior.

Indeed, whether attempting to link violent video games with psychological and neurological harm or with violent, aggressive, and antisocial behavior, all of the

studies that California and Senator Yee cite suffer from inherent and fundamental methodological flaws.

- *The survey of aggressive behavior.* The courts below carefully considered this survey and correctly discredited it because the questions it posed are simply not valid indicators for actual violent or aggressive behavior and because it fails to account or control for other variables that have been proven to affect the behavior of minors.
- *The laboratory experimental study of aggression.* This study, too, was rightly discounted by the courts below because it relies on proxies for aggression that do not correlate with aggressive behavior in the real world.
- *The "meta-analysis" of video game violence research.* A meta-analysis combines the results of many other studies on a particular subject. But the accuracy and utility of any meta-analysis depends on the quality of the underlying studies themselves. Put another way, a meta-analysis of scientifically unreliable studies cannot cure the studies' flaws. Here, the meta-analysis on which Senator Yee relies was compromised because it was based on studies that used invalid measures of aggression.
- *"Longitudinal" studies of aggression.* A longitudinal study analyzes participants on many occasions over an extended period. The studies that Senator Yee cites are not longitudinal because they observed participants on only a few occasions and over just a short period of time. Additionally, those studies both failed to account for other variables that may explain aggressive behavior and used invalid measures of aggression.
- *Neuroscience studies.* These studies supposedly show a connection between playing violent video games and altered brain activity. The courts below properly concluded that they do not. Further, the neuroscience studies are rooted in fundamentally flawed statistical methodologies and do not address the cause of brain activation and deactivation in children.

U.S. Supreme Court, 2010.

Methodological flaws are only the beginning of the studies' problems. Both California and Senator Yee repeatedly exaggerate the statistical significance of the studies' findings, failing to inform the Court of express disclaimers and cautionary statements in the studies about the nature of their findings.

Finally, California and Senator Yee ignore a weighty body of scholarship, undertaken with established and reliable scientific methodologies, debunking the claim that the video games California seeks to regulate have harmful effects on minors.

Argument

I. California's Asserted Interest in Preventing Psychological and Neurological Harm to Minors Is Not Supported by Any Reliable, Let Alone, Substantial Evidence.

A. California's Studies Do Not Show a Causal Link, or Even a Correlation, Between Playing Violent Video Games and Psychological or Neurological Harm to Minors.

California's ban on the sale and rental of violent video games to minors rests on the same flawed studies that court after court has rejected. Pet. Br. 52–56; Pet. App. 27a–32a, 63a–64a; *Entertainment Software Ass'n v. Blagojevich,* 404 F. Supp. 2d 1051, 1059–1067 (N.D. Ill. 2005), *aff'd* 469 F.3d 641 (7th Cir. 2006); *Interactive Digital Software Ass'n v. St. Louis County,* 329 F.3d 954, 958–59 (8th Cir. 2003); *American Amusement Machine Ass'n v. Kendrick,* 244 F.3d 572, 578–79 (7th Cir. 2001) ("AAMA"); *Entertainment Software Ass'n v. Foti,* 451 F. Supp. 2d 823, 832 (M.D. La. 2006); *Entertainment Software Ass'n v. Hatch,* 443 F. Supp. 2d 1065, 1069–70 & n.2 (D. Minn. 2006); *Entertainment Software Ass'n v. Granholm,* 426 F. Supp. 2d 646, 652–54 (E.D. Mich. 2006). The courts were right to reject these studies because they do not even establish the "correlation" between violent video games and psychological harm to minors that California says exists, let alone the causation of harm that, as respondent explains, the First Amendment requires. Nor do the studies show a connection between playing violent video games and violent or aggressive behavior of minors, which explains why California disclaimed that interest below.

First, California points to a 2004 study by Douglas Gentile of approximately 600 eighth-and ninth-grade students. Pet. Br. 52–53 (citing JA 600). These students completed surveys that asked questions about the types of video games they preferred and how "violent" they were. (The survey did not provide any definition of "violent.")

The survey also recorded how often the students played the games; the students' hostility level; how often they had argued with teachers during the past year; their average grades; and whether they had been in a physical fight in the past year. JA 613–15. From the survey answers, Gentile concluded that "[a]dolescents who expose themselves to greater amounts of video game violence" were more hostile and reported getting into more arguments with teachers and physical fights and performing poorly in school. JA 601.

Although California relies heavily on the Gentile survey, Pet. Br. 52–53, it has absolutely no relevance here. The survey examines only the purported connection between video game violence and "aggressive behavior" or "physical aggression" towards third parties. Pet. Br. 53. It does not study, and says nothing about, the psychological or neurological harm allegedly caused to those who play violent video games, which is the only interest that California defended below and thus is the only interest that is properly before this Court. Pet. App. 24a.

Even if the Gentile survey were relevant, it simply does not say what California says it does. California states that the survey "suggest[s] a causal connection between playing violent video games and aggressive behavior." Pet. Br. 53. It does no such thing. The survey makes absolutely no finding that exposure to violent video games leads to physical aggression. To the contrary, it explicitly cautions against making that inference: "It is important to note . . . that this study is limited by *its correlational nature. Inferences about causal direction should be viewed with caution.*" JA 638 (emphasis added); see also JA 632–33 ("Are young adolescents more hostile and aggressive because they expose themselves to media violence, or do previously hostile adolescents prefer violent media? Due to the correlational nature of this study, we cannot answer this question directly").

Beyond that, the Gentile survey is rife with methodological flaws that undermine even the suggested correlation. For example, the measures of "aggressive behavior" that Gentile employed are highly suspect. Having an argument with a teacher—without any further exploration into the nature of the event—does not even suggest violent or aggressive behavior. And simply asking students whether they had been in a fight—again, without any further analysis of the event—is not a valid indicator for violent or aggressive behavior.

Additionally, there are many factors that may influence youth violence or aggressive behavior, including: family violence, antisocial personality traits, and association with delinquent peers. *See* Herrenkohl et al., *Risk Factors for Violence and Relational Aggression in Adolescence,*

22 Journal of Interpersonal Violence 386 (2007); *see also* Savage, *The Role of Exposure to Media Violence in the Etiology of Violent Behavior: A Criminologist Weighs In,* 51 American Behavioral Scientist 1123, 1127 (2008) ("A focus on media violence literature, where we might find some correlations in a subset of studies, would lead to an exaggerated view of the importance of media violence in the etiology of violent behavior if we ignore the empirical evidence on other individual factors and situational factors."). Because Gentile's survey failed to control for, or even consider, those other variables, its conclusion that there is a correlation between video games and hostility to third parties lacks scientific grounding. In fact, controlling for gender alone removes most of the variance from which Gentile finds a correlation. Ferguson, *Blazing Angels or Resident Evil? Can Violent Video Games Be a Force for Good?,* 14 Review of General Psychology 74–75 (2010). In other words, the correlation Gentile claims to find is equally explainable by the effect of gender: boys tend to play more violent video games and tend to be more aggressive. *Id.*

Second, California points to a 2004 study of 130 college students by Craig Anderson. Pet. Br. 53 (citing JA 479, 493–94). That study measured the blood pressure of students before, during, and after playing selected video games and had students take a "word completion" test after playing selected video games. JA 497. Based on the resulting measurements, Anderson concluded that the students' blood pressure increased while playing certain video games he labeled "violent" and that game play "increase[d] . . . the accessibility of aggressive thoughts." JA 507.

The Anderson study is no help to California, because it does not show that a rise in students' blood pressure has any relationship to whether violent video games cause psychological or neurological harm. Nor does California show how "aggressive thoughts" leads to psychological harm.

Laboratory experiments, like Anderson's, that measure aggression immediately following the playing of a video game are common in the field of media effects research. *See generally* Kutner & Olson, supra, at 73–74. And like Anderson's, these experiments rely on proxies for *real* aggressive or violent behavior, such as the participants' willingness to administer blasts of white noise against an unseen (and non-existent opponent). Freedman, *supra,* at 60–63. The problem is that the proxies bear no relationship to whether someone is going to act aggressively or violently in the real world. Kutner & Olson, *supra,* at 73–74. Similarly, giving participants words with blank spaces and evaluating whether they make "aggressive" or "non-aggressive" words with the letters they fill in (i.e.,

"explo_e" could be completed as "explore" or "explode"), as Anderson did in his experiment, JA 496, has no known validity for measuring aggressive behavior (or even aggressive thinking).

Third, California points to a 2004 study of fourth- and fifth-grade students by Jeanne Funk, and claims it "found that playing violent video games was correlated with lower empathy as well as stronger pro-violence attitudes." Pet. Br. 53 (citing JA 705–06). But the Funk study specifically disclaimed any proof of causality. JA 730. As Funk admitted, the children in her study whose scores indicated lower empathy or stronger pro-violence attitudes may simply have been drawn to violent video games. *Id.* Moreover, the small sample size—just 150 children—and the failure to control for or consider any other variables undermine even the study's tentative conclusion of a correlation between violent video games and proviolence attitudes.

B. The Additional Studies Cited by Senator Yee Do Not Support California's Ban on the Sale and Rental of Violent Video Games to Minors.

Senator Yee's brief boldly declares that "science confirms that violent video games are harmful to minors." Yee Br. 10. But the studies he discusses do not show that.

Senator Yee leans heavily on a one-page statement by some researchers, who did not join his amicus brief. Yee Br. 11. That statement focuses on whether violent video games increase the likelihood of "aggressive behavior," which is the interest that California disclaimed below. Pet. App. 24a. With respect to the interest that California defended below—whether violent video games cause psychological or neurological harm to minors—the statement offers only one line at its tail end expressing concern about aggressive "thinking," aggressive "feelings," desensitization, and a decrease in "pro-social" behavior. But if the First Amendment means anything, it means government cannot ban speech to stop thoughts or feelings, and certainly not to promote "pro-social" behavior.

Aside from his reliance on the one-page statement of scholars, Senator Yee refers to "recent research," "new data," and "hundreds of studies" regarding the effects of violent video games. Yee Br. 5, 6. But there rarely are citations in Senator Yee's brief to support these broad assertions.

Read carefully, the "recent research" and "new data" that Senator Yee offers boils down to (1) a meta-analysis conducted by Craig Anderson, (2) a book co-authored by Anderson and Douglas Gentile, (3) certain purported "longitudinal studies," (4) broad policy statements of the American Academy of Pediatrics and the American Psychological Association, and (5) a few neuroscience studies.

None of these sources provides substantial evidence that violent video games cause psychological or neurological harm to minors or lead to violent, aggressive, or antisocial behavior in minors.

1. *Anderson Meta-analysis.*   This recent study is labeled a "meta-analysis" of video game violence research. Anderson et al., *Violent Video Game Effects on Aggression, Empathy and Prosocial Behavior in Eastern and Western Countries: A Meta-Analytic Review*, 136 Psychological Bulletin 151 (2010). "Meta-analysis" is a research technique that merges the results of many studies on a particular topic using statistical analysis.

The accuracy and usefulness of this tool necessarily depends, however, on the choice and quality of the studies that are merged for analysis, and the "end-product will never be better than the individual studies that make up the meta-analysis." Anderson's study is an example of how a meta-analysis can simply compound the methodological flaws in the underlying studies.

For example, Anderson's meta-analysis combines studies that used methods for measuring aggression that have not been proven to be valid. Ferguson & Kilburn, *Much Ado About Nothing: The Misestimation and Overinterpretation of Violent Video Game Effects in Eastern and Western Nations: Comment on Anderson et al.*, 136 Psychological Bulletin 174, 175–76 (2010). By incorporating those studies into his analysis, Anderson replicated their methodological flaws in his meta-analysis, severely eroding the reliability of its findings.

Additionally, the process by which Anderson selected the studies for inclusion in the meta-analysis casts serious doubt on the results. Anderson reasonably included some unpublished studies in his meta-analysis given the risk of publication bias in the field of violent video game effects research. But the process by which Anderson selected unpublished studies—he included his own unpublished work and the work of others whose conclusions mirror his, and excluded a wealth of unpublished studies from a contrary perspective—injected more, not less, bias into the analysis. Ferguson & Kilburn, *supra*, at 175.

Notably, Senator Yee fails to mention that the methodology of Anderson's meta-analysis was resoundingly criticized in the very same issue of the journal in which the meta-analysis was first published. Ferguson & Kilburn, *supra*.

Leaving the methodological flaws aside, Anderson's meta-analysis does not support Senator Yee's sweeping claims that it contains "definitive findings" and "unequivocal evidence" that "prove[s]" playing violent video games increases aggressive thoughts and behavior. Yee Br. 26, 28. That is because the estimated "effect size" between playing violent video games, on the one hand, and aggressive behavior, on the other, that Anderson identified is minimal. Anderson et al., *supra*, at 170. An "effect size" estimate represents the proportion of shared variance between two variables. It is, roughly speaking, the degree to which one variable can predict the other improving upon chance alone. For example, an effect size of 1% means that knowing variable x (playing violent video games) for an individual would be 1% better than chance alone in predicting whether that individual was likely to engage in aggressive or violent behavior. In contrast, an effect size of 100% means that the variable is a fully accurate predictor.

In his meta-analysis, Anderson concedes that the estimated effect size between playing violent video games and aggressive behavior is "small," specifically, 0.152 or 2.31%. Anderson et al., *supra*, at 170. Thus, the effect size that Anderson himself calculates—far from being a significant "causal risk factor," Yee Br. 26—means that playing violent video games is only 2.31% better than chance alone at predicting whether that individual will engage in aggressive behavior. And even that insignificant effect size is likely inflated because Anderson's study did not control for well-accepted risk factors for aggressive behavior, such as the influence of peers and family. Ferguson & Kilburn, *supra*, at 177.

Finally, other meta-analytic research that incorporated studies with valid and reliable methodologies, properly accounted for publication bias, and controlled for "third" variables have found little evidence that violent video games cause psychological harm (or any other harm) to minors.

For example, in a 2009 study published in the Journal of Pediatrics, Dr. Christopher Ferguson and Dr. John Kilburn conducted a meta-analytic review of studies that considered the impact of violent media on aggressive behavior. They relied on studies that used well-validated measures for assessing aggressive behavior, properly corrected for publication bias, and controlled for well-accepted risk factors for aggressive behavior. Ferguson & Kilburn, *Public Health Risks, supra*, at 759–60. The results suggest that the overall effect for exposure to media violence (both television and video game violence) was less than 1%. *Id.* at 761. Thus, the authors concluded that the results of their study "do not support the conclusion that media violence leads to aggressive behavior." *Id.* at 759.

In another recent meta-analytic study, Dr. John Sherry concluded that while there are researchers in the field who "are committed to the notion of powerful effects," they have been unable to prove such effects;

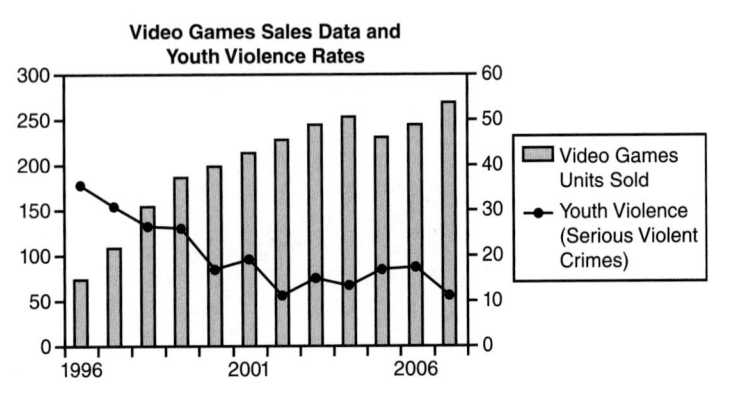

Video Games Sales Data and Youth Violence Rates

(Source: Ferguson & Olson et al., *Violent Video Games, Catharsis Seeking, Bullying, and Delinquency: A Multivariate Analysis of Effects*, Crime & Delinquency 5 (2010))

that studies exist that seem to support a relationship between violent video games and aggression but other studies show no such relationship; and that research in this area has employed varying methodologies, thus "obscuring clear conclusions." Sherry, *Violent Video Games and Aggression: Why Can't We Find Effects?*, Mass Media Effects Research: Advances Through Meta-Analysis 231, 232 (2007); see also Sherry, *The Effects of Violent Video Games on Aggression: A Meta-Analysis*, 27 Human Communication Research 409–31 (2001). Although Dr. Sherry "expected to find fairly clear, compelling, and powerful effects," based on assumptions he had formed regarding video game violence, he did not find them. Sherry, *Violent Video Games, supra*, at 231, 245. Instead, he found only a small relationship between playing violent video games and short-term arousal or aggression and further found that this effect lessened the longer one spent playing video games. *Id.* at 243–45.

Such small and inconclusive results prompted Dr. Sherry to ask: "[W]hy do some researchers continue to argue that video games are dangerous despite evidence to the contrary?" *Id.* at 244. Dr. Sherry further noted that if violent video games posed such a threat, then the increased popularity of the games would lead to an increase in violent crime. *Id.* But that has not happened. Quite the opposite, during the same period that video game sales, including sales of violent video games, have risen, youth violence has dramatically declined.

2. Anderson and Gentile Book. Senator Yee touts a "recent book" (Yee Br. 16–17), co-authored by Anderson and Gentile, that asserts there are "reasons to expect" larger effects from exposure to violent video games because of their interactive nature. Anderson, Gentile, & Buckley, *Violent Video Game Effects on Children and Adolescents: Theory, Research, and Public Policy* 135 (Oxford Univ. Press

2006). But that assertion rests on the same old research of Anderson and Gentile that has been rejected as fundamentally flawed by every court that has considered it. Pet. App. 29a, 64a; *see, e.g., Blagojevich*, 404 F. Supp. 2d at 1063 ("Dr. Anderson also has not provided evidence to show that video games . . . are any more harmful than violent television, movies, Internet sites or other speech-related exposure.").

3. Longitudinal Studies. A longitudinal study examines a subject on several occasions over an extended period of time. *See* Kutner & Olson, *supra*, at 68–69. Both Anderson and Gentile (the main proponents of the idea that violent video games have harmful effects on minors) acknowledged in the record below that "there is a 'glaring empirical gap' in video game violence research due to 'the lack of longitudinal studies'" (Anderson) and that therefore "longitudinal research is needed" (Gentile). Pet. App. 28a, 30a.

Senator Yee claims that this gap has now been closed: according to Senator Yee, longitudinal studies of violent video games have been done and have proven harmful effects. Yee Br. 26. But Senator Yee provides no citations to support this proposition.

Amici are aware of one recent study of students in the United States and Japan that Anderson has described as "longitudinal" data that "confirm[s]" that playing violent video games is an "important causal risk factor for youth aggression." Anderson et al., *Longitudinal Effects of Violent Video Games in Aggression in Japan and the United States*, 122 Pediatrics 1067 (2008). But there is nothing "longitudinal" about this study. Rather than studying participants multiple times over extended periods, it surveyed participants only twice and with only a few months lag in between. Additionally, the flaws that taint Anderson's other research (*e.g.*, failing to control for "third" variables and using measures of aggression that have not been proven reliable) recur in this study. Finally, Anderson's sweeping assertion of a causal connection is belied by the study's insignificant effect sizes (between .152 and .075, or 0.5% and 2.3%).

4. *Policy Statements.* Senator Yee cites policy statements of two organizations, the American Academy of Pediatrics and the American Psychological Association, that violence in the media generally is a risk to minors. Yee Br. 10–12. But these pronouncements indict violence in *all* media, not just video games, and thus, if acted upon, would open the door to sweeping governmental restrictions on speech in films and on the Internet that even California does not propone.

Further, broad organizational pronouncements, like those in the policy statements that Senator Yee cites, are not based on a serious analysis of the relevant scientific evidence. See, e.g., Freedman, *supra*, at 9 ("Although they have all made unequivocal statements about the effects of media violence, it is almost certain that not one of these organizations conducted a thorough review of the research. They have surely not published or made available any such review."). The lack of any detailed analysis underpinning the statements is illustrated by (a) the American Academy of Pediatrics' assertion that *"[m]ore than 3500 research studies* have examined the association between media violence and violent behavior; all but 18 have shown a positive relationship,"* American Academy of Pediatrics, *Media Violence,* 108 Pediatrics 1222 (2001), emphasis added (cited at Yee Br. 11), and (b) an assertion in a 2000 joint statement of medical and psychological groups that *"well over 1000 studies . . .* point overwhelmingly to a causal connection between media violence and aggressive behavior in some children,"* JA 378, emphasis added (quoted at Pet. Br. 44). The rub is that there have not been over 3500—or even over 1000—scientific studies done on this topic. And the studies that have been conducted do not reach the uniform or "overwhelming" conclusion that the organizations claim they do. Freedman, *supra*, at 9; *see also* Kutner & Olson, *supra*, at 78. Finally, it is telling that the citations in the policy statements on which Senator Yee relies are to the flawed studies that were incorporated into Anderson's meta-analysis.

5. *Neuroscience Research.* California's ban on the sale and rental of violent video games to minors is based on an assumption that "[e]xposing minors to depictions of violence in video games . . . makes those minors more likely . . . to experience a reduction of activity in the frontal lobes of the brain." Pet. App. 8a. In both the trial court and the court of appeals, California relied on research by William Kronenberger that purported to identify a connection between violent video games and altered brain activity using functional magnetic resonance imaging ("fMRI") technology. Pet. App. 3la. But every single court to review Kronenberger's fMRI research, including the courts below, have found no such connection. *Id.; See, e.g., Blagojevich,* 404 F. Supp. 2d at 1063–65; *Granholm,* 426 F. Supp. 2d at 653. California has now abandoned all reliance on Kronenberger's fMRI research or any other fMRI study.

Senator Yee, however, invokes Kronenberger's fMRI research, as well as a handful of other neuroscience articles, claiming that they show "a critical link" between virtual violence and altered brain functioning Yee Br. 24. They do no such thing.

To begin with, Senator Yee fails to acknowledge the intense debate in the scientific community, widely reported in both the academic and popular press, regarding whether fMRI technology is being misused and its results being exaggerated. *See, e.g.,* Lehrer, *Picturing Our Thoughts,* The Boston Globe, Aug. 17, 2008; Vul et al., *Puzzlingly High Correlations in fMRI Studies of Emotion, Personality, and Social Cognition,* 4 Perspectives on Psychological Science 274 (2009); *see also* Hotz, *The Brain, Your Honor, Will Take the Witness Stand,* The Wall Street Journal, Jan. 15, 2009 (reporting scholars' criticism that fMRI brain scans cannot be used as legal evidence because they are "easily manipulated" and "can't be trusted yet"); Begley, *Of Voodoo and the Brain,* Newsweek, Jan. 31, 2009 (reporting scholars' claim that many published fMRI studies show "voodoo correlations," methods and analysis so poor that they must be redone); Begley, *Brain Imaging and (More) Voodoo, But Politer,* Newsweek, April 27, 2009 (asking "isn't it time the fMRI community came to grips with the growing criticism of its methods"); Hamilton, *False Signals Cause Misleading Brain Scans,* National Public Radio, July 7, 2009 (reporting "furious debate" as to whether flaws in statistical analysis have made fMRI results "appear stronger than they really are" and that "even the strongest defenders of fMRI acknowledge that there are problems"); Sanders, *Trawling the Brain,* ScienceNews, Dec. 19, 2009 (describing growing concern in scientific community as to fMRI's reliability and warning that "the singing of fMRI's praises ought to be accompanied by a chorus of caveats"); Logothetis, *What We Can Do and What We Cannot Do with fMRI,* Nature, June 2008 ("[F]undamental questions concerning the interpretation of fMRI data abound, as the conclusions drawn often ignore the actual limitations of the methodology.").

As many scholars have cautioned, fMRI studies of brain activation have inherent methodological issues that make them difficult to understand and interpret. In a typical fMRI experiment, a subject is placed in a tube-shaped machine (just like the one used for an ordinary MRI test), told to lie perfectly still and then to perform some experimental task, such as looking at an image and making a decision. Magnets detect the ratio of the change between oxygenated and deoxygenated blood in a specific region of the brain. A complicated statistical analysis is then used to turn that signal into an "activation" in the brain. The underlying assumption is that active neurons require more oxygen to work and, therefore, more oxygen means greater neuronal activity.

A central problem, however, is that while fMRI studies may indicate areas of the brain that decrease in activation during a task, deactivations that may occur simultaneously are not well understood and, thus, are only tentatively discussed in published fMRI studies. *See, e.g.,* Kalbfleish, *Getting to the Heart of the Brain: Using Cognitive Neuroscience to Explore the Nature of Human Ability and Performance,* 30 Roeper Review 165 (2007). Additionally, it is not yet understood how brain activation is influenced by neural development in children. *Id.*

Further, because fMRI studies depend on statistical analysis, errors in the method or procedure of that analysis may undermine the reliability of the results. *See* Vul et al., *supra.* A recent study surveyed 55 fMRI studies on brain activation and emotion, personality, and social cognition and found that, in about half of these studies, the methods and analysis were so flawed that the results were "entirely spurious correlations." *Id.* at 274.

On top of the inherent limitations of fMRI research generally, the particular fMRI studies that Senator Yee cites—three studies conducted in part by Kronenberger and one study conducted by Rene Weber—have their own specific flaws and their results are so inconclusive that they do not remotely support the asserted link between playing video games and altered brain functioning.

The Kronenberger articles—each of which expressly states that it was funded by a grant from the anti-media violence Center for Successful Parenting—set forth findings that are so qualified as to render them meaningless.

In the most recent Kronenberger study, *see* Yee Br. 21 (citing Hummer et al., *Short-Term Violent Video Game Play by Adolescents Alters Prefontal Activity During Cognitive Inhibition,* 13 Media Psychology 136 (2010)), forty-five adolescents were divided into two groups, with one group playing a car racing video game and the other group playing a shooting game. After thirty minutes of play, each participant was subjected to an fMRI scan, during which they were required to press a button for each letter that was displayed, except for the letter x, for which there was no response. Looking at the resulting data, Kronenberger and his co-authors made the broad conclusion that there were lower activity levels for the shooting game in regions of the brain "*thought to be involved*" in cognitive inhibition." *Id.* at 147 (emphasis added).

As a threshold matter, this study cannot possibly support California's claim that violent video game cause harm to minors because a decrease in activity in an area of the brain is not necessarily a negative effect and, instead, may indicate nothing more than expertise in a practiced task. *See, e.g.,* Poldrack et al., *The Neural Correlates of Motor Skill Automaticity,* 25 Journal of Neuroscience 5356 (2005). The mere fact that the brain changes as it responds to stimuli does not prove that the stimuli are harmful.

Additionally, the study's own express qualifications undercut its findings. The authors admitted that the two video games chosen differed in ways other than the presence or absence of violent content and thus created "potential confounds" for the results. Hummer et al., *supra,* at 149.

The two other studies conducted in part by Kronenberger did not consider exposure to video games specifically, just "media violence" generally, and thus do not support California's claim that violent *video games* cause harm to minors. See Kronenberger et al., *Media Violence Exposure and Executive Functioning in Aggressive and Control Adolescents,* 61 Journal of Clinical Psychology 725, 726 (2005) (cited at Yee Br. 21); Mathews et al., *Media Violence Exposure and Frontal Lobe Activation Measured by Functional Magnetic Resonance Imaging in Aggressive and Nonaggressive Adolescents,* 29 Journal of Computer Assisted Tomography 287 (2005) (cited at Yee Br. 22). More importantly, each study is expressly announced to be inconclusive. For example, in their study of media violence and "executive functioning," Kronenberger and his colleagues explicitly warn that the results are only "preliminary" and "should be viewed with caution." Kronenberger et al., *supra,* at 726," *see also* Mathews et al., *supra,* at 291–92 (explaining study's "limitation" is that it "did not evaluate other brain regions involved in emotional control"; authors recommended "further study" to evaluate "the entire system involved in aggressive behavior").

Senator Yee fares no better in his reliance on the Weber fMRI study. Yee Br. 24 (citing Weber et al., *Does Playing Violent Video Games Induce Aggression? Empirical Evidence of a Functional Magnetic Resonance Imaging Study,* 8 Media Psychology 39 (2006)). The Weber study involved thirteen adult men who were observed playing a supposedly violent video game for an hour. The study examined brain activity patterns that were similar to those seen in a previous study of individuals "imagin[ing] scenarios involving aggressive behavior." *Id.* at 42–43, 53. What those patterns mean, however, is not explained by the science. Nor do the patterns demonstrate any real-world connection between the "imagin[ings]" and violence or harmful neurological effect. And Senator Yee fails to explain how this limited study of a small pool of adult men substantiates the sweeping assertions about minors' neurological functioning on which California's law depends.

C. California and Senator Yee Ignore the Large Body of Empirical Evidence That Shows No Causal Connection, or Even a Correlation, Between Violent Video Games and Harm to Minors.

California and Senator Yee ignore a wealth of recent empirical evidence disabusing the notion that violent video games are harmful to minors. Here is just a snapshot of that body of scholarship:

- A study of 603 Hispanic youths (ages ten to fourteen), recently published in The Journal of Pediatrics, examined various risk factors for youth violence, including video game violence, delinquent peer association, family conflict, depression, and others. Ferguson et al., *A Multivariate Analysis of Youth Violence and Aggression: The Influence of Family, Peers, Depression, and Media Violence,* 155 Journal of Pediatrics 904 (2009). The children listed television shows and video games and rated how often they viewed or played the media—a reliable and valid method of evaluating violent media exposure. *Id.* at 905. The children were then evaluated using the Child Behavior Checklist, a well-researched and well-validated tool for measuring behavioral problems in children and adolescents. *Id.* A statistical analysis of the results revealed that exposure to video games had a negligible effect size and was not predictive of youth violence and aggression. *Id.* at 906.
- A study of 1,254 seventh- and eighth-grade students examined the influence of exposure to violent video games on delinquency and bullying behavior. Ferguson & Olson et al., *supra.* The Entertainment Software Ratings Board ratings were employed as a standardized measure of participants' exposure to violence in video

games. *Id.* at 8. The study applied a multivariate statistical method that considered other factors that might be predictive of aggressive behavior (such as level of parental involvement, support from others, and stress). *Id.* at 7–8. This study did not use abstract measures of aggression, but instead focused on specific negative behaviors such as delinquency and bullying. *Id.* at 8, 9. A statistical analysis revealed insignificant effect sizes between exposure to violent video games and delinquency or bullying. *Id.* at 11, 12. The authors accordingly concluded that exposure to such games was not predictive of delinquency or bullying. *Id.*

- A study of 213 participants examined the influence of violent video game play on aggressive behavior. Williams & Skoric, *Internet Fantasy Violence,* 72 Communication Monographs 217 (2005). The 213 participants were divided into a 75-person treatment group that played a single game, Asheron's Call 2, a type of "massively multi-player online role-playing game" that is "highly violent" and has "a sustained pattern of violence," for at least five hours over a one-month period, and a 138-person control group that did not play the game. *Id.* at 221, 224. Participants then completed self-reported questionnaires that included a range of demographic, behavioral, and personality variables. *Id.* at 225. Aggression-related beliefs were measured according to the Normative Beliefs in Aggression general scale, a well-validated scale for measuring beliefs about the acceptability of aggression, and aggressive social interactions were measured using specific behavioral questions. Both measurement techniques had been successfully used in previous studies of violent television and video game effects. *Id.* The results of this study found no effects associated with aggression caused by playing violent video games. *Id.* at 228.

These studies are just the tip of the iceberg. They rate barely a mention in Senator Yee's brief, which disparages them as "alleged 'scientific studies'" that involved "small sample size, poor test conditions and chance." Yee Br. 27. That is wrong. The studies employed large sample sizes, long-standing and validated measures of aggression, and superior statistical controls. Ironically, the studies also include the work of researchers whom California and Senator Yee cite favorably. For example, as noted above, California relies on the research of Jeanne Funk. Pet Br. 53 (citing JA 705–06). But, in a separate study that California does not mention, Funk "fail[ed] to find" even a correlation between violent video games and aggressive emotions and behavior. *See* Funk et al., *Aggression and Psychopathology in Adolescents With a Preference for Violent Electronic Games,* 28 Aggressive Behavior 134 (2002). Notably, this second Funk study employed the Child Behavior Checklist, which is a better validated measure of aggression than measures utilized in the studies on which California and Senator Yee rely.

At minimum, the scholarship that California and Senator Yee ignore belies the notion that the "substantial evidence of causation" standard imposes an "insurmountable hurdle" on science or legislatures. Pet. Br. 52. These studies show unequivocally that the causation research can be done, and, indeed, has been done. The problem confronting California and Senator Yee thus is not the constitutional standard; it is simply their inability to meet that standard in this case because validated scientific studies prove the opposite, leaving no empirical foundation for the assertion that playing violent video games causes harm to minors.

Conclusion

For the foregoing reasons, the judgment of the court of appeals should be affirmed.

Respectfully submitted.

Michael C. Small
Katharine J. Galston
Akin, Gump, Strauss,
Hauer & Feld LLP

Patricia A. Millett
Counsel of Record
Akin, Gump, Strauss,
Hauer & Feld LLP

Attorneys for Amici Curiae

September 17, 2010

Patricia A. Millett is an attorney in Washington, D.C., at the law firm of Akin Gump Strauss Hauer & Feld LLP, where she heads the firm's Supreme Court practice and coheads the firm's national appellate practice. She has argued a total of 31 cases before the U.S. Supreme Court (the most of any woman in history) and approximately 35 in the courts of appeals. She has briefed scores of cases in the Supreme Court and appellate courts across the nation.

EXPLORING THE ISSUE

Does Research Confirm That Violent Video Games Are Harmful to Minors?

Critical Thinking and Reflection

1. The U.S. Constitution's First Amendment prohibits making any law that infringes on freedom of speech. What are your thoughts about video games being viewed as a form of free speech?
2. In light of the fact that government controls the sale of alcohol and tobacco to minors, what are the arguments for and against similar governmental control of the sale of violent video games to minors?
3. In what ways is the practice of playing violent video games similar to and different from watching violent movies? What are your thoughts about the possibility that exposure to violence can lead to desensitization to violence?
4. How would you go about designing a research project to study the effects of playing violent video games on minors? How you would go about determining causality, rather than correlation?
5. After reading the criticisms of the research studies cited in these briefs, what are some of the methodological limitations evident in the studies cited? If you were conducting such research, how would you try to overcome these limitations?

Is There Common Ground?

It would seem safe to offer the conjecture that adults as a rule do not want to put children in harm's way. As a society we strive to project humans from birth from being exposed to dangerous threats in the environment. Laws dictate that children must be protected in car seats, that house paint must be lead-free to prevent brain damage from accidental ingestion, and that tobacco and alcohol sales to children are prohibited. Thus, the argument could be made that if violent video games have a detrimental effect on children, efforts should be made by society to keep minors away from these media. But how do we go about determining that these video games are indeed detrimental to a child's development?

The authors of the brief pointing to the detrimental effects on children of violent video games believe that they have summarized compelling evidence that unwanted behavioral and neurological changes result from playing these games. However, in light of the great methodological challenges involved in studying this issue, is the research cited all that convincing? Has sufficient research been conducted to assess the extent to which there might be a differential impact between watching violent movies and playing violent video games? What about the effect on a child of seeing graphic images of war on the news in

which real people are being blown to pieces in war zones? Do such images lead these impressionable children toward being more aggressive themselves?

The author of the brief on the opposing side of the argument pokes holes in the research positing a connection between playing violent video games and engaging in aggressive behavior. She raises some compelling arguments about the limitations of these research studies, and contests the extent to which such research should be the basis for drawing conclusions about speculative causality. What is not addressed in this brief, however, is the question "how violent is too violent?" Perhaps "shooting" an alien is acceptable, but what about raping an innocent victim? Most people would be critical of video games in which horrifying acts of torture and assault are glorified, but what is the threshold of violent acts that should be kept out of the games played by children?

Create Central

www.mhhe.com/createcentral

Additional Resources

Hamilton, J. (2011). *Video Games*. Detroit, MI: Greenhaven Press.

Kirsh, S. J. (2006). *Children, Adolescents, and Media Violence: A Critical Look at the Research*. Thousand Oaks, CA: Sage Publications.

Kutner, L., & Olson, C. K. (2008). *Grand Theft Childhood: The Surprising Truth about Violent Video Games and What Parents Can Do*. New York, NY: Simon & Schuster.

Singer, D. G., & Singer, J. L. (2012). *Handbook of Children and the Media*. Los Angeles, CA: Sage.

Internet References . . .

American Society of Child and Adolescent Psychiatry

http://www.aacap.org/aacap/Families_and_Youth/
Facts_for_Families/Facts_for_Families_Pages/
Children_and_Video_Games_Playing_with_
Violence_91.aspx

Entertainment Software Association

http://www.theesa.com/facts/violence.asp

Media Education Foundation

http://www.mediaed.org/cgi-bin/commerce.
cgi?preadd=action&key=175

Selected, Edited, and with Issue Framing Material by:
Richard P. Halgin, *University of Massachusetts, Amherst*

ISSUE

Must Mentally Ill Murderers Have a Rational Understanding of Why They Are Being Sentenced to Death?

YES: American Psychological Association, American Psychiatric Association, and National Alliance on Mental Illness, from "Brief for *Amici Curiae* American Psychological Association, American Psychiatric Association, and National Alliance on Mental Illness in Support of Petitioner," U.S. Supreme Court (2007)

NO: Greg Abbott et al., from "On Writ of Certiorari to the United States Court of Appeals for the Fifth Circuit: Brief for the Respondent," U.S. Supreme Court (2007)

Learning Outcomes

After reading this issue, you will be able to:

- Understand the concept of "rational understanding" as it is used in the American legal system.
- Discuss the ways in which mental illness can impair an individual's ability to understand right from wrong, as well as the rationale for being punished following wrongful behavior.
- Understand the meaning and purpose of retribution as it is used in the American legal system.
- Discuss the reasons why professional associations (e.g., the American Psychological Association and American Psychiatric Association) would submit an *amicus curiae* brief to the Court.
- Critically evaluate the extent to which it is possible to accurately assess malingering in the case of an accused murderer.

ISSUE SUMMARY

YES: The American Psychological Association, the American Psychiatric Association, and the National Alliance on Mental Illness collaborated in the preparation of an *amicus curiae* brief pertaining to the case of Scott Panetti, who was sentenced to death for murder. In this brief, the argument is made that mentally ill convicts should not be executed if their disability significantly impairs their capacity to understand the nature and purpose of their punishment or to appreciate why the punishment is being imposed on them.

NO: In his position as Attorney General of Texas, Greg Abbott argued the case of *Scott Louis Panetti, Petitioner v. Nathaniel Quarterman, Director, Texas Department of Criminal Justice, Correctional Institutions Division, Respondent.* Attorney General Abbott asserts that punishment for murder does not depend on the rational understanding of the convicted individual, but rather on the convict's moral culpability at the time the crime was committed.

F or hundreds of years, debate has raged about how to respond as a society to criminal acts committed by mentally ill individuals. Within the American legal system much of the discussion has focused on the insanity defense, with the debate intensifying in the 1980s following John Hinckley's attempt to assassinate President Ronald Reagan. Hinckley, who was obsessed with the actress

Jodie Foster, believed that if he killed the president, Jodie Foster would be so impressed that she would fall in love and marry him. When the case went to trial, Hinckley was ruled insane and was sent to a psychiatric hospital rather than to prison. Subsequent to this case, Congress passed the Insanity Defense Reform Act of 1984, which made it much more difficult for a defendant to be acquitted on the basis of the insanity plea. Concurrently, there was a sea change in America, at least in certain states, regarding the appropriateness of the death penalty for horrific acts such as murder. With the reduced likelihood of being acquitted on the basis of insanity, questions emerged about the ethics of executing individuals who lack an understanding of their criminal act or a realization that they are being sentenced to death because of this act.

The complexity of the issue of executing the mentally ill received special scrutiny as a result of the case of Scott Panetti that was heard by the U.S. Supreme Court in 2007. In 1992, Panetti murdered his mother-in-law and father-in-law while his wife and his daughter watched. Panetti, who had a lengthy history of mental illness and psychiatric hospitalizations during which he was treated for intense delusions and hallucinations, was nevertheless sentenced to death in Texas. In 2003, Panetti petitioned the Texas state court to determine his competency for execution, but this court ruled him competent. When Panetti brought his case to a higher level, the federal district court found fault with the earlier ruling and summoned three psychologists and a psychiatrist, all of whom concurred that Panetti suffered from mental illness characterized by impaired cognitive process and delusions consistent with schizoaffective disorder. Even with this startling evidence of disturbance, the court ruled that Panetti was competent to be executed. Panetti's case then went to the Fifth Circuit, and the argument was put forth that a previous U.S. Supreme Court ruling (*Ford v. Wainwright*) required that Panetti not only be aware of the fact that he would be executed, but also that he have a rational understanding of *why*. Panetti asserted that he was being executed because he preached the gospel, not because of his murders.

The American Psychological Association, the American Psychiatric Association, and the National Alliance on Mental Illness collaborated on the submission to the Supreme Court of an *amicus curiae* (a document submitted by an uninvolved party in which opinion or advice is offered to the court). This brief provided information to the court about serious mental illness and the nature of symptoms in some individuals, namely that individuals with psychotic conditions such as that of Panetti may experience delusions and a disrupted understanding of reality; also, they may be unable to connect events or

understand cause and effect (i.e., the connection between murder and punishment).

According to the *amicus* brief, mentally ill convicts are not competent to be executed if they have a disability that significantly impairs their capacity to understand the nature and purpose of their punishment, or to appreciate why the punishment is being imposed on them. People with schizophrenia and schizoaffective disorder may not be able to rationally understand the reasons for their execution sentence. Convinced of the reality of their delusions, they cannot grasp the essential truth: that their impending execution is retribution for their crimes. Executing a prisoner who cannot appreciate why he or she is being executed does not further the retributive purpose of the death penalty.

In the *amicus* brief it is argued that the Eighth Amendment forbids the execution of individuals who are unaware of the punishment they are about to suffer *and why they are to suffer it*. The Constitution requires that, before a prisoner is deemed competent to be executed, the prisoner must be aware of (1) the fact that he or she will be put to death, and (2) the reason for that sentence, namely society's retribution for the prisoner's criminal acts.

The brief contends that Scott Panetti belongs to the class of mentally ill persons who suffer from severe psychotic disorders that impede cognitive functioning in some respects, while leaving other aspects relatively unimpaired. Such individuals suffer from delusions: false beliefs that cannot be corrected by reasoning and that usually involve a misinterpretation of perceptions or experiences. Such people may possess the ability to comprehend and understand facts about the subject of their delusions, but they are often unable to appreciate the personal significance of those facts or to reason about them in a logical way. Psychotic disorders such as schizophrenia distort the mind in certain ways while leaving other functions generally intact. While the *process* of the person's thinking appears normal, the *content* of the thoughts defies accepted reality. The Fifth Circuit's approach permits the execution of severely delusional individuals even though they believe they are to be executed *for something other than their crimes*, notwithstanding the State's assertions to the contrary.

On the other side of the argument are the points raised by Attorney General Abbott, including the assertion that the court should reject the proposition that a murderer must possess a rational understanding of the reasons for execution, to render death an acceptable punishment under the Eighth Amendment to the Constitution (cruel and unusual punishment). Mr. Abbott argued that capital punishment in such cases should not rest on whether or not a convict has rational understanding, but rather on the convict's moral culpability at the time the crime was committed by this person.

Mr. Abbott argues that the viability of retribution as a permissible theory of punishment depends not on the rational understanding that a convict may or may not have, but rather on the convict's moral culpability at the time he or she committed the crime. He therefore contends that the Court should reject the proposition that a capital convict must possess a "rational understanding" of the reasons for execution to render death an acceptable punishment under the Eighth Amendment. Such a standard is not tailored to the particular interests at stake in the post-sentencing phase of capital proceedings, it invites malingering and abuse, and it is not necessary to advance the retributive and deterrent justifications for the death penalty.

According to Abbott, given the high rate of serious mental illness among homicide defendants, granting psychiatric exemptions could leave very few individuals eligible for the death penalty. The conceded objective of the submitted brief, Abbott states, is not simply avoiding the inhumanity of executing a person who is truly insane, but rather removing from death row as large a class of capital convicts as reasonably possible, and thus exempting vast numbers of convicted murderers from execution. Requiring a "deep" or "meaningful" appreciation of the State's reasons for imposing the death penalty would create an even greater risk that the Court's test could be circumvented through malingering or abuse.

In the U.S. Supreme Court ruling on this case, a split court overturned the death sentence. In a sharp rebuke to lower courts, the justices ruled 5 to 4 that Panetti was not shown to possess sufficient understanding of why he was to be put to death for murdering his wife's parents in 1992. Justice Clarence Thomas was joined by Justices Roberts, Scalia, and Alito in dissent, calling the ruling a "half-baked holding that leaves the details of the insanity standard for the District Court to work out."

YES

American Psychological Association, American Psychiatric Association, and National Alliance on Mental Health

Brief for *Amici Curiae* American Psychological Association, American Psychiatric Association, and National Alliance on Mental Illness in Support of Petitioner

The American Psychological Association is a voluntary, nonprofit, scientific and professional organization with more than 155,000 members and affiliates, and is the major association of psychologists in the nation.

The American Psychiatric Association, with more than 36,000 members, is the nation's leading organization of physicians who specialize in psychiatry.

The National Alliance on Mental Illness was founded in 1979 and is the nation's largest grassroots organization dedicated to improving the quality of life of persons living with serious mental illness and their families.

Members of *amici* are regularly called before courts to participate in competency hearings. *Amici* therefore have both pertinent expertise and a strong interest in the establishment of legal competency standards consistent with the best scientific knowledge about individuals suffering from mental illness.

In 2003, the American Bar Association established a Task Force on Mental Disability and the Death Penalty, which included mental health professionals who are members and representatives of *amici*. The Task Force was convened in light of this Court's decision in *Atkins* to address unresolved issues concerning application of the death penalty to persons suffering from impaired mental conditions. In 2005, the Task Force presented a series of recommendations.

[T]he Task Force identified several situations in which the death penalty should not be applied to individuals with mental illness. One category encompasses individuals who, though having been determined competent to stand trial and sentenced to death, suffer from a severe mental disorder or disability that renders them incompetent to understand the nature and purpose of the death penalty. This category would include, for example, individuals whose mental illness worsens in material respects after imposition of valid sentences.[1] Based on the Task Force Report *amici* and the American Bar Association recommended, in substantially similar form, that the death penalty should not be applied to such persons.[2]

Introduction and Summary of Argument

The Fifth Circuit, in this case and in *Barnard v. Collins*, 13 F.3d 871 (5th Cir. 1994), has adopted a very narrow construction of this Court's decision in *Ford*, a construction that permits the execution of individuals whose severe mental illness precludes them from understanding that the State is putting them to death as retribution for their crimes. The Fifth Circuit recognized that Scott Panetti suffers from schizoaffective disorder, a severe form of psychosis, and that as a direct result he "suffer[s] from paranoid delusions that his [sentence of] execution was the result of a conspiracy against him and not his crimes." *Panetti v. Dretke*, 448 F.3d 815, 819 (5th Cir. 2006). The court of appeals nevertheless deemed Panetti competent to be executed under *Ford*.

Amici respectfully submit that the Fifth Circuit's approach is inconsistent with the reasoning of the controlling opinions in *Ford*. Scientific knowledge about schizophrenia and schizoaffective disorder supports the conclusion that persons in Panetti's condition cannot rationally understand the reasons for their execution. Convinced of the reality of their delusions, they simply cannot grasp the essential truth: that their impending execution is retribution for their crimes. Where the prisoner cannot appreciate the reason, his execution cannot further the retributive purpose of the death penalty any more than if the prisoner, as in *Ford*, suffers delusions that he can never be executed at all. As explained further in this brief, for these reasons *amici* American Psychological Association, American Psychiatric Association, and the National Alliance on Mental Illness each has resolved that a prisoner is not competent to be executed if he "has a mental disorder or disability that significantly impairs his or her capacity to understand the nature and purpose of the punishment, or to appreciate the reason for its imposition in the prisoner's own case." *See, e.g.,* American Psychological Association Council of Representatives, APA Policy Manual: N. Public Interest (2001) (incorporating policy adopted by the Council of Representatives in February 2006), *available at.* . . . *Amici*'s approach, which is consistent with *Ford*, requires reversal of the Fifth Circuit here.

In Part I of this brief, *amici* explain that individuals who, like Panetti, suffer from severe psychotic disorders such as schizophrenia or schizoaffective disorder, frequently suffer from bizarre delusions that disrupt their understanding of reality. These delusional beliefs are genuine and often unshakeable, withstanding all attempts to introduce logic or contrary evidence. When they attach to the State's reasons for carrying out the mentally ill prisoner's execution, such delusions can deny the prisoner all rational understanding about "why" he is to be executed. In such a circumstance, proceeding with the execution would not further the purposes of the death penalty. In Part II, *amici* explain that mental health experts can assist the courts in identifying prisoners with mental illness who suffer delusions that preclude them from understanding the actual reasons for their execution. Mental health professionals routinely evaluate patients for the presence of delusional beliefs and generate reliable conclusions as to how those delusions impact the patients' ability to rationally understand information.

Argument

I. The Fifth Circuit's Interpretation of *Ford v. Wainwright* Fails to Protect a Class of Severely Mentally Ill Prisoners, in Contravention of the Purposes That Animated *Ford*

A. In *Panetti* and *Barnard*, *the Fifth Circuit Has Interpreted and Applied* Ford *Very Narrowly*

In 1986, this Court held that the Eighth Amendment forbids the execution of individuals suffering from mental illness that renders them incompetent. *Ford v. Wainwright*, 477 U.S. 399 (1986). The Court relied on common law to support its interpretation of the Eighth Amendment and identified several reasons why the execution of the insane is unacceptable in a civilized society. *Id.* at 409–410.[3] As one justification, the Court "seriously question[ed] the retributive value of executing a person who has no comprehension of why he has been singled out and stripped of his fundamental right to life." *Id.* at 409. Yet, while suggesting that the Constitution prevents the execution of a prisoner who lacks "comprehension of why he has been singled out" for death, the Court did not provide a substantive test for defining insanity in this context. Justice Powell attempted to do so, in a separate concurring opinion largely devoted to explaining his disagreements with the procedural protections set forth by the four-justice plurality. Justice Powell noted that "today, as at common law, one of the death penalty's critical justifications, its retributive force, depends on the defendant's awareness of the penalty's existence and purpose." *Id.* at 421 (Powell, J., concurring). Accordingly, he concluded that "the Eighth Amendment forbids the execution . . . of those who are unaware of the punishment they are about to suffer *and why they are to suffer it.*" *Id.* at 422 (emphasis added). Justice Powell recognized that the Constitution requires, as a minimum before a prisoner may be deemed competent to be executed, that the prisoner be aware of both the fact that he will be put to death and the reason for that: society's retribution for his criminal acts.

In the case at bar, the Fifth Circuit . . . has ruled that the Constitution permits the execution of a severely delusional man who has no awareness of the true reason for his execution. In upholding Panetti's death sentence, the court of appeals expressly ruled that the Constitution does not bar the execution of an individual "suffer[ing] from paranoid delusions that his execution was the result of a conspiracy against him *and not his crimes.*" *Panetti v. Dretke*, 448 F.3d 815, 819 (5th Cir. 2006) (emphasis added). Panetti understands that he has been found guilty of murder and faces execution, but holds the unequivocal and delusional belief that the State is using his crimes as a pretext, and that its real motivation is "to prevent him from preaching the Gospel." *Id.* at 816 (citing *Panetti v. Dretke*, 401 F. Supp. 2d 702, 709 (W.D. Tex. 2004)). Relying on *Barnard*, the court of appeals found Panetti's recognition of the State's *articulated* reason for his execution adequate to satisfy the standard set forth in Justice Powell's *Ford* concurrence, despite the court's recognition that Panetti's delusional thinking denies him awareness that the stated rationale is genuine. *Panetti*, 448 F.3d at 819 (noting that "Justice Powell did not state that a prisoner must 'rationally understand' the reason for his execution, only that he must be 'aware' of it").

B. Panetti Is Readily Identifiable as Suffering from Delusions That Commonly Accompany Schizophrenia and Schizoaffective Disorder

Scott Panetti is not an anomaly who by some odd quirk can correctly comprehend the fact of his execution and the State's explanation for it yet who breaks with reality when he ascribes the State's true motivation to a fantastical conspiracy or bizarre purpose. Rather, he is readily recognizable as belonging to the class of mentally ill persons who suffer from severe psychotic disorders that impede their cognitive functioning in some respects while leaving other aspects relatively unimpaired.[4] Such people may possess the ability to comprehend and understand facts about the subject of their delusions, but they are often unable to appreciate the personal significance of those facts or to reason about them in a logical way.

1. Individuals who suffer from delusions firmly hold false, illogical beliefs that cannot be corrected with reason and that interfere with their ability to interpret ordinary experiences. In the scientific literature, individuals such as Panetti are commonly described as suffering from delusions: false beliefs that cannot be corrected by reasoning and that usually involve a misinterpretation of perceptions or experiences. Such delusions are often characterized by flaws in logical thinking that prevent those who suffer from them from making the right connections between ideas and from testing their beliefs about the world in ways that would enable them to determine the veracity of those beliefs.

Delusional thinking forms part of various psychotic disorders. A delusion has been defined as:

> A false belief based on incorrect inference about external reality that is firmly sustained despite what almost everyone else believes and despite what constitutes incontrovertible and obvious proof or evidence to the contrary. The belief is not one ordinarily accepted by other members of the person's culture or subculture (e.g., it is not an article of religious faith). When a false belief involves a value judgment, it is regarded as a delusion only when the judgment is so extreme as to defy credibility.

American Psychiatric Association, *Diagnostic and Statistical Manual of Mental Disorders* 821 (4th ed. text rev. 2000) (hereinafter DSM-IV-TR).

Delusional thinking is a hallmark symptom of schizophrenia[5] and of related psychotic disorders, such as schizoaffective disorder.[6] It may also occur as a symptom of mood disorders such as depressive disorders or bipolar disorders.[7] It is particularly pronounced in what is known as the Paranoid Type of Schizophrenia. DSM-IV-TR 313-314. The essential feature of this type of schizophrenia is "the presence of prominent delusions or auditory hallucinations in the content of a relative preservation of cognitive functioning and affect." *Id.* at 313. Typically, persons with this condition suffer from delusions that are categorized as *persecutory* and/or *grandiose*. *Id.* A persecutory delusion, generally speaking, is a delusion whose theme involves a conspiracy or other form of malicious obstruction to thwart the individual's goals. *Id.* at 325. A grandiose delusion is one whose central theme involves the patient possessing a great yet unrecognized talent, sometimes accompanied by the belief that the patient has a special relationship with a prominent person or bears a special message from a deity. *Id.* The two types of delusions are often intertwined: persons experiencing persecutory delusions may reason that, as one textbook puts it, "they must be very important if so much effort is spent on their persecution." Robert Cancro & Heinz E. Lehmann, *Schizophrenia: Clinical Features*, in *Kaplan & Sadock's Comprehensive Textbook of Psychiatry* 1187 (7th ed. 2000).[8]

Psychotic disorders such as schizophrenia distort the mind in certain ways while leaving other functions generally intact. As noted above, an individual with paranoid schizophrenia may possess "a relative preservation of cognitive functioning." DSM-IV-TR 313. Yet such a person, plagued by a delusional psychotic disorder, may have no ability to apply his cognitive functions to test the veracity of the conclusions that he draws; while the *process* of a person's thinking appears normal, the *content* of the thoughts defies accepted reality. For example, a person who is under the delusion that he is the basketball player Michael Jordan may be unable to "test reality" in a way that would disprove his belief. Michael Jordan is tall, athletically gifted, widely recognized, and wealthy. Even after it is pointed out to the delusional person that he possesses none of these characteristics "and even if the person *agrees* that he does not" he may persist in his belief that he is in fact Michael Jordan.

Such persons may understand much of the world around them and have real intelligence. Yet their delusional thought process may consistently lead them to wildly incorrect results. As one psychiatry textbook explains:

> Disturbances of thinking and conceptualization are one of the most characteristic features of

schizophrenia. The feature common to all manifestations of schizophreni[c] thought disorder is that patients think and reason . . . according to their own intricate private rules of logic. Schizophrenic patients may be highly intelligent, certainly not confused, and they may be painstaking in their abstractions and deductions. But their thought processes are strange and do not lead to conclusions based on reality or universal logic.

Cancro & Lehmann, *supra*, at 1189. Thus, a person suffering from schizophreniaor schizoaffective disorder may know that he has committed a crime; tha the death penalty is imposed on persons who commit such crimes; and that the State has asserted he will be put to death because he committed that crime; and yet be absolutely and unwaveringly certain that his execution is not in fact a response to his crime but is instead an effort to prevent him from preaching the Gospel.

2. Panetti suffers from grandiose, persecutory delusions that disrupt his understanding of the purpose of his execution. Based upon the record and findings in this case, Panetti clearly falls into this framework. He is not incoherent: the district court found that "at least some of the time, Panetti is capable of communicating, and apparently understanding, in a coherent fashion." *Panetti*, 401 F. Supp. 2d at 708. As one of the State's experts concluded, Panetti possessed a "capacity to understand the Bible, to understand history, movies." *Id.* Indeed, he represented himself at trial, cross-examined witnesses, and applied for subpoenas.

Yet, in the decade preceding his crime, Panetti was hospitalized with diagnoses that included schizophrenia, schizoaffective disorder, and bipolar disorder—all serious mental disorders that, in his case, were accompanied by psychotic symptoms such as auditory hallucinations and delusions of persecution and grandiosity. Pet. 3. While defending himself at trial, he exhibited a wide array of delusional behaviors. His cross-examination tended to be rambling and illogical, and he attempted to subpoena John F. Kennedy, Pope John Paul II, and Jesus Christ. Although Panetti knows that the State claims it intends to execute him for the murders that he committed, he believes in the words of one of the experts who examined him that "God had nullified it, God had forgiven him, God had wiped the slate clean." *Panetti*, 401 F. Supp. 2d at 707. And the district court credited testimony from one of the State's experts who concluded that:

> Panetti does not even understand that the State of Texas is a lawfully constituted authority, but rather, he believes the State is in league with the forces of evil that have conspired against him. [That expert's] testimony is consistent with that of Dr. Conroy, Dr. Rosin, and Dr. Silverman, each of whom testified Panetti believes the real reason he is to be executed is for preaching the Gospel.

Id. at 712; *see also id.* at 707 (Panetti suffers from "grandiosity and a delusional belief system in which he believes himself to be persecuted for his religious activities and beliefs"). As reflected in the findings and the testimony below, therefore, Panetti is able to draw some logical connections but suffers from textbook persecutory and grandiose delusions centered around religion that render him deeply disturbed and deny him any genuine understanding of the reason for his execution.

Although the record does not reflect the methods employed by the doctors who examined Panetti, it is likely that his delusional belief withstood all attempts to "test reality" by confronting him with contrary evidence. A person who is captive to such a delusion would likely be unconvinced by evidence that, for example (1) the State does not, in fact, seek to execute people for preaching the Gospel and (2) the State has certainly not sought to execute others whose preaching is heard by many more than Panetti's.[9]

C. Contrary to the Rationale of Ford, *by Permitting the Execution of Prisoners Who Suffer from Psychotic Delusions, the Fifth Circuit's Approach Permits Executions That Do Not Further the Death Penalty's Retributive Purpose*

Insisting that the death penalty must serve its core retributive purpose in every case, Justice Powell wrote in *Ford* that "the Eighth Amendment forbids the execution . . . of those who are unaware of the punishment they are about to suffer and why they are to suffer it." 477 U.S. at 422. In *Panetti*, the Fifth Circuit held that "'awareness,' as that term is used in *Ford*, is not necessarily synonymous with 'rational understanding.'" *Panetti*, 448 F.3d at 821. Accordingly, the court of appeals allowed the execution of an individual who believes that the State's expressed reason for his execution is merely a pretext for the true reason: to stop him from preaching Gospel. The Fifth Circuit's approach fails to recognize the force of the delusions that characterize psychotic disorders such as Panetti's, and thus, contrary to *Ford*, permits executions where the retributive purpose of the death penalty is not served.

As a simple linguistic matter, "awareness of why" a person is to suffer the death penalty might arguably be construed to include mere "awareness of *what the State has claimed as a reason."* But that circumscription of Justice Powell's test otherwise makes little sense. There are individuals, like Panetti, who know what the State says but believe just as surely that the State's claim is not true. The Fifth Circuit's approach permits the execution of such severely delusional individuals even though they believe they are to be executed for *something other than their crimes*, notwithstanding the State's assertions to the contrary.

The Fifth Circuit's standard makes some forms of severe delusion about one's impending execution matter, while others do not. For example, an individual capable of repeating back the State's stated reasons for the execution may not be executed if he believes that his execution is impossible (as in *Ford*), but may be executed if he considers it possible or certain but entirely misapprehends why the death penalty is actually being applied to him. Yet both individuals suffer from debilitating delusional thinking about their forthcoming execution and therefore the retributive purpose of the death penalty is not served in either circumstance. Indeed, Justice Powell plainly recognized that the prisoner's awareness of the "why" was as important to the legitimacy of the execution as his awareness of the "whether." Nor does it appear that the retributive purpose is served more fully when the State executes a person whose delusions cause him entirely to disbelieve the State's asserted rationale than when it executes one who cannot comprehend that rationale in the first place.

Indeed, of the various grounds articulated by the *Ford* majority, none supports privileging one sort of fundamental delusion about an impending execution over another. Whether the ground is that "the execution of an insane person simply offends humanity," 477 U.S. at 407, or that such an execution "provides no example to others," *id.*, or that "it is uncharitable to dispatch an offender into another world, when he is not of a capacity to fit himself for it," *id.*, or that "madness is its own punishment," *id.*, or that executing an insane person serves no retributive purpose, *id.*; *see also id.* at 422 (Powell, J., concurring), there is no reason to spare one individual beset by a delusion regarding whether death awaits or the State's purported reasons for imposing the penalty, yet to execute another individual plagued by a different yet equally irrational delusion regarding the same subject.

D. All Three Amici Have Adopted a Common Position on This Issue

For these reasons, with respect to competency to be executed, *amici* and the American Bar Association have respectively adopted substantively identical versions of a recommendation proposed by the Task Force on Mental Disability and the Death Penalty:

If, after challenges to the validity of the conviction and death sentence have been exhausted and execution has been scheduled, a court finds that a prisoner has a mental disorder or disability that significantly impairs his or her capacity to understand the nature and purpose of the punishment, or to appreciate the reason for its imposition in the prisoner's own case, the sentence of death should be reduced to a lesser punishment.[10]

This recommendation, *amici* submit, draws the proper line between individuals who are competent to be executed and those who are not. The recommendation recognizes that it is impossible to draw a meaningful line among the myriad delusions that may fog an individual's understanding of his pending execution, or the reasons for it.

Specifically, under the recommendation, awareness of the "why" of an execution necessarily includes understanding the reason the death penalty is being applied in one's own case. The Report of the Task Force, which explains the reasoning that underlies each recommendation, stated that an offender who has been sentenced to die

must "appreciate" its personal application in the offender's own case—that is, why it is being imposed *on the offender*. This formulation is analogous to the distinction often drawn between a "factual understanding" and a "rational understanding" of the reason for the execution. If, as is generally assumed, the primary purpose of the competence-to-be-executed requirement is to vindicate the retributive aim of punishment, then offenders should have more than a shallow understanding of why they are being executed.

Recommendation and Report on the Death Penalty and Persons with Mental Disabilities, 30 Mental & Physical Disability L. Rep. 668, 675 (2006). In short, it does not fulfill the retributive purpose of the death penalty to execute an individual, like Panetti, who has no rational understanding as to why the punishment is being imposed on him. For that reason, the Fifth Circuit's ruling should be reversed.[11]

II. Mental Health Professionals Can Reliably Identify the Nature and Extent of an Individual's Rational Understanding of an Impending Execution and Routinely Make Similar Assessments in Other Judicial Contexts

In the case at bar, the experts for the State and for the defense largely concurred in the most important aspects of their assessments. *Panetti v. Dretke*, 401 F. Supp. 2d 702, 707–708, 712 (W.D. Tex. 2004) (all experts testified that Panetti possesses cognitive functionality with respect to certain topics and communications, yet suffers delusions, including the belief that he will be executed for preaching the Gospel). Disagreements were limited to the degree, and not existence, of Panetti's delusions pertaining to the reason for his impending execution, *Panetti v. Dretke*, 448 F.3d 815, 817 (5th Cir. 2006), and thus the parties' dispute has focused on the impact of Panetti's functional deficiencies on the ultimate question of "competence to be executed," which is a legal, not a scientific or medical, question.

Expert agreement in this area can be attributed to two factors: first, the underlying scientific and clinical concepts, the nature of psychotic delusions, and the concept of "rational understanding" are well established; second, when the diagnosis is made through an evaluation of the prisoner's currently presenting condition, no extrapolation is needed to assess the prisoner's condition at a remote time in the past.[12] Indeed, the expert consensus on Panetti's diagnosis is consistent with studies showing that mental health professionals using structured interviews and assessing present-oriented functional capacities typically have very high levels of agreement. *See, e.g.*, Gary B. Melton, *et al.*, *Psychological Evaluations for the Courts: A Handbook for Mental Health Professionals and Lawyers* 138 (2d ed. 1997). Thus, mental health experts can provide testimony that can meaningfully inform judicial decisions about competency to be executed with established procedures that have a record of producing reliable, consistent results.

Conclusion

Amici submit that the Fifth Circuit's competence for execution standard permits the execution of individuals who lack any meaningful understanding of the nature and purpose of their punishment, contrary to this Court's decision in *Ford*. *Amici* urge this Court to reverse the judgment of the Fifth Circuit.

Notes

1. Both parties have consented to the filing of this brief. No counsel for a party authored any part of this brief. No person or entity other than *amici* and their counsel made any monetary contribution to the preparation or submission of this brief.

2. In addition to the recommendation discussed in text, the Task Force presented, and *amici* and the ABA adopted, recommendations relating to persons with mental retardation and equivalent impairments of intellectual and adaptive functioning, persons who were mentally ill at the time of the offense, and persons not competent to seek or assist counsel in post-conviction proceedings. *See Recommendation and Report on the Death Penalty and Persons with Mental Disabilities*, 30 Mental & Physical Disability L. Rep. 668, 668 (2006).

3. *Amici* gratefully acknowledge the assistance of Richard J. Bonnie, J.D., Joel A. Dvoskin, Ph.D., Kirk S. Heilbrun, Ph.D., and Diane T. Marsh, Ph.D., in the preparation of this brief.

4. The term "appreciate" approximates the term "rationally understand." *See* Norman G. Poythress, *et al.*, *Adjudicative Competence: The MacArthur Studies* 112 (2002); *see also Martin v. Dugger*, 686 F. Supp. 1523, 1569–1573 (S.D. Fla. 1988).

5. Justice Powell concurred in parts one and two of Justice Marshall's opinion, 477 U.S. at 418, creating a majority for the holding that "the Eighth Amendment prohibits a State from carrying out a sentence of death upon a prisoner who is insane." *Id.* at 409.

6. *Amici* of course have not examined Panetti in person; rather, *amici* rely upon the facts as set forth in the record and on Panetti's prior mental health evaluations.

7. Schizophrenia is typically defined as encompassing two or more of the following five symptoms: (1) delusions; (2) hallucinations; (3) disorganized speech; (4) grossly disorganized or catatonic behavior; and (5) negative symptoms, *i.e.*, affective flattening (diminished emotional expressiveness), alogia (poverty of speech), or avolition (inability to initiate and persist in goal-oriented activities). DSM-IV-TR 299–301, 312.

8. Schizoaffective disorder essentially consists of schizophrenic symptoms coupled with, at some point, either a major depressive episode, a manic episode, or a mixed episode (*i.e.*, an episode in which the individual alternates between major depressive and manic symptoms). DSM-IV-TR 319–323.

9. *See generally* DSM-IV-TR 345–428; *see also id.* at 327 (discussing Mood Disorders With Psychotic Features).

10. It is important to distinguish delusional beliefs from beliefs that are merely wrong. An individual who believes that her husband is cheating on her may be mistaken, but her view may not be delusional, depending upon the facts that she adduces to support her belief. But, the individual who, in one reported case, based such a belief solely on the presence of a red car outside of her apartment, is clearly delusional.

See Adolfo Pazzagli, *Delusion, Narrative, and Affects,* 34 J. of the Am. Acad. of Psychoanalysis & Dynamic Psychiatry 367, 370 (2006).

11. The record in *Barnard* is much more sparse than in *Panetti;* accordingly, it is difficult to assess the true nature of Barnard's delusions. Because the state court found that Barnard tended to blame his conviction on "a conspiracy of Asians, Jews, Blacks, homosexuals, and the Mafia," 13 F.3d at 876, it is likely that his beliefs would have withstood efforts to test reality by presenting him with evidence that (1) those five groups do not, in fact, work in concert, (2) there is no reason why those groups would have any motive to do him harm, and (3) most fundamentally, those groups do not control the judicial system, and thus did not bring about his conviction.

12. American Psychological Association Council of Representatives, APA Policy Manual: N. Public Interest (2001) (incorporating policy adopted by the Council of Representatives in February 2006), *available at. . . . Mentally Ill Prisoners on Death Row: Position Statement*, American Psychiatric Association (2005), *available at. . . .* The National Alliance on Mental Illness adopted an earlier version of this language. *Public Policy Platform of the National Alliance on Mental Illness* 50 (8th ed. 2006), *available at. . . .* The ABA adopted a later version of this proposal with a different final clause. *Recommendation and Report on the Death Penalty and Persons with Mental Disabilities,* 30 Mental & Physical Disability L. Rep. 668, 668 (2006).

AMERICAN PSYCHOLOGICAL ASSOCIATION (APA) aims to improve psychology as a science and as a profession. As the United States' representative of psychology, the APA aspires to advance education, health, and human welfare by liberally supporting all branches of psychology and psychological research, advancing research methods, and improving psychologists' conduct, education, and ethics standards. The APA also advocates for psychology at the federal level through three directorates: education, public interest, and science. The APA works with federal agencies when they reformulate legislation and regulations of psychological interest. www.apa.org

AMERICAN PSYCHIATRIC ASSOCIATION (APA) is an international society working to ensure that all persons with mental disorders receive humane care and effective, accessible psychiatric diagnosis and treatment. In addition to supporting the prevention, diagnosis, and treatment of mental illness and working toward greater funding for education and psychiatric research, the APA educates lawmakers about a variety of issues, including the insanity defense. www.psych.org/

NATIONAL ALLIANCE ON MENTAL ILLNESS (NAMI) is dedicated to eliminating mental illness and improving the lives of mentally ill persons and their families. NAMI takes a strong stance on public policy issues that affect the mentally ill and their loved ones. The alliance supports the insanity defense, favoring both volitional and cognitive standards. www.nami.org/

Greg Abbott et al.

 **NO**

On Writ of Certiorari to the United States Court of Appeals for the Fifth Circuit: Brief for the Respondent

Statement of the Case

A. The Crime

Scott Louis Panetti has led a troubled and violent life. Between 1981 and 1992, Panetti was hospitalized on multiple occasions and variously diagnosed with substance abuse and dependence, personality disorders, depression, chronic undifferentiated schizophrenia, and schizoaffective disorder. JA 339–41;1 Federal Petition for Writ of Habeas Corpus, No. 1:99-CV-00260 (W.D. Tex. Sept. 7, 1999) (hereinafter "Federal Petition") (Ex. 14). Although his doctors initially treated him only with therapy, they later placed him on medication, which proved effective in controlling his mental illness. *Id.*, at 462–63 (noting in 1986 that, while taking medication, Panetti "shows no evidence of thought disorder" and "was not paranoid in his attitude"), 466 (observing in 1990 that, after Panetti was stabilized on his medication, he displayed no evidence of "any delusions or any psychotic thinking, or any suicidal or homicidal ideations").

Panetti married his second wife, Sonja, in 1988, and they had a daughter the following year. 31.RR.61. In August 1992, Sonja separated from Panetti because of his drinking and physical threats. 31.RR.62. She took their daughter, then three years old, to live with her parents, Amanda and Joe Alvarado. 31.RR.60-61. Panetti later called to threaten Sonja and his in-laws, saying he would kill both her and the Alvarados or burn down their house. 31.RR.64. On September 2, 1992, in response to these threats, Sonja obtained a protective order against Panetti. 31.RR.65-66; 41.RR (SX 91).

Six days later, Panetti awoke before dawn, 33.RR.695, shaved his head, 31.RR.95-96, and dressed himself in camouflage, 33.RR.679. Arming himself with a rifle, a sawed-off shotgun, 33.RR.696, and several knives, 33.RR.706-07, Panetti drove to the Alvarados' house, 33.RR.696. When he arrived, Panetti broke his shotgun trying to shatter a sliding glass door near Sonja's bed. 31.RR.69; 33.RR.717. He chased Sonja out of the house and confronted her in the front yard, 33.RR.704, hitting her face with the butt of his rifle, 31.RR.73.

Although Sonja managed to retreat into the house and lock the front door, Panetti shot the lock off and cornered Joe and Amanda Alvarado in the kitchen. 31.RR.42-43; 33.RR.705. He asked Sonja, who was standing in the adjoining hallway, who she would like to see die first. 31.RR.84. Using his rifle, Panetti then shot and killed Joe Alvarado. 31.RR.84. Sonja begged Panetti not to kill her mother, 31.RR.91, but Panetti pressed the rifle against Amanda Alvarado's chest and pulled the trigger, 32.RR.417-18, killing her and spraying Sonja and their daughter with blood, 31.RR.91. Then his rifle jammed. 31.RR.92.

Panetti grabbed Sonja and their daughter and walked them out to his Jeep. 31.RR.92-93. He drove them back to his bunkhouse, 31.RR.94, where he had them wash off the blood, 31.RR.96. When Sonja asked if she could go check on her parents, he responded: "I just shot your parents. No more mommy, no more daddy; get that through your head." 31.RR.96-97. He then forced Sonja to read the protective order aloud. 31.RR.97-98. Sonja asked Panetti if he planned to shoot her and her daughter. 31.RR.98. He replied that he had not yet decided. 31.RR.98.

At dawn, Panetti allowed both Sonja and their daughter to leave the bunkhouse, telling Sonja that he planned to stay there and "shoot two or three policemen" before taking his own life. 31.RR.101. Panetti surrendered to police that afternoon. 31.RR.241. Later the same day, Panetti confessed to the murders, recounting the details of the crime to police. 33.RR.692-737. When asked if he thought that his mental condition excused his behavior, Panetti replied, "it doesn't excuse me from any of that. You know, I made my bed and I'm going to lie in it. . . . I f***ed up. I feel a lot of remorse." 33.RR.734-35; see also JA 208.

Dr. Michael Lennhoff, a psychiatrist, interviewed Panetti several times at the local jail. Panetti stated that he had followed his drug regimen over the preceding year, but he later confessed that he had not taken his medication for one week before the murders. Federal Petition Ex. 14, at 431, 436. Although Dr. Lennhoff noted that Panetti exhibited genuine mental illness, he also concluded that "Panetti may have wanted to impress me with how mentally disturbed he is, perhaps in an exaggerated way." *Id.*, at 434. After a later meeting, Dr. Lennhoff felt that Panetti was "still trying to impress me as not having committed a deliberate crime." *Id.*, at 436.

B. Panetti's Exhaustively Affirmed Conviction and Sentence and the Rejection of His Alleged Incompetence to Stand Trial and to Waive Counsel

Panetti was charged with capital murder. 1.CR.8. The trial court appointed Dr. E. Lee Simes, a psychiatrist, to evaluate Panetti's competence for trial. JA 9. Dr. Simes noted that, despite Panetti's delusional thinking, "his overall story was quite consistent and insightful." JA 13. In particular, Dr. Simes observed that Panetti understood why he was facing capital-murder charges, the significance of those charges, and the significance of the punishment he might receive. JA 13. Panetti also displayed ability to process questions and information and to assist in his defense. JA 13. Dr. Simes concluded that Panetti was competent to stand trial. JA 13.

In April 1994, Panetti moved for a competence hearing. 2.CR.236-41. In the first trial-competence hearing, the jury deadlocked at four for incompetent, three for competent, and five undecided. 3.CR.295-96; 10.RR.379.2. At the second trial-competence hearing, the jury found Panetti competent to stand trial. 13.RR.206-07.

Eight months later, Panetti sent the trial judge a letter explaining that he had stopped taking all medication and, as a result, was "restored to sanity"; he had dismissed his attorneys; he felt competent to represent himself; he did not intend to "act like a lawyer" in his trial; and he would be able to prove that he was insane at the time of the murders. 3.CR.360. Panetti's attorneys then moved to withdraw as his counsel. 3.CR.363–64.

The trial court called a pretrial hearing to inquire further into Panetti's expressed desire to represent himself. 15.RR.5. The judge told Panetti that he personally did not want Panetti to represent himself, 15.RR.10, and asked Panetti's attorneys to confer privately with Panetti about waiving counsel, 15.RR.11. After this consultation, Panetti's attorneys reported that they did not think Panetti should represent himself, but that was his "clear intent." 15.RR.12–13. Panetti confirmed that he wanted to represent himself because he had the right to do so

under Texas law and the United States Constitution, and that he was "fully aware" of the penalty for the charges against him. 15.RR.18. Panetti then executed a voluntary waiver of counsel. 3.CR.369. The district attorney informed the court that, because the State was "concerned about protecting the Defendant's rights," he did not want Panetti's attorneys to withdraw. 15.RR.24. When the court reexamined Panetti about his decision, Panetti replied, "I understand everything that's been going on today, sir. I do, however, feel a little bit insulted that I have been asked the same question so many times, Your Honor." 15.RR.25–28. The court held that Panetti had voluntarily and intelligently exercised his right to represent himself and then appointed standby counsel for Panetti. 15.RR.29–30.

At trial, Panetti entered a plea of not guilty by reason of insanity. 31.RR.24. In his rambling opening statement, Panetti informed the jury that he had been diagnosed with paranoid schizophrenia and manic depression in 1986, and that he believed only an insane person could prove the insanity defense. 31.RR.28–29. As Panetti explains in his brief, he exhibited bizarre and incoherent behavior throughout his trial. Panetti Br. 11–15. He did call as witnesses two psychiatrists who had previously treated him, 38.RR.1567–1616, and endeavored to establish through one that, when he did not take his medication, his mental illness could prevent him from distinguishing right and wrong, 38.RR.1574–75. The jury nonetheless found Panetti guilty of capital murder and sentenced him to death. 7.CR.1041–44; 38.RR.1685; 39.RR.102. The Texas Court of Criminal Appeals (CCA) affirmed Panetti's conviction and sentence, *Panetti v. Texas*, No. 72,230 (Tex. Crim. App. Dec. 3, 1997) (unpublished), and the Court denied certiorari, 525 U.S. 848 (1998) (Mem.). Panetti then filed a state habeas petition raising fourteen claims, including whether he was competent to stand trial and competent to waive counsel. State Petition for Writ of Habeas Corpus, No. 3310-A, at 3–4 (Tex. Crim. App. June 19, 1997). The CCA denied relief. (pp. 1–5)

In sum, one jury and four courts rejected Panetti's trial-incompetence claim; one court found him competent to waive counsel and four courts rejected his collateral challenge to that determination; and another jury and two courts rejected his insanity defense. No judge or jury has ever found him incompetent.

C. Panetti's Efforts to Prove Incompetence to Be Executed in State and Federal Court

Once an execution date was set, Panetti filed a motion in the state trial court under Texas Code of Criminal Procedure

Article 46.05 asserting incompetence to be executed. JA 355. After concluding that Panetti had failed to make a substantial showing of incompetence, the state court denied his Article 46.05 motion, JA 355, and the CCA dismissed his appeal, *Ex parte Panetti*, No. 74,868 (Tex. Crim. App. Jan. 28, 2004) (*per curiam*) (unpublished).

Panetti then filed a habeas petition in federal district court, asserting that *Ford v. Wainwright*, 477 U.S. 399 (1986), prohibited his execution. JA 355–56. The district court granted a stay of execution and allowed Panetti an opportunity to present his renewed allegations to the state trial court. JA 357.

In response to Panetti's second Article 46.05 motion, the state court appointed two neutral experts, Dr. George Parker and Dr. Mary Anderson, to assess Panetti's competence to be executed. JA 59. After conducting a joint interview of Panetti, Drs. Parker and Anderson filed a report documenting their observations and conclusions. JA 70–76. This report reflects Panetti's hostility to Drs. Parker's and Anderson's questions, his tendency toward religious conversation, his attempted manipulation of the interview process, and his general refusal to cooperate with the court-appointed experts. JA 70–73, 75.

Because of Panetti's refusal to cooperate, Drs. Parker and Anderson also relied on several sources of collateral data—including prison records; letters that Panetti had recently written to friends and family; court documents, including documents relating to other competence determinations; discussions with prison staff; and another expert evaluation of Panetti—to help form their relevant opinions. JA 73–75. Based on these data and their personal observations, Drs. Parker and Anderson concluded that Panetti (1) "knows that he is to be executed, and that his execution will result in his death" and (2) "has the ability to understand the reason he is to be executed." JA 75.

In response, Panetti filed a detailed submission criticizing Drs. Parker and Anderson's methodology and contrasting their conclusions with those in a psychiatric evaluation that Panetti had previously presented to the court. JA 79–98. After considering that submission, the state court again denied relief under Article 46.05. JA 99.

Panetti then sought habeas relief in the federal district court, JA 375, which concluded that the state court's determination of Panetti's competence to be executed was not entitled to AEDPA deference because Panetti allegedly failed to receive constitutionally sufficient process, JA 359–61. After granting Panetti's motions for appointment of counsel, discovery, and funds for expert and investigative assistance, JA 358, the district court held an evidentiary

hearing on competence, JA 362. At the hearing, Panetti presented expert testimony[.]" (pp. 5–7)

"All of the expert witnesses agreed that Panetti suffers from some degree of mental illness." Although some of the experts labeled this illness schizophrenia or schizoaffective disorder, *e.g.*, JA 144–45, 205, they were collectively unable to agree on a single diagnosis, see JA 239, 313.[1]

The experts did agree, however, that Panetti has the capacity to—and does, in fact—understand that he will be executed. JA 147–48, 207, 236, 243, 245.[2]

Further expert testimony established Panetti's specific understanding that he committed the murders. Indeed, Dr. Rosin testified that Panetti recounted details of his activity on the day of the murders and expressed sorrow for having committed the crime. JA 208; see also JA 148–49 (Dr. Conroy's testimony that Panetti believed that God had forgiven him for killing the Alvarados and had "wiped the slate clean"). Dr. Silverman testified to uncertainty about whether Panetti knows that he killed the Alvarados, but only because Panetti steadfastly refused to answer his questions on this topic. JA 221.

Several experts also concluded that Panetti's delusions created a false sense of the true reason for his execution. *E.g.*, JA 149, 156, 202, 209 (testimony from Drs. Conroy and Rosin that Panetti believes his execution was ordered to prevent him from preaching the Gospel). Importantly, however, these same experts testified that Panetti understands that the State's stated reason for his execution is punishment for capital murder. JA 157, 214.

Dr. Parker testified that portions of Panetti's responses to the experts execution-competence examinations could be attributed to malingering, see JA 241–43; see also, *e.g.*, JA 174, 177, 181 (noting additional reports of Panetti's suspected malingering in the past), and Drs. Parker and Anderson each specifically testified that Panetti has the capacity to understand the reason for his execution, JA 245, 247, 303–04. Both Dr. Parker and Dr. Anderson emphasized that Panetti was deliberately manipulative and uncooperative during his interview with them. JA 239–40, 244–46, 271, 300, 303, 312–14; accord JA 75. They based their ultimate conclusions on Panetti's overall cognitive functionality, as demonstrated through letters he wrote to friends and family, his logical responses to interview questions, and his ability to understand such things as history and movies. JA 242–43, 302–04.

Dr. Parker's suspicions of malingering were corroborated by evidence of psychiatric evaluations conducted in the two years following Panetti's capital trial. For example, Dr. Michael Gilhousen noted that loosening of Panetti's thought processes "appeared to be intentional on his part to create the impression of mental illness." JA 167, II-30. After another interview, Dr. Gilhousen described Panetti's behavior as "obviously manipulative and theatrical." JA 171–72, II-20. Another doctor expressed the belief that Panetti's switching among different voices was "contrived . . . to impress us or lead us to believe that he did have alter personalities." JA 170, II-41.

After hearing all the evidence, the federal district court made three factual findings. First, based on the expert's agreement, the court concluded that Panetti is aware that he will be executed. JA 372.

Second, the district court found that Panetti is aware that he committed both murders. JA 372. The court based this conclusion on Dr. Conroy's and Dr. Rosin's testimony that Panetti knows that he murdered the Alvarados. JA 372. Although the court recognized that Dr. Silverman's testimony cast doubt on this conclusion, the court discounted that testimony, noting that it was based on Panetti's limited responses during his interview with Dr. Silverman. JA 372.

Third, the district court found that Panetti understands the State's stated reason for execution. JA 372. The court based this finding on the testimony of Drs. Conroy and Rosin, and discounted Dr. Silverman's contrary testimony for the same reason. JA 372–73.

Additionally, the district court recounted Dr. Parker's and Dr. Anderson's assessments that "some portion of Panetti's behavior could be attributed to malingering," and it expressly concluded that, although all of the experts had agreed Panetti had "some degree" of mental illness, their testimony collectively "casts doubt on the extent of Panetti's mental illness and symptoms." JA 363.

Finally, the district court noted Dr. Cunningham's testimony that "suggests" that Panetti's delusions prevent him from understanding that Texas is a lawfully constituted authority and lead him to believe that the State "is in league with the forces of evil that have conspired against him," and it observed that this testimony was consistent with the testimony of Panetti's other experts. JA 373. The court made no finding, however, whether these delusions were genuine or the partial product of malingering, because the court deemed it irrelevant to the question of whether Panetti "knows the reason for his execution" within the meaning of the court of appeals's execution-competence test. JA 373.

Based on these factual findings, the district court concluded that Panetti is competent to be executed. JA 373. Although the court denied Panetti's habeas petition, it stayed his execution pending appeal, JA 373, and granted a certificate of appealability, *Panetti v. Dretke*, No.

04-CA-042 (W.D. Tex. Nov. 4, 2004). The court of appeals affirmed the district court's denial of habeas relief, *Panetti v. Dretke*, 448 F.3d 815 (CA5 2006); JA 374–84, and the Court granted certiorari, JA 387.

Summary of the Argument

In devoting fully half of his brief to his statement of the case, Panetti endeavors to focus the Court's attention on his lengthy mental-health history, explaining that "incompetency runs like a fissure through every proceeding in this case." Panetti Br. 6. But that fissure has been mostly sealed once and for all by the conclusive determinations of state and federal courts repeatedly rejecting Panetti's direct and collateral challenges to adverse rulings on his insanity defense, his competence to stand trial, and his competence to waive counsel. For that reason, Panetti correctly concedes that, as a matter of law, he is now presumed competent to be executed. *Ibid.*

The state court, the district court, and the court of appeals have all concluded that Panetti has failed to overcome that presumption. The district court found as a factual matter that Panetti knows that he murdered the Alvarados, that he will be executed, and that the State's stated reason for executing him is that he committed two murders. Panetti has not challenged those factual findings on appeal. (pp. 7–11)

"Both Panetti's and his *amici's* proposed standards, which require that a convict rationally understand" the reasons for his execution, are fundamentally flawed. Given the inherent subjectivity and manipulability of such a standard, capital murderers could as a routine matter claim a lack of "rational understanding" through malingering or refusing to cooperate with experts. (p. 12) . . . "Finally, the retributive and deterrent interests served by the death penalty—focused primarily as they are on society at large rather than the capital murderer—do not demand the "rational understanding" that Panetti urges.

The Court should instead adopt a clear and objective test for execution competence. Specifically, the Court should hold that a mentally ill capital convict is incompetent to be executed only if, because of his illness, he lacks the *capacity* to recognize that his punishment (1) is the result of his being convicted of capital murder and (2) will cause his death. This standard controls for the malingering or uncooperative convict, is appropriately tailored to the execution stage of capital proceedings, and serves the twin goals of retribution and deterrence that justify capital punishment. Applying this standard, the Court should hold that Panetti is competent to be executed. (pp. 12–13)

Argument

II. Even if AEDPA Deference Does Not Apply, Panetti's Execution Does Not Violate the Eighth Amendment

Only if the Court concludes that the AEDPA does not bar habeas review should it reach Panettis claim that the court of appeals employed the wrong legal standard for execution competence. Although *Ford* held that the Eighth Amendment proscribes execution of the "insane," 477 U.S., at 409–10, the Court did not define "insanity" or otherwise delineate the constitutional threshold of competence to be executed, *id.*, at 418 (Powell, J., concurring in the judgment), a question which remains unresolved.

Before turning to the merits of that claim, two issues bear emphasis. **First**, there is no dispute that, under *Ford*, executing the insane violates the Eighth Amendment. Executing the insane was forbidden at common law, and it is forbidden today." (p. 19) . . . "And **second**, there is no dispute that, like many capital defendants, Panetti suffers from some degree of mental illness." (p. 19)

"The only legal question before the Court on the merits of this case is what is the definition of "insanity"— that is, what must a court find to conclude that a capital murderer is constitutionally incompetent to be executed." (p. 19)

Although execution of the "insane" was deemed cruel and unusual in 1971, *Ford*, 477 U.S., at 406–08, the common law did not then draw fine distinctions in mental ability, and thus did not delineate any precise competence standard. Consequently, the standards of the common law are, at best, inconclusive. Likewise, a survey of modern state legislation offers indefinite guidance, as it yields no consensus at all on the mental faculty a capital murderer must possess at the time of his execution. Finally, in the exercise of its independent judgment, the Court should reject the proposition that a capital convict must possess a "rational understanding" of the reasons for his execution to render death an acceptable punishment under the Eighth Amendment. Such a standard is not tailored to the particular interests at stake in the postsentencing phase of capital proceedings, invites malingering and abuse, and is not necessary to advance the retributive and deterrent justifications for the death penalty.

For all of these reasons, the Court should reject Panetti's and his *amici*'s proposed execution-competence standards." (pp. 20–21)

C. The Court Should Hold That the Appropriate Constitutional Standard for Competence to Be Executed Is Whether a Defendant Has the Capacity to Recognize That His Punishment Is the Result of His Being Convicted of Capital Murder and Will Cause His Death. (p. 33)

"Both Panetti's and his *amici*'s proposed execution-competence standards are deeply flawed. The State urges the Court to reject those proposals and instead adopt a clearer and more objective test. Specifically, the Court should hold that a mentally ill capital convict is incompetent to be executed only if, because of his illness, he lacks the *capacity* to recognize that his punishment (1) is the result of his being convicted of capital murder and (2) will cause his death.

The State's proposed standard—derived from *Ford* and the Court's Eighth Amendment jurisprudence—prevents the execution of the truly incompetent, while at the same time (1) incorporating essential safeguards against malingering and noncooperation with psychological examiners, (2) being specifically tailored to the postsentencing phase of capital proceedings, and (3) effectively advancing the modern penological interests behind the death penalty.

1. **Because of the inherent uncertainties and subjectivity of psychiatric testing, and the risks of malingering and abuse, any standard for competence to be executed should be rigorous and clear."** (pp. 33–34)

"The Court has often noted the difficulties that attend even the most skilled psychiatric diagnoses. "[P]sychiatrists disagree widely and frequently on what constitutes mental illness [and] on the appropriate diagnosis to be attached to given behavior and symptoms." *Ake v. Oklahoma*, 470 U.S. 68, 81 (1985). For that reason, "a particularly acute need for guarding against error inheres in a determination that 'in the present state of the mental sciences is at best a hazardous guess however conscientious.'" *Ford*, 477 U.S., at 412 (plurality op.) (quoting *Solesbee v. Balkcom*, 339 U.S. 9, 23 (1950) (Frankfurter, J., dissenting)). As Justice Powell explained,

"Unlike issues of historical fact, the question of petitioner's sanity calls for a basically subjective judgment. And unlike a determination of whether the death penalty is appropriate in a particular case, the competency determination depends substantially on expert analysis in a discipline fraught with 'subtleties and nuances.'" *Id.*, at 426 (Powell, J., concurring in the judgment) (quoting *Addington v. Texas*, 441 U.S. 418, 430 (1979)) (citations omitted).

Just last Term, the Court observed that the medical definitions of mental illness "are subject to flux and disagreement," and that such diagnoses "may mask vigorous debate within the profession about the very contours of the mental disease itself." *Clark v. Arizona*, 126 S.Ct. 2709, 2722, 2734 (2006). "[T]he consequence of this professional ferment," the Court noted, "is a general caution in treating psychological classifications as predicates for excusing otherwise criminal conduct." *Id.*, at 2734.

Not only are psychiatric diagnoses subjective and frequently conflicting, they are by their nature subject to change. *Atkins* and *Roper* were predicated on constant variables: if a defendant is fifteen or seventeen or twenty at the time of the crime, that age at that instant is fixed and unchanging; likewise, if an individual is of normal intelligence throughout his or her life, that person cannot be expected later to become mentally retarded. In contrast, if a person is sane yesterday and today, that does not mean he or she will be sane tomorrow. As Justice O'Connor cautioned in *Ford*, that mutability carries with it serious risks of malingering:

> "[T]he *potential for false claims and deliberate delay* in this context is *obviously enormous*. This potential is exacerbated by a unique feature of the prisoner's protected interest in suspending the execution of a death sentence during incompetency. By definition, this interest can *never* be conclusively and finally determined: Regardless of the number of prior adjudications of the issue, until the very moment of execution the prisoner can claim that he has become insane sometime after the previous determination to the contrary." 477 U.S., at 429 (O'Connor, J., concurring in part and dissenting in part) (citations omitted) (first two emphases added).[3]

Finally, unlike with age or retardation, capital murderers facing execution may have some ability to voluntarily choose to render themselves incompetent to be executed simply by ceasing to take their medication. Indeed, in the case at bar, the evidence indicates that Panetti's medication had been largely successful in controlling his mental illness, Federal Petition Ex. 14, at 462–63, but that he willingly chose to stop taking it, *id.*, at 431, 436; 3.CR.360.

Panetti's proposed "rational understanding" standard has no basis in the Court's precedent and would invite abuse. (pp. 34–36)

   a. **A "rational understanding" inquiry would engraft Fifth and Sixth Amendment concerns on an Eighth Amendment test.**

Although Panetti uses the phrase loosely, "rational understanding" is a specific term of art; it describes the core of several pre-sentencing competence tests. "Rational understanding" was introduced in *Dusky*, in which the Court defined the test for competence to stand trial as whether the defendant has "sufficient present ability to consult with his lawyer with a reasonable degree of rational understanding" and has "a rational as well as factual understanding of the proceedings against him." 362 U.S., at 402 (quotation marks omitted); see also *Godinez v. Moran*, 509 U.S. 389, 398 (1993) (concluding that the "rational understanding" test should also be used to measure a defendant's competence to plead guilty and to waive the right to counsel). (p. 37)

"[A] 'rational understanding' is necessary to ensure that defendants do not foolishly or mistakenly relinquish valuable constitutional rights. A defendant faced with such choices must be able to understand the nature and object of the proceedings against him, to consult with counsel, and to assist in preparing his defense." *Drope*, 420 U.S., at 171.

But a capital convict, unlike a capital defendant, has substantially fewer rights, and there are no significant strategic choices left for him to make. See *Herrera v. Collins*, 506 U.S. 390, 399 (1993) (explaining that the presumption of innocence disappears after conviction and listing numerous constitutional rights that defendants enjoy but that convicts do not); *Barefoot v. Estelle*, 463 U.S. 880, 887–88 (1983) (discussing the "secondary and limited" nature of federal habeas proceedings); see also *Ford*, 477 U.S., at 421 (Powell, J., concurring in the judgment) (noting that, because the Court's decisions already recognize . . . that a defendant must be competent to stand trial, . . . the notion that a defendant must be able to assist in his defense is largely provided for"). Assuming that a convict is competent to be executed, only the remote possibilities of clemency or commutation—processes that call for no significant strategic decisions by a convict—can prevent the sentence from being carried out.

b. Panetti's conception of "rational understanding" is far too expansive.

Panetti's argument is, in fact, even more aggressive than one for inclusion of only a pure "rational understanding" component. Although he invokes that phrase throughout his brief, the substantive requirement that Panetti asks the Court to incorporate is actually a version of the heightened "knowing and voluntary" requirement that the Court has held applicable, over and above the "rational understanding" competence component, with respect to a defendant's decision to plead guilty or to waive his right to counsel. *Godinez*, 509 U.S., at 400–01 & n.12; *Faretta v. California*, 422 U.S. 806, 835 (1975).

As *Godinez* explained, "knowing and voluntary" is not part of any competence test; it is an additional safeguard designed to ensure not merely that a defendant has the *capacity* to understand trial proceedings, but rather that he "*actually does* understand the significance and consequences of a particular decision and whether the decision is uncoerced." 509 U.S., at 401, n.12 (emphasis added). (pp. 38–39)

"[R]equiring a "deep" or "meaningful" appreciation of the State's reasons for imposing the death penalty would create an even greater risk that the Court's test could be circumvented through malingering or abuse. See *supra* Part II.C.1." (p. 39)

When viewed in light of the overall death-row population, Panetti's proposal is especially problematic. As a matter of common understanding, most individuals who commit heinous murders are, almost by definition, not entirely sane. Although estimates vary, some sources indicate that as many as 70 percent of death-row inmates suffer from some form of schizophrenia or psychosis. Nancy S. Horton, Restoration of Competency for Execution: Furiosus Solo Furore Punitur, 44 Sw. L.J. 1191, 1204 (1990) (citing Amnesty International, United States of America: the Death Penalty 108–09 (1987)); see JA 142 (expert testimony that most of the convicts in federal Bureau of Prisons hospitals are schizophrenic). Many, if not most, schizophrenics exhibit the type of delusional thinking that Panetti has been observed to exhibit. See Douglas Mossman, *Atkins v. Virginia: A Psychiatric Can of Worms*, 33 N.M. L. Rev. 255, 280 (2003); APA Br. 8 (noting that "[d]elusional thinking is a hallmark symptom of schizophrenia" (citing DSM-IV-TR 299–301, 312)).[4] Accordingly, Panetti's "rational understanding" requirement would be applied to a population that is, in significant part, delusional—and thus necessarily *irrational*. See APA Br. 9, n.11." (p. 40)

[T]he introduction of Panetti's ill-defined—and inherently indefinite—"rational understanding" component would render the execution-competence standard substantially overinclusive. See Mossman, *supra*, at 289 ("Given the high rate of serious mental illness among homicide defendants, granting psychiatric exemptions could leave very few individuals eligible for the death penalty.").

Nor is this potential for exempting vast numbers of convicted murderers from execution an unintended consequence of Panetti's and his *amici*'s proposed test. Indeed, *amicus* APA is nothing if not candid, explaining that both its own position and the ABA's is that "an individual who is found incompetent to face the death penalty" should not have his sentence "merely suspended," but should "have his sentence *permanently commuted* to a non-capital punishment." APA Br. 17, n.15 (emphasis added). Thus, the conceded objective of these *amici* (and the predictable consequence of their proposed test) is not simply avoiding the inhumanity of executing a person who is truly insane, but rather removing from death row as large a class of capital convicts as reasonably possible.[5] (pp. 40–41)

Application of the State's proposed test will advance the modern penological interests behind the death penalty.

The Court has recently confirmed that retribution and deterrence are capital punishment's two predominant social purposes. *Roper*, 543 U.S., at 571 (citing *Gregg v. Georgia*, 428 U.S. 153, 183 (1976) (joint opinion of Stewart, Powell, and Stevens, JJ.)); accord *Atkins*, 536 U.S., at 318–19. As shown below, application of the State's proposed test will advance each of those interests.[6]

a. The State's test will further the retributive purpose of punishment.

Retribution aims either "to express the community's moral outrage or . . . to right the balance for the wrong to the victim." *Roper*, 543 U.S., at 571; see *Atkins*, 536 U.S., at 319 (explaining that retribution is "the interest in seeing that the offender gets his 'just deserts' "). The Court has repeatedly emphasized the societal focus of retribution. See, *e.g.*, *Thompson v. Oklahoma*, 487 U.S. 815, 836 (1988); see also *Schriro v. Summerlin*, 542 U.S. 348, 360 (2004) (Breyer, J., dissenting); *Gregg*, 428 U.S., at 183–84 (joint opinion of Stewart, Powell, and Stevens, JJ.). Panetti misunderstands the societal nature of retribution, erroneously equating it with vengeance. Panetti Br. 46 & n.33. (p. 43)

i. The retributive justification for punishment necessarily precedes any execution-competence analysis.

The viability of retribution as a permissible theory of punishment depends not on the "rational understanding" that a convict may or may not have, see *supra* Part II.C.2; cf. Panetti Br. 46, but rather on the convict's moral culpability at the time he committed his crime, *Enmund v. Florida*, 458 U.S. 782, 800–01 (1982) (reflecting that "personal responsibility and moral guilt" define a criminal's level of culpability and concluding that execution of one convict for murders that he did not personally commit failed to serve the retributive goal of punishment). (p. 44)

[I]n the present context the question of culpability will already have been conclusively—and affirmatively—resolved. The issue is not whether the Constitution permits society to *impose* the death penalty on a criminal who was, for some reason, less culpable at the time of his crime, cf. *Roper*, 543 U.S., at 556, 578; *Atkins*, 536 U.S., at 306–08, 321, but rather whether an unquestionably valid death sentence may be *carried out* against a criminal who has subsequently become mentally ill, see *Ford*, 477 U.S., at 425 (Powell, J., concurring in the judgment). This is so because any convict to whom the execution-competence test is applied will necessarily have been adjudicated both sane at the time of his offense and competent to stand trial, removing any doubts about culpability that might in some cases arise from mental illness.

> ### ii. There are substantial problems with the wholly personal view of retribution that Panetti advances. (pp. 44–45)

"Relying heavily on nonjudicial sources, Panetti asserts that retribution requires a condemned prisoner to have a subjective appreciation of the moral impropriety of his criminal conduct and to "suffer the anguish" of knowing the reason for his fate. Panetti Br. 45. (p. 45)

Putting aside its lack of support in case law, there are significant problems with Panetti's mind-of-the-criminal approach. First, tailoring the execution competence test to the innermost thoughts of capital convicts would present substantial practical problems. It is difficult to imagine how anyone other than the convict himself could accurately assess whether he truly appreciates the magnitude of his moral wrong—at least with respect to a convict who is willing to lie about such things. And under Panetti's proposed test, it would be remarkably easy for a convict to feign his way out of a death sentence.

Second, allowing the execution-competence test to be shaped primarily by a personal, subjective view of the retributive rationale would prevent the execution of convicts who genuinely lack moral qualms about their crimes. It cannot be that amoral capital convicts should be excused from death sentences based on amorality alone. Yet Panetti's proposed standard would yield that result. (p. 46)

D. Under Both the State's Proposed Test and the Test That the Court of Appeals Applied, Panetti Is Competent to Be Executed. (p. 48)

Under the State's proposed test, Panetti could properly be held incompetent to be executed only if, because of mental illness, he lacked the capacity to recognize that his punishment (1) is the result of his being convicted of capital murder and (2) will cause his death. To the extent, this test varies from that applied by the court of appeals, any such variances are immaterial to the result because, as shown below, the record establishes that Panetti is competent to be executed under either standard.

First of all, it is undisputed that Panetti has the capacity to recognize that the punishment he faces is death. Indeed, the experts all agreed and the district court expressly found that, as a factual matter, "Panetti is aware he is to be executed," JA 363, 372; accord JA 373. Panetti did not oppose this conclusion in the district court, see JA 367, 372, did not challenge it in the court of appeals, and does not challenge it here. Therefore, Panetti is unquestionably "[]aware of the punishment [he is] about to suffer," JA 379 (quoting *Ford*, 477 U.S., at 422 (Powell, J., concurring in the judgment))" (p. 48–49).

The only question that remains is whether Panetti has the capacity to recognize that his punishment is the result of his being convicted of capital murder, or, under the court of appeals's analysis, whether he is aware of why he is to be executed, JA 379. The record establishes that Panetti passes each of these prongs as well.

Dr. Parker and Dr. Anderson each testified that Panetti has the capacity to understand that he is being executed for the murders of which he was convicted. JA 245, 247 (testimony of Dr. Parker), 303–04 (testimony of Dr. Anderson); accord JA 75 (joint report of Drs. Parker and Anderson), and the district court explicitly concluded that "[t]here is evidence in the record to support a finding that Panetti is *capable* of understanding the reason for his execution," JA 367. Again, Panetti does not challenge this conclusion. And under the State's proposed test, it is irrelevant that these witnesses "were unable to reach a formal conclusion that [Panetti] did, in fact, understand" the reason for his execution. JA 364. For the reasons already noted, it is the *capacity* to understand—rather than actual demonstration of understanding—that defines the minimal level of competence needed to satisfy this prong of the State's proposed test. See *supra* Part II.C.3.

And with respect to the court of appeals's test, the district court accurately noted that two of Panetti's own execution-competence experts testified that, "despite his delusions, Panetti understands [that] the State's stated reason for seeking his execution is for his murders." JA 366; see also JA 157 (testimony of Dr. Conroy); JA 214 (testimony of Dr. Rosin). Thus, not only did the district court explicitly find that "Panetti is aware he committed the murders that serve as the basis for his execution," JA 372, but the court further found that "Panetti understands the State's stated reason for executing him is that he committed two murders," JA 372.

The district court also correctly concluded that the alternative sense of "understand" embodied in Panetti's proposal did not match the court of appeals's standard. JA 369 (p. 49–50).

In sum, the record establishes that Panetti: (1) has the capacity to recognize that his punishment will cause his death (and does in fact does recognize this), and (2) has the capacity to recognize that his punishment is the result of his being convicted of capital murder (or, within the meaning of the court of appeals's test, is aware of why he is to be executed). Taken together, these facts conclusively establish Panetti's competence to be executed under both the court of appeals's test and the State's proposed test.

Conclusion

The judgment of the court of appeals should be affirmed. (p. 50)

Notes

1. Citations to the transcript of Panetti's capital-murder trial are noted as "RR" ("Reporters Record"). Citations to the States exhibits admitted into evidence during those proceedings are noted as "SX" ("State Exhibit"). Citations to the pleadings, orders, and motions filed in the trial court are noted as "CR" ("Clerk's Record"). Citations to the federal district court's hearing on execution competence are noted as "FH" ("Federal Hearing"). Citations to the joint appendix filed in this Court are noted as "JA."

2. Panetti incorrectly reports the final vote as nine-to-three in favor of incompetence. Panetti Br. 8, n.6. That vote occurred earlier in the deliberations. 3.CR.290.

3. Dr. Conroy noted that "the major portion of our population in our inpatient units in federal Bureau of Prisons hospitals are diagnosed with some form of schizophrenia," JA 142, and Dr. Silverman opined that most schizophrenics are competent to be executed, JA 227.

4. Lay testimony corroborated this point. Major Miller testified that Panetti cooperated with him in going over the State's pre-execution forms, JA 281, II-42–53, and demonstrated his understanding of the forms' questions about disposition of assets, choice of last meal, and the like. JA 287–88. Additional lay testimony reflected Panetti's demonstrated ability to communicate coherently—and politely—with prison staff. *E.g.*, 1 FH 193–96 (testimony of Terri Hill); 1 FH 200 (testimony of Victoria Williams).

5. In so noting, Justice O'Connor echoed the concerns of Hale, who, some three centuries earlier, likewise urged courts to guard against the potential for "great fraud" concerning those claiming incompetence. 1 Hale, *supra*, at 35; Legal Historians Br. 15, n.8.

6. Indeed, one death-row study of a limited population noted that half of the profiled inmates exhibited delusional tendencies, which included persecutory delusions (*e.g.*, inmate's belief that he was target of a Jewish conspiracy). Barbara A. Ward, Competency for Execution: Problems in Law and Psychiatry, 14 Fla. St. U. L. Rev. 35, 39–40 & n.26 (1986) (citing Bluestone & McGahee, Reaction to Extreme Stress: Impending Death by Execution, 119 Am. J. Psychiatry 393, 393 (1962)). Other inmates in the study coped with their predicament through obsessive rumination, "thinking furiously about other things, such as appeals, religion, or philosophy." *Ibid.*

GREG ABBOTT was reelected as the 50th attorney general of Texas on November 7, 2006. Prior to his election as attorney general, Greg Abbott served as a justice on the Texas Supreme Court and as a state district judge in Harris County.

EXPLORING THE ISSUE

Must Mentally Ill Murderers Have a Rational Understanding of Why They Are Being Sentenced to Death?

Critical Thinking and Reflection

1. In murder cases in which the assertion is made that an individual's crime was attributable to mental illness, complex questions arise about how to assess the legitimacy of the accused person's psychiatric symptoms. If you were a member of a jury in such a case, what kind of evidence would you deem necessary so that a determination could be made about the accused person's psychological functioning?

2. In criminal cases involving mentally ill individuals, several debates have emerged about the condition of the accused within the context of the trial. A particularly thorny issue pertains to whether the accused should be taken off all antipsychotic medication for the trial, so that the court can see this individual in a nonmedicated state (possibly similar to the functional level at the time of the crime). Discuss the benefits and problems of this option.

3. Some proponents of the death penalty would argue that people who engage in violent murder should be executed, regardless of whether they are mentally ill, if for no reason other than ridding society of such people. Discuss the moral implications of this stance.

4. Forensic specialists have worked diligently for years to develop assessment measures to determine whether people accused of a crime are malingering (faking symptoms for an ulterior motive). If you were given the task of developing such an instrument, what kind of data would you look for?

5. Discuss the hypothetical situation in which a convicted murderer understands the nature of his crime but has no understanding of what the death penalty means or why it would be associated with the crime he had committed. Discuss the moral dilemmas inherent in a decision to execute such an individual.

6. After reading the criticisms of the research studies cited in these briefs, what are some of the methodological limitations evident in the studies cited? If you were conducting such research, how would you try to overcome these limitations?

Is There Common Ground?

Related to the debate under consideration in these two selections is the legal concept of insanity, and the defense that is sometimes invoked to defend an accused murderer. The insanity defense refers to the argument presented by a lawyer acting on behalf of the client that, because of a mental disorder, the client should not be held legally responsible for criminal actions. In an attempt to develop uniform standards for the insanity defense, the American Law Institute published guidelines in 1962 stating that people are not responsible for criminal behavior if at the time of the crime their mental disorder prevented them from appreciating the wrongfulness of their behavior or from exerting the necessary willpower to control an irresistible impulse.

In the case of Panetti, the heart of the debate was not so much whether he was insane at the time he committed the murders, but whether he understood why he had been sentenced to execution. He asserted that he was being executed because he preached the gospel, not because of the murders. Thus, even though both sides of the debate respect the insanity defense, they disagree with the notion that the convicted murderer must have a rational understanding of his sentence to death.

Create Central

www.mhhe.com/createcentral

Additional Resources

Bartol, C. R., & Bartol, A. M. (2012). *Current Perspectives in Forensic Psychology and Criminal Behavior.* Thousand Oaks, CA: SAGE.

Bohm, R. M. (2012). *Deathquest, Fourth Edition: An Introduction to the Theory and Practice of Capital Punishment in the United States.* Waltham, MA: Anderson Publishing.

Perlin, M. L. (2013). *Mental Disability and the Death Penalty: The Shame of the States.* Lanham, MD: Rowman & Littlefield.

Internet References . . .

American Constitution Society for Law and Policy

https://www.acslaw.org/

Criminal Justice Legal Foundation

http://www.cjlf.org/

National Alliance on Mental Illness

www.nami.org

Selected, Edited, and with Issue Framing Material by:
Richard P. Halgin, *University of Massachusetts, Amherst*

ISSUE

Does Research Confirm That Abortion Is a Psychologically Benign Experience?

YES: APA Task Force on Mental Health and Abortion, from "Mental Health and Abortion," *Report of the APA Task Force on Mental Health and Abortion,* American Psychological Association (2008)

NO: Priscilla K. Coleman, from "Critique of the APA Task Force on Abortion and Mental Health," AAPLOG (2008)

Learning Outcomes
After reading this issue, you will be able to: • Understand the methodology used by the Task Force of the American Psychological Association to review published studies on the mental health of women who had undergone abortions.   • Critically evaluate the conclusions drawn regarding the mental health of women postabortion, giving consideration to the strengths and limitations of the studies reviewed.   • Discuss the role of political ideology that might be reflected on both sides of the debate regarding the psychological effects of abortion.   • Consider the methodological challenges involved in conducting research on possible psychological effects of abortion.   • Discuss the ways in which cultural factors might influence the psychological impact of abortion.

ISSUE SUMMARY

YES: The APA Task Force (TFMHA) reviewed the empirical literature and concluded that for women who have an unplanned pregnancy, the risk of mental health problems is no greater than the risk for women who deliver an unplanned pregnancy.

NO: Professor Priscilla K. Coleman contends that the TFMHA analysis of the evidence reflects politically motivated bias in the selection of studies, analysis of the literature, and the conclusions derived.

Perhaps no other issue in American judicial history has sparked as much debate and controversy as the Supreme Court decision in 1973 in the case of *Roe v. Wade,* in which the Court determined a woman's right to abortion. This decision, based on the constitutional right to privacy, sparked an uproar of dissension that has continued for four decades, and has involved several spheres of American society including religion, politics, health care, and economics. Proponents of a woman's right to choose have ardently sought to fend off efforts to reduce or eradicate access to abortion. Opponents of abortion have engaged in a wide range of activities aimed at convincing Americans that abortion is not only morally wrong, but psychologically hazardous to the women who undergo this procedure. The term postabortion syndrome emerged in the 1980s to characterize detrimental psychological symptoms that may follow the experience of abortion. Over the past few decades, several studies have been conducted in an effort to assess the psychological effects of undergoing an abortion. Periodically, reviews of these research studies have been conducted. For example, in 1987 President

Reagan instructed Surgeon General C. Everett Koop to issue a report on the health effects of abortion. Although the report lacked compelling conclusions one way or the other, controversy and political positioning escalated as a result. The American Psychological Association then stepped in to summarize the research, which culminated in a 1990 article in *Science* concluding that scientific studies did not point to adverse psychological effects from abortion. Nevertheless, the controversy refused to go away, and in 2007 the American Psychological Association appointed yet another task force to review the literature.

In an effort to assess the psychological effects of abortion on women, the American Psychological Association commissioned a task force to review all research on this topic. The 2008 APA Task Force on Mental Health and Abortion was chaired by Brenda Major, Ph.D., Professor of Psychology at UC Santa Barbara. Dr. Major was one of the co-authors of the 1990 *Science* article, and the first author of a 2000 article in the prestigious *Archives of General Psychiatry*, which examined women's psychological responses following abortion. In the 2008 report, the TFMHA reviewed the empirical literature and concluded that for women who have an unplanned pregnancy, the risk of mental health problems is no greater than the risk for women who deliver an unplanned pregnancy. In drawing this conclusion from the research, they highlight methodological problems inherent in the research that pointed to detrimental psychological effects following abortion.

The TFMHA evaluated all empirical studies published in English in peer-reviewed journals post-1989 that compared the mental health of women who had an induced abortion to the mental health of comparison groups of women ($N = 50$) or that examined factors that predict mental health among women who have had an elective abortion in the United States ($N = 23$). The Task Force urged caution in drawing conclusions from research pointing to psychiatric disorders in women who had abortions. In pointing out methodological problems, for example, it is noted that Fergusson et al. (2008) (1) did not measure wantedness of pregnancy, (2) used a comparison group of women who had never been pregnant, (3) used a very small sample of 48, (4) did not control for number of prior abortions or births, and (5) conducted the study in New Zealand. Also, a study by Gilchrist et al. (1995), which

stood out for its methodological rigor, concluded that once psychiatric disorders prior to pregnancy were taken into account, the rate of total psychiatric disorder was no higher after termination of an unplanned pregnancy than after childbirth. The most methodologically strong studies showed that interpersonal concerns, including feelings of stigma, perceived need for secrecy, exposure to antiabortion picketing, and the perception or anticipation of low social support for the abortion decision, negatively affected women's postabortion psychological experiences.

Dr. Priscilla Coleman, Associate Professor of Human Development and Family Studies at Bowling Green State University, takes aim at the TFMHA report, asserting that it reflects an extensive, politically motivated bias in the selection of studies reviewed, analysis of the literature, and conclusions drawn. Dr. Coleman contends that bias is evident even in the choice of Task Force members, and she contends that the conclusion drawn in the report does not follow from the literature reviewed.

According to Dr. Coleman, the TFMHA conveniently restricts its review to studies conducted in the United States, thereby eliminating at least 40 studies, including a large Swedish study of 854 women in which rates of negative experiences were considerably higher than in previously published studies using more superficial assessments. Furthermore, Dr. Coleman asserts, the TFMHA fails to highlight methodological strengths of research pointing to adverse psychological effects of abortion. For example, the study by Fergusson et al. (2008) (1) was longitudinal, (2) included comprehensive mental health assessments, (3) had lower estimated abortion concealment rates than previous studies, (4) used a sample representing 80–83 percent of a group of 630 subjects, and (5) used extensive controls. She goes on to state that TFMHA essentially bases the final conclusion of the report on a study by Gilchrist et al. (1995) which has a number of ignored flaws: (1) the response rate is not reported; (2) there are very few controls for confounding variables; (3) the study had a problematically high attrition rate; and (4) no standardized measures of mental health diagnoses were used, and the diagnoses were reported by general physicians, not psychiatrists. Dr. Coleman concludes that the power attributed to cultural stigmatization of women's abortion-related stress is unsupported, as there have been few well-designed studies that support this claim.

Mental Health and Abortion

Executive Summary

The Council of Representatives of the American Psychological Association charged the Task Force on Mental Health and Abortion (TFMHA) with "collecting, examining, and summarizing the scientific research addressing the mental health factors associated with abortion, including the psychological responses following abortion, and producing a report based upon a review of the most current research." In considering the psychological implications of abortion, the TFMHA recognized that abortion encompasses a diversity of experiences. Women obtain abortions for different reasons; at different times of gestation; via differing medical procedures; and within different personal, social, economic, and cultural contexts. All of these may lead to variability in women's psychological reactions following abortion. Consequently, global statements about the psychological impact of abortion on women can be misleading.

The TFMHA evaluated all empirical studies published in English in peer-reviewed journals post-1989 that compared the mental health of women who had an induced abortion to the mental health of comparison groups of women (N-50) or that examined factors that predict mental health among women who have had an elective abortion in the United States (N-23). This literature was reviewed and evaluated with respect to its ability to address four primary questions: (1) Does abortion cause harm to women's mental health? (2) How prevalent are mental health problems among women in the United States who have had an abortion? (3) What is the relative risk of mental health problems associated with abortion compared to its alternatives (other courses of action that might be taken by a pregnant woman in similar circumstances)? and (4) What predicts individual variation in women's psychological experiences following abortion?

A critical evaluation of the published literature revealed that the majority of studies suffered from methodological problems, often severe in nature. Given the state of the literature, a simple calculation of effect sizes or count of the number of studies that showed an effect in one direction versus another was considered inappropriate. The quality of the evidence that produced those effects must be considered to avoid misleading conclusions. Accordingly, the TFMHA emphasized the studies it judged to be most methodologically rigorous to arrive at its conclusions.

The best scientific evidence published indicates that among adult women who have an *unplanned pregnancy* the relative risk of mental health problems is no greater if they have a single elective first-trimester abortion than if they deliver that pregnancy. The evidence regarding the relative mental health risks associated with multiple abortions is more equivocal. Positive associations observed between multiple abortions and poorer mental health may be linked to co-occurring risks that predispose a woman to both multiple unwanted pregnancies and mental health problems.

The few published studies that examined women's responses following an induced abortion due to fetal abnormality suggest that terminating a wanted pregnancy late in pregnancy due to fetal abnormality appears to be associated with negative psychological reactions equivalent to those experienced by women who miscarry a wanted pregnancy or who experience a stillbirth or death of a newborn, but less than those who deliver a child with life-threatening abnormalities.

The differing patterns of psychological experiences observed among women who terminate an unplanned pregnancy versus those who terminate a planned and wanted pregnancy highlight the importance of taking pregnancy intendedness and wantedness into account when seeking to understand psychological reactions to abortion.

None of the literature reviewed adequately addressed the prevalence of mental health problems among women in the United States who have had an abortion. In general, however, the prevalence of mental health problems observed among women in the United States who had a single, legal, first-trimester abortion for nontherapeutic reasons was consistent with normative rates of comparable mental health problems in the general population of women in the United States.

Nonetheless, it is clear that some women do experience sadness, grief, and feelings of loss following termination of a pregnancy, and some experience clinically significant disorders, including depression and anxiety. However, the TFMHA reviewed no evidence sufficient to support the claim that an observed association between abortion history and mental health was caused by the abortion per se, as opposed to other factors.

This review identified several factors that are predictive of more negative psychological responses following first-trimester abortion among women in the United States. Those factors included perceptions of stigma, need for secrecy, and low or anticipated social support for the abortion decision; a prior history of mental health problems; personality factors such as low self-esteem and use of avoidance and denial coping strategies; and characteristics of the particular pregnancy, including the extent to which the woman wanted and felt committed to it. Across studies, prior mental health emerged as the strongest predictor of postabortion mental health. Many of these same factors also predict negative psychological reactions to other types of stressful life events, including childbirth, and, hence, are not uniquely predictive of psychological responses following abortion.

Well-designed, rigorously conducted scientific research would help disentangle confounding factors and establish relative risks of abortion compared to its alternatives as well as factors associated with variation among women in their responses following abortion. Even so, there is unlikely to be a single definitive research study that will determine the mental health implications of abortion "once and for all" given the diversity and complexity of women and their circumstances. . . .

Summary and Conclusions

The empirical literature on the association between abortion and mental health has been asked to address four primary questions: (1) Does abortion cause harm to women's mental health? (2) How prevalent are mental health problems among women in the United States who have had an abortion? (3) What is the relative risk of mental health problems associated with abortion compared to its alternatives (other courses of action that might be taken by a pregnant woman in similar circumstances)? and (4) What predicts individual variation in women's psychological experiences following abortion? As discussed above, the first question is not scientifically testable from

an ethical or practical perspective. The second and third questions obscure the important point that abortion is not a unitary event, but encompasses a diversity of experiences. That said, in the following section we address what the literature reviewed has to say with respect to the last three questions.

The Relative Risks of Abortion Compared to Its Alternatives

The TFMHA identified 50 papers published in peer-reviewed journals between 1990 and 2007 that analyzed empirical data of a quantitative nature on psychological experiences associated with induced abortion, compared to an alternative. These included 10 papers based on secondary analyses of two medical record data sets, 15 papers based on secondary analyses of nine public data sets, 19 papers based on 17 studies conducted for the primary purpose of comparing women who had first-trimester abortions (or an abortion in which the trimester was unspecified) with a comparison group, and 6 studies that compared women's responses following an induced abortion for fetal abnormality to women's responses following other reproductive events. These studies were evaluated with respect to their ability to draw sound conclusions about the relative mental health risks associated with abortion compared to alternative courses of action that can be pursued by a woman facing a similar circumstance (e.g., an unwanted or unintended pregnancy).

A careful evaluation of these studies revealed that the majority suffered from methodological problems, sometimes severely so. Problems of sampling, measurement, design, and analyses cloud interpretation. Abortion was often underreported and underspecified and in the majority of studies, wantedness of pregnancy was not considered. Rarely did research designs include a comparison group that was otherwise equivalent to women who had an elective abortion, impairing the ability to draw conclusions about relative risks. Furthermore, because of the absence of adequate controls for co-occurring risks, including systemic factors (e.g., violence exposure, poverty), prior mental health (including prior substance abuse), and personality (e.g., avoidance coping style), in almost all of these studies, it was impossible to determine whether any observed differences between abortion groups and comparison groups reflected consequences of pregnancy resolution, preexisting differences between groups, or artifacts of methodology. Given this state of the literature, what can be concluded about relative risks from this body of research?

One approach would be to simply calculate effect sizes or count the number of published papers that suggest adverse effects of abortion and those that show no adverse effects (or even positive effects) of abortion when compared to an alternative course of action (e.g., delivery). Although tempting, such approaches would be misleading and irresponsible, given the numerous methodological problems that characterize this literature, the many papers that were based on the same data sets, and the inadequacy of the comparison groups typically used. Given this state of the literature, the TFMHA judged that the best course of action was to base conclusions on the findings of the studies identified as most methodologically rigorous and sound.

Of the studies based on medical records, the most methodologically rigorous studies were conducted in Finland. The largest and strongest of these examined the relative risk of death within a year of end of pregnancy associated with abortion versus delivery (Gissler et al., 2004b). It demonstrated that the relative risk differs depending on how cause of death is coded. Compared to women who delivered, women who had an abortion had lower rates of direct pregnancy-related deaths (cause of death was directly related to or aggravated by the pregnancy or its management, but not from accidental or incidental causes) but higher rates of pregnancy-associated deaths (deaths occurring within one year from end of pregnancy, regardless of whether deaths are pregnancy-related). When therapeutic abortions were excluded from the category of pregnancy-associated deaths, however, this latter difference was not significant. Across both the Medi-Cal and Finland record-based studies, a higher rate of violent death (including accidents, homicide, and suicide) was observed among women who had an abortion compared to women who delivered. This correlational finding is consistent with other evidence indicating that risk for violence is higher in the lives of women who have abortions and underscores the importance of controlling for violence exposure in studies of mental health associated with pregnancy outcome.

With respect to the studies based on secondary analyses of survey data, the conclusions regarding relative risk varied depending on the data set, the approach to the design of the study, the covariates used in analyses, the comparison group selected, and the outcome variables assessed. Analyses of the same data set (the NLSY) with respect to the same outcome variable (depression) revealed that conclusions regarding relative risk differed dramatically depending on the sampling and exclusion criteria applied.

The strongest of the secondary analyses studies was conducted by Fergusson et al. (2006). This study was based on a representative sample of young women in Christchurch, NZ, was longitudinal (although Fergusson also reported concurrent analyses), measured postpregnancy/abortion psychiatric morbidity using established diagnostic categories, and controlled for mental health prior to the pregnancy in prospective analyses. Fergusson et al. compared women who terminated a pregnancy to women who delivered or had not been pregnant. The prospective analyses reported by Fergusson et al. are most informative. These analyses compared number of total psychiatric disorders among women who had an abortion prior to age 21 to number of total psychiatric disorders among women who had delivered a child by age 21 or among women who had never been pregnant by age 21, controlling for prepregnancy mental health and other variables that differed initially among the three groups. In these analyses, women who had one or more abortions prior to age 21 had a significantly higher number of total psychiatric disorders by age 25 than women who had delivered or had never been pregnant by age 21. This study thus suggests that women who have one or more abortions at a young age (<21) are at greater relative risk for psychiatric disorder compared to women who deliver a child at a young age or women who do not get pregnant at a young age.

There are several reasons why caution should be used in drawing the above conclusion from this study. First and most importantly, Fergusson et al. (2006) did not assess the *intendedness or wantedness* of the pregnancy. As noted earlier, approximately 90% of pregnancies that are aborted are unintended, compared to only 31% of those that are delivered (Henshaw, 1998). Thus, although these were young women, it is reasonable to assume that at least some of the women in the delivery group were delivering a planned and wanted child. Delivery of a planned and wanted child would be expected to be associated with positive outcomes and is not a viable option for women facing an unintended pregnancy. Second, the other comparison group used by Fergusson et al.—women who had never been pregnant—is not a viable option for women already facing an unintended pregnancy. Third, the prospective analyses were based on only 48 women who had abortions, an extremely small sample. Fourth, the study did not control for number of prior abortions or births. Fifth, the study focused on women who had one or more abortions at a young age (<21 years), limiting its generalizability to younger women; younger age has been linked in some studies to more negative psychological experiences following abortion (e.g., Major et al., 2000). Finally, this study was conducted in New Zealand, a country with more restrictive abortion regulations than those in the United States. Because the focus of APA is on mental health in the United States, it may thus be less useful as a basis for drawing conclusions about relative risks of abortion for US. women.

The TFMHA also reviewed and evaluated 19 papers based on 17 studies conducted tor the primary purpose of comparing women who had first-trimester abortions (or an abortion in which trimester was unspecified) with a comparison group on a mental health relevant variable. These studies varied widely in methodological quality and cultural context. Although most of the studies showed no significant differences between the psychological experiences of women who had an induced first-trimester abortion and women in a variety of comparison groups once important covariates (e.g., marital status, age) were controlled, most also were characterized by methodological deficiencies. These included problems of sampling, measurement, design, analyses, and inappropriate comparison groups. Thus, as a group, these studies also do not provide good answers to questions of relative risk or prevalence.

One study, however, stood out from the rest in terms of its methodological rigor. This study was conducted in the United Kingdom by the Royal College of General Practitioners and the Royal College of Obstetricians and Gynecologists (Gilchrist et al., 1995). It was longitudinal, based on a representative sample, measured postpregnancy/abortion psychiatric morbidity using established diagnostic categories, controlled for mental health prior to the pregnancy as well as other relevant covariates, and compared women who terminated an unplanned pregnancy to women who pursued alternative courses of action. In prospective analyses, Gilchrist et al. compared postpregnancy psychiatric morbidity (stratified by prepregnancy psychiatric status) of four groups of women, all of whom were faced with an unplanned pregnancy: women who obtained abortions, who did not seek abortion, who requested abortion but were denied, and who initially requested abortion but changed their mind. The researchers concluded that once psychiatric disorders prior to the pregnancy were taken into account, the rate of total reported psychiatric disorder was no higher after termination of an unplanned pregnancy than after childbirth.

This study provides high-quality evidence that among women faced with an unplanned pregnancy, the relative risks of psychiatric disorder among women who terminate the pregnancy are no greater than the risks among women who pursue alternative courses of action. What appears to be a discrepancy between the conclusions

of this study and those of Fergusson et al. (2006) is likely due to differences in sampling and study design. First and most importantly, Gilchrist et al. (1995) restricted their study to women identified by their family doctor as having an "unplanned" pregnancy, whereas Fergusson et al. did not assess the intendedness of the pregnancy, as noted above.

Consequently, the comparison groups used by Gilchrist et al. are more appropriate for addressing the question of relative risk of negative psychological experiences following elective abortion *compared to other courses of action women in similar circumstances (i.e., facing an unplanned pregnancy) might take*. Second, the Gilchrist et al. study was not restricted to women who became pregnant at a young age; hence the sample is more representative of women who seek abortion. Third, differences in abortion sample size were dramatic. The prospective analyses by Gilchrist et al. were based on an abortion sample of 6,410 women, as compared to 48 in the Fergusson et al. study. Fourth, unlike the study by Fergusson et al., the Gilchrist et al. study controlled for number of prior abortions and births. For these reasons, the TFMHA had more confidence in arriving at conclusions about relative risk based on the findings of Gilchrist et al. Nonetheless, it should be noted that the abortion context in the United Kingdom may differ from that in the United States, weakening generalization to the U.S. context.

The TFMHA reviewed six studies that compared women's responses following an induced abortion for fetal abnormality to women's responses following other reproductive events. These studies were based on extremely small samples often characterized by high attrition rates and low response rates. Nonetheless, these studies suggest that terminating a wanted pregnancy, especially late in pregnancy, can be associated with negative psychological experiences comparable to those experienced by women who miscarry a wanted pregnancy or experience a stillbirth or death of a newborn, but less severe than those experienced by women who deliver a child with a severe abnormality. At least one study also suggests that the majority of women who make this difficult choice do not regret their decision (e.g., Kersting et al., 2005). As a group, these studies of responses to termination of a wanted pregnancy for fetal abnormality underscore the importance of considering the wantedness of the pregnancy, as well as the reason for and timing of the abortion, in studying its psychological implications. Interpretation of prevalence of psychological distress and relative risk is clouded when researchers lump together under the category of "abortion" women who abort a wanted pregnancy for reasons of fetal anomaly with women who have an elective abortion of an unplanned and unwanted pregnancy.

In summary, although numerous methodological flaws prevent the published literature from providing unequivocal evidence regarding the relative mental health risks associated with abortion per se compared to its alternatives (childbirth of an unplanned pregnancy), in the view of the TFMHA, the best scientific evidence indicates that the relative risk of mental health problems among adult women who have an unplanned pregnancy is no greater if they have an elective first-trimester abortion than if they deliver that pregnancy (Gilchrist et al., 1995).

The evidence regarding the relative mental health risks associated with multiple abortions is more equivocal. One source of inconsistencies in the literature may be methodological, such as differences in sample size or age ranges among samples. Positive associations observed between multiple abortions and poorer mental health (e.g., Harlow et al., 2004) also may be due to co-occurring risks that predispose a woman to both unwanted pregnancies and mental health problems.

Terminating a wanted pregnancy late in pregnancy due to fetal abnormality appears to be associated with negative psychological experiences equivalent to those experienced by women who miscarry a wanted pregnancy or experience a stillbirth or the death of a newborn.

Prevalence of Mental Health Problems Among U.S. Women Who Have an Abortion

A second question this literature has been used to address concerns the prevalence of mental health problems among women in the United States who have had an abortion. As noted at the outset of this report, research capable of adequately addressing this question requires at minimum: (1) a clearly defined, agreed upon, and appropriately measured mental health problem (e.g., a clinically significant disorder, assessed via validated criteria); (2) a sample representative of the population to which one wants to generalize (e.g., women in the United States); and (3) knowledge of the prevalence of the same mental health problem in the general population, equated with the abortion group with respect to potentially confounding factors. None of the studies reviewed met all these criteria and hence provided sound evidence regarding prevalence. Few of the U.S. studies assessed clinically significant disorders with valid and reliable measures or physician diagnosis. In those studies that did use clinically relevant outcome measures, sampling strate-

gies were inadequate to address the question of prevalence in the larger U.S. population either because the samples were biased, highly selected, geographically restricted or failed to use appropriate sampling weights. Furthermore, because of the lack of adequate control for co-occurring risks, the extent to which the incidence of mental health problems associated with abortion was due to the procedure versus to potentially confounding factors, such as poverty, poorer prior mental health, etc., was impossible to establish.

Given these caveats, however, the prevalence of mental health problems observed among women in the United States who had a single, legal, first-trimester abortion for nontherapeutic reasons appeared to be consistent with normative rates of comparable mental health problems in the general population of women in the United States. Consider, for example, the overall prevalence of depression among women in the NLSY, a longitudinal national survey of a cohort of men and women aged 14–21 years in 1979. Among *all* women in the NLSY, irrespective of reproductive history and without controlling for any covariates, 22% met criteria for depression in 1992 (i.e., scored above the clinical cutoff on the CES-D). Among women who reported one abortion, the corresponding percentage was 23%. Among women who reported multiple abortions, however, the percentage was higher; 31% met criteria for depression (see Table). A similar pattern was reported by Harlow et al. (2004) in their study of a representative sample of women in the Boston metropolitan area.

To say that women *in general* do not show an increased incidence of mental health problems following a single abortion, however, does not mean that no women experience such problems. Abortion is an experience often hallmarked by ambivalence and a mix of positive and negative emotions is to be expected (Adler et al., 1990; Dagg, 1991). Some women experience beneficial outcomes, whereas others experience sadness, grief, and feelings of loss following the elective termination of a pregnancy. Some women experience clinically significant outcomes, such as depression or anxiety. However, the TFMHA reviewed no evidence sufficient to support the claim that an observed association between abortion history and a mental health problem was caused by the abortion per se, as opposed to other factors. As observed throughout this report, unwanted pregnancy and abortion are correlated with preexisting conditions (e.g., poverty), life circumstances (e.g., exposure to violence, sexual abuse), problem behaviors (e.g., drug use), and personality characteristics (e.g., avoidance style of coping with

Population estimates of proportion of all women and women identified as having been pregnant exceeding CES-D clinical cutoff score, National Longitudinal Survey of Youth: 1992.

Group (N)	CES-D>15
All women (unweighted N = 4401)	22%
No abortion ever	21%
Ever abortion	25%
One abortion	23%
Multiple abortions	31%
All women ever pregnant + (unweighted N = 3503)	23%
No abortion ever	23%
Ever abortion	25%
One abortion	22%
Multiple abortions	31%

Notes: + Includes pregnancies ending in miscarriages.
No covariates are controlled.

negative emotion) that can have profound and long-lasting negative effects on mental health. Differences in prevalence of mental health problems or problem behaviors observed between women who have had an abortion and women who have not may be primarily accounted for by these preexisting and ongoing differences among groups.

Predictors of Individual Variation in Responses Following Abortion

A third issue addressed in the literature on abortion and mental health concerns individual variation in women's psychological experiences following abortion. The TFMHA reviewed 23 papers based on 15 data sets that were based solely on samples of women who had abortions in the United States, but that otherwise met inclusion criteria. These noncomparison group studies typically focused on predictors of individual variation in response. They were of two major types: (1) prospective or concurrent studies that usually included preabortion measures of psychological adjustment and risk factors and one or more postabortion assessments of adjustment and (2) retrospective studies that assessed women's perceived reactions to the event and current level of psychological functioning several years after the abortion. The retrospective studies had serious methodological problems that made interpretation

of their findings difficult. The prospective studies, despite limitations of high attrition, geographically limited samples, and potential confounds that were not measured, provided valuable information about sources of variation in individual women's psychological experiences and, to a more limited extent, mental health problems subsequent to abortion.

The most methodologically strong studies in this group showed that interpersonal concerns, including feelings of stigma, perceived need for secrecy, exposure to antiabortion picketing, and low perceived or anticipated social support for the abortion decision, negatively affected women's postabortion psychological experiences. Characteristics of the woman also predicted more negative psychological experiences after first-trimester abortion, including a prior history of mental health problems, personality factors such as low self-esteem and low perceived control over her life, and use of avoidance and denial coping strategies. Feelings of commitment to the pregnancy, ambivalence about the abortion decision, and low perceived ability to cope with the abortion prior to its occurrence also predicted more negative postabortion responses. Across studies, prior mental health emerged as the strongest predictor of postabortion mental health (Major et al., 2000). Type of abortion procedures, at least those used in the first trimester, did not appear to be related to postabortion psychological well-being or mental health.

In considering these risk factors, it is important to recognize that many of the same factors shown to be associated with more negative postabortion psychological experiences also predict more negative reactions to other types of stressful life events, including childbirth (e.g., low perceived social support, low self-esteem, low self-efficacy, avoidance coping). For instance, low perceived social support and low self-esteem also are risk factors for postpartum depression (Beck, 2001; Logsdon & Usui, 2001). Most risk factors are not uniquely predictive of psychological experiences following abortion. Women characterized by one or more such risk factors might be equally (or more) likely to experience negative psychological reactions if they pursued an alternative course of action (motherhood or adoption).

Conclusions and Future Research

Based on our comprehensive review and evaluation of the empirical literature published in peer-reviewed journals since 1989, this Task Force on Mental Health and Abortion concludes that the most methodologically sound research indicates that among women who have a single, legal, first-trimester abortion of an unplanned pregnancy for nontherapeutic reasons, the relative risks of mental health problems are no greater than the risks among women who deliver an unplanned pregnancy. This conclusion is generally consistent with that reached by the first APA task force (Adler et al., 1990).

This report has highlighted the methodological failings that are pervasive in the literature on abortion and mental health. This focus on methodological limitations raises the question of whether empirical science is capable of informing understanding of the mental health implications of and public policy related to abortion. Some policy questions cannot be definitively answered through empirical research because they are not pragmatically or ethically possible.

Other questions, however, are amenable to the methods of well-designed, rigorously conducted scientific research. For example, empirical research can identify those women who might be more or less likely than others to show adverse or positive psychological outcomes following an abortion. Well-designed research can also answer questions of relative risk and prevalence. What would this research look like?

Such research would use methods that are prospective and longitudinal and employ exacting sampling methods (including the use of sampling weights that allow proper generalization back to the populations to whom the conclusions are being applied). Careful attention would be paid to adequately assessing preexisting and co-occurring conditions such as marital status, domestic violence, age, socioeconomic status, parity, prior mental health, and prior problem behaviors as well as other situations that are known to be associated with both differential utilization of abortion and mental health problems. Importantly, comparison groups would be selected so as to be equivalent to the abortion group on all variables other than abortion history. Critical variables such as intendedness and wantedness of the pregnancy would be assessed, and abortion status verified objectively (not only through

self-report). Careful use of covariance or similar adjustment techniques (applied to pre-defined covariates) would be employed. Precision of measurement (both in terms of specification of outcome measure and psychometric adequacy of the measurements) would also be guaranteed. Positive psychological responses and experiences as well as negative mental health would be assessed. Repeated assessment of responses over time would be made to assess relevant changes, positive and negative, in the trajectory of responses following abortion. Samples sufficiently large to guarantee adequate power to detect effects that are present would be used, and attention would be paid to effect-size estimation in addition to the simple reliance on null hypothesis statistical testing.

Research that met the above scientific standards would help to disentangle confounding factors and establish relative risks of abortion compared to its alternatives. Even so, there is unlikely to be a single definitive research study that will determine the mental health implications of abortion "once and for all" as there is no "all," given the diversity and complexity of women and their circumstances. Important agendas for future research are to further understand and alleviate the conditions that lead to unwanted pregnancy and abortion and to understand the conditions that shape how women respond to these life events, with the ultimate goal of improving women's lives and well-being.

APA Task Force on Mental Health and Abortion consisted of Brenda Major (Chair), Mark Appelbaum, Linda Beckman, Mary Ann Dutton, Nancy Felipe Russo, and Carolyn West. The American Psychological Association (APA) is a 150,000-member scientific and professional organization that represents psychology in the United States. The mission of the APA is to advance the creation, communication, and application of psychological knowledge to benefit society and improve people's lives.

Priscilla K. Coleman

 **NO**

Critique of the APA Task Force on Abortion and Mental Health

The charge of the APA Task Force on Abortion and Mental Health was to collect, examine, and summarize peer-reviewed research published over the last 17 years pertaining to outcomes associated with abortion.

Evidence described below indicates an extensive, politically motivated bias in the selection of studies, analysis of the literature, and in the conclusions derived by the Task Force. As opposed to bringing light to a complex literature, the misleading report carries enormous potential to hinder scientific understanding of the meaning of abortion in women's lives. The report should be recalled and at a minimum, the conclusion changed. There is sufficient data in the world's published literature to conclude that abortion increases risk of anxiety, depression, substance use, and suicide. At this juncture, the APA cannot be trusted to provide accurate assimilation of information.

Problematic Features of the Report Substantiated in This Critique

The conclusion DOES NOT follow from the literature reviewed

When comparing reviews of the literature there is selective reporting

Avoidance of quantification

Biased selection of Task Force members and possibly reviewers

Power attributed to cultural stigmatization in women's abortion-related stress is unsupported

Selection criteria resulted in dozens of studies indicating negative effects being ignored

Methodologically based selection criteria as opposed to geographic locale should have been employed and consistently applied

Shifting standards of evaluation of studies presented based on the conclusion's fit with a pro-choice agenda

The Conclusion (in Italics Below) Does Not Follow from the Literature Reviewed

"The best scientific evidence published indicates that among adult women who have an unplanned pregnancy the relative risk of mental health problems is no greater if they have a single elective first-trimester abortion than if they deliver that pregnancy."

They also note "Rarely did research designs include a comparison group that was otherwise equivalent to women who had an elective abortion, impairing the ability to draw conclusions about relative risks."

They are essentially basing the final conclusion of the entire report on one study by Gilchrist et al. (1995), which has a number of ignored flaws. The three studies that I authored or co-authored with unintended pregnancy delivered as a comparison group indicated that abortion was associated with more mental health problems. A few flaws of the Gilchrist study are highlighted below:

1. The response rate was not even provided.
2. Very few controls for confounding third variables. The comparison groups may very well have differed systematically with regard to income, relationship quality including exposure to domestic violence, social support, and other potentially critical factors.
3. On page 247, the authors report retaining only 34.4% of the termination group and only 43.4% of the group that did not request a termination at the end of the study. The attrition rate is highly problematic as are the differential rates of attrition across the comparison groups. Logically, those traumatized are less likely to continue in a study.
4. No standardized measures for mental health diagnoses were employed and evaluation of the

From Priscilla K. Coleman (August 13, 2008).

psychological state of patients was reported by general practitioners, not psychiatrists. The GPs were volunteers and no attempt was made to control for selection bias.

When Comparing Reviews of the Literature There Is Selective Reporting

A review of Bradshaw and Slade (2003) in the report ignores this statement from the abstract: "Following discovery of pregnancy and prior to abortion, 40–45% of women experience significant levels of anxiety and around 20% experience significant levels of depressive symptoms. Distress reduces following abortion, but up to around 30% of women are still experiencing emotional problem after a month."

Also ignored from Bradshaw and Slade (2003) is the following: "The proportion of women with high levels of anxiety in the month following abortion ranged from 19% [to] 27%, with 3–9% reporting high levels of depression. The better quality studies suggested that 8–32% of women were experiencing high levels of distress."

Coleman is quoted from a testimony given in South Dakota rather than quoting from the two reviews she has published in prestigious peer-reviewed journals.

There is a claim that other reviews such as those of Coleman and a very strong quantitatively based one by Thorp et al. (2003) are incorporated, but the conclusions of these reviews are avoided entirely.

Avoidance of Quantification

The authors of this report avoid quantification of the numbers of women likely to be adversely affected by abortion. This seems like an odd omission of potentially very useful, summary information. There is consensus among most social and medical science scholars that a minimum of 10% to 30% of women who abort suffer from serious, prolonged negative psychological consequences (Adler et al., 1992; Bradshaw & Slade, 2003; Major & Cozzarelli, 1992; Zolese & Blacker 1992). With nearly 1.3 million U.S. abortions each year in the U.S. (Boonstra et al., 2006), the conservative 10% figure yields approximately 130,000 new cases of mental health problems each year.

In the report, the authors note "Given the state of the literature, a simple calculation of effect sizes or count of the number of studies that showed an effect in one direction versus another was considered inappropriate." What??? Too few studies to quantify, but a sweeping conclusion can be made?

Biased Selection of Task Force Members and Reviewers

No information whatsoever is provided in the report regarding how the Task Force members were selected. What was done to assure that the representatives do not all hold similar ideological biases? What was the process for selecting and securing reviewers? How many were offered the opportunity? Did any decline? How was reviewer feedback incorporated into revising the document? . . . very minimally from this reviewer's vantage point. Disclosure of this information is vital for credibility and accountability purposes.

Power Attributed to Cultural Stigmatization in Women's Abortion-Related Stress Is Unsupported

There are few well-designed studies that have been conducted to support this claim. In fact, many studies indicate that internalized beliefs regarding the humanity of the fetus, moral, religious, and ethical objections to abortion, and feelings of bereavement/loss often distinguish between those who suffer and those who do not (see Coleman et al., 2005 for a review).

Selection Criteria Resulted in Dozens of Studies Indicating Negative Effects Being Ignored

According to the report "The TFMHA evaluated all empirical studies published in English in peer-reviewed journals post-1989 that compared the mental health of women who had an induced abortion to the mental health of comparison groups of women (N=50) or that examined factors that predict mental health among women who have had an elective abortion in the United States (N=23)."

Note the second type of study is conveniently restricted to the U.S. resulting in elimination of at least 40 studies. As a reviewer, I summarized these and sent them to the APA. There is an insufficient rationale (cultural variation) for exclusively focusing on U.S. studies when it comes to this type of study.

Introduction of this exception allowed the Task Force to ignore studies like a large Swedish study of 854 women one year after an abortion, which incorporated a semi-structured interview methodology requiring 45–75 minutes to administer (Soderberg et al., 1998). Rates of negative experiences were considerably higher than in previously published studies relying on more superficial assessments. Specifically, 50–60% of the women experienced emotional distress of some form (e.g., mild depression, remorse or guilt feelings, a tendency to cry without cause, discomfort upon meeting children), 16.1% experienced serious emotional distress (needing help from a psychiatrist or psychologist or being unable to work because of depression), and 76.1% said that they would not consider abortion again (suggesting indirectly that it was not a very positive experience).

Methodologically Based Selection Criteria as Opposed to Geographic Locale Should Have Been Employed and Consistently Applied

If the Task Force members were interested in providing an evaluation of the strongest evidence, why weren't more stringent criteria employed than simply publication of empirical data related to induced abortion, with at least one mental health measure in peer-reviewed journals in English on U.S. and non-U.S. samples (for one type of study)? Employment of methodological criteria in selection would certainly have simplified the task of evaluation as well. Sample size/characteristics/representativeness, type of design, employment of control techniques, discipline published in, etc. are logical places to begin. I am shocked to not see the development of criteria that reflect knowledge of this literature.

Shifting Standards of Evaluation of Studies Presented Based on the Conclusion's Fit with a Pro-Choice Agenda

There are numerous examples of studies with results suggesting no negative effects of abortion being reviewed less extensively and stringently than studies indicating adverse effects. Further the positive features of the studies suggesting abortion is a benign experience for most women are highlighted while the positive features of the studies revealing adverse outcomes are downplayed or ignored. All the studies showing adverse effects were published in peer-reviewed journals, many in very prestigious journals with low acceptance rates. Clearly then, the studies have many strengths, which outweigh the limitations.

The same standards and criteria are simply not applied uniformly and objectively in the text, and I could literally write pages and pages pointing out examples of this blatantly biased survey of the literature. A few examples are provided below:

a. The Medi-Cal studies are sharply criticized for insufficient controls; however with the use of a large socio-demographically homogeneous sample many differences are likely distributed across the groups. Moreover, the strengths of the study include use of actual claims data (diagnostic codes assigned by trained professionals), which eliminate the problems of simplistic measurement, concealment, recruitment, and retention, which all are serious shortcomings of many post-abortion studies. The authors of the Medi-Cal Studies also removed all cases with previous psychological claims and analyzed data using an extended time frame, with repeated measurements enabling more confidence in the causal question. . . .

b. Results of the Schmiege and Russo (2005) study are presented as a superior revision of the Reardon and Cougle (2002) study, yet none of the criticism that was publicly leveled against the former study on the BMJ website is described. I contributed to this Rapid Response dialogue, and I reiterate a few of my comments here: "The analyses presented in Table 3 of the article do not incorporate controls for variables identified as significant predictors of abortion (higher education and income and smaller family size). These associations between pregnancy outcome and depression are troubling since lower education and income and larger family size predicted depression (see Table 4). Without the controls, the delivery group, which is associated with lower education and income and larger families, will have more depression variance erroneously attributed to pregnancy resolution. Among the unmarried, white women, 30% of those in the abortion group had scores exceeding the clinical cut-off for depression, compared to 16% of the delivery group. Statistical significance is likely to have been achieved with the controls instituted. This group is important to focus on as unmarried, white women represent the segment of the U.S. population obtaining the majority of abortions. Failure to convey the most scientifically defensible information is inexcusable when the data set contains the necessary variables. I strongly urge the authors to run these analyses. Curiously, in all the comparisons throughout the article, the authors neglect to control for family size without any explanation."

c. Fergusson and colleagues' (2006) study had numerous positive methodological features: (1) longitudinal in design, following women over several years; (2) comprehensive mental health assessments employing standardized diagnostic criteria of DSM III-R disorders; (3) considerably lower estimated abortion concealment rates than found in previously published studies; (4) the sample represented between 80% [and] 83% of the original cohort of 630 females; and (5) the study used extensive controls. Variables that were statistically controlled in the primary analyses included maternal education, childhood sexual abuse, physical abuse, child neuroticism, self-esteem, grade point average, child smoking, history of depression, anxiety, and suicidal ideation, living with parents, and living with a partner. Very little discussion in the report is devoted to the positive features of this study and the limitations, which are few compared to most published studies on the topic, are emphasized.

d. Attrition as a methodological weakness is downplayed because the studies with the highest attrition rates (those by Major et al.) are also the ones that provide little evidence of negative effects and are embraced despite attrition as high as 60%. Common sense suggests that those who are most adversely affected are the least likely to want to think about the experience and respond to a questionnaire. Research indicates that women who decline to participate or neglect to provide follow-up data are more likely to be negatively impacted by an abortion than women who continue participating (Soderberg, Anderson, Janzon, & Sjoberg, 1997).

Suffice to say, there is clear evidence of bias in reporting and in keeping with the rather transparent agenda of discrediting studies showing negative effects regardless of their true methodological rigor.

I strongly recommended evaluating only studies that met stringent inclusion criteria and then summarizing the studies in table format in such a way that the reader can quickly note the strengths and limitations of every study in a non-biased manner. Picking and choosing particular criteria from a large assortment of methodological criteria to evaluate various studies is inappropriate, suggestive of bias, and obfuscates the informative literature that is currently available. Lack of uniform application of evaluation standards creates a warped perception of the relative contributions of the studies.

The following quote by the editors of the *Canadian Medical Association Journal* (CMAJ) would have been insightful to the Task Force members as they incorporated feedback and endeavored to produce a report in keeping with their charge of objective assessment: "The abortion debate is so highly charged that a state of respectful listening on either side is almost impossible to achieve. This debate is conducted publicly in religious, ideological and political terms: forms of discourse in which detachment is rare. But we do seem to have the idea in medicine that science offers us a more dispassionate means of analysis. To consider abortion as a health issue, indeed as a medical 'procedure,' is to remove it from metaphysical and moral argument and to place it in a pragmatic realm where one deals in terms such as safety, equity of access, outcomes and risk–benefit ratios, and where the prevailing ethical discourse, when it is evoked, uses secular words like autonomy and patient choice." (CMAJ, 2003. p. 93)

PRISCILLA K. COLEMAN is an associate professor of human development and family studies at Bowling Green State University. Her research interests focus on socioemotional development in early childhood, parenting issues, and the psychological effects of the abortion experience.

EXPLORING THE ISSUE

Does Research Confirm That Abortion Is a Psychologically Benign Experience?

Critical Thinking and Reflection

1. Reviews of the literature on psychological consequences of abortion, and critiques of these reviews, are labeled by many as politically biased. What steps would you recommend for assembling a task force that would be free from bias on this topic?
2. Imagine that you are a researcher with a large grant to study the psychological experiences of women following abortion. What variables would be especially important to consider in the design of such a study?
3. Imagine that you are a clinician who is consulting with a woman who is considering an elective abortion and asks for reading recommendations on the topic of what she might experience after going through the procedure. What considerations would influence the publications that you recommend?
4. Priscilla K. Coleman criticizes the TFMHA on the basis that the review was restricted to studies conducted in the United States. What are the pros and cons of covering research studies on this topic that were conducted in non-U.S. countries?
5. The TFMHA report contends that negative postabortion psychological experiences are more likely attributable to interpersonal concerns such as feelings of stigma and low perceived or anticipated social support for the abortion decision. How would you go about assessing the extent to which psychological difficulties following abortion are due to concerns about stigma rather than due to emotional distress about the experience itself?

Is There Common Ground?

The issue of abortion has been one of the most hotly debated topics of the past half century and has been addressed from many vantage points, including legal, psychological, medical, political, and human rights perspectives. Political campaigns at all levels of government have been influenced by a candidate's stance on the abortion issue, with vehement assertions on both sides of the debate about the ethics and impact of abortion.

In the field of psychology, a major focus has been placed on understanding the emotional impact of abortion on a woman. Studying this variable is understandably challenging because researchers face the difficult task of inquiring about a very personal issue, and they realize that even asking questions about a woman's attitude about the experience and the psychological impact of abortion can in itself be emotionally provocative. The APA Task Force reviewed research studies published post-1989 in peer-reviewed journals and concluded that for women who have an unplanned pregnancy, the risk of mental health problems is no greater than the risk for women who deliver an unplanned pregnancy. The Task Force was critical of the methodology of some studies that pointed in the other direction. Contesting the conclusions of the Task Force, Dr. Coleman also zeroes in on methodological limitations of the published studies. We can predict that controversy regarding the psychological impact of abortion will not abate. Thus, the door remains open for the development of methodologically rigorous studies to assess the various ways in which women respond psychologically to abortion.

Create Central

www.mhhe.com/createcentral

Additional Resources

Macleod, C. (2011). *Adolescence, Pregnancy and Abortion: Constructing a Threat of Degeneration.* London: Routledge.

Perrucci, A. C. (2012). *Decision Assessment and Counseling in Abortion Care: Philosophy and Practice.* Lanham, MD: Rowman & Littlefield.

Schwarz, S. D., & Latimer, K. (2012). *Understanding Abortion: From Mixed Feelings to Rational Thought.* Lanham, MD: Lexington Books.

Tooley, M. (2009). *Abortion: Three Perspectives.* New York, NY: Oxford University Press.

Internet References . . .

Afterabortion.com

www.afterabortion.com

National Abortion Federation

https://www.prochoice.org/

Planned Parenthood

http://www.plannedparenthood.org/health-topics/
pregnancy/thinking-about-abortion-21519.htm

Women on Web

https://www.womenonweb.org/en/page/537/do-you-
require-psychological-counseling-after-you-have-
had-an-abortion

Selected, Edited, and with Issue Framing Material by:
Richard P. Halgin, *University of Massachusetts, Amherst*

ISSUE

Is the Use of Aversive Treatment an Inhumane Intervention for Psychologically Disordered Individuals?

YES: Laurie Ahern and Eric Rosenthal, from *Torture Not Treatment: Electric Shock and Long-Term Restraint in the United States on Children and Adults with Disabilities at the Judge Rotenberg Center,* Mental Disability Rights International (2010)

NO: Matthew L. Israel, from *Aversives at JRC: A Better Alternative to the Use of Drugs, Restraint, Isolation, Warehousing, or Expulsion in the Treatment of Severe Behavior Disorders,* Judge Rotenberg Center (2010)

Learning Outcomes

After reading this issue, you will be able to:

- Critically evaluate the pros and cons of using aversive treatments such as the Graduated Electronic Decelerator (GED) device on individuals with severe behavioral disorders.
- Discuss the argument that aversive treatments are forms of torture.
- Understand the debate about whether withholding aversive treatments from disabled individuals is a form of discrimination, because they would be deprived access to interventions which might help them control their behavior.
- Consider whether the infliction of pain can be justified on moral grounds as a form of psychological intervention.
- Consider the threshold for determining a possible justification for administering aversive treatments (e.g., head banging, eye gouging, interpersonal assault, etc.).

ISSUE SUMMARY

YES: Laurie Ahern and Eric Rosenthal, writing on behalf of Mental Disability Rights International (MDRI), characterize the intentional infliction of pain at JRC as human rights abuses.

NO: Psychologist Matthew Israel, director of the Judge Rotenberg Center (JRC), responds to the MDRI with insistence that JRC is using behavioral methods to save individuals from their treatment-resistant, life-threatening disorders.

One of the most heartbreaking experiences for parents of emotionally disordered children is to see these fragile youngsters engage in self-injurious and even self-mutilating behaviors such as head banging, self-punching, and even manually pulling out teeth. Many of these children are also aggressive, sometimes to the point of life-threatening violence. In these extreme cases, parents desperately seek out solutions so that the well-being of these troubled children can be protected. Traditional therapeutic interventions are customarily the first line of treatment, as parents turn to mental health professionals for therapy for themselves and their children. When talking approaches prove to be of limited value, medications are likely to be recommended. For some children, however, even the most potent of antipsychotic medications may be ineffective in reducing self-destructive behaviors. Feeling exhausted, bewildered, and frightened, the guardians of these very disturbed individuals seek out the options of last resort, which sometimes involve behavioral interventions involving the use of physical restraints and aversive conditioning. A leader in the application of such procedures is the Judge Rotenberg Center (JRC) in Canton, MA, which has been at the center of controversy for the four decades that it has been in operation.

On behalf of Mental Disability Rights International (MDRI), human rights activists Laurie Ahern and Eric Rosenthal prepared a scathing critique of the behavioral techniques used at JRC, which they label "torture" rather than treatment. This report was submitted to the United Nations along with a request that the UN initiate an inquiry into what are described as "abusive practices perpetrated against residents of JRC." MDRI contends that the severe pain and suffering perpetrated against children and adults with disabilities violates the UN Convention Against Torture.

MDRI asserts that no population is more vulnerable to abuse than children with disabilities detained in an institution. For this population, the use of electric shock in the form of the Graduated Electronic Decelerator (GED), long-term restraint, and other aversives used by JRC constitute human rights violations that are even more serious than corporal punishment in a school. They assert that the GED is used to administer shock for behaviors that are not problematic, such as getting out of one's seat or nagging other students. According to MDRI, aversive interventions such as the GED device are used with children with all kinds of disabilities, many without self-injurious behaviors.

MDRI contends that behavioral programming at JRC is not sufficiently monitored by appropriate professionals at the school, and in many cases the level of background and preparation of staff are not sufficient for overseeing the intensive treatment of children with challenging emotional and behavioral disorders. While the infliction of pain may stop a person from engaging in a specific behavior while being subject to a course of aversive treatment, aversive treatment cannot treat an underlying emotional disorder or intellectual disability.

Dr. Matthew Israel, founding director of JRC, expresses strong objection to the MDRI claims, citing the fact that for the last four decades JRC has used safe intensive behavioral therapy to treat the most severe forms of behavior disorders, and has freed hundreds of individuals from disturbing alternatives such as excessive sedation, restraint, seclusion, and institutional warehousing. The claim is made that JRC's 24-hour behavioral system works effectively for individuals for whom every other treatment has failed. In these individuals, positive behaviors replace the prior behaviors of self-abuse, aggression, and destruction.

According to Dr. Israel, under state and federal law, nondisabled individuals have the right to choose aversive therapy to treat behavioral problems such as smoking and drinking. To deny persons with developmental or behavioral/psychiatric disabilities the same right to treat their behavior problems with aversives would be to impose an invidious form of discrimination against those unfortunate enough to suffer from such disabilities. Instead of using problematic interventions (e.g., cocktails of mind-numbing drugs, restraint, take-downs, isolation, warehousing, expulsion), Dr. Israel explains that JRC employs a corrective consequence in the form of a 2-second shock to the skin. This treatment, which feels like a hard pinch, Dr. Israel notes, has been validated in the scientific literature, is extremely effective, and has no significant adverse side effects.

Dr. Israel contends that all of the students at JRC have at least one thing in common—they suffer from severe behavior disorders that could not be effectively treated by the many other treatment programs and psychiatric hospitals they had been in prior to coming to JRC. JRC uses extraordinary safeguards. Each individual's treatment program that includes the use of skin shock must be preapproved by a physician and by the parent, must be included in the student's Individualized Education Program or Individual Health Plan, must be approved by a human rights committee and a peer review committee, and must be individually preapproved and reviewed at regular intervals by a Massachusetts Probate Court Judge. Techniques of behavior modification and applied behavior analysis involve analyzing the causes of problematic behaviors, eliminating triggering events, rewarding desired behaviors, and applying corrective consequences for undesired behaviors.

YES ↵

Laurie Ahern and Eric Rosenthal

Torture Not Treatment: Electric Shock and Long-Term Restraint in the United States on Children and Adults with Disabilities at the Judge Rotenberg Center

Introduction

The Judge Rotenberg Center (JRC) was founded by psychologist Matthew Israel almost 40 years ago in California when it was known then as the Behavior Research Institute (BRI). According to Israel, the school's philosophy is based on the work of renowned behaviorist B.F. Skinner.[2] In the 1950s, Israel was a student of Skinner's at Harvard University, and today he is a self-proclaimed devotee of radical behaviorism.

In 1981, a 14 year old boy died face down, tied to his bed. JRC (then known as BRI) was not held responsible for the boy's death, but the death resulted in an investigation by California's Department of Social Services. California issued a critical report the following year, citing widespread abuse of children at the facility and the state of California greatly limited the use of punishment as treatment.[3] The facility was then moved to Rhode Island and then again to Canton, Massachusetts, where it is located today.

Today, JRC boasts a main campus with a school and offsite residential apartments with 24 hour staffing. The facility serves as a residential school for children with disabilities, as well as a residential facility for adults. There are approximately 200 children and adults at JRC at any given time,[4] with costs paid for by state and local school districts and state agencies serving adults with disabilities at approximately $220,000 per year, per person. People with disabilities living at the JRC residential center mostly come from New York and Massachusetts, and seven other states.

The Judge Rotenberg Center Program

The program of "behavior modification" and "aversive treatment" and the rationale for its use is spelled out on JRC's website. The theory of behavior modification is that every human being responds to positive rewards or negative punishments and that all behavior can be manipulated through a combination of rewards and punishments. Using this approach, "rewards" and "punishments" constitute treatment.[5] Treatment entails the infliction of pain. JRC is clear that this approach "differs markedly" from "traditional approaches" to mental health care.[6] The website boasts that "JRC is probably the most consistently behavioral treatment program in existence."

JRC maintains that the same form of reward and punishment works for anyone, justifying a "near-zero rejection policy" for admission.[7] As a result:

> . . . we really pay relatively little attention to psychiatric diagnosis which are essentially labels for groups of behaviors. . . . Of the first two students we worked with, one was labeled autistic and one was labeled schizophrenic.[8]

The implication of this approach is a highly unorthodox program for treatment and education. All residents, regardless of diagnosis or history, are subjected to the same behavior modification techniques of reward and punishment. The use of traditional psychological therapies and/or medication is virtually non-existent at JRC.[9] Psychotropic medications are rarely used.[10] According to JRC, seventy percent of educational instruction in the school consists of solitary work on a computer referred to by JRC as "self-paced programmed instruction."[11] . . .

Early on, punishments—known as aversives—were used to control the behavior of people who were called severely "mentally retarded" and children with autism. Punishments included pinching, spatula spankings, water sprays, muscle squeezes, forced inhalation of ammonia and helmets which battered the brain with inescapable white noise.[24]

In the late 1980s, JRC began using SIBIS (Self-Injurious Behavior Inhibiting System) machines on students, as an alternative to spanking, squeezing and pinching. The machine, developed in 1985, produced a 0.2 second shock of 2.02 milliamps on the arms or legs of the recipient, with the intention of stopping self-injurious behaviors in children with autism and other developmental disabilities. Controversial from the outset and shunned by advocates, the use of SIBIS was largely abandoned in the 1990s in favor of "positive-based" practices.[25]

Over the years, JRC has found that an individual who responds to low levels of electricity may become "adapted" to pain and "needs a stronger stimulation."[26] The 12 year old nephew of Massachusetts State Representative Jeffrey Sanchez was diagnosed with autism and was a student at JRC in 1989 when JRC began using the SIBIS machine. As described in testimony before the Massachusetts legislature,[27] one day he received more than 5,000 shocks to stop his behaviors—to no avail. When the manufacturer of SIBIS refused JRC's request to provide them with a stronger and more painful shock machine, JRC developed its own mechanism for administering shock, the Graduated Electronic Decelerator (GED). The GED is a remotely controlled device that can be strapped to an individual's back or another part of the body with electrodes attached to the torso, arms, legs, hands and feet. The GED administers 15.5 milliamps of electricity. A stronger version, the GED-4, subjects an individual to a shock of 45.5 milliamps. Both may be used up to 2.0 seconds. The director of JRC, Matthew Israel, describes the shock as "very painful."[28] Sanchez's nephew is now 31 years old and remains at JRC. According to testimony before the Massachusetts Legislature in November 2009, he is still tethered to the GED shock machine.[29]

JRC also uses physical restraints as a form of aversive treatment, sometimes simultaneously with electric shock.[30] The GED and restraints are sometimes combined because it is necessary to stop a person from ripping the GED pack off his or her body. Other times, physical restraints may be added to the use of the GED when the aversive power of electricity alone is not sufficient. As described on the JRC website, "[T]he safest way to do this is to use mechanical restraint to contain the student, in a prone position, on a flexible plastic restraint platform that has been specially designed for the purpose."[31] It is worth noting that, outside JRC, the use of any "prone" (face down) restraints are widely considered to be inherently dangerous, and many states have banned any form of prone restraints in the mental health context.[32] . . .

Critique of Aversive Treatment from Research and Policy

What's wrong with punishments is that they work immediately, but give no long-term results. The responses to punishment are either the urge to escape, to counterattack or a stubborn apathy.

—B.F. Skinner interview, *The New York Times*, 1987[36]

. . . The NY Psychological Association Task Force, which reviewed NYSED's report, raised particular concerns about the use of aversives at JRC without careful attention to the patients' diagnosis. They point out that for certain children—in particular abuse or trauma survivors—aversives can be particularly dangerous.[45] Other researchers have warned that "restraints and seclusion should never be used with children who present with certain psychological or medical characteristics. . . . Contraindications for the use of seclusion and restraints with children include a history of sexual abuse, physical abuse, or neglect and abandonment."[46]

. . . While the infliction of pain may stop a person from engaging in a specific behavior while being subject to a course of aversive treatment, aversive treatment cannot treat an underlying emotional disorder or intellectual disability. A review of the research found that "the implementation of punishment-based procedures, including those that incorporate noxious stimulation, do not guarantee long-term reductive effects in the treatment of severe disorders."[48] The alleviation of symptoms only takes place while aversives are in place, leaving a person subject to this painful treatment over a long period of time. This is why JRC has had to create increasingly strong systems for administering pain and shock. JRC's website candidly acknowledges that aversives only bring about the temporary alleviation of symptoms. . . .

Findings: The Use of Aversives at JRC

Electric Shock

As described above, JRC's stated reason for the use of electric shocks is behavior modification and punishment.[57] Children and adults at JRC are routinely subject to electric shock, receiving multiple skin shocks on their legs, arms, hands, feet, fingers and torsos for behaviors such as getting out of their seats, making noises, swearing or not following staff directions.[58] The homemade shock devices, invented by the school's founder, Matthew Israel, and manufactured at the school, are carried by students in backpacks with electrodes attached to their skin.[59] The shock is administered remotely by minimally trained staff—some with only two weeks of training.[60] Students never know when they will receive a jolt or where on their body they will be shocked. Some children are subjected to dozens of shocks over the course of a day. The April 2009 report by the Massachusetts Department of Mental Retardation (DMR), found that of the 109 children subjected to electric skin shocks, 48 had been receiving the shocks for 5 years or more.[61] . . .

Restraints

Some problem behaviors can be controlled and prevented by putting the student into continual manual or mechanical restraint. To manually restrain a vigorous young man can take the efforts of many staff members and is inevitably a dangerous exercise. Putting a student in continuing restraints is much more cruel than changing his/her behavior quickly with a powerful positive reward program that is supplemented with occasional two-second skin shocks.

—JRC website, Frequently Asked Questions

JRC refers to physical restraints as "limitation of movement" (LOM), and this is a core part of its aversive treatment program. According to the JRC website, some students receive shocks while strapped prone to a platform board in 4-point mechanical restraints.[75] Restraints are used in combination with the GED to stop a person from ripping off the GED pack while receiving painful electrical impulses.[76] Restraints may also be used to increase the level of pain and discomfort when electric shock alone is not adequate to produce the behavior changes sought by JRC.[77]

A nurse at the facility is responsible for monitoring abrasions due to restraints, according to the NYSED. Depending on the recommendations of the nurse, "a student may be restrained in a prone, seated, or upright position."[78] As described by the NYSED investigators:

With mechanical movement limitation the student is strapped into/onto some form of physical apparatus. For example, a four-point platform board designed specifically for this purpose; or a helmet with thick padding and facial grid that reduces sensory stimuli to the ears and eyes. Another form of mechanical restraint occurs when the student is in a five-point restraint in a chair. **Students may be restrained for extensive periods of time (e.g. hours or intermittently for days)** [emphasis added] when restraint is used as a punishing consequence. Many students are required to carry their own "restraint bag" in which the restraint straps are contained.[79]

MDRI's investigation suggests that restraints may last even longer than reported by the NYSED team. A former patient, a mother, a former teacher at JRC, and an attorney who represented clients at JRC all informed MDRI that children are restrained for weeks and months at a time. . . .

MDRI interviews indicate that students are likely to be restrained after they are admitted and before they go before a court to determine whether they can be subject to Level III aversive treatment. These findings are supported by the findings of the New York State and Massachusetts evaluation teams.[90] These findings raise concerns that restraints may used to pressure or coerce individuals into consenting to the GED. . . .

According to the NYSED evaluation team:

It is during this initial restrictive placement at JRC that the frequency of behaviors is documented for purposes of obtaining a substituted judgment for the use of Level III aversive procedures. . . . In this setting, interactions with students involved little to no instruction; staff primarily attended to students' negative behaviors and employed the use of physical and mechanical restraints at a high frequency and for extended periods of time.[91]

The Massachusetts Certification Team found that restraints were used without being included in treatment plans.[92] According to one observer from the Massachusetts team, "the more JRC used these interventions, the more aggressive the students became."[93] . . .

Provocation of Bad Behavior

One component of treatment at JRC is referred to as the behavioral rehearsal lesson (BRL).[95] Students are restrained and GED administered as the student is forcibly challenged to do the behavior the punishment seeks to eliminate. JRC students are sometimes induced to exhibit a behavior for which they will receive a shock punishment. Students endure surprise mock attacks and threatened stabbings by staff, which compel them to react with aggression, fear or screaming—deemed unacceptable or inappropriate behavior—for which they are subject to more shock for their reactions.

Former students report BRLs as particularly terrifying and some staff describe BRLs as "difficult to participate in and dramatic to watch."[96]

It was reported by a JRC staff member that one of the BRL episodes involved holding a student's face still while a staff person went for his mouth with a pen or pencil threatening to stab him in the mouth while repeatedly yelling "You want to eat this?"

—June 2006 report on JRC by New York State Education Department[97]

The worst thing ever was the BRLs. They try and make you do a bad behavior and then they punish you. The first time I had a BRL, two guys came in the room and grabbed me—I had no idea what was going on. They held a knife to my throat and I started to scream and I got shocked. I had BRL's three times a week for stuff I didn't even do. It went on for about six months or more. I was in a constant state of paranoia and fear. I never knew if a door opened if I would get one. It was more stress than I could ever imagine. Horror.

—MDRI interview with former JRC student[98]

Food Deprivation

In addition to the use of electric shock, restraints, mock stabbings and assaults as a means of punishment, JRC uses dangerous food deprivation techniques to further abuse children, adding to the environment of fear, pain, punishment and control. Collectively known as "Loss of Privileges" or "LOPs," the abuses are masked in clinical sounding terminology. The "Contingent Food Program" (CFP) and the "Specialized Food Program" (SFP) include the systematic withholding of food as a form of punishment.[99] The CFP "is widely applied and designed to motivate students to be compliant."[100] If children or adolescents exhibit any behaviors not tolerated by JRC staff, a portion of food is withheld during the day. **Food not earned during the day is then given to the child in the evening, "which consists of mashed food sprinkled with liver powder."**[101] The SFP is "more restrictive" for those whose behavior does not improve—there is no make-up food given at the end of the day.[102] . . .

Other LOPs include limitations and restrictions with regard to visits to the school's store, television viewing, bedtime, and permission to talk with other students. And some LOPs result in even harsher consequences. One former student reported that she was forced to eat her dinner tied to a chair, alone in her room, for almost a month—LOPs she earned for talking in class without raising her hand.[105]

When we first visited JRC, she had a beautiful room with a TV and stereo. Within one month, she only had a mattress on the floor.

—MDRI interview with mother of a former JRC student[106]

Stopping work for more than 5 seconds and you would lose points and get LOPs. I sat in front of the computer all day, other than lunch. And we couldn't have a social conversation with any staff member.

—MDRI interview with former JRC student[107]

Creating Social Isolation

To further maintain strict control, socialization among students, between students and staff, and among staff, is also extremely limited.[108] For students, socialization with other peers must be earned. Children spend their school days in classrooms facing the walls and staring at a computer screen. Using self-teaching software, conversations and discussions are virtually non-existent and getting up from a chair or attempting to leave the classroom without permission could result in a shock or other form of punishment. . . .

Additionally, staff is not allowed to carry on any personal conversations with the students and all are under 24 hour video surveillance. Employees must also sign a confidentiality agreement at the beginning of their tenure with JRC, effectively barring them from ever talking about what they observe or participate in at the school—including the use of GEDs—or face legal action against them by the school.[111]

You are sworn to secrecy. It is like a secret society. We had to sign a paper that if we said anything that would harm their reputation, they would prosecute you. If you talked bad about the school, everything is taped. If we needed to talk, we had to go outside.

—MDRI interview with former JRC employee[112]

Aversives for Harmless Behavior

One of the critiques of the GED identified by the NYSED evaluation team is that it is used on behaviors that "the district did not consider problematic for a student that they had placed at JRC (i.e. getting out of seat, nagging)."[113] Indeed, the NYSED evaluators found that:

Many of the students observed at JRC were not exhibiting self-abusive/mutilating behaviors, and their IEP's had no indication that these behaviors existed. However, they were still subject to Level III aversive interventions, including the use of the GED device. The review of the NYS students' records revealed that Level III interventions are used for behaviors including 'refuse to follow staff directions'; 'failure to maintain a neat appearance', 'stopping work for more than 10 seconds', interrupting others', 'nagging', 'whispering and/or moving conversation away from staff', 'slouch in chair'. . . .[114]

The observations of the NYSED evaluators were mirrored by a former teacher at JRC.[115] According to this teacher, children are routinely given shock for behaviors as normal or innocuous as reacting in fear when witnessing other students getting shocked; attempting to remove electrodes from their skin; tearing a paper cup; blowing bubbles with saliva; standing up out of a seat without permission; going to the bathroom in one's pants; or asking to go to the bathroom more than five times, which is considered an inappropriate verbal behavior.[116]

MDRI interviewed a teacher and a former JRC student who told similar stories:

> One girl who was blind, deaf and non-verbal was moaning and rocking. Her moaning was like a cry. The staff shocked her for moaning. Turned out she had broken a tooth. Another child had an accident in the bathroom and was shocked.

—MDRI interview with former JRC teacher[117]

> I felt terrible for the kids with autism getting shocked. This one 13 year old girl with autism kept getting the GED. They get it for verbal inappropriate behaviors. They made noises, that's how they communicate. They are non-verbal but they would get more shocks. The poor girl would hurt herself a lot.

—MDRI interview with former JRC student who was also getting shocked[118]. . .

Deaths and Subsequent Legal Challenges

From the outset, Israel's treatment for children with disabilities was controversial and the focus of much media attention. This was especially true when the magnitude and severity of punishments being perpetrated against children came to light or when an unexplained death occurred at the facility, of which there have been six. As previously described, it was a death at the facility in 1980 that resulted in the virtual ban on the use of aversives in California.

In 1990, the Massachusetts DMR conducted an exhaustive investigation on the horrific death of a 19 year old, a young woman diagnosed with severe mental retardation, who also died at the facility. The report states that the staff and administration committed acts against her that were "egregious" and "inhumane beyond all reason" and violated "universal standards of human decency."[196] The young woman, who was unable to speak, became ill and refused to eat, attempted to vomit and made sounds and noises that were not usual for her. For this she was

punished repeatedly as the staff translated her actions as misbehaviors. In the hours leading up to her death from a perforated stomach and ulcers, the investigation found that she endured "8 spankings, 27 finger pinches, 14 muscle squeezes" and was forced to smell ammonia and eat "either vinegar mix, or jalapeno peppers or hot sauce."[197]

Prior to her death, she had been subjected to the school's punishment of withholding food for being unable to do school work on the computer or getting wrong answers, despite having the mental capacity of a pre-schooler. At times she was limited to 300 calories per day.

In the end, DMR concluded that there was not enough evidence to link the punishments to her death.

The Massachusetts Office for Children (OFC) ordered the closure of JRC. The school and its parents sued the OFC and appealed the closure. A state administrative law judge ruled that the school could remain open but limited the use of aversives during the litigation.[198]

In 1986, in the midst of the OFC litigation, JRC (then called the Behavior Research Institute) brought one of its most self-abusive students before the Bristol County Probate Court (MA) and Chief Judge Ernest Rotenberg (for whom the school is now named) for a substituted judgment hearing to allow JRC to use aversive treatments on the student. Judge Rotenberg found in JRC's favor and JRC began to bring each student they felt needed aversives before Judge Rotenberg for approval.

Despite the objections of the OFC, Judge Rotenberg was eventually given judicial authority over all pending legal actions between the OFC, JRC and parents of students and a settlement was reached. In the December 1986 agreement, aversives were permitted with a court-ordered treatment plan, and a monitor must report to the court on the clients' treatment.[199]. . .

New York's Attempts to Limit Use of Aversives

New York State sends more of its children to JRC than any other state. As a result of questions and concerns by NY lawmakers regarding the use of punishment at JRC, specifically electric shock and restraint, the NYSED sent a review team to JRC in April and May 2006. The team included NYSED staff and three behavioral psychologists. One visit was announced; the other was unannounced. The NYSED review team reported a litany of abuses involving the most painful of punishments used by JRC. Following the publication of the NYSED report, New York held public hearings. As a result, NYSED adopted restrictive new regulations that would phase out new cases where aversive treatment would be approved.[206] Before New York could implement these new regulations, parents representing children at the school challenged the regulations in federal court, claiming they have a right to subject their children to Level III aversives. They claim that such treatment is necessary for their children to receive an appropriate education as required by IDEA. The federal court has ordered a stay on the implementation of New York's regulations until the substantive issues under IDEA are heard.[207]

A summary of the NYSED review team findings include:

- Level III punishments are given to children with all kinds of disabilities, many without self-injurious behaviors;
- Level III punishments are given for swearing, nagging and failure to maintain a neat appearance;
- The use of electric shock skin devices raises health and safety concerns;
- The withholding of food as punishment could pose risks affecting growth and development;
- Delayed punishment practices are used so that subjects may not be able to comprehend any relationship between a punishment and a behavior;
- The JRC setting discourages social interactions;
- There is insufficient academic and special education instruction;
- JRC compromises the privacy and dignity of students.[208]

Ultimately, the NYSED's review team concluded that the effects of the punishment on children at JRC are increased fear, anxiety or agression.[209]

One of the findings of the NYSED review team was that "behavioral programming at JRC is not sufficiently monitored by appropriate professionals at the school and in many cases the level of background and preparation of staff is not sufficient to oversee the intensive treatment of children with challenging emotional and behavioral disorders."[210]

The reality is that JRC staff may have had even less training than was represented to the NYSED review team. In May 2006, the Massachusetts Division of Professional Licensure found that JRC had improperly claimed that fourteen JRC clinicians were trained as licensed psychologists. In a consent agreement with the Board of Registration of Psychologists, JRC paid $43,000 in fines.[211] Dr. Matthew Israel, the Director of JRC, was personally fined $29,600 and was reprimanded by the Board.[212]

Recent Incidents of Abuse

In August 2007, an investigation of JRC was conducted by the Massachusetts Department of Early Education and Care (EEC)—the licensing agency for JRC residences—following the unauthorized administering of shock to two boys at their JRC residence. According to the report, one boy received 29 electric shocks, and the other received 77 shocks within a three hour time period.[213] The incident occurred when a former JRC student phoned the residence in the middle of the night, pretending to be a staff person, and ordered the residence staff to use shocks on the sleeping adolescents. EEC investigators interviewed the boys and staff and reviewed video footage and found that both boys had been awoken from their sleep when they received the shock; both boys had additional shocks when they were strapped to a 4-point restraint board; both were in transport restraints (legs and waist) while they were in their beds; and one of the boys did not have the required Level III court approval for restraints in his record. Neither boy was evaluated by any medical staff until the following day after the incident, despite asking for a nurse and complaining of pain.

> *Staff reported that it is not atypical for a resident to say that they have injuries following a GED application. It was reported that typically staff would not call a nurse when a resident voices that he is in pain from a GED application and described it as a pinch.*

The EEC report stated that staff observed that the "skin was off" and there were "fresh marks" on the calf of one of the boys, who complained of leg pain. It was later diagnosed as a stage two ulcer. These wounds were located at the same site that the resident had received the shock.

The EEC investigation further concluded that:

- staff was physically abusive toward the residents;
- the staff was unable to provide for the safety and well being of a child;
- staff lacked necessary training and experience;
- staff used poor judgment;
- staff failed to provide a safe environment;
- staff failed to follow policies regarding medical treatment;
- staff were neglectful in the care of residents.

The incidents of unlawful restraint of the boys at the JRC residence would never have been discovered had EEC not been investigating the unauthorized shock "prank.". . .

Conclusions and Recommendations

. . . **No population is more vulnerable to abuse than children with disabilities detained in an institution.** This population needs the strongest level of international protection to protect them against abuse. For this population, the use of electric shock, long-term restraint, and other aversives used by JRC constitutes human rights violations that are even more serious than corporal punishment in a school, where children eventually go home to friends and family in the community. The UN Special Rapporteur on Torture has stated that corporal punishment constitutes inhuman and degrading treatment. For a population detained in an institution, such as JRC, the vulnerability is much greater—and the experience of pain and suffering is likely more extreme. Thus, severe pain perpetrated against this population should be viewed as fully tantamount to torture. According to Nowak, "[t]he powerlessness of the victim is the essential criterion which the drafters of the Convention had in mind when they introduced the legal distinction between torture and other forms of ill-treatment."[225] . . .

A flat ban on the use of electricity or long-term use of restraints to treat or modify behavior would be the best way to prevent future abuse. Such a ban would be consistent with federal policy and best practice in the field of behavior modification that strongly supports positive behavioral supports instead of painful aversives. Such a ban would be consistent with what CAT has called for to protect people in custody in a law enforcement context. In 2000, as described above, CAT recommended that the United States "abolish electro-shock stun belts and restraint chairs as methods of restraining those in custody since 'their use almost invariably leads to breaches of article 16 of the Convention [defining inhumane and degrading treatment].'"[226]

This year, CAT will be conducting its fifth periodic review and report of the United States of America and its compliance with the UN Convention against Torture. In its last review of the US in 2006, CAT's report made a number of recommendations to the US government with regard to torture, including a concern they voiced over the use of electro-shock devices: *"restricting it to substitution for lethal weapons and eliminate the use of these devices to restrain persons in custody. . . ."*[227] In this year's review by CAT, in their list of issues of concern, they again bring up the use of electro-shock devices and ask the government if they have restricted its use as a substitution for lethal weapons only, as recommended in CAT's previous observations. And they ask point blank, "Are such devices still used to restrain persons in custody?"[228] CAT has also asked

for updated information on steps taken to "address the concern about the conditions of detention of children" with a particular emphasis on the use of excessive force.[229] And finally CAT asks:

> *Please describe steps taken to end the practice of corporal punishment in schools, in particular of mentally and/or physically disabled students.*[230]

This year, the United States human rights record is being scrutinized by the United Nations as part of a process known as "universal periodic review" under all the human rights conventions the United States has ratified. The United States report to the United Nations should include detailed information on the use of force against children with disabilities at JRC.

Since the United States legal system has failed to protect children and adults with disabilities, **MDRI brings this urgent appeal to the UN Special Rapporteur on Torture and recommends:**

- The UN Special Rapporteur on Torture should demand a full international accounting by the United States government of the abusive practices being perpetrated at the facility;
- The use of electric shock and long-term restraints should be brought to an immediate halt as a form of behavior modification or treatment;
- New federal law should be adopted to completely ban the infliction of severe pain for so-called therapeutic purposes in any context;
- Torture as treatment should be banned and prosecuted under criminal law. . . .

Notes

2. Matthew L. Israel, History of JRC, 1971–1985: Beginnings, Philosophy and Early Growth, *available at* http://www.judgerc.org/history.html (last visited April 8, 2010).

3. Jennifer Gonnerman, *School of Shock,* 32 Mother Jones, 36,41 (Sept.–Oct. 2007).

4. The number of students is an average taken from a legislative hearing.

5. Matthew L. Israel, Frequently Asked Questions, "Supplementary aversives at JRC—13. How is an aversive defined and which aversives are considered acceptable?" Judge Rotenberg Center, *available at* http://www.judgerc.org/ (last visited April 8, 2010).

6. Matthew L. Israel, *supra* note 2, at 1971–1985: Beginnings, Philosophy and Early Growth.

7. *Id.*

8. *Id.*

9. *Id.*

10. *Id.*, at 1971–1985: Beginnings, Philosophy and Early Growth—No or minimal use of psychotropic medication.

11. Matthew L. Israel, Distinguishing Features of the Judge Rotenberg Center, Judge Rotenberg Center, *available at* http://www.judgerc.org/ (last visited April 20, 2010).

24. Matthew L. Israel, *supra* note 2.

25. Sharon Lohrmann-O'Rourke and Perry A. Zirkel, *The Case Law on Aversive Interventions for Students with Disabilities,* 65 Exceptional Children 101 (Fall 1998).

26. Matthew L. Israel, *supra* note 5, at "Is it true that one of the consequences JRC uses is to administer several GED applications, over a half-hour period during which a student may be restrained on a restraint board?"

27. Patricia Wen, *Showdown over shock therapy testimony moves some critics; new bill would limit, not ban, treatment,* The Boston Globe 1 (Jan. 17, 2008), *available at* http://www.boston.com/news/local/articles/2008/01/17/showdown_over_shock_therapy/.

28. Paul Kix, *The Shocking Truth,* Boston Magazine Online 3 (2008), *available at* http://www.bostonmagazine.com/articles/the_shocking_truth/.

29. Patricia Wen (2008), *supra* note 27, at 1.

30. Matthew L. Israel, *supra* note 5, at "The use of restraint as an aversive consequence."

31. Matthew L. Israel, *supra* note 5, at "Multiple Applications of GED Combined with Restraint as an Aversive."

32. Gregory D. Kutz, Seclusions and Restraints: Selected Cases of Death and Abuse at Public and Private Schools and Treatment Centers, US Government Accountability Office, GAO-09-719T 4 (2009).

36. Daniel Goleman, *Embattled Giant of Psychology Speaks His Mind,* N.Y. Times, Aug. 25, 1987, at C1 and C3.

45. NY Psychological Association Task Force (2006), *supra* note 37, at 13.

46. *Id.* at 11, *quoting* D. Day, "A review of the literature on restraints and seclusion with children and youth: toward the development of a perspective in practice" (2000), *available at* http://rccp.connell.edu/pdfs/Day.pdf (retrieved July 26, 2006).

48. Frank L. Bird & James K. Luiselli, "Positive behavioral support of adults with developmental disabilities: assessment of long-term adjustment and habilitation following restrictive treatment histories," 31 Journal of Behavior Therapy and Experimental Psychiatry 5, 7 (2000).

57. Matthew L. Israel., Use of Skin Shock as a Supplementary Aversive, Judge Rotenberg Center, para. 1 (2002), *available at* http://www.judgerc.org/ (last visited April 21, 2010).

58. Matthew L. Israel (2002), *supra* note 57, at 1990-date: Development of the GED and GED-4 Devices.

59. *Id.*

60. Certification Team, *Report of the Certification Team on the Application of the Judge Rotenberg Education Center for Level II Behavior Modification Certification,* Commonwealth of Massachusetts, Executive Office of Health & Human Services, Department of Mental Retardation 10 (April 27, 2009) (on file with author).

61. *Id.*

75. Matthew L. Israel, *supra* note 5, at "Is it true that one of the consequences JRC uses is to administer several GED applications, over a half-hour period during which a student may be restrained on a restraint board?" See also, Jennifer Gonnerman (2007), *supra* note 3, at 38.

76. Matthew L. Israel, *supra* note 5, at "Multiple applications of the GED skin shock."

77. Matthew L. Israel, *supra* note 5.

78. NYSED Review Team (2006), *supra* note 17, at 8.

79. *Id.*

90. Certification Team (2009), *supra* note 60, at 32. *See also,* NYSED Review Team (2006), *supra* note 17, at 5.

91. NYSED Review Team (2006), *supra* note 17, at 6.

92. Certification Team (2009), *supra* note 60, at 32.

93. *Id.*

95. Matthew L. Israel, *supra* note 5, at "1. Is it true that at JRC a staff member will sometimes prompt a student to begin to engage in a problem behavior and then arrange an aversive for that? 2. Is there any professional support in the literature for that procedure?"

96. NYSED Review Team (2006), *supra* note 17, at 19.

97. *Id.*

98. MDRI Interview (2009).

99. NYSED Review Team (2006), *supra* note 17, at 10.

100. *Id.*

101. *Id.*

102. *Id.*

105. MDRI Interview (2009).

106. MDRI Interview (2009).

107. MDRI Interview (2009).

108. NYSED Review Team (2006), *supra* note 17, at 24.

111. Jennifer Gonnerman (2007), *supra* note 62, at 46–47.

112. MDRI Interview (2009).

113. NYSED Review Team (2006), *supra* note 17, at 14.

114. *Id.*

115. Greg Miller, *Response to Dr. Matthew Israel's letter entitled "Outrage Over Jennifer Gonnerman's Article, 'School of Shock'* (Sept. 4, 2007) (posted on Mother Jones comment blog for "School of Shock" article) *available at* http://motherjones.com/politics/2007/08/school-shock?page=4.

116. *Id.*

117. MDRI Interview (2009).

118. MDRI Interview (2009).

196. Letter from Disability Advocates, Addendum to A Call to Action to Eliminate the Use of Aversive Procedures and Other Inhumane Practices, 6 (Sept. 2009), *citing* Coalition for the Legal Rights of People with Disabilities, 6 The Communicator 1 (1995).

197. *Id.*

198. Matthew L. Israel, *supra* note 2, at "1985–1987 Failed Attempt by Office for Children to close JRC."

199. *Behavior Research Institute v. Mary Kay Leonard,* Sup. Ct. Dept. of the Trial Ct., and Prob. and Fam. Ct. of the Dept. of the Trial Ct., Docket No. 86E-0018-GI, Settlement Agreement (December 12, 1986). Under the settlement agreement, aversive procedures are only permitted with a court-ordered "substituted judgment" treatment plan. In presenting requesting a court-ordered "substituted judgment" treatment plan, the petitioner must show (1) the client's inability to provide informed consent and (2) "target behaviors" to be treated; what procedures will be used to treat the target behaviors; foreseeable adverse side-effects; professional discipline of staff members; prognosis should the procedures be implements; opinions of the client's family; client's previous treatment at BRI or elsewhere; description of appropriate behaviors; client's IEP. The settlement agreement requires a monitor to report to the court on the client's treatment. The court will also appoint a doctor to oversee BRI's compliance.

206. Rick Karlin, *Regents set to reject use of electric shock,* Albany Times Union, January 9, 2007.

207. *Jeanette Alleyne v. N. Y. State Educ. Dep't,* No. 1:06-cv-00994-GLS (N.D.N.Y 2010) (memorandum-decision and order to the parties).

208. NYSED Review Team (2006), *supra* note 17, at 2–3.

209. *Id.*

210. NYSED Review Team (2006), *supra* note 17, at 11.

211. Massachusetts Office of Consumer Affairs and Business Regulation, "Judge Rotenberg Center clinicians fined $43,000, Consent agreement with Board of Psychologists Reached," Oct. 9, 2006, *available at* http://www.arcmass.org/AversivesPress/tabid/592/Default.aspx#JRCfine

212. Abbie Ruzicka, *Rotenberg Center director fined over clinicians' titles,* The Boston Globe, October 7, 2009.

213. Investigation Report, Massachusetts Department of Early Education and Care 4, November 1, 2007.

225. Nowak & MacArthur (2008), *supra* note 124, at 76–77.

226. Committee Against Torture, Conclusions and Recommendations of the Committee against Torture: United States of America, 15 May 2000, A/55/44, para. 180(c).

227. Committee Against Torture, Conclusions and Recommendations of the Committee Against Torture: United States of America, 18 May 2006, CAT/C/USA/CO/2, para. 35.

228. Committee Against Torture, List of issues prior to the submission of the fifth periodic report of UNITED STATES OF AMERICA 9, 20 Jan. 2010, CAT/C/USA/Q/5.

229. *Id.*

230. *Id.*

Laurie Ahern is the president of Mental Disabilities Rights International (MDRI). She worked for 10 years as a newspaper editor and investigative reporter. Ms. Ahern is the former cofounder and codirector of the federally funded National Empowerment Center, and former vice president of the U.S. National Association of Rights Protection and Advocacy. She has written and lectured extensively on psychiatric recovery and self-determination, and has won several awards and honors for her efforts to improve conditions for, and attitudes toward, people with psychiatric disabilities.

Eric Rosenthal is the founder and executive director of Mental Disabilities Rights International (MDRI), and is also vice president of the United States International Council on Disability. He has served as a consultant to the World Health Organization, UNICEF, and the U.S. National Council on Disability. Rosenthal has won awards for his human advocacy efforts on behalf of people with disabilities.

Matthew L. Israel    **NO**

Aversives at JRC: A Better Alternative to the Use of Drugs, Restraint, Isolation, Warehousing, or Expulsion in the Treatment of Severe Behavior Disorders[1]

Why Behavior Modification Treatment, Including Aversives in Some Cases, Is Needed

The Judge Rotenberg Educational Center (JRC)[2,3,4], founded in 1971, is a residential education and treatment program in Canton, MA that provides behavior modification therapy, essentially without the use of psychotropic drugs, for 215 special needs children and adults from 7 different states. All of the students have at least one thing in common—they suffer from severe behavior disorders that could not be effectively treated by the many previous treatment programs and psychiatric hospitals they had been in prior to coming to JRC. Because of its zero-rejection, zero-expulsion policy, JRC serves the largest collection of individuals with difficult-to-treat self-abusive, aggressive and severely harmful behaviors in the country. JRC saves individuals from the mental and emotional pain, crippling disabilities, permanent injuries and even death caused by their otherwise untreatable behavior disorders. Before coming to JRC, many students were confined for years in psychiatric or correctional facilities or were living on the streets.

The students who are treated at JRC have shown, prior to admission to JRC, self-abusive behaviors such as: gouging out their eyes, causing near-blindness; smearing feces; head-banging to the point of causing detached retinas and blindness[5] or even stroke[6]; skin scratching to the point of fatal blood and bone infection; pulling out their own adult teeth[7]; running into a street filled with moving cars; or suicidal actions such as attempting to hang oneself, swallowing razor blades, taking a drug overdose, and jumping out of a moving vehicle or off of a building. Some students have shown violent aggression such as biting, hitting, kicking, punching, and head butting others.

Some have pushed a parent down a flight of stairs, raped someone, tried to strangle a parent while the parent was driving, and beat a peer so severely that plastic surgery was required. Some have attempted to injure or kill others—for example, by pushing a child into oncoming traffic, smothering a sibling, stabbing a teacher, or slicing a peer's throat. Some have attacked police and therapists. Some have set their homes on fire, lit a fire in school, and lit themselves or family members on fire. Some have engaged in prostitution, been involved in gangs, and assaulted others with weapons such as a machete and chainsaw.

The following letter, which was written by the parents of a student who, prior to her treatment at JRC, had detached both of her retinas through self-abusive head-poking, illustrates what such behavior problems mean to a family. This letter was sent to legislators who were considering a proposed bill in the Massachusetts legislature to ban the use of aversives:

To Whom it May Concern:

We would like to tell you about our daughter, Samantha, and how the Judge Rotenberg School in Canton Massachusetts has saved her life.

We first discovered Samantha was different when she was about 2 years old. She would not relate well to others, had very little speech, and would stare at her hands or small objects for hours at a time. She also had frequent tantrums, and cried often. She began with early intervention, and over the next ten years, she went to four specialized schools for autistic children. In addition to her schooling, numerous therapists, and teachers came to our house to work with Samantha after hours, most of which was paid for out of our own funds. All these schools worked closely with her in small groups, and on a one to one basis, using learning trials, and positive reinforcement. In addition to this, Samantha was under the care of a psychiatrist, and given several different psychotropic medications.

Despite, all these well caring professionals working with our daughter, Samantha progressively deteriorated. Over the years, she became more violent. She would attack us, other children, and her teachers. She would bite, scratch, kick, hit, pinch, and head-butt. In addition she became more self-abusive. She would throw herself on the floor, hit herself, and throw herself against hard objects. She constantly had marks, and bruises on her from her own self abuse. We were also prisoners in our own home, as we could not take her anywhere, due to her behaviors; this had an impact on our other children as well. The final straw came when she hit herself in her head with such force, that she detached both retinas of her eyes, and was virtually blind. This has subsequently required 6 eye surgeries to repair, and her vision is still far from normal. The Anderson School, where she was at the time, told us they could not handle her, and asked us to find another school. This is when we learned about the Judge Rotenberg School (JRC), and the GED device.

Within several weeks of getting treated with the GED device, a miracle happened; Samantha stopped hitting herself, and stopped her violent behavior. She appeared much happier. She was able to be weaned off all of her psychotropic medications.

There was a period of deterioration. In June 2006, aversive treatment became a big issue in New York State. A law was passed prohibiting the use of the GED for antecedent behaviors, leading up to more aggressive behaviors. Samantha became more aggressive, and angry. Some of her old behaviors returned. An injunction to this law was obtained several months later, and the GED was then able to be applied as indicated in the JRC program. Samantha improved, and was happier, and no longer aggressive towards herself or others. This was proof that she needs an ongoing program that includes the GED.

Recently, Samantha had another challenge. Due to a congenital condition, she had to undergo complex orthopedic surgery on both legs to correct a balance problem, and prevent future arthritis. JRC was absolutely wonderful. They accompanied her to all her appointments at the Boston Children's Hospital. She remained in the hospital for 6 days after her surgery. JRC had staff members in her room 24 hours a day, during her entire stay in the hospital. In her post operative period, the staff was with her in her residence at all times, and met her every need. She had to be non-weight bearing for 6 weeks post op, and the JRC staff helped her and transported her to school, and to all her post operative doctor's appointments. One of the most remarkable things about her surgical experience, is through all her pain and all her frustration of not being able to walk, she remained calm, and pleasant. This proves the durability of this program at JRC. If she was anywhere else, surely her old behaviors would have returned, and may have affected her post operative outcome.

Sometimes, we feel that JRC is the most misunderstood place in the world. Samantha has now been at JRC for over 5 years, and we have seen nothing but love and affection for her on the part of the entire staff. They appear to have the same love for all the students at the school. The GED is given only after the failure of positive reinforcement programs, and only after the approval of a judge. It is given carefully, and under strict protocols. Everything done at this school and in the residences is video monitored. The program is 100 percent transparent, and has nothing to hide.

The bottom line is that this program helped, and continues to help our daughter where all other programs have failed. Our daughter is a different person than 5 years ago. She is happy, able to concentrate and learn, and fun to be with. She is on no psychotropic medications.

JRC takes only the most difficult kids that have failed at other programs, and make successes of a large number of them. Many of these children have life threatening behaviors, before arriving at JRC. Everything there is done out of love, not cruelty. We believe our daughter would be dead, or in an institution heavily sedated if it were not for this wonderful school, and caring staff. Many other parents feel the same.

Sincerely,
Mitchell Shear, MD, and Marcia Shear[8]

Fortunately, behavioral psychology has developed a treatment for problematic behaviors such as Samantha's self-abuse. The treatment is called "behavior modification" or "applied behavior analysis." Simply put, this involves analyzing the causes of the problematic behaviors, eliminating events that "trigger" the occurrence of the behaviors, arranging rewards for desired behaviors, and applying corrective consequences (consequences designed to decrease problem behaviors, or *aversives)* for undesired behaviors.

JRC's treatment relies overwhelmingly on the use of positive procedures such as rewards and educational procedures. In fact, JRC has created a unique Yellow Brick Road Reward Area[9] for its students that is found in no other program. However, in the case of 22% of its school-age population (and 41% of its total population), these procedures are not sufficiently effective to treat severe problem behaviors. JRC's experience in this respect is fairly consistent with the scientific literature. Thee major literature reviews show that positive-only procedures are effective in only 50–60% of the cases[10] (JRC's positive programming is able to achieve better results than the literature reports because of JRC's cutting edge reward programs.)

For individuals who do not respond to positive-only procedures, most treatment facilities do the following: administer a cocktail of mind-numbing, sometimes addicting, dangerous, and often ineffective psychotropic drugs; use restraint, take-downs, isolation rooms, and/or warehousing (doing nothing); or expel the student, leaving the parent with no options at all[11]. Instead of using these alternatives, all of which are problematic, JRC employs a corrective consequence ("aversive") in the form of a 2-second shock to the surface of the skin, typically of an arm or leg. This treatment, which feels like a hard pinch, has been extensively validated in the scientific literature (113 published papers since the 1960s[12]), is extremely effective[13], and has no significant adverse side effects[14]. For some individuals it is only required at the beginning of their treatment and can be faded out gradually as their behaviors improve. Even in the minority of cases where it is necessary, it is used rarely (the median number of applications per week at JRC is 0 and the mean is 3), and its use is initiated only after trying positive-only procedures for an average of 11 months. JRC uses this procedure only with an extensive and extraordinary list of safeguards[15]. For example, each individual's treatment program that includes the use of skin shock must be pre-approved by a physician, the parent (who can revoke this consent at any time), included in the student's IEP or IHP, approved by a human rights committee and a peer review committee. It also must be individually pre-approved and reviewed at regular intervals by a Massachusetts Probate Court Judge.[16,17]

JRC has been licensed or approved continuously, throughout its 39-year history, by the state education, developmental disabilities and child care departments of Rhode Island and Massachusetts. The Massachusetts Department of Developmental Services ("DDS") has granted and renewed, ever since 1986, JRC's special certification to use aversive behavioral procedures. More than 15 different judges of the Massachusetts Probate and Family Court have, during the last 25 years, approved individual petitions, by guardians on behalf of incompetent children and adults at JRC, to allow the use of aversive therapy in individual behavior modification treatment programs[18]. Thousands of loving parents—including professors at Harvard and NYU, as well as psychiatrists and pediatricians—have entrusted the care and habilitation of their children to JRC.[19] Former JRC students have voluntarily come before legislative committees to testify that JRC saved their lives.[20]

Certain well-intentioned, but ill-informed advocates object to JRC's use of skin shock and are constantly seeking regulations and legislation to ban the use of aversives. Because JRC is the leading example of a program willing to supplement positive behavioral supports, such as rewards, with skin shock as an aversive, in cases where the person cannot be effectively treated without them, JRC has become the focus of attacks by anti-aversive advocates. Characteristically, these persons are unwilling to rationally weigh the risks or intrusiveness of skin shock aversives against the benefits, and to consider whether using such aversives might be a better choice than the alternatives. They simply ignore the small population of people who cannot be effectively treated with psychotropic drugs and positive behavioral supports alone, and who are being warehoused and drugged into submission. In some cases, these anti-aversives advocates have been so dogmatic that they have contributed to a child's death through self-abuse rather than allow him to receive life-saving therapy that includes aversives[21].

Under state and federal law, non-disabled individuals have the right to choose aversive therapy to treat behavioral problems such as smoking and drinking. To deny persons with developmental or behavior/psychiatric disabilities the same right to treat their behavior problems with aversives would be to impose an invidious form of discrimination against those unfortunate enough to suffer from such disabilities.

The Mental Disabilities Rights International (MDRI) Report

The authors of the MDRI Report have a strong philosophical opposition to aversives. Like other anti-aversive advocates, they are unwilling to use a rational risks-versus-benefits analysis in evaluating the use of aversives. Presumably, even if treatment with behavioral skin shock were the only treatment that could save a child from maiming or killing himself or herself, they would oppose its use. Indeed, Dr. Fredda Brown, one of the key persons who provided information to the authors of the MDRI Report was involved in just such a case.[22] In that case, a young man who was maiming himself through self-abusive scratching until he received effective treatment with behavioral skin shock at JRC. Unfortunately, anti-aversive advocates persuaded his parents that he no longer needed that treatment and could live in a supported apartment where aversives would no longer be available. Without aversives, however, his self-abusive scratching (causing blood and bone infection and eventual paralysis) resumed and caused him a painful and premature death at the age of 25.

Almost all of the persons listed as sources for the information for the MDRI Report have testified in Massachusetts for bills that would, if passed, ban the use of aversives. After trying, unsuccessfully to pass such bills for 24 years, the proponents of these bills now are looking to the United Nations Rapporteur on Torture for help with their political cause.

Because of the authors' strong philosophical opposition to aversives, what they refer to as an "investigation" was simply not that. They never visited JRC, never sought to discuss their concerns with JRC's clinicians or staff, never spoke to the hundreds of parents who are pleased with what JRC has been able to accomplish for their children, never advised JRC of their investigation or invited JRC to respond to their concerns, and never interviewed current or former students who have been pleased with the results of their treatment at JRC, including the use of aversives.

MDRI's "investigation" consisted largely of the following: finding and using unverified negative accusations available on the internet; taking selective quotations from the JRC website given by parents and students in *support* of JRC's use of aversives, and fraudulently revising those portions to make up false or misleading statements designed to make the authors appear to be *negative* toward JRC's treatment; soliciting information from an individual who, according to an August 29, 2006 police report, claimed to have placed a "whistle blower" inside JRC;[23] soliciting as many negative quotes as possible from persons who are opposed to JRC; accepting and publishing anonymous accusations without researching whether there was any truth to them; taking selective quotations from reports by a state agency that has a philosophical opposition to aversives (and that is currently being sued by a group of JRC parents in the Federal District Court of Northern New York) without any reference to JRC's responses to those accusations, all of which are available on JRC's website;

and presenting as facts, outdated, re-hashed, and long-since refuted accusations, some of which are now as much as 30–40 years old.

Here are a few examples of the poorly researched, false and misleading statements in the MDRI Report. More can be found in JRC's full response to the MDRI Report.

1. **"The Judge Rotenberg Center (JRC) was founded . . . in California . . . was then moved to Rhode Island."** (p. 6) This is an example of the shoddiness of the MDRI authors' research, even in simply reporting what they found in JRC's publicly available website. JRC's website clearly states that JRC was started in Cranston, Rhode Island.[24]

2. **"in 1981 [in California], a 14 year-old boy died face down . . ."** [bracketed material supplied] (p. 6) JRC was not operating a program in California in 1981 and was not responsible for this boy's care and treatment.

3. **"What's wrong with punishments is that they work immediately, but give no long-term results . . ."** B.F. Skinner interview The New York Times, 1987. (p. 10) This is another example of MDRI's misleading the reader by providing incomplete misinformation. Subsequent to the interview referred to, Skinner issued a statement on punishment that clarified his position regarding the usefulness of punishment in the treatment of certain behaviors. In this statement he wrote:

   > [s]ome autistic children, for example, will seriously injure themselves or engage in other excessive behavior unless drugged or restrained, and other treatment is then virtually impossible. If brief and harmless aversive stimuli, made precisely contingent on self-destructive or other excessive behavior, suppress the behavior and leave the children free to develop in other ways, I believe it can be justified.[25]

4. **"I would be frequently restrained and placed in a small room . . ."** (p. 17 of the full MDRI Report) Again, MDRI has fraudulently taken out of context a small part of a longer statement that is very supportive toward JRC and toward the use of the GED skin shock.[26] By selecting and rearranging words, MDRI makes it seem like a critical statement. The words as quoted were not what the student actually said. Notably absent from the words that MDRI chose to quote are the following words, *"About the GED, it saved my life,"* which appear as the first sentence in the final paragraph of the letter. The full statement,

a letter from a former JRC student, Brian Avery, is re-printed below. The words taken out of context are indicated by bold font.

My name is Brian Avery and I was a student at JRC from September 1998 to January 2004. Prior to me entering JRC at age 12, I was in and out of several psychiatric hospitals and failed in two alternative educational settings.

My behavioral problems really began to escalate when I was 8 or 9 years old. I was on several medications including Tegretol, Haldol, Ritalin, Risperdal, Depekote, Prozac and Paxil. At age 10, my behavior become dangerously out of control. While in school, I would climb on furniture, climb under furniture, mouth off at the teacher, run out of the classroom and would have to be chased down by school staff. I would disrespect authority figures, yell, swear, exhibit inappropriate sexual behaviors in school. I would even try to stab myself with a pencil. I would become physically aggressive with my teachers and would have to be confined in a small padded room. In December of 1996 I was moved from a co-ed class with a 10:2 student/ teacher ratio to another elementary school a few towns over and placed in a all male class with a 6:2 student/teacher ratio. That change delivered little improvement in my behavior and academic progress. At home, I spent most of my time sleeping or being a couch potato, a debilitating side effect of all the medication I was taking. During the time that I was awake, I would disrespect my parents, be aggressive towards my parents and siblings, throw tantrums, destroy property, and would spend hours on end crying. In November of 1996, I spend three weeks in a psychiatric hospital. In February of 1998, and also in May of that year, I spent another three weeks in a psychiatric hospital. After my third hospitalization, my parents and school district finally came to the conclusion that I needed to be placed in a residential school. After visiting numerous schools in New York, Pennsylvania, New Jersey, and Massachusetts, my parents chose JRC.

In September of 1998, I was placed at JRC. Within three months of being at JRC, I was taken off all of my medication. My first few months at JRC were very depressing. For the first month or so of being at JRC, my behavior was much more under control than it had been for a very long time. However, once I became acclimated to the program, my behavior began to deteriorate. I would once again display the same

inappropriate behaviors that I did in public school. ***I would be frequently restrained and placed in a small room.*** *JRC would employ an elaborate scheme of behavior contracts and punishments (not the temporary skin shock). Such contracts included earning a small snack and 10 minutes of free time for going an hour without exhibiting inappropriate behaviors, earning a preferred breakfast for completing my morning routine without incident, being able to order take out for going a full day without displaying inappropriate behavior, being able to attend the weekly BBQ and go on field trips for going a week without displaying inappropriate behavior, and so on. Punishments that JRC would employ involve me spending the day in a small room with a staff person whom I was forbidden from socializing with, going to bed at 7 pm, having to do schoolwork or chores on the weekend without being able to socialize with my housemates. Other punishments included being deprived of foods that were rewards. For example, if everyone else were having pizza, I would be served peanut butter and jelly. I would also be put through a ball task, which involved me needing to place 250 foam balls, one at a time, into a trash can while wearing mitts, a task that is very unpleasant. Although I would have occasional bouts of progress (staying on contract for two months at one point), I made no sustainable progress in 1998 through most of 1999. In the fall of 1999, JRC and my parents had decided that it was time to give the GED a try. I reluctantly agreed to the GED and decided not to fight JRC's attempt to place me on the device. I figured that although unpleasant, the GED would deter me from displaying behaviors that would result in me being restrained and losing out on the rewards that came with the program.*

In December of 1999, I was placed on the GED. For the first month or so that I was on the GED, I displayed few inappropriate behaviors, however, once I became acclimated to the fact that I was on the device and was aware of what the GED felt like, I would start displaying lots of more minor behaviors that were not treated with the GED. Once on the GED, instances of me acting out became fewer and more far in between. Although when my contract was broken, I would display lots of inappropriate behaviors, but I would be selective as to not exhibit GED behaviors, although I would occasionally slip up and receive a GED application. By the spring of 2001, it had been several months since my previous major behavioral incident. JRC then began to rapidly fade me off the GED (although the fading process started nearly a year prior, bouts of behavioral episodes impeded the fading process). In July of 2001, I was completely faded from the GED and was moved into a less restrictive residence (apartment), with a student/staff ratio of 4:1. In the apartment, I enjoyed many privileges, such as grocery shopping, going on weekly field trips to the movies, to the arcade, YMCA, local parks etc. I even attended a few sporting events, including the Providence Bruins, Harlem Globetrotters, and even a Red Sox-Yankees game at Fenway Park. I was also given independence to move about the residence and school unsupervised. All of these were privileges I could not even dream of prior to being placed on the GED. From September 2001–September 2002, I would have a few bouts of behavioral incidents and was placed on and off the GED. However, in October of 2002, I was faded from the GED for good. In the fall of 2002, I attended a culinary class at Blue Hills Technical school, and in November I worked in the computer department as an in school job. Also, I began preparing for the New York Regents exams, and in 2003 I began taking the Regents exams. In the fall of 2003, it became clear to JRC, my parents, and school district that I had accomplished all I could while at JRC and in January 2004 I was transitioned back to public school in New York and mainstreamed.

I moved to Florida in August of 2004 and graduated from high school with honors in May 2005. Since then, I took and passed a couple of college courses and had a few jobs, including a seasonal position working for a bank as a data capture specialist, a job that I obtained because of my quick typing skills that I acquired while at JRC.

About the GED, it saved my life. There are lots of opponents to this controversial, yet potentially life-saving treatment, and understandably so. For someone who has never had the kind of problems I had nor has dealt with anyone who has my kind of problems, when hearing about the GED for the first time, it is only natural to cry torture. However, in reality, being on the GED is a much nicer alternative than being warehoused in a hospital, incarcerated, or being doped up on psychotropic drugs to the point of oblivion. A brief 2-second shock to the surface of the skin sure beats out spending my days restrained and drugged up on drugs and not making any academic progress. I did not like being on the GED when I felt like acting up because it prevented

me from being able to do so. But in the end, I'm thankful for the GED because of the enormous progress I made with it and have continued to make once I no longer needed it.

Some people may wind up spending the majority of their life at JRC while being able to enjoy the benefits and privileges the program has while others, like myself, are able to go on to live an independent life. The bottom line is, if those who opposed the GED had their way, I would currently be locked up and heavily medicate at a hospital or in jail or possibly even dead. So for those who have set out to ban the GED please don't.

Thank you very much

Sincerely,

Brian Avery

5. **"I refused to allow the GED . . ." (p. 18 of the full MDRI Report)** This is another example of MDRI fraudulently taking a very positive and supportive statement off of JRC's website and editing it to make it appear to be saying something negative about JRC. This statement comes from the testimony of Ricardo Mesa, the father of a current JRC student. Mr. Mesa's full testimony is given below.[27] To illustrate how blatantly out of context this quote is, the full testimony is reproduced here and the words taken out of context are shown in bold font. Notably absent from the words that the MDRI Report chose to quote are the words, *"What means something is that I have a daughter who has a life now . . . and is happy."*

I have a daughter, Nicole, who went to JRC in 2004. She's still at JRC in the adult services and she was diagnosed with autism and later Landau-Kleffner Syndrom. As the years went by she got progressively worse. She had brain surgery to remove the epilepsy, which helped with her receptive language. But her behavior continued to be extremely severe. To the point that she would constantly punch her eyes like this {demonstrates} constantly. And I used to be a martial Arts instructor and I used to block and there was no way you could block those punches. Those were hard punches to the eyes. She was doing about a thousand a week. We had to pad the entire room, in her bedroom, she lived with us, she still lives with us. We had to, um, we couldn't go anywhere, we couldn't go on vacation, we couldn't. . . . At nights we would hear her banging her head constantly, all night long.

*She would run out, pinching constantly, her face, her body her breasts, black and blue. You get the picture. She went to the May Center, she went to the LCDC Center, she went to Lighthouse, she went to Perkins School for the Blind, she went to the behavioral program, the neuro-behavioral program at the May Center. These are all excellent programs with very devoted teachers and excellent staff. They couldn't help her. They couldn't stop her. Finally, the Boston School District, the ETL suggested JRC because of some of the progress she had seen from some of the children and I went to see it. We decided to send her over there. And I refused to allow the GED. Because it just, it's so counter-intuitive, I love my daughter, so **I refused to allow it.** And they were fine with it. They allowed me to keep her in the school. They used other methods to try to keep her safe, the restraints, the arm splints and so forth. But Nicole was not making any progress. When she'd come home it was the same story. I agreed after a long time and the hardest day of my life was going before Judge Souten (sp) and asking for them to allow her to use the GED. I told my wife, "We will give them one month. If I don't see immediate progress, she's off it." They put her on the GED, she had a few applications the first day. A few days went by and she had one more. And from that point on she's had an application once every three months, two months and they were usually for very severe behaviors. I don't allow them to use it for any other type of behavior. That contradicts prior testimony {gesturing about someone behind him.} They are fine with it. They have not asked me to take her out of there. Because of that, now she gets one maybe once every year, six months. I mean it's been a long, long time. I can't even recall. She lives at home with us. At home she doesn't wear the GED. It's there in the house and I remind her, that if I see the antecedents, I tell her, "You're going to have to wear the GED." She's fine with it. She has to dress well to go to school. She takes really good care of herself. The staff is extremely loving to her. Always has been, that's one of the things I love. I know them well. My wife knows them very well. We've been able to go to a vacation to Florida every year and Virginia Beach, we are able to go to the movies, we are able to go to dinner together, we have a life. And she lives with us. And that's the way I want it. My biggest fear is that we'll lose all of this ground we've made. That she might return to those horrible days, when she was hurting herself so badly. She knocked out my wife a couple of times with*

headbutts, this was before the GED. And if she were to go back to that stage, it would be just a matter of time before we would have to put her in an institution, or, she wouldn't be able to live with us. So, you know, I really, I know there's a lot of emotion in all of this. A lot of these are articles that have been written, I spoke one time to a reporter all about my daughter and the Boston Globe and the only thing they did, was post "Torture Versus Love." Not one word about what I told them about my daughter was in that article. You can't believe everything you read. And there's a public outcry, against this and exaggerations about what they are doing at the school. I can't speak for anybody else, but I can speak for my daughter and for my life. And I am not a crazy person, or an uninformed person. I am an accountant and I am also an ordained permanent Deacon with the Archdiocese of Boston. I work very closely with Cardinal Law, I mean Cardinal Sean O'Malley. I studied psychology when I was in school. All of that doesn't mean anything. What means something is that I have a daughter who has a life now. I taught her how to ride a bicycle, who can go swimming, who can go on vacation, who goes to school and comes home and is happy.

Particularly disturbing is the authors' willingness to distort testimonial material from JRC's own website, as shown in items 4 and 5 above. The authors took words out of context, made up statements that were not made by the persons who gave the testimonials, and represented the material to be negative comments about JRC and/or skin shock aversives. If the authors were so willing to falsify statements that can be so easily checked—just by going to the JRC website—how much have they distorted the many other accusations in the MDRI Report that were made anonymously and whose accuracy cannot be checked?

In summary, the MDRI Report is a false, misleading, sensationalized, and one-sided account of JRC that is worthy only of a tabloid. It is not a serious or accurate piece of reporting or investigation. One fervently hopes that this Report is an aberration, and not representative of the standards used by MDRI for its other work on both the national and international fronts.

Notes

1. For a more detailed presentation of the material in this document, see pp. 1–50 of JRC's complete Reply to MDRI Report, available at www.judgerc .org/MDRIReportResponse.pdf.

2. JRC's website, at www.judgerc.org, contains a wealth of information. Additional information about aversives can be found at www.effectivetreatment .org.

3. See http://judgerc.org/parents_journey.wmv ("Parents' Journey") for film clips showing some of these types of behavior problems, and giving an overview of how JRC uses positive reward and educational procedures, supplemented with aversives when necessary, in treating these behaviors.

4. JRC's Board of Directors contains five Ph.D. level behavioral psychologists, three of whom are college professors, and one of whom is the President-elect of the Association for Behavior Analysis International, the leading professional organization of behavioral psychologists.

5. JRC currently has such a student who at one point, prior to attending JRC, had detached both retinas due to head-hitting and knee-to-head. Her previous placement, a program that used positive-only treatment procedures, was unable to stop the behavior. Supplementary skin shock at JRC was successful in treating the behavior and thereby enabling the retinas to be re-attached. The young lady is now thriving. See below for photos of this student before and after her treatment at JRC, and for a letter from her parents.

6. JRC currently has a student who is only 16 years old, but who has engaged in head-hitting so forcefully that he has caused himself to have a stroke. His physician has advised JRC that in all probability continued head-banging will cause a fatal brain hemorrhage.

7. JRC currently has a student who has pulled out all but 14 of his adult teeth.

8. This and other letters from JRC parents may be found on the JRC website at http://www.judgerc.org/ parentletters.html#letter66.

9. See http://judgerc.org/yellowbrickroad.html.

10. Carr, E. G., Robinson, F., Taylor, J. & Carlson, J. (1990). Positive approaches to the treatment of severe behavior problems in persons with developmental disabilities. In: *National Institute of Mental Health Consensus Development Conference* (pp. 231–341). NIH Publication No. 91-2410. And see Carr, E. G., Horner, R. H., Turnbull, A. P., Marquis, J. G., Magito McLaughlin, D., McAtee, M. L., Smith, C. E., Anderson Ryan, K., Ruef, M. B., & Doolabh, A. (1999). *Positive behavior support for people with developmental disabilities: A research synthesis.* Washington, D.C.: American Association of Mental Retardation. Full text available at http:// www.judgerc.org/PositiveBehaviorSupport.pdf.   And see Horner, R. H., Carr, E. G., Strain, P. S., Todd,

A .W., and Reed, H. K. (2002). Problem behavior interventions for young children with autism: A research synthesis. *Journal of Autism and Developmental Disorders, 32,* 423–445.

11. Israel, M. L., Blenkush, N. A., von Heyn, R. E., and Sands, C. C. Seven Case studies of individuals expelled from positive-only programs (2010). *The Journal of Behavior Analysis of Offender and Victim Treatment and Prevention, 2* (1), 20–36. Full text available at http://www.judgerc.org/SevenCaseStudies .pdf. See also http://www.judgerc.org/posonlyprograms. pdf (contains documentary proof of the assertion that well-known positive-only programs expel students whose behaviors prove to be too severe to be treated with positive-only treatment procedures).

12. See http://www.effectivetreatment.org/bibliography.html.

13. Israel, M. L., Blenkush, N. A., von Heyn, R. E., & Rivera, P. M. (2008). Treatment of aggression with behavioral programming that includes supplementary skin-shock. *The Journal of Behavior Analysis of Offender and Victim Treatment and Prevention, 1* (4), 119–166. Full text available at http:// www.judgerc.org/AggressionPaper.pdf.

14. van Oorsouw, W. M. W. J., Israel, M. L., von Heyn, R. E., & Duker, P. C. (2008). Side effects of contingent shock treatment. *Research in Developmental Disabilities, 29,* 513–523. Full text available at http://www.judgerc.org/SideEffectsContingent.pdf.

15. See "Safeguards for the Use of Aversives with Students at JRC," a paper that may be found in Appendix F in JRC's full response to the MDRI Report, at http://www.judgerc.org/MDRIReportResponse .pdf.

16. In these adversarial hearings, the judge appoints an independent attorney to represent the interests of the student, as distinct from the interests of the parent or JRC. That attorney is given funds to hire an expert who evaluates the student and his/her treatment needs and advises the attorney as to JRC's proposed treatment program. At the hearing, the judge decides whether the student is competent to make his/her own treatment decisions, and whether, if incompetent, he/she would have chosen to use aversives to treat the problem behavior.

17. All programs that educate children with difficult behaviors use aversives but either hide them or give them different names (e.g., "emergency procedures" or "reactive procedures"). If a program administers a "take-down" every time a child is aggressive, this may function as an aversive. The same applies to "time-out" procedures or seclusion procedures that are administered as consistent consequences for certain behaviors. Holding a

young autistic child still for 30–60 seconds against his/her will is a frequently used aversive. Physical "redirection" procedures or physical "prompts" that are accompanied with a hard squeeze on the shoulder or arm can also function as "hidden" aversives. A loud shouted "NO!" can be a terrifying aversive for young child. A spank on the buttocks is a common aversive that parents sometimes use. Monetary fines, bad grades, point losses, losses of privileges, ignoring, and signs of disapproval can also function as aversives. It is not the case that JRC uses aversives and other programs do not. Rather, JRC chooses to use a safer and more effective aversive (skin shock) than these other procedures, and is willing to label it for what it really is—an aversive. For an explanation of what aversives are, how and why they are used and the reasons why skin shock is so much more effective than, and preferable to, other aversives, *see* Israel, M. L. (2008). *Primer on Aversives.* Full text available at www.judgerc.org/aversivesprimer.pdf.

18. A brief summary of the legal status of aversives at JRC may be found at http://judgerc.org/LegalBasisAversives.pdf.

19. *See* http://www.judgerc.org/intensivetreatment.html#State_House_Testimonies,_November_2009 and http://www.judgerc.org/Comments/parents_AV.html.

20. *Id.*

21. A young man from New York had been maiming himself through self-abusive scratching until he was placed at JRC where he received effective treatment with behavioral skin shock. Unfortunately, anti-aversive advocates persuaded his parents that he no longer needed that treatment and could live in a supported apartment where aversives would no longer be available. Without aversives, however, his self-abusive scratching (causing blood and bone infection and eventual paralysis) resumed and caused him a painful and premature death at the age of 25. See Note 5 in JRC's Response to MDRI Report at *persons already enjoy when they use aversives to treat behaviors such as excessive smoking or drinking* http://www.judgerc.org/MDRIReportResponse.pdf.

22. Dr. Brown, a zealous advocate of deinstitutionalization and an anti-aversive supporter, was instrumental in the removal from JRC in the late 1990s of a student named James Velez. James suffered from a debilitating compulsion to scratch and gouge his skin with his fingernails—a behavior that caused serious blood and bone infections and caused him to require a wheelchair. At JRC his behavior improved sufficiently to enable him to get out of the wheelchair. His self-mutilation was drastically reduced, his skin bone infections cleared to the point where he could have some skin grafts, and he was even able to attend classes at a local public high school with having to wear his GED skin shock device. Unfortunately the anti-aversive advocates, advised by Dr. Brown persuaded James' parents that he no longer needed the behavioral structure or aversives of JRC.

James was then removed from JRC against JRC's advice. The advocates who removed him were so hostile to JRC that they refused to even communicate with JRC's medical director about what James' medical needs were, and refused to discuss with JRC's clinicians what his treatment needs were. JRC was unable to even find out where James was living. The anti-aversive advocates were so eager to remove him from JRC that they removed him even before there was a group home or supported apartment ready for him in New York, his home state. As a result he spent 2 years in a ward for developmentally disabled persons at the Brooklyn Development Center.

Eventually James was moved into a supported apartment in Brooklyn operated by an agency that was opposed to the use of aversives. After moving into his apartment, James was invited by the anti-aversive advocates to tell his story at a Boston conference of TASH, an advocacy organization that is strongly opposed to aversives. (Jan Nisbet, one of the other persons providing information for the MDRI Report is a former President of TASH.) James' life story to this point was chronicled in a manner quite sympathetic to the anti-aversive advocates, in four front page articles that ran in the *New York Times* in June and December 1997. Copies of the four *New York Times* articles, James' obituary, and a proposed OpEd piece about James by Dr. Israel are attached hereto in Appendix J. (This Appendix may be found in JRC's full response to the MDRI Report, at www.judgerc.org/MDRIReportResponse.pdf.)

At his shared apartment James' behavioral consultant was Dr. Brown. Devoid of the behavioral structure and aversives that had served him at JRC, James resumed his scratching, had to use a wheelchair once again, and within about 13 months was hospitalized and nearly died from a leg infection. By February, 1999 he was paralyzed and by October 1999 he was dead at the age of 25, due to infections of the blood and spine caused by the very behaviors JRC had been able to successfully control through the use of skin shock. Characteristically, the anti-aversive advocates showed no remorse over his death or second thoughts as to the wisdom of removing from JRC the one program that had gotten him out of a wheelchair, made him healthy again, and kept him alive. The director of the supervised apartment program in which he died is quoted in his obituary as saying, "Things turned out not to be so simple as we first thought. For the last few years, though, I think that James had the best life that he could have. If that's what this experiment proves, that's a lot. . . . He had the life he wanted . . . James paved the way."

After James' death, when Dr. Brown came to JRC to testify against the use of aversives in the treatment program of another student, Dr. Israel invited her to his office to discuss the case. She refused and marched out of his office when the subject was raised.

23. A copy of the police report may be found in Appendix A of JRC's full response to the MDRI Report, at www.judgerc.org/MDRIReportResponse. pdf. Note that even a fellow JRC-accuser admitted, "I guess we know the whistle blower is not reliable."

24. *See* http://judgerc.org/history.html.

25. Skinner, B. F. A Statement on Punishment. *APA Monitor*, June 1988, p. 22. Full text available at http://www.judgerc.org/Griffin1988Skinnerpunishment statementAJMR.pdf.

26. Letter from former JRC Student Brian Avery, received June 7, 2009. This statement in its entirety appears on JRC's website at http://judgerc.org/ Comments/stultr15.html.

27. Testimony of Father of a JRC Student to Massachusetts Legislative Committee, October 27, 2009. Available in its entirety testimony at: http://judgerc.org/ StateHouseTestimonies/42.%20Ricardo%20Mesa%20 State%20House%20Testimony%2011.4.09.wmv.

Matthew L. Israel is a psychologist who currently serves as director of the Judge Rotenberg Center (JRC), which he founded in 1971 as the Behavior Research Institute. Dr. Israel studied psychology under the late B. F. Skinner as an undergraduate, graduate student, and a postdoctoral fellow at Harvard University. In the 1960s, he was involved in several initiatives using behavioral interventions with disturbed children. JRC is a special needs school in Canton, Massachusetts, serving individuals from the age of 3 through adulthood. For nearly four decades, JRC has provided education and treatment to emotionally disturbed individuals with conduct, behavioral, emotional, and/or psychiatric problems, as well as to individuals with developmental delays and autistic-like behaviors.

EXPLORING THE ISSUE

Is the Use of Aversive Treatment an Inhumane Intervention for Psychologically Disordered Individuals?

Critical Thinking and Reflection

1. In cases in which traditional interventions such as counseling and medication have been ineffective, what options would you recommend to the parents of children who engage in dangerous aggression toward themselves or others?
2. What considerations should be given to the question of how much is too much when it comes to the use of aversive techniques?
3. Imagine that you have been appointed by the governor to conduct an objective evaluation of the ethics of techniques such as those used at JRC. What factors would you include in your evaluation?
4. Assume that you've been awarded a large grant to compare the effectiveness of the JRC techniques to other interventions. What kind of study would you design?
5. What are your thoughts about the emotional effects on the clinicians who administer the aversive techniques to clients?

Is There Common Ground?

When considering the almost unimaginable behaviors of some profoundly disturbed people, one's heart goes out to the family members whose loved one engages in acts that are dangerous to the body, and possibly fatal. Seemingly uncontrollable impulses to gouge out an eye, yank out a tooth, bite through one's skin, or assault another person are horrifying to observe. For individuals with profound intellectual disability or extreme forms of psychological disturbance, traditional forms of behavior therapy may be ineffective. Both MDRI and Dr. Israel would certainly support any intervention that can effectively control such behaviors, and both parties would support using the least intrusive and restrictive procedures possible. The goal of individuals on both sides of this argument is to protect human beings from harm. MDRI believes that aversives such as the GED go too far, and deprive humans of their basic rights. Dr. Israel contends that thoughtful policies and careful procedures have been established to protect the rights of these disabled individuals, and he cites the pleas of family members to help their loved ones acquire the skills they need to refrain from engaging in self-injurious behaviors.

Create Central

www.mhhe.com/createcentral

Additional Resources

Kallert, T. W. (2011). *Coercive Treatment in Psychiatry.* Oxford: Wiley-Blackwell.

Kallert, T. W., Mezzich, J. E., & Monahan, J. (2011). *Coercive Treatment in Psychiatry: Clinical, Legal and Ethical Aspects.* Hoboken, NJ: John Wiley & Sons.

Mcsherry, B. (2013). *Coercive Care: Rights, Law and Policy.* Taylor & Francis.

Reichow, B. (2011). *Evidence-Based Practices and Treatments for Children with Autism.* New York, NY: Springer Science+Business Media, LLC.

Internet References . . .

Citizens Commission on Human Rights

http://www.cchr.org/about-us/mental-health-declaration-of-human-rights.html

National Alliance on Mental Illness

http://www.nami.org/

The Association for Science in Autism Treatment

http://www.asatonline.org/

National Institute of Child Health and Human Development

https://www.nichd.nih.gov/Pages/index.aspx

Selected, Edited, and with Issue Framing Material by:
Richard P. Halgin, *University of Massachusetts, Amherst*

ISSUE

Should Gay Conversion Therapy Be Prohibited by Law?

YES: **Pan American Health Organization,** from "'Cures' for An Illness That Does Not Exist," PAHO (2012)

NO: **International Federation for Therapeutic Choice,** from "What Research Does and Does Not Say about the Possibility of Experiencing 'Harm' by Persons Who Receive Therapeutic Support for Unwanted Same-Sex Attractions or 'Sexual Orientation Change Efforts (SOCE)'?" *Core Issues Trust* (2014)

Learning Outcomes
After reading this issue, you will be able to: • Understand changing views in the mental health field about homosexuality over the past half-century. • Discuss whether research findings support the effectiveness of gay conversion therapies. • Consider the argument that individuals have the right to self-determination, even if choosing a potentially ineffective or harmful intervention. • Discuss whether gay conversion therapy should fall under the purview of law, and whether different standards should apply to the provision of such therapy to minors. • Understand the ethical issues for professionals who provide gay conversion therapy.

ISSUE SUMMARY

YES: PAHO asserts that there is no scientific evidence for the effectiveness of sexual reorientation efforts, and that efforts aimed at changing non-heterosexual orientations lack medical justification. The PAHO statement views "conversion therapies" as threats to personal autonomy and to personal integrity.

NO: In an article approved by the International Federation for Therapeutic Choice, Philip M. Sutton contends that it is a violation of some clients' right to "self-determination" and a potential for harm, not to offer—let alone forbid—professional care for unwanted same-sex attraction via sexual orientation change efforts (SOCE).

A few decades ago the *Diagnostic and Statistical Manual of Mental Disorders* listed homosexuality as a mental disorder in the category of sexual deviations. In 1973, social norms, the views of some experts, and an active gay community in the United States led the American Psychiatric Association to remove homosexuality from the DSM, despite the fact that some psychiatrists strongly opposed this change. Although homosexuality per se was dropped, when DSM-III was published in 1980, "ego-dystonic homosexuality" was included as a mental disorder, characterized by a persistent lack of heterosexual arousal which the individual experienced as interfering with his or her ability to initiate or maintain wanted heterosexual relationships, and persistent distress due to a pattern of unwanted homosexual arousal. Some critics viewed this new label as a continuation of prejudicial and demeaning attitudes toward gay and lesbian individuals, in that homosexuality was still being viewed as pathological. Many gays and lesbians continued to feel stigmatized and marginalized in society.

In what seems disturbing by contemporary standards, so-called interventions were developed in the 1960s involving aversive conditioning techniques in which individuals would be administered electric shock or nausea-inducing drugs when they became sexually aroused during the presentation of same-sex erotic images. Some techniques involved covert sensitization in which individuals were instructed to imagine vomiting or being shocked when they felt aroused in response to such stimuli. Alternatively, they might be instructed to conjure a heterosexual fantasy while masturbating in a technique known as masturbatory reconditioning.

Even though the diagnostic label ego-dystonic homosexuality was removed from the DSM in 1986, some mental health professionals and members of the clergy continued to promote techniques aimed at sexual reorientation. Terms such as "reparative therapy" and "sexual orientation conversion" were used to describe such efforts. For example, men undergoing such treatment may have been instructed to engage in stereotypically masculine activities such as sports while avoiding pursuits of interest to gays such as visiting museums or attending opera. They would have been instructed to spend more time with heterosexual men so that they could better learn how to talk and act like them. While engaging in these pursuits, including dating and having sex with women, they would participate in therapy groups in which they would obtain and provide support in order to prevent relapse to their undesired homosexual thoughts and behaviors.

In time, several professional mental health associations questioned conversion techniques, and advised members to refrain from using such techniques. The debate about the ethics of such interventions continues to brew, however, because some argue that they can be effective for some people. According to this view, every individual has the right to self-determination. People have the right to pursue a change in their sexual orientation, and it is no one's business other than their own. The response to this argument is the assertion that these individuals have been persuaded to seek a "cure" for something that is neither a disease nor inherently changeable. By seeking change through a conversion therapy, critics of such techniques argue that these individuals are putting themselves at risk of psychological harm and the providers of such therapy are therefore engaging in unethical practice. Those who practice these interventions, however, assert that they carry little risk of harm and that homosexuality is not fixed for life.

The discussion about gay conversion therapies has become much broader than concern about its effectiveness. In recent years, attention has shifted to the question of whether such interventions should be outlawed, a debate that has emerged in various states and countries and in political party platform discussions. In 2013, the national spotlight was on New Jersey Governor Chris Christie, who signed a law outlawing gay conversion therapy for minors, expressing concerns about the risks of trying to change a young person's sexual orientation. He asserted that such risks should outweigh worries that the government is setting limits on parental choice by obstructing their options for pursuing sexual orientation change for their children.

The Pan American Health Organization (PAHO) of the World Health Organization (WHO) asserts that efforts aimed at changing non-heterosexual orientations lack medical scientific justification because homosexuality is not a pathological condition. Rather, homosexuality is a natural variation of human sexuality that lacks any intrinsically harmful effect on the health of the individual or those close to him or her. PAHO characterizes sexual orientation as an integral personal characteristic that cannot be changed. Although some individuals may limit the expression of their sexual orientation in terms of behavior, PAHO argues that there is no scientific evidence for the effectiveness of sexual reorientation efforts in changing the inherent trait.

PAHO highlights the risks associated with participating in such interventions, and cites research suggesting a detrimental impact of these efforts. Many individuals experience depression, anxiety, insomnia, feelings of guilt and shame, and even suicidal thoughts and behavior. They argue that by communicating to gay and lesbian individuals that they have a "defect" which they should change, professionals using such techniques are violating medical ethics because of the harm resulting from their work.

Arguing against criticisms of gay conversion therapies, Philip M. Sutton, director of the International Federation for Therapeutic Choice, points out that the disturbing therapeutic approaches described above have been abandoned in the western world, being replaced by "talking therapies." He states that the American Psychological Association itself could find no scientifically rigorous studies of sexual orientation change efforts (SOCE) that would point to a definitive conclusion about whether SOCE is safe or harmful. He points to efforts of organizations such as the International Federation for Therapeutic Choice and the National Association for Research and Therapy of Homosexuality to minimize the potential harmfulness of such techniques and enhance the potential helpfulness of professional care for unwanted same-sex attraction. Speaking against legislation that would outlaw SOCE, Sutton contends that it would be a violation of individuals' right to self-determination, and a potential for them to be harmed, "for not offering—let alone forbidding professional care" for their unwanted same-sex attraction. Sutton would ask why a married man with children should not be allowed to seek help to hold his family together.

Pan American Health Organization

"Cures" for an Illness That Does Not Exist: Purported therapies aimed at changing sexual orientation lack medical justification and are ethically unacceptable

Introduction

Countless human beings live their lives surrounded by rejection, maltreatment, and violence for being perceived as "different." Among them, millions are victims of attitudes of mistrust, disdain and hatred because of their sexual orientation. These expressions of homophobia are based on intolerance resulting from blind fanaticism as well as pseudo-scientific views that regard non-heterosexual and non-procreative sexual behavior as "deviation" or the result of a "developmental defect."

Whatever its origins and manifestations, any form of homophobia has negative effects on the affected people, their families and friends, and society at large. There is an abundance of accounts and testimonies of suffering; feelings of guilt and shame; social exclusion; threats and injuries; and persons who have been brutalized and tortured to the point of causing injuries, permanent scars and even death. As a consequence, homophobia represents a public health problem that needs to be addressed energetically.

While every expression of homophobia is regrettable, harms caused by health professionals as a result of ignorance, prejudice, or intolerance are absolutely unacceptable and must be avoided by all means. Not only is it fundamentally important that every person who uses health services be treated with dignity and respect; it is also critical to prevent the application of theories and models that view homosexuality as a "deviation" or a choice that can be modified through "will power" or supposed "therapeutic support".

In several countries of the Americas, there has been evidence of the continued promotion, through supposed "clinics" or individual "therapists," of services aimed at "curing" non-heterosexual orientation, an approach known as "reparative" or "conversion therapy."[1] Worryingly, these services are often provided not just outside the sphere of public attention but in a clandestine manner. From the perspective of professional ethics and human rights protected by regional and universal treaties and conventions such as the American Convention on Human Rights and its Additional Protocol ("Protocol of San Salvador")[2], they represent unjustifiable practices that should be denounced and subject to corresponding sanctions.

Homosexuality as a Natural and Non-Pathological Variation

Efforts aimed at changing non-heterosexual sexual orientations lack medical justification since homosexuality cannot be considered a pathological condition.[3] There is a professional consensus that homosexuality represents a natural variation of human sexuality without any intrinsically harmful effect on the health of those concerned or those close to them. In none of its individual manifestations does homosexuality constitute a disorder or an illness, and therefore it requires no cure. For this reason homosexuality was removed from the relevant systems of classification of diseases several decades ago.[4]

The Ineffectiveness and Harmfulness of "Conversion Therapies"

Besides the lack of medical indication, there is no scientific evidence for the effectiveness of sexual re-orientation efforts. While some persons manage to limit the expression of their sexual orientation in terms of conduct, the orientation itself generally appears as an integral personal characteristic that cannot be changed. At the same time, testimonies abound about harms to mental and physical health resulting from the repression of a person's sexual orientation. In 2009, the American Psychological Association conducted a review of 83 cases of people who had been subject to "conversion" interventions.[5] Not only was it impossible to demonstrate changes in subjects' sexual orientation, in addition the study found that the intention to change sexual orientation was linked to depression, anxiety, insomnia, feelings of guilt and shame, and even suicidal ideation and behaviors. In light of this evidence, suggesting to patients that they suffer from a "defect" and that they ought to change constitutes a violation of the first principle of medical ethics: "first, do no harm." It affects the right to personal integrity as well as the right to health, especially in its psychological and moral dimensions.

Reported Violations of Personal Integrity and Other Human Rights

As an aggravating factor, "conversion therapies" have to be considered threats to the right to personal autonomy and to personal integrity. There are several testimonies from adolescents who have been subject to "reparative" interventions against their will, many times at their families' initiative. In some cases, the victims were interned and deprived of their liberty, sometimes to the extent of being kept in isolation during several months.[6] The testimonies provide accounts of degrading treatment, extreme humiliation, physical violence, aversive conditioning through electric shock or emetic substances, and even sexual harassment and attempts of "reparative rape," especially in the case of lesbian women. Such interventions violate the dignity and human rights of the affected persons, independently of the fact that their "therapeutic" effect is nil or even counterproductive. In these cases, the right to health has not been protected as demanded by the regional and international obligations established through the Protocol of San Salvador and the International Covenant on Economic, Social, and Cultural Rights.

Conclusion

Health professionals who offer "reparative therapies" align themselves with social prejudices and reflect a stark ignorance in matters of sexuality and sexual health. Contrary to what many people believe or assume, there is no reason—with the exception of the stigma resulting from those very prejudices—why homosexual persons should be unable to enjoy a full and satisfying life. The task of health professionals is to not cause harm and to offer support to

patients to alleviate their complaints and problems, not to make these more severe. A therapist who classifies non-heterosexual patients as "deviant" not only offends them but also contributes to the aggravation of their problems. "Reparative" or "conversion therapies" have no medical indication and represent a severe threat to the health and human rights of the affected persons. They constitute unjustifiable practices that should be denounced and subject to adequate sanctions and penalties.

The Long History of Psychopathologization

For centuries, left-handed persons suffered because the use of the left hand ("sinister" in Latin) was thought to be associated with disaster. These people were regarded as carriers of misfortune and as having a "constitutional defect." Until relatively recently, there were attempts to "treat" and "correct" this supposed defect, causing suffering, humiliation, learning difficulties and difficulties in adapting to daily life in the affected persons.

Recommendations

To Governments:

Homophobic ill-treatment on the part of health professionals or other members of health care teams violates human rights obligations established through universal and regional treaties. Such treatment is unacceptable and should not be tolerated.

"Reparative" or "conversion therapies" and the clinics offering them should be reported and subject to adequate sanctions.

Institutions offering such "treatment" at the margin of the health sector should be viewed as infringing the right to health by assuming a role properly pertaining to the health sector and by causing harm to individual and community well-being.[7]

Victims of homophobic ill-treatment must be treated in accordance with protocols that support them in the recovery of their dignity and self-esteem. This includes providing them treatment for physical and emotional harm and protecting their human rights, especially the right to life, personal integrity, health, and equality before the law.

To Academic Institutions:

Public institutions responsible for training health professionals should include courses on human sexuality and sexual health in their curricula, with a particular focus on respect for diversity and the elimination of attitudes of pathologization, rejection, and hate toward non-heterosexual persons. The participation of the latter in teaching activities contributes to the development of positive role models and to the elimination of common stereotypes about non-heterosexual communities and persons.

The formation of support groups among faculty and within the student community contributes to reducing isolation and promoting solidarity and relationships of friendship and respect between members of these groups. Better still is the formation of sexual diversity alliances that include heterosexual persons.

Homophobic harassment or maltreatment on the part of members of the faculty or students is unacceptable and should not be tolerated.

To Professional Associations:

Professional associations should disseminate documents and resolutions by national and international institutions and agencies that call for the de-psychopathologization of sexual diversity and the prevention of interventions aimed at changing sexual orientation.

Professional associations should adopt clear and defined positions regarding the protection of human dignity and should define necessary actions for the prevention and control of homophobia as a public health problem that negatively impacts the enjoyment of civil, political, economic, social, and cultural rights.

The application of so-called "reparative" or "conversion therapies" should be considered fraudulent and as violating the basic principles of medical ethics. Individuals or institutions offering these treatments should be subject to adequate sanctions.

To the Media:

The representation of non-heterosexual groups, populations, or individuals in the media should be based on personal respect, avoiding stereotypes or humor based on mockery, ill-treatment, or violations of dignity or individual or collective well-being.

Homophobia, in any of its manifestations and expressed by any person, should be exposed as a public health problem and a threat to human dignity and human rights.

The use of positive images of non-heterosexual persons or groups, far from promoting homosexuality (in virtue of the fact that sexual orientation cannot be changed), contributes to creating a more humane and diversity-friendly outlook, dispelling unfounded fears and promoting feelings of solidarity.

Publicity that incites homophobic intolerance should be denounced for contributing to the aggravation of a public health problem and threats to the right to life, particularly as it contributes to chronic emotional suffering, physical violence, and hate crimes.

Advertising by "therapists," "care centers," or any other agent offering services aimed at changing sexual orientation should be considered illegal and should be reported to the relevant authorities.

To Civil Society Organizations:

Civil society organizations can develop mechanisms of civil vigilance to detect violations of the human rights of non-heterosexual persons and report them to the relevant authorities. They can also help to identify and report persons and institutions involved in the administration of so-called "reparative" or "conversion therapies."

Existing or emerging self-help groups of relatives or friends of non-heterosexual persons can facilitate the connection to health and social services with the goal of protecting the physical and emotional integrity of ill-treated individuals, in addition to reporting abuse and violence.

Fostering respectful daily interactions between persons of different sexual orientations is enriching for everyone and promotes harmonic, constructive, salutary, and peaceful ways of living together.

Notes

1. Human Rights Committee (2008). Concluding Observations on Ecuador (CCPR/C/ECU/CO/5), paragraph 12. <http://www2.ohchr.org/english/bodies/hrc/docs/co/CCPR.C.ECU.CO.5.doc>

Human Rights Council (2011). Discriminatory Laws and Practices and Acts of Violence Against Individuals Based on Their Sexual Orientation and Gender Identity (A/HRC/19/41), paragraph 56. <http://www.ohchr.org/Documents/HRBodies/HRCouncil/RegularSession/Session19/A-HRC-19-41_en.pdf>

Human Rights Council (2011). Report of the Special Rapporteur on the Right of Everyone to the Enjoyment of the Highest Attainable Standard of Physical and Mental Health (A/HRC/14/20), paragraph 23. <http://www2.ohchr.org/english/bodies/hrcouncil/docs/14session/A.HRC.14.20.pdf>

United Nations General Assembly (2001). Note by the Secretary-General on the Question of Torture and Other Cruel, Inhuman or Degrading Treatment or Punishment (A/56/156), paragraph 24. <http://www.un.org/documents/ga/docs/56/a56156.pdf>

2. The human rights that can be affected by these practices include, among others, the right to life, to personal integrity, to privacy, to equality before the law, to personal liberty, to health, and to benefit from scientific progress.

3. American Psychiatric Association (2000). Therapies Focused on Attempts to Change Sexual Orientation (Reparative or Conversion Therapies): Position Statement. <http://www.psych.org/Departments/EDU/Library/APAOfficialDocumentsandRelated/PositionStatements/200001.aspx>

   Anton, B. S. (2010). "Proceedings of the American Psychological Association for the Legislative Year 2009: Minutes of the Annual Meeting of the Council of Representatives and Minutes of the Meetings of the Board of Directors". American Psychologist, 65, 385–475. <http://www.apa.org/about/governance/council/policy/sexual-orientation.pdf>

   Just the Facts Coalition (2008). Just the Facts about Sexual Orientation and Youth: A Primer for Principals, Educators, and School Personnel. Washington, DC. <http://www.apa.org/pi/lgbc/publications/justthefacts.html>

4. World Health Organization (1994). International Statistical Classification of Diseases and Related Health Problems (10th Revision). Geneva, Switzerland.

   American Psychiatric Association (2000). Diagnostic and Statistical Manual of Mental Disorders (4th ed., text revision). Washington, DC.

5. APA Task Force on Appropriate Therapeutic Responses to Sexual Orientation (2009). Report of the Task Force on Appropriate Therapeutic Responses to Sexual Orientation. Washington, DC. <http://www.apa.org/pi/lgbt/resources/therapeutic-response.pdf>

6. Taller de Comunicación Mujer (2008). Pacto Internacional de Derechos Civiles y Políticos: Informe Sombra. <http://www.tcmujer.org/pdfs/Informe%20Sombra%202009%20LBT.pdf>

   Centro de Derechos Económicos y Sociales (2005). Tribunal por los Derechos Económicos, Sociales y Culturales de las Mujeres. <http://www.tcmujer.org/pdfs/TRIBUNAL%20DESC%20ECUADOR%20MUJERES.pdf>

7. See General Comment No. 14 by the Committee on Economic, Social, and Cultural Rights with regards to the obligation to respect, protect and comply with human rights obligations on the part of States parties to the International Covenant on Economic, Social, and Cultural Rights.

THE PAN AMERICAN HEALTH ORGANIZATION **(PAHO),** founded in 1902, is the world's oldest international public health agency. It provides technical cooperation and mobilizes partnerships to improve health and quality of life in the countries of the Americas. PAHO is the specialized health agency of the Inter-American System and serves as the Regional Office for the Americas of the World Health Organization (WHO). Together with WHO, PAHO is a member of the United Nations system.

International Federation for Therapeutic Choice  **NO**

What Research Does and Does Not Say about the Possibility of Experiencing "Harm" by Persons Who Receive Therapeutic Support for Unwanted Same-Sex Attractions or "Sexual Orientation Change Efforts (SOCE)"[1]

Abstract

In recent years, national and international medical and mental health associations typically have emphasized the potential harmfulness of professional care for unwanted same-sex attraction and behavior (SSA or homosexuality). During 2012 and 2013, state legislatures in the U.S. and legislative bodies in other countries either have passed or are considering passing laws which would penalize professionals who provided professional care for unwanted SSA—to minors and/or adults—the loss of the license to practice. This paper was written as a response to the present situation in the United Kingdom. The paper reviews the universal ethics of all medical and mental health professionals to avoid harm and do good (non-maleficence/malfeasance and beneficence); discusses the documented potential for harm when using *every* mental health treatment for *every* presenting problem; clarifies steps taken by the *Alliance for Therapeutic Choice and Scientific Integrity* (ATCSI) and its international division, the *International Federation for Therapeutic Choice* (IFTC), to promote ethical professional care for unwanted SSA; clarifies the injustice and presumed ideological biases of the medical and mental health associations' warning about the potential for harm for psychotherapy only for unwanted SSA and not all approaches; and documents that the research purporting to show this harmfulness, in the research authors own words, does not do so. Recommendations to promote scientific integrity in the conduct and reporting of relevant research are offered.

Introduction

It has come to the attention of the International Federation for Therapeutic Choice (IFTC) that the UK Parliament will soon be debating the merits of the proposed Private Member's Bill *Counsellors and Psychotherapists (Regulation) Bill no. 14120*, (http://www.publications.parliament.uk/pa/bills/cbill/2013-2014/0120/14120.pdf) which would amend *Section 60 of the Health Act 1999 (Regulation of health care and associated professions)* as follows: "The [*Code of ethics for registered counsellors, therapists and psychotherapists*] must include a prohibition on gay to straight conversion therapy." The *Complaints and disciplinary procedures of the Code* would be amended as follows: "(2) A practitioner found by the Council to have breached . . . that section of the code relating to prohibition of gay to straight conversion therapy shall result in permanent removal from the register."

This information came to our attention when reading a professional statement by the United Kingdom's Association of Christian Counsellors (ACC, 2014) and a news report of this statement in *The Guardian* (Strudwick, 13 January 2014). Both the ACC statement and Guardian report made serious allegations about the great risk for "harm" to persons who receive "reparative or conversion therapy," what the American Psychological Association (APA) has chosen to call "Sexual Orientation Change Efforts (SOCE)" (APA, 2009).

Members of the IFTC (www.therapeutic-choice.org/) and the IFTC's parent organization, the *Alliance for Therapeutic Choice and Scientific Integrity* (ATCSI; www.therapeuticchoice.com) and like-minded licensed medical and mental health professionals, refer to such therapy as licensed professional care to "change"—i.e., manage, diminish or resolve—unwanted same-sex attractions (SSA) and behavior. Such professional care may include educational guidance, counseling, therapy and/or medical services.

Specifically, the ACC statement declared: "we do not endorse Reparative or Conversion Therapy" because of "the potential to create harm" and "in the interests of public safety." The report in *The Guardian* commented:

> Research by the US clinical psychologists Ariel Shidlo and Michael Schroeder . . . found 'conversion therapy' *usually* led to worsened mental health, self-harm and suicide attempts . . . such treatment *routinely* led to worsened (sic) self-harm, thoughts of suicide and suicide attempts (emphasis added).[2]

The ACC statement and Guardian story reflect the views of four leading mental and medical health professional associations in the UK. The British Medical Association (2010) voted at its Annual Representative Meeting that "'conversion therapy' for homosexuality . . . is discredited and harmful to those 'treated'." The British Association for Counselling and Psychotherapy (2013) mentions the PAHO/WHO (2012) position statement that practices "such as conversion or reparative therapies . . . represent a severe threat to the health and human rights of the affected persons" (p. i).

Similarly, the Royal College of Psychiatrists (n.d.) states that "we know from historical evidence that treatments to change sexual orientation that were common in the 1960s and 1970s were very damaging" and specifically mentions that the 2002 "Shidlow (sic) and Schroeder" study showed that such treatment resulted in "considerable harm." And the UK Council for Psychotherapy (2010) asserts that a person who undergoes "therapy that aims to change or reduce same sex attraction" is at risk for "considerable emotional and psychological cost."

These and other recent **allegations that the harmfulness of "SOCE" has been proven scientifically are simply false** (Rosik, 2013a, 2013b, 2013c, 2013d, 2013e). Warnings by national mental health associations of the "potential harmfulness of 'SOCE'" are unscientific, professionally irresponsible, and misleading, if not dishonest.[3] These observations are explained below.

1. **First, *do no harm*. Then *do as much good as you can*.** Avoiding and minimizing harm (nonmaleficence, nonmalfeasance) and doing good for those one serves (beneficence) are the foundational principles of ethical care by all mental—and medical—health care professionals. As an illustration, the first Principle of the American Psychological Association's *Ethical Principles of Psychologists and Code of Conduct* (2010) states:

   Principle A: Beneficence and Nonmaleficence: Psychologists strive to benefit those with whom they work and take care to do no harm. In their professional actions, psychologists seek to safeguard the welfare and rights of those with whom they interact professionally and other affected persons

2. ***Every* approach to medical and mental health care has the potential for harmful—or at least unwanted—side effects. And no approach is guaranteed to work for any particular patient or client, even if "taken or used as directed."**

   Lambert (2013) reports that reviews "of the large body of psychotherapy research, whether it concerns broad summaries of the field or outcomes of specific disorders and specific treatments" lead to the conclusion that, while all clients do not report or show benefits, "psychotherapy has proven to be highly effective" for many clients (p. 176). Unfortunately, the research "literature on negative effects" also offers "substantial . . . evidence that psychotherapy can and does harm a portion of those it is intended to help." These include "the relatively consistent portion of adults (5% to 10%) and a shockingly high proportion of children (14% to 24%) who deteriorate while participating in treatment" (p. 192). Such findings have been reported in the therapeutic and scientific communities for over three decades (Lambert, 2013; Lambert & Ogles, 2004; Lambert & Bergin, 1994; Lambert, Bergin and Collins, 1977; Lambert, Shapiro & Bergin, 1986; Nelson, Warren, Gleave, & Burlingame, 2013; Warren, Nelson, Mondragon, Baldwin, & Burlingame, 2010).

   As Rosik (2013c) has written,

   > Any discussion of alleged harms simply must be placed in the broader context of psychotherapy outcomes in general. . . . Deterioration rates would need to be established for professionally conducted change-oriented therapy ("SOCE") significantly beyond 10% for adults and 20% for youth in order for claims of approach-specific harms to be substantiated.

In this light, it is unfortunate that the UK Association of Christian Counsellors (2014) has the following ethical guideline for membership: # 5.5. *"Members should avoid any action which might cause harm to a client."* If any—and every—action that *may* occur in counseling *"might* cause harm to a client," how does the ACC envision any of its counselors ever attempting to serve their clients? Their position is not science but wishful thinking. As Rosik (2013e) has noted:

> Reasonable clinicians and mental-health association representatives should agree that anecdotal accounts of harm constitute no basis upon which to prohibit a form of psychological care. If this were not the case, the practice of any form of psychotherapy could place the practitioner at risk of regulatory discipline, as research indicates that 5 to 10% of all psychotherapy clients report deterioration and as many as 50% experience no reliable change during treatment (Hansen, Lambert, & Forman, 2002; Lambert & Ogles, 2004).

3. **The IFTC and ATCSI have taken steps to minimize the potential harmfulness and enhance the potential helpfulness of professional care for unwanted SSA through the *Practice Guidelines for the Treatment of Unwanted Same-Sex Attractions and Behavior* (NARTH, 2010). (See Appendix A—below—for the short form of the *Practice Guidelines*.)**

These *Practice Guidelines* were formally adopted in 2008 and published in 2010. Their purpose is to guide the ethical practice of "change-oriented" professional mental and mental health care for unwanted SSA. The *Practice Guidelines* have been written, published and used to educate medical and mental health professionals—as well as concerned nonprofessionals—about how to enhance the helpfulness and avoid any harmfulness of providing professional care for unwanted SSA.

For example, *Practice Guideline # 5* advises: *"At the outset of treatment, clinicians are encouraged to provide clients with information on change-oriented processes and intervention outcomes that is both accurate and sufficient for informed consent."*

Concerning potential harmfulness, *Practice Guideline # 6* states: "Clinicians are encouraged to utilize accepted psychological approaches to psychotherapeutic interventions that minimize the risk of harm when applied to clients with unwanted same-sex attractions."

As many of the "therapists" who reportedly provided "conversion therapy" to persons interviewed by Shidlo and Schroeder (2002) were not professionally trained or licensed (see Point 5 below), *Practice Guideline #11* is especially relevant: *"Clinicians are encouraged to increase their knowledge and understanding of the literature relevant to clients who seek change, and to seek continuing education, training, supervision, and consultation that will improve their clinical work in this area."*

Translations of the short form of the *Practice Guidelines for the Treatment of Unwanted Same-Sex Attractions and Behavior* are available, so far, in Chinese, French, German, Italian, Polish, Russian, and Spanish. Translations of the long form are available in Polish and Spanish, as well. These translations may be retrieved from http://www.narth.com/#!about3/c1k2y

4. *"There are no scientifically rigorous studies of recent SOCE that would enable us to make a definitive statement about whether recent SOCE is safe or harmful and for whom"* (American Psychological Association, 2009, p. 83). In the same document, the APA states further: "None of the recent research . . . meets methodological standards that permit conclusions regarding efficacy or safety (APA, 2009, p. 2.) APA similarly emphasizes that "recent SOCE research cannot provide conclusions regarding efficacy or safety" (p. 3). The APA offered these conclusions *after* having reviewed all relevant research to date, including the study by Shidlo and Schroeder (2002).

5. **In the authors' own words, the Shidlo and Schroeder (2002) study does *"not provide information on the incidence and prevalence of failure, success, harm, help, or ethical violations in conversion therapy"* (p.249), i.e., "SOCE".**

Shidlo and Schroeder acknowledge that *how* they conducted their study limits what any reports of "harm" given by the participants in their study may mean. The authors accurately describe their research as an "exploratory study . . . based on the retrospective accounts of consumers" who are asked to talk about what their therapists did and what the consumers experienced "on average . . . 12 years ago" (p. 250). The authors acknowledge that, like all research using this method, the reports of the alleged consumers' perspectives on their experience of therapy "may not accurately reflect" what actually happened. Shidlo and Schroeder discuss the potential limitations of the accuracy of the reports of their consumers, in light of the earlier findings of Rhodes, Hill, Thompson, and Elliott (1994) that "retrospective data from clients" are subject to "misunderstandings" about what happened years earlier in psychotherapy. As actual former clients try to make sense of the events of their experience of therapy, they may unknowingly change the details of their story (Rhodes, et al., p. 481).

Additional problems with how the Shidlo and Schroeder study was conducted further erode the scientific credibility and significance of any of its results.

▸ Initial participants of the study were recruited with the following advertisement:

> Have you gone through counseling or therapy where you were encouraged to become heterosexual or ex-gay? The National Lesbian and Gay Health Association wants to hear from you. The organization is conducting research for a project entitled "Homophobic Therapies: Documenting the Damage." (Shidlo & Schroeder, 2002, Appendix A)

Such a recruitment statement is an example of research based more on ideology than on objective, scientific inquiry.

▸ There is *no* evidence—*besides* the interviewees' claims—that:

- They *actually participated* in a "conversion therapy" ("SOCE").
- They *actually experienced* the harms they claimed to have.
- Any actual harm did not preexist their experience of "conversion therapy" ("SOCE").
- Any actual harm occurred *as a result of*, *during* or *after*, the sessions of "SOCE," instead of as a result of an experience outside of "therapy."

▸ While approximately two-thirds of the "therapists" reported by the presumed former clients were described as "licensed mental health practitioners," one third of the "therapists" were "unlicensed counselors," including "peer counselors, religious counselors, and unli-

censed therapists." Shidlo and Schroeder did not clarify what kinds of "harm" were associated with which kind of therapist. This study does not—and cannot based on how it was designed and conducted—show that, if consumers were harmed, this resulted from the actions of licensed mental health professionals who provided "conversion therapy" (i.e., professional "SOCE") vs. nonprofessional caregivers.

▸ Ironically, a careful reading of the report of this study, which admittedly was intended to "document the harm" experienced by consumers of "SOCE," also showed the opposite result. In particular, the results suggest that pre-existing suicidality was at least managed, not induced by the participants' experience of "SOCE" (Whitehead, 2010, pp. 161–165).

▸ Several studies published during the past two years which also were intended to document the harm of receiving such professional care suffer from the same methodological difficulties as the Shidlo and Schroeder (2002) study and offer no better evidence in support of the harmfulness claim (Rosik, 2014).

6. **Medical and mental health professionals, and their patients and clients, would not allow the kind of "evidence" provided by the Shidlo and Schroeder (2002) study to prevent them from receiving wanted treatment for any other concern.**

Imagine how someone who has experienced a helpful medical or mental health-care product or service would feel, if their product or service were forbidden them based on the kind of information provided by the Shidlo and Schroeder (2002) study. Otherwise satisfied customers would be refused the chance to continue—and willing new consumers to start—receiving these products for services based on complaints—but no clear evidence—of harmful side effects. Those complaining would not have to prove that they actually received the products or treatment—or that they had used them as directed. The complainers would not have to prove that they actually experienced the side effects they claimed, or that the side effects did not already exist prior to their treatment. Nor, would complainers have to prove who they received the product or service from, while admitting that some of the care providers were professionally licensed, but as many as a third were not.

Most people would not accept their favorite pain reliever or medical treatment being taken off the market based on such minimal "evidence." Retrospective ("anecdotal") reports—based on what allegedly happened an average of 12 years ago—are not an acceptable standard of "evidence" for stopping or preventing others from receiving care which *has* been found helpful—by some. The various professional organizations which are so quick to accept the truthfulness of any complaints about the harmfulness of "SOCE" are also too quick to deny the validity of over a century of professional reports which document wanted changes in same-sex attraction and behavior (APA, 2009; NARTH, 2009; Phelan, 2014).

As a rule, IFTC, ATCSI and allied mental health professionals do *not* attempt to "cure" same-sex attractions and behaviors. Rather, we agree that change in sexual orientation is not typically categorical in nature and observe that clients may experience changes on a continuum that is personally meaningful and satisfying (NARTH, 2012). While not agreeing that "SOCE" is or may be beneficial, even the APA (2009) admits that "the recent research on sexual orientation identity diversity illustrates that sexual behavior, sexual attraction, and sexual orientation identity are labeled and expressed in many different ways, some of which are fluid" (p. 14, cf. p. 2). Fluidity in sexuality, sexual orientation, sexual orientation identity, and relationships—without professional assistance—seems especially true among adolescents (p. 76) and women (p. 63; cf. Diamond, 2009), and has been documented as occurring among men as well (Laumann, et al., 1994).

7. **There is a violation of some clients' right to "self-determination" and a potential for harm, for not offering—let alone forbidding—professional care for unwanted SSA ("SOCE") to persons who freely choose to seek such care.**

Another foundation for ethical, beneficial practice is respect for clients' and patients' right to "self-determination." As *Principle E: Respect for People's Rights and Dignity* of the APA (2010) Ethical Principles states: "Psychologists respect the dignity and worth of all people, and the rights of individuals to privacy, confidentiality, and *self-determination*" (emphasis added). Surely, this must include the

rights of persons to choose to manage or resolve same-sex attractions and behaviors.

Also, there would be appear to be the potential for grave harm caused to some people by neglecting to provide such care for those who want it. There are significant medical and psychological health risks which co-occur with engaging in same-sex behavior (CDC, 2014; NARTH, 2009, III. Response to APA Claim: There Is No Greater Pathology in the Homosexual Population than in the General Population, p. 53–87; Whitehead, 2010).

Anecdotal and correlational studies clearly document that sexual abuse and other emotionally traumatic events are more common in the childhoods of persons with sexual minority attractions and behaviors than those with heterosexual (Austin et al., 2008; Corliss, Cochran, & Mays, 2002; Friedman et al., 2011; Lehavot, Molina, & Simoni, 2012; Stoddard, Dibble, & Fineman, 2009; Steed & Templer, 2010; Tomeo, Templer, Anderson, & Kotler, 2001; Wells, Magnus, McGee, & Beautrais, 2011). Sexual abuse in particular has been shown to precede the development of Gender nonconformity (Alanko, et al., 2008; Roberts, Glymour, & Koenen, 2103) as well as of same-sex attractions and behavior for some persons (Fields, Malebranche, & Feist-Price, 2008; Walker, Archer, and Davies, 2005).

While further research is needed to clarify the extent of any causal connection between traumatic childhood events and the development of SSA and behavior, their co-occurrence is undeniable. Professional compassion warrants assisting those who want to try to manage and resolve SSA behaviors—and the underlying feelings and experiences which may motivate them.

8. **Moving forward, it is necessary that national and world medical and mental health associations deal with the issue of therapeutic choice concerning unwanted same-sex attraction in a professionally responsible manner with scientific integrity.**

Persistent warnings that professional "SOCE" have "the potential to harm" those who receive them are misleading and disserve the general public. Organizations like the American Psychological Association, The World Medical Association, and—most recently—the Association of Christian Counselors in the UK, in effect deceive the public when they—not inaccurately—warn that there is a *potential* for harm, but then do not qualify this warning by clarifying that (1) *all* mental health services for all personal and interpersonal concerns have this risk *and* (2) that responsible science has not yet shown whether the degree of risk for professional "SOCE" is greater, the same as, or less than the risk for all other psychotherapies.

Overall, we agree with Shidlo and Schroeder (2002) that more *"complementary research (is) needed."* Such research ideally *"would include interviews with sexual orientation conversion therapists and analysis of psychotherapy sessions by independent third-party observers."* In the absence of such clear, reliable and valid scientific evidence, it is difficult to avoid the conclusion that professional organizations like the American Psychological Association, the UK Association of Christian Counselors, various state and national government legislatures, and even media such as *The Guardian,* are working to prevent mental health professionals from offering educational guidance, counseling and therapeutic care for persons with unwanted same-sex attraction and behavior based on ideological and not scientific or professional grounds. Persons who experience unwanted same-sex attractions and behaviors deserve the right to receive professional care to try to change (i.e., manage, diminish or resolve) these feelings and actions if they choose to do so.

Notes

1. A version of this document was published in February, 2014 by Core Issues Trust. Retrieve from http://www.core-issues.org/uploads/IFTC%20 Sutton%20Paper%2021%20Feb%202014.pdf. A version of this document also has been accepted for publication by *Linacre Quarterly.*

2. This report was retrieved on 15 January 2014. When attempting to retrieve this report again on 6 February 2014, the link no longer worked. Instead, a report by the same name was retrieved from http://www.theguardian.com/world/2014/jan/13/ christian-therapists-stop-conversion-therapy-turn-gay-patients-straight. In this revised *Guardian* report, the claims of "harm" due to "conversion therapy" are described as follows: "Research by the US clinical psychologists Ariel Shidlo and Michael Schroeder has shown such treatment routinely led to worsened

mental health, self-harm, thoughts of suicide and suicide attempts."

3. The IFTC (2011, 2012, 2013) has offered interventions at the Organization for Security and Co-operation in Europe (OSCE) Office of Democratic Institutions and Human Rights (ODIHR) Human Dimension Implementation Meeting (HDIM) in Warsaw, Poland on these and related concerns.

References

Alanko, K., Santitila, P., Sato, B., Jem, P., Johansson, A., et al. (2011). Testing causal models of the relationship between childhood gender atypical behavior and parent-child relationship. *British Journal of Developmental Psychology, 29*, 214–233. doi: 10.1348/2044-835X.002004

American Psychological Association (2010). *Ethical Principles of Psychologists and Code of Conduct.* Washington, DC: Author. Retrieved from http://apa.org/ethics/code/index.aspx

American Psychological Association, Task Force on Appropriate Therapeutic Responses to Sexual Orientation (2009). *Report of the APA Task Force on Appropriate Therapeutic Responses to Sexual Orientation.* Washington, D.C.: American Psychological Association. Retrieved from http://www.apa.org/pi/lgbt/resources/therapeuticresponse.pdf

Association of Christian Counselors (2014). *An ACC statement to its members January 2014.* Retrieved from http://www.acc-uk.org/pdfs/ACC%20statement%20to%20its%20members%20January%202014.pdf.

Austin, S. B., Jun, H., Jackson, B., Spiegelman, D., Rich-Edwards, J., Corliss, H. L., & Wright, R. J. (2008). Disparities in child abuse victimization in lesbian, bisexual, heterosexual women in the Nurses' Health Study II. *Journal of Womens Health, 17*, 597–606. doi: 10.1089/jwh.2007.0450

British Association for Counselling and Psychotherapy (2013). *Ethical Framework for Good Practice in Counselling & Psychotherapy.* Retrieved from http://www.itsgoodtotalk.org.uk/assets/docs/BACP-Ethical-Framework-for-Good-Practice-in-Counselling-and-Psychotherapy_1360076878.pdf

British Medical Association (2010). *Policy group: Annual Representative Meeting, 2010.* Retrieved from http://web2.bma.org.uk/bmapolicies.nsf/searchresults?OpenForm&Q=conversion+therapy~ 8~50~Y

Centers for Disease Control and Prevention (CDC), National Center for HIV/AIDS, Viral Hepatitis, STD, and TB Prevention, Division of STD Prevention (January, 2014). *Sexually Transmitted Disease Surveillance 2012.* Retrieved from http://www.cdc.gov/std/stats12/Surv2012.pdf

Corliss, H. I., Cochran, S. D., & Mays, V. M. (2002). Reports of parental maltreatment during childhood in a United States population-based survey of homosexual, bisexual, and heterosexual adults. *Child Abuse & Neglect, 26,* 1165–1178.

Friedman, M. S., Marshal, M. P., Guadamuz, T. E., Wei, C., Wong, C. F., Sacwyc, E. M., & Stall, R. (2011). A meta-analysis of disparities in childhood sexual abuse, parental physical abuse, and peer victimization among sexual minority and sexual nonminority individuals. *American Journal of Public Health, 101,* 1481–1494. doi: 10.2105/AJPH.2009.190009

Diamond, L. M. (2009). *Sexual Fluidity: Understanding Women's Love and Desire.* Cambridge, MA: Harvard University Press.

Fields, S. D., Malebranche, D., & Feist-Price, S. (2008). Childhood sexual abuse in black men who have sex with men: Results from three qualitative studies. *Cultural Diversity and Ethnic Minority Psychology, 14,* 385–390. doi: 10.1037/1099-9809.14.4.385

Hansen, N. B., Lambert, M. J., & Forman, E. M. (2002). The psychotherapy dose-response effect and its implications for treatment delivery services. *Clinical Psychology: Science and Practice, 9,* 329–343. doi:10.1093/clipsy.9.3.329

International Federation for Therapeutic Choice (IFTC, 2011). Intolerance and Discrimination Against Medical and Mental Health Professionals, Researchers, and Educators Threaten the Freedoms of the Professionals and Those Whom They Serve. *Journal of Human Sexuality,* Volume 4, 136–140 (November, 2012). Retrieve from http://www.scribd.com/doc/174191760/Journal-of-Human-Sexuality-Vol-IV.

International Federation for Therapeutic Choice (IFTC, 2012). Legally Sanctioned Intolerance and Discrimination Threatens the Freedom of Medical and Mental Health Professionals and Researchers to Provide—and Potential Patients or Clients to Receive—Freely Sought Education, Guidance, Therapy and Other Professional Care. *Journal of Human Sexuality,* Volume 5, 112–119 (December, 2013).

Retrieved from http://www.narth.com/#!iftc-reports/c1qbu

International Federation for Therapeutic Choice (IFTC, 2013). Legally Sanctioned Intolerance and Discrimination Threatens the Freedom of Medical and Mental Health Professionals and Researchers to Provide—and Potential Patients or Clients to Receive—Freely Sought Education, Guidance, Therapy and Other Professional Care. Retrieved from http://www.narth.com/#!iftc-reports/c1qbu

Jones, S. L., Rosik, C. H., Williams, R. N., & Byrd, A. D. (2010). A Scientific, Conceptual, and Ethical Critique of the Report of the APA Task Force on Sexual Orientation. *The General Psychologist, 45*(2), 7–18. Retrieved from http://www.apa.org/divisions/div1/news/fall2010/Fall%202010%20TGP.pdf

Lahavot, K., Molina, Y., & Simoni, J. M. (2012). Childhood trauma, adult sexual assault, and adult gender expression among lesbian and bisexual women. *Sex Roles, 67,* 272–284. doi: 10.1007/s11199-012-0171-1

Lambert, M. (2013). The efficacy and effectiveness of psychotherapy. In Michael J. Lambert (Ed.) *Bergin and Garfield's Handbook of Psychotherapy and Behavior Change* (6th edition), pp. 169–218. Hoboken, NJ: Wiley.

Lambert, M. J., & Bergin, A. E., (1994). The effectiveness of psychotherapy. In S. L. Garfield & A. E. Bergin (Eds.), *Handbook of Psychotherapy and Behavior Change* (4th edition, pp. 143–189). New York, NY: Wiley.

Lambert, M. J., Bergin, A. E., & Collins, J. L. (1977). Therapist induced deterioration in psychotherapy patients. In A. S. Gurman & A. M. Razin (Eds.), *Effective psychotherapy: A handbook of research* (pp. 452–81). New York: Pergamon Press.

Lambert, M. J., & Ogles, B. M. (2004). *The efficacy and effectiveness of psychotherapy.* New York, NY: Wiley.

Lambert, M. J., Shapiro, D. A., & Bergin, A. E. (1986). The effectiveness of psychotherapy. In S. L. Garfield & A. E. Bergin (Eds.), *Handbook of Psychotherapy and Behavior Change* (3rd edition, pp. 157–211). New York, NY: Wiley.

Laumann, E. O, Gagnon, J. H., Michael, R. T., & Michaels, S. (1994). *The social organization of sexuality.* Chicago: University of Chicago Press.

National Association for Research and Therapy of Homosexuality (NARTH) Scientific Advisory

Committee (2009). What research shows: NARTH's response to the American Psychological Association's (APA) claims on homosexuality. *Journal of Human Sexuality*, 1, 1–128. Retrieved from http://www.scribd.com/doc/115507777/Journal-of-Human-Sexuality-Vol-1 Summary of *Journal of Human Sexuality Volume* 1 retrieved from http://www.scribd.com/doc/125145105/Summary-of-Journal-of-Human-Sexuality-Volume-1.

National Association for Research and Therapy of Homosexuality *(NARTH)*, Task Force on Practice Guidelines for the Treatment of Unwanted Same-Sex Attractions and Behavior (2010). *Practice Guidelines for the Treatment of Unwanted Same-Sex Attractions and Behavior. Journal of Human Sexuality*, 2, 5–65. Retrieved from http://www.scribd.com/doc/115506183/Journal-of-Human-Sexuality-Vol-2). The *Practice Guidelines* themselves may also be retrieved from http://www.scribd.com/doc/115508811/NARTH-Practice-Guidelines

National Association for Research and Therapy of Homosexuality (2012). *NARTH Statement on Sexual Orientation Change.* Approved by the NARTH Board of Directors on January 25, 2012. Retrieved from: http://www.narth.com/2012/01/narth-statement-on-sexual-orientation-change/%29#!about1/c1wab)

Nelson, P. L., Warren, J. S., Gleave, R. L., & Burlingame, G. M. (2013). Youth psychotherapy change trajectories and early warning system accuracy in a managed care setting. *Journal of Clinical Psychology*, 69, 880–895. doi: 10.1002/jclp.21963

Pan American Health Organization (17 May 2012). *"Cures" for an illness that does not exist.* Retrieved from http://www.paho.org/hq/index.php?option=com_content&view=article&id=6803 &itemid=1926&lang=en

Phelan, J. E. (2014). *Successful Outcomes of Sexual Orientation Change Efforts (SOCE): An Annotated Bibliography.* Charleston, SC: Practical Application Publications (Phelan Consultants LLC.)

Rhodes, R. H., Hill, C. E., Thompson, B. J., & Elliott, R. (1994). Client retrospective recall of resolved and unresolved misunderstanding of events. *Journal of Counseling Psychology*, 41, 473–483.

Roberts, A. L., Glymour, M. M., & Koenen, K. C. (2013). Does maltreatment in childhood affect sexual orientation in adulthood? *Archives of Sexual Behavior*, 42, 161–171. doi: 10.1007/s10508-012-0021-9

Rosik, C. H. (2012). Did the American Psychological Association's *Report on Appropriate Therapeutic Responses to Sexual Orientation* Apply Its Research Standards Consistently? A Preliminary Examination. *Journal of Human Sexuality*, 4, 70–85. Retrieved from http://www.scribd.com/doc/174191760/Journal-of-Human-Sexuality-Vol-IV

Rosik, C. H. (2013a). Countering a One-Sided Representation of Science: NARTH Provides the "Rest of the Story" for Legal Efforts to Challenge Anti-Sexual Orientation Change Efforts (SOCE) Legislation. *Journal of Human Sexuality*, 5, 120–164.

Rosik, C. H. (2013b). Fact-Checking California Senate Bill 1172. *Journal of Human Sexuality*, 5, 94–102. Retrieved from http://www.narth.com/#!narth-analysis-of-soce-ban/c1q8f

Rosik, C. H. (2013c). *NARTH Response to the WMA Statement on Natural Variations of Human Sexuality* (December 23, 2013). Retrieved from http://www.narth.com/#!world-medical-association---narth/c4c6

Rosik, C. H. (2013d). California Senate Bill 1172: A Scientific and Legislative Travesty—A Look at the Bill's Misuse of Science. *Journal of Human Sexuality*, 5, 83–93. Retrieved from http://www.narth.com/#!narth-analysis-of-soce-ban/c1q8f

Rosik, C. H. (2013e). The (Complete) Lack of a Scientific Basis for Banning Sexual-Orientation Change Efforts (SOCE) with Minors. *Journal of Human Sexuality*, 5, 103–111. Retrieved from http://www.narth.com/#!narth-analysis-of-soce-ban/c1q8f

Rosik, C. H. (2014). The Reincarnation of Shidlo and Shroeder (2002): New Studies Introduce Anti-SOCE Advocacy Research to the Next Generation. *Journal of Human Sexuality*, 6, in press. Retrieve from http://www.narth.com/#!reincarnation-of-shidlo--/c1tch

Royal College of Psychiatrists (n.d.), *Psychiatry and LGB People: Psychotherapy and reparative therapy for LGB people.* Retrieved from www.rcpsych.ac.uk/rollofhonour/specialinterestgroups/gaylesbian/submissiontothecofe/psychiatryandlgbpeople.aspx

Shidlo, A., & Schroeder, M. (2002). Changing sexual orientation: A consumer's report. *Professional Psychology: Research and Practice, 33*(3), 249–259. Retrieved from http://antigayfactcheck.files.wordpress.com/2012/10/changing_so_consumers_report_ashidlo_pprp_2002_249-259.pdf.

Steed, J. J., & Templer, D. I. (2010). Gay men and lesbian women with molestation history: Impact on sexual orientation and experience of pleasure. *The Open Psychological Journal, 3*, 36–41. doi: 10.2174/1874350101003010036

Stoddard, J. P., Dibble, S. I., & Fineman, N. (2009). Sexual and physical abuse: A comparison between lesbians and their heterosexual sisters. *Journal of Homosexuality, 56,* 407–420. doi: 10.1080/00918360902821395

Strudwick, P. (2014). Christian counsellors ban therapy aimed at 'converting' gay patients. *The Guardian,* (Monday 13 January 2014). Retrieved from: http://www.theguardian.com/world/2014/jan/13/christian-therapists-stop-conversion-therapy-turn-gay-patients-straight

Tomeo, M. E., Templer, D. L., Anderson, S., & Kotler, D. (2001). Comparative data of childhood and adolescent molestation in heterosexual and homosexual persons. *Archives of Sexual Behavior, 30,* 535–541.

UK Council for Psychotherapy (2010). *UKCP's Ethical Principles and Codes of Professional Conduct: Guidance on the Practice of Psychological Therapies that Pathologise and/or Seek to Eliminate or Reduce Same Sex Attraction.* Retrieved from http://www.psychotherapy.org.uk/index.php?id=428

United Kingdom Parliament. Counsellors and Psychotherapists (Regulation) Bill. Retrieved on 15 Jan 2014 from: http://www.publications.parliament.uk/pa/bills/cbill/2013-2014/0120/14120.pdf

Walker, J., Archer, J., & Davies, M. (2005). Effects of rape on men: A descriptive analysis. *Archives of Sexual Behavior, 14,* 69–80. doi: 10.1007/s10508-005-1001-0

Warren, J. S., Nelson, P. L., Mondragon, S. A., Baldwin, S. A., & Burlingame, G. M. (2010). Youth psychotherapy change trajectories and outcomes in usual care: Community mental health versus managed care settings. *Journal of Counseling and Clinical Psychology, 78*(2), 144–155. doi: 10.1037/a0018544

Wells, J. E., McGee, M. A., & Beautrais, A. L. (2011). Multiple aspects of sexual orientation: Prevalence and sociodemographic correlates in a New Zealand National Survey. *Archives of Sexual Behavior, 40,* 155–168. doi: 10.1007/s10508-010-9636-x

Whitehead, N. E. (2010). Homosexuality and Co-Morbidities: Research and Therapeutic Implications. *Journal of Human Sexuality, 2, 124–175.* Retrieved from http://www.scribd.com/doc/115506183/Journal-of-Human-Sexuality-Vol-2

Appendix A:

Practice Guidelines for the Treatment of Unwanted Same-Sex Attractions and Behaviors

In December, 2008, at its annual strategic planning meeting, the National Association for Research and Therapy of Homosexuality (NARTH)'s Board of Directors formally accepted the following *Practice Guidelines for the Treatment of Unwanted Same-Sex Attractions and Behaviors.* Their purpose is to educate and guide mental health professionals, who affirm the right of clients to pursue change of unwanted same-sex (homosexual) attraction and behavior (SSA), so that these professionals may provide competent, ethical, and effective guidance and care to those who seek it.

The goals of the *Practice Guidelines* are twofold: (1) to promote professional practice that maximizes positive outcomes and reduces the potential for harm among clients who seek change-oriented intervention for unwanted same-sex attractions and behavior, and (2) to provide information that corrects stereotypes or mischaracterizations of change-oriented intervention and those who seek it. These guidelines reflect the state of the art in the practice of guidance and psychotherapy with same-sex-attracted clients who want to decrease homosexual functioning and/or increase heterosexual functioning.

Attitudes Toward Clients Who Seek Change

Guideline 1. *Clinicians are encouraged to recognize the complexity and limitations in understanding the etiology of same-sex attractions.*

    Guideline 2. *Clinicians are encouraged to understand how their values, attitudes, and knowledge about homosexuality affect their assessment of and intervention with clients who present with unwanted same-sex attractions and behavior.*

    Guideline 3. *Clinicians are encouraged to respect the value of clients' religious faith and refrain from making disparaging assumptions about their motivations for pursuing change-oriented interventions.*

    Guideline 4. *Clinicians are encouraged to respect the dignity and self-determination of all their clients, including those who seek to change unwanted same-sex attractions and behavior.*

Treatment Considerations

Guideline 5. *At the outset of treatment, clinicians are encouraged to provide clients with information on change-oriented*

processes and intervention outcomes that is both accurate and sufficient for informed consent.

Guideline 6. *Clinicians are encouraged to utilize accepted psychological approaches to psychotherapeutic interventions that minimize the risk of harm when applied to clients with unwanted same-sex attractions.*

Guideline 7. *Clinicians are encouraged to be knowledgeable about the psychological and behavioral conditions that often accompany same-sex attractions and to offer or refer clients for relevant treatment services to help clients manage these issues.*

Guideline 8. *Clinicians are encouraged to consider and understand the difficult pressures from culture, religion, and family that are confronted by clients with unwanted same-sex attractions.*

Guideline 9. *Clinicians are encouraged to recognize the special difficulties and risks that exist for youth who experience same-sex attractions.*

Education

Guideline 10. *Clinicians are encouraged to make reasonable efforts to familiarize themselves with relevant medical, mental health, spiritual, and religious resources that can support clients in their pursuit of change.*

Guideline 11. *Clinicians are encouraged to increase their knowledge and understanding of the literature relevant to clients who seek change, and to seek continuing education, training, supervision, and consultation that will improve their clinical work in this area.*

As do all professional guidelines, the preceding *Practice Guidelines* were written in order to supplement accepted principles of psychotherapy, not to replace them. As *guidelines*, they are aspirational and intended to facilitate the continued, systematic development of the profession and to help assure a high level of professional practice by clinicians.

The clinical and scientific research which supports each of the *Practice Guidelines* is explained in detail in Volume 2 of NARTH's *Journal of Human Sexuality (JHS)*. A copy of JHS Volume 2 may be retrieved from http://www.scribd.com/doc/115506183/Journal-of-Human-Sexuality-Vol-2 and the complete *Practice Guidelines* may be retrieved from http://www.scribd.com/doc/115508811/NARTH-Practice-Guidelines. Translations of the short form of the *Practice Guidelines* (*Guidelines* only without explanation) are available, so far, in Chinese, French, German, Italian, Polish, Russian, and Spanish. These translations may be retrieved from http://www.narth.com/#!about3/c1k2y

PHILIP M. SUTTON, PHD, is the director of the International Federation for Therapeutic Choice. He is licensed as a psychologist in Michigan and Ohio and as a marriage and family therapist, clinical social worker, and school psychologist in Indiana. Dr. Sutton is a therapist in private practice in South Bend, Indiana, and serves professionally at Sacred Heart Major Seminary in Detroit, and at the Samaritan Counseling Center in Benton Harbor, Michigan.

EXPLORING THE ISSUE

Should Gay Conversion Therapy Be Prohibited by Law?

Critical Thinking and Reflection

1. How should clinicians respond to clients who come to therapy for the purpose of changing their sexual orientation?
2. What role should mental health professionals play in the public arena when legislation is being debated about outlawing gay conversion therapy?
3. Should laws and standards regarding gay conversion therapy differ when involving minors versus adults?
4. What is a reasonable response to the assertion that individuals who pursue sexual orientation change have the right to self-determination?
5. Should mental health professionals who conduct gay conversion therapy be found in violation of professional ethics?

Is There Common Ground?

Although PAHO and Philip M. Sutton have opposing views about whether gay conversion therapy should be outlawed, both parties would concur about the fact that many gay and lesbian individuals suffer profound distress. However, they would differ in their views about this distress should be managed and resolved. PAHO discusses the profound impact of homophobia on gays and lesbians, on their families and friends, and on society at large; many gay and lesbian individuals speak of their suffering, feelings of guilt and shame, social isolation, as well as threats and injuries. Who would choose such a difficult path in life?

Dr. Sutton acknowledges the distress of individuals who have same-sex attraction, and argues that their distress for some individuals can be alleviated by providing them with interventions aimed at changing their thoughts, feelings, and identity. He acknowledges that every approach to medical and mental health care has the potential for harmful or unwanted side effects, and it should be up to the individual to have the autonomous right to choose whether or not to participate in professional care for unwanted same-sex attractions, feelings, behavior, and/or identity.

Create Central

www.mhhe.com/createcentral

Additional Resources

APA Task Force on Appropriate Therapeutic Responses to Sexual Orientation. (2009). *Report of the Task Force on Appropriate Therapeutic Responses to Sexual Orientation*. Washington, DC: American Psychological Association.

Drescher, J., & Zucker, K. J. (2006). *Ex-Gay Research: Analyzing the Spitzer Study and Its Relation to Science, Religion, Politics, and Culture*. New York, NY: Harrington Park Press.

Dynes, W. R. (2014). *The Homophobic Mind*. Wayne R. Dynes Publisher.

International Federation for Therapeutic Choice (IFTC, 2011). Intolerance and discrimination against medical and mental health professionals, researchers, and educators threaten the freedoms of the professionals and those whom they serve. *Journal of Human Sexuality, 4*, 136–140 (November, 2012). Retrieved from http://www.scribd.com/doc/174191760/Journal-of-Human-Sexuality-Vol-IV.

Shidlo, A., & Schroeder, M. (2002). Changing sexual orientation: A consumer's report. *Professional Psychology: Research and Practice, 33*, 249–259.

Internet References . . .

Alliance for Therapeutic Choice and Scientific Inquiry

http://www.therapeuticchoice.com

American College of Pediatricians

http://www.acpeds.org/

American Counseling Association

http://www.counseling.org/news/updates/2013/
01/16/ethical-issues-related-to-conversion-or-
reparative-therapy

American Psychiatric Association

http://www.psychiatry.org/mental-health/people/
lgbt-sexual-orientation

American Psychological Association

http://apa.org/topics/lgbt/index.aspx

Core Issues Trust

http://www.core-issues.org

Selected, Edited, and with Issue Framing Material by:
Richard P. Halgin, *University of Massachusetts, Amherst*

ISSUE

Is Forced Treatment of Seriously Mentally Ill Individuals Justifiable?

YES: Samuel J. Brakel and John M. Davis, from "Overriding Mental Health Treatment Refusals: How Much Process Is 'Due'?" *Saint Louis University Law Journal* (2007)

NO: James B. Gottstein, from "How the Legal System Can Help Create a Recovery Culture in Mental Health Systems," *Leading the Transformation to Recovery* (2005)

Learning Outcomes

After reading this issue, you will be able to:

- Discuss the role of the law in determining whether mentally ill individuals can be treated against their will, with particular attention to constitutional limits on involuntary commitment and forced drugging.
- Critically evaluate the benefits and risks known to be associated with antipsychotic medications.
- Discuss the history of treatment for mentally ill individuals in the United States during the past half century, with particular consideration of the move away from approaches that were inhumane.
- Understand the meaning of civil commitment and the procedures associated with this process.
- Consider alternative options to involuntary treatment that would be viewed as humane as well as effective.

ISSUE SUMMARY

YES: Attorney Samuel J. Brakel and psychiatrist John M. Davis assert that society has a responsibility to take care of seriously mentally ill individuals who are incapable of making an informed decision about their need for care and treatment.

NO: Attorney James B. Gottstein contends that forced treatment of mentally ill citizens represents a curtailment of liberty which leads many people down a road of permanent disability and poverty.

The deinstitutionalization movement that began in the final quarter of the twentieth century was regarded as an important positive trend in the treatment of seriously mentally ill people. Although some patients who were transferred to community programs and halfway houses thrived in a less restrictive environment, other patients became lost in the maze, with many becoming homeless and destitute. In response to the social crisis following deinstitutionalization, some social critics have called for more aggressive efforts to reach out to seriously mentally ill people so that they can be provided with badly needed care, even if these individuals resist such solicitous efforts. A controversy has raged about whether therapeutic treatment should be forced upon seriously mentally ill people.

In the first reading, attorney Samuel Brakel argues that many citizens with profound mental illness are incapable of caring for themselves, and will resist treatment because they do not view themselves as mentally ill. According to Brakel, interventions such as psychiatric medication can have a markedly beneficial impact on the lives of mentally ill people; without such treatment, many individuals will not only be at risk, but will also be deprived of experiencing a better quality of life. Attorney Brakel believes that mental health professionals should be allowed to initiate treatment over a patient's objection in instances involving seriously ill individuals who cannot be convinced to accept treatment voluntarily.

According to Brakel, what unknowing critics see as an "orgy of pill pushing" is no more than a reflection of the reality that, without drugs as the base treatment for schizophrenia and other psychotic disorders, there is no hope for improvement. Talk and behavior therapy, by themselves, are useless treatment methods for schizophrenia, and may be harmful if used to the exclusion of needed pharmacology. Many people suffering from psychosis have a neurological inability to appreciate that they are sick and need treatment (a condition called anosognosia). These people will resist treatment because they do not view themselves as mentally ill.

Brakel asserts that, if a patient cannot be convinced to accept prescribed treatment, the physician should be allowed to initiate treatment over the patient's objection with minimal legal interference. Studies show that patients who adhere to *continued* drug treatment benefit on virtually all important personal and social measures. Both the old and new antipsychotic drugs used in treatment are highly efficacious and without the purported negative side effects portrayed by anti-psychiatry alarmists. Individuals who are appropriately treated have lower rates of rehospitalization, criminal recidivism, and violent behavior. Also, they experience improved quality of life because of a reduction in symptoms, an improvement in functioning, more appropriate use of the mental health system, and a reduced likelihood of homelessness.

In the second reading, Attorney James B. Gottstein argues vehemently against the idea of forcing treatment upon unwilling citizens. He argues that myths about mental illness need to be debunked, while efforts are made to provide more humane, effective, recovery-oriented, and noncoercive interventions. Gottstein contends that it is easier for the system to lock people up and drug them into submission than it is to engage them in a much more humane process of recovery. He advocates spending time with them to develop a therapeutic relationship, and thus being able to engage troubled individuals with voluntary humane alternatives leading to recovery. He asserts that forced drugging simply cannot be scientifically proven to be in a person's best interest. Furthermore, information is lacking about the long-term effectiveness or the possible harm associated with these drugs.

According to Gottstein, mental patients are not by definition incapable of making rational decisions; nor are they necessarily less competent than nonmentally ill medical patients. As posited by the United States Supreme Court, involuntary commitment does nothing to enhance autonomy, but rather represents a "massive curtailment of liberty." Rather than providing remarkable opportunities for growth and autonomy, the system of forced psychiatry leads a tremendous number of people down a road to permanent disability and poverty.

YES

Samuel J. Brakel and John M. Davis

Overriding Mental Health Treatment Refusals: How Much Process Is "Due"?

Abstract

Getting mental health treatment to patients who need it is today a much belegaled enterprise. This is in part because law makers have a skewed view of the enterprise, in particular the treatment of patients with antipsychotic medications. The properties and uses of these medications are misunderstood by many in the legal community, while the drugs' undesirable side-effects are typically overstated and the remedial effects undersold when not outright ignored. One specific legal effect has been to accord to mental patients a substantively outsized right to refuse treatment that comes with a correspondingly action-stifling dose of procedural safeguards, this despite the patients' frequent lack of capacity to exercise the right wisely and the bad personal and systemic consequences that flow from that. The purpose of this article is to provide better balanced and accurate evidence of the properties of antipsychotic drugs so as to convince law makers and advocates for the mentally disabled that it is safe to roll back some of the more counterproductive legal strictures on the effort to provide mental health treatment. . . .

I. Introduction

In 1991 the above listed authors published an article in the *Indiana Law Review* titled "Taking Harms Seriously: Involuntary Mental Patients and the Right to Refuse Treatment."[1] In it we argued that the extension to involuntarily committed mental health patients of a legal right to refuse mental health treatment (at least in the sense of its being protected by potentially multiple judicial hearings), was a legal/logical anomaly and one that had bad consequences for those patients who exercised the right, not to mention their fellow patients, the hospital doctors and the institutions in which the patients were (ware)housed. We felt, somewhat naively perhaps, that the reason the law was askew stemmed from the lack of good medical

information on the part of lawyers, judges and legislators and that rectifying the situation required the presentation in an appropriate legal forum of such information. Everyone's eyes would be opened and the law would change in the direction warranted by our confidence in the medical facts—*i.e.*, that the antipsychotic drugs predominantly used in treatment were highly efficacious and without anywhere near the negative side-effects profiles portrayed by antipsychiatric alarmists. There has been some success in the realization of this hope, though pinning much or any of it on the publication/dissemination of a legal academic article would be presumptuous.[2] There has been progress in the law in the sense that the cases and statutes today are somewhat more likely than a decade or so ago to reflect an appropriate appreciation of what the medications can do (and what they won't do), in multiple contexts. Whether the issue is civil commitment and treatment (inpatient or outpatient), or treatment in the criminal justice-mandated context of competency commitments (whether pretrial or presentence) or post-conviction treatment in the prison setting, medical authority to medicate unwilling patients has overall expanded while judicial review has been relegated to a lesser and later ("postdeprivation") role—a realignment of power that one would surmise has much to do with better knowledge of the (large) benefits vs. (relatively small) costs in potential negative consequences of the medications.

At the same time, however, there has been some jurisprudential backsliding as well, including at the U.S. Supreme Court level, (p. 5) . . . where a small number of decisions have been handed down and some language articulated that seems to give new life to what one had hoped was the moribund view of psychotropic drugs as predominantly harmful and the accompanying disbelief in the competence and integrity of doctors to appropriately prescribe them.

Given the thus still uneven, not to say precarious, lay of the legal landscape on treatment refusals, we feel it is timely to do a reprise of sorts of our 1991 article and

From *bepress Legal Series,* Year 2007 Paper 1964, 2007. Reprinted with permission of the Saint Louis University Law Journal © 2008 St. Louis University School of Law, St. Louis, Missouri.

to present once again what we believe is a true picture of the risks and benefits of antipsychotic medications. It is a picture that in many respects is and can be more optimistic than before, consistent with another set of major advances over the last 10–15 years in psychiatric medicine (in particular, the development of the so-called atypicals, a new line of antipsychotic drugs with higher benefit potential and fewer risks than the "old" medications, and continuing improvement in their usage). . . .

We will begin by presenting the new medical data because (1) it is the most significant (new) element in the debate on the matter of treatment rights, including the right to refuse it and (2) it immediately makes more intelligible what that debate is about as well as what our preferences/biases as authors are and from where these derive. We will present the research and anecdotal results documenting the heightened efficacy and the reduced possibility of untoward effects of the new antipsychotic drugs. This section of the paper will include information, new information to the extent it has been developed, on the harms, both personal and institutional, that result from withholding for legal reasons treatment that is medically indicated—in short we will present some indication at least of the costs of an inefficient legal treatment refusal regime, one that makes any conscientious and medically justified attempt to override the patient's resistance to treatment cumbersome to the point of impractical, if not impossible. . . .

II. Of Typicals and Atypicals: The Old and New Medical Data

We begin this section on the new medical data by summarizing what we said in the old article. Under the heading "Separating Myth from Reality" we first reported on a review we conducted of the legal literature on the use of psychotropic drugs—law journals as well as judicial opinions—concluding that the vast bulk of it was woefully, even willfully, misinformed about the both the drugs' risks and benefits.[3] The prevalence and severity of negative (side-) effects were almost uniformly overstated, alleged misuse of "drugging" by state physicians was played up as rampant if not the norm (embellishments/inventions ranging from the charge that drugs were administered mostly for administrative convenience or punishment to the suggestion by analogy that it might be or at least risked being done to suppress political dissent), while the huge health benefits of proper drug usage for people with serious mental illness got no play at all (the whole helping rationale behind psychiatric treatment being simply ignored).[4] We

wrote of the characteristic internal referencing aspect of this legal literature where reliance for authority was not on original medical publications but almost exclusively on a few biased analyses written by non-physicians or one or two radical antipsychiatry doctors, leading to an inevitable repetition of false information and myth or even, as in the legal cases ruled by common law precedent, the outright transformation of medical myth into legal fact.[5] . . .

One area where the law needs to adjust is the treatment of patients with antipsychotic drugs. When these drugs were first discovered in the early 1950's they were referred to as tranquilizers. The first antipsychotic drug, chlorpromazine, did have considerable sedative properties. Thence came the charge that the drugs "dulled the senses" or that they were a convenient chemical straight-jacket. But even the early drugs did not act by sedation. Like the newer drugs their action is to counteract psychosis by blocking excessive dopamine in the brain, a hormone-like substance whose release in abnormal quantities is associated with "positive" psychiatric symptoms such as hallucinations and delusions.[6] While the drugs may quiet a highly agitated and excited patient, they also help restore apathetic, affect-less patients.[7] The restoration is in the nature of a regaining of cognitive skills, ideally as close as possible to normal premorbid thinking and functioning. . . .

Treatment with antipsychotic drugs is the hallmark of psychiatric treatment of patients suffering from schizophrenia and other major mental disorders. In no institution today, whether the remaining state facilities, private general hospitals or specialized facilities, the medical schools, or for that matter in the doctor's office, is psychological or psychosocial treatment alone provided. Treatment is always given with drugs. It is not true that wealthy patients get verbal psychotherapy while poor patients are drugged. The wealthy get drugs *plus* psychotherapy. Medication dispensation and management have become primary aspects of psychiatric treatment for mentally ill patients of all classes and cultures. What is seen by unknowing critics as an orgy of pill pushing is no more than a reflection of the reality that without drugs as the base treatment for schizophrenia and other psychotic disorders there is no hope for improvement. Talk and behavior therapy are still provided, but such therapy builds on the substantial degree of cognitive and emotional restoration that can be achieved with medication. Often its focus is on developing the patient's and even the family's coping skills, to sharpen recognition of the onset of an episode of the conditions, stresses that signal vulnerability, and what to do in the face of them. . . . By themselves however these treatment methods are useless for schizophrenia, potentially harmful even, particularly if used to the exclusion of needed pharmacology.[8]

Prior to the early 1950s most schizophrenic patients spent much of their life in state insane asylums. Since schizophrenia's onset is typically in adolescence, the illness took away most of the patients' normal lives. In the early 1950s, 50% of the hospital beds in the country were in massive state mental facilities located in rural areas.[9] Up to half a million mental patients filled these beds.[10] When chlorpromazine was discovered in 1953 its use spread quickly throughout the world in two or three years. Violence in state hospitals in the United States dropped by 90% almost overnight.[11] The number of patients in hospitals began to drop year by year with comparable alacrity. Today the total [number] of patients in state mental hospitals throughout the United States is less than 10% of what it was in the mid-1950s and the facilities themselves have almost completely disappeared, been restructured for new use or torn down.[12]

When good care is available and patients take their medication the majority of them can return to work or school and be productive members of society. Unfortunately, many schizophrenic patients do not have access to high quality care. The emptying of the state hospitals was accompanied by the realization that much of the treatment burden would now fall on community, mostly outpatient, programs. But the will or wherewithal to create a community treatment system equal to the task never materialized. The result is that the hope of full social rehabilitation, a theoretical possibility for many schizophrenic patients, is realized in all too few cases. For other patients it is worse than that. They may get brief treatment in a hospital or, more likely today, in a jail but they will stop taking their medication once released. Their lives will spiral downward to where episodes of active schizophrenia grow more frequent and worse and recovery is less complete with each episode. Eventually the disease process may flatten out but by then too often alcoholism, drug abuse and homelessness will have become dominant if not permanent features of the patient's existence.[13] What used to be the back wards of hospitals for these patients have today become the back streets and jails. As presently structured, the law and the courts provide little in the way of relief from this pattern.

Schizophrenia is not normally thought of as a fatal illness. The average life expectancy of schizophrenic patients is lower than that of the normal population, but many live into old age. Much of the shorter life span is attributable to a high suicide rate among people suffering from schizophrenia, as well as accidental death and the negative lifestyle effects of those who are not well cared

for. In that respect, it is relevant to note that schizophrenic patients not receiving drugs die at a rate ten times higher than patients on medication.[14] . . .

[T]here is today a great deal more documented evidence of the concept of anosognosia.[15] More than just an assertion that mentally ill people sometimes lack full awareness of or adequate insight into their illness and distinct from denial as a psychologically-based defense tactic, the term is meant to describe a "biologically-based" or even "neurological" inability on the part of the sick person to appreciate that he/she is sick and needs treatment, which is a characteristic of the illness itself. It is said to afflict some 47%–57% of schizophrenic patients[16] with implications not just for health and behavior (as mentioned, untreated mental illness is strongly related to psychiatric deterioration and violence) but of course also the law's assessment of a treatment refuser's 'competence' and the desirability/wisdom of honoring his or her wishes. . . .

We also wrote of the costs of treatment delayed or denied because of the law's overprotections: individual clinical costs such as mental deterioration and the inability to recapture such psychiatric loss; institutional costs and harms on the order of increased violence in hospitals on the part of untreated patients and its effect on compliant patients and care givers; and the direct financial costs of warehousing patients before they can be treated, as well as legal process expenditures in judicially or administratively resolving treatment refusal disputes.[17]

Finally, we wrote of the "true risks of side effects" of the antipsychotic drugs (the first-generation drugs of that time), noting that on the one hand all drugs have side effects, and on the other, that as measured by both their efficacy (high but underappreciated) and their asserted bad effects (grossly overstated as to seriousness, general prevalence and particular risk to the patient or patient class) the antipsychotics predominantly used were relatively benign.[18] (p. 13) . . . [T]he risk of death from untreated psychosis, drawn from hospital studies documenting large numbers of deaths from lethal catatonia, suicide, accidents, infection and other harms that used to befall chronically psychotic patients in predrug days, was infinitely larger than from the antipsychotic drugs, a situation we analogized to the benefits of penicillin which exponentially increased medical survival rates in homes, hospitals and on the battle fields despite the fact that an allergic reaction to the drug can on occasion be fatal.[19] (p. 13) . . . To anticipate arguments about autonomy or (even) free speech, we emphasized, as we do today, the restorative properties of the drugs; that the evidence of cognitive/perceptual restoration to premorbid "normal" mental processing was substantial for many patients treated with the drugs; and the bearing this in turn should have on which of the patient's choices in what mental state to honor.[20]

This was the state of the medication treatment art in regard to what have since been called the "typicals" (i.e., haloperidol, chlorpromazine, thioridazine, fluphenazine, perphenazine), the "old," "conventional" antipsychotic drugs that in the early 1990s began to be replaced by a newer line of pharmaceuticals called (of course) the "atypicals" (the forerunner clozapine and later olanzapine, quetiapine, risperidone, ziprasidone, and aripiprazole). Trials and other research on the atypicals tended to show substantial efficacy gains as well as a marked reduction in the prevalence and seriousness of undesirable side effects. . . .

The evidence also continues to accumulate and solidify that all drugs, old or new, produce major gains and help safeguard against psychiatric loss which occurs in the absence of treatment and cannot be recouped even after treatment is initiated. Recent studies document disturbingly high percentages of untreated mental illness or treatment that is interrupted against medical advice (this, in a context where the law's preoccupation continues, anachronistically, to be with alleged unneeded and unwanted treatment). A 2001 report of a National Comorbidity Survey conducted between 1990 and 1992 found that fewer than 40% of a cohort of seriously mentally ill patients received stable treatment, with the primary reason for failure to seek treatment or failing to continue being the subjects' unwillingness or inability to see the need.[21] The prognosis for these patients is a diminishing chance of amelioration or recovery as relapses mount and symptoms increase in acuity, severity (negative symptoms in particular) and resistance to remediation.[22] At the same time, studies on adherence to drug treatment, many conducted in the context of attempts to evaluate the merits of so-called outpatient commitment (OPC),[23] show the benefits of treatment and especially *continued* treatment (even for the minimally symptomatic) on virtually all important personal and social measures: i.e., reduced hospital recidivism and reduced criminal recidivism/violent behavior,[24] as well as reduced victimization;[25] quality of life improvements such as measured by reduced psychiatric symptomatology and better functioning;[26] and systemic gains in terms of less discordant and more appropriate use of the mental health and correctional systems, respectively, for mentally ill people who come into contact with the law as well as appreciable gains in housing situations (reductions in homelessness).[27]

Finally, as mentioned, new findings and confirmation of older study results on anognosia, which document the relationship between schizophrenia and lack of insight as one of the latter being a neurological function/

symptom of the former,[28] provide strengthening support for a best-medical-interests decision making model in mental health matters. The implications of the concept of anognosia for treatment adherence/compliance are self-evident. A person who believes he is not sick will resist treatment at all stages and levels. To the extent the implications for the person's mental health (negative, as they would be for most any untreated somatic illness) are not equally self-evident, they have been described and documented in studies such as those cited in the preceding paragraph. Last, while the details may ultimately bedevil some or many, we believe no spelling out is required of anognosia's implication *in principle* regarding the need for and propriety of the option of (legal) coercion in mental health treatment. Much as we might want, desirable as it may seem, we cannot afford to limit mental health treatment to its entirely voluntary provision and acceptance.

These then are the contemporary medical facts against whose backdrop we proceed with the analysis in the remainder of the paper.

III. Once Again: What Is the Legal Debate About?

. . . All patients have a legally, even constitutionally, protected right to refuse treatment. There is no disagreement on this and need not be. Nor, despite its constitutionally protected status, is there any doubt that this right of a patient (p. 17) . . . in some situations must yield to superior interests, in particular the interests of treating doctors and/or those they represent. The "issue" is how much/what kind of process must be observed to override the patient's refusal, should that be considered medically necessary. This is where opinions, both legal and lay, diverge. And the legal/medical context in which the refusal is asserted will have everything to do with what the answer is or, better, as there is no consensus here, what we think the answer ought to be. This is the crux of the matter. . . .

VI. Legislative Process and Progress

Reports by groups favoring psychiatric intervention when needed such as the Treatment Advocacy Center (TAC)[29] suggest that in regard to inpatient commitment observable strides have been made nationally—i.e., jurisdiction by jurisdiction—to impart a more medically-oriented/*parens patriae* perspective and, if not replace, to at least supplement the danger-to-others/police power focus of the earlier statutes. This has been accomplished via a revival of the need for treatment standard to suffice for commitment and an accompanying refocus of the legal lens on indicators such as psychiatric treatment history, recent decompensation, deterioration or destabilization, or even mere risk of such—all of which avoid, conceptually, the implicit emergency/police power strictures that dominate the dangerousness formulation, and should help us move away in practice from the consequent futile pattern of repetitive one-at-a-time, typically post-crisis, interventions.

As for outpatient commitment statutes, the concept underlying them is not new, but they have over the past few years swept the country in terms of increased visibility and use.[30] The objective of these laws, at least partly met according to early studies,[31] is to ensure treatment for those who otherwise resist, avoid, stop, slip-through-the-cracks-of, and "recycle" through the mental health and criminal justice systems, to their own as well as their fellow citizens' detriment. More, and especially earlier, treatment for more people who need it is the aspiration here, as is the continuation of treatment already begun given the proven benefits of adherence/compliance and the well-documented negatives associated with the interruption or cessation of the treatment regimen. The concept's ancillary virtue . . . "is that it is and has been correctly perceived by many as a lesser infringement on patients' liberty than having the treatment need met by inpatient hospitalization (or the 'police need' for segregation met by incarceration)." In other words, it is a concept on which people of differing political/philosophical persuasion and orientation—*i.e.*, those on opposite sides of the traditional advocacy divide—should be able to agree.[32] . . .

A. Increased Treatment Focus in Commitment Statutes

1. Persistence of Dangerousness as the Sole Commitment Criterion (and Four Deviations)

It is the view, correct in our opinion, that for determining the need for psychiatric intervention it is both apposite and sufficient to use psychiatric standards and terms, and not those of law enforcement. The law is not asking a secondary question here such as it does in the context of, say, the insanity defense, where the psychiatric input is meant to address cognitive or volitional capacity so as to help resolve the ultimate legal issue of accountability/culpability, or any of a number of issues where the law seeks psychiatric consultation as it were via testimony on so-called penultimate issues.[33] This is direct and ultimate: it is about treatment and treatability. The question can both be posed and answered directly, in medical terms.[34] . . .

[A] growing number of states are passing statutory provisions that premise involuntary hospitalization on a finding by the committing court that the individual proposed therefore lacks capacity to make treatment decisions. . . . Such laws collapse the inquiry into need for hospitalization with the (to us, self-evident) need to be treated once hospitalized and thereby avoid the anomaly of legally sustainable treatment refusals. . . .

B. Outpatient "Commitment" Laws

The judicial power to order treatment outside the institutional context has today been formalized in the laws of all but eight states in the U.S. with the passages of what are generally, if oxymoronically, known as outpatient commitment statutes.

VII. The ADA, *Olmstead* and the "Conversion" of Justice Kennedy

It must be remembered that for the person with severe mental illness who has no treatment, the most dreaded of confinements can be the imprisonment inflicted by his own mind, which shuts reality out and subjects him to the torment of voices and images beyond our powers to describe. . . . It is a common phenomenon that a patient functions well with medication, yet, because of the mental illness itself, lacks discipline or capacity to follow the regime the medication requires.[35] . . .

Conclusions

We believe that for civil commitment . . . and commitment for restoration to trial competence both the substantive standards and procedures can and should be medical. As we said at the outset, every patient or proposed patient has a right to refuse treatment if he/she does not want it. That is to say, patients as other citizens should be able to articulate their objection to prescribed treatment and that objection, if made, should be heard. Moreover, the physician who is responsible for treating the patient should try to convince the patient that the course prescribed is best for him/her or propose another course or courses that the patient finds more palatable but that, despite perhaps being suboptimal, still work(s). In short, we support the kind of therapist/patient dialogue about therapy that we will presume takes place in any hospital, community treatment center or doctor's office to the extent the patient's mental condition permits.[36]

However, if the patient cannot be convinced to accept the prescribed treatment, rejecting it and any plausible alternative courses (including trial and error), the physician should be allowed to initiate treatment over the patient's objection with minimal legal interference. That is, the only substantive criterion that need or should inform the physician's decision to proceed to treat is medical need/propriety. Inquiries into the patient's dangerousness, the government's (compelling) interest in prosecuting or any similarly diversionary issues should not be required. Procedurally, in-house medical review of the initial treatment decision should suffice to allow the primary physician to go ahead. The purpose after all of each of these commitments, simply stated even if not always simple to achieve, is to restore mental health and functioning as much and as quickly as possible. . . .

Judges cannot be and should not be the baseline decision makers in any of these institutional (or non-institutional), post-legal judgment phases of the treatment process. Forced treatment can begin once the medical reviewer has approved the treating physician's recommendation. Post-deprivation judicial review, after treatment has been initiated and limited by the professional judgment rule, is all the law should call for at this juncture.[37]

Notes

1. Samuel J. Brakel & John M. Davis, *Taking Harms Seriously: Involuntary Mental Patients and the Right to Refuse Treatment*, 25 IND. L. REV. 429 (1991).

2. Indeed, it would be demonstrably wrong. (1) What success there is has been slow in coming and uneven. (2) The article has not been cited with great frequency, its appeal apparently being limited mostly to the already converted. And (3) the achievement of significant legal change tends to require a combination of many factors and forces, among which academic writings may play a role but not usually a prominent one. . . .

3. Brakel & Davis, *supra*, note 1, at 437–438 and notes.

4. *Ibid.*

5. *Id.* at 438–440, especially note 33, citing *In re* the Mental Commitment of M.P., 510 N.E. 2d 645 (IN 1987) and *In re* Orr, 531 N.E. 2d 64 (IL 1988) as textbook examples. The earlier Indiana case had made reference to a "virtually undisputed allegation that a person medicated with antipsychotic drugs has a 50% risk of contracting tardive dyskinesia." This in fact highly disputable, if not plain erroneous (the much less alarming facts were not widely known at the time), allegation was then cited by the Illinois court in a subsequent decision as a "fact" "found" by the Indiana Supreme Court. . . .

6. There are imaging data today from living schizophrenic patients that show excessive dopamine release in the brain when the patient is having hallucinations and delusions, as well as of the blocking effect on dopamine receptors when antipsychotics are administered. *See* A. Abi-Dargam, R. Gil, J. Krystal *et al.*, *Increased Striatal Dopamine Transmission in Schizophrenia: Confirmation in a Second Cohort*, 155 *AM. J. PSYCHIATRY* 761 (1998); A. Bartolomeis, D.R. Weinberger, N. Weisenfeld *et al.*, *Schizophrenia Is Associated with Elevated Amphetamine-Induced Synaptic Dopamine Concentrations: Evidence from a Novel Positron Emission Tomography Method*, 94 *PROC. NAT'L. ACAD. SCI. U.S.A.* 2569 (1997).

7. The amotivational, apathetic, poor social skills aspects of schizophrenia are its so-called negative symptoms. Combined with cognitive/executive defects, these deficits contribute greatly to poor social and vocational functioning among people with the illness. But today's drugs can go a long way toward remedying these deficits and we have an understanding, albeit imperfect, of how they work. S. R. Marder, J. M. Davis & G. Chouinard, *The Effects of Risperidone on the Five Dimensions of Schizophrenia Derived by Factor Analysis: Combined Results of the North American Trial*, 58 *J. CLIN. PSYCHIATRY* 538 (1997); J.M. Davis & N. Chen, *Clinical Profile of an Atypical Antipsychotic: Risperidone*, 28 *SCHIZOPHRENIA BULLETIN* 43 (2002). . . .

8. It is less a matter of psychosocial treatments having no place or a lesser place in the treatment of severe mental illness today than that the treatments are entirely different. They *capitalize* today on the gains in thinking and functioning that can be achieved by the medications, as distinct from trying the impossible, which is to achieve these gains directly through verbal or behavioral therapy. *See Osherhoff v. Chestnut Lodge, Inc.* 62 Md. App. 519, 490 A.2d 720 (1985) for an early case—the reported court case merely affirms an arbitration award for allegedly negligent treatment that took place in 1979—involving the recognition that verbal therapy as such is ineffective in treating mental illness with substantial biological components, in this instance a psychotic depressive reaction, and that the failure on the part of the defendant to initiate psychopharmacologic treatments may constitute negligence. The defendant institution, Chestnut Lodge, was a facility famous for furthering psychoanalytic theory and practice, having trained a number of prominent American psychiatrists of this school, a fact which seems to have influenced the diagnosis its staff made of the plaintiff's mental health problems as much as the treatment course that was pursued in the face of unmistakable evidence that the patient was getting worse rather than better.

9. E. Fuller Torrey, *OUT OF THE SHADOWS* (1997).

10. *Ibid. See* also, H. Brill & R.E. Patton, *Population Fall in New York State Mental Hospitals in First Year of a Large-Scale Use of Tranquilizing Drugs*, 114 *AM. J. PSYCHIATRY* 509 (1957).

11. See Brill & Patton, *supra*, note 28.

12. *See OUT OF THE SHADOWS, supra*, note 27. The lawyer author of this paper conducted social/legal research in the early 1970's at Kankakee State Hospital 30 miles south of Chicago at a time when it housed some 4,000 patients. Within a few years the hospital was a relic, empty of mentally ill patients and in the process of being converted, to the extent possible, to other uses.

13. The neuropsychological deficits and the loss of grey matter seem to get worse after the patient's first psychotic episode and there is strong evidence that failure to treat the first episode with antipsychotic drugs leads to substantially worse outcome, in terms of repeat episodes and recovery therefrom, in the following five years. There is beginning evidence that at least some of the second-generation drugs in particular are effective in blocking the progression of these deficits and losses. K. Kasai, M.E. Shenton *et al., Progressive Decrease of Left Superior Temporal Gyrus Grey Matter Volume in Patients with First-Episode Schizophrenia*, 160 *AM. J. PSYCHIATRY* 156 (2003); W. Cahn, H.E. Hulshoff Poll *et al., Brain Volume Changes in First-Episode Schizophrenia: A One-Year Follow-Up Study*, 59 *ARCH. GEN. PSYCHIATRY* 1002 (2002). Moreover, a large study carried out in Finland, based on that country's central register, found that the risk of untreated schizophrenic patients dying was 10 times higher than that of patients on medication. J. Tiihonen, K. Wahlbeck *et al., Effectiveness of Antipsychotic Treatments in a Nationwide Cohort of Patients in Community Care after First Hospitalization Due to Schizophrenia and Schizoaffective Disorder: Observational Follow-Up Study*, 333 *BRITISH MED. J.* 224 (2006).

14. *Ibid. . . .*

15. Researchers most prominently identified with the concept of anosognosia, through studies conducted in the early 1990s, are psychologist Xavier Amador at Columbia University in New York and psychiatrist Anthony David at the Institute of Psychiatry in London (UK). Psychiatrist Joseph McEvoy of the University of Pittsburgh however first explicitly linked the characteristic to the illness in the 1980s. Joseph P. McEvoy *et al., Why Must Some Schizophrenic Patients Be Involuntarily Committed? The Role of Insight*, 30 *COMPR. PSYCHIATRY* 13 (1989); Joseph P. McEvoy *et al., Measuring Chronic Schizophrenic Patients' Attitudes Toward Their Illness and Treatment*, 32 *HOSP. COMMUNITY PSYCHIATRY* 856 (1981).

16. Xavier Amador *et al., Awareness of Illness in Schizophrenia and Schizoaffective and Mood Disorders*, 51 *ARCHIVES GEN. PSYCHIATRY* 826 (1994); Xavier Amador *et al., Awareness Deficits in Neurological Disorders and Schizophrenia* (abstract), 24 *SCHIZOPHRENIA RES.* 96 (1997). . . .

17. *Id.* at 453–461, under "Research Findings on the Harms Resulting from Delayed Treatment."

18. *Id.* at 461–467. . . .

19. *Ibid. . . .*

20. *Id.* at 465. . . .

21. Ronald C. Kessler, Patricia A. Berglund, Martha L. Bruce *et al., The Prevalence and Correlates of Untreated Serious Mental Illness*, 36 *HEALTH SERVICES RESEARCH* 978 (2001).

22. *E.g.,* Diana O. Perkins, Hongbin Gu, Kalina Boteva & Jeffrey A. Lieberman, *Relationships Between Duration of Untreated Psychosis and Outcome in First-Episode Schizophrenia: A Critical Review and Meta Analysis*, 162 *AM. J. PSYCHIATRY* 1785 (2005); D.A.W. Johnson, G. Pasterski, L. Ludlow *et al., The Discontinuance of Maintenance Neuroleptic Therapy in Chronic Schizophrenic Patients: Drug and Social Consequences*, 67 *ACTA PSYCHIATR. SCAND.* 339 (1983); Charles M. Beasley, Jr., Virginia K. Sutton, Cindy C. Taylor *et al., Is Quality of Life Among Minimally Symptomatic Patients with Schizophrenia Better Following Withdrawal or Continuation of Antipsychotic Treatment?* 26 *J. OF CLINICAL PSYCHOPHARMACOLOGY* 40 (2006).

23. See section on this topic *infra*. . . .

24. Jeffrey W. Swanson, Randy Borum, Marvin S. Swartz, Virginia A. Hiday *et al., Can Involuntary Outpatient Commitment Reduce Arrests Among Persons with Severe Mental Illness?* 28 *CRIM. JUSTICE AND BEHAVIOR* 156 (2001); Jeffrey W. Swanson, Marvin S. Swartz, Randy Borum, Virginia A. Hiday *et al., Involuntary Outpatient Commitment and Reduction of Violent Behaviour in Persons with Severe Mental Illness*, 176 *BRITISH J. OF PSYCHIATRY* 324 (2000); Marvin S. Swartz, Jeffrey W. Swanson, H. Ryan Wagner, Barbara J. Burns *et al., Can Involuntary Outpatient Commitment Reduce Hospital Recidivism?: Findings from a Randomized Trial with Severely Mentally Ill Individuals*, 156 *AM. J. PSYCHIATRY* 1968 (1999).

25. Virginia A. Hiday, Marvin S. Swartz, Jeffrey W. Swanson, Randy Borum & H. Ryan Wagner, *Impact of Outpatient Commitment on Victimization of People with Severe Mental Illness*, 159 *AM. J. PSYCHIATRY* 1403 (2002).

26. Jeffrey W. Swanson, Marvin S. Swartz, Eric B. Elbogen *et al., Effects of Involuntary Outpatient Commitment on Subjective Quality of Life in Persons with*

Severe Mental Illness, 21 BEHAV. SCIENCES AND THE LAW 473 (2003).

27. Haya Ascher-Svanum, Douglas E. Faries, Baojin Zhu et al., *Medication Adherence and Long-Term Functional Outcomes in the Treatment of Schizophrenia in Usual Care*, 67 J. OF CLINICAL PSYCHIATRY 453 (2006).

28. See Amador and McEvoy articles, *supra*. Also, Joseph P. McEvoy, Paul S. Appelbaum, L. Joy Apperson *et al., Why Must Some Schizophrenic Patients Be Involuntarily Committed? The Role of Insight*, 30 COMPR. PSYCHIATRY 13 (1989); Anthony S. David, *Insight and Psychosis*, 156 BRITISH J. OF PSYCHIATRY 798 (1990); Xavier F. Amador, David H. Strauss, Scott A. Yale & Jack M. Gorman, *Awareness of Illness in Schizophrenia*, 17 SCHIZOPHRENIA BULLETIN 113 (1991); Faith B. Dickerson, John J. Boronow, Norman Ringel & Frederick Parente, *Lack of Insight Among Outpatients with Schizophrenia*, 48 PSYCHIATRIC SERVICES 195 (1997); Xavier F. Amador & Regina A. Seckinger, *The Assessment of Insight: A Methodological Review*, 27 PSYCHIATRIC ANNALS 798 (1997); Graig Goodman, Gabriella Knoll, Victoria Isakov & Henry Silver, *Insight into Illness in Schizophrenia*, 46 COMPR. PSYCHIATRY 284 (2005).

29. See the *CATALYST* (Newsletter of the Treatment Advocacy Center) Spring/Summer 2004. TAC also maintains a website, www.psychlaws.org, on which it provides, *e.g.*, updates on the latest legislative reforms. TAC advocates refer to the process as "assisted outpatient treatment" (AOT) which apart from deemphasizing the nonconsensual aspects of "outpatient commitment" also has the advantage of avoiding its oxymoronic quality, the term commitment being associated with confinement in an institution, *i.e.*, being an *in*patient.

30. *Ibid.*

31. *CATALYST,* Spring/Summer 2005 at 7 and 15. The latter page presents "real-world results" on New York's Kendra's law under the title "Kendra's Law families and participants laud program: Report shows sharp reductions in hospitalizations, incarcerations, homelessness." The TAC group points to a number of other studies supporting the notion that the outpatient commitment laws have achieved their intended effects: Guido Zanni & Leslie deVeau, *Inpatient Stays Before and After Outpatient Commitment*, 37 HOSP. & CMTY PSYCHIATRY 941 (1986); M.R. Munetz *et al., The Effectiveness of Outpatient Civil Commitment*, 47 Psychiatric Services 1251 (1996); B.M. Rohland, *The Role of Outpatient Commitment in the Management of Persons with Schizophrenia*, IOWA CONSORTIUM FOR MENTAL HEALTH SERVICES, TRAINING, AND RESEARCH (1998); and Gustavo A. Fernandez & Sylvia Nygard,

Impact of Involuntary Outpatient Commitment on the Revolving-Door Syndrome in North Carolina, 41 HOSP. & CMTY PSYCHIATRY 1001 (1990). Later studies in North Carolina have been especially persuasive in documenting positive effects of mandated outpatient treatment in various respects. *See* (the titles are indicative) Marvin S. Swartz, Jeffrey W. Swanson, H. Ryan Wagner *et al., Can Involuntary Outpatient Commitment Reduce Hospital Recidivism?* 156 AM. J. PSYCHIATRY 1986 (1999); Jeffrey W. Swanson, Marvin S. Swartz, R. Borum *et al., Involuntary Outpatient Commitment and Reduction in Violent Behaviour in Persons with Severe Mental Illness*, 176 BRIT. J. PSYCHIAT. 224 (2000); Jeffrey W. Swanson, R. Borum, Marvin S. Swartz *et al., Can Involuntary Outpatient Commitment Reduce Arrests among Persons with Severe Mental Illness?* 28 CRIM. JUSTICE & BEHAVIOR 156 (2001); Virginia A. Hiday, Marvin S. Swartz, Jeffrey W. Swanson *et al., Impact of Outpatient Commitment on Victimization of People with Severe Mental Illness*, 159 AM. J. PSYCHIAT. 1403 (2002). . . .

32. In theory at least. A recent article by Richard J. Bonnie and John Monahan, *From Coercion to Contract: Reframing the Debate on Mandated Community Treatment for People with Mental Disorders*, 29 LAW AND HUMAN BEHAVIOR 485 (2005), confirms (by the title alone) that there is much less agreement on the value of the concept than its proponents once optimistically believed. See also note 277, *supra*. . . .

33. The law has gone back and forth on whether it is appropriate for mental health experts to offer testimony on ultimate legal issues, with the post-Hinckley reforms following the acquittal by reason of insanity of President Reagan's would-be assassin, enacted in 1984 for the federal courts, leading the way toward the currently dominant position of disallowing it.

34. It has been pointed out innumerable times by both judges and legal commentators that commitment is a social/legal decision rather than a medical one, but this does not alter the fact that medical criteria and medical facts are what that social/legal decision should be heavily based on. . . .

35. *Id.* at 609–610.

36. The law is allowed to, should in fact, assume basic medical/institutional realities including such that there ordinarily is communication about treatment prospects and plans between therapist and patient. As distinct from case law drawn from litigation where worst-case evidence is introduced, the statutory or regulatory law ordinarily need not and should not be written based on worst-case scenarios. *Cf.* the discussion of *Rennie v. Klein* in the text, *supra*, . . . where we reproduce the administrative regulation—

presumptively a codification of practices—guiding doctors in New Jersey on how to approach patients who resist prescribed treatment. Substantively, the regulation in fact incorporates the least intrusive/least restrictive principle and its procedural mandates suggest abundant deference to the patient's preferences via the physician's stated obligation to discuss alternatives with the patient, to try make the patient understand and to encourage voluntary acceptance (with the help of relatives and friends if so indicated) before seeking approval from the hospital medical director to proceed over the patient's objections. . . .

37. Postdeprivation judicial review should suffice because (1) judges have no expertise in medical matters and therefore should not be baseline (first-instance) decision makers and (2) the costs in time and treatment foregone, deflection of resources, and institutional bad effects of the judiciary's failing to show proper deference to medical professionals are large.

Samuel J. Brakel is the CEO and education director for the Isaac Ray Forensic Group, a group that provides psychological and forensic psychiatric services in its mission to attain justice and public safety. Attorney Brakel, author of *Law and Psychiatry in the Criminal Justice System* (2001), has faculty appointments at Rush Medical College and DePaul University College of Law and continues to publish widely in the area of mental health law.

John M. Davis is Gillman Professor of Psychiatry and Research Professor of Medicine at the University of Illinois, Chicago. His research focuses on schizophrenic spectrum disorders, mood disorders, obsessive-compulsive disorder, premenstrual dysphoric disorder, and the biology of major mental illnesses.

James B. Gottstein   → **NO**

How the Legal System Can Help Create a Recovery Culture in Mental Health Systems

Summary

The purpose of this paper is to show how strategic litigation can and should be a part of efforts to transform mental health systems to a culture of recovery. Currently, involuntary commitment and forced drugging are by far the "path of least resistance" when society is faced with someone who is disturbing and their thinking does not conform to society's norms.[1] In other words, it is far easier for the system to lock people up and drug them into submission, than it is to spend the time with them to develop a therapeutic relationship and thus able to engage the person with voluntary humane alternatives leading to recovery.[2] I estimate that 10% of involuntary commitments in the United States and none of the forced drugging under the *parens patriae* doctrine[3] are legally justified. This presents a tremendous opportunity to use litigation to "encourage" the creation of voluntary, recovery-oriented services.[4]

In my view, though, in order to be successful various myths of mental illness need to be debunked among the general public and humane, effective recovery oriented, noncoercive alternatives must be made available. . . . The thesis of this paper is that strategic litigation (and public education) are likely essential to transforming the mental health system to one of a recovery culture. . . .

For example, debunking the myth among the general public that people do not recover from a diagnosis of serious mental health illness can encourage the willingness to invest in recovery-oriented alternatives. Similarly, having successful, recovery-oriented alternatives will help in debunking the myth that people don't recover from serious mental illness. In like fashion, judges and even counsel appointed to represent psychiatric defendants believe the myth "if this person wasn't crazy, she would know these drugs are good for her" and therefore don't let her pesky rights get in the way of doing the "right thing," i.e., forced drugging. The myth of dangerousness results in people being locked up. In other words, the judges and lawyers reflect society's views and to the extent that society's views change, the judges and lawyers' responses will change to suit. That leads to taking people's rights more seriously. The converse is true as well. Legal cases can have a big impact on public views. *Brown v. Board of Education*,[5] which resulted in outlawing segregation is a classic example of this. Finally, the involuntary mental illness system[6] operates largely illegally, including through its failure to offer less restrictive alternatives.[7] Thus, litigation can force the creation of such alternatives. At the same time, as a practical matter, the availability of acceptable (to the person) recovery-oriented alternatives are necessary for anyone to actually be able to get such services when faced with involuntary commitment and forced drugging.

The Involuntary Mental Illness System Operates Largely Illegally

Involuntary "treatment"[8] in the United States largely operates illegally in that court orders for forced treatment are obtained without actual compliance with statutory and constitutional requirements. One of the fundamental constitutional rights that is ignored in practice is that of a "less restrictive alternative."[9] Thus, enforcement of this right through the courts can be instrumental in bringing about change. First, I will discuss the key constitutional principles. . . .

Constitutional Limits on Involuntary Commitment

The United States Supreme Court has recognized for a long time that involuntary civil commitment is a "massive curtailment of liberty"[10] requiring substantive due process protection:

> Freedom from bodily restraint has always been at the core of the liberty protected by the Due Process Clause from arbitrary governmental action. "It is clear that commitment for any purpose constitutes a significant deprivation of liberty that requires due process protection."[11]

Constitutional Limits on Forced Drugging

The United States Supreme Court has also held a number of times that being free of unwanted psychiatric medication is a fundamental constitutional right.[15] In the most recent case, *Sell*, the United States Supreme Court reiterated:

> [A]n individual has a "significant" constitutionally protected "liberty interest" in "avoiding the unwanted administration of antipsychotic drugs."[16] . . .

The Massachusetts Supreme Judicial Court has held people have the absolute right to decline medication unless they are incompetent to make such a decision and if they are incompetent they cannot be medicated against their will except by a court made Substituted Judgment Decision that includes the following factors:

1. The patient's expressed preferences regarding treatment.
2. The strength of the incompetent patient's religious convictions, to the extent that they may contribute to his refusal of treatment.
3. The impact of the decision on the ward's family—this factor being primarily relevant when the patient is part of a closely knit family.
4. The probability of adverse side effects.
5. The prognosis without treatment.
6. The prognosis with treatment.
7. Any other factors which appear relevant. . . .

[I]n *Rivers v. Katz*,[24] decided strictly on common law and constitutional due process grounds, New York's highest court held a person's right to be free from unwanted antipsychotic medication is a constitutionally protected liberty interest:

> [I]f the law recognizes the right of an individual to make decisions about . . . life out of respect for the dignity and autonomy of the individual, that interest is no less significant when the individual is mentally or physically ill.

We reject any argument that the mere fact that appellants are mentally ill reduces in any manner their fundamental liberty interest to reject antipsychotic medication. We likewise reject any argument that involuntarily committed patients lose their liberty interest in avoiding the unwanted administration of antipsychotic medication.

If . . . the court determines that the patient has the capability to make his own treatment decisions, the State shall be precluded from administering antipsychotic drugs. If, however, the court concludes that the patient lacks the capacity to determine the course of his own treatment, the court must determine whether the proposed treatment is narrowly tailored to give substantive effect to the patient's liberty interest, taking into consideration all relevant circumstances, including the patient's best interests, the benefits to be gained from the treatment, the adverse side effects associated with the treatment and any less intrusive alternative treatments. The State would bear the burden to establish by clear and convincing evidence that the proposed treatment meets these criteria. . . .

[I]n practice, people's rights are not being honored.[25] There are other states which have just as good legal rights and some that don't under state law, but the common denominator in all of them is whatever rights people have, they are uniformly ignored. . . .

In *Sell*, decided in 2003, the United States Supreme Court held someone could not be force drugged to make them competent to stand trial unless:

1. The court finds that *important* governmental interests are at stake.
2. The court must conclude that involuntary medication will *significantly further* those concomitant state interests.
3. The court must conclude that involuntary medication is *necessary* to further those interests. The court must find that any alternative, less intrusive treatments are unlikely to achieve substantially the same results.
4. The court must conclude that administration of the drugs is *medically appropriate*, i.e., in the patient's best medical interest in light of his medical condition. The specific kinds of drugs at issue may matter here as elsewhere. Different kinds of antipsychotic drugs may produce different side effects and enjoy different levels of success.

(italics in original) These are general constitutional principles and should apply in the civil context. Thus, for example, while in *Sell*, the "*important* governmental interest" is in bringing a criminal defendant to trial, the governmental interest in the civil context is (supposedly) the person's best interest, i.e., the *parens patriae* doctrine.[26]

With respect to the second requirement that the forced drugging "will *significantly further*" those interests, the question in the competence to stand trial context is whether the forced drugging is likely to make the person competent to stand trial, while in the civil context, the question is whether it is in the person's best interest or is the decision the person would make if he or she were competent.

The third requirement that the forced drugging must be *necessary* and there is no less restrictive alternative is hugely important in the civil context because it is a potential lever to require less restrictive (i.e., non-drug, recovery-oriented alternatives). It is important to note here that failure to find these alternatives does not give the government the right to force drug someone. If a less restrictive alternative could be made available, the forced drugging is unconstitutional.[27] . . .

The fourth requirement is also very important because it essentially requires the state to prove the drugging is in the person's best interest and not merely recite "professional judgment."

The take-away message is, in my view, people are constitutionally entitled to noncoercive, nondrugging, recovery-oriented alternatives before involuntary commitment and forced drugging can occur and even then forced drugging can only constitutionally occur if it is in the person's best interest. There are a couple of ways to look at this since the reality is so far from what the law requires. One is to see it as a tremendous opportunity to improve the situation. The other is that there are forces operating to totally defeat people's rights. Both are true and this paper suggests there are actions that can be taken to have people's rights honored that can play a crucial part in transforming the mental health system to one of a recovery culture.

Proper Procedures and Evidentiary Standards

Mentioned above are the United States Supreme Court rulings that involuntary commitment can occur only pursuant to proper procedures and evidentiary standards. In contrast to this legal requirement, involuntary commitment and forced drugging proceedings can quite fairly be characterized as a sham, a farce, Kangaroo Courts, etc., in the vast majority of cases.[29] . . .

Proper Procedures . . .

Proper evidentiary standards. . . . [I]involuntary commitment is constitutionally permissible only if the person is a harm to self or others as a result of a "mental illness." In *Addington v. Texas*[33] the United States held that this has to be proven by "clear and convincing evidence," which is less than "'beyond a reasonable doubt,'" but more than the normal "preponderance of the evidence"[34] standard in most civil cases. . . .

The truth is psychiatric testimony as to a person's dangerousness is highly unreliable with a high likelihood of overestimating dangerousness.

> The voluminous literature as to the ability of psychiatrists (or other mental health professionals) to testify reliably as to an individual's dangerousness in the indeterminate future had been virtually unanimous: "psychiatrists have absolutely no expertise in predicting dangerous behavior—indeed, they may be less accurate predictors than laymen—and that they usually err by overpredicting violence."[37]

This is the primary reason why I estimate only 10% of involuntary commitments are legally justified. If people were only involuntarily committed when it can be shown, by clear and convincing evidence, under scientifically reliable methods of predicting the requisite harm to self or others, my view is 90% of current commitments would not be granted.

With respect to forced drugging, one of the prerequisites is the person must be found to be incompetent to decline the drug(s). Here, too, psychiatrists, to be kind, overestimate incompetence.

> [M]ental patients are not always incompetent to make rational decisions and are not inherently more incompetent than nonmentally ill medical patients.[38] . . .

The reason why I believe no forced drugging in the civil context is legally justified is it simply cannot be scientifically proven it is in a person's best interest.[40] It would make this paper even more too long than it already is to fully support this assertion, but some will be presented. First, there is really no doubt the current overreliance on the drugs is at least doubling the number of people becoming defined by the system as chronically mentally ill with it recently being estimated it has increased the rate of disability due to "mental Illness" six-fold.[41] In the case where we litigated the issue in Alaska, the trial court found:

> The relevant conclusion that I draw from [the evidence presented by the Respondent's experts] is that there is a real and viable debate among qualified experts in the psychiatric community regarding whether the standard of care for treating schizophrenic patients should be the administration of antipsychotic medication.

⚜

> [T]here is a viable debate in the psychiatric community regarding whether administration of this type of medication might actually cause damage to her or ultimately worsen her condition.[42]

A recent study in Ireland concluded the already elevated risk for death in schizophrenia due to the older neuroleptics was doubled with the newer, so-called "atypical" neuroleptics, such as Zyprexa and Risperdal.[43] More information on these drugs can be found on PsychRights' website. . . .

In sum, my view is the state can never (or virtually never) actually meet its burden of proving forced drugging is in a person's best interest (assuming that is required) because of the lack of long-term effectiveness and great harm they cause. Again, this raises the question of why forced drugging is so pervasive and what might be done about it. In other words, it is an opportunity for strategic litigation playing a key role in a transformation to a recovery-oriented system.

Corrupt Involuntary Mental "Treatment" System

As set forth above, people are locked up under judicial findings of dangerousness and force drugged based on it being in their best interests without any legitimate scientific evidence of either dangerousness or the drugs being in a person's best interests. As Professor Michael Perlin has noted:

> [C]ourts accept . . . testimonial dishonesty, . . . specifically where witnesses, especially expert witnesses, show a "high propensity to purposely distort their testimony in order to achieve desired ends." . . .
>
> Experts frequently . . . and openly subvert statutory and case law criteria that impose rigorous behavioral standards as predicates for commitment. . . .
>
> This combination . . . helps define a system in which (1) dishonest testimony is often regularly (and unthinkingly) accepted; (2) statutory

and case law standards are frequently subverted; and (3) insurmountable barriers are raised to insure that the allegedly "therapeutically correct" social end is met. . . . In short, the mental disability law system often deprives individuals of liberty disingenuously and upon bases that have no relationship to case law or to statutes.[44]

In other words, testifying psychiatrists lie,[45] the trial (but generally not appellate) courts don't care, and lawyers assigned to represent defendants in these cases, are "woefully inadequate—disinterested, uninformed, roleless, and often hostile. A model of "'paternalism/best interests'" is substituted for a traditional legal advocacy position, and this substitution is rarely questioned."[46] Counsel appointed to represent psychiatric defendants is more often than not, actually working for the other side, or barely put up even a token defense, which amounts to the same thing.[47]

No one in the legal system is taking psychiatric defendants' rights seriously, including the lawyer appointed to represent the person. There are two reasons for this: The first is the belief that "if this person wasn't crazy, she'd know this is good for her." The second is the system is driven by irrational fear. All the evidence shows people who end up with psychiatric labels are no more likely to be dangerous than the general population and that medications increase the overall relapse rate, yet society's response has been to lock people up, and whether locked up or not, force them to take these drugs.[48] . . .

The Requirement and Necessity of Alternatives

Hopefully it is apparent from the foregoing that people should be allowed (less restrictive) alternatives when they are faced with forced drugging. The same is basically true of involuntary commitment.[55] These alternatives, I suggest, should primarily include noncoercive, for sure, and nondrug alternatives that are known to lead to recovery for many people.[56] The reality is likely a "which came first, the chicken or the egg?" situation, because judges will be reluctant to deny petitions for forced drugging on the basis that a less restrictive alternative could be made available, but in fact is not available. Thus, the actual availability of alternatives is important. However, where sufficient legal pressure is applied, the courts will simply not be able to order forced drugging. I know these are contradictory statements, but that is why they reinforce each other as set forth above (and below).

[A]s set forth above, everyone has the absolute constitutional right to decline psychiatric drugs, with one exception, which is if they are incompetent to do so. Currently, the competency determinations are not legitimate and Advance Directives are ignored. One reason I would posit, is that the system simply does not know what else to do with people so the system deals with it by finding people incompetent when they are not. . . .

The Importance of Public Opinion

It is perhaps easier to see how Public Education and the Availability of Alternatives reinforce each other. Alternatives to the hopelessness driven, medication only, stabilization-oriented system are not available because our society believes it is the only possibility, in spite of all kinds of evidence to the contrary. Thus, to the extent effective alternatives become known to society in general, these alternatives will become desired by society because they produce much more desired outcomes. Not only do people get better, but huge amounts of money will be saved by more than halving the number of people who become a permanent ward of government. At the same time, having successful Alternatives will show society that they are viable. Thus, as with the Availability of Alternatives and Honoring Legal Rights, they reinforce each other. . . .

Interplay Between Public Education and Honoring Legal Rights

As set forth above, the judges and even the lawyers representing people facing forced psychiatry accept the current societal view that people need to be locked up and forcibly drugged for society's and the person's own safety and best interests. To the extent society becomes aware this is not true, the judicial system will reflect that and be much more willing to honor people's rights. . . .

Requirements for Successful Litigation—Attorneys & Expert Witnesses

The building blocks for mounting successful strategic litigation are recruiting attorneys who will put forth a serious effort to discharge their ethical duties to their clients and expert witnesses who can prove the junk science behind current "treatment" and the effectiveness of recovery-oriented alternatives.

Types of Legal Actions . . .

Establishing the Right to Effective Assistance of Counsel

If people's rights were being honored, the problem of forced psychiatry would be mostly solved and this would absolutely force society to come up with alternatives—hopefully recovery oriented. Thus, challenges to the effectiveness of counsel should be made. In light of the current state of affairs, there seems little downside to trying to get the United States Supreme Court to hold it is a right under the United States Constitution. I also believe that ethics complaints should be brought against the attorneys who do not discharge their duty to zealously represent their clients. If every involuntary commitment and forced drugging hearing were zealously represented, each case should take at least half a day. In my view it takes that long to fully challenge the state's case and present the patient's. This, in itself, would encourage the system to look for alternatives (the "path of least resistance" principle).

Challenges to State Proceedings

States that proceed under the "professional judgment" rule should be challenged. The right to state paid expert witnesses should be pursued. The right to less restrictive alternatives should be pursued. Challenges to "expert witness" opinion testimony regarding dangerousness and competence should be made. Challenges to *ex parté* proceedings should be made. There are a myriad of challenges that can be made in the various states, depending on the statutes and procedures utilized in them.[58] . . .

Public Attitudes

Even though this paper is about the court's potential role in transforming mental health systems to a recovery culture, it seems worthwhile to also make a few comments about changing public attitudes. There is an historic opportunity right now to make substantial inroads against the Psychopharmacology/Psychiatric hegemony because of the revelations in the media regarding dangerous, ineffective drugs, but this must be seized or it will be lost. **A serious public education program must be mounted.**

An Effective Public Relations Campaign

In the main, perhaps unduplicated for any other issue, the power of the Psychopharmacology/Psychiatric hegemony has so controlled the message that the media tends not to even acknowledge there is another side. For most issues, the media will present at least one spokesperson from each side. However, when the latest questionable breakthrough in mental illness research or "treatment" is announced, the other side is not even presented. One might want to pass this off as Big Pharma advertising money infecting the news departments, but I think that is way too simplistic and perhaps even largely untrue. . . .

Alternatives

It also seems worthwhile to spend a little bit of space here on creating alternatives. Ultimately, in order to be successful, alternatives need to be funded by the public system.[75] One argument in its favor that should be attractive to government (but has not heretofore been) in the current system is breaking the bank. As Whitaker has shown, the disability rate for mental illness has increased six-fold since the introduction of Thorazine.[76] Making so many people permanently disabled and financially supported by the government, rather than working and supporting the government, is not only a huge human tragedy, but is also a massive, unnecessary governmental expense.

One of the simplest, but very important things that should be done is to compile a readily accessible, accurate, list of existing alternatives and efforts to get them going. I have seen lists of alternatives, but then I hear that this program or that is really not a true nondrugging and/or noncoercive alternative. It would be extremely helpful for there to be a description of each such program with enough investigation to know what is really happening. . . .

Conclusion

A final word about the importance of the potential role of the courts and the forced psychiatry issue. While it is true that many, even maybe most, people in the system are not under court orders at any given time, it is my view that the forced psychiatry system is what starts a tremendous number of people on the road to permanent disability (and poverty) and drives the whole public system. Of course, coercion to take the drugs is pervasive outside of court orders too, but again I see the legal coercion as a key element. If people who are now being dragged into forced psychiatry were given noncoercive, recovery-oriented options, they would also become available for the people who are not subject to forced psychiatry. I hope this paper has conveyed the role that strategic litigation can play in transforming mental health systems to a culture of recovery.

Notes

1. By phrasing it this way, I am not disputing that people become psychotic. I have been there. . . . However, there are lots of degrees—a continuum, if you will—and there are different ways of looking at these unaccepted ways of thinking, or altered states of consciousness. So, what I mean by this terminology is that people are faced with involuntary commitment and forced drugging when two conditions exist: One, they are bothering another person(s), including concern about the risk of suicide or other self-harm, and two, they are expressing thoughts that do not conform to those accepted "normal" by society. Of course, this ignores the reality that a lot of both are often trumped up, especially against people who have previously been subjected to the system.

2. The system believes it is also less expensive, but the opposite is actually true. The overreliance on neuroleptics and, increasingly, polypharmacy, has at least doubled the number of people who become permanently reliant on government transfer payments. In *Anatomy of an Epidemic: Psychiatric Drugs and the Astonishing Rise of Mental Illness in America,* which is available at. . . . Robert Whitaker demonstrates the rate of disability has increased six-fold since the introduction of Thorazine in the mid '50s. The Michigan State Psychotherapy Project demonstrated extremely more favorable long-term outcomes for those receiving psychotherapy alone from psychotherapists with *relevant* training and experience. The short-term costs were comparable to the standard treatment and the long-term savings were tremendous. This study can be found at. . . .

3. "Parens Patriae" is legal Latin, literally meaning "parent of his or her country." *Black's Law Dictionary,* seventh edition defines it as "the state in its capacity as provider of protection to those unable to care for themselves." It is invoked with respect to minors and adults who are deemed incompetent to make their own decisions. In the context of forced drugging under the *parens patriae* doctrine, it basically is based on the notion, "If you weren't crazy, you'd know this was good for you."

4. At the same time there are impediments to doing so, primarily the lack of legal resources.

5. U.S. 294, 75 S.Ct. 753, 99 L.Ed. 1083 (1955).

6. In light of the system basically creating massive numbers of people who become categorized as chronically mentally ill, I call it the mental illness system, rather than the mental health system.

7. By saying the mental illness system operates largely illegally I mean that to the extent people are locked

up and forcibly drugged when the statutory and constitutional requirements are not being met, that is illegal. Of course, this is done by filing paperwork and getting court orders, which looked at another way, makes it legal.

8. "Treatment" is in quotes because it is both (1) pretty clear the current, virtually exclusive reliance on psychiatric drugs by the public mental illness system hinders recovery for the vast majority of people, and (2) if it isn't voluntary, it isn't treatment.

9. *See*, e.g., *Sell v. United States*, 539 U.S. 166 (2003). However, not everyone agrees with my legal analysis of the right to the least restrictive alternative.

10. *Humphrey v. Cady*, 405 U.S. 504 (1972).

11. *Addington v. Texas*, 441 U.S. 418 (1979).

15. *Mills v. Rogers*, 457 U.S. 291 (1982); *Washington v. Harper*, 494 U.S. 210 (1990; *Riggins v. Nevada*, 504 U.S. 127 (1992); and *Sell v. United States*, 539 U.S. 166 (2003).

16. *Sell v. United States*, 539 U.S. 166, 177-8 (2003), citing to the Due Process Clause, U.S. Const., amend. 5, and *Washington v. Harper*, 494 U.S. 210, 110 S.Ct. 1028 (1990).

24. *Rivers v. Katz*, 495 N.E.2d 337, 341-3 (NY 1986).

25. *See*, Mental Hygiene Law Court Monitoring Project: Part 1 of Report: Do Psychiatric Inmates in New York Have the Right to Refuse Drugs? An Examination of Rivers Hearings in the Brooklyn Court, which can be accessed on the Internet at. . . .

26. I say, "supposedly," because in truth, controlling the person's behavior is a primary interest. "Police power" justification, which actually is based on controlling dangerous behavior, has also been used to justify forced drugging. *See*, *Rivers v. Katz*, 495 N.E.2d 337, 343 (NY 1986). However, the behavior presumably has to be very extreme to invoke "police power" and is not normally the stated basis for seeking forced drugging orders. It has been suggested there is an important government interest in ending indeterminate commitment and returning the individual to society, which can be done most effectively if the person is required to take the prescribed drugs. However, this is not the basis normally asserted and I would argue it is not a sufficient interest to override a person's rights to decline the drugs, particularly in light of the physical harms they cause.

27. There are likely limits on this, such as there being no requirement for Herculean efforts or where the cost is prohibitive. *See*, e.g., *Mathews v. Eldridge*, 424 U.S. 319, 334–35 (1976). . . .

29. An example is described in the recent Alaska Supreme Court brief we filed in *Wetherhorn v. Alaska Psychiatric Institute*, which can be found on the Internet at. . . .

33. 441 U.S. 418 (1979).

34. "Preponderance of the evidence," means more likely than not or, put another way, it only requires the balance to be slightly more on one side than the other. Yet another way to look at it is it just has to be more than 50% likely. . . .

37. Michael L. Perlin, *Mental Disability Law: Civil and Criminal*, §2A-4.3c, p. 109 (2d. Ed. 1998), footnotes omitted. *See*, also, Morris, Pursuing Justice for the Mentally Disabled, 42 San Diego L. Rev. 757, 764 (2005) ("Recent studies confirm . . . that psychotic symptoms, such as delusions or hallucinations, currently being experienced by a person, do not elevate his or her risk of violence.")

38. Perlin, "And My Best Friend, My Doctor/Won't Even Say What It Is I've Got: The Role And Significance Of Counsel In Right To Refuse Treatment Cases," 42 *San Diego Law Review* 735, 746–7 (2005), citing to Thomas Grisso & Paul S. Appelbaum, *The MacArthur Treatment Competence Study. III: Abilities of Patients to Consent to Psychiatric and Medical Treatments*, 19 *Law & Hum. Behav.* 149 (1995). . . .

40. While I believe this is true in the forced drugging context in terms of meeting the legal burden of justifying overriding a person's right to decline the medications, and I know this paper comes off as a polemic against psychiatric drugs, I absolutely believe people also have the right to choose to take them. I do think people should be fully informed about them, of course, which is normally not done, but that is a different issue. Not surprisingly, in a study of people who have recovered after being diagnosed with serious mental illness, those who felt the drugs helped them, used them in their recovery and those that didn't find them helpful, didn't use the drugs in their recovery. "How Do We Recover? An Analysis of Psychiatric Survivor Oral Histories," by Oryx Cohen, in *Journal of Humanistic Psychology*, Vol. 45, No. 3, Summer 2005, 333–35, which is available on the Internet at. . . .

41. Anatomy of an Epidemic: Psychiatric Drugs and the Astonishing Rise of Mental Illness in America, by Robert Whitaker, *Ethical Human Psychology and Psychiatry*, Volume 7, Number I: 23–35 Spring 2005, which can be accessed on the Internet at. . . .

42. Order, in *In the Matter of the Hospitalization of Faith Myers*, Anchorage Superior Court, Third Judicial District, State of Alaska, Case No. 3AN-03-277 PR,

March 14, 2003, pp. 8, 13, which can be accessed on the Internet at. . . .

43. Prospective analysis of premature mortality in schizophrenia in relation to health service engagement: a 7.5-year study within an epidemiologically complete, homogeneous population in rural Ireland, by Maria G. Morgan, Paul J. Scully, Hanafy A. Youssef, Anthony Kinsellac, John M. Owensa, and John L. Waddingtona, *Psychiatry Research* 117 (2003) 127–135, which can be found on the Internet at. . . .

44. *The ADA and Persons with Mental Disabilities: Can Sanist Attitudes Be Undone? Journal of Law and Health*, 1993/1994, 8 *JLHEALTH* 15, 33–34.

45. "It would probably be difficult to find any American Psychiatrist working with the mentally ill who has not, at a minimum, exaggerated the dangerousness of a mentally ill person's behavior to obtain a judicial order for commitment." Torrey, E. Fuller. 1997. *Out of the Shadows: Confronting America's Mental Illness Crisis*, New York: John Wiley and Sons, page 152. Dr. Torrey goes on to say this lying to the courts is a good thing. Of course, lying in court is perjury. Dr. Torrey also quotes psychiatrist Paul Applebaum as saying when "confronted with psychotic persons who might well benefit from treatment, and who would certainly suffer without it, mental health professionals and judges alike were reluctant to comply with the law," noting that in "'the dominance of the commonsense model,' the laws are sometimes simply disregarded."

46. Perlin, *"And My Best Friend, My Doctor/Won't Even Say What It Is I've Got": The Role And Significance Of Counsel In Right To Refuse Treatment Cases*, 42 *San Diego Law Review* 735, 738 (2005).

47. This is a violation of professional ethics. For example, the Comment to the Model Rules of Professional Conduct for attorneys, Rule 1.3, includes, "A lawyer should pursue a matter on behalf of a client despite opposition, obstruction or personal inconvenience to the lawyer, and take whatever lawful and ethical measures are required to vindicate a client's cause or endeavor. A lawyer must also act with commitment and dedication to the interests of the client and with zeal in advocacy upon the client's behalf."

48. "Kendra's Law" in New York is a classic example of this. There a person who had been denied numerous attempts to obtain mental health services pushed Kendra in front of a moving subway and when he was grabbed, said something like "now maybe I will get some help." The response was to pass an outpatient commitment law requiring people to take psychiatric drugs or be locked up in the hospital. This is a characterization, but when this was challenged, New York's high court ruled Kendra's Law didn't require people to take the drugs; that all it did was subject people to "heightened scrutiny" for involuntary commitment if they didn't. *See, In the Matter of K.L.*, 806 N.E.2d 480(NY 2004). . . .

55. Many state statutes certainly require it, and I would suggest it is constitutionally required as well.

56. *See*, Effective Non-Drug Treatments, which can be found on the Internet at. . . .

58. For example, I have identified a lot of things under Alaska law where I think valid challenges to what is going on can and should be made. . . .

75. However, I am also in favor of non-system alternatives.

76. *See*, Anatomy of an Epidemic: Psychiatric Drugs and the Astonishing Rise of Mental Illness in America, which is available at. . . .

James B. Gottstein is a psychiatric rights lawyer from Anchorage, Alaska, where he has practiced law for over 25 years. Gottstein is the president of numerous organizations, including the Law Project for Psychiatric Rights (PsychRights), which he cofounded in 2002; Peer Properties, Inc., which he cofounded in 2002 to offer peer-run housing for mentally ill people in bad living situations; Soteria-Alaska, Inc., an organization that offers noncoercive and mostly nondrug alternatives to psychiatric hospitalization, which he cofounded in 2003; and CHOICES, Inc., which he also cofounded in 2003 to make available peer-run services that particularly support the right of people to choose whether or not to take psychiatric drugs. Gottstein has also been a member of the board of directors for the National Association for Rights Protection and Advocacy since 2005, acting as president in 2006, and he has been on the board of directors of the International Center for the Study of Psychiatry and Psychology since 2006. http://psychrights.org/about/Gottstein.htm

EXPLORING THE ISSUE

Is Forced Treatment of Seriously Mentally Ill Individuals Justifiable?

Critical Thinking and Reflection

1. What legal protections can be put in place, and what specific procedures followed, to protect the right of individuals to make choices affecting their psychological and physical well-being?
2. What arguments can be made to support the idea that mental health professionals should be accorded the legal right to administer treatments against the will of a mentally ill person?
3. To what extent should family members of a seriously mentally ill individual be given the right to approve treatment for a loved one who is resisting such intervention?
4. In cases in which an involuntarily treated patient begins to recover from symptoms, how should decisions be made by mental health professionals to respect the prerogative of the patient to stop the treatment?
5. How would you go about designing a study to evaluate the psychological impact on individuals for whom treatment has been involuntarily administered?

Is There Common Ground?

In both articles the authors are advocating on behalf of humane care of severely mentally ill individuals. There is agreement about the fact that American history is tainted by horrifying inhumane treatments in mental hospitals up until the second half of the twentieth century. As mentioned by attorneys Brakel and Davis, prior to the 1950s most people with schizophrenia spent much of their life in state insane asylums, with close to a half-million individuals filling these beds. The introduction of antipsychotic medications such as chlorpromazine brought with it optimism that psychotically disturbed patients could be effectively treated, but this hope was naïve. These drugs were seen as an easy solution to the centuries-old problem of how to control the harmful and bizarre behaviors of psychotically disturbed individuals. The initial hope for these drugs was simplistic, in that no one realized that these medications could cause harmful physical side effects, some of which would involve irreversible neurological damage. Fortunately, over the course of the past several decades, considerable advances have been made in the development of medications with less severe side effects.

The deinstitutionalization movement that was active in the 1970s had a profound effect on moving psychologically disturbed individuals out of mental hospitals and into community settings where they could be treated and supported in less restrictive and more humane contexts. However, many of these individuals fell through the cracks, becoming homeless, malnourished, and psychotically disturbed once again. In consideration of these realities, both articles struggle with the question of how to take care of psychologically disturbed individuals who are incapable of self-care. To what extent should their rights to autonomy be respected, particularly when their life may be at risk? These are thorny questions that professionals in the fields of law and mental health continue to address.

Create Central

www.mhhe.com/createcentral

Additional Resources

Kallert, T. W. (2011). *Coercive Treatment in Psychiatry*. Oxford: Wiley-Blackwell.

Kallert, T. W., Mezzich, J. E., & Monahan, J. (2011). *Coercive Treatment in Psychiatry: Clinical, Legal and Ethical Aspects*. Hoboken, NJ: John Wiley & Sons.

Mcsherry, B. (2013). *Coercive Care: Rights, Law and Policy*. Taylor & Francis.

Internet References . . .

American Constitution Society for Law and Policy

http://www.acslaw.org/

Citizens Commission on Human Rights

http://www.cchr.org/about-us/mental-health-declaration-of-human-rights.html

Mental Health Law.US

http://www.mentalhealthlaw.us/

National Alliance on Mental Illness

http://www.nami.org/

Selected, Edited, and with Issue Framing Material by:
Richard P. Halgin, *University of Massachusetts, Amherst*

ISSUE

Is Pornography Harmful?

YES: **Pamela Paul**, from "The Cost of Growing Up on Porn," washingtonpost.com (2010)

NO: **Megan Andelloux**, from "Porn: Ensuring Domestic Tranquility of the American People," Original Work (2011)

Learning Outcomes
After reading this issue, you should be able to: • Explain the limitations and difficulties in defining "pornography."   • Describe some of the recent research that has been done on pornography.   • Critique research methods on the effects of pornography.   • Discuss specific reasons why pornography might be considered harmful, or beneficial.

ISSUE SUMMARY

YES: Pamela Paul, author of *Pornified: How Pornography Is Transforming our Lives, Our Relationships, and Our Families*, argues that studies declaring the harmlessness of pornography on men are faulty, and that consequences of porn consumption can be seen in the relationships men have with women and sex.

NO: Megan Andelloux, sexuality educator and founder of the Center for Sexual Pleasure and Health, argues that the benefits of porn on American society outweigh the questionable consequences. Andelloux outlines several arguments for how porn may be beneficial.

"The Internet is for porn!" Or, so sings a muppet from the hit Broadway show *Avenue Q*. As in-home access to the Internet has risen, so has access to a seemingly unlimited supply of pornography. But is pornography harmful? And whom, if anyone, does it harm? While the debate over erotic and explicit material is nothing new, the widespread availability of online pornography has raised new concerns about an old issue.

Debates over pornography in the United States have largely focused on the perceived negative impact of porn versus free-speech arguments that oppose censorship of any kind. While many see this conflict as a feminist issue, even feminists can find themselves on opposing sides of the argument. In the 1970s and 1980s, an often intense academic debate (referred to as the feminist sex wars) raged between "radical feminists" and a new school of feminist thinkers who labeled themselves "sex-positive." Radical feminists, such as Andrea Dworkin and Catharine MacKinnon, opposed pornography. Sex-positive feminists were weary of calls for censorship and alarmed by anti-porn feminists who were now allied with the conservative movement they saw as in opposition to women's liberation.

A key part of the debate hinges on the effects of the consumption of pornography. Opponents point to researchers who have found connections between porn and a decrease in compassion toward rape victims and the support of violence against women. Recently several popular authors (including Pamela Paul, whose essay is featured in this issue) have warned against the negative impact easily accessible porn can have on relationships, masculinity, and femininity.

On the other hand, supporters of porn point to other studies that show no significant correlation between sexually explicit material and attitudes that are supportive of violence against women. Anti-censorship advocates like Nadine Strossen and sex-positive feminists like Susie Bright and Violet Blue have written about the ways pornography can empower both performers and viewers. The growing market for feminist and queer erotica, featuring films produced and directed by women such as Candida Royalle, Tristan Taormino, and Jayme Waxman, suggests women are supporting porn in increasing numbers.

While the feminist sex wars cooled over time, the debate was never settled—thanks in large part to the ambiguous definition of porn. What, exactly, is pornography? Is there a line between art and pornography? Between pornography and obscenity? In 1964 Supreme Court Justice Potter Stewart, in an opinion stating the scope of obscenity laws should be limited, famously said of hard-core porn, "I know it when I see it." Nearly 50 years later, controversial porn producer Max Hardcore was sentenced to 46 months in prison (though the sentence was later reduced) for violating federal obscenity laws by distributing his films and promotional material via mail and over the Internet.

The issue of pornography and its potential harms, particularly in reinforcing the subjugation and humiliation of females, is a perplexing one. Efforts to censor speech, writing, and pictorial material (including classical art) have been continuous throughout American history. The success of censorship efforts depends mainly on the dominating views in the particular era in which the efforts are being made, and on whether conservative or liberal views dominate during that period. In the conservative Victorian era, morals crusader Anthony Comstock persuaded Congress to adopt a broadly worded law banning "any book, painting, photograph, or other material design, adapted, or intended to explain human sexual functions, prevent conception, or produce abortion." That 1873 law was in effect for almost a hundred years, until the U.S. Supreme Court declared its last remnants unconstitutional by allowing the sale of contraceptives to married women in 1963 and to single women in 1972.

In 1986, a pornography commission headed by then-Attorney General Edwin Meese maintained that the "totality of evidence" clearly documented the social dangers of pornography and justified severe penalties and efforts to restrict and eliminate it. At the same time, then-Surgeon General C. Everett Koop arrived at conclusions that opposed those of the Meese commission. Koop stated that "Much research is still needed in order to demonstrate that the present knowledge [of laboratory studies] has significant real world implications for predicting [sexual] behavior.

It is doubtful that Justice Stewart, the feminists of the 1970s, or the Meese commission could have foreseen the impact of the Internet and "smart phones" (such as iPhones, Androids, and Blackberries) on the availability or distribution of porn. The seemingly unlimited availability of free hard-core porn at our fingertips has been cited by many as a need for further restrictions. The implications of porn consumption, however, are still hotly debated. While accurate statistics are difficult to come by, there is no debating porn's popularity or billion dollar revenues.

As you read the selections, think about how *you* define pornography. Does it need to be explicit to be considered pornographic? How should feminist, gay, lesbian, or queer-produced porn that portrays people of various genders and body types enjoying sex be viewed in the conversation? What about erotic novels, like *Fifty Shades of Gray*, or paintings, illustrations, and sculptures depicting nudity or sex? Should soft-core porn be treated the same way as hard-core? What about animated scenes of nudity or sexual intercourse that are often depicted in video games? Consider your own porn-viewing habits, or the habits of people you know. Do you think it has had an impact on your (or your friends') attitudes toward women, men, or sex in general? If you believe pornography to be harmful, do you feel it is more damaging to women or men? Do you believe society would benefit from restricting or banning some types of sexually explicit material? Where would you draw the line (or lines) in deciding something was illegal?

In the following selections, Pamela Paul, author of *Pornified: How Pornography Is Transforming Our Lives, Our Relationships, and Our Families*, calls into question the findings of a Canadian researcher who found that viewing pornography had no negative effects on men in his sample. Megan Andelloux, sexuality educator and founder of the Center for Sexual Pleasure and Health, argues that pornography is not only healthy, but it is a valuable part of the fabric of American society.

YES ↵

Pamela Paul

The Cost of Growing Up on Porn

Guess what, guys? Turns out pornography—the much-maligned bugaboo of feminists, prigs and holy rollers—is nothing more than good, not-so-dirty fun.

The proof comes from the University of Montreal, where recent research showed that connoisseurs easily parse fantasy from reality, shudder at the idea of dating a porn star (what would Maman think?) and wholeheartedly support gender equality. "Research contradicts anti-pornography zealots," gloated a column's headline in the *Calgary Sun.*

So, I've been contradicted. Presumably, I'm one of the zealots in question. My anti-porn fanaticism took the form of a 2005 book, "Pornified," in which I dared to offer evidence that all is not well in the era of Internet porn. Today, 20-somethings, teenagers and even—sorry to break it to you, parents—tweens are exposed to the full monty of hard-core pornography.

Wasn't it time someone asked some obvious questions? What will happen now that the first generation of men raised on Internet porn is making its way onto the marriage market? What influence does the constant background blare of insta-porn have on their ideas about women and monogamous relationships?

The answers I found to those questions were less than cheering. In dozens of interviews with casual and habitual porn users, I heard things such as: "Real sex has lost some of its magic." "If I'm looking like eight or 10 times a day, I realize I need to do something to build my confidence back up." "My wife would probably think I was perverted and oversexed if she knew how much I looked at it every day."

In the years since I wrote the book, I have heard from dozens of readers who described the negative effects of porn. One was a student at Berkeley, who observed that "ever more deplorable acts needed to be satiated" and noted: "As a child, we are exposed to things that we may not realize have formative effects. As adults, many times we simply continue without questioning." (Women, it seems, also turn to iVillage.com, where a board devoted to "relationships damaged by pornography" contains more than 32,280 messages to date.)

Yet there's still so much we don't know. Perhaps we can learn from the scintillating news out of Montreal. Let's have a closer look at that—oops!—turns out there is no study. Simon Louis Lajeunesse, a postdoctoral student and associate professor at the university's School of Social Work, has yet to publish a report. His findings, such as they exist, were based on interviews with 20 undergraduate males who detailed their views on sex, gender and pornography in one to two lickety-split hours.

Granted, it's qualitative, not quantitative, research, but the brevity of the interviews is concerning. While reporting "Pornified," I felt the need for more than four hours with many of my 100 interviewees. Of course, my guys could talk anonymously to a disembodied voice on the phone; the poor fellows in Montreal had to sit down and look a male social worker in the eye before confessing a penchant for three-ways. Lajeunesse asked 2,000 men before he found 20 willing subjects. Most of them, he said, were referred by women in their lives. Hmm.

And just how did Lajeunesse learn that pornography hadn't affected their views of said women? Why, he asked and they said so! "My guys want to have equal relationships, equal income, equal responsibility domestically," Lajeunesse told me. Color me dubious, but I hardly think most men would own up to discriminating against women, spurred on by porn or not.

To be fair, researching the relationship between men and pornography isn't easy. My methods had flaws, too. The most methodologically sound study would involve gathering a sample of men, scheduling regular sessions to view online porn, and comparing their subsequent sexual attitudes and behaviors with those of a control group that did not use pornography. Through a series of measures—interviews, questionnaires, observations—the data would be collected and analyzed by a team of objective academics.

That's not going to happen now, though it once did. Back in 1979, Jennings Bryant, a professor of communications at the University of Alabama, conducted one of the most powerful peer-reviewed lab studies of the effects of porn viewing on men. Summary of results: not good. Men who consumed large amounts of pornography were less likely to want daughters, less likely to support women's equality and more forgiving of criminal rape. They also grossly overestimated Americans' likelihood to engage in group sex and bestiality.

Yet Bryant's research (conducted with colleague Dolf Zillmann) was carried out long before the Internet brought on-demand porn to a computer screen near you. So why no update? Other than a spate of research in the '80s and '90s that attempted to link pornography with violence (results: inconclusive), nobody has looked at the everyday impact of hard-core porn. "That's a catch-22 with most studies about media effects," Bryant told me. "If you can't demonstrate that what you're doing to research participants is ultimately beneficial and not detrimental, and you can't eradicate any harm, you're required not to do that thing again."

Every university has a review board for the protection of human subjects that determines whether a study is ethically up to snuff. "It is commonly the case that when you get studies as clear as ours, human subjects committees make it difficult to continue to do research in that area," Bryant explained. "Several graduate students at the time wanted to follow up, but couldn't get permission." In other words, the deleterious effects were so convincing, ethics boards wouldn't let researchers dip human subjects back into the muck.

No matter—people will take care of that on their own. As one young man explained, after mentioning that "porn may have destroyed my relationship with my girlfriend" in an e-mail: "I always feel that I'm over porn, but I find myself keep coming back to it. There seems to be an infinite number of porn sites with limitless variations, one never becomes bored with it. . . . It's a very difficult habit to break."

Or as one 27-year-old female lawyer noted recently: "All of my girlfriends and I expect to find histories of pornographic Web sites on our computers after our boyfriends use it. They don't bother erasing the history if you don't give them a lot of hell." The implications troubled her. "I fear we are losing something very important—a healthy sexual worldview. I think, however, that we are using old ideas of pornography to understand its function in a much more complex modern world."

Of the many stories I've heard revealing the ways in which young men struggle with porn, I offer here just one, distilled, from a self-described "25 year old recovering porn-addict" who wrote to me in October. "Marc" began

looking at his father's magazines at age 11, but soon, he wrote, he "turned to the Internet to see what else I could find." This "started off as simply looking at pictures of naked women. From there, it turned into pictures of couples having sex and lesbian couples. When I got into watching videos on the Internet, my use of porn skyrocketed." At 23, he began dating a woman he called "Ashley." "However, since Ashley's last boyfriend had been a sex/porn addict, I was quick to lie about my use of porn. I told her that I never looked at it. But after 5–6 months, Ashley discovered a hidden folder on my computer containing almost a hundred porn clips. She was devastated."

Marc and Ashley broke up, got back together and spent several months traveling in India. He continued to look at porn behind her back, and on a trip to Las Vegas, he got lap dances despite promising not to. Ashley broke up with him again. "I had never thought about the adverse effects of my use of porn. . . . I want to change. I want to be a respectful human being towards all human beings, male and female. I want to be a committed and loving boyfriend to Ashley."

This is hardly solid lab research. But it is one of many signs of pornography's hidden impact. And flimsy "if only it were true!" research isn't an acceptable substitute for thorough study. An entire generation is being kept in the dark about pornography's effects because previous generations can't grapple with the new reality. Whether by approaching me (at the risk of peer scorn) after I've spoken at a university or via anonymous e-mails, young people continue to pass along an unpopular message: Growing up on porn is terrible. One 17-year-old who had given up his habit told me that reading about porn addicts "was like reading a horrifying old diary, symptoms, downward spirals, guilt, hypocrisy, lack of control, and the constant question of to what degree fantasy is really so different from reality. I felt like a criminal, or at the very least, a person who would objectively disgust me."

Let's not ignore people like him, even if it's tempting to say, as one headline did, "All men watch porn, and it is not bad for them: study."

That's just one more fantasy warping how we live our real lives.

PAMELA PAUL is a journalist and author. Her books include *Parents, Inc.*, and *Pornified: How Pornography Is Damaging Our Lives, Our Relationships, and Our Families.*

Megan Andelloux

NO

Porn: Ensuring Domestic Tranquility of the American People

Pornography. Images of happy people rolling over one another, flashes of arched backs, moans that cannot be ignored, and giggles pouring from the mouths of stars. Out of the corner of the eye a flash of skin on the monitor catches our attention and draws us in. Porn has become ubiquitous on the Internet in the modern day, but its existence has graced the surface of the Earth since humans first began tracing stick figures on cave walls. One of its earliest forms comes to us from the town of Santillana del Mar, in the Cantabria region of northern Spain during the Upper Paleolithic Period.[1] Coital scenes were drawn out on cave walls 40,000 years ago depicting oral sex, voyeurism, and sex for the sake of fun! Records of these "graphic" images coming from France, Portugal, and Egypt beg the question: did rulers like the great Pharaoh Ramses have to hide his papyrus porn from the royal court? Were our ancestors riddled with angst and shame about the potential damage of gazing at naked bodies drawn on scrolls? Probably not. The danger of depicting human nudity wasn't a social concern until the middle of the 18th century, when the written word made erotica available to the common man.[2] Suddenly, politicians, clergy members, and authority figures of all types decried the erotic word and spread fear of its supposed dangerous and corrupting influence. Today, alas, we still face the same argument: Is pornography harmful?

Not all porn is created equal, but it is a form of speech that has been and must continue to be protected in our society. What may be found offensive by one citizen or group of citizens should not dictate whether or not the rest of society is to be allowed free access to it, lest tyranny of minority opinion rule the day. It's clear the American court systems agree.[3] If the US Supreme found that the Westboro Baptist Church's hate speech is to be afforded protection, how could one ever think to outlaw pornography's message of pleasure? Porn virtually embodies everything the founders envisioned when they penned "the right to life, liberty, and the pursuit of happiness!"

It's been reported that over 372 million websites are devoted to displaying images of people having sex of one sort or another.[4] There are untold thousands of magazines, flash drives, comic strips, and pornographic images that circulate around us every day. Porn is a major part of our American culture, and it could be argued that watching porn is America's real pastime. Now before I start getting hate mail for an inflammatory statement like that, let me point out that regardless of a person's religious preference or political affiliation, about 36% of the American population uses porn at least once a month.[5] One would never know it because very few people publicly claim to enjoy pornography. It's understandable why. Acknowledging that you watch pornography is tantamount to identifying yourself as a "pervert" in our society.

It is astonishing that 40 years after a conservative administration spent years and millions of dollars trying to find a correlation between violence and porn (which they were unable to do), and show that porn has damaging effects on individuals and their personal relationships (which they have not), Americans are still shamed when they enjoy such a basic, ancient part of our humanity.

So, when we have hard, reputable data that tens of millions of Americans have watched porn in the past month, that our crime rates are lower when we have access to it,[6] that the most prevalent images *by far* are of adults having sex,[7] and that the performers in the field like the work they do,[8] why then is porn still vilified? It's because a group of highly motivated, yet select few people yell hard, long, and loud. They shame both people who watch and the actors who perform in porn. They portray those who stand up for porn as being misguided, or as duped by the industry itself, and browbeat people with their opinion that looking at images of people having sex is somehow immoral. We rarely hear that using porn is beneficial, empowering and a healthy choice in sexual development, exploration and expression.

Let's look at why pornography is indeed, good for society and individuals.

Pornography Shows Human Beings as Being Sexual Creatures

Pornography exposes sexual desire, and it is unashamed of what it produces. It shows the lust, the yearning, and the appreciation of other human bodies and their sexual energy. Pornography rejoices in the very things society works so hard to suppress.

Whether stumbled upon or sought out intentionally, porn is a part of society because we enjoy it. People derive pleasure seeing other people be sexual. Porn helps individuals explore behaviors they may feel alone in experiencing, such as fetishes, non-heterosexuality, or even simple masturbation. The anti-porn folks are right in at least one thing: We do learn from the images. Although, the moral crusaders will then go on to argue that we in the audience are without free will and are forced to mimic the most degrading images we see in pornographic films. But just as I will continue to come to a full stop at the next red light I see despite having enjoyed *The French Connection* last night, free will gives us the option to imitate movie scenes or not at will. Nearly everyone is sexual. Porn helps us to share in our sexuality without overriding or sublimating it.

> "Old, young, black, white, male, female, trans, pretty, ugly, tall, short, big, little, all types are represented on screen. A wider variety of body types are welcome on the porn screen as opposed to mainstream media representations of love, sex and romance. We may not look like Angelina Jolie, but we can find someone on a porn screen who looks a lot like we do, having a fun time and living to tell the tale. That's no small thing."
>
> —*Nina Hartley*
> *Porn Performer, Sex Educator*

Pornography Shows the Wide Variety of Human Sexual Desires and Actions

Porn gives hope to those who feel alone and/or sexually isolated. Queers, women, the elderly, or any marginalized group can see, with full representation, that there may be others out there, sexual like they are.

> "I started performing in pornography so that I could participate in what I felt is much needed visibility of queer sexuality, gender expressions, and

sex-positive behaviors and culture. My work reflects the minority/marginalized communities that I am a part of, while allowing me to connect with a universal audience who can all appreciate great sex."
>
> —*Jiz Lee, Feminist Porn Award's Boundary Breaker and AVN Nominated Best New Web Star*

And now with amateur porn being the highest accessed sexually explicit material,[9] we have more evidence of the sex-lives of average Americans! We have proof that it's not just the "evil" porn industry that wants ejaculation scenes or spankings. We see normal bodies on film, flaws and all, having the best most creative sex.

And rather than a for-profit corporation behind the production, amateur porn has become the sexual art of folk. It's Bob and Jane playing here, or Jane and Jane, or Bob and Bob—beer belly, thick legs, short hair and . . . all frolicking around in sexual bliss.

> "Porn has afforded me the ability to feel out my sexuality without the fear of rejection or humiliation."
>
> —*Mark Farlow*

Ethically made pornography is a sub-genre of porn comprised of actors who are paid living wages for depiction of realistic sex. Ethically made pornography allows a performer to participate as more than just an actor in the sexual act being depicted. Ethical porn is an emerging powerful field within the adult market. The individuals and companies behind this movement seek out participants who DON'T look like the typical porn-stars. The ultimate goal seems to be to bring real sex to the masses. Some notable companies in this field include:

- Comstock Films
- Pink and White Productions
- Good Releasing
- Fatale Media
- Reel Queer Productions
- Sir Video
- Tristan Taormino's Expert Guide Series
- Nina Hartley's Guide Series

> "Independent and feminist porn especially can be an incredible validation for those who don't see their own desires reflected in mainstream media."
>
> —*Alison Lee, Good For Her Feminist Porn Awards*

Pornography Is a Risk Reduction Method It Is the Safest of Safe Sex

Watching porn is one of the safest ways to explore sexuality. There is no risk of STI transmissions, no risk of an unwanted pregnancy, no risk of feeling disappointed by the way our body performed, no risk of cheating, and no risk of violence. Human beings fantasize about forbidden fruit. We often wonder what it would be like to be with someone of the same gender, experience a threesome, engage in anal play, explore power dynamics, or talk dirty to our lover. Porn lets us find out, risk-free.

"Pornography can be a great way for people to explore their sexuality and fantasies without affecting others in society. Through pornography, they are able to jump their pizza delivery person or proposition their car dealer without actually disturbing others."

—Shanna Katz, Sexologist

Pornography Gives Access to Sex Information to All

While pornography isn't the best way to educate individuals on how to have sex, it does grant access to sexual information. It allows a great number of people to see what it means to have oral sex, pull-my-hair-play, or cis-gendered experiences. They say a picture is worth a thousand words. There is a clear difference between reading about it in a book and seeing it live in front of you, where you can watch the emotions, see the actual behaviors that take place, and process that information in a different way.

A person may feel titillated or disgusted, intrigued or off put, but all of these feelings are important parts of the learning process. What better starting point could one have when making decisions about the type of sexual behavior one wants to engage in?

I'm not arguing that pornography pretends to be educational. But it does purport to be experiential. Not everyone goes to college, nor do they have access to a sex educator, nor sex education programs, nor even a well stocked sex-ed self-help bookshelf. Accessing pornography can often be the first guidepost pointing the way to what one may want to do (or not do) in bed. The experience that porn brings, surrogate to real life as it may be, helps create a more informed decision making process.

"We know that many people turn to porn for sex information because there is a dearth of sex ed media. So even if we're making a movie that is in no way intended to be primarily educational, (that is, porn) we want to show sex as people actually have it."

—Carol Queen, Good Releasing Films

Pornography Encourages Conversations to Take Place about Sex

Hate it or love it, pornography is part of America.

Whether you call the risqué PETA commercial banned from prime-time porn, or find Charlie Sheen's latest sexual adventures pornographic, porn can start a conversation. We can turn to our neighbor or friend and ask, with all good intentions and proper decorum, "What do you think about Sasha Grey going into mainstream movies? Do you think she's going to make it? Why?" These probing questions serve a vital public service of allowing us to learn the sexual attitudes of our neighbors and friends.

American culture doesn't speak openly about sexuality yet harbors a judgmental attitude. Knowing the sexual mores of our peers can be vital for our social well-being. With the pornography industry putting "sexy time" out there for everyone to see and critique, seize the opportunity and talk about it!

"Viewing porn was helpful to convey what turned me on (and off) to my partner, ultimately making the sex and relationship stronger."

—Kim Chanza

Myth-Busting

In cultures that have access to pornography, violent crimes rates decreased. Yes, decreased. The US Government shows there is no correlation between violence and having access to and watching pornography.

The media routinely blares headlines bearing shocking titles such as "Porn made him sodomize his child!" Therefore, one would think that porn contributes to all manner of bad outcomes. The facts show, however, that pornography has been established not to increase rates of sexual violence. In 1970, the President's Commission on Obscenity and Pornography (also known as The Lockhart Report) found no link between pornography and delinquent or criminal behavior among youth and adults.[10] William B. Lockhart, Dean of the University of Minnesota Law School and chairman of the commission, famously said that before his work with the commission he had favored control of obscenity for both children and adults, but had changed his mind as a result of scientific studies done by commission researchers.

Similarly, in 1984 the Metro Toronto Task Force on Public Violence against Women and Children failed to demonstrate a link between pornography and sex crimes,[11] as did the 1994 US National Research Council Panel on Understanding and Preventing Violence.[12] Even the Meese Report, a famously biased hand-picked group of anti-pornography advocates hired by Ronald Reagan to prove the damaging effects of pornography failed to show any hard evidence. In fact, they got more than they bargained for when they hired Canadian sociologist Edna F. Einsiedel to summarize the current scientific studies linking pornography and violence. Her conclusion was that "No evidence currently exists that actually links fantasies with specific sexual offenses; the relationship at this point remains an inference.[13]"

Those talking heads who cling to the canard that porn leads to violence, rape, sexual assault, or child molestation are preaching from emotion, not facts. They fear what horrors "might" come to pass, and their fear is contagious. Terrifying tales without background or prelude are woven in the media to provoke a base response in their audience. Unfortunately, American history is littered with examples of just such emotional arguments being more powerful than well-reasoned counterparts. Witness the Salem witch trials, Japanese internment camps during WWII, or the sordid history of the House Un-American Activities Committee.

The anti-porn community (be it conservative religious or liberal feminist) stuffs the news media with anecdotal evidence of the danger posed by porn. Anecdotal evidence is of course the least reliable type of scientific data; one person, with a pretty face and a sob-story, can be more convincing than stacks of peer-reviewed journal articles. Though it can be moving to hear stories such as "Porn made me masturbate all day," or, "Porn made me see people as if they were naked," porn has not been actually shown to cause any such behavior.

Porn is an easy target for attack, but here is the thing: Humans have free will. We can choose to act one way or another, but pornography does not force us to do evil.

In all seriousness, rape and sexual assault are caused by violent antisocial tendencies, complete disregard for another's rights, and pure self-interest. To pin it on porn relieves the rapist of the guilt and blame.

One may not like certain aspects of pornography, but that discomfort should not restrict other's access to it. A society that produces legal pornography, a people that have access to pornography, is a sexually healthy nation. Pornography, a blessing of liberty, creates for us a more perfect union.

Resources

- Feminists for Free Expression
- ACLU
- Woodhull Freedom Foundation
- National Coalition for Sexual Freedom
- Free Speech Network
- Society for the Scientific Study of Sexuality
- America's War on Sex, Marty Klein
- Planned Parenthood of Western Washington, Pornography: Discussing Sexually Explicit Images, Irene Peters, Ph.D.

References

1. Cave paintings show aspects of sex beyond the reproductive. (2006, May 2). *Dominican Today*, Retrieved from http://www.dominicantoday.com/dr/people/2006/5/2/12982/Cave-paintings-show-aspects-of-sex-beyond-the-reproductive.

2. Carroll, J. L. (2007). *Sexuality now*. Belmont, CA: Wadsworth.

3. Corry v. Stanford University, Case No. 740309 (Cal. Super. Ct. 1995); Dambrot v. Central Michigan University, 839 F. Supp. 477 (E.D. Mich. 1993); Doe v. University of Michigan, 721 F. Supp. 852 (E.D. Mich. 1989).

4. Joseph, M. (Producer). (2007). *Internet porn* [Web]. Available from http://www.good.is/post/internet-Porn.

5. Media Metrix Demographic Profile—Adult. (2008, June). comScore

6. Kendall, T. D. (2006). Pornography, rape, and the internet. *Proceedings of the law and economics seminar* Stanford, CA: http://www.law.stanford.edu/display/images/dynamic/events_media/Kendall%20cov er%20+%20paper.pdf.

7. Diamond, M. (2009). Pornography, public acceptance, and sex related crime: a review. *International Journal of Law and Psychiatry* 32 (2009) 304–314; corrected with Corrigendum IJLP 33 (2010) 197–199.

8. Paulie & Pauline. (2010). *Off the set: porn stars and their partners*. Glen Rock, NJ: Aural Pink Press.

9. Klein, M. (2006). *America's war on sex: the attack on law, lust, and liberty.* Santa Barbara, CA: Praeger.

10. The Commission on Obscenity and Pornography, (1970). *President's commission on obscenity and pornography.* Washington, DC: U.S. Government Printing Office.

11. Task Force on Public Violence against Women and Children, Final Report (1984). *Metro Toronto.* Toronto, Canada.

12. Reiss, A. J., & Roth, A. J. National Research Council, (1993). *Understanding and preventing violence.* Washington, DC: National Academy Press.

13. United States Attorney General, Commission on Pornography. (1986). *Attorney general's commission on pornography.* Washington, DC.

MEGAN ANDELLOUX, a certified sexologist and sexuality educator, is the director of the Center for Sexual Pleasure and Health, a sexuality resource center for adults in Pawtucket, Rhode Island. Ms. Andelloux lectures at major universities, medical schools, and conferences on issues surrounding sexual freedom and the politics of pleasure.

EXPLORING THE ISSUE

Is Pornography Harmful?

Critical Thinking and Reflection

1. What types of harm or benefits could result from consuming pornography?
2. Do you think that the ways men and women consume pornography are different? Explain.
3. How has technology changed the way porn is consumed?

Is There Common Ground?

Is there the potential for middle ground between vehemently anti-porn and resoundingly pro-porn camps? Is all porn bad and inherently harmful? How does the age of the viewer impact the potential for harm? There does appear to be general consensus that child pornography is harmful. However, defining child pornography may prove just as challenging as defining all porn. And should the viewer's age be taken into account? At what age should the line be drawn? 12? 16? 18? 21? Is there a difference between a 14-year-old watching online porn versus a 24-year-old? Should two high school students "sexting" each other be viewed the same way as a much older adult looking at nude images or video of a high school student?

In his book, *America's War on Sex*, Marty Klein reports that 50 million Americans use legal adult pornography. A 2013 *Huffiington Post* article reported that 30 percent of all data transmitted on the Internet is porn, and that porn websites are visited more frequently than Amazon, Netflix, and Twitter combined. Most people do not publicly acknowledge their use of pornography, and many even adopt shameful attitudes about it. So, in this way, the arguments presented by Paul and Andelloux may reflect American attitudes and experiences, in general. The common ground may be that people will continue to consume pornography, while many—even the same consumers of pornography—will be silent about it, or condemn it.

Create Central

www.mhhe.com/createcentral

Additional Resources

Blue, V. (2006). *The Smart Girl's Guide to Porn*. San Fransisco, CA: Cleis Press.

Klein, M. (2012). *America's War on Sex*. Santa Barbara, CA: Praeger.

Levy, A. (2006). *Female Chauvinist Pigs: Women and the Rise of Raunch Culture*. New York, NY: Free Press.

Nathan, D. (2007). *Pornography*. Toronto, ON: Groundwood Press.

Paul, P. (2006). *Pornified: How Pornography Is Transforming Our Lives, Our Relationships, and Our Families*. New York, NY: Holt.

Sarracino, C. & Scott, K.M. (2009). *The Porning of America: The Rise of Porn Culture, What It Means, and Where We Go from Here*. Boston, MA: Beacon Press.

Internet References . . .

Academia Does Porn

This article describes a brand new peer-reviewed academic journal devoted to pornography.

www.salon.com/2013/05/03/academia_does_porn/

Cindy Gallop Wants to Change the Future of Porn

Cindy Gallop, creator of www.makelovenotporn.com, shares some of her thoughts on intimacy, pornography, social media, and how these things will come together in the future.

www.businessinsider.com/make-love-not-porn-cindy-gallop-2013-4

Porn Study: Does Viewing Explain Doing—Or Not?

This is a discussion of a new study investigating the relationship between porn use, risky behavior, and erectile dysfunction.

www.psychologytoday.com/blog/cupids-poisoned-arrow/201304/porn-study-does-viewing-explain-doing-or-not

The History of Pornography No More Prudish than the Present

A history of pornography from the ancient to the current.

www.livescience.com/8748-history-pornography-prudish-present.html

Selected, Edited, and with Issue Framing Material by:
Richard P. Halgin, *University of Massachusetts, Amherst*

ISSUE

Should the United States Be More Restrictive of Gun Ownership?

YES: Barack Obama and Joe Biden, from "Gun Control," remarks delivered at South Court Auditorium, The White House, Washington, DC (2013)

NO: Jeffrey Goldberg, from "The Case for More Guns (and More Gun Control)," *The Atlantic Magazine* (2012)

Learning Outcomes

After reading this issue, you will be able to:

- Discuss current gun ownership restrictions in the United States.
- Assess the threats gun pose to society.
- Describe efforts by the Obama administration to limit gun ownership.
- Explain why some argue that society would be safer with more guns.
- Identify key political players in the battle over gun control.

ISSUE SUMMARY

YES: President Barack Obama and Vice President Joe Biden, speaking in the wake of the Newtown shooting, discuss why America needs to take a more proactive stance in limiting control to guns to prevent further mass shootings.

NO: Columnist Jeffrey Goldberg presents an argument that Americans own plenty of guns to protect themselves but will only be able to prevent mass shootings if they are more readily able to carry them at all times.

Should Americans have the right to self-defense? Does the Second Amendment not give all Americans a fundamental right to bear arms in order to protect themselves and their property in the pursuit of life and liberty? Without guns, rebellion against a tyrannical government would not have been possible and the American Revolution would not mark the beginning of America's independence from England. In fact, search and seizure of firearms and ammunition were a major catalyst for events leading to the American Revolution. While the Second Amendment laid the foundation for gun rights in America, it was not until recently that courts began to clarify exactly who the Second Amendment impacts. Without such clarification, state and local governments have been slowly stripping away access to firearms and therefore a citizen's right to

self-defense with false claims of more guns equals more violence.

The Second Amendment, ratified in 1791, states, "A well-regulated militia, being necessary to the security of a free State, the right of the people to keep and bear Arms, shall not be infringed." Proponents of gun control believe the word "militia" was specifically used to guarantee the right of states to have an armed militia, like our current National Guard. Of course, opponents of gun control believe it to be an individual right to bear arms and a denial of access to guns is unconstitutional. Prior to *District of Columbia v. Heller* in 2008, the Supreme Court had not reviewed a Second Amendment case since *United States v. Miller* in 1939, which did not answer if the Second Amendment was an individual right or one specifically held by the state militia. Without a Supreme Court standing on the issue, states and local governments spent nearly 70 years with little authoritative guidance and have been able to push gun restrictions to the edge, including all out handgun bans in places like the District of Columbia and the city of Chicago.

In 2008, *District of Columbia v. Heller* finally answered the question as to individual rights granted by the Second Amendment. In 1976 the District of Columbia banned all handguns within the district, and all long guns had to be disassembled and a trigger lock used at all times, ultimately defeating the usefulness of a firearm for self-defense in one's home. In siding with *Heller*, the Supreme Court showed that such stringent controls are unconstitutional and obstruct a person's right of self-defense. The *Heller* case was a monumental movement to solidifying the individual right to bear arms, at least at the federal level, but did not express whether the case was enforceable against the states. In 2010, the Supreme Court heard the case of *McDonald v. Chicago*, in which the Supreme Court ruled that the Second Amendment was enforceable against the state under the Privileges and Immunities Clause of the Fourteenth Amendment. *District of Columbia v. Heller* and *McDonald v. Chicago* have been two of the most influential cases in decades to address the right to bear arms, but as is often the result with major court decisions, the rulings have raised many new questions.

The problem with imposing excessive gun bans like those in Chicago and the District of Columbia is that they may not do much to actually reduce crime. Instead, they hinder the law-abiding citizen's right to self-defense, and at best create unreasonable barriers to access firearms. According to a Harvard study by Don Kates and Gary Mauser, Russia's gun controls are so stringent that very few civilians have access to firearms, yet as of 2002 Russia had the highest murder rate of any developed country. Russia is not alone, ownership of any gun in Luxembourg is minimal and handguns are banned, yet they have a murder rate nine times that of countries with high gun ownership such as Germany, Norway, Switzerland, and Austria. In 1996, Australia banned most guns and made the defensive use of a firearm illegal, which resulted in armed robberies rising 51 percent, unarmed robberies by 37 percent, assaults by 24 percent, and kidnappings by 43 percent in the four years following the ban. England has fared no better, during the late 1990s handguns were banned resulting in a 40 percent increase in firearm-related crimes, yet hundreds of thousands of guns were confiscated from law-abiding citizens. Countries like Australia and England are proving when stringent gun restrictions are imposed, and the right to self-defense is taken away, there are only two people with access to guns: the government and criminals.

The idiom "guns don't kill people, people kill people" is being tested in public opinion in the United States every time a mass shooting occurs within the nation's borders. In recent months, we have experienced two such incidents that returned gun control to the federal agenda. First, on July 20, 2012, James Eagan Holmes killed 12 people and injured 70 others during a mass shooting at a Century theater in Aurora, Colorado during a late screening of *The Dark Knight Rises*. Less than five months later, Adam Lanza shot and killed twenty school children and six adults at Sandy Hook Elementary School in Newtown, Connecticut. He also killed his mother. By the time Lanza took his own life with police closing in, it had become the second deadliest mass shooting by an individual gunman in the history of the United States. In both Aurora and Newtown, there were concerns raised about gun control: how did these men gain access to weapons despite displaying signs of mental illness? Why do we have semiautomatic weapons available? Is there any way to prevent possible criminals from getting access to guns without preventing Americans from protecting themselves?

Speaking after a mass shooting in the Navy Yard, President Obama explained: "By now . . . it should be clear that the change we need will not come from Washington. . . . Change will come the only way it ever has come, and that's from the American people. . . . Part of what wears on . . . is the sense that this has happened before," the president said. "What wears on us, what troubles us so deeply, as we gather here today is this senseless violence that took place in the Navy Yard echoes other recent tragedies. . . . I do not accept that we cannot find a common sense way to preserve our traditions, including our basic Second Amendment freedoms and the rights of law-abiding gun owners while at the same time reducing the gun violence that unleashed so much mayhem on a regular basis." Yet the National Rifle Association remains a significant obstacle to any gun control in the United States. With strong membership numbers, funds, and a knack for lobbying, even after a string of massacres, the NRA has successfully prevented any new restrictions to gun ownership.

In the following selections, we hear from President Barack Obama and Vice President Joe Biden who in the aftermath of the Sandy Hook shooting took to a microphone to ask Americans to be more proactive in trying to limit access to guns in order to prevent future death. Opposing our chief executives is Jeffrey Goldberg, who claims Americans have plenty of guns but need better capabilities for carrying them on their person if they plan to prevent massacres.

YES

Barack Obama and Joe Biden

Gun Control

THE VICE PRESIDENT: Before I begin today, let me say to the families of the innocents who were murdered 33 days ago, our heart goes out to you. And you show incredible courage—incredible courage—being here. And the President and I are going to do everything in our power to honor the memory of your children and your wives with the work we take up here today.

It's been 33 days since the nation's heart was broken by the horrific, senseless violence that took place at Sandy Hook Elementary School—20—20 beautiful first-graders gunned down in a place that's supposed to be their second sanctuary. Six members of the staff killed trying to save those children. It's literally been hard for the nation to comprehend, hard for the nation to fathom.

And I know for the families who are here that time is not measured in days, but it's measured in minutes, in seconds, since you received that news. Another minute without your daughter. Another minute without your son. Another minute without your wife. Another minute without your mom.

I want to personally thank Chris and Lynn McDonald, who lost their beautiful daughter, Grace, and the other parents who I had a chance to speak to, for their suggestions and for—again, just for the courage of all of you to be here today. I admire the grace and the resolve that you all are showing. And I must say I've been deeply affected by your faith, as well. And the President and I are going to do everything to try to match the resolve you've demonstrated.

No one can know for certain if this senseless act could have been prevented, but we all know we have a moral obligation—a moral obligation—to do everything in our power to diminish the prospect that something like this could happen again.

As the President knows, I've worked in this field a long time—in the United States Senate, having chaired a committee that had jurisdiction over these issues of guns and crime, and having drafted the first gun violence legislation—the last gun violence legislation, I should say. And I have no illusions about what we're up against or how hard the task is in front of us. But I also have never seen the nation's conscience so shaken by what happened at Sandy Hook. The world has changed, and it's demanding action.

It's in this context that the President asked me to put together, along with Cabinet members, a set of recommendations about how we should proceed to meet that moral obligation we have. And toward that end, the Cabinet members and I sat down with 229 groups—not just individuals, representing groups—229 groups from law enforcement agencies to public health officials, to gun officials, to gun advocacy groups, to sportsmen and hunters and religious leaders. And I've spoken with members of Congress on both sides of the aisle, had extensive conversations with mayors and governors and county officials.

And the recommendations we provided to the President on Monday call for executive actions he could sign, legislation he could call for, and long-term research that should be undertaken. They're based on the emerging consensus we heard from all the groups with whom we spoke, including some of you who are victims of this god-awful occurrence—ways to keep guns out of the wrong hands, as well as ways to take comprehensive action to prevent violence in the first place.

We should do as much as we can, as quickly as we can. And we cannot let the perfect be the enemy of the good. So some of what you will hear from the President will happen immediately; some will take some time. But we have begun. And we are starting here today and we're going to resolve to continue this fight.

During the meetings that we held, we met with a young man who's here today—I think Colin Goddard is here. Where are you, Colin? Colin was one of the survivors of the Virginia Tech massacre. He was in the classroom. He calls himself one of the "lucky seven." And he'll tell you he was shot four times on that day and he has three bullets that are still inside him.

And when I asked Colin about what he thought we should be doing, he said, "I'm not here because of what happened to me. I'm here because of what happened to me keeps happening to other people and we have to do something about it."

Obama, Barack and Biden, Joe. Remarks delivered at South Court Auditorium, The White House, Washington, DC, on January 16, 2013.

Colin, we will. Colin, I promise you, we will. This is our intention. We must do what we can now. And there's no person who is more committed to acting on this moral obligation we have than the President of the United States of America.

Ladies and gentlemen, President Barack Obama. (Applause.)

THE PRESIDENT: Thank you, everybody. Please have a seat. Good afternoon, everybody.

Let me begin by thanking our Vice President, Joe Biden, for your dedication, Joe, to this issue, for bringing so many different voices to the table. Because while reducing gun violence is a complicated challenge, protecting our children from harm shouldn't be a divisive one.

Over the month since the tragedy in Newtown, we've heard from so many, and, obviously, none have affected us more than the families of those gorgeous children and their teachers and guardians who were lost. And so we're grateful to all of you for taking the time to be here, and recognizing that we honor their memories in part by doing everything we can to prevent this from happening again.

But we also heard from some unexpected people. In particular, I started getting a lot of letters from kids. Four of them are here today—Grant Fritz, Julia Stokes, Hinna Zeejah, and Teja Goode. They're pretty representative of some of the messages that I got. These are some pretty smart letters from some pretty smart young people.

Hinna, a third-grader—you can go ahead and wave, Hinna. That's you—(laughter.) Hinna wrote, "I feel terrible for the parents who lost their children . . . I love my country and [I] want everybody to be happy and safe."

And then, Grant—go ahead and wave, Grant. (Laughter.) Grant said, "I think there should be some changes. We should learn from what happened at Sandy Hook . . . I feel really bad."

And then, Julia said—Julia, where are you? There you go—"I'm not scared for my safety, I'm scared for others. I have four brothers and sisters and I know I would not be able to bear the thought of losing any of them."

These are our kids. This is what they're thinking about. And so what we should be thinking about is our responsibility to care for them, and shield them from harm, and give them the tools they need to grow up and do everything that they're capable of doing—not just to pursue their own dreams, but to help build this country. This is our first task as a society, keeping our children safe. This is how we will be judged. And their voices should compel us to change.

And that's why, last month, I asked Joe to lead an effort, along with members of my Cabinet, to come up with some concrete steps we can take right now to keep our children safe, to help prevent mass shootings, to reduce the broader epidemic of gun violence in this country.

And we can't put this off any longer. Just last Thursday, as TV networks were covering one of Joe's meetings on this topic, news broke of another school shooting, this one in California. In the month since 20 precious children and six brave adults were violently taken from us at Sandy Hook Elementary, more than 900 of our fellow Americans have reportedly died at the end of a gun—900 in the past month. And every day we wait, that number will keep growing.

So I'm putting forward a specific set of proposals based on the work of Joe's task force. And in the days ahead, I intend to use whatever weight this office holds to make them a reality. Because while there is no law or set of laws that can prevent every senseless act of violence completely, no piece of legislation that will prevent every tragedy, every act of evil, if there is even one thing we can do to reduce this violence, if there is even one life that can be saved, then we've got an obligation to try.

And I'm going to do my part. As soon as I'm finished speaking here, I will sit at that desk and I will sign a directive giving law enforcement, schools, mental health professionals and the public health community some of the tools they need to help reduce gun violence.

We will make it easier to keep guns out of the hands of criminals by strengthening the background check system. We will help schools hire more resource officers if they want them and develop emergency preparedness plans. We will make sure mental health professionals know their options for reporting threats of violence—even as we acknowledge that someone with a mental illness is far more likely to be a victim of violent crime than the perpetrator.

And while year after year, those who oppose even modest gun safety measures have threatened to defund scientific or medical research into the causes of gun violence, I will direct the Centers for Disease Control to go ahead and study the best ways to reduce it—and Congress should fund research into the effects that violent video games have on young minds. We don't benefit from ignorance. We don't benefit from not knowing the science of this epidemic of violence.

These are a few of the 23 executive actions that I'm announcing today. But as important as these steps are, they are in no way a substitute for action from members of Congress. To make a real and lasting difference, Congress, too, must act—and Congress must act soon. And I'm calling on Congress to pass some very specific proposals right away.

First: It's time for Congress to require a universal background check for anyone trying to buy a gun. (Applause.)

The law already requires licensed gun dealers to run background checks, and over the last 14 years that's kept 1.5 million of the wrong people from getting their hands on a gun. But it's hard to enforce that law when as many as 40 percent of all gun purchases are conducted without a background check. That's not safe. That's not smart. It's not fair to responsible gun buyers or sellers.

If you want to buy a gun—whether it's from a licensed dealer or a private seller—you should at least have to show you are not a felon or somebody legally prohibited from buying one. This is common sense. And an overwhelming majority of Americans agree with us on the need for universal background checks—including more than 70 percent of the National Rifle Association's members, according to one survey. So there's no reason we can't do this.

Second: Congress should restore a ban on military-style assault weapons, and a 10-round limit for magazines. (Applause.) The type of assault rifle used in Aurora, for example, when paired with high-capacity magazines, has one purpose—to pump out as many bullets as possible, as quickly as possible; to do as much damage, using bullets often designed to inflict maximum damage.

And that's what allowed the gunman in Aurora to shoot 70 people—70 people—killing 12 in a matter of minutes. Weapons designed for the theater of war have no place in a movie theater. A majority of Americans agree with us on this.

And, by the way, so did Ronald Reagan, one of the staunchest defenders of the Second Amendment, who wrote to Congress in 1994, urging them—this is Ronald Reagan speaking—urging them to "listen to the American public and to the law enforcement community and support a ban on the further manufacture of [military-style assault] weapons." (Applause.)

And finally, Congress needs to help, rather than hinder, law enforcement as it does its job. We should get tougher on people who buy guns with the express purpose of turning around and selling them to criminals. And we should severely punish anybody who helps them do this. Since Congress hasn't confirmed a director of the Bureau of Alcohol, Tobacco and Firearms in six years, they should confirm Todd Jones, who will be—who has been Acting, and I will be nominating for the post. (Applause.)

And at a time when budget cuts are forcing many communities to reduce their police force, we should put more cops back on the job and back on our streets.

Let me be absolutely clear. Like most Americans, I believe the Second Amendment guarantees an individual right to bear arms. I respect our strong tradition of gun ownership and the rights of hunters and sportsmen. There are millions of responsible, law-abiding gun owners in America who cherish their right to bear arms for hunting, or sport, or protection, or collection.

I also believe most gun owners agree that we can respect the Second Amendment while keeping an irresponsible, law-breaking few from inflicting harm on a massive scale. I believe most of them agree that if America worked harder to keep guns out of the hands of dangerous people, there would be fewer atrocities like the one that occurred in Newtown. That's what these reforms are designed to do. They're common-sense measures. They have the support of the majority of the American people.

And yet, that doesn't mean any of this is going to be easy to enact or implement. If it were, we'd already have universal background checks. The ban on assault weapons and high-capacity magazines never would have been allowed to expire. More of our fellow Americans might still be alive, celebrating birthdays and anniversaries and graduations.

This will be difficult. There will be pundits and politicians and special interest lobbyists publicly warning of a tyrannical, all-out assault on liberty—not because that's true, but because they want to gin up fear or higher ratings or revenue for themselves. And behind the scenes, they'll do everything they can to block any common-sense reform and make sure nothing changes whatsoever.

The only way we will be able to change is if their audience, their constituents, their membership says this time must be different—that this time, we must do something to protect our communities and our kids.

I will put everything I've got into this, and so will Joe. But I tell you, the only way we can change is if the American people demand it. And by the way, that doesn't just mean from certain parts of the country. We're going to need voices in those areas, in those congressional districts, where the tradition of gun ownership is strong to speak up and to say this is important. It can't just be the usual suspects. We have to examine ourselves and our hearts, and ask ourselves what is important.

This will not happen unless the American people demand it. If parents and teachers, police officers and pastors, if hunters and sportsmen, if responsible gun owners, if Americans of every background stand up and say, enough; we've suffered too much pain and care too much about our children to allow this to continue—then change will come. That's what it's going to take.

In the letter that Julia wrote me, she said, "I know that laws have to be passed by Congress, but I beg you to try very hard." (Laughter.) Julia, I will try very hard. But she's right. The most important changes we can make depend on congressional action. They need to bring these proposals up for a vote, and the American people need to make sure that they do.

Get them on record. Ask your member of Congress if they support universal background checks to keep guns out of the wrong hands. Ask them if they support renewing a ban on military-style assault weapons and high-capacity magazines. And if they say no, ask them why not. Ask them what's more important—doing whatever it takes to get a A grade from the gun lobby that funds their campaigns, or giving parents some peace of mind when they drop their child off for first grade? (Applause.)

This is the land of the free, and it always will be. As Americans, we are endowed by our Creator with certain inalienable rights that no man or government can take away from us. But we've also long recognized, as our Founders recognized, that with rights come responsibilities. Along with our freedom to live our lives as we will comes an obligation to allow others to do the same. We don't live in isolation. We live in a society, a government of, and by, and for the people. We are responsible for each other.

The right to worship freely and safely, that right was denied to Sikhs in Oak Creek, Wisconsin. The right to assemble peaceably, that right was denied [to] shoppers in Clackamas, Oregon, and moviegoers in Aurora, Colorado. That most fundamental set of rights to life and liberty and the pursuit of happiness—fundamental rights that were denied to college students at Virginia Tech, and high school students at Columbine, and elementary school students in Newtown, and kids on street corners in Chicago on too frequent a basis to tolerate, and all the families who've never imagined that they'd lose a loved one to a bullet—those rights are at stake. We're responsible.

When I visited Newtown last month, I spent some private time with many of the families who lost their children that day. And one was the family of Grace McDonald. Grace's parents are here. Grace was seven years old when she was struck down—just a gorgeous, caring, joyful little girl. I'm told she loved pink. She loved the beach. She dreamed of becoming a painter.

And so just before I left, Chris, her father, gave me one of her paintings, and I hung it in my private study just off the Oval Office. And every time I look at that painting, I think about Grace. And I think about the life that she lived and the life that lay ahead of her, and most of all, I think about how, when it comes to protecting the most vulnerable among us, we must act now—for Grace. For the 25 other innocent children and devoted educators who had so much left to give. For the men and women in big cities and small towns who fall victim to senseless violence each and every day. For all the Americans who are counting on us to keep them safe from harm. Let's do the right thing. Let's do the right thing for them, and for this country that we love so much.

BARACK OBAMA served as U.S. Senator for Illinois prior to defeating John McCain in the 2008 presidential election to become the 44th President of the United States. He is the first African American to hold the position. In 2012, President Obama defeated Republican challenger Mitt Romney to win a second term.

JOE BIDEN is Vice President of the United States. He is a member of the Democratic Party and was a United States Senator from Delaware from January 3, 1973, until his resignation on January 15, 2009, following his election to the Vice Presidency. In 2012, Biden was elected to a second term alongside Obama.

Jeffrey Goldberg  **NO**

The Case for More Guns (and More Gun Control)

How Do We Reduce Gun Crime and Aurora-Style Mass Shootings When Americans Already Own Nearly 300 Million Firearms? Maybe by Allowing More People to Carry Them

The Century 16 Cineplex in Aurora, Colorado, stands desolate behind a temporary green fence, which was raised to protect the theater from prying eyes and mischief-makers. The parking lots that surround the multiplex are empty—weeds are pushing through the asphalt—and the only person at the theater when I visited a few weeks ago was an enervated Aurora police officer assigned to guard the site.

I asked the officer whether the building, which has stood empty since the night of July 20, when a former graduate student named James E. Holmes is alleged to have killed 12 people and wounded 58 others at a midnight showing of *The Dark Knight Rises*, still drew the curious. "People drive by to look," he said, but "not too many." The Aurora massacre is noteworthy, even in the crowded field of mass shootings, as one of the more wretched and demoralizing in the recent history of American violence, and I was surprised that the scene of the crime did not attract more attention. "I guess people move on," he said.

I walked up a slight rise that provided an imperfect view of the back of Theater 9, where the massacre took place, and tried to imagine the precise emotions the victims felt as the gunfire erupted.

"The shooting started at a quiet moment in the movie," Stephen Barton told me. He was shot in the opening fusillade. "I saw this canister-type thing, a smoking object, streak across the screen. I thought it was a kid with fireworks playing a prank."

Barton is 22 years old. He had been preparing to leave for Russia this fall on a Fulbright scholarship. "The first feeling I remember was bewilderment. I don't remember having a single thought before I was shot, because I was shot early on. I was sitting in the middle of the row,

toward the back. I got blasted in my head, neck, and face—my whole upper body—by shotgun pellets."

As he lay wounded on the floor by his seat, he said, his bafflement gave way to panic. "I had this unwillingness to accept that this was actually happening. I wanted to believe that there was no way that someone in the same room as me was shooting at people," he said. "So it was disbelief and also this really strong feeling that I'm not ready to die. I'm at someone else's mercy. I've never felt more helpless."

In the chaos of smoke and gunshots, Barton saw the emergency exit door open, and managed to escape into the parking lot. "If I hadn't seen that door, I might not have made it," he said.

I left the theater and drove into Denver, to meet a man named Tom Mauser, who lost a son in the 1999 massacre at Columbine High School, 19 miles from the Aurora theater.

Daniel Mauser, who was 15 years old when he died, tried to hide from the Columbine killers, Eric Harris and Dylan Klebold. Harris found the boy under a table in the school library. A classmate told *The Denver Post* shortly after the massacre, "Eric shot him once, and Daniel pushed chairs at him to try to make him stop, and Eric shot him again."

After the murder of his son, Tom Mauser became a gun-control activist. In the days after Columbine, advocates of more-stringent controls of firearms thought they could feel a shift in the culture. People were disgusted that Harris and Klebold, neither of whom was of the legal age to buy firearms, had found a way to acquire guns: an 18-year-old woman, a friend of the two shooters, bought three weapons legally at a gun show, where federal background checks were not required.

After Columbine, Colorado closed its "gun-show loophole," but efforts to close the loophole on the national level failed. The National Rifle Association and other anti-gun-control groups worked diligently to defend the loophole—misnamed, because while *loophole* suggests a small opening not easily negotiated, about 40 percent of all legal gun sales take place at gun shows, on the Internet, or through more-informal sales between private sellers and buyers, where buyers are not subject to federal background checks. Though anti-loophole legislation passed the U.S. Senate, it was defeated in the House of Representatives. On top of that, the 1994 ban on sales of certain types of semiautomatic weapons, known as the assault-weapons ban, expired in 2004 and was not reauthorized.

After the Aurora shooting, gun-control activists who expected politicians to rise up in outrage were quickly disappointed. Shortly after the massacre, John Hickenlooper, the Democratic governor of Colorado, suggested that stricter gun laws would not have stopped the shooter. "If there were no assault weapons available and no this or no that, this guy is going to find something, right?," Hickenlooper said. "He's going to know how to create a bomb."

Hickenlooper's statement helped Mauser realize that his side was losing the fight. "I had deep anger when I heard that," he told me. "I heard the same kinds of statements from some people after Columbine: 'Well, you know, they had bombs, too.' The fact is that the deaths were from guns."

Mauser believes the public has grown numb to mass violence. "People say 'How tragic' and then move on," he said. "They're told by their governor, their political leaders, that there's no solution. So they don't see a solution out there."

According to a 2011 Gallup poll, 47 percent of American adults keep at least one gun at home or on their property, and many of these gun owners are absolutists opposed to any government regulation of firearms. According to the same poll, only 26 percent of Americans support a ban on handguns.

To that 26 percent, American gun culture can seem utterly inexplicable, its very existence dispiriting. Guns are responsible for roughly 30,000 deaths a year in America; more than half of those deaths are suicides. In 2010, 606 people, 62 of them children younger than 15, died in accidental shootings.

Mauser expresses disbelief that the number of gun deaths fails to shock. He blames the American attachment to guns on ignorance, and on immaturity. "We're a pretty new nation," he told me. "We're still at the stage of rebellious teenager, and we don't like it when the government tells us what to do. People don't trust government to do what's right. They are very attracted to the idea of a nation of individuals, so they don't think about what's good for the collective."

Mauser said that if the United States were as mature as the countries of Europe, where strict gun control is the norm, the federal government would have a much easier time curtailing the average citizen's access to weapons. "The people themselves would understand that having guns around puts them in more danger."

There are ways, of course, to make it at least marginally more difficult for the criminally minded, for the dangerously mentally ill, and for the suicidal to buy guns and ammunition. The gun-show loophole could be closed. Longer waiting periods might stop some suicides. Mental-health professionals could be encouraged—or mandated—to report patients they suspect shouldn't own guns to the FBI-supervised National Instant Criminal Background Check System, although this would generate fierce opposition from doctors and patients. Background checks, which are conducted by licensed gun shops, have stopped almost 1 million people from buying guns at these stores since 1998. (No one knows, of course, how many of these people gave up their search for a gun, and how many simply went to a gun show or found another way to acquire a weapon.)

Other measures could be taken as well. Drum-style magazines like the kind James Holmes had that night in Aurora, which can hold up to 100 rounds of ammunition and which make continuous firing easy, have no reasonable civilian purpose, and their sale could be restricted without violating the Second Amendment rights of individual gun owners.

But these gun-control efforts, while noble, would only have a modest impact on the rate of gun violence in America.

Why?

Because it's too late.

There are an estimated 280 million to 300 million guns in private hands in America—many legally owned, many not. Each year, more than 4 million new guns enter the market. This level of gun saturation has occurred not because the anti-gun lobby has been consistently outflanked by its adversaries in the National Rifle Association, though it has been. The NRA is quite obviously a powerful organization, but like many effective pressure groups, it is powerful in good part because so many Americans are predisposed to agree with its basic message.

America's level of gun ownership means that even if the Supreme Court—which ruled in 2008 that the Second Amendment gives citizens the individual right to own firearms, as gun advocates have long insisted—suddenly reversed itself and ruled that the individual ownership of handguns was illegal, there would be no practical way for a democratic country to locate and seize those guns.

Many gun-control advocates, and particularly advocates of a total gun ban, would like to see the United States become more like Canada, where there are far fewer guns per capita and where most guns must be registered with the federal government. The Canadian approach to firearms ownership has many attractions—the country's firearm homicide rate is one-sixth that of the U.S. But barring a decision by the American people and their legislators to remove the right to bear arms from the Constitution, arguing for applying the Canadian approach in the U.S. is useless.

Even the leading advocacy group for stricter gun laws, the Brady Campaign to Prevent Gun Violence, has given up the struggle to convince the courts, and the public, that the Constitution grants only members of a militia the right to bear arms. "I'm happy to consider the debate on the Second Amendment closed," Dan Gross, the Brady Campaign's president, told me recently. "Reopening that debate is not what we should be doing. We have to respect the fact that a lot of decent, law-abiding people believe in gun ownership."

Which raises a question: When even anti-gun activists believe that the debate over private gun ownership is closed; when it is too late to reduce the number of guns in private hands—and since only the naive think that legislation will prevent more than a modest number of the criminally minded, and the mentally deranged, from acquiring a gun in a country absolutely inundated with weapons—could it be that an effective way to combat guns is with more guns?

Today, more than 8 million vetted and (depending on the state) trained law-abiding citizens possess state-issued "concealed carry" handgun permits, which allow them to carry a concealed handgun or other weapon in public. Anti-gun activists believe the expansion of concealed-carry permits represents a serious threat to public order. But what if, in fact, the reverse is true? Mightn't allowing more law-abiding private citizens to carry concealed weapons—when combined with other forms of stringent gun regulation—actually reduce gun violence?

This thought has been with me for nearly two decades. On December 7, 1993, a bitter and unstable man named Colin Ferguson boarded an eastbound Long Island Rail Road train at the Jamaica, Queens, station. As the train pulled into the Merillon Avenue station in Nassau County, Ferguson pulled out a Ruger 9 mm pistol he had bought legally in California (which had a 15-day waiting period) and began walking down the aisle, calmly shooting pas-

sengers as he went. He killed six people and wounded 19 others before three passengers tackled him while he was reloading.

I had been an LIRR commuter not long before this happened, and I remember clearly my reaction to the slaughter, and I remember as well the reaction of many New York politicians. Much of the political class, and many editorialists, were of the view that the LIRR massacre proved the need for stricter gun control, and even for the banning of handguns. I shared—and continue to share—the view that muscular gun-control regulations, ones that put stumbling blocks in front of criminals seeking firearms, are necessary. But I was also seized by the thought that, had I been on the train, I would much rather have been armed than unarmed. I was not, and am not, under the illusion that a handgun would have necessarily provided a definitive solution to the problem posed by Colin Ferguson. But my instinct was that if someone is shooting at you, it is generally better to shoot back than to cower and pray.

Would a civilian firing back at Ferguson have wounded or killed innocent people? Quite possibly yes. Is that a risk potential victims quaking under train seats or classroom desks might accept? Quite possibly yes. Especially when you consider the massacres that have been prevented or interrupted by armed civilians before the police arrived.

Many of the worst American massacres end not in the capture of the gunman but in his suicide. In the 2007 mass shooting at Virginia Tech, for instance, the gunman, Seung-Hui Cho, killed himself as the police were set to capture him. But in other cases, massacres were stopped early by the intervention of armed civilians, or off-duty or retired police officers who happened to be nearby.

In 1997, a disturbed high-school student named Luke Woodham stabbed his mother and then shot and killed two people at Pearl High School in Pearl, Mississippi. He then began driving toward a nearby junior high to continue his shooting spree, but the assistant principal of the high school, Joel Myrick, aimed a pistol he kept in his truck at Woodham, causing him to veer off the road. Myrick then put his pistol to Woodham's neck and disarmed him. On January 16, 2002, a disgruntled former student at the Appalachian School of Law in Grundy, Virginia, had killed three people, including the school's dean, when two students, both off-duty law-enforcement officers, retrieved their weapons and pointed them at the shooter, who ended his killing spree and surrendered. In December 2007, a man armed with a semiautomatic rifle and two pistols entered the New Life Church in Colorado Springs and killed two teenage girls before a church member, Jeanne Assam—a former Minneapolis police officer and a volunteer church security guard—shot and wounded the gunman, who then killed himself.

And so I put a question to Stephen Barton, who described feeling helpless in the Aurora theater: Would he rather have been armed, or at least been in the theater with armed patrons, when the massacre started?

"Intuitively it makes sense for people to have that reaction, to want to defend themselves," he said. "It's easy to say that if more people had guns to defend themselves, they could take criminals down, but I don't think concealed-carry weapons are the answer." In a dark and crowded theater, he said, facing someone wearing bullet-resistant armor on much of his body, a gun, even in trained hands, would have been unlikely to do much good.

I put to Tom Mauser a variation of the question I had asked Barton. What if a teacher or an administrator inside Columbine High School had been armed on the day of the massacre? Unlike the theater in Aurora, the school was brightly lit, and not as densely packed. If someone with a gun had confronted Harris and Klebold in the library, he or she would have been able, at the very least, to distract the killers—perhaps even long enough for them to be tackled or disarmed.

"That kind of speculation doesn't solve anything," Mauser said. "I don't know if that person might have shot my son accidentally."

But the worst thing that could have happened to Daniel Mauser did, in fact, happen. The presence in the Columbine library of a well-trained, armed civilian attempting to stop the killers could hardly have made the situation worse. Indeed, the local police—who waited 45 minutes to enter the school, while a SWAT team assembled—were severely criticized for the delay.

But Mauser remained implacable. "We know that if the country adopts this vision that everyone should be armed—that administrators and janitors in school are armed, that people are walking around armed—we won't be safe," Mauser told me. "In Aurora, if five people in that theater had guns, they could have just ended up shooting each other or innocent people in the crossfire. It just makes sense that if people are walking around armed, you're going to have a high rate of people shooting each other."

Earlier this year, a man who was upset with the anti-gay-rights position of the Family Research Council entered the group's Washington, D.C., headquarters and allegedly shot and wounded the building manager (who subsequently tackled the gunman). At the time, Washington's mayor, Vincent Gray, said: "We don't need to make more guns available to people. . . . The more access they have, the more they threaten people."

The District of Columbia does not allow for concealed carry, though its residents can now apply for a license allowing them to keep handguns at home, thanks to the 2008 Supreme Court ruling in a case brought on behalf of a D.C. man who wanted a gun for self-protection.

I called Gray to ask him about his assertion that more guns mean more violence, noting that he himself travels the city with armed police bodyguards, a service not afforded the typical Washington resident. "Well, first of all, I've never even seen the guns that the security people have. When I travel outside the city, I don't have security. I would be fine without security," he said. "But we have 3,800 police officers to protect people. They may not be at someone's side at every moment, but they're around."

I asked him whether he could envision a scenario in which an armed civilian might be able to stop a crime from occurring. "There are those who believe that if they have a weapon, they can combat crime, but I don't think that way," he said.

The police, of course, have guns to stop crime. So why couldn't a well-trained civilian also stop crime? "If you have a gun on you, that's just another opportunity to use it," Gray said. "It's the temptation of the moment. I just think the opportunity is there to create more violence."

In 2004, the Ohio legislature passed a law allowing private citizens to apply for permits to carry firearms outside the home. The decision to allow concealed carry was, of course, a controversial one. Law-enforcement organizations, among others, argued that an armed population would create chaos in the streets. In 2003, John Gilchrist, the legislative counsel for the Ohio Association of Chiefs of Police, testified, "If 200,000 to 300,000 citizens begin carrying a concealed weapon, common sense tells us that accidents will become a daily event."

When I called Gilchrist recently, he told me that events since the state's concealed-carry law took effect have proved his point. "Talking to the chiefs, I know that there is more gun violence and accidents involving guns," he said. "I think there's more gun violence now because there are more guns. People are using guns in the heat of arguments, and there wouldn't be as much gun violence if we didn't have people carrying weapons. If you've got people walking around in a bad mood—or in a divorce, they've lost their job—and they get into a confrontation, this could result in the use of a gun. If you talk to emergency-room physicians in the state, [they] see more and more people with gunshot wounds."

Gilchrist said he did not know the exact statistics on gun-related incidents (or on incidents concerning concealed-carry permit holders specifically, because the state keeps the names of permit holders confidential).

He says, however, that he tracks gun usage anecdotally. "You can look in the newspaper. I consciously look for stories that deal with guns. There are more and more articles in *The Columbus Dispatch* about people using guns inappropriately."

Gilchrist's argument would be convincing but for one thing: the firearm crime rate in Ohio remained steady after the concealed-carry law passed in 2004.

It is an unexamined assumption on the part of gun-control activists that the possession of a firearm by a law-abiding person will almost axiomatically cause that person to fire it at another human being in a moment of stress. Dave Kopel, the research director of the libertarian-leaning Independence Institute, in Denver, posits that opposition to gun ownership is ideological, not rational. "I use gay marriage as an analogue," he said. "Some people say they are against gay marriage because they think it leads to worse outcomes for kids. Now, let's say in 2020 all the social-science evidence has it that the kids of gay families turn out fine. Some people will still say they're against it, not for reasons of social science, but for reasons of faith. That's what you have here in the gun issue."

There is no proof to support the idea that concealed-carry permit holders create more violence in society than would otherwise occur; they may, in fact, reduce it. According to Adam Winkler, a law professor at UCLA and the author of *Gunfight: The Battle Over the Right to Bear Arms in America*, permit holders in the U.S. commit crimes at a rate lower than that of the general population. "We don't see much bloodshed from concealed-carry permit holders, because they are law-abiding people," Winkler said. "That's not to say that permit holders don't commit crimes, but they do so at a lower rate than the general population. People who seek to obtain permits are likely to be people who respect the law." According to John Lott, an economist and a gun-rights advocate who maintains that gun ownership by law-abiding citizens helps curtail crime, the crime rate among concealed-carry permit holders is lower than the crime rate among police officers.

Today, the number of concealed-carry permits is the highest it's ever been, at 8 million, and the homicide rate is the lowest it's been in four decades—less than half what it was 20 years ago. (The number of people allowed to carry concealed weapons is actually considerably higher than 8 million, because residents of Vermont, Wyoming, Arizona, Alaska, and parts of Montana do not need government permission to carry their personal firearms. These states have what Second Amendment absolutists refer to as "constitutional carry," meaning, in essence, that the Second Amendment is their permit.)

Many gun-rights advocates see a link between an increasingly armed public and a decreasing crime rate. "I think effective law enforcement has had the biggest impact on crime rates, but I think concealed carry has something to do with it. We've seen an explosion in the number of people licensed to carry," Lott told me. "You can deter criminality through longer sentencing, and you deter criminality by making it riskier for people to commit crimes. And one way to make it riskier is to create the impression among the criminal population that the law-abiding citizen they want to target may have a gun."

Crime statistics in Britain, where guns are much scarcer, bear this out. Gary Kleck, a criminologist at Florida State University, wrote in his 1991 book, *Point Blank: Guns and Violence in America*, that only 13 percent of burglaries in America occur when the occupant is home. In Britain, so-called hot burglaries account for about 45 percent of all break-ins. Kleck and others attribute America's low rate of occupied-home burglaries to fear among criminals that homeowners might be armed. (A survey of almost 2,000 convicted U.S. felons, conducted by the criminologists Peter Rossi and James D. Wright in the late '80s, concluded that burglars are more afraid of armed homeowners than they are of arrest by the police.)

Others contend that proving causality between crime rates and the number of concealed-carry permits is impossible. "It's difficult to make the case that more concealed-carry guns have led to the drop in the national crime rate, because cities like Los Angeles, where we have very restrictive gun-control laws, have seen the same remarkable drop in crime," Winkler told me. (Many criminologists tend to attribute America's dramatic decrease in violent crime to a combination of demographic changes, longer criminal sentencing, innovative policing techniques, and the waning of the crack wars.)

But it is, in fact, possible to assess with some degree of accuracy how many crimes have been stopped because the intended victim, or a witness, was armed. In the 1990s, Gary Kleck and a fellow criminologist, Marc Gertz, began studying the issue and came to the conclusion that guns were used defensively between 830,000 and 2.45 million times each year.

In only a minority of these cases was a gun fired; the brandishing of a gun in front of a would-be mugger or burglar is usually enough to abort a crime in progress. Another study, the federal government's National Crime Victimization Survey, asked victims of crimes whether they, or someone else, had used a gun in their defense. This study came up with a more modest number than Kleck and Gertz, finding 108,000 defensive uses of firearms a year.

All of these studies, of course, have been contested by gun-control advocates. So I asked Winkler what he thought. He said that while he is skeptical of the 2.45 million figure, even the smaller number is compelling: 108,000 "would represent a significant reduction in criminal activity."

Universities, more than most other institutions, are nearly unified in their prohibition of licensed concealed-carry weapons. Some even post notices stating that their campuses are gun-free zones. At the same time, universities also acknowledge that they are unable to protect their students from lethal assault. How do they do this? By recommending measures that students and faculty members can take if confronted by an "active shooter," as in the massacre at Virginia Tech.

These recommendations make for depressing reading, and not only because they reflect a world in which random killing in tranquil settings is a genuine, if rare, possibility. They are also depressing because they reflect a denial of reality.

Here are some of the recommendations:

- Wichita State University counsels students in the following manner: "If the person(s) is causing death or serious physical injury to others and you are unable to run or hide you may choose to be compliant, play dead, or fight for your life."
- The University of Miami guidelines suggest that when all else fails, students should act "as aggressively as possible" against a shooter. The guidelines, taken from a Department of Homeland Security directive, also recommend "throwing items and improvising weapons," as well as "yelling."
- Otterbein University, in Ohio, tells students to "breathe to manage your fear" and informs them, "You may have to take the offensive if the shooter(s) enter your area. Gather weapons (pens, pencils, books, chairs, etc.) and mentally prepare your attack."
- West Virginia University advises students that if the situation is dire, they should "act with physical aggression and throw items at the active shooter." These items could include "student desks, keys, shoes, belts, books, cell phones, iPods, book bags, laptops, pens, pencils, etc."
- The University of Colorado at Boulder's guidelines state, "You and classmates or friends may find yourselves in a situation where the shooter will accost you. If such an event occurs, quickly develop a plan to attack the shooter. . . . Consider a plan to tackle the shooter, take away his weapon, and hold him until police arrive."

It is, of course, possible to distract a heavily armed psychotic on a suicide mission by throwing an iPod at him, or a pencil. But it is more likely that the psychotic would respond by shooting the pencil thrower.

The existence of these policies suggests that universities know they cannot protect their students during an armed attack. (At Virginia Tech, the gunman killed 30 students and faculty members in the 10 minutes it took the police to arrive and penetrate the building he had blockaded.) And yet, these schools will not allow adults with state-issued concealed-carry permits to bring their weapons onto campus, as they would be able to almost anywhere else. "Possession or storage of a deadly weapon, destructive device, or fireworks in any form . . . is prohibited," West Virginia University's policy states.

To gun-rights advocates, these policies are absurd. "The fact that universities are providing their faculties and students with this sort of information is, of course, an admission that they can't protect them," Dave Kopel told me. "The universities are unable to protect people, but then they disable people from protecting themselves."

It is also illogical for campuses to advertise themselves as "gun-free." Someone bent on murder is not usually dissuaded by posted anti-gun regulations. Quite the opposite—publicly describing your property as gun-free is analogous to posting a notice on your front door saying your home has no burglar alarm. As it happens, the company that owns the Century 16 Cineplex in Aurora had declared the property a gun-free zone.

"As a security measure, it doesn't seem like advertising that fact is a good idea," Adam Winkler says of avowedly gun-free campuses, though he adds that "advertising a school's gun-free status does provide notice to potentially immature youth that they're not allowed to have guns."

In Colorado, the epicenter of the American gun argument, the state supreme court recently ruled that the University of Colorado must lift its ban on the carrying of concealed handguns by owners who have been licensed by local sheriffs. (The university has responded by requiring students who own guns to move to a specified housing complex.) The ruling has caused anxiety among some faculty. The chairman of the faculty assembly, a physics professor named Jerry Peterson, told the Boulder *Daily Camera*, "My own personal policy in my classes is if I am aware that there is a firearm in the class—registered or unregistered, concealed or unconcealed—the class session is immediately canceled. I want my students to feel unconstrained in their discussions."

Peterson makes two assumptions: The first is that he will know whether someone is carrying a concealed weapon in class. The second is that students will feel frightened about sharing their opinions if a gun is present. (I could find no evidence that any American educational institution has ever seen fatalities or serious gun-related injuries result from a heated classroom discussion.)

Claire Levy, a Colorado state legislator, says she intends to introduce a bill that would ban guns once again. "If discussions in class escalated," she argues, "the mere fact that someone is potentially armed could have an inhibiting effect on the classroom, This is genuinely scary to faculty members." The push to open up campuses to concealed-carry permit holders, Levy says, is motivated by ideological gun-rights advocacy, rather than an actual concern for campus safety. Guns, even those owned by licensed and trained individuals, she insists, would simply make a campus more dangerous. "American campuses are the safest places to be in the whole world," she said. "The homicide rate on campuses is a small fraction of the rate in the rest of the country. So there's no actual rational public-safety reason that anyone would need to bring a gun on campus."

However, the University of Colorado's own active-shooter recommendations state:

> Active harming incidents have occurred at a number of locations in recent years, and the University of Colorado is not immune to this potential. While the odds of this occurring at CU are small, the consequences are so potentially catastrophic it makes sense for all students, staff, faculty and visitors to CU to consider the possibility of such an incident occurring here.

In making her argument against concealed-carry weapons to me, Levy painted a bit of a contradictory picture: On the one hand, campuses are the safest places in the country. On the other hand, campus life is so inherently dangerous that the introduction of even licensed guns could mean mayhem. "You're in this milieu of drugs and alcohol and impulsive behavior and mental illness; you've got a population that has a high propensity for suicide," she told me. "Theft is a big concern, and what if you had a concealed-carry gun and you're drinking and become violent?"

For much of the population of a typical campus, concealed-carry permitting is not an issue. Most states that issue permits will grant them only to people who are at least 21 years old. But the crime-rate statistics at universities that do allow permit holders on campus with their weapons are instructive. An hour north of Boulder, in Fort Collins, sits Colorado State University. Concealed carry has been allowed at CSU since 2003, and according to James Alderden, the former sheriff of Larimer County,

which encompasses Fort Collins, violent crime at Colorado State has dropped since then.

Despite the fact that CSU experienced no violent incidents involving concealed-carry permit holders, the university governing board voted two years ago to ban concealed carry. The ban never went into effect, however, because the state appeals court soon ruled against a similar ban at the University of Colorado, and because Sheriff Alderden announced that he would undermine the ban by refusing to process any violator in the county jail, which serves the university's police department.

Alderden, who recently retired, told me that opponents of concealed carry "make an emotional argument rather than a logical one. No one could show me any study that concealed carry leads to more crime and more violence. My idea of self-defense is not those red rape phones on campus, where you get to the phone and tell someone you're getting raped. I have a daughter, and I'd rather have her have the ability to defend herself. I'm not going to violate a citizen's right to self-defense because someone else has an emotional feeling about guns."

Though Colorado is slowly shading blue, Alderden said he believes most of its residents "still don't rely on the government to protect them." He added: "Maybe in Boulder they do, but most people believe they have a right to self-defense."

Boulder may be the locus of left-wing politics in Colorado, but it is also home to the oversubscribed Boulder Rifle Club, which I visited on a bright early-fall morning with Dave Kopel, of the Independence Institute. The existence of the rifle club surprised me, given Boulder's reputation. But Kopel argued that gun ownership and sport shooting are not partisan phenomena, and he made the plausible assertion that Boulder is home to "the largest population of armed vegans in America."

I wanted to understand from Kopel the best arguments against government intervention in gun ownership, and Kopel wanted to fire some of the many handguns he owns, so we alternately talked and shot. Kopel brought with him a bag of guns: a Ruger Mark II .22 LR pistol; a Springfield Armory XD-9 9 mm; a Glock 9 mm; a Springfield Armory 1911 tactical-response pistol (similar to a Colt .45); and a Ruger Alaskan .45 revolver, powerful enough to drop a bear. The Ruger Alaskan is the most powerful weapon we used, but the act of firing even a .22 underscores for most thinking people the notion that firing a gun is a serious business. Kopel argued that a law-abiding citizen is less likely to get into a confrontation after a traffic accident or an exchange of insults if he or she is carrying a weapon: "You're aware of the power you have, and you naturally want to use that power very carefully."

I expressed to Kopel my concern that the overly lax standards some states set for concealed-carry permitting means that the occasional cowboy gets passed through the system. Florida—which has among the most relaxed standards for gun permitting, and granted a license to George Zimmerman, who famously killed Trayvon Martin, apparently during an exercise in freelance vigilantism—is a case in point. (Zimmerman has pled not guilty, claiming he shot Martin in self-defense.) Applicants in Florida must submit to a background check, take a brief class, and pay $112 to obtain a license.

In Colorado, the standards are slightly more stringent. Permit seekers must submit to criminal checks, fingerprinting, and safety classes, but in addition, they must pass what James Alderden referred to as the "naked man" rule: if a local sheriff learns that a person has no criminal record, and has not been deemed mentally ill, but nevertheless was, say, found naked one night in a field howling at the moon, the sheriff is granted the discretion to deny that person a permit.

Kopel argued, correctly, that Florida, like Colorado, has seen a drop in crime since 1987, when it started granting concealed-carry permits—which suggests to him that permit holders are not, in the main, engaging in crime sprees or taking the law into their own hands. But for Kopel, the rigor, or laxity, of the permitting process from state to state is not his principal concern, because he believes that in most cases, the government has no right to interfere with an adult's decision to buy or carry a weapon. Those who seek to curtail gun rights, he insists, are promoting the infantilization of Americans.

"If they get their way," he said of the anti-gun forces, "people who are the victims of violent crimes wouldn't be able to fight back; women who are abused couldn't protect themselves; criminals will know that their intended victims, who have no access to the black market, will be unable to defend themselves.

"It's more than that," he went on. "Telling the population that they are incapable of owning a tool that can be dangerous means you are creating a population that loses its self-reliance and increasingly sees itself as wards of the state."

James Alderden put it another way: "Your position on concealed-carry permits has a lot to do with your position on the reliability and sanity of your fellow man."

The ideology of gun-ownership absolutism doesn't appeal to me. Unlike hard-line gun-rights advocates, I do not believe that unregulated gun ownership is a defense against the rise of totalitarianism in America, because I do not think that America is ripe for totalitarianism. (Fear of

a tyrannical, gun-seizing president is the reason many gun owners oppose firearms registration.)

But I am sympathetic to the idea of armed self-defense, because it does often work, because encouraging learned helplessness is morally corrupt, and because, however much I might wish it, the United States is not going to become Canada. Guns are with us, whether we like it or not. Maybe this is tragic, but it is also reality. So Americans who are qualified to possess firearms shouldn't be denied the right to participate in their own defense. And it is empirically true that the great majority of America's tens of millions of law-abiding gun owners have not created chaos in society.

A balanced approach to gun control in the United States would require the warring sides to agree on several contentious issues. Conservative gun-rights advocates should acknowledge that if more states had stringent universal background checks—or if a federal law put these in place—more guns would be kept out of the hands of criminals and the dangerously mentally unstable. They should also acknowledge that requiring background checks on buyers at gun shows would not represent a threat to the Constitution. "The NRA position on this is a fiction," says Dan Gross, the head of the Brady Campaign. "Universal background checks are not an infringement on our Second Amendment rights. This is black-helicopter stuff." Gross believes that closing the gun-show loophole would be both extremely effective and a politically moderate and achievable goal. The gun lobby must also agree that concealed-carry permits should be granted only to people who pass rigorous criminal checks, as well as thorough training-and-safety courses.

Anti-gun advocates, meanwhile, should acknowledge that gun-control legislation is not the only answer to gun violence. Responsible gun ownership is also an answer. An enormous number of Americans believe this to be the case, and gun-control advocates do themselves no favors when they demonize gun owners, and advocates of armed self-defense, as backwoods barbarians. Liberals sometimes make the mistake of anthropomorphizing guns, ascribing to them moral characteristics they do not possess. Guns can be used to do evil, but guns can also be used to do good. Twelve years ago, in the aftermath of Matthew Shepard's murder, Jonathan Rauch launched a national movement when he wrote an article for *Salon* arguing that gay people should arm themselves against violent bigots. Pink Pistol clubs sprang up across America, in which gays and lesbians learn to use firearms in self-defense. Other vulnerable groups have also taken to the idea of concealed carry: in Texas, African American women represent the largest percentage increase of concealed-carry permit seekers since 2000.

But even some moderate gun-control activists, such as Dan Gross, have trouble accepting that guns in private hands can work effectively to counteract violence. When I asked him the question I posed to Stephen Barton and Tom Mauser—would you, at a moment when a stranger is shooting at you, prefer to have a gun, or not?—he answered by saying, "This is the conversation the gun lobby wants you to be having." He pointed out some of the obvious flaws in concealed-carry laws, such as too-lax training standards and too much discretionary power on the part of local law-enforcement officials. He did say that if concealed-carry laws required background checks and training similar to what police recruits undergo, he would

be slower to raise objections. But then he added: "In a fundamental way, isn't this a question about the kind of society we want to live in?" Do we want to live in one "in which the answer to violence is more violence, where the answer to guns is more guns?"

What Gross won't acknowledge is that in a nation of nearly 300 million guns, his question is irrelevant.

JEFFREY GOLDBERG is a national correspondent for *The Atlantic* Magazine and a recipient of the National Magazine Award for Reporting. Author of the book *Prisoners: A Story of Friendship and Terror*, Goldberg also writes the magazine's advice column.

EXPLORING THE ISSUE

Should the United States Be More Restrictive of Gun Ownership?

Critical Thinking and Reflection

1. What are the arguments for placing greater restrictions on gun ownership in the United States? Which argument do you believe is most persuasive, why?
2. What are the arguments for loosening present restrictions on gun ownership in the United States? Which argument do you believe is most persuasive, why?
3. Do you believe mass tragedies like those in Aurora and Newtown can ever be prevented? Why or why not?
4. Cities like Chicago, which have some of the strictest gun control laws in the country, have the highest rates of gun violence in the United States. How does this happen? How can it be prevented?
5. Do you believe the Second Amendment is properly applied and understood in the United States? Why or why not?

Is There Common Ground?

While it may seem that lines are clearly drawn in the sand when it comes to gun control in the United States, in reality there is great potential for middle ground to be discovered. Throughout the history of guns in America, compromises have been reached. There are certain restrictions and purchasing protocols in place currently trying to assure that malintenioned individuals struggle to gain access to a firearm. In another vein, across the country concealed carry laws are becoming prominent, permitting skilled individuals to keep their piece on their person at all times. What these examples show is that both sides of the argument have made certain sacrifices already.

But there are concerns that are perhaps more difficult to bridge the gap on. Those opposed to gun control, for example, routinely point to the fact that criminals are not likely to obey any form of law passed related to access to weapons. In this scenario, law abiding citizens could find themselves vulnerable as only lawbreakers maintain firearms. At the same time, those in favor of curbing access will seemingly always have a fresh mass shooting to use when driving home key arguments. Few Americans are on the fence with regards to gun control and consequently the sharpness of opinions leads one to believe that middle ground may be more difficult to realize than we originally expected.

Create Central

www.mhhe.com/createcentral

Additional Resources

Gregg L. Carter, *Gun Control in the United States: A Reference Handbook* (ABC-CLIO, 2006)

Saul Cornell, *A Well-Regulated Militia: The Founding Fathers and the Origins of Gun Control in America* (Oxford University Press, 2008)

John R. Lott Jr., *More Guns, Less Crime: Understanding Crime and Gun Control Laws* (University of Chicago Press, 2010)

Robert Spitzer, *The Politics of Gun Control* (Paradigm, 2011)

Craig Whitney, *Living with Guns: A Liberal's Case for the Second Amendment* (PublicAffairs, 2012)

Internet References . . .

Brady Campaign to Prevent Gun Violence (BCPGV)

www.handguncontrol.org

Coalition to Stop Gun Violence (CSGV)

www.gunfree.org

National Criminal Justice Reference Service

www.ncjrs.gov/App/Topics/Topic.aspx?topicid=87

National Rifle Association

www.nra.org

Revolution PAC

www.revolutionpac.com

Selected, Edited, and with Issue Framing Material by:
Richard P. Halgin, *University of Massachusetts, Amherst*

ISSUE

Should "Recreational" Drugs Be Legalized?

YES: **Bryan Stevenson**, from "Drug Policy, Criminal Justice, and Mass Imprisonment," paper presented to the Global Commission on Drug Policies (2011)

NO: **Charles D. Stimson**, from "Legalizing Marijuana: Why Citizens Should Just Say No," *Heritage Foundation Legal Memorandum* (2010)

Learning Outcomes

After reading this issue, you will be able to:
- Identify different interpretations of what should be classified as recreational drugs.
- Explain how individual choices can impact public well-being.
- Discuss the potential long-term health effects of drug usage.
- Explain why some argue that using certain drugs is not risky behavior.
- Identify the possible impacts to law enforcement of legalizing or not legalizing recreational drugs.

ISSUE SUMMARY

YES: Law professor Bryan Stevenson focuses on how the criminalization of drugs has led to mass imprisonment with negative consequences for law enforcement.

NO: Charles D. Stimson, former Deputy Assistant Secretary of Defense, explains that marijuana is not safe and makes more sense than the prohibition of alcohol did in the early 1900s. Further, he demonstrates that the economic benefits would not outweigh the societal costs.

Prohibition is a word Americans associate with the prohibition of liquor, which was adopted as a national policy with the ratification of the Eighteenth Amendment to the U.S. Constitution in 1920 and repealed with the adoption of the Twenty-first Amendment in 1933. Many states had earlier banned whiskey and other intoxicating beverages, and some states have had various restrictions since repeal.

Similarly, certain categories of illicit drugs were banned in some states prior to the passage of the Controlled Substance Act in 1970, which made the prohibition a national policy. Unlike the Prohibition Amendment, this was achieved by an Act of Congress. Many claimed then, and many still do today, that to do this in the absence of a constitutional amendment exceeds the power of the national government. Nevertheless, it has been upheld by the federal courts and has continued to function for more than four decades.

The principal substances that are banned include opium, heroin, cocaine, and marijuana. Marijuana is also known as cannabis (the plant from which it is obtained) and by a variety of informal names, most familiarly "pot." Its use dates back several thousand years, sometimes for religious or medical purposes. However, it is a so-called recreational drug that a United Nations committee characterized as "the most widely used illicit substance in the world." Because opium, heroin, and cocaine are more powerful, more addictive, and less prevalent, advocates of legalization often restrict their appeal to removing the ban on marijuana.

In the 50 years following an international convention in 1912 that urged the restriction of dangerous drugs, the use in the United States of illicit drugs other than marijuana was consistently below 1/2 of 1 percent of the population, with cocaine rising somewhat in the counter culture climate that began in the late 1950s. Illicit drug use was widely promoted as mind-expanding and relatively harmless. It is estimated that its use peaked in the 1970s. Present estimates for drugs other than marijuana suggest that between 5 and 10 percent of the population at least occasionally engages in the use of some illicit drugs.

In 2006, there were approximately 1.9 million drug arrests in the United States. Of these, 829,625 (44 percent of the total) were marijuana arrests. During the past two decades, the price of marijuana has gone down, its potency has increased, and it has become more readily available. Further, it has begun being mixed with other substances, increasing the potential for unintended side effects.

Studies, principally conducted in Sweden, Holland, and other nations with more tolerant drug policies, conclude that social factors influence drug use. Apart from peer pressure, particularly in the use of marijuana, hard drugs generally become more common in times of higher unemployment and lower income. Apart from cannabis, which is easily grown, the illicit character of hard drugs makes them expensive, but the profit motive induces growers, distributors, and "pushers" to risk arrest and punishment. It has been estimated that as many as one-sixth of all persons in federal prisons have been convicted of selling, possessing, or using marijuana.

The movement to legalize these drugs, often with a focus on marijuana, has existed as long as their prohibition, but in recent years has won recruits from both liberal and conservative ranks. As with the prohibition of alcohol, experience with the unintended consequences of prohibition of drugs led some to wonder whether this has not only failed to eliminate their use but has increased public health problems. Under the Prohibition Amendment, people drank unlicensed alcohol, often adulterated by the addition of poisonous substances. Illicit drug prohibition has led to the sale of toxic ingredients added to the drugs resulting in more impure and more dangerous products. Drug users injecting the drugs employ dirty reused needles that spread HIV and hepatitis B and C. While illicit drug use has never rivaled the widespread public acceptance of alcohol, their use has been extensive enough to spawn new networks of organized crime, violence related to the drug market, and the corruption of law enforcement and governments. We have recently witnessed this in the drug gang wars in Mexico that have slipped over into the American southwest.

Milton Friedman, who was America's most influential conservative economist, reached the interesting conclusion that drug prohibition has led to the rise of drug cartels. His reasoning was that only major retailers can handle massive shipments, own aircraft fleets, have armed troops, and employ lawyers and methods of eluding and bribing the police. Consequently, law enforcement as well as competition drives out smaller, less ruthless, and less efficient drug dealers.

The economic cost of legislating and attempting to enforce drug prohibition is very high. When the national policy went to effect, the federal cost was $350 million in 1971. Thirty-five years later in 2006, the cost was $30 billion. To this should be added the revenue that could be obtained if marijuana were subject to taxation. If it were taxed at the same rate as alcohol or tobacco, it has been estimated that it would yield as much as $7.7 billion. It may be, as advocates of legalization suggest, that the financial costs exceed the damages that the drugs themselves cause.

Against these arguments for repeal, those who support the war on drugs claim that prohibitive drug laws suppress drug use. Compare the large majority of Americans who consume legal alcohol with the very much smaller proportion who use illicit drugs. The Drug Enforcement Administration (DEA) has demonstrated that people under the influence of drugs are more than six times more likely to commit homicides than people looking for money to buy drugs. Drug use changes behavior and causes criminal activity. Cocaine-related paranoia frequently results in assaults, drugged driving, and domestic violence. These crimes are likely to increase when drugs are more readily available.

The point that liberalization advocates miss is that the illicit drugs are inherently harmful. In the short term, illicit drugs cause memory loss, distorted perception, a decline of motor skills, and an increased heart rate and anxiety. Particularly for young people, drug use produces a decline in mental development and motivation, as well as a reduced ability to concentrate in school.

The United States Centers for Disease Control and Prevention has concluded that although there are more than seven times more Americans who use alcohol than drugs, during a single year alone (2000), there were almost as many drug-induced deaths (15,8520) as alcohol-induced (18, 539). The DEA concludes that drugs are "far more deadly than alcohol." This is true even for marijuana, which is deemed more potent than it was a generation ago. It contains more than 400 chemicals (the toxicity of some is clear and of many others is unknown) and one marijuana cigarette deposits four times more tar than a filtered tobacco cigarette.

The widespread support for medicinal marijuana seems to be changing public attitudes toward potential legalization. Colorado and Washington voters have sent a message that their respective states will exercise their rights under the Constitution legalizing the recreational use of marijuana. This process began with the legalization of medical marijuana in over a dozen states, opening the doors of debate with regards to the benefits of marijuana and dispelling some misconceptions. Party support has increased across the board. Republican support increased from 33 percent to 35 percent between November 2012 and October 2013, with Democratic changes increases from 61 percent to 65 percent and Independents from 50 percent to 62 percent within the same time period respec-tively. While marijuana is still illegal at the federal level, the Obama administration has made it clear that they will not go after users in states that choose to legalize. A memo sent from Attorney General Eric Holder to all U.S. attorneys informs them the federal government will not intervene with state laws as long as the states follow cer-tain protocols and guidelines in regulating product. Per-haps the tides are actually changing.

In the following selections, Bryan Stevenson, Execu-tive Director of the Equal Justice Initiative, focuses on how the criminalization of drugs has led to mass imprisonment with negative consequences for law enforcement. Charles D. Stimson argues, on the other hand, that marijuana is by no means the safe drug some make it out to be and that the economic benefits of legalization will not be able to surmount the societal costs.

YES

Bryan Stevenson

Drug Policy, Criminal Justice, and Mass Imprisonment

The last three decades have witnessed a global increase in the criminalization of improper drug use. Criminalization has resulted in increased use of harsh punitive sanctions imposed on drug offenders and dramatic increases in rates of incarceration. These policies have had limited impact on eliminating or reducing illegal drug use and may have resulted in adverse consequences for social and community health. The criminal justice system has proved to be an ineffective forum for managing or controlling many aspects of the drug trade or the problem of illegal drug usage. In recent years, some progress has been reported when governing bodies have managed drug use and addiction as a public health problem which requires treatment, counseling and medical interventions rather than incarceration. Primarily as a result of drug policy, the number of people currently incarcerated worldwide is at an all time high of ten million.

In the United States, the prison population has increased from 300,000 in 1972 to 2.3 million people today. One in 31 adults in the United States is in jail, prison, on probation or parole. The American government currently spends over 68 billion dollars a year on incarceration. Drug Policy and the incarceration of low-level drug offenders is the primary cause of mass incarceration in the United States. [Forty percent] of drug arrests are for simple possession of marijuana. There is also evidence that drug enforcement has diverted resources from law enforcement of violent crimes and other threats to public safety.

Incarceration of low-level drug offenders has criminogenic effects that increase the likelihood of recidivism and additional criminal behavior. Enforcement of drug policy against low-level users and small scale trafficking has been racially biased and fueled social and political antagonisms that have undermined support of drug policy.

Growing evidence indicates that drug treatment and counseling programs are far more effective in reducing drug addiction and abuse than is incarceration. Needle exchange, compulsory treatment, education, counseling, drug substitutes like Methadone or Naxolene have proved highly effective in reducing addiction, overdose and the spread of HIV and Hepatitis C.

The last three decades have witnessed a global increase in the criminalization of improper drug use. Criminalization has resulted in increased use of harsh punitive sanctions imposed on drug offenders and dramatic increases in rates of incarceration. These policies have had limited impact on eliminating or reducing illegal drug use and may have resulted in adverse consequences for social and community health. The criminal justice system has proved to be an ineffective forum for managing or controlling many aspects of the drug trade or the problem of illegal drug usage. In recent years, some progress has been reported when governing bodies have managed drug use and addiction as a public health problem which requires treatment, counseling and medical interventions rather than incarceration. Most experts agree that drug-related HIV infection, the spread of infectious diseases like Hepatitis C and related public health concerns cannot be meaningfully addressed through jail and imprisonment and are often aggravated by policies which are primarily punitive. This paper briefly reviews this issue and identifies some of the costs of over-reliance on incarceration and outlines new strategies.

Criminal Justice Policy and Increased Use of Sanctions and Incarceration for Low-Level Drug Offenders

The Criminalization of Drugs and the Legacy of Mass Imprisonment

Criminalization of possession and illegal use of drugs compounded by mandatory sentencing and lengthy prison sanctions for low-level drug use has become the primary cause of mass incarceration. The global prison population has skyrocketed in the last three decades with ten million people worldwide now in jails and prisons. The extraordinary increase in the number of people now incarcerated has had tremendous implications for state and national governments dealing with global recession and a range of economic, social and political challenges. Research indicates that resources that would otherwise be spent on development, infrastructure, education and health care have been redirected over the last two decades to incarcerating drug offenders, many of whom are low-level users. The trend toward mass incarceration has been especially troubling in the United States. In the last thirty-five years, the number of U.S. residents in prison has increased from 330,000 people in jails and prisons in 1972 to almost 2.3 million imprisoned people today. The United States now has the highest rate of incarceration in the world.

Over five million people are on probation and parole in America. Currently, one out of 100 adults is in jail or prison and one out of 31 adults is in jail, prison on probation or parole. The consequences of increased incarceration and penal control strategies have been dramatic and costly. Many states spend in excess of $50,000 a year to incarcerate each prisoner in a state prison or facility, including non-violent, low-level drug offenders. Corrections spending by state and federal governments has risen from $6.9 billion in 1980 to $68 billion in 2006 in America. During the ten year period between 1985 and 1995, prisons were constructed at a pace of one new prison opening each week.

The economic toll of expansive imprisonment policies has been accompanied by socio-political consequences as well. Mass incarceration has had discernible impacts in poor and minority communities which have been disproportionately impacted by drug enforcement strategies. Collateral consequences of drug prosecutions of low-level offenders have included felon disenfranchisement laws, where in some states drug offenders permanently lose the right to vote. Sociologists have also recently observed that the widespread incarceration of men in low-income communities has had a profound negative impact on social and cultural norms relating to family and opportunity. Increases in the imprisonment of poor and minority women with children have now been linked with rising numbers of displaced children and dependents. Drug policy and the over-reliance on incarceration is seen by many experts as contributing to increased rates of chronic unemployment, destabilization of families and increased risk of reincarceration for the formerly incarcerated.

There are unquestionably serious consequences for community and public health when illegal use of drugs is widespread. Addiction and other behavioral issues triggered by drug abuse have well known consequences for individuals, families, communities and governing bodies trying to protect public safety. Governing bodies are clearly justified in pursuing policies and strategies that disrupt the drug trade and the violence frequently associated with high-level drug trafficking. Similarly, drug abuse is a serious problem within communities that threatens public health and merits serious attention. However, some interventions to address drug abuse are now emerging as clearly more effective than others. Consequently, interventions that reduce drug dependence and improve the prospects for eliminating drug addiction and abuse are essential if measurable improvements on this issue are to be achieved in the coming years.

Drug Policy and the Criminal Justice System

Many countries have employed the rhetoric of war to combat the drug trade. While there are countries where violent drug kingpens have created large militias that have necessitated more militarized responses from law enforcement, most drug arrests are directed at low-level users who have been the primary targets in the "war on drugs." States have criminalized simple possession of drugs like marijuana and imposed harsh and lengthy sentences on people arrested. Small amounts of narcotics, unauthorized prescription medicines and other drugs have triggered trafficking charges that impose even lengthier prison sentences. The introduction of habitual felony offender laws has exacerbated drug policy as it is not uncommon for illegal drug users to accumulate multiple charges in a very short period of time. Under the notorious "three strikes laws" that have become popular in America, drug offenders with no history of violence may face mandatory minimum sentences in excess of 25 years in prison. Thousands of low-level drug offenders have been sentenced to life imprisonment with no chance of parole as a result of these sentencing laws.

In the United States, drug arrests have tripled in the last 25 years, however most of these arrests have been for simple possession of low-level drugs. In 2005, nearly 43% of all drug arrests were for marijuana offenses. Marijuana possession arrests accounted for 79% of the growth in drug arrests in the 1990s. Nearly a half million people are in state or federal prisons or a local jail for a drug offense, compared to 41,000 in 1980. Most of these people have no history of violence or high-level drug selling activity.

The "war on drugs" has also generated indirect costs that many researchers contend have undermined public safety. The federal government has prioritized spending and grants for drug task forces and widespread drug interdiction efforts that often target low-level drug dealing. These highly organized and coordinated efforts have been very labor intensive for local law enforcement agencies with some unanticipated consequences for investigation of other crimes. The focus on drugs is believed to have redirected law enforcement resources that have resulted in more drunk driving, and decreased investigation and enforcement of violent crime laws. In Illinois, a 47% increase in drug arrests corresponded with a 22% decrease in arrests for drunk driving. Florida researchers have similarly linked the focus on low level drug arrests with an increase in the serious crime index.

In prison, as a result of the increased costs of incarceration, most drug addicts are less likely to receive drug treatment and therapy. The increasing costs of mass imprisonment have eliminated funds for treatment and counseling services even though some of these services have proved to be very effective. In 1991, one in three prison inmates was receiving treatment while incarcerated, today the rate is down to one in seven. The decline of treatment and counseling services makes re-offending once released much more likely. This is one of the ways in which incarceration and criminal justice intervention has proved costly and less effective than other models of managing illegal drug use.

Racially Discriminatory Enforcement of Drug Laws

In the United States, considerable evidence demonstrates that enforcement of drug policy has proved to be racially discriminatory and very biased against the poor. America's criminal justice system is very wealth sensitive which makes it difficult for low-income residents to obtain equally favorable outcomes as more wealthy residents when they are charged with drug crimes. Targeting communities of color for enforcement of drug laws has added to the problems of racial bias in American society and generated some of the fiercest debates about the continuing legacy of racial discrimination. Illegal use of drugs is not unique to communities of color and rates of offending are not higher in these communities than they are in nonminority communities. African Americans comprise 14% of regular drug users in the United States, yet are 37% of those arrested for drug offenses and 56% of those incarcerated for drug crimes. Black people in the United States serve almost as much time in federal prison for a drug offense (58.7 months) as whites serve for a violent crime (61.7 months), primarily as a result of the racially disparate sentencing laws such as the 100-1 crack powder cocaine

disparity. For years, the sentences for illegal possession or use of crack cocaine, which is more prevalent in communities of color, were 100 times greater than possession or use of equivalent amounts of powder cocaine, leading to dramatically longer prison sentences for African Americans. In 2010, Congress amended this law and reduced the disparity from 100-1 to 12-1. However, the failure to make the law retroactive has left the costly and troubling racial disparities uncorrected. Hispanic people are also disproportionately at much greater risk of arrest and prosecution for drug crimes than are whites in the United States.

Discriminatory enforcement of drug laws against communities of color has seriously undermined the integrity of drug policy initiatives and frequently these policies are perceived as unfair, unjust and targeted at racial minorities. Enforcement of drug laws tends to be directed at low-income communities or residential and social centers where residents have less political power to resist aggressive policing and engagement. Even some reforms aimed at shielding low-level drug offenders from incarceration have been skewed against the poor and people of color. Some data show that people of color are more likely to be redirected back to the criminal courts if drug court personnel have discretion. Similarly, many community-based programs that permit drug offenders to avoid jail or prison have significant admission fees and costs that many poor people simply cannot afford. Discriminatory enforcement of drug policy has undermined its effectiveness and legitimacy and contributed to continuing dysfunction in the administration of criminal justice.

There Is Growing Evidence that Drug Treatment Is More Cost Effective than Incarceration and Incapacitation Strategies

One of the clear consequences of mass incarceration directed at low level drug offenders has been to acculturate and socialize illegal drug users into criminality through extended incarceration. This criminogenic effect has been seen in studies that examined rates of recidivism among drug offenders who are given probation and not sent to jail or prison and drug offenders who are incarcerated for the same offenses. In purely human terms, these findings reveal that incarceration may be dramatically more costly than other approaches.

However, the economic analysis of approaches to low level drug offending that avoid incarceration are even more compelling. Whatever the measure, data indicates that drug treatment is more cost effective than incarceration. In California, a study has recently shown that spending on drug treatment is eight times more likely to reduce drug consumption than spending on incarceration. Corresponding decreases in drug-related crime were also documented when comparing drug treatment programs with incarceration. In a RAND analysis study, treatment was estimated to reduce crime associated with drug use and the drug trade up to 15 times as much as incarceration. These findings have been reflected in other studies that have also found that drug treatment is more cost effective in controlling drug abuse and crime than continued expansion of the prison system when looking at low level drug offenders.

Consequently, many states have now started to shift their management of drug offenders to drug courts that have discretion to redirect people who illegally use drugs away from jail or prison and into community-based treatment, counseling and therapeutic interventions. The early signs suggest that these innovations are saving states millions of dollars and accomplishing improved public safety. For the first time in 38 years, 2010 saw a slight decrease in the national state prison population in the United States. Significant reductions will need to continue to deal with a global recession and decreasing resources available for incarceration.

New and More Effective Strategies for Managing Low-Level Drug Offenders Are Emerging

Proponents of "Harm Reduction" have long argued that a more effective way to combat illegal drug use is to spend more on public education, treatment and interventions that view illegal drug use as a public health problem rather than continued spending on incarceration and harsh sanctions. Supporters of harm reduction acknowledge that the use of incarceration and sanctions will be necessary when illegal drug trafficking or distribution threatens public safety, however, they contend that most drug arrests don't directly implicate public safety. States are beginning to recognize the benefits associated with harm reduction and in recent years have begun to reallocate resources with surprisingly good outcomes.

Sentencing Reform

In recent years, states have begun to retreat from mandatory sentences and other harsh strategies for enforcing drug laws and moved to alternative models that involve probation, treatment, counseling and education. Between 2004 and 2006, at least 13 states expanded drug treatment or programs which divert drug offenders away from jail or prison into community-based programs. States like Michigan have recently amended statutes that required a mandatory sentence of life imprisonment without parole for distribution of cocaine or heroin. With over 5 million people on probation or parole in the United States, drug use on parole or probation has become the primary basis by which thousands of people are returned to prison. These technical violations of parole or probation account for as many as 40% of new prison admissions in some jurisdictions. In recent years, states have restricted the length of incarceration imposed when formerly incarcerated people test positive for recent drug use. These new statues . . . incarcerated drug users into drug therapy and counseling programs.

The federal government has amended mandatory sentencing laws for drug offenders and seen a dramatic reduction in the number of people facing long-term incarceration for low-level drug use. These sentencing reforms are considered critical to containing the costs of mass imprisonment in the United States and for generating resources necessary to approach drug addiction and abuse as a public health problem.

Drug courts have also emerged in the last decade to play a critical role in redirecting low-level drug offenders away from traditional, punitive models of intervention for illegal drug use. Drug courts have been set up in hundreds of communities. Court personnel have discretion to order drug treatment and community-based programs where offenders must receive counseling and treatment and receive education concerning drug addiction and abuse. By shielding thousands of drug offenders from incarceration and transfer to overcrowded prisons, drug courts have reduced the collateral consequences of illegal drug use, saved millions of dollars and had more favorable outcomes for people who have been identified as illegally using drugs. Drug court participants can avoid a criminal record and all the disabling collateral consequences associated with a criminal record.

Reducing the penalties for some low-level drug crimes, giving judges more discretion to avoid unwarranted and lengthy mandatory sentences and retreating from the rhetoric of war and unscientific policy analysis could substantially reduce incarceration rates and provide additional resources for treatment options that are more effective at eliminating drug abuse.

Medical and Public Health Models for Drug Abuse Intervention

The risk of criminal prosecution has had many unintended consequences, especially for people with addiction problems who also have critical medical issues that require treatment and intervention. HIV infection and AIDS continue to threaten many countries with tragic and devastating effect. Intravenous drug users are primary targets for infection and have extremely elevated risks of illness from sharing needles. Rather than facilitating less hazardous practices for this community, criminal justice interventions have forced people with addiction underground and infection rates have spiraled. Providing clean needles and other strategies associated with needle exchange have had a significant impact on reducing the rate of HIV infection and offering people with addiction issues an opportunity for treatment. Creating safe zones where people struggling with drug addiction can safely come has also greatly increased the ability of public health officials to provide education, counseling and treatment opportunities that are scientifically proven to be effective to the population with the greatest needs. For example, where needle-exchange has been implemented, the results have been extremely promising for controlling illegal drug use and reducing public health threats.

Policies that make it permissible for people to safely admit to drug addiction problems are well established to be more effective at managing drug addiction. In 2006, there were 26,000 deaths in the United States from accidental drug overdose, the highest level ever recorded by the Centers for Disease Control. Accidental death through overdose is currently the leading cause of injury-related death for people between the ages of 35–54. This extraordinarily high level of death through overdose can only be meaningfully confronted with public education efforts and improving treatment options for people who are abusing drugs.

Criminalization has created huge and complex obstacles for people motivated to eliminate their drug dependence to seek or obtain necessary health care and support. When public health options are made available, studies have reported dramatic declines in drug dependence, mortality and overdose. Medical developments have proved extremely effective in reducing drug dependence and addiction. A range of maintenance therapies are available for people with addiction problems. Methadone maintenance has been cited as the primary intervention strategy for people with heroin addiction. Drugs like Naloxone have been utilized in an extremely effective manner to save lives when people ingest too many opiates. However, these very cost effective treatments are not possible without providing safe opportunities to report drug and overdose issues to health care providers who are free to treat rather than arrest people with addiction and drug dependence.

Mass imprisonment, the high economic and social costs of incarcerating low-level drug offenders and the ineffectiveness of criminalization and punitive approaches to drug addiction have had poor outcomes in many countries. Governing bodies have available dozens of new, scientifically tested interventions which have been proved to lower rates of drug abuse and addiction without incarceration. Reducing illegal drug use and disrupting the sometimes violent drug trade will require new and more effective strategies in the 21st century. The politics of fear and anger that have generated many of these policies must be resisted and adoption of scientifically established treatment protocols that have been found effective and successful should be pursued vigorously.

Bryan Stevenson is a faculty member of the New York University School of Law and executive director of the Equal Justice Initiative, an organization that focuses on criminal justice reform.

Charles D. Stimson

 **NO**

Legalizing Marijuana: Why Citizens Should Just Say No

The scientific literature is clear that marijuana is addictive and that its use significantly impairs bodily and mental functions. Marijuana use is associated with memory loss, cancer, immune system deficiencies, heart disease, and birth defects, among other conditions. Even where decriminalized, marijuana trafficking remains a source of violence, crime, and social disintegration.

Nonetheless, this November, California voters will consider a ballot initiative, the Regulate, Control and Tax Cannabis Act of 2010 (RCTCA), that would legalize most marijuana distribution and use under state law. (These activities would remain federal crimes.) This vote is the culmination of an organized campaign by pro-marijuana activists stretching back decades.

The current campaign, like previous efforts, downplays the well-documented harms of marijuana trafficking and use while promising benefits ranging from reduced crime to additional tax revenue. In particular, supporters of the initiative make five bold claims:

1. "Marijuana is safe and non-addictive."
2. "Marijuana prohibition makes no more sense than alcohol prohibition did in the early 1900s."
3. "The government's efforts to combat illegal drugs have been a total failure."
4. "The money spent on government efforts to combat the illegal drug trade can be better spent on substance abuse and treatment for the allegedly few marijuana users who abuse the drug."
5. "Tax revenue collected from marijuana sales would substantially outweigh the social costs of legalization."

As this paper details, all five claims are demonstrably false or, based on the best evidence, highly dubious.

Further, supporters of the initiative simply ignore the mechanics of decriminalization—that is, how it would directly affect law enforcement, crime, and communities. Among the important questions left unanswered are:

- How would the state law fit into a federal regime that prohibits marijuana production, distribution, and possession?
- Would decriminalization, especially if combined with taxation, expand market opportunities for the gangs and cartels that currently dominate drug distribution?
- Would existing zoning laws prohibit marijuana cultivation in residential neighborhoods, and if not, what measures would growers have to undertake to keep children from the plants?
- Would transportation providers be prohibited from firing bus drivers because they smoke marijuana?

No one knows the specifics of how marijuana decriminalization would work in practice or what measures would be necessary to prevent children, teenagers, criminals, and addicts from obtaining the drug.

The federal government shares these concerns. Gil Kerlikowske, Director of the White House Office of National Drug Control Policy (ONDCP), recently stated, "Marijuana legalization, for any purpose, is a non-starter in the Obama Administration." The Administration—widely viewed as more liberal than any other in recent memory and, for a time, as embodying the hopes of pro-legalization activists—has weighed the costs and benefits and concluded that marijuana legalization would compromise public health and safety.

California's voters, if they take a fair-minded look at the evidence and the practical problems of legalization, should reach the same conclusion: Marijuana is a dangerous substance that should remain illegal under state law.

The Initiative

The RCTCA's purpose, as defined by advocates of legalization, is to regulate marijuana just as the government regulates alcohol. The law would allow anyone 21 years of age or older to possess, process, share, or transport up to one full ounce of marijuana "for personal consumption." Individuals could possess an unlimited number of living and harvested marijuana plants on the premises where they were grown. Individual landowners or lawful occupants of private property could cultivate marijuana plants "for personal consumption" in an area of not more than 25 square feet per private residence or parcel.

The RCTCA would legalize drug-related paraphernalia and tools and would license establishments for on-site smoking and other consumption of marijuana. Supporters have included some alcohol-like restrictions against, for example, smoking marijuana while operating a vehicle. Finally, the act authorizes the imposition and collection of taxes and fees associated with legalization of marijuana.

Unsafe in Any Amount: How Marijuana Is Not Like Alcohol

Marijuana advocates have had some success peddling the notion that marijuana is a "soft" drug, similar to alcohol, and fundamentally different from "hard" drugs like cocaine or heroin. It is true that marijuana is not the most dangerous of the commonly abused drugs, but that is not to say that it is safe. Indeed, marijuana shares more in common with the "hard" drugs than it does with alcohol.

A common argument for legalization is that smoking marijuana is no more dangerous than drinking alcohol and that prohibiting the use of marijuana is therefore no more justified than the prohibition of alcohol. As Jacob Sullum, author of *Saying Yes: In Defense of Drug Use*, writes:

> Americans understood the problems associated with alcohol abuse, but they also understood the problems associated with Prohibition, which included violence, organized crime, official corruption, the erosion of civil liberties, disrespect for the law, and injuries and deaths caused by tainted black-market booze. They decided that these unintended side effects far outweighed whatever harms Prohibition prevented by discouraging drinking. The same sort of analysis today would show that the harm caused by drug prohibition far outweighs the harm it prevents, even without taking into account the value to each individual of being sovereign over his own body and mind.

At first blush, this argument is appealing, especially to those wary of over-regulation by government. But it overlooks the enormous difference between alcohol and marijuana.

Legalization advocates claim that marijuana and alcohol are mild intoxicants and so should be regulated similarly; but as the experience of nearly every culture, over the thousands of years of human history, demonstrates, alcohol is different. Nearly every culture has its own alcoholic preparations, and nearly all have successfully regulated alcohol consumption through cultural norms. The same cannot be said of marijuana. There are several possible explanations for alcohol's unique status: For most people, it is not addictive; it is rarely consumed to the point of intoxication; low-level consumption is consistent with most manual and intellectual tasks; it has several positive health benefits; and it is formed by the fermentation of many common substances and easily metabolized by the body.

To be sure, there are costs associated with alcohol abuse, such as drunk driving and disease associated with excessive consumption. A few cultures—and this nation for a short while during Prohibition—have concluded that the benefits of alcohol consumption are not worth the costs. But they are the exception; most cultures have concluded that it is acceptable in moderation. No other intoxicant shares that status.

Alcohol differs from marijuana in several crucial respects. First, marijuana is far more likely to cause addiction. Second, it is usually consumed to the point of intoxication. Third, it has no known general healthful properties, though it may have some palliative effects. Fourth, it is toxic and deleterious to health. Thus, while it is true that both alcohol and marijuana are less intoxicating than other mood-altering drugs, that is not to say that marijuana is especially similar to alcohol or that its use is healthy or even safe.

In fact, compared to alcohol, marijuana is not safe. Long-term, moderate consumption of alcohol carries few health risks and even offers some significant benefits. For example, a glass of wine (or other alcoholic drink) with dinner actually improves health. Dozens of peer-reviewed medical studies suggest that drinking moderate amounts of alcohol reduces the risk of heart disease, strokes, gallstones, diabetes, and death from a heart attack. According to the Mayo Clinic, among many others, moderate use of alcohol (defined as two drinks a day) "seems to offer some health benefits, particularly for the heart." Countless articles in medical journals and other scientific literature confirm the positive health effects of moderate alcohol consumption.

The effects of regular marijuana consumption are quite different. For example, the National Institute on Drug Abuse (a division of the National Institutes of Health) has released studies showing that use of marijuana has wide-ranging negative health effects. Long-term marijuana consumption "impairs the ability of T-cells in the lungs' immune system to fight off some infections." These studies have also found that marijuana consumption impairs short-term memory, making it difficult to learn and retain information or perform complex tasks; slows reaction time and impairs motor coordination; increases heart rate by 20 percent to 100 percent, thus elevating the risk of heart attack; and alters moods, resulting in artificial euphoria, calmness, or (in high doses) anxiety or paranoia. And it gets worse: Marijuana has toxic properties that can result in birth defects, pain, respiratory system damage, brain damage, and stroke.

Further, prolonged use of marijuana may cause cognitive degradation and is "associated with lower test scores and lower educational attainment because during periods of intoxication the drug affects the ability to learn and process information, thus influencing attention, concentration, and short-term memory." Unlike alcohol, marijuana has been shown to have a residual effect on cognitive ability that persists beyond the period of intoxication. According to the National Institute on Drug Abuse, whereas alcohol is broken down relatively quickly in the human body, THC (tetrahydrocannabinol, the main active chemical in marijuana) is stored in organs and fatty tissues, allowing it to remain in a user's body for days or even weeks after consumption. Research has shown that marijuana consumption may also cause "psychotic symptoms."

Marijuana's effects on the body are profound. According to the British Lung Foundation, "smoking three or four marijuana joints is as bad for your lungs as smoking twenty tobacco cigarettes." Researchers in Canada found that marijuana smoke contains significantly higher levels of numerous toxic compounds, like ammonia and hydrogen cyanide, than regular tobacco smoke. In fact, the study determined that ammonia was found in marijuana smoke at levels of up to 20 times the levels found in tobacco. Similarly, hydrogen cyanide was found in marijuana smoke at concentrations three to five times greater than those found in tobacco smoke.

Marijuana, like tobacco, is addictive. One study found that more than 30 percent of adults who used marijuana in the course of a year were dependent on the drug. These individuals often show signs of withdrawal and compulsive behavior. Marijuana dependence is also responsible for a large proportion of calls to drug abuse help lines and treatment centers.

To equate marijuana use with alcohol consumption is, at best, uninformed and, at worst, actively misleading. Only in the most superficial ways are the two substances alike, and they differ in every way that counts: addictiveness, toxicity, health effects, and risk of intoxication.

Unintended Consequences

Today, marijuana trafficking is linked to a variety of crimes, from assault and murder to money laundering and smuggling. Legalization of marijuana would increase demand for the drug and almost certainly exacerbate drug-related crime, as well as cause a myriad of unintended but predictable consequences.

To begin with, an astonishingly high percentage of criminals are marijuana users. According to a study by the RAND Corporation, approximately 60 percent of arrestees test positive for marijuana use in the United States, England, and Australia. Further, marijuana metabolites are found in arrestees' urine more frequently than those of any other drug.

Although some studies have shown marijuana to inhibit aggressive behavior and violence, the National Research Council concluded that the "long-term use of marijuana may alter the nervous system in ways that do promote violence." No place serves as a better example than Amsterdam.

Marijuana advocates often point to the Netherlands as a well-functioning society with a relaxed attitude toward drugs, but they rarely mention that Amsterdam is one of Europe's most violent cities. In Amsterdam, officials are in the process of closing marijuana dispensaries, or "coffee shops," because of the crime associated with their operation. Furthermore, the Dutch Ministry of Health, Welfare and Sport has expressed "concern about drug and alcohol use among young people and the social consequences, which range from poor school performance and truancy to serious impairment, including brain damage."

Amsterdam's experience is already being duplicated in California under the current medical marijuana statute. In Los Angeles, police report that areas surrounding cannabis clubs have experienced a 200 percent increase in robberies, a 52.2 percent increase in burglaries, a 57.1 percent increase in aggravated assault, and a 130.8 percent increase in burglaries from automobiles. Current law requires a doctor's prescription to procure marijuana; full legalization would likely spark an even more acute increase in crime.

Legalization of marijuana would also inflict a series of negative consequences on neighborhoods and communities. The nuisance caused by the powerful odor of mature marijuana plants is already striking California municipalities. The City Council of Chico, California, has released a report detailing the situation and describing how citizens living near marijuana cultivators are disturbed by the incredible stink emanating from the plants.

Perhaps worse than the smell, crime near growers is increasing, associated with "the theft of marijuana from yards where it is being grown." As a result, housing prices near growers are sinking.

Theoretical arguments in favor of marijuana legalization usually overlook the practical matter of how the drug would be regulated and sold. It is the details of implementation, of course, that will determine the effect of legalization on families, schools, and communities. Most basically, how and where would marijuana be sold?

- Would neighborhoods become neon red-light districts like Amsterdam's, accompanied by the same crime and social disorder?
- If so, who decides what neighborhoods will be so afflicted—residents and landowners or far-off government officials?
- Or would marijuana sales be so widespread that users could add it to their grocery lists?
- If so, how would stores sell it, how would they store it, and how would they prevent it from being diverted into the gray market?
- Would stores dealing in marijuana have to fortify their facilities to reduce the risk of theft and assault?

The most likely result is that the drug will not be sold in legitimate stores at all, because while the federal government is currently tolerating medical marijuana dispensaries, it will not tolerate wide-scale sales under general legalizational statutes. So marijuana will continue to be sold on the gray or black market.

The act does not answer these or other practical questions regarding implementation. Rather, it leaves those issues to localities. No doubt, those entities will pass a variety of laws in an attempt to deal with the many problems caused by legalization, unless the local laws are struck down by California courts as inconsistent with the underlying initiative, which would be even worse. At best, that patchwork of laws, differing from one locality to another, will be yet another unintended and predictable problem arising from legalization as envisioned under this act.

Citizens also should not overlook what may be the greatest harms of marijuana legalization: increased addiction to and use of harder drugs. In addition to marijuana's harmful effects on the body and relationship to criminal conduct, it is a gateway drug that can lead users to more dangerous drugs. Prosecutors, judges, police officers, detectives, parole or probation officers, and even defense attorneys know that the vast majority of defendants arrested for violent crimes test positive for illegal drugs, including marijuana. They also know that marijuana is the starter drug of choice for most criminals. Whereas millions of Americans consume moderate amounts of alcohol without ever "moving on" to dangerous drugs, marijuana use and cocaine use are strongly correlated.

While correlation does not necessarily reflect causation, and while the science is admittedly mixed as to whether it is the drug itself or the people the new user associates with who cause the move on to cocaine, heroin, LSD, or other drugs, the RAND Corporation reports that marijuana prices and cocaine use are directly linked, suggesting a substitution effect between the two drugs. Moreover, according to RAND, legalization will cause marijuana prices to fall as much as 80 percent. That can lead to significant consequences because "a 10-percent decrease in the price of marijuana would increase the prevalence of cocaine use by 4.4 to 4.9 percent." As cheap marijuana floods the market both in and outside of California, use of many different types of drugs will increase, as will marijuana use.

It is impossible to predict the precise consequences of legalization, but the experiences of places that have eased restrictions on marijuana are not positive. Already, California is suffering crime, dislocation, and increased drug use under its current regulatory scheme. Further liberalizing the law will only make matters worse.

Flouting Federal Law

Another area of great uncertainty is how a state law legalizing marijuana would fit in with federal law to the contrary. Congress has enacted a comprehensive regulatory scheme for restricting access to illicit drugs and other controlled substances. The Controlled Substances Act of 1970 prohibits the manufacture, distribution, and possession of all substances deemed to be Schedule I drugs—drugs like heroin, PCP, and cocaine. Because marijuana has no "currently accepted medical use in treatment in the United States," it is a Schedule I drug that cannot be bought, sold, possessed, or used without violating federal law.

Under the Supremacy Clause of the Constitution of the United States, the Controlled Substances Act is the supreme law of the land and cannot be superseded by state laws that purport to contradict or abrogate its terms. The RCTCA proposes to "reform California's cannabis laws in a way that will benefit our state" and "[r]egulate cannabis like we do alcohol." But the act does not even purport to address the fundamental constitutional infirmity that it would be in direct conflict with federal law. If enacted and unchallenged by the federal government, it would call into question the government's ability to regulate all controlled substances, including drugs such as Oxycontin, methamphetamine, heroin, and powder and crack cocaine. More likely, however, the feds would challenge the law in court, and the courts would have no choice but to strike it down.

Congress has the power to change the Controlled Substances Act and remove marijuana from Schedule I. Yet after decades of lobbying, it has not, largely because of the paucity of scientific evidence in support of a delisting.

California, in fact, is already in direct violation of federal law. Today, its laws allow the use of marijuana as a treatment for a range of vaguely defined conditions, including chronic pain, nausea, and lack of appetite, depression, anxiety, and glaucoma. "Marijuana doctors" are listed in the classified advertising sections of newspapers, and many are conveniently located adjacent to "dispensaries." At least one "doctor" writes prescriptions from a tiny hut beside the Venice Beach Boardwalk.

This "medical marijuana" law and similar ones in other states are premised on circumvention of the Food and Drug Administration (FDA) approval process. "FDA's drug approval process requires well-controlled clinical trials that provide the necessary scientific data upon which FDA makes its approval and labeling decisions." Marijuana, even that supposedly used for medicinal purposes, has been rejected by the FDA because, among other reasons, it "has no currently accepted or proven medical use."

The lack of FDA approval means that marijuana may come from unknown sources, may be adulterated with foreign substances, or may not even be marijuana at all. Pot buyers have no way to know what they are getting, and there is no regulatory authority with the ability to go after bogus manufacturers and dealers. Even if one overlooks its inherently harmful properties, marijuana that is commonly sold is likely to be far less safe than that studied in the lab or elsewhere.

Marijuana advocates claim that federal enforcement of drug laws, particularly in jurisdictions that allow the use of medical marijuana, violates states' rights. The Supreme Court, however, has held otherwise. In 2002, California resident Angel Raich produced and consumed marijuana, purportedly for medical purposes. Her actions, while in accordance with California's "medical marijuana" law, clearly violated the Controlled Substances Act, and the local sheriff's department destroyed Raich's plants. Raich claimed that she needed to use marijuana, prescribed by her doctor, for medical purposes. She sued the federal government, asking the court to stop the government from interfering with her right to produce and use marijuana.

In 2006, the Supreme Court held in *Gonzales vs. Raich* that the Commerce Clause confers on Congress the authority to ban the use of marijuana, even when a state approves it for "medical purposes" and it is produced in small quantities for personal consumption. Many legal scholars criticize the Court's extremely broad reading of the Commerce Clause as inconsistent with its original meaning, but the Court's decision nonetheless stands.

If the RCTCA were enacted, it would conflict with the provisions of the Controlled Substances Act and invite extensive litigation that would almost certainly result in its being struck down. Until that happened, state law enforcement officers would be forced into a position of uncertainty regarding their conflicting obligations under federal and state law and cooperation with federal authorities.

Bogus Economics

An innovation of the campaign in support of RCTCA is its touting of the potential benefit of legalization to the government, in terms of additional revenues from taxing marijuana and savings from backing down in the "war on drugs." The National Organization for the Reform of Marijuana Laws (NORML), for example, claims that legalization "could yield California taxpayers over $1.2 billion per year" in tax benefits. According to a California NORML Report updated in October 2009, an excise tax of $50 per ounce would raise about $770 million to $900 million per year and save over $200 million in law enforcement costs per year. It is worth noting that $900 million equates to 18 million ounces—enough marijuana for Californians to smoke one billion marijuana cigarettes each year.

But these projections are highly speculative and riddled with unfounded assumptions. Dr. Rosalie Liccardo Pacula, an expert with the RAND Corporation who has studied the economics of drug policy for over 15 years, has explained that the California "Board of Equalization's estimate of $1.4 billion [in] potential revenue for the state is based on a series of assumptions that are in some instances subject to tremendous uncertainty and in other cases not validated." She urged the California Committee on Public Safety to conduct an honest and thorough cost-benefit analysis of the potential revenues and costs associated with legalizing marijuana. To date, no such realistic cost-benefit analysis has been done.

In her testimony before the committee, Dr. Pacula stated that prohibition raises the cost of production by at least 400 percent and that legalizing marijuana would cause the price of marijuana to fall considerably—much more than the 50 percent price reduction incorporated into the state's revenue model. Furthermore, she noted that a $50-per-ounce marijuana tax was not realistic, because it would represent a 100 percent tax on the cost of the product.

Under the state scheme, she testified, there would be "tremendous profit motive for the existing black market providers to stay in the market." The only way California could effectively eliminate the black market for marijuana, according to Dr. Pacula, "is to take away the substantial profits in the market and allow the price of marijuana to fall to an amount close to the cost of production. Doing so, however, will mean substantially smaller tax revenue than currently anticipated from this change in policy."

The RCTCA, in fact, allows for so much individual production of marijuana that even the Board of Equalization's $1.4 billion per year revenue estimate seems unlikely. Under the law, any resident could grow marijuana for "personal use" in a plot at home up to 25 square feet in size. One ounce of marijuana is enough for 60 to 120 marijuana cigarettes. One plant produces one to five pounds, or 16 to 80 ounces, of marijuana each year, and 25 square feet of land can sustain about 25 plants. Therefore, an individual will be able to produce 24,000 to 240,000 joints legally each year.

Not only is this more than any individual could possibly consume; it is also enough to encourage individuals to grow and sell pot under the individual allowance. Who would buy marijuana from a state-regulated store and pay the $50 tax per ounce in addition to the sale price when they can either grow it themselves or buy it at a much lower price from a friend or neighbor? In this way, the RCTCA undermines its supporters' lavish revenue claims.

Other Negative Social Costs

In addition to its direct effects on individual health, even moderate marijuana use imposes significant long-term costs through the ways that it affects individual users. Marijuana use is associated with cognitive difficulties and influences attention, concentration, and short-term memory. This damage affects drug users' ability to work and can put others at risk. Even if critical workers—for exam-

ple, police officers, airline pilots, and machine operators—used marijuana recreationally but remained sober on the job, the long-term cognitive deficiency that remained from regular drug use would sap productivity and place countless people in danger. Increased use would also send health care costs skyrocketing—costs borne not just by individual users, but also by the entire society.

For that reason, among others, the Obama Administration also rejects supporters' economic arguments. In his speech, Kerlikowske explained that tax revenue from cigarettes is far outweighed by their social costs: "Tobacco also does not carry its economic weight when we tax it; each year we spend more than $200 billion and collect only about $25 billion in taxes." If the heavy taxation of cigarettes is unable even to come close to making up for the health and other costs associated with their use, it seems doubtful at best that marijuana taxes would be sufficient to cover the costs of legalized marijuana—especially considering that, in addition to the other dangers of smoking marijuana, the physical health effects of just three to four joints are equivalent to those of an entire pack of cigarettes.

Other claims also do not measure up. One of the express purposes of the California initiative is to "put dangerous, underground street dealers out of business, so their influence in our communities will fade." But as explained above, many black-market dealers would rationally choose to remain in the black market to avoid taxation and regulation. Vibrant gray markets have developed throughout the world for many products that are legal, regulated, and heavily taxed. Cigarettes in Eastern Europe, alcohol in Scandinavia, luxury automobiles in Russia, and DVDs in the Middle East are all legal goods traded in gray markets that are wracked with violence. In Canada, an attempt at a $3 per pack tax on cigarettes was greeted with the creation of a black market that "accounted for perhaps 30 percent of sales."

Further, even if the RCTCA were to pass, marijuana would remain illegal in the entire United States under federal law while taxed only in California, a situation that would strengthen both California's gray market and the nationwide black market in illegal drugs. Fueled by generous growing allowances and an enormous supply in California, criminal sales operations would flourish as excess California marijuana was sold outside the state and, at the same time, out-of-state growers attempted to access the more permissive market inside the state.

In sum, legalization would put additional strain on an already faltering economy. In 2008, marijuana alone was involved in 375,000 emergency room visits. Drug overdoses already outnumber gunshot deaths in America and are approaching motor vehicle crashes as the nation's leading cause of accidental death. It is true that taxing marijuana sales would generate some tax revenue, but the cost of handling the influx of problems resulting from increased use would far outweigh any gain made by marijuana's taxation. Legalizing marijuana would serve only to compound the problems already associated with drug use.

Social Dislocation and Organized Crime

The final two arguments of those favoring legalization are intertwined. According to advocates of legalization, the government's efforts to combat the illegal drug trade have been an expensive failure. Consequently, they argue, focusing on substance abuse and treatment would be a more effective means of combating drug abuse while reducing the violence and social ills stemming from anti-drug enforcement efforts.

There is no doubt that if marijuana were legalized, more people, including juveniles, would consume it. Consider cigarettes: While their purchase by people under 18 is illegal, 20 percent of high school students admit to having smoked cigarettes in the past 30 days. Marijuana's illegal status "keeps potential drug users from using" marijuana in a way that no legalization scheme can replicate "by virtue of the fear of arrest and the embarrassment of being caught." With increased use comes increased abuse, as the fear of arrest and embarrassment will decrease.

Legalization advocates attempt to create in the minds of the public an image of a typical "responsible" user of marijuana: a person who is reasonable and accountable even when under the influence of marijuana. And for those few that don't fit that image? Society will treat them and restore them to full health. The facts, however, are much uglier.

The RAND Corporation projects a 50 percent increase in marijuana-related traffic fatalities under the RCTCA. That alone should weigh heavily on California voters this fall. In a 2008 national survey, approximately 3 million Americans 12 years old or older started using illicit drugs in the past year—almost 8,000 new users per day. The most commonly used illicit drug is marijuana, especially among the 20 million Americans over 12 who were users in 2008. In California, 62 percent of all marijuana treatment cases are already individuals under 21. Legalization will increase the number of underage users.

Keeping marijuana illegal will undoubtedly keep many young people from using it. Eliminate that criminal

sanction (and moral disapprobation), and more youth will use the drug, harming their potential and ratcheting up treatment costs.

Educators know that students using marijuana underperform when compared to their non-using peers. Teachers, coaches, guidance counselors, and school principals have seen the negative effect of marijuana on their students. The Rev. Dr. D. Stuart Dunnan, Headmaster of Saint James School in St. James, Maryland, says of marijuana use by students:

> The chemical effect of marijuana is to take away ambition. The social effect is to provide an escape from challenges and responsibilities with a like-minded group of teenagers who are doing the same thing. Using marijuana creates losers. At a time when we're concerned about our lack of academic achievement relative to other countries, legalizing marijuana will be disastrous.

Additionally, making marijuana legal in California will fuel drug cartels and violence, particularly because the drug will still be illegal at the national level. The local demand will increase in California, but reputable growers, manufacturers, and retailers will still be unwilling—as they should be—to produce and distribute marijuana. Even without the federal prohibition, most reputable producers would not survive the tort liability from such a dangerous product. Thus, the vacuum will be filled by illegal drug cartels.

According to the Department of Justice's National Drug Threat Assessment for 2010, Mexican drug trafficking organizations (DTOs) "have expanded their cultivation operations in the United States, an ongoing trend for the past decade. . . . Well-organized criminal groups and DTOs that produce domestic marijuana do so because of the high profitability of and demand for marijuana in the United States."

Legalize marijuana, and the demand for marijuana goes up substantially as the deterrence effect of law enforcement disappears. Yet not many suppliers will operate legally, refusing to subject themselves to the established state regulatory scheme—not to mention taxation—while still risking federal prosecution, conviction, and prison time. So who will fill the void?

Violent, brutal, and ruthless, Mexican DTOs will work to maintain their black-market profits at the expense of American citizens' safety. Every week, there are news articles cataloguing the murders, kidnappings, robberies, and other thuggish brutality employed by Mexican drug gangs along the border. It is nonsensical to argue that these gangs will simply give up producing marijuana when it is legalized; indeed, their profits might soar, depending on the actual tax in California and the economics of the interstate trade. While such profits might not be possible if marijuana was legalized at the national level and these gangs were undercut by mass production, that is unlikely ever to happen. Nor does anyone really believe that the gangs will subject themselves to state and local regulation, including taxation. And since the California ballot does nothing to eliminate the black market for marijuana—quite the opposite, in fact—legalizing marijuana will only incentivize Mexican DTOs to grow more marijuana to feed the demand and exploit the black market.

Furthermore, should California legalize marijuana, other entrepreneurs will inevitably attempt to enter the marketplace and game the system. In doing so, they will compete with Mexican DTOs and other criminal organizations. Inevitably, violence will follow, and unlike now, that violence will not be confined to the border as large-scale growers seek to protect their turf—turf that will necessarily include anywhere they grow, harvest, process, or sell marijuana. While this may sound far-fetched, Californians in Alameda County are already experiencing the reality of cartel-run marijuana farms on sometimes stolen land, protected by "guys [who] are pretty heavily armed and willing to protect their merchandise."

It is not uncommon for drugs with large illegal markets to be controlled by cartels despite attempts to roll them into the normal medical control scheme. For instance, cocaine has a medical purpose and can be prescribed by doctors as *Erythroxylum coca*, yet its true production and distribution are controlled by drug cartels and organized crime. As competition from growers and dispensaries authorized by the RCTCA cuts further into the Mexican DTOs' business, Californians will face a real possibility of bloodshed on their own soil as the cartels' profit-protection measures turn from defensive to offensive.

Thus, marijuana legalization will increase crime, drug use, and social dislocation across the state of California—the exact opposite of what pro-legalization advocates promise.

Conclusion

Pro-marijuana advocates promoting the Regulate, Control and Tax Cannabis Act of 2010 invite Californians to imagine a hypothetical and idyllic "pot market," but America's national approach to drug use, addiction, and crime must be serious, based on sound policy and solid evidence.

In 1982, President Ronald Reagan adopted a national drug strategy that took a comprehensive approach consisting of five components: international cooperation, research, strengthened law enforcement, treatment and rehabilitation, and prevention and education. It was remarkably successful: Illegal drug use by young adults dropped more than 50 percent.

Reagan was right to make drug control a major issue of his presidency. Illegal drugs such as marijuana are responsible for a disproportionate share of violence and social decline in America. Accordingly, federal law, representing the considered judgment of medical science and the nation's two political branches of government, takes the unequivocal position that marijuana is dangerous and has no significant beneficial uses.

California cannot repeal that law or somehow allow its citizens to contravene it. Thus, it has two options. By far the best option is to commit itself seriously to the federal approach and pursue a strategy that attempts to prevent illegal drug use in the first place and reduce the number of drug users. This may require changes in drug policy, and perhaps in sentencing guidelines for marijuana users charged with simple possession, but simply legalizing a harmful drug—that is, giving up—is not a responsible option.

The other option is to follow the above path in the short term while conducting further research and possibly working with other states in Congress to consider changes in federal law. Although those who oppose the legalization of marijuana have every reason to believe that further, legitimate scientific research will confirm the dangers of its use, no side should try to thwart the sober judgment of the national legislature and sister states.

In short, no state will likely be allowed to legalize marijuana on its own, with such serious, negative cross-state spillover effects. Yet even if California could act as if it were an island, the legalization route would still end very badly for the Golden State. There is strong evidence to suggest that legalizing marijuana would serve little purpose other than to worsen the state's drug problems—addiction, violence, disorder, and death. While long on rhetoric, the legalization movement, by contrast, is short on facts.

Charles D. Stimson is a senior legal fellow in the Center for Legal & Judicial Studies at The Heritage Foundation. Before joining The Heritage Foundation, he served as deputy assistant secretary of defense, as a local, state, federal, and military prosecutor, and as a defense attorney and law professor.

EXPLORING THE ISSUE

Should Recreational Drugs Be Legalized?

Critical Thinking and Reflection

1. How harmful are illegal drugs? Are they more dangerous than alcohol? Can we distinguish among them?
2. Is the history of prohibition of alcohol relevant in revealing the consequences of prohibition? Are the indicted substances sufficiently different so that comparisons are not useful?
3. In view of crowded prisons, should we consider alternative means of punishment for some categories of drug offenders? Does prohibition inspire its violation?
4. Why shouldn't we have a civil right to do what may be harmful to ourselves?
5. Do you believe there would be a larger societal impact if recreational drugs were to be legalized? If so, what could it be? If not, why not?

Is There Common Ground?

Advocates of legalization mostly believe that it must be accompanied by restraints on drug usage. Just as alcohol is subject to restrictions regarding its manufacturing and sale, and states vary in their requirements regarding the sale of alcohol, so legal drugs may be subject to strict controls. Absolute libertarians will dissent, arguing that there should be no regulation, but a vast majority of Americans would disagree. It would be likely that legalization would involve laws on purity of contents and other requirements that apply to alcohol and other legal drugs.

It is possible that supporters of prohibition may distinguish among the illicit drugs based on present awareness of their different effects. Defenders of drug prohibition might consent to the sale of medical marijuana, due to the claim that its use can reduce the pain of certain diseases. However, the experience in California and elsewhere is that licensing medical marijuana is likely to lead to the easy medical dispensing of medical marijuana to persons who are not legally entitled to it.

Perhaps the true common ground has already begun to emerge. States are able to legalize within their boundaries and not fear federal crackdowns so long as they regulate the drug within federal guidelines. While such a measure works well for the time being, questions will arise in 2016 when a new president takes office. After all, the current set-up keeps recreational drugs illegal at the federal level and relies on policy memos from a political appointee. For the states to feel safe in their status, it will be necessary for a clearer relationship to develop between federal and state authorities on these issues so enforcement does not ultimately become a political whim of the sitting president.

Create Central

www.mhhe.com/createcentral

Additional Resources

Jonathan P. Caulkins, Angela Hawken, Beau Kilmer, and Mark A. R. Kleiman, *Marijuana Legalization: What Everyone Needs to Know* (Oxford University Press, 2012)

Larry Gaines, *Drug, Crimes, & Justice* (Waveland Press, 2002)

Internet References . . .

Citizens Against Legalizing Marijuana

www.calmca.org/about/

Gallup

www.gallup.com/poll/165539/first-time-americans
-favor-legalizing-marijuana.aspx

Marijuana Policy Project

www.mpp.org/

**National Organization for the Reform of
Marijuana Laws**

http://norml.org/

Public Broadcasting Service

www.pbs.org/wnet/need-to-know/ask-the-experts
/ask-the-experts-legalizing-marijuana/15474/

Selected, Edited, and with Issue Framing Material by:
Richard P. Halgin, *University of Massachusetts, Amherst*

ISSUE

Are Energy Drinks with Alcohol Dangerous Enough to Ban?

YES: Don Troop, from "Four Loko Does Its Job with Efficiency and Economy, Students Say," *The Chronicle of Higher Education* (2010)

NO: Jacob Sullum, from "Loco Over Four Loko," *Reason Magazine* (2011)

Learning Outcomes
After reading this issue, you should be able to:
• Discuss the health implications of energy drinks.
• Discuss the argument that energy drinks should be banned from sale and distribution.
• Assess the reason for the drink's popularity among college students.

ISSUE SUMMARY

YES: *The Chronicle of Higher Education* journalist Don Troop argues that the combination of caffeine and alcohol is extremely dangerous and should not be sold or marketed to college students and young people.

NO: Journalist and editor of *Reason Magazine* Jacob Sullum disagrees and claims that alcoholic energy drinks should not have been targeted and banned since many other products are far more dangerous.

Energy drinks such as Four Loko are alcoholic beverages that originally also contained caffeine and other stimulants. These products have been the object of legal, ethical, and health concerns related to companies supposedly marketing them to underaged consumers and the alleged danger of combining alcohol and caffeine. After the beverage was banned in several states, a product reintroduction in December 2010 removed caffeine and the malt beverage is no longer marketed as an energy drink.

In 2009, companies that produced and sold caffeinated alcohol beverages were investigated, on the grounds that their products were being inappropriately advertised to an underage audience and that the drinks had possible health risks by masking feelings of intoxication due to the caffeine content. Energy drinks came under major fire in 2010, as colleges and universities across the United States began to see injuries and blackouts related to the drink's consumption. Colleges such as the University of Rhode Island banned this product from their campus that year. The state of Washington banned Four Loko after nine university students, all under 20, from Central Washington University became ill after consuming the beverage at a nearby house party. The Central Washington college students were hospitalized and one student, with extremely high blood alcohol content, nearly died.

Following the hospitalization of 17 students and 6 visitors in 2010, Ramapo College of New Jersey banned the possession and consumption of Four Loko on its campus. Several other colleges also prohibited the sale of the beverages. Many colleges and universities sent out notices informing their students to avoid the drinks because of the risk associated with their consumption.

Other efforts to control the use of energy drinks have been under way. The Pennsylvania Liquor Control Board sent letters to all liquor stores urging distributors to discontinue the sale of the drink. The PLCB also sent letters to all colleges and universities warning them of the dangers of the product. While the board has stopped short of a ban, it has asked retailers to stop selling the drink until U.S. Food and Drug Administration (FDA) findings prove the products are safe. Several grocery chains have voluntarily removed energy beverages from their stores. In Oregon, the sale of the restricted products carried a penalty of 30-day suspension of liquor license.

The U.S. FDA issued a warning letter in 2010 to four manufacturers of caffeinated alcohol beverages stating that the caffeine added to their malt alcoholic beverages is an "unsafe food additive" and said that further action, including seizure of their products, may occur under federal law. The FDA determined that beverages that combine caffeine with alcohol, such as Four Loco energy drinks, are a "public health concern" and couldn't stay on the market in their current form. The FDA also stated that concerns have been raised that caffeine can mask some of the sensory cues individuals might normally rely on to determine their level of intoxication. Warning letters were issued to each of the four companies requiring them to provide to the FDA in writing within 15 days of the specific steps the firms will be taking. Prior to the FDA ruling, many con-

sumers bought and hoarded large quantities of the beverage. This buying frenzy created a black market for energy drinks, with some sellers charging inflated prices. A reformulated version of the drink was put on shelves in late 2010. The new product had exactly the same design as the original, but the caffeine had been removed.

Effective February 2013, cans of Four Loko carry an "Alcohol Facts" label. The label change is part of a final settlement between the Federal Trade Commission and Phusion Projects, the manufacturer of Four Loko. The company still disagrees with the commission's allegations, but said in a statement that the agreement provides a practical way for the company to move ahead. The FTC claimed that ads for Four Loko inaccurately claimed that a 23.5-ounce can contain the alcohol equivalent of one to two cans of beer. In fact, the FTC says, it's more like four to five beers. In the YES and NO selections, Don Troop argues that the combination of caffeine and alcohol is extremely dangerous and should not be sold or marketed to college students and young people. Journalist and editor of *Reason Magazine* Jacob Sullum disagrees and claims that alcoholic energy drinks should not have been targeted and banned since many other products are far more dangerous.

YES ⬅   **Don Troop**

Four Loko Does Its Job with Efficiency and Economy, Students Say

It's Friday night in this steep-hilled college town, and if anyone needs an excuse to party, here are two: In 30 minutes the Mountaineers football team will kick off against the UConn Huskies in East Hartford, Conn., and tonight begins the three-day Halloween weekend.

A few blocks from the West Virginia University campus, young people crowd the aisles of Ashebrooke Liquor Outlet, an airy shop that is popular among students. One rack in the chilled-beverage cooler is nearly empty, the one that is usually filled with 23.5-ounce cans of Four Loko, a fruity malt beverage that combines the caffeine of two cups of coffee with the buzz factor of four to six beers.

"That's what everyone's buying these days," says a liquor store employee, "Loko and Burnett's vodka," a line of distilled spirits that are commonly mixed with nonalcoholic energy drinks like Red Bull and Monster to create fruity cocktails with a stimulating kick.

Four Loko's name comes from its four primary ingredients—alcohol (12 percent by volume), caffeine, taurine, and guarana. Although it is among dozens of caffeinated alcoholic drinks on the market, Four Loko has come to symbolize the dangers of such beverages because of its role in binge-drinking incidents this fall involving students at New Jersey's Ramapo College and at Central Washington University. Ramapo and Central Washington have banned Four Loko from their campuses, and several other colleges have sent urgent e-mail messages advising students not to drink it. But whether Four Loko is really "blackout in a can" or just the highest-profile social lubricant of the moment is unclear.

Just uphill from Ashebrooke Liquor Outlet, four young men stand on a porch sipping cans of Four Loko—fruit punch and cranberry-lemonade. All are upperclassmen except for one, Philip Donnachie, who graduated in May. He says most Four Loko drinkers he knows like to guzzle a can of it at home before meeting up with friends, a custom that researchers in the field call "predrinking."

"Everyone that's going to go out for the night, they're going to start with a Four Loko first," Mr. Donnachie says, adding that he generally switches to beer.

A student named Tony says he paid $5.28 at Ashebrooke for two Lokos—a bargain whether the goal is to get tipsy or flat-out drunk. Before the drink became infamous, he says, he would see students bring cans of it into classrooms. "The teachers didn't know what it was," Tony says, and if they asked, the student would casually reply, "It's an energy drink."

Farther uphill, on the sidewalk along Grant Avenue, the Tin Man from *The Wizard of Oz* carries a Loko—watermelon flavor, judging by its color. Down the block a keg party spills out onto the front porch, where guests sprawl on a sofa and flick cigarette ashes over the railing. No one here is drinking Four Loko, but most are eager to talk about the product because they've heard that it could be banned by the federal government as a result of the student illnesses.

Research Gap

That's not likely to happen anytime soon, according to the Food and Drug Administration.

"The FDA's decision regarding the regulatory status of caffeine added to various alcoholic beverages will be a high priority for the agency," Michael L. Herndon, an FDA spokesman, wrote in an e-mail message. "However, a decision regarding the use of caffeine in alcoholic beverages could take some time." The FDA does not consider such drinks to be "generally recognized as safe." A year ago the agency gave 27 manufacturers 30 days to provide evidence to the contrary, if it existed. Only 19 of the companies have responded.

Dennis L. Thombs is chairman of the Department of Social and Behavioral Sciences at the University of North Texas Health Science Center, in Fort Worth. He knows a great deal about the drinking habits of young people.

Last year he was the lead author on a paper submitted to the journal *Addictive Behaviors* that described his team's study of bar patrons' consumption of energy drinks and alcohol in the college town of Gainesville, Fla. After interviewing 802 patrons and testing their blood-alcohol content, Mr. Thombs and his fellow researchers concluded that energy drinks' labels should clearly describe the ingredients, their amounts, and the potential risks involved in using the products.

But Mr. Thombs says the government should have more data before it decides what to do about alcoholic energy drinks.

"There's still a big gap in this research," he says. "We need to get better pharmacological measures in natural drinking environments" like bars.

He says he has submitted a grant application to the National Institutes of Health in hopes of doing just that.

"Liquid Crack"

Back at the keg party in Morgantown, a student wearing Freddy Krueger's brown fedora and razor-blade glove calls Four Loko "liquid crack" and says he prefers not to buy it for his underage friends. "I'll buy them something else," he says, "but not Four Loko."

Dipsy from the *Teletubbies* says the people abusing Four Loko are younger students, mostly 17- and 18-year-olds. He calls the students who became ill at Ramapo and Central Washington "a bunch of kids that don't know how to drink."

Two freshmen at the party, Gabrielle and Meredith, appear to confirm that assertion.

"I like Four Loko because it's cheap and it gets me drunk," says Gabrielle, 19, who seems well on her way to getting drunk tonight, Four Loko or not. "Especially for concerts. I drink two Four Lokos before going, and then I don't have to spend $14 on a couple drinks at the stadium."

Meredith, 18 and equally intoxicated, says that although she drinks Four Loko, she favors a ban. "They're 600 calories, and they're gross."

An interview with Alex, a 19-year-old student at a religiously affiliated college in the Pacific Northwest, suggests one reason that the drink might be popular among a younger crowd. In his state and many others, the laws that govern the sale of Four Loko and beer are less stringent than those for hard liquor.

That eases the hassle for older friends who buy for Alex. These days that's not a concern, though. He stopped drinking Four Loko because of how it made him feel the next day.

"Every time I drank it I got, like, a blackout," says Alex. "Now I usually just drink beer."

DON TROOP is a senior editor of the *Chronicles of Higher Education,* which covers state policy, as well as economic development, town-and-gown relations, fund raising and endowments, and other financial issues at the campus level.

Jacob Sullum  **NO**

Loco Over Four Loko: How a Fruity, Brightly Colored Malt Beverage Drove Politicians to Madness in Two Short Years

In a column at the end of October, *The New York Times* restaurant critic Frank Bruni looked down his nose at Four Loko, a fruity, bubbly, brightly colored malt beverage with a lower alcohol content than Chardonnay and less caffeine per ounce than Red Bull. "It's a malt liquor in confectionery drag," Bruni wrote, "not only raising questions about the marketing strategy behind it but also serving as the clearest possible reminder that many drinkers aren't seeking any particular culinary or aesthetic enjoyment. They're taking a drug. The more festively it's dressed and the more vacuously it goes down, the better."

Less than two weeks after Bruni panned Four Loko and its déclassé drinkers, he wrote admiringly of the "ambition and thought" reflected in hoity-toity coffee cocktails offered by the Randolph at Broome, a boutique bar in downtown Manhattan. He conceded that "there is a long if not entirely glorious history of caffeine and alcohol joining forces, of whiskey or liqueurs poured into after-dinner coffee by adults looking for the same sort of effect that Four Loko fans seek: an extension of the night without a surrender of the buzz."

Like Bruni's distaste for Four Loko, the moral panic that led the Food and Drug Administration (FDA) to ban the beverage and others like it in November, just two years after it was introduced, cannot be explained in pharmacological terms. As Brum admitted and as the drink's Chicago-based manufacturer, Phusion Projects, kept pointing out to no avail, there is nothing new about mixing alcohol with caffeine. What made this particular formulation intolerable—indeed "adulterated," according to the FDA—was not its chemical composition but its class connotations: the wild and crazy name, the garish packaging, the low cost, the eight color-coded flavors, and the drink's popularity among young partiers who see "blackout in a can" as a recommendation. Those attributes made

Four Loko offensive to the guardians of public health and morals in a way that Irish coffee, rum and cola, and even Red Bull and vodka never were.

The FDA itself conceded that the combination of alcohol and caffeine, a feature of many drinks, that remain legal, was not the real issue. Rather, the agency complained that "the marketing of the caffeinated versions of this class of alcoholic beverage appears to be specifically directed to young adults," who are "especially vulnerable" to "combined ingestion of caffeine and alcohol."

Because Four Loko was presumed to be unacceptably hazardous, the FDA did not feel a need to present much in the way of scientific evidence. A grand total of two studies have found that college-students who drink alcoholic beverages containing caffeine (typically bar- or home-mixed cocktails unaffected by the FDA's ban) tend to drink more and are more prone to risky behavior than college students who drink alcohol by itself. Neither study clarified whether the differences were due to the psychoactive effects of caffeine or to the predispositions of hearty partiers attracted to drinks they believe will help keep them going all night. But that distinction did not matter to panic-promoting politicians and their publicists in the press, who breathlessly advertised Four Loko while marveling at its rising popularity.

This dual function of publicity about an officially condemned intoxicant is familiar to anyone who has witnessed or read about previous scare campaigns against stigmatized substances, ranging from absinthe to *Salvia divinorum*. So is the evidentiary standard employed by Four Loko alarmists: If something bad happens and Four Loko is anywhere in the vicinity, blame Four Loko.

The National Highway Traffic Safety Administration counted 13,800 alcohol-related fatalities in 2008. It did not place crashes involving Four Loko drinkers in a special category. But news organizations around the country, primed to perceive the drink as unusually dangerous, routinely did. Three days before the FDA declared Four Loko illegal, a 14-year-old stole his parents' SUV and crashed it into a guardrail on Interstate 35 in Denton, Texas. His girlfriend, who was not wearing a seat belt, was ejected from the car and killed. Police, who said they found a 12-pack of beer and five cans of Four Loko in the SUV, charged the boy with intoxication manslaughter. Here is how the local Fox station headlined its story: "'Four Loko' Found in Deadly Teen Crash."

Likewise, college students were getting sick after drinking too much long before Four Loko was introduced in August 2008. According to the federal government's Drug Abuse Warning Network, more than 100,000 18-to-20-year-olds make alcohol-related visits to American emergency rooms every year. Yet 15 students at two colleges who were treated for alcohol poisoning after consuming excessive amounts of Four Loko were repeatedly held up as examples of the drink's unique dangers.

If all alcoholic beverages had to satisfy the reckless college student test, all of them would be banned. In a sense, then, we should be grateful for the government's inconsistency. With Four Loko, as with other taboo tipples and illegal drugs, there is little logic to the process by which the scapegoat is selected, but there are noticeable patterns. Once an intoxicant has been identified with a disfavored group—in this case, heedless, hedonistic "young adults"—everything about it is viewed in that light. Soon the wildest charges seem plausible: Four Loko is "a recipe for disaster," "a death wish disguised as an energy drink," a "witch's brew" that drives you mad, makes you shoot yourself in the head, and compels you to steal vehicles and crash them into things.

The timeline that follows shows how quickly a legal product can be transformed into contraband once it becomes the target of such over-the-top opprobrium. Although it's too late for Four Loko, lessons gleaned from the story of its demise could help prevent the next panicky prohibition by scaremongers who criminalize first and ask questions later.

June 2008: Anheuser-Busch, under pressure from 11 attorneys general who are investigating the brewing giant for selling the caffeinated malt beverages Tilt and Bud Extra, agrees to decaffeinate the drinks. "Drinking is not a sport, a race, or an endurance test," says New York Attorney General Andrew Cuomo, who will later be elected governor. "Adding alcohol to energy drinks sends exactly the wrong message about responsible drinking, most especially to young people."

August 2008: Phusion Projects, a Chicago company founded in 2005 by three recent graduates of Ohio State University, introduces Four Loko, which has an alcohol content of up to 12 percent (depending on state regulations); comes in brightly colored, 23.5-ounce cans; contains the familiar energy-drink ingredients caffeine, guarana, and taurine; and is eventually available in eight fruity, neon-hued varieties.

September 2008: The Center for Science in the Public Interest (CSPI), a pro-regulation group that is proud of being known as "the food police," sues MillerCoors Brewing Company over its malt beverage Sparks, arguing that the caffeine and guarana in the drink are additives that have not been approved by the FDA. "Mix alcohol and stimulants with a young person's sense of invincibility," says CSPI's George Hacker, "and you have a recipe for disaster. Sparks is a drink designed to mask feelings of drunkenness and to encourage people to keep drinking past the point at which they otherwise would have stopped. The end result is more drunk driving, more injuries, and more sexual assaults."

December 2008: In a deal with 13 attorneys general and the city of San Francisco, MillerCoors agrees to reformulate Sparks, removing the caffeine, guarana, taurine, and ginseng. Cuomo says caffeinated alcoholic beverages are "fundamentally dangerous and put drinkers of all ages at risk."

July 2009: *The Wall Street Journal* reports that Cuomo, Connecticut Attorney General Richard Blumenthal (now a U.S. senator), California Attorney General Jerry Brown (now governor), and their counterparts in several other states are investigating Four Loko and Joose, a close competitor. The National Association of Convenience Stores says the two brands are growing fast now that Tilt and Sparks have left the caffeinated malt beverage market.

August 2009: To demonstrate the threat that Four Loko poses to the youth of America, Blumenthal cites an online testimonial from a fan of the drink: "You just gotta drink it and drink it and drink it and drink it and not even worry about it because it's awesome and you're just partying and having fun and getting wild and drinking it." *The Chicago Tribune* cannot locate that particular comment on Phusion Projects' website, but it does find this: "I'm having a weird reaction to Four that makes me want to dance in my bra and panties. Please advise."

September 2009: Eighteen attorneys general ask the FDA to investigate the safety of alcoholic beverages containing caffeine.

November 2009: The FDA sends letters to 27 companies known to sell caffeinated alcoholic beverages, warning them that the combination has never been officially approved and asking them to submit evidence that it is "generally recognized as safe," as required by the Food,

Drug, and Cosmetic Act. In addition to Phusion Projects, the recipients include Joose's manufacturer, United Brands; Charge Beverages, which sells similar products; the PINK Spirits Company, which makes caffeinated vodka, rum, gin, whiskey, and sake; and even the Ithaca Beer Company, which at one point made a special-edition stout brewed with coffee. "I continue to be very concerned that these drinks are extremely dangerous," says Illinois Attorney General Lisa Madigan, "especially in the hands of young people."

February 2010: In a feature story carried by several newspapers under headlines such as "Alcopops Only Look Innocent and Can Hook Kids," Kim Hone-McMahan of the *Akron Beacon Journal* outlines one scenario in which these extremely dangerous drinks might end up in tiny hands: "Intentionally or by accident, a child could grab an alcoholic beverage that looks like an energy drink, and hand it to Mom to pay for at the register. Without taking a closer look at the label, Mom may think it's just another brand of nonalcoholic energy beverage." It does seem like the sort of mistake that Hone-McMahan, who confuses fermented malt beverages with distilled spirits and warns parents about an alcoholic energy drink that was never actually introduced, might make. She explains that the combination of alcohol and caffeine "can confuse the nervous system," producing "wired, wide-awake drunks."

July 12, 2010: Sen. Charles Schumer (D-N.Y.) urges the Federal Trade Commission to investigate Four Loko and products like it. "It is my understanding that caffeine-infused, flavored malt beverages are becoming increasingly popular among teenagers," he writes. "The style and promotion of these products is extremely troubling." Schumer complains that the packaging of Joose and Four Loko is "designed to appear hip with flashy colors and funky designs that could appeal to younger consumers."

July 29, 2010: Schumer, joined by Sens. Dianne Feinstein (D-Calif.), Amy Klobuchar (D-Minn.), and Jeff Merkley (D-Ore.), urges the FDA to complete its investigation. "The FDA needs to determine once and for all if these drinks are safe, and if they're not, they ought to be banned," says Schumer, right before telling the FDA the conclusion it should reach: "Caffeine and alcohol are a dangerous mix, especially for young people."

August 1, 2010: After a crash in St. Petersburg, Florida, that kills four visitors from Orlando, police arrest 20-year-old Demetrius Jordan and charge him with drunk driving and manslaughter. The *St. Petersburg Times* reports that Jordan, who "had been drinking liquor and a caffeinated alcoholic beverage and smoking marijuana prior to the crash," "may have been going in excess of 80 mph when he crashed into the other vehicle." It notes that a "can of Four Loko was found on the floor of the back seat."

August 5, 2010: In a follow-up story, the *St. Petersburg Times* reports that "Four Loko, the caffeine-fueled malt liquor that police say Demetrius Jordan downed before he was accused of driving drunk and killing four people, is part of a new breed of beverages stirring controversy across the country." It quotes Bruce Goldberger, a toxicologist at the University of Florida, who declares, "I don't think there's a place for these beverages in the marketplace." The headline: "Alcohol, Caffeine: A Deadly Combo?"

August 12, 2010: The *Orlando Sentinel*, catching up with the *St. Petersburg Times,* shows it can quote Goldberger too. "It's a very bad combination having alcohol, plus caffeine, plus the brain of a young person," he says. "It's like a perfect storm." The headline: "Did High-Octane Drink Fuel Deadly Crash?"

September 2010: Peter Mercer, president of Ramapo College in Mahwah, New Jersey, bans Four Loko and other caffeinated malt beverages from campus after several incidents in which a total of 23 students were hospitalized for alcohol poisoning. Just six of the students were drinking Four Loko. Mercer later tells the Associated Press, "There's no redeeming social purpose to be served by having the beverage."

October 9, 2010: In a story about nine gang members who tied up and tortured a gay man after luring him to an abandoned building in the Bronx by telling him they were having a party, the *New York Daily News* plays up the detail that they "forced him to guzzle four cans" of the Four Loko he had brought with him. "The sodomized man couldn't give police a clear account of what he'd gone through," the paper reports, "possibly because of the Four Loko he was forced to drink."

October 10, 2010: In a follow-up story, the *Daily News* reports that Four Loko, a "wild drink full of caffeine and booze," "is causing controversy from coast to coast," citing the deadly crash in St. Petersburg.

October 13, 2010: Police in New Port Richey, Florida, arrest Justin Barker, 21, after he breaks into an old woman's home, trashes the place, strips naked, defecates on the floor, and then breaks into another house, where he falls asleep on the couch. Barker says Four Loko made him do it.

October 15, 2010: Calling Four Loko "a quick and intense high that has been dubbed 'blackout in a can,'" the Passaic County, New Jersey, *Herald News* notes the Ramapo College ban and quotes Mahwah Police Chief James Batelli. "The bottom line on the product is it gets you very drunk, very quick," he says. "To me, Four Loko is just a dangerous substance." The "blackout in a can" sobriquet, obviously hyperbolic when applied to a beverage that contains less alcohol per container than a bottle of wine, originated with Four Loko fans who considered it high praise; one of their Facebook pages is titled "four lokos are blackouts in a can and the end of my morals."

October 19, 2010: Bruce Goldberger, who co-authored one of the two studies linking caffeinated alcohol to risky behavior, tells the *Pittsburgh Post-Gazette* "the science is clear that consumption of alcohol with caffeine leads to risky behaviors." Mary Claire O'Brien, the Wake Forest University researcher who co-authored the other study, expresses her anger at the FDA. "I'm mad as a hornet that they didn't do something in the first place," she says, "and I'm mad as a hornet that they haven't done anything yet."

October 20, 2010: Based on a single case of a 19-year-old who came to Temple University Hospital in Philadelphia with chest pains after drinking Four Loko, ABC News warns that the stuff, which contains about one-third as much caffeine per ounce as coffee, can cause fatal heart attacks in perfectly healthy people. "That was the only explanation we had," says the doctor who treated the 19-year-old, before extrapolating further from his sample of one: "This is a dangerous product from what we've seen. It doesn't have to be chronic use. I think it could happen to somebody on a first-time use."

October 25, 2010: Citing the hospitalization of nine Central Washington University students for alcohol poisoning following an October 8 party in Roslyn where they drank Four Loko along with beer, rum, and vodka, Washington Attorney General Rob McKenna calls for a ban on caffeinated malt liquor. "The wide availability of the alcoholic energy drinks means that a single mistake can be deadly," he says. "They're marketed to kids by using fruit flavors that mask the taste of alcohol, and they have such high levels of stimulants that people have no idea how inebriated they really are." McKenna's office cites Ken Briggs, chairman of the university's physical education department, who says Four Loko is known as "liquid cocaine" as well as "blackout in a can," and with good reason, since it is "a binge drinker's dream."

October 26, 2010: McKenna's reaction to college students who drank too much Four Loko, like Peter Mercer's at Ramapo, attracts national attention. A Pennsylvania E.R. doctor quoted by *The New York Times* calls Four Loko "a recipe for disaster" and "one of the most dangerous new alcohol concoctions I have ever seen."

November 1, 2010: The Pennsylvania Liquor Control Board asks retailers to stop selling Four Loko, which is produced at the former Rolling Rock brewery in Latrobe,

because it may "pose a significant threat to the health of all Pennsylvanians." State Rep. Robert Donatucci (D-Philadelphia) says "there is overriding circumstantial evidence that this combination may be very dangerous," and "until we can determine its effect on people and what kind of danger it may present, it should be yanked from the shelves."

November 3, 2010: Two Chicago aldermen propose an ordinance that would ban Four Loko from the city where its manufacturer is based. "I think it is completely irresponsible," says one, "to manufacture and market a product that can make young people so intoxicated so fast."

November 4, 2010: The Michigan Liquor Control Commission bans 55 "alcohol energy drinks," including Four Loko, Joose, a "hard" iced tea that no longer exists, a cola-flavored variety of Jack Daniel's Country Cocktails, and an India pale ale brewed with yerba mate. "With all the things that are happening, it's very alarming," explains commission chairwoman Nida Samona. "It's more serious than any of us ever imagined."

November 8, 2010: Oklahoma's Alcoholic Beverage Laws Enforcement Commission bans Four Loko from the state "in light of the growing scientific evidence against alcohol energy drinks, and the October 8th incident involving Four Loko in Roslyn, Washington."

November 9, 2010: NPR quotes Washington State University student Jarod Franklin as an authority on Four Loko's effects. "We would start to lose those inhibitions," he says, "and then [it would be like], 'How did you get a broken knuckle?' 'Oh, I punched through a three-inch layer of ice [because] you bet me I couldn't.'"

November 10, 2010: The Washington State Liquor Control Board bans beverages that "combine beer, strong beer, or malt liquor with caffeine, guarana, taurine, or other similar substances." Gov. Christine Gregoire, who recommended the ban, explains her reasoning: "I was particularly concerned that these drinks tend to target young people. Reports of inexperienced or underage drinkers consuming them in reckless amounts have given us cause for concern. . . . By taking these drinks off the shelves we are saying 'no' to irresponsible drinking and taking steps to prevent incidents like the one that made these college students so ill."

Sen. Schumer urges the New York State Liquor Authority to "immediately ban caffeinated alcoholic beverages." He says drinks like Four Loko "are a toxic, dangerous mix of caffeine and alcohol, and they are spreading like a plague across the country." Schumer claims "studies have shown that caffeinated alcoholic beverages raise unique and disturbing safety concerns, especially for younger drinkers." While they "can be extremely hazardous for teens and adults alike," he says, they "pose a unique danger because they target young people" with their "vibrantly colored aluminum can colors and funky designs."

November 12, 2010: A CBS station in Baltimore reports that two cans of Four Loko caused a 21-year-old Maryland woman to "lose her mind," steal a friend's pickup truck, and crash it into a telephone pole, killing herself.

A CBS station in Philadelphia reports that a middle-aged suburban dad "spiraled into a hallucinogenic frenzy" featuring "nightmarish delusions" after drinking a can and a half of Four Loko. "It was like he was stuck inside a horror movie and he couldn't get out and I couldn't get him out," the man's wife says. "In his mind, he had harmed all of our kids and he had to kill me and kill himself so that we could go to heaven to take care of them. Next thing I know, he was having convulsions [and] making gurgling sounds as if someone were choking him, and then he stopped breathing."

Connecticut Attorney General Blumenthal urges the FDA to "impose a nationwide ban on these dangerous and potentially deadly drinks."

November 14, 2010: Under pressure from Gov. David Paterson and the state liquor authority, Phusion Projects agrees to stop shipping Four Loko to New York. "We have an obligation to keep products that are potentially hazardous off the shelves," says the liquor authority's chairman.

Bruce Goldberger tells the *New Haven Register* Four Loko is "a very significant problem" for the "instant gratification generation." The kids today, he says, "text, they have iPhones, and they can access the Internet any minute of their life. And now, they can get drunk for literally less than $5, and they can get drunk very rapidly."

November 15, 2010: WBZ, the CBS affiliate in Boston, reports that the Massachusetts Alcoholic Beverages Control Commission plans to ban Four Loko. According to WBZ, commission officials say the drink—a fermented malt beverage with an alcohol content of 12 percent, compared to 40 percent or more for distilled spirits—"is really not a malt liquor, but a much more potent form of hard liquor, like vodka." The commission's chairman explains that the ban is aimed at protecting consumers who cannot read: "We are concerned that people who are drinking these alcoholic beverages are not aware of the ingredients which are contained in them."

The New York Times reports that Four Loko "has been blamed for several deaths over the last several months," including that of a 20-year-old sophomore at Florida State University in Tallahassee who "started playing with a

gun and fatally shot himself after drinking several cans of Four Loko over a number of hours." Richard Blumenthal tells the *Times* "there's just no excuse for the delay in applying standards that clearly should bar this kind of witch's brew." Mary Claire O'Brien argues that Four Loko is guilty until proven innocent: "The addition of the caffeine impairs the ability of the drinker to tell when they're drunk. What is the level at which it becomes dangerous? We don't know that, and until we can figure it out, the answer is that no level is safe."

November 16, 2010: Phusion Projects says it will reformulate Four Loko, removing the caffeine, guarana, and taurine. "We have repeatedly contended—and still believe, as do many people throughout the country—that the combination of alcohol and caffeine is safe," the company's founders say. "We are taking this step after trying—unsuccessfully—to navigate a difficult and politically charged regulatory environment at both the state and federal levels."

The Arizona Republic reports that an "extremely intoxicated" 18-year-old from Mesa crashed her SUV into a tree after "playing 'beer pong' with the controversial caffeinated alcoholic beverage Four Loko." The headline: "Caffeine, Alcohol Drink Tied to Crash."

Reporting on a lawsuit against Phusion Projects by the parents of the FSU student who shot himself after drinking Four Loko, ABC News quotes Schumer, who avers, "It's almost a death wish disguised as an energy drink."

November 17, 2010: The FDA and the Federal Trade Commission send warning letters to Phusion Projects, United Brands, Charge Beverages, and New Century Brewing Company, which makes a caffeinated lager called Moonshot. The agency says their products are "adulterated," and therefore illegal under the Food, Drug, and Cosmetic Act, because they contain an additive, caffeine, that is not generally recognized as safe in this context. But the FDA does not conclude that all beverages combining alcohol and caffeine are inherently unsafe. It focuses on these particular companies because they "seemingly target the young adult user." Federal drug czar Gil Kerlikowske approves the FDA's marketing-based definition of adulteration, saying "these products are designed, branded, and promoted to encourage binge drinking."

NPR correspondent Tovia Smith reports that "many college students say they agree with the FDA that alcoholic energy drinks do result in more risky behavior, like drunk driving or sexual assaults." Smith presents one such student, Ali Burak of Boston College, who says "it seems like every time someone wakes up in the morning and regrets the night before it's usually because they had Four Loko."

November 20, 2010: In a *Huffington Post* essay, David Katz, director of Yale University's Prevention Research

Center, explains why "anyone who is for sanity and safety in marketing" should welcome the FDA's ban. "Combining alcohol and caffeine is—in one word—crazy," he writes. "Don't do it! It has an excellent chance of hurting you, and a fairly good chance of killing you." His evidence: the Maryland car crash in which a woman who had been drinking Four Loko died after colliding with a telephone pole. "It's hard to imagine any argument for such products," Katz concludes. "It's also hard to imagine anyone objecting to a ban of such products."

Jacob Sullum is a journalist and editor of *Reason Magazine*.

EXPLORING THE ISSUE

Are Energy Drinks with Alcohol Dangerous Enough to Ban?

Critical Thinking and Reflection

1. Why were energy drinks with caffeine banned?
2. Why are caffeinated energy drinks so popular among college students?
3. Describe why the drinks are dangerous and how they contributed to deaths among some college students.

Is There Common Ground?

Four Loco and other energy drinks provide the effects of caffeine and sugar, but there is little or no evidence that a wide variety of other ingredients have any impact on the body. A variety of physiological and psychological effects, however, have been blamed on energy drinks and their components. Excess use of energy drinks may produce mild-to-moderate euphoria primarily due to the stimulant properties of caffeine. The drinks may also cause agitation, anxiety, irritability, and sleeplessness.

Ingestion of a single energy drink will not lead to excessive caffeine intake, but consumption of two or more drinks over the course of a day can. Ginseng, guarana, and other stimulants are often added to energy drinks and may bolster the effects of caffeine. Negative effects associated with caffeine consumption in amounts greater than 400 mg include nervousness, irritability, sleeplessness, increased urination, abnormal heart rhythms, and upset stomach. By comparison, a cup of drip coffee contains about 150 mg of caffeine. Caffeine in energy drinks can cause the excretion of water from the body to dilute high concentrations of sugar entering the blood stream, leading to dehydration.

In the United States, energy drinks have been linked with reports of emergency room visits due to heart palpitations and anxiety. The beverages have been associated with seizures due to the crash following the high energy that occurs after ingestion. In the United States, caffeine dosage is not required to be on the product label for food, unlike drugs, but some advocates are urging the FDA to change this practice.

Drinking one 24-ounce can of Four Loko provides the alcoholic kick of four beers and the caffeine buzz of a strong cup of coffee. Drinking one quickly makes someone pretty drunk and reasonably awake, and able to drink more. As a result, college students seem particularly drawn to it, which has landed some in hospitals. But should Four Loko be banned state-by-state as a result? Banning Four Loko might prevent some people, especially some college students, from hurting themselves or others. But does it improve people's judgment or otherwise empower them to protect themselves?

Create Central

www.mhhe.com/createcentral

Additional Resources

The party's over. (2010, November 25). *Nature, 475.*

Siegel, S. (2011). The Four-Loko effect. *Perspectives on Psychological Science, 6*(4), 357–362.

Wood, D. B. (2010, November 19). Four Loko: Does FDA's caffeinated alcoholic beverage ban go too far? *Christian Science Monitor*, p. N.PAG.

Internet References . . .

Energy Drinks—American Association of Poison Control Centers

www.aapcc.org/alerts/energy-drinks

Food and Drug Administration

www.fda.gov

National Institute on Drug Abuse (NIDA)

www.nida.nih.gov